The Bull Ring Uncovered

The Bull Ring Uncovered

Excavations at Edgbaston Street, Moor Street, Park Street and The Row, Birmingham, 1997–2001

Catharine Patrick and Stephanie Rátkai

edited by Stephanie Rátkai

With contributions by David Barker, Ian Baxter, Lynne Bevan, Bob Burrows, Simon Buteux, Marina Ciaraldi, Sheila Hamilton-Dyer, James Grieg, David Higgins, Mike Hodder, Rob Ixer, Rachel Ives, Steve Litherland, Erica Macey-Bracken, Helen Martin, Quita Mould, Matthew Nicholas, David Orton, Chris Patrick, Eleanor Ramsay, David Smith and David Williams.

Principal illustrations by Nigel Dodds. Studio photography by Graham Norrie.

Oxbow Books

Published by
Oxbow Books, Oxford

© Cathy Patrick and Stephanie Rátkai, and the individual authors 2009

ISBN 978-1-84217-285-8

A CIP record of this book is available from the British Library

This book is available direct from

Oxbow Books, Oxford
(Phone: 01865-241249; Fax: 01865-794449)

and

The David Brown Book Company
PO Box 511, Oakville, CT 06779, USA
(Phone: 860-945-9329; Fax: 860-945-9468)

or from our website

www.oxbowbooks.com

Front cover: Sculptor Laurence Broderick's 5 tonne bronze bull, situated at the heart of the Bullring development, seen here with some of Birmingham's past inhabitants and the spire of St Martin's visible in the background.

Back cover: Reflections of the Bullring.

Cover design by Nigel Dodds and Amanda Forster.

Printed and bound at Gomer Press
Llandysul, Wales

Contents

Summary

The archaeological excavations in the historic centre of Birmingham uncovered evidence of some prehistoric and Roman activity but primarily evidence of occupation from the 12th through to the 19th centuries. They provided a wealth of both artefactual and environmental information, hitherto unknown for the city, as well as structural evidence for domestic buildings and features, and industrial processes.

From the outset, it was determined that the final excavation volume would integrate fully the various specialist artefactual and environmental reports together with cartographic and documentary evidence in order to provide as rounded a picture of life and work in Birmingham in the medieval and post-medieval periods as possible.

The environmental evidence was important in highlighting how wet much of Birmingham was, with numerous springs, watercourses and pools of standing water. The town was also surprisingly well wooded for much of its history. Plant and pollen remains provided corroborative evidence for the presence of the numerous gardens shown on 18th-century maps and gave some indication of diet through the ages. Links between Birmingham and heathland to the west were also evidenced in the plant and pollen record.

Excavation revealed substantial remains of Birmingham's medieval industrial past and revealed the importance and longevity of tanning, which is of importance both regionally and nationally, and the manufacture of hemp and linen yarn or cloth. Metal working and pottery production were also attested in this period. Although tanning continued in the late medieval and early post-medieval periods, the focus of industrial activity at this time seems to have shifted from the market area around St Martin's Church down the hill towards the valley floor of the River Rea where water could more effectively be utilised. The importance of livestock, particularly cattle, was markedly apparent in the medieval and early post-medieval periods. Stock rearing, with tanning and associated trades, seems to have been intertwined with Birmingham's pre-eminence as a centre for the sale of drove cattle. The roots of this trade in beasts may go back to the 12th century. Tanning continued throughout the post-medieval period and tanyards and later skinyards were a mainstay of Edgbaston Street until the early 19th century.

Evidence for metal working in the Bull Ring area became more manifest in the 17th century and seems to have been more concentrated along Park Street in particular and also on Moor Street rather than on Edgbaston Street, where tanning was pre-eminent. The earlier metal-working industries on Park Street were associated with smithing and cutlering and it is only in the 18th century that brass founding became well established there. This volume also provides one of the rare opportunities to analyse metal-working debris of this period. An adjunct to cutlering, was the production of bone and ivory handles, offcuts from which were found at Edgbaston Street and Park Street. A cut section of elephant tusk from Edgbaston Street, a surprise find, was further evidence of ivory working in the post-medieval period.

Most of the artefactual evidence was concerned with industrial processes, with comparatively few items of personal adornment or domestic life. However, a number of artefacts, both medieval and post-medieval, hinted at affluence amongst residents around the Bull Ring. A significant corpus of clay pipes was recorded for the first time in Birmingham, which is of importance both regionally and nationally. There was little archaeological evidence of Birmingham's 'toy trade', although evidence of 18th-century bone and mother-of-pearl button making was found at Edgbaston Street and Park Street. Debris from an 18th-century glassworks was unearthed at Edgbaston Street.

The excavations were not without their mysteries. The anomalous burial of two individuals at Park Street, probably in the medieval period, is difficult to understand, as is the presence of a rock crystal swivel seal bearing a heraldic device seemingly associated with an aristocrat.

Overall, the excavations have proved invaluable for many reasons, not least because of the remarkable survival of below-ground archaeology in a heavily developed industrial city. They have demonstrated the presence of industrial activities and their locations, hitherto unrecorded in the documentary sources, and have given insights into the topographic development and day-to-day lives of the people of Birmingham for over 800 years.

Foreword

The Birmingham Alliance

Throughout history, Birmingham has been a leading centre of trade and market innovation. One of its earliest known transformations, in the 1100s, turned it from a village into a thriving market town. Later, in the 18th century, it was described as 'the first manufacturing town in the world' and in the 19th century its industrial greatness earned it the soubriquet 'the city of a thousand trades'. In the 1960s it became one of the country's most celebrated examples of revolutionary urban planning, which brought with it the opening of the old Bull Ring shopping centre. At the time, it was one of world's largest shopping centres outside America and an exemplar of shopping centre design.

Today Birmingham is undergoing yet another transformation. The city is seeing billions of pounds of new investment, and the opening of the new 110,000m² Bullring[1] in September 2003 has been a major milestone in reviving the city's status as a leading European retail capital.

The opening of Bullring has brought over 130 different retailers together in a new central focus of shopping, leisure and entertainment. Its creation is part of a long continuum of Birmingham's history as a major trading centre. Not only has the archaeological work confirmed the site as the historic heart of the city, but through Bullring it will continue to be so.

Sited beneath the spire of St Martin's Church, this historic centre for market trading began life in 1166 when the city was awarded a charter giving it the right to have its own market. Since then, the site's existence as a market has continued to the present day. The opening of the old Bull Ring shopping centre in 1964 brought the location international prestige as one of Europe's largest and most modern shopping complexes. Almost forty years on, the 26-acre site is again the centre of innovation, this time as the home of the largest retail-led urban regeneration project in Europe: Bullring. The construction of this latest manifestation of Birmingham's transformation has brought startling and exciting discoveries. New evidence, unearthed during archaeological digs commissioned by the Birmingham Alliance over three and a half years as part of Bullring's regeneration, has provided new perspectives on the city's history.

The Birmingham Alliance is privileged to have been part of the process which has allowed so much more knowledge of the city's history to become known. The dedication of the team of archaeologists from the University of Birmingham during their time of discovery has been outstanding. Special thanks must be made to Mike Hodder, Birmingham City Council's planning archaeologist, and also to Catharine Patrick, of CgMs Consulting, the archaeological consultant to The Birmingham Alliance. It is their efforts which have brought about this book – another vital chapter of Birmingham's fascinating history.

Jon Emery, Hammerson; Neil Varnham, Henderson Global Investors; Bob de Barr, Land Securities

---

[1]   The name Bullring is used here to refer specifically to the 2003 development.

Foreword: The Bull Ring Uncovered

The Leader of Birmingham City Council

Birmingham has always been a progressive city, responding to changing requirements. The new Bullring is part of Birmingham's Renaissance since the closing years of the 20th century and brings the historic centre of Birmingham into the 21st century.

The archaeological excavations at the Bull Ring have revealed nine centuries of progress and change in Birmingham and have overturned previous perceptions of the city's history. Pits and ditches, pottery and bone, and seeds and pollen, have provided remarkable details about life and work in the historic centre of Birmingham. They reveal Birmingham's origins as a 12th-century market town with a deer park alongside it; the 13th-century expansion of the town, including the construction of two new roads; medieval industries, including leather tanning, pottery making and textile processing as well as metal working; and the 18th-century gardens of grand houses, replaced by industries and back-to-back houses as the better-off moved out to the suburbs.

The Bull Ring excavations not only demonstrated the wealth of surviving remains of the city's past but also how they can be properly investigated without preventing or delaying new development. The Birmingham Alliance has enthusiastically embraced the integration of archaeology with new development to the benefit of the people of Birmingham, adding value to their development by increasing public interest and appreciation, and setting a fine example for other developers to follow. This has been achieved through the development partnership fostered by the City Council, working together with developers and their agents, which promotes quality development that the people of Birmingham can own and be proud of. It includes making sure that remains of the city's historic development are not swept away without record while we are building a new Birmingham.

In the Bullring, the City Council's aims of encouraging major, high quality development and at the same time safeguarding the city's past have come together. The Bullring shows how archaeological work will be successfully achieved in future developments in the city centre and elsewhere in Birmingham to the benefit of developers, the citizens of Birmingham, and visitors.

Interpretation panels in the Bullring briefly describe the results of the excavations to modern shoppers: this report contains detailed descriptions and analysis which demonstrate the importance of the archaeological remains for Birmingham and beyond.

Councillor Mike Whitby
Leader of Birmingham City Council

Acknowledgements

The Bull Ring excavations and subsequent analysis and report were sponsored by The Birmingham Alliance, the developers of the Bull Ring. Sincere thanks to all at The Birmingham Alliance who ensured that the archaeological investigations were smoothly integrated into the pre-construction programme and who helped make the project a success. The archaeological investigations were monitored by Dr Michael Hodder for Birmingham City Council; the Park Street investigations and post-excavation programme were also monitored by Jim Hunter and Catharine Patrick at CgMs Consulting on behalf of The Birmingham Alliance. The fieldwork was managed by Iain Ferris of Birmingham Archaeology.

The fieldwork staff were:
Edgbaston Street – Cathy Patrick (director), Yianni Altsitzoglou, Gino Bellavia, Julie Candy, Mary Duncan, Emma Hancocks, Chris Hewitson, John Hovey, Steve Litherland, Edward Newton, Chris Patrick, Ellie Ramsey, Elidh Ross, Jon Sterenberg, Sarah Watt and Christine Winter.

Moor Street – Cathy Patrick (director) Bob Burrows (supervisor), Mary Duncan, John Halsted, Roy Krakowicz, Helen Martin, John la Niece, Chris Patrick and Ellie Ramsey.

Park Street – Bob Burrows (director), Helen Martin (supervisor), Kate Bain, Sabina Belim, Suzie Blake, Richard Cherrington, Melissa Conway, Nathan Flavell, Suzanne Gailey, Emma Hancox, Chris Hewitson, Mark Hewson, Roy Krakowicz, Erica Macey-Bracken, Phil Mann, Charlotte Nielson, Dave Priestley, Sally Radford, Ellie Ramsey, Andy Rudge, Jon Sterenberg, Sarah Weatherall, Josh Williams, Steve Williams, Danni Wooton.

Chris Patrick carried out The Row project with the assistance of Gino Bellavia, John Hovey, Chris Hewitson, Ellie Ramsey and Christine Winter.

The initial stages of the post-excavation programme were managed by Iain Ferris and Annette Hancocks. Later stages of the post-excavation programme were managed by Simon Buteux and Amanda Forster. Processing of artefacts was managed by Lynne Bevan, Annette Hancocks and Erica Macey-Bracken. The illustrations were prepared by Nigel Dodds, John Halsted and Bryony Ryder. Studio photographic images were taken by Graham Norrie.

The assistance of Steve Litherland and Toni and George Demidowicz with the documentary sources is gratefully acknowledged. Amanda Forster undertook the formatting and technical editing of the volume and Della Hooke undertook the final copy editing.

Cathy Patrick would particularly like to thank:
Jon Emery, Mel Evans, Vic Michel and Simon Wallis at The Alliance, Sara Boonham at Gardiner and Theobald, Kimber Heath at Benoy, Mike Nisbet at Gardiner and Theobald Management Services, the Site Managers at Balfour Beatty Construction, Controlled Demolition, Shepherd Construction and Sir Robert McAlpine and the drivers at St Clements Plant Hire.

Thanks also to the archaeological specialists who have contributed to this publication and who have helped to enhance our understanding of Birmingham's archaeological and historical development. In addition, George and Toni Demidowicz have provided valuable access to their research, as has Paul Davies.

Especial thanks to Dr Mike Hodder, Planning Archaeologist, Birmingham City Council, for his tireless enthusiasm in promoting the city's archaeology which has always helped to drive the team forward.

Stephanie Rátkai would like to thank the following:
The Staff of Birmingham Archives and Birmingham Local Studies, Quita Mould and Roy Thomson for their expertise in all aspects of tanning and hide curing, Glennys Wilde (Birmingham Museum and Art Gallery) for her help with the identification of glass and the swivel-seal, Geoff Egan (Museum of London) for information on cutlery manufacture, John Hunt for answering various historical queries and Margaret Bonham for generously

sharing her in-depth knowledge of Birmingham's history. Thanks are also due to Nigel Baker, David Barker, Paul Belford, Megan Brickley, Hilary Cool, David Dungworth, Della Hooke, Rob Ixer, Steve Linnane and Martin Lambert, Managing Director of Henry Shaw and Sons Ltd.

Thanks are due to Simon Buteux who laid the groundwork for this volume and without whom it would have been impossible to attain such a high standard, to Mike Hodder for his unswerving enthusiasm and support for Birmingham's archaeology and to Alex Jones and Caroline Raynor of Birmingham Archaeology for their support.

Special thanks are due to Nigel Dodds for work on cartographic sources, mapping and pictorial evidence of historic Birmingham and to Amanda Forster who worked tirelessly and good-humouredly on the technical editing and referencing.

Ian L. Baxter would like to thank:
Sheila Hamilton-Dyer for her observations on the Edgbaston Street turkey bones and Umberto Albarella for providing a pre-publication draft of his paper on tannery evidence.

Marina Ciaraldi would like to thank:
James Greig for his helpful advice during the identification of the plant remains and Allan Hall for his help with the identification of bark sclereids, and for his comments on some of the samples from Edgabston Street. I would also like to thank Mike Hodder for his many comments and suggestions on the documentary evidence for hemp and flax cultivation in Birmingham.

James Greig gratefully acknowledges:
the support of English Heritage and of The University of Birmingham during part of the time while this work was being done and Marina Ciaraldi kindly made her macrofossil results available for comparison with the pollen data.

Illustration acknowledgements
We are grateful to the Birmingham Alliance who provided the photograph for the front cover design, and to Amanda Forster for the background photograph used on the back cover. Mike Hodder kindly provided photographs of the Park Street and Moor Street excavations in progress. ACS Ltd., Ireland, gave permission to reproduce illustrations from the Ardee Street report (Fig. 2.28) and Birmingham Public Libraries gave permission to reproduce Joseph William Pickering's photograph of Park St, 1867 (Fig. 4.32).

The Bull Ring Excavations and Archaeology in Birmingham City Centre: an Overview

Michael Hodder
Planning Archaeologist, Birmingham City Council

The archaeological excavation in Edgbaston Street in 1999 (on the site now occupied by the Indoor Market) was, amazingly, the first ever large-scale archaeological excavation in Birmingham city centre. It and the other excavations undertaken between 1997 and 2001 in advance of the Bull Ring development revealed extensive and well-preserved remains of life and work in the historic core of Birmingham from the 12th to the 20th centuries. This overview considers the Bull Ring excavations in the wider context of the archaeology of the city centre as a whole, in terms of the processes, the implications of the results for the future management of the archaeological resource, and the overall achievement of the excavations.

The process

The recovery of archaeological remains of Birmingham's past as part of the Bull Ring redevelopment was achieved through the structured and sequential process established as national best practice. This process is reflected in Birmingham City Council's archaeology policies which are in turn derived from central government guidance in PPG16 (Department of the Environment 1990).

At the Bull Ring, the process began with desk-based archaeological assessments in which existing information was considered for each part of the development site. This information included an extensive desk-based archaeological assessment of the Digbeth/ High Street Deritend/ High Street Bordesley frontage which had been commissioned by the City Council itself in 1995 (Litherland *et al.* 1995) to provide information from which to consider development proposals and to reduce uncertainty about archaeological implications amongst potential developers and investors. The archaeological desk-based assessments indicated where archaeological

remains were likely to survive and, conversely, where they were unlikely to survive.

Following desk-based assessment, evaluation by excavated trenches would normally be required before determination of a planning application, but this was not possible on the Edgbaston Street, Moor Street and Park Street sites because they were inaccessible. Planning conditions were therefore imposed requiring archaeological evaluation by trenching followed by the submission of a mitigation strategy to the City Council for approval. The mitigation strategy included substantial archaeological excavation before commencement of development followed by post-excavation analysis and publication, which is an essential and integral part of the process.

The information derived from the Bull Ring excavations and all other archaeological work in Birmingham is incorporated into the Sites and Monuments Record, the City Council's archaeological database. Birmingham City Council's Archaeology Strategy, adopted as Supplementary Planning Guidance in 2003 (Birmingham City Council 2004), includes specific reference to the city centre, and archaeology is included in other documents such as conservation area character appraisals and management plans.

Management of the archaeological resource

The excavations at the Bull Ring and other sites in the city centre demonstrate the good survival of archaeological features and deposits and their potential to provide much new information about Birmingham's medieval and post-medieval development. The extent and quality of survival of archaeological deposits in the Bull Ring area exceeded previous expectations of potential survival, which were based on the results of a watching brief alongside High Street Deritend in 1953 (Sherlock 1957), observations at the Birmingham Moat site between 1973 and 1975 (Watts 1980), and small-scale excavations at the Old Crown in 1994 (Litherland *et al.* 1994), High Street Bordesley in 1995 (Jackson and Rátkai 1995; Cook and Rátkai 1995), and Hartwell Smithfield Garage in 1996 (Litherland and Moscrop 1996). At Edgbaston Street, Park Street and Moor Street there was a sequence of deposits from the 12th or 13th century through to the 20th century, represented by intercutting features and accumulated layers. The structural remains included organic material such as the wooden planks lining water tanks at Park Street, and objects included pottery, animal bone, industrial residues and plant and insect remains – in fact, exactly the type of features and deposits regarded as characteristic of 'urban archaeology' and represented on a larger scale at places like York.

In addition to the sites listed above, the survival of archaeological remains from the medieval and post-medieval periods in Birmingham city centre has been demonstrated, following the commencement of the Bull Ring excavations, at the Custard Factory, Gibb Street (Mould 2001a), Bordesley Street (Tavener 2000), Floodgate Street (Williams 2002), Rea Street (Williams 2003), High Street Deritend (Martin 2004), Heath Mill Lane (Ramsey 2004), the Masshouse area (*e.g.* Kracowicz and Rudge 2004), High Street Bordesley (Martin 2005), Upper Dean Street (Martin and Rátkai 2005), and the Freeman Street area (Hayes 2006), and we can confidently predict that such deposits survive throughout Digbeth, Deritend and Bordesley. Although deposits investigated so far have been of medieval and post-medieval date, the possibility of future discoveries of prehistoric and Roman remains must not be discounted.

Because Birmingham has not been regarded as a 'historic town' it has never been the subject of detailed urban archaeological surveys like, for example, that undertaken for nearby Shrewsbury. Following the Bull Ring and other excavations, an analysis and synthesis of all the archaeological information from the city centre so far, including deposit modelling and prediction, is now needed as part of the management of the archaeological resource in a development context. It is also essential for future management that the below-ground archaeological deposits are regarded as a component of the historic environment as a whole, which in Birmingham city centre includes medieval and post-medieval street patterns and property boundaries as well as historic buildings, and that protection of the historic environment is regarded as part of sustainable development (Office of the Deputy Prime Minister 2005, 2).

Archaeological remains in Bull Ring and in most of the city centre as a whole have so far been preserved 'by record' through excavation in advance of development, rather than *in situ*, but this has resulted in a huge gain in information which has far outweighed any benefit of *in situ* preservation. Increasing archaeological data enables closer prediction of the likely archaeological impact of subsequent developments on nearby sites, contributing to the response to development proposals through the planning process and enabling the aims of further archaeological work as part of the planning process to be better focused, and therefore more cost- and information-effective.

It can be anticipated that similarly well-preserved archaeological remains survive in areas adjoining and near to those hitherto excavated. The Bullring development has acted as a catalyst for further development in this part of Birmingham, and over the next few years there will be extensive new development in the area extending northwards from the Digbeth/ High Street Deritend/ High Street Bordesley frontage (known as Eastside in current planning terms), and to the south of the frontage (the Irish Quarter). Where these sites are affected by development which would damage or destroy archaeological remains it is important that excavation takes place in advance of such development. The excavation must be of sufficient extent to properly understand and record the surviving remains, including those of post-medieval date, and strategies for on-site sampling and subsequent analysis must ensure that the maximum potential of environmental evidence and industrial residues is realised.

As well as building up a picture of the historical development of Birmingham as a whole, inter-site comparisons draw attention to gaps in knowledge and ambiguities or uncertainties. These contribute to the formulation of research frameworks which in turn inform and guide strategies for future archaeological work in the city centre and elsewhere. All of this future work is likely to be undertaken as part of the development process.

The achievement

In addition to overturning previous perceptions that what is now the city centre was relatively insignificant until the post-medieval period and that the survival of archaeological deposits would in any case be poor because of the intensity of later development, the cumulative archaeological evidence from the Bull Ring excavations and from other excavations in the city centre considerably augments, and in some cases challenges, the picture of the past derived from documentary sources. The physical evidence provided by archaeological remains, whose interpretation may be debated but whose existence is indisputable, has on the one hand augmented and on the other contradicted previous assertions about Birmingham's past often based on weak and unsubstantiated arguments derived from the scant documentation available.

A particular contribution of the Bull Ring excavations to our knowledge of medieval and post-medieval Birmingham is the information provided by environmental evidence and industrial debris. Prior to the Bull

Ring excavations, the only environmental evidence for the medieval and post-medieval periods in Birmingham city centre consisted of seeds and pollen from the 1970s work at Birmingham Moat (Greig in Watts 1980). The archaeological evidence for medieval and post-medieval industries, other than surviving 18th- and 19th-century buildings and structures, consisted only of waste pottery from the Old Crown and High Street Deritend (Sherlock 1957; Litherland *et al.* 1994), debris from button manufacturing in High Street Deritend (Symons 1984), and, at Birmingham Moat, hemp seeds indicating processing for textile manufacture and fragments of muffle kiln in which clay pipes were fired (Watts 1980, 48).

The Bull Ring excavations demonstrated how, through implementation of the City Council's policies in accordance with central government advice, substantial archaeological work can take place without preventing or compromising major new development. This process ensured that the archaeological work was smoothly integrated into the development programme because its extent, and therefore the time required for it and its cost, could be closely estimated. Successful implementation of this process has involved close co-operation at every stage between the developers, their archaeological and other consultants and contractors, and the Council's planning archaeologist and other officers.

Proper management of the city's archaeology through the planning process ensures efficient implementation of the requirements and ensures that archaeological best value is achieved in terms of information retrieval, analysis and dissemination.

1 Introduction

Catharine Patrick

Before the mid-1990s, archaeology in Birmingham did not have a high profile. Historical research (Holt 1985) had suggested that Birmingham was an important example of an industrially based medieval town but there was little in the way of excavated evidence to support this. Archaeology can provide an important and contrasting source to the traditional documentary record, even for the 18th and 19th centuries – both in terms of the evidence provided by standing buildings and in terms of the buried evidence of the lives of the urban residents. This evidence becomes progressively more important the further back in time one goes, particularly in Birmingham, where relatively few medieval documents have survived for the town.

The historic memory of the Bull Ring is not represented by buildings – these were replaced by the Bull Ring development of the '60s and '70s – nor is it represented by documents. The historic memory is instead represented by buried remains – yards, pits, wells, postholes, ovens, ditches and gullies – all of which can yield dating evidence and clues to the profession and status of the town's inhabitants, and provide a glimpse of what it must have been like to live in the Bull Ring in the medieval period.

This publication focuses on archaeological sites at Edgbaston Street, Moor Street, Park Street and The Row, which are all located within the historic Bull Ring market area of Birmingham, close to the focal point of St Martin's Church (Figs 1.1–1.4).

Geology and topography

This part of Birmingham developed on a prominent sandstone ridge about 1.2km wide. The ridge is part of the Birmingham Plateau, a geographical zone consisting of mainly Triassic rocks covered with glacial clays and gravels. The Bull Ring lies on this ridge (between 110m–120m AOD) to the east of the conjectured Birmingham fault, overlooking a steep slope leading down via Digbeth to the lower lying and wet, marl-lined valley of the River Rea (VCH Warwickshire VII 1964).

The geology and natural topography of Birmingham are important for an understanding of the early development of the town. A good supply of water is essential to a medieval market town – it is needed for human consumption, for the watering of animals, and to drive mills, and is an essential ingredient, often in quantity, for many early crafts and industries. For early Birmingham, an important source of water was provided by springs that rose at the junction of the water-bearing Bromsgrove Sandstone Formation (formerly known as Keuper Sandstone) of the Birmingham ridge with the impervious Mercia Mudstone along the line of the Birmingham fault. These springs were the source of a number of rivulets that flowed generally southeastwards down the slope from the ridge and into the River Rea. Suitably modified and canalised, these springs and watercourses supplied the two medieval moats, Parsonage Moat and the Lord of the Manor's (or Birmingham) Moat, which were amongst the earliest features of Birmingham's topography. The watercourses also strongly influenced the layout of the early town. For example, the watercourse that connected Parsonage Moat with the Lord of the Manor's Moat formed the southern boundary of the built-up area until the early 19th century (see Fig. 1.2).

Another major topographic influence on the development of the town was the rural road system which existed before the town developed. On the high ground where St Martin's Church and the Bull Ring now stand, and where a market place was established in the 12th century, a number of local and long distance roads converged and then crossed the Rea floodplain via a single corridor, the Digbeth–Deritend–Bordesley route.

Together, the natural topography, watercourses and rural road network were important factors in shaping the

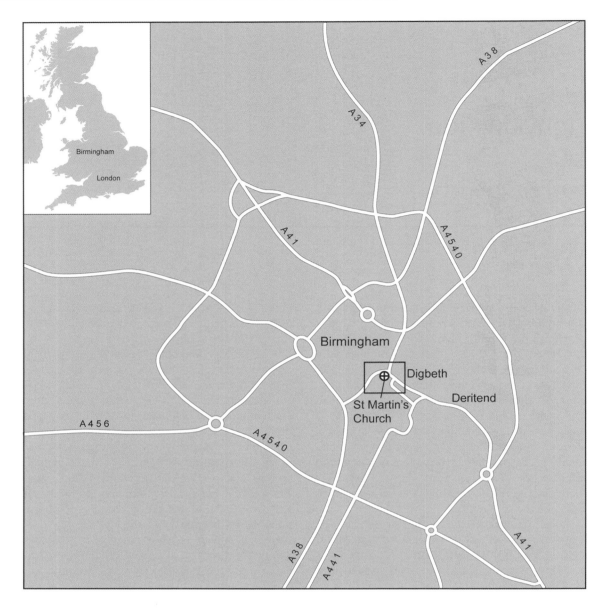

Fig. 1.1 Location of Birmingham.

development of the town. The town grew through the successive development of land parcels along the old roads and the insertion of new streets, generally roughly at right angles to the old roads, which created new land parcels for development. This street pattern then became fossilised and survived in recognisable form into the 19th century. Only with the coming of the railway, in the 19th century, and then the extraordinary road schemes and redevelopment of the 20th century, did this pattern become substantially obscured (see Figs 1.2–1.4).

Moor Street and Park Street – both the focus of excavations described in this report – represent 'insertions' into the pre-existing road network. Edgbaston Street – the third major site described in the report – is likely to have earlier origins.

In Birmingham, as elsewhere, the typical medieval urban property plot, known as a burgage ('town person's') plot, is long and thin, laid out at right angles to the street frontage. The rationale for this is simple: space on the street frontage was at a premium. The main building, perhaps a residence and/ or shop, would be situated on the frontage, while the strip of land behind, the backplot, could be used for a variety of purposes – market gardening, keeping animals, industrial activities of various kinds, and waste disposal. Much of the archaeological evidence uncovered in the Bull Ring excavations relates to this sort of 'backplot' activity.

While the front of the plot would be defined by the road, the back end of the plot might be defined by a ditch or watercourse. Plots with a ready source of water to

Fig. 1.2 Location map showing excavated areas overlaid on 18th century map (Bradford 1750).

hand were particularly valuable. It has been noted that 'the provision of watered plots is a recurrant feature of nascent urban settlements and, in particular, early markets' (Baker 1995). Livestock could be grazed and watered close to the market – there would be a particular demand for such plots from the town's butchers – while related industries such as the tanning of hides would demand a good supply of water.

This pattern certainly seems to be true of early Birmingham. The plots fronting onto Edgbaston Street terminated in the watercourse connecting Parsonage Moat and the Lord of the Manor's Moat; extensive evidence of tanning was uncovered in the archaeological excavations there. At Moor Street and Park Street, a large ditch marked the far end of the backplots fronting onto the market place and the upper end of Digbeth respectively. The ditch not only defined the original town boundary

but also the edge of a deer park – Little Park or Over Park – that lay to the north and east of the early town. From the environmental evidence, a watercourse may have run along this ditch or it may simply have collected pools of standing water. Likewise, the environmental remains from a second ditch at Park Street, running at right angles to the above and defining the back end of the burgage plots running down from Park Street, indicate that it was also waterlogged. However, at Moor Street and Park Street the ditches were backfilled in the 13th century, which would seem to indicate that whatever the quantity of water they may have supplied to the burgage plots it was not considered of sufficient importance to keep them open. Park Street does seem to have had a number of water-filled ponds and tanks, which presumably provided some or all of the necessary water requirements. This is in stark contrast to Edgbaston Street, where the water-

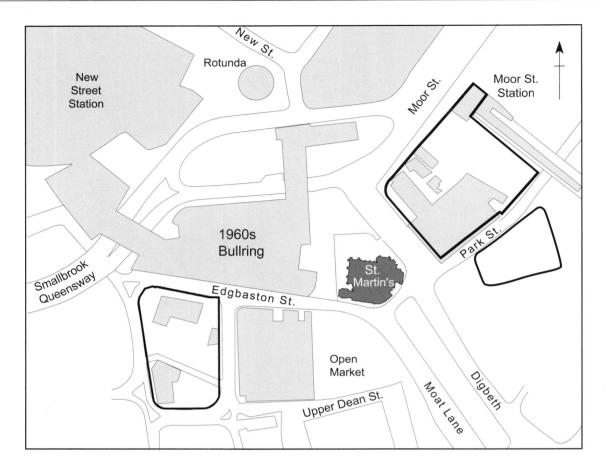

Fig. 1.3 Location map showing excavated areas in relation to the 1960s Bullring.

course was kept open until the late 18th or early 19th centuries. However, both the Moor Street and Park Street ditches produced plant and insect remains that provide important insights into the environment and the uses to which the ditches and adjacent land were put.

Background to the excavations

Edgbaston Street, Moor Street, Park Street and The Row represent part of the historic centre of Birmingham around St Martin's Church. Research (Holt 1985; Baker 1995) suggested that evidence for the growth of Birmingham from the Middle Ages onwards was likely to be found in the immediate vicinity of the Bull Ring. The Lord of the Manor's Moat, the smaller Parsonage Moat and their associated watercourses lie close by, and Edgbaston Street was one of the earliest streets to be laid out in the town. The notable persistence of property boundaries within the Bull Ring area suggested a high potential for the survival of archaeological deposits. It was predicted that there would be intense structural activity along the street frontages and a build-up of occupation deposits and rubbish pits within the yards and backplots to the rear. Excavation bore these sugges-

tions out and extensive, well-preserved medieval deposits were located, generally at a depth of 1.60–3m below the present-day ground level.

The position of Moor Street and Park Street – close to the medieval and post-medieval market place – meant that archaeological deposits found there would be likely to reflect the area's trading status. It was hoped that the archaeological evidence would help to date more precisely the insertion of the two streets into the town plan, and characterise the complexity and type of later developments.

The deposits and features identified by the archaeological investigations on all of the sites have revealed a sequence of development probably commencing soon after the granting of a market charter in the 12th century. In addition, information was gained pertaining to the economic activities which were crucial to the development of this part of Birmingham, beginning in the medieval period and continuing through the important transitional phases of the early post-medieval and later periods. The significance of industry to Birmingham in the medieval and early post-medieval periods cannot be emphasised too strongly.

The below-ground archaeology of the city centre has

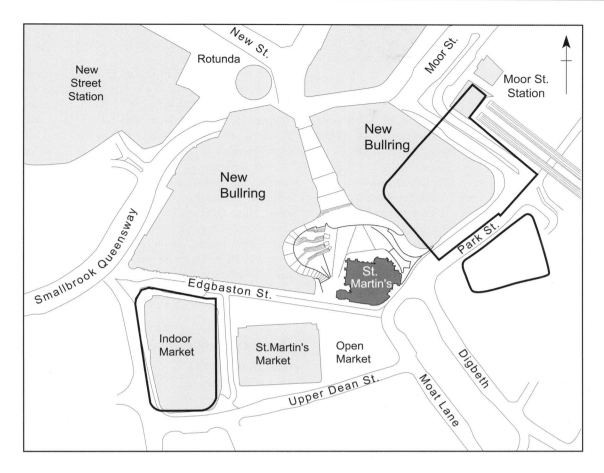

Fig. 1.4 Location map showing excavated areas overlaid on modern Bullring.

furthered our understanding of the chronology and form of Birmingham's growth and has provided evidence to help to resolve vitally important questions concerning Birmingham's early development. It has shed light on the historical development of this area from the Middle Ages up to the present day. The value of the archaeological resource in this area should not be underestimated, as Holt notes: 'archaeology alone has the potential to offer a truly comprehensive early history of this part of Birmingham' (Holt 1995).

Historical background

In 1086, at the time of the Domesday Book, Birmingham was only one of several small agricultural settlements within the area of the present-day city. Over the ensuing centuries this settlement evolved into a thriving trading, manufacturing and industrial town. The principal early stimulus to this development occurred in 1166 when the lord of the manor purchased a charter from the Crown allowing him to hold a weekly market and charge tolls. The charter probably legalised a pre-existing market and, as elsewhere, was no doubt obtained in an effort by the lord to create a new town around the market and enhance

the value of his property through the generation of rents. Plots of building land, exclusion from tolls and privileged access to the market were offered to those who settled in the town (Holt 1985), and in the case of Birmingham this proved to be a very successful venture, signalling the rapid urbanisation of the settlement. By 1300, Birmingham and the wider region of Warwickshire had experienced a period of massive population growth and Birmingham had grown to become one of a network of market centres manufacturing and distributing goods. Lay Subsidies dating to the 1320s and 1330s show that Birmingham was the third largest town in Warwickshire after Warwick and Coventry (Holt 1985). However, Birmingham's significance lay not in the presence of a castle (like Tamworth), nor as an administrative or religious centre (like Coventry, Shrewsbury or Stafford), but instead in its development as a trading and industrial centre for its evolving hinterland. The location of the triangular market place to the north of the manor house was probably part of this deliberate enhancement of Birmingham's trading facilities.

The origins of Birmingham's two moats – the Lord of the Manor's Moat and Parsonage Moat – and their original relationship to each other are not clear but they

are likely to have been important foci of rural development, and it has been suggested that they originally
represented the manorial site and its 'home farm' (Baker
1995).

The 1166 charter refers to the market being held in
the *castrum* and this may be the earliest surviving
reference to the Lord of the Manor's Moat. Stonework
recovered during excavation of the moat (Watts 1980)
has been dated to the 12th century, with parallels at
Sandwell Priory, Wenlock Priory and Buildwas Abbey
(pers. comm. Richard Morris). The market may have had
a rival in Deritend *c*.1200 which, albeit temporarily, tried
to capture some of Birmingham's trade (Holt 1995).

It is likely that St Martin's Church was built by the
mid-12th century under the sponsorship of the lord of the
manor. Architectural fragments dating to the 12th century
have been found in the church, within a later rebuild.
Descriptions, but no drawings, of these fragments survive.
The economic success of the town allowed the church to
be rebuilt on a larger scale around the middle of the 13th
century (Holt 1985).

A survey of the lordship of Birmingham made in 1553
(Bickley and Hill 1891) details all the tenancies in the
town, but it seldom gives the size of a property or its
position within the town. The survey mentions a deer
park and Tanners Row, which has been taken to mean
Digbeth although the description would also be equally
applicable to Edgbaston Street and Holme Park.

Nigel Baker (1995) has produced a preliminary town
plan analysis of the development of Birmingham, mainly
based upon interpretation of the Bradford map of 1750/
51 (surveyed 1750, published the following year) and
subsequent Ordnance Survey maps. His analysis has
suggested that the principal features of the Birmingham
town plan, which includes streets, street frontage lines,
sites of public buildings, and property boundaries
surveyed in the early 18th century, have probably not
changed significantly since the area was first laid out for
settlement following the granting of the market charter.

As described above, the growth of Birmingham was
characterised by the successive development of land
parcels along the major pre-urban roads, and the insertion
of new roads laid out across the interstices of the existing
network. Baker suggests that Moor Street and Park Street
were cut through an already built-up frontage on the
northeast side of the Bull Ring and that their purpose
would have been to extend settlement behind that axial
route (Baker 1995). The regular shape of the land parcel
which these two streets define suggests that they were
probably inserted as part of a single phase of town
planning. The consequent creation of fresh building land
may be seen within the context of an increased demand
for house-plots within the rapidly expanding market
town. Both Holt and Baker conclude that much of the
central area of Birmingham, including the Moor Street,
Park Street and Bull Ring area, was laid out sometime
before *c*.1400. Given the limitations of the documentary

and cartographic record, archaeological evidence is the
only source for defining more precisely the early development of the town.

The founding of a Priory or Hospital at the northern
limit of the medieval town was in keeping with contemporary urban development (Cullum 1993). As for the
town itself, medieval documents for the Priory are scarce,
although one document does record that land was given
to the Priory in 1286. The Priory precinct was located at
the northern extent of Dale End, which runs roughly
parallel to Moor Street and Park Street. This is a street
which represented a continuation of the main north-south
axial route through Digbeth, the Bull Ring and High
Street, and which fed north from the triangular market
place. The later insertion of an arterial route from Dale
End and High Street to the northwest (Bull Street) is
likely to reflect the capacity of a priory to act as a stimulus
for further planned medieval urban development (Palliser
1993).

Previous archaeological work

Prior to the 1970s, very little archaeological work had
been done in Birmingham city centre. Construction work
for the fish market to the north of the Bull Ring in the
1880s revealed a stone passageway and chamber, while a
series of objects reputedly originating from the Lord of
the Manor's Moat, including a medieval ring, was already
published (Oswald 1951).

Some examination of surviving below-ground archaeological deposits at the manorial moat site was carried
out between October 1973 and June 1975, during
development of the present-day Wholesale Market (Watts
1980). However, this development preceded the introduction of measures which have enabled large-scale
archaeological excavation to take place as a condition of
development (the Department of the Environment's 1990
Planning Policy Guidance note 16). As a consequence,
although much relevant information was recovered, the
work resembled more a present-day 'watching brief'
during construction than an open-area excavation. In this
instance, Lorna Watts and a small team, working on
behalf of the City Museum, monitored construction
groundworks and recorded the survival of 'islands' of
archaeology within the concrete pile foundation pits.
Despite difficult conditions, this watching brief clearly
demonstrated the survival not just of the ditch of the
manorial moat, which was waterlogged and contained
preserved wooden stakes, but also of substantial dressed
sandstone footings and walls belonging to 13th-century
structures on the moat platform. The walls survived to
over 2m in height with a buttress on the outside of the
south wall. No evidence for the date of the moat's
construction was found as most of the fills were post-
medieval. Watts also noted that the 19th-century construction of the market had scoured away important
occupation deposits from the moat platform itself.

Archaeological investigations associated with the Bull Ring redevelopment

Edgbaston Street was the first site to be excavated in advance of the Bull Ring development, with various episodes of excavation between 1997 and 1999. These excavations demonstrated the extensive survival of medieval and early post-medieval settlement and industrial features (dating from the 12th century through to the 20th century). The Moor Street site was the second major site to be excavated as part of the development, in 2000.

Smaller scale work took place elsewhere as the Bull Ring development progressed. In 1999 trial trenching immediately to the east of The Row Market found pockets of medieval survival between later 19th-century cellaring (Hovey 1999); this was followed up by a watching brief (Ramsey 2000). A watching brief (Patrick 2000 and this volume) was also carried out during the construction of a new street, The Row, which runs approximately east to west from Moat Lane to Upper Dean Street. This new street cuts across the northwestern side of the medieval manorial moat.

Trial trenching work was carried out at Manzoni Gardens and in the Open Markets in 2000 (Burrows and Mould 2000a; Burrows and Mould 2000b). Here all the archaeological remains were shown to have been scoured away by development, the only surviving early feature being a well cut into the sandstone ridge and located close to the present-day boundary of St Martin's Churchyard.

A desk-based assessment in 1997 for the Martineau Galleries development (Litherland and Mould 1997) suggested the potential for survival of medieval deposits to the north of the Bull Ring. However, subsequent archaeological monitoring of geotechnical work and service pits in 1998 and 2000 found no surviving archaeology, but did record the natural sandstone ridge less than 1m below the present ground surface in Dale End (Mould 2001c).

In 2001, evaluation by means of trial trenching at Park Street was more productive, demonstrating extensive survival of medieval and later deposits. The evaluation was followed by area excavations in the same year and Park Street forms the third of the major sites described in this volume. At the same time as the excavations at Park Street, major excavations were also carried out near by in the churchyard of St Martin's, in advance of landscaping works. The results of these latter excavations, which provided fascinating insights into the lives and deaths of the parishioners of St Martin's in the 18th and 19th centuries (Brickley *et al.* 2006), form a companion volume to this one.

Collectively, these investigations make the most significant contribution to our understanding of Birmingham's historic development since the recording of the Lord of the Manor's Moat by Lorna Watts in the early 1970s.

Excavation and research aims

All of the major excavated sites offered an opportunity to study a more-or-less unbroken sequence of activity from the 12th century through to the 20th century.

The aims of the evaluation and excavation work, determined at the outset of the investigations, were to:

- 'preserve by record' any significant surviving medieval and post-medieval remains
- determine the character, development and chronology of the archaeological remains
- define the morphology of the settlement and of any industrial remains
- set the archaeological results in their historical context
- relate the site data to the early development of Birmingham
- contribute to the understanding of domestic and industrial activity within medieval and post-medieval Birmingham
- examine the pottery chronology and place evidence of pottery production within its local and regional context
- place evidence of tanning within its local and regional context
- reconsider the role of industry in the city, in both the medieval and post-medieval periods
- examine the dynamics of urbanism through an examination of changing functions and varying degrees of intensity of use of land in the medieval and post-medieval periods.

To a very considerable extent, these aims have been achieved.

Excavation method

The excavation method employed for all three major sites – Edgbaston Street, Moor Street and Park Street – was broadly the same. The modern overburden and concrete surfaces were removed by a 360 degree excavator, with a toothed and toothless bucket, under archaeological supervision. Spoil was stockpiled on site. The uppermost horizon of archaeological features and deposits revealed by machining was hand-cleaned and a base plan of features was prepared.

Machine excavation was carried out in two stages. The first stage was to remove modern overburden down to a distinct horizon noted at all three sites, the so-called Phase 3 'cultivation soil', a dark layer of silty-clay sand dating to the 18th century, which generally sealed the earlier features. Any features cutting this horizon were excavated and the soil layer was itself sampled before being removed. The second stage was to mechanically remove the 'cultivation soil' to the top of surviving earlier post-medieval (Phase 2) and medieval (Phase 1) deposits and features.

Sampling by hand excavation comprised not less than 50% of discrete features. A higher percentage of discrete features was excavated where more information was required to achieve a full understanding of the date, character and function of an individual feature or group of features. Features of probable industrial function were fully excavated, whilst linear features not associated with settlement were sampled to determine their form, function and date, and to determine the stratigraphic sequence. Excavation of linear features associated with settlement comprised a minimum of 25%. All datable features were sampled for environmental analysis, with 20-litre samples being taken from non-waterlogged deposits and 30-litre samples from waterlogged deposits. Deeply stratified deposits or large features were multi-sampled.

Recording was by means of pre-printed pro-formas for contexts and features, supplemented by plans (at 1:20 and 1:50), sections (at 1:10 and 1:20), monochrome print and colour slide photography. Subject to the permission of the landowner, it is intended to deposit the paper and finds archive in an archive store approved by the Planning Archaeologist for Birmingham City Council.

At Edgbaston Street, Area B, the movement of skins and hides from one tanning pit to another over a period of almost 500 years had caused deposits to spill over from one feature to the next, making excavation in plan practically impossible. These features were instead recorded and sampled by a series of excavated sections, which is a departure from normal procedure. A similar approach was adopted for the series of pits and ditches at the Park Street site.

Phasing

To facilitate comparison between the sites, which are in fact elements of the same urban landscape, a common system of phasing has been adopted for Edgbaston Street and Moor Street (see below). Park Street is broadly the same but has subdivisions of Phase 3. Five phases of activity have been distinguished, mainly on the basis of the date of the pottery.

Edgbaston Street and Moor Street

Phase 1: 12th–14th century
Phase 2: 15th–16th century
Phase 3: 17th–18th century

Phase 4: 19th century
Phase 5: 20th century

Park Street

Phase 1: 12th–14th century
Phase 2: 15th–16th century
Phase 3.1: Late 16th–early 18th century
Phase 3.2: c.1720/30–1760
Phase 3.3: c.1760–1800/1810
Phase 4: 19th century
Phase 5: 20th century

2   Land to the South of Edgbaston Street: Investigations 1997–1999

Catharine Patrick and Stephanie Rátkai

with a contribution from Steve Litherland

Background to the excavations

Today, the location of the Edgbaston Street excavations is underneath the new Indoor Market to the south of Edgbaston Street (Fig 1.4). Before redevelopment began here, land use comprised a multi-storey office block, two warehouses and a restaurant, which were demolished, and the rest of the street block was made up of rough car parking for the markets (Fig 1.3). The street block was still bisected by a narrow lane called Smithfield Passage that followed the line of a former medieval watercourse, and from here the ground level rose gradually towards the Edgbaston Street frontage.

A desk-based assessment of the site was carried out in 1995 (Mould and Litherland 1995b), and in 1997 two areas became available for evaluation by means of trial-trenching. Trench 1 was located at the western end of Edgbaston Street (Fig. 2.1). It extended to the south from the street frontage in order to test for surviving deposits relating to the former Parsonage Moat. However, several cellars had truncated any earlier remains and subsequent comparison and re-scaling of various historic maps with modern Ordnance Survey editions indicated that the moat actually lay a little further to the west, under what is now Pershore Street.

The second trench excavated at this time, Trench 5 in the overall scheme for site evaluation, was located immediately to the south of Smithfield Passage. Its purpose was to test for deposits relating to the watercourse that originally linked Parsonage Moat with the Lord of the Manor's Moat. This trench demonstrated that the profile, primary fills and later backfill of the watercourse did survive. As a consequence, more extensive excavation to the south of Smithfield Passage followed on directly, with the aim of recovering further evidence of the watercourse. This involved the excavation of four further transects (Transects A–D) across the line of the watercourse (see Fig 2.1).

Four larger areas were opened up for excavation; Areas A–C lying to the north of Smithfield Passage and Area D to the south (Fig. 2.1).

Historical profile

by Steve Litherland and Catharine Patrick

As outlined in the introduction, Peter de Birmingham was actively promoting the status of his lordship in the 12th century, principally by gaining a market charter, and probably also by sponsoring St Martin's Church. Edgbaston Street formed a primary component of his town planning, forming the lower end of a triangle of streets laid out around the market and St Martin's Church. While it is possible that Edgbaston Street was a remnant of an earlier road system, after the laying out of the market place this thoroughfare connected the market, church and manor house with a network of local and regional routes serving Edgbaston, Dudley and Worcester to the west.

Edgbaston Street would have carried mainly local traffic from the southwest to and from the main axial route represented by High Street and Digbeth and it would have been one of the earliest streets to be developed in the town. Its limits were defined by Parsonage Moat to the west and the Lord of the Manor's Moat to the east.

Edgbaston Street broadly follows part of the *c*.115m contour of the sandstone ridge that overlooks the Rea valley to the south. It is situated roughly two-thirds of the way up this hill and is also located just above the conjectural line of the Birmingham fault. Around the fault, several springs, issuing as water running off the hill, could not pass from the permeable sandstone into the impermeable Mercia Mudstone. These springs were harnessed to feed the Parsonage Moat situated at the west end of Edgbaston Street and also the Manorial Moat (*i.e.* the Lord of the Manor's Moat) towards the east end (Fig.

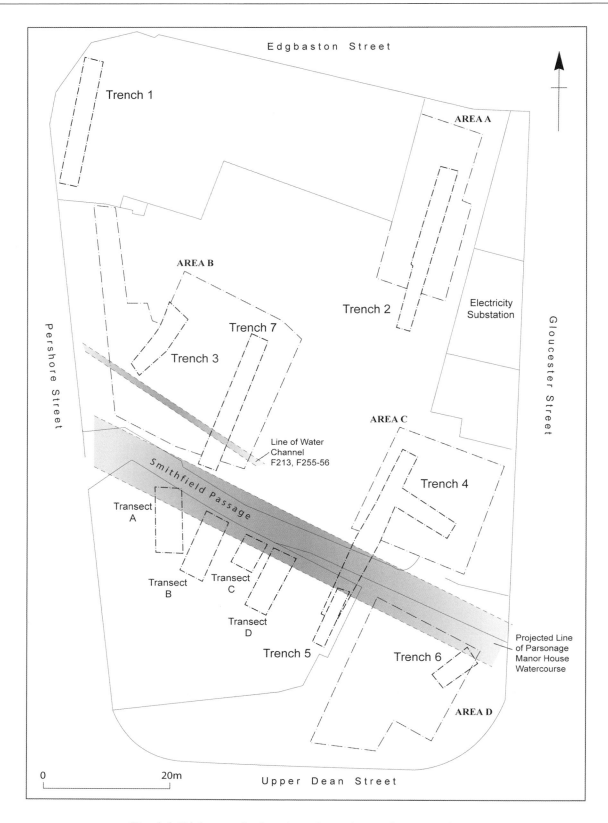

Fig. 2.1 Edgbaston St: location of trenches and excavated areas.

2.2). The two moats were also directly linked by a watercourse, which by the later 18th century was linked to two other water channels, the Pudding Brook and the Dirty Brook (the latter basically an open sewer).

The watercourse linking the two moats formed the back boundary of an irregular series of properties running down the slope from Edgbaston Street, and it was the westernmost portion of these plots, situated between the former line of Gloucester Street to the east and the surviving line of Pershore Street to the west, that was targeted for excavation. The area immediately to the east of Gloucester Street lay under the former Rag Market building, where extensive cellaring had destroyed the archaeological deposits.

The provision of watered plots next to a market would have been particularly attractive to tradesmen such as butchers as livestock could be grazed and watered close to the market. The watercourse might also attract industrial enterprise, such as tanning. So the Edgbaston properties were likely to have been much sought after for their trading and market frontages and ready access to fresh water behind, and doubtless they continued to be so long after the de Birmingham family lost control of the manor in the 16th century.

There is evidence to suggest that the Black Death severely affected Edgbaston Street (McKenna 2005, 14). As a result, new tenancies were created by Fulke de Birmingham and there followed a rapid recovery, with properties given over to tanners, skinners, graziers, butchers, weavers, and flax and yarn dressers. The importance of a plentiful and easily available source of water to most of these trades is clear.

The 1500s were a difficult time for the administration of the town giving rise to three surveys, the most comprehensive of which, that of 1553, was only 're-discovered' in the 1880s and formed the basis for a conjectural map compiled by William Bickley, who translated the document, and Joseph Hill, who wrote copious background notes to accompany the publication of the survey (Bickley and Hill 1891). While the precise location of some of the holdings outlined on the map has been questioned and further corroborative evidence is often desirable, nevertheless certain general points may be inferred from the 1553 survey with reasonable confidence.

By 1553, Edgbaston Street was certainly one of the more heavily developed streets in Birmingham, along with High Street, Corn Cheaping, Well Street (Upper Digbeth), and the Shambles in the market place. Most of the property in Edgbaston Street was held as free burgages, and some important families were represented who also owned other property around the town. These included the Holt (Holte) family, later of Aston Hall, who also held the Malt Mill, William Phillips (Phillippes, an ancestor of the Inges according to Hill), William Booth (Bothe, a knight), and Richard Wythal (who was probably a tanner).

As late as the early 19th century the limits of the town here were probably much the same as in medieval times. The Manorial Moat, Parsonage Moat and their associated watercourses still formed the southern boundary of the town. Throughout most of the 18th century the view from here remained overwhelmingly rural. Nearest the town were gardens and small enclosures, some of which were used as drying grounds by hide curers (note the 'gibbet-like' posts depicted on Westley's view of 1732, see Fig. 2.2), and others contained osier pits where willow was soaked to make it supple for basket weaving. Beyond these were larger fields and enclosures that were once part of the Holme Park, which stretched from the Manor House down to water meadows by the banks of the River Rea.

By the time of Ackerman's panoramic view of 1847 the block from Edgbaston Street to Bromsgrove Street had been fully developed (see Fig. 16.8). The oblique line of Smithfield Passage, which follows the line of the old watercourse, is still clear, although fronted on both sides by buildings.

Development up to the 18th century was hindered partly by the restrictive policies of the landowners involved. Dr Sherlock, Bishop of London (1678–1761), even went so far as to debar his successors from granting building leases by the terms of his last will and testament. This was because he thought that 'his land was valuable, and if built upon, his successor at the extirpation of the term would only have the rubbish to carry off'. It took an Act of Parliament sponsored by one of Sherlock's successors, Sir Thomas Gooch, to overcome this bar on development in 1766. However, a greater hindrance was probably the rather waterlogged nature of this area and the availability and development of more desirable land elsewhere in the town centre (pers. comm. Toni Demidowicz).

In 1731 the only development to the southwest of the Lord of the Manor's Moat was a group of what appear to be farm buildings. However, this began to change once Sir Thomas Gooch, a major landowner, whose estates extended south from Edgbaston Street into the area which had been medieval parkland, was granted an Act of Parliament in which he was given permission to cut streets from his estate and lease out parcels of land. The fairly immediate outcome of this was the construction of Jamaica Row and Moat Row to the southeast and southwest of the Lord of the Manor's Moat. This development was of mixed use comprising domestic retail and industrial buildings and is shown on Hanson's map of 1778 (Fig. 2.3). However, development to the south of the Edgbaston Street backplots, beyond the watercourse, was minimal other than the division of land into garden plots. Clearly, as Birmingham expanded and burgeoned, there was a ready market for fresh garden produce in her markets. The situation still more or less pertained in the early 19th century, since Sherriff's map of 1808 (Fig. 2.4) shows the area to be still predominantly gardens and

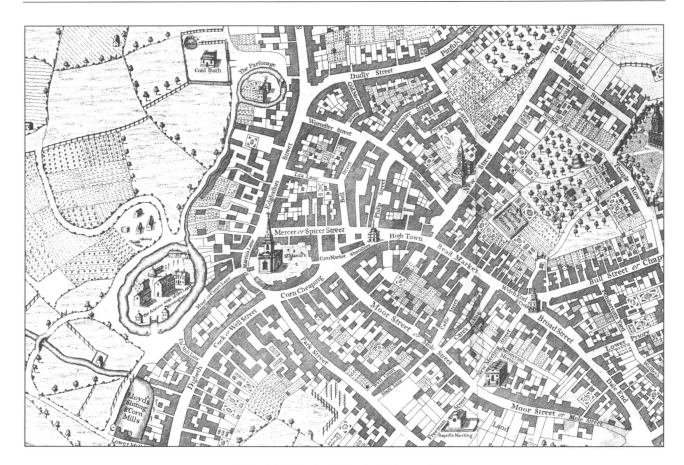

Fig. 2.2 Detail of Westley's Map 1731.

osier beds. By the mid- to late 1820s this area was becoming built up.

During the 18th century several trades are listed in the Birmingham directories for Edgbaston Street. Sketchley's 1770 Directory indicates several butchers, a skinner, a fellmonger and leather workers, button makers, various shop keepers including ironmongers, grocers and drapers, tailors and peruke makers, a basket maker and several publicans. Unlike Park Street, metal-working trades such as smithing and brass founding were not well represented – in fact only one smith is listed on the whole street (pers. comm. Stephanie Rátkai). An apothecary and a surgeon, an attorney and an excise officer were also listed for Edgbaston Street along with several merchants, including Sampson Lloyd who had originally owned No. 18 Park Street (see Litherland and Rátkai, Chapter 4). The Edgbaston Street site included or adjoined the site of Hawkers glassworks which was built in 1777–8. The glassworks had gone by 1786–7, although Glasshouse Court is marked on Sheriff's Map of 1808 (Fig 2.4). Documentary evidence from 18th- and 19th-century rate books (pers. comm. Toni Demidowicz) suggests that in more or less the same area as the Edgbaston Street excavations was a large holding under single proprietorship until the late 17th century. This holding was subsequently multiply sub-let, several lessees being

skinners. At some point, probably in the late 18th century, the Welch family, also skinners (although termed 'leather dressers' in the 1808 Directory: pers. comm. Toni Demidowicz), managed to appropriate a large holding here, which is shown on Sherriff's map of 1808 as Welch's Skinyard. The term skinyard could be used for a variety of processes (see below).

Development continued during the 19th century, and it was at this time that the watercourses were culverted and these and other remnants of the medieval townscape disappeared. The driving force behind this was the rapid rise in the population of the town, which rocketed from around 23,000 in 1731 to around 170,000 in 1831. In 1815 the Manorial Moat was sold by Thomas Gooch to the town commissioners, the buildings were rapidly demolished (including the associated thread mill, once the Malt Mill, in Upper Mill Lane) and the moat filled in. Following a short construction programme, the Smithfield Market opened on the 5th of April 1817 for the sale of cattle, horses, sheep and pigs. A decade later the Parsonage Moat also disappeared under a turnpike road connecting Worcester Street and Bromsgrove Street, which is now called Pershore Street. A contemporary map (not illustrated here) shows how the new street cut through the southeast corner of 'Reverend Curtis' St Martin's Parsonage'. Property deeds of the 1830s and

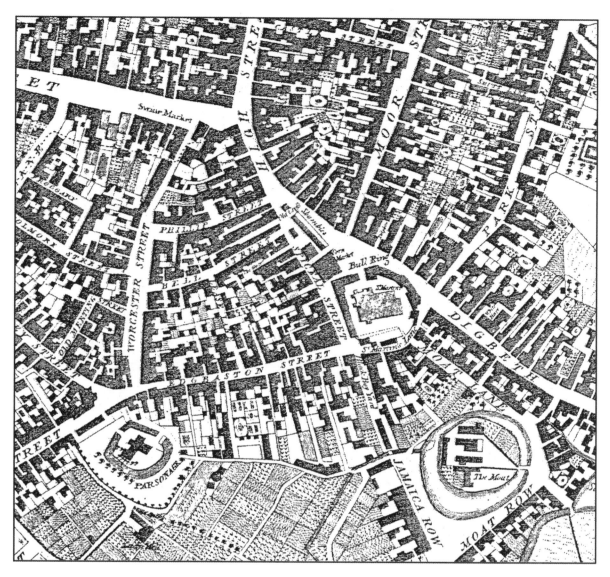

Fig. 2.3 Detail of Hanson's Map 1778.

1840s describe the subsequent build up of structures along the newly created street frontage. At some point between the mid-1820s and the mid-1830s Gloucester Street, running south from Edgbaston Street, close to and more or less parallel with Jamaica Row, was constructed. By the time of Jobbins' 1838 map, Gloucester Street was in place and the southern Edgbaston Street backplots had been cleared of buildings and replaced by narrow ribbon-like developments along the southern street frontage and along the north side of Smithfield Passage (pers. comm. Stephanie Rátkai).

Development of the Gooch estate in this vicinity continued into the 1830s and 1840s and became the home of a vibrant and diverse multi-skilled population working around the market in associated trades and in the growing industry of 'Birmingham Toys'. Aspects of the documented history of these working-class people and their housing have been intensively studied as part of the

conservation of the 'back-to-backs' on Hurst and Inge Street near by (Demidowicz 1994).

This speculative early Victorian development can be contrasted with the large Queen Anne and Georgian houses that continued to line Edgbaston Street. An advertisement from 1765 (Aris Gazette) described one of the houses, probably of this period, as a

handsome large commodious house, consisting of a large warehouse with a counting house behind it, two good parlours, a hall, two staircases, a china pantry, three large chambers, each having light and dark closet, many of each of them large enough to hold a bed, a spacious dining room, wainscoted, six good upper chambers with closets, a kitchen, pantry, four large cellars in one of which is a pump, a brewhouse with a pump, and an oven to bake bread, a good stable with a loft over it, a coach house and a large garden, with a canal, and other conveniences thereto belonging...

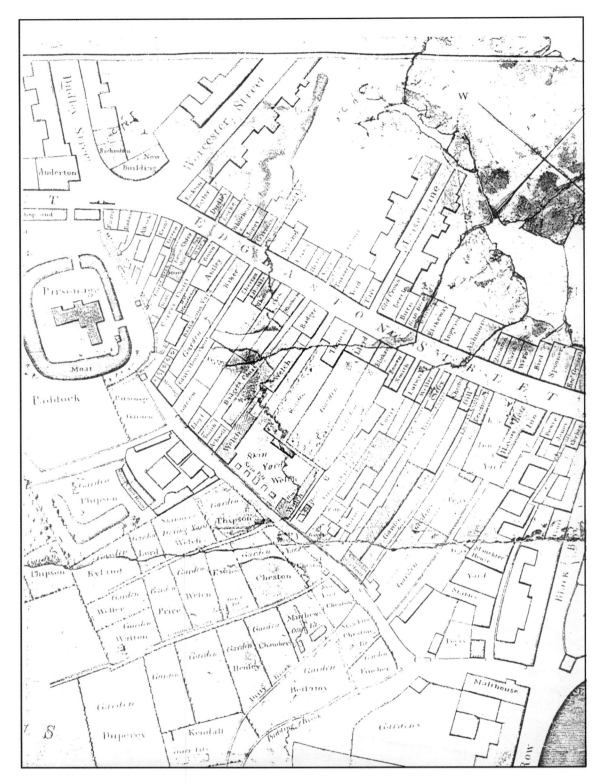

Fig. 2.4 Detail of Sheriff's Map 1808.

One of the party walls of a house of this period survived adjacent to Gloucester Street until the latest development and provided useful information about potential archaeological survival along the Edgbaston Street frontage, which was proved by the excavation of Area A where several medieval features had survived. The status of Edgbaston Street increasingly declined during the 19th century; the large houses were subdivided and came to resemble in character the other properties in the vicinity of the market, which were clearly working class. However this decline also reflects a general trend witnessed at Park St for the 'middle classes' to move out of the Bull Ring area to new developments such as Old Square and Colmore Row (pers. comm. Toni Demidowicz) and later in the late 18th–early 19th centuries into the suburbs. This period marks the beginnings of the break from home and work being interrelated or interdependent, as it had been from the medieval period onwards, towards the division between home and the workplace. This process was however piecemeal (see Cattell *et al.* 2002, 23), with family concerns and small workshops still in evidence alongside small-scale concerns carried on in the courts, essentially one-man operations, and purely domestic occupation. This pattern is perhaps most famously seen in the Jewellery Quarter, Birmingham (Cattell *et al.* 2002).

Another reason for change was the massive growth of the urban population in the 19th century, associated with social changes brought about by the Industrial Revolution. The urban poor were forced to live in unsanitary, and often old, properties commonly situated in courts built behind the more substantial properties lining the street frontages. This situation only began to be seriously addressed during Joseph Chamberlain's leadership of the Town Council, which corresponded with broader changes in the economic shape of Birmingham, particularly brought about by enhanced rail links. These firmly established the status of the 19th-century wholesale markets situated over the former Birmingham Moat, which continued to grow both in size and importance throughout the 19th century. Later, in the 20th century, the markets suffered set-backs associated with changes in the economic infrastructure of the country as a whole, and in addition they suffered from bomb damage during the war. The overall effect was such that by the late 1950s, when the economy began to expand again, the area as a whole was ripe for extensive redevelopment. Smallbrook Queensway became a crucial element of the Inner City Ring Road, while Edgbaston Street was downgraded further, essentially performing the modern function of a medieval back lane servicing the 1960s Bull Ring Shopping Centre. The wholesale markets, with one of the first grants of European Economic Community Regional Aid, were one of the last parts of the general market complex to be redeveloped in the 1970s, and it was during this work that archaeological investigations on the Lord of the Manor's Moat took place (Watts 1980).

Excavation results

Phase 1: 12th–14th centuries

The original ground level sloped down southwards from Edgbaston Street, following the natural gradient of the sandstone ridge on which the town was established. Erosion of the soft sandstone produced deposits of soft sand and pebbles at the southern end of Areas A and B. Relatively thin patches of waterlogged organic material overlying the subsoil in Area C suggested that this area was substantially drier than Area D to the south. The presence of a tree bole (F352) suggested a former wooded landscape. In Area D the ground was wet, with patches of marshy ground. The area seems originally to have been wooded, as is evidenced by a number of tree boles. This interpretation is supported by the results of analysis of the plant macroremains and pollen (see Ciaraldi, Chapter 12, and Greig, Chapter 13).

Area A (Fig. 2.5, 2.6 colour & 2.7)
Area A lay towards the Edgbaston Street frontage. In the central third of Area A the subsoil (1002) was overlaid by a thin silt-sand layer (1074). A concentration of features survived against the eastern edge of the excavation area. A square pit (F123) had a recut (F105) and a smaller square cut at its base (F149) (Figs 2.5, 2.6 colour & 2.7; Fig. 2.8, S1). The sides of the pit were vertically cut, with no slumping, which suggests that it may originally have been lined.

The insect fauna and pollen remains associated with the fills 1011 and 1012 (see Fig. 2.8, S1) of this pit are informative (see Greig, Chapter 13, and Smith, Chapter 14). The insect fauna is typical of human settlement, but also includes species that are associated with decaying prepared timbers – strengthening the conjecture that the pit was originally wood-lined. Smith (*ibid.*) suggests that the pit held mouldering vegetation as well as decaying timbers, which could be consistent with a period of abandonment. Both the insect fauna and pollen suggest that the pit periodically served as a water cistern or tank. The high percentage of woodland pollen – which is unusual for an occupied site – might be accounted for by this pollen having been brought in with the timber for the lining, although Greig also suggests that it might be the result of a period of abandonment. The pollen analysis also showed the presence of grassland; the large numbers of bracken spores present may have resulted from the use of bracken for animal bedding.

In addition to a stone roof tile, the fills of the pit recut (F105) contained a substantial quantity of medieval pottery. The uppermost infilling (1010) contained an almost complete straight-sided cooking pot (Fig. 2.9, colour; Fig. 7.1.19), which may not have been a discard but may have been deliberately placed in the pit for an unknown function (see Rátkai, Chapter 7). The pottery evidence suggests that the pit was backfilled in the 13th century, possibly before *c.*1250.

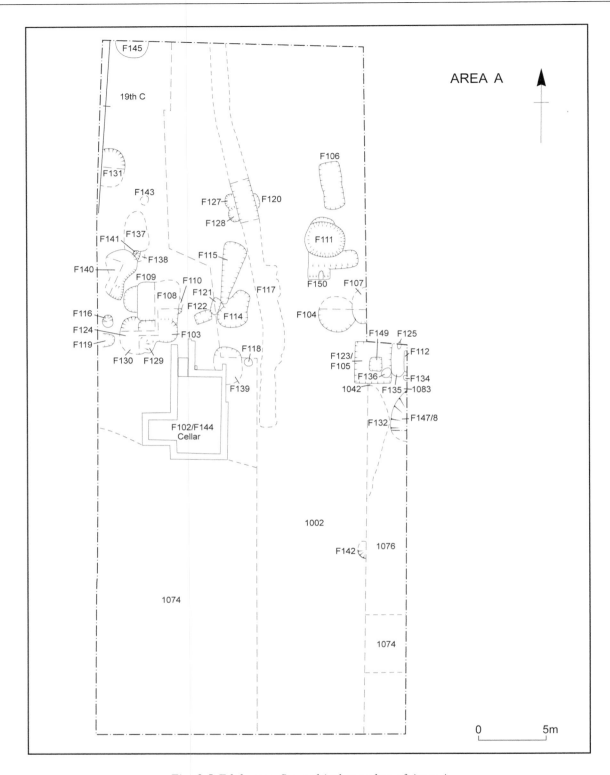

Fig. 2.5 Edgbaston St: multi-phase plan of Area A.

Immediately to the east of the square pit, one half of a steeply cut sub-circular pit (F147), which again had a recut (F148), was recorded. The ceramic evidence suggests that this pit was early, with backfilling possibly occurring in the late 12th century but certainly before the

mid-13th century. The recut F148 contained no finds. A series of three post-holes or possibly small pits (F134, F135 and F136) was aligned east-west. All of these features cut into a charcoal-flecked sandy silt layer (1042). A further four post-holes (F118, F121, F142 and

Fig. 2.7 Area A; phase plans.

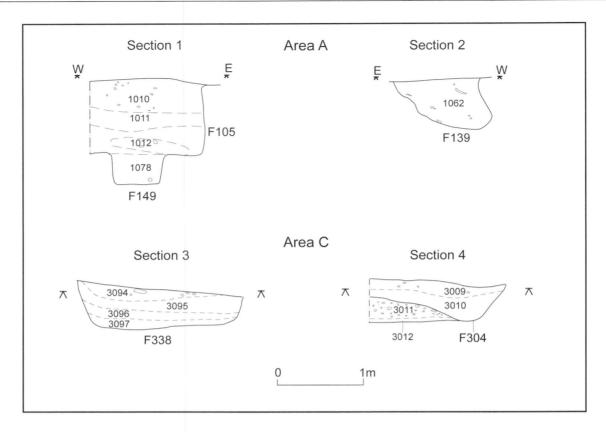

Fig. 2.8 Area A and Area C sections.

F143) were recorded across the excavation area. Post-hole F121 to the east of F110 contained two cooking pot sherds in Fabric cpj1 and cpj12 (Fig. 7.6.126) and F143, a small chip of reduced Deritend ware.

Towards the western boundary, an oven (F109) survived as a clay-lined cut with a tile floor (Fig. 2.10, colour). A clay 'plug' was located near the base of the oven. The absence of charcoal and the presence of an unburnt clay lining completely covering the tiles suggests that the oven may not have been used. However, the upper backfill (1023) did contain a quantity of heat-shattered stones. Pottery comprised two whiteware jug sherds and two sherds from an iron-poor jug (Fabric ip8) which may be later medieval in date. Two fragments of worked bone, probably an offcut from the manufacture of knife plates (Bevan *et. al.*, Chapter 8), were recovered from one of the oven's fills (1028). However, bone-working debris was mainly confined to Phase 3 pits and the examples from F109 may therefore be intrusive. A second clay-lined feature (F110) may have been related to the oven (F109), but its only partial survival prevents further comparison and there were no finds from its fill.

Area B (Figs 2.11, colour & 2.12–2.16)
Area B was situated immediately to the north of Smithfield Passage adjacent to Pershore Street (see Fig. 2.1). The survival of Phase 1 activity extended over a large part of the area (see Fig. 2.11, colour and Fig.

2.12). A brown organic clay-silt occupation horizon overlay the subsoil. Towards the southern edge of the area, the orange gravel-sand subsoil (2247) was overlaid by bands of water-deposited sand (2017, 2018 and 2036). These may represent the continuation southeast of an early – partially silted-up – water channel (recorded as F213, F255 and F256; see Fig. 2.13), which fed into the larger watercourse linking the Lord of the Manor's Moat with Parsonage Moat. The water channel had a rounded profile and appeared to be a natural feature. The insect fauna from 2036 suggest that the water channel was filled with decaying settlement waste. Pottery was only found in F256 and dated to the 13th century. Interestingly, sherds from the same vessel were found in the water channel and in one of the tanning pits (F229), providing a link between this water source and its use in the tanning industry.

Extending north from the water channel and water-course was a small number of tanning pits (F224, F226, F227, F228, Fig. 2.14, S1 and F218/ F232, F229 and F233, Fig. 2.11). These were large, rectangular features measuring up to 5m in length and 0.80m in depth which were variously wood-lined, clay-lined, or simply cut into the subsoil. One of the pits (F224) had the remains of a wooden beam at its base. A number had stake-holes associated with them. The majority of tannery remains were contained within one plot of land – the limits of which were still bounded by Phase 3 brick walls.

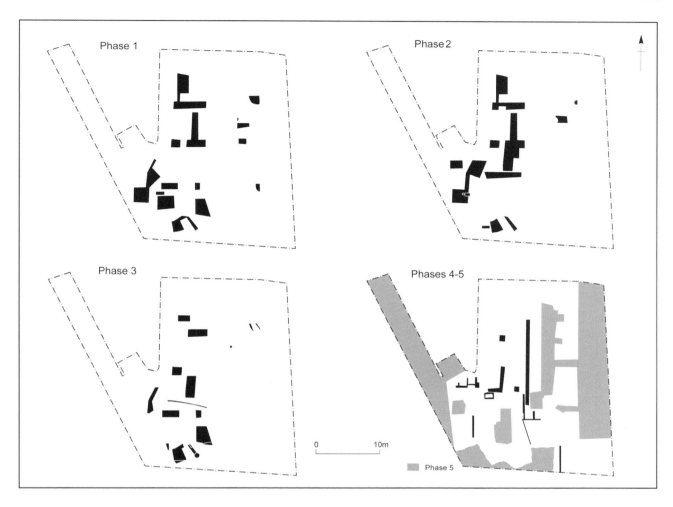

Fig. 2.12 Area B; phase plans.

The plant macroremains and insect fauna from pit F218/ F232 confirm that water from the nearby watercourse was being used to fill the tanning pits. The presence of bark scleroids – which are consistent with the production of tanning liquor – and of 'bark beetles' associated with bark or timber attests to the presence of the tanning industry. The recovery of fragments of decomposed leather also demonstrates this material's contemporary production (see Ciaraldi, Chapter 12, and Smith, Chapter 14). The range of insect fauna suggests that the pits would have remained open for a long period of time which is in line with the tannery continuing in use to Phase 3.

Further Phase 1 survival was recorded in a second plot of land to the east (see Fig. 2.12), including a large rectangular-shaped tanning pit (F237) and a cluster of features represented by an east-west aligned V-shaped gully (F265), its recut (F270) and a steeply cut subcircular pit (F266), shown on Fig. 2.15, S1 and Fig. 2.16. Neither F265 nor F270 contained pottery but the clay-silt backfill of F270 contained leather offcuts. F266 contained three medieval cooking pot sherds. Insect fauna from the

gully (F265) and pit (F266) was characteristic of human settlement and associated rotting waste.

Three pits (F267–F269) were recorded at the eastern limit of the excavated area (Fig. 2.12). Two of the pits (F267 and F268) were sealed by a thin layer of grey sand-silt (2230) before being cut by the third larger pit (F269). None of these contexts contained pottery or other artefacts apart from F268, which contained four sherds of pottery unlikely to be later than the 13th century. These comprised a mudstone-tempered ware jug sherd with roller stamp decoration and three cooking pots sherds (Fabric cpj1).

Area C (Figs 2.17, 2.18 colour & 2.19)
A cluster of three features – a north-south aligned gully (F350), a small pit (F352) and a larger pit (F351) – survived against the northern edge of the excavated area (Fig. 2.17; Fig. 2.18, colour and Fig. 2.19). The gully (F350) was filled with a fine grey-silt (3151) and was cut by the larger pit (F351). The truncated remains of three more pits (F306–F308) were recorded in section only. A whetstone or rubbing stone was recovered from the fill of

Fig. 2.13 Area B; photograph showing location of sections and major features, Phase 1.

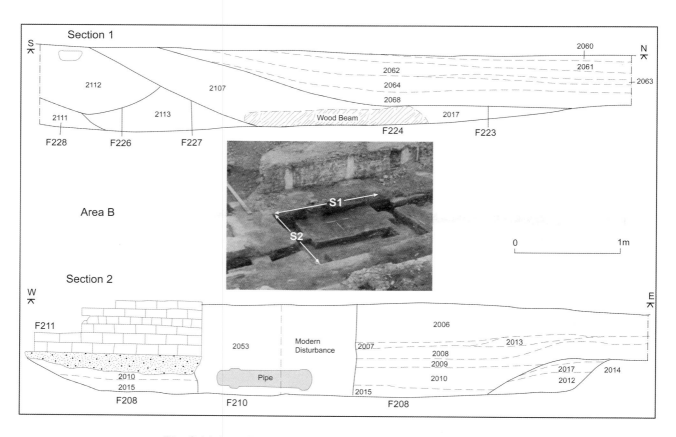

Fig. 2.14 Area B; section of F224, Phase 1 and F208, Phase 2.

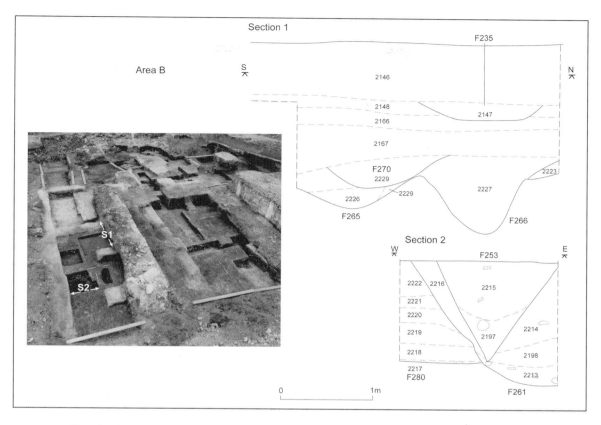

Fig. 2.15 Area B; section of F266, showing associated features, and of ditch F253.

Fig. 2.16 Area B; Phase 1 features, F265 and F266.

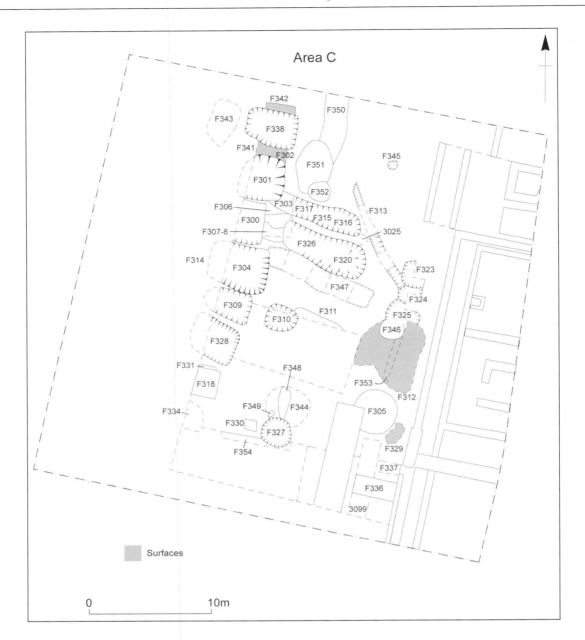

Fig. 2.17 Area C; multi-phase plan.

pit F308. A thin occupation layer (3025) and an organic layer (3115, 3165) were recorded 2m to the south. A shallow rectangular pit (F348) and a post-hole (F349) survived to the west of a Phase 3 well (F327).

Area D (not illustrated)
A tree bole (F426) and two peaty, organic layers overlying the subsoil (recorded as 4031, 4032, 4049 and 4050) represent the earliest remains in this area. There were no artefactual finds from these layers and it is possible that these organic layers pre-date the Phase 1 establishment of the town. Charcoal and whipworm, indicators of human habitation, for example, do not appear until the

middle sample in the monolith. The plant macroremains and pollen analysis show that this area was characterised by some woodland cover and wetland vegetation, although the insect fauna is more characteristic of open and disturbed land. There is clear evidence that this was a marshy area with pools of shallow water and that the area was subject to periodic flooding up to and including the first part of Phase 3. The presence of parasites in the pollen samples and specific species of insect fauna associated with settlement waste attests to a low level of human activity within the area.

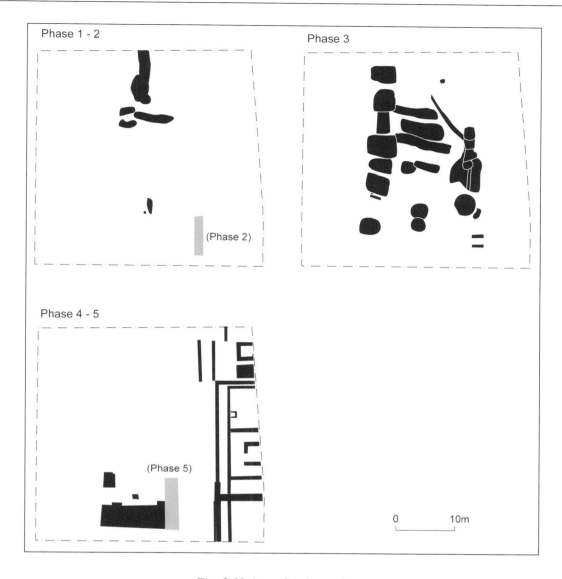

Fig. 2.19 Area C; phase plans.

Transects A–D (Fig. 2.1)

A watercourse ran northwest-southeast across this area joining Parsonage Moat with the Lord of the Manor's Moat (see Fig. 1.2). Unlike channel F213/ F255/ F256 in Area B (see above), the watercourse had a flat base and straight sides suggesting that it had been a deliberate construction, probably regulating the course of a pre-existing natural watercourse or spring. Phase 1 primary and lower fills were represented by waterlogged, peaty deposits and gleyed black clays contexts (5043), (5051), (5110), (5401) and (5402). These were sampled extensively for waterlogged plant remains, pollen and insect remains (see Ciaraldi, Chapter 12; Greig, Chapter 13; Smith, Chapter 14) which suggest that the watercourse was free, but slow-flowing, possibly due to the reed beds and aquatic plants which were also recorded. The presence of a few trees was noted and this is supported by the evidence of tree boles in the adjacent excavated areas.

The watercourse was adjacent to an open landscape with some hedgerows in Phase 1 and it is likely that this represents the backplots extending from Edgbaston Street and the open land to the south of the watercourse. The insect fauna gives a strong indication that animals were being kept on this land, supporting the suggestion that land at Edgbaston Street served as a stocking yard to rest and water animals prior to their sale at the Bull Ring market.

The insect fauna is characteristic of dense urban settlement, whilst specific human activity in this phase is indicated by the presence of cereals and hemp, which was used for making rope and canvas. Some sewage and urban contamination of the watercourse is also suggested by the pollen and insect fauna remains – the occupants of Edgbaston Street were not averse to throwing their household waste into the nearby watercourse.

Phase 2: 15th–16th centuries

Area A (Figs 2.5, 2.6 colour & 2.7)

In Area A, the only evidence of Phase 2 activity was a discrete layer (1083) against the eastern edge of the site, close to the Phase 1 pit and recut (F123 and F105, see Figs 2.5 and 2.6, colour). That there was some activity in this phase is evidenced by Phase 2 pottery found residually in Phase 3 contexts. This formed a minimum of 15% of the Phase 3 pottery. This may indicate that activity concentrated more towards the street frontage, evidence for which has been lost through later development. Alternatively, the plot could have been temporarily abandoned or the focus could have shifted to more industrial concerns at the back end of the plot, like those witnessed in Area B.

Area B (Figs 2.20–2.23)

The tannery established in Phase 1 continued in use throughout Phase 2, incorporating a number of tanning pits, most of which can be seen on Fig. 2.20 (F208, F209, F214, F217, F223, F230 and F279). Although the pits were cleared out at intervals, the entire contents of the pits were not always removed, resulting in multi-phase pit fills in some instances. A clay lining was recorded for two of the pits (F214 and F223). The wooden lining of F208 partially survived on its southern edge (see Figs

2.21 and 2.22, and Fig. 2.14, S2). Tanning pit F214 also had two stake-holes (F219 and F220) on its eastern edge, whilst tanning pit F279 had three (F276–F278, see Fig. 2.23).

Finds from the pits and associated fills offer glimpses of the various activities occurring on and around the area. The recovery of perinatal and unweened calves and of perinatal sheep from pits F214, F223 and layer 2196 suggests that livestock were kept on the site. Pit F208 contained a whetstone (see Fig. 8.12.2), which was broken at one end but which had a carved and decorated terminal at the other, possibly dating to the 15th century (see Bevan and Ixer, Chapter 8). The fill of this pit contains mainly early Phase 3 pottery, although there is some Phase 2 material in it and there is no reason why pit F208 could not have been dug in Phase 2 and continued in use through to Phase 3. The upper fill of pit F214 contained a fragment of seam *i.e.* a small strip of leather with stitching holes (see Macey-Bracken and Mould, Chapter 8). A palmate antler tine and an oyster shell fragment were also recovered from this pit and leather offcuts were found in F217.

Activity on either side of the tannery was limited. Only three other features, a pit (F222), a post-hole (F221) and a 1m-deep north-south aligned linear (F254), which heavily truncated the earlier Phase 1 water channel, were

Fig. 2.20 Area B; photograph illustrating major Phase 2 features and sections.

Fig. 2.21 Area B; Phase 2 tanning pit F208.

recorded to the west. Pit F222 contained two sherds from a coarseware jar of later 16th- or early 17th-century date. Pottery from the linear was probably more or less contemporary with that from F222. Some interesting ceramic evidence, including drinking vessels, and vessels for storage and food preparation (see Rátkai, Chapter 7), was recovered from a series of layers recorded across Area B including 2035, which sealed the backfill of tanning pit F214.

Area C (Figs 2.17 & 2.18 colour)
Phase 2 activity is limited to a single occupation layer (3099; see Figs 2.17 and 2.18, colour) at the southern limit of the excavation area – immediately to the north of the watercourse. This layer contained three quite large sherds from a cooking pot (Fig. 7.5.117), a reduced Deritend ware cooking pot, and a late oxidised ware jug (Fig. 7.7.147).

Area D
No Phase 2 activity was recorded in this area, although two late oxidised sherds were recovered from the machining layer 4019.

Transects A–D
No Phase 2 activity was recorded in this area.

Fig. 2.22 Area B; Phase 2 tanning pit F208 showing surviving wooden lining.

Fig. 2.23 Area B; Phase 2 plan detail showing drainage gullies (F239 to F242) and tanning pit (F280).

Phase 3: 17th–18th centuries

Area A (Figs 2.5–2.8, Fig. 2.24, colour)

Phase 3 is characterised by a concentration of intercutting sub-rectangular steep-sided and bell-shaped pits (F103, F106, F108, F119, F120, F122, F124, F127–F131, F137–F141 and F145; *e.g.* see Fig. 2.24, colour), along with a feature which, from its form, is identified as a kiln (F114/F115), and two post-holes (F116 and F125) in the northern half of Area A (see Fig. 2.5). One of the pits (F141) had the remains of a wooden stake *in situ*, another (F129) contained part of a 17th-century glass beaker base (Orton and Rátkai, Chapter 8, Fig. 8.3.4), another (F108) contained fragments of two possible marble floor tiles or facing stones which may be intrusive (see Bevan and Ixer, Chapter 8), whilst four others (F120, F127, F128 and F145) had a concentration of tiles within their fills. The fill of pit F139 (see Fig. 2.8, S2) included a glazed crested ridge tile. These bell-shaped pits find a parallel in the concave pits at Park St (see Burrows *et al.*, Chapter 4) and are thought to have an industrial use possibly associated with metal working. The similar nature of all the feature backfills – a grey-black, charcoal-flecked silt-

sand with mortar and brick fragments – suggests not only building demolition but also a deliberate large-scale backfilling event and reorganisation of the area. The pottery, clay pipe and vessel glass seem to indicate that all this backfilling took place in the early 18th century, after which a 'dark earth' or 'cultivation soil' (1005) and (1076) built up across the site, covering Area A, possibly indicating that the plot was used for market gardening. This coincides with documented changes in landowner-ship (see historical profile, above). Similar soil horizons have also been recorded in Phase 3 contexts at Moor Street (see Burrows *et al.*, Chapter 3) and Park Street (see Burrows *et al.*, Chapter 4), and also at Wrottesley Street (Jones 2000) and Upper Dean Street (Martin and Rátkai 2005), although these soils were not all con-temporaneous or necessarily cultivation soils (see Rátkai, Chapter 7).

Area B (Figs 2.25–2.27)

The tannery continued to be used, and expanded again during this phase, with additional pits being cut (*e.g.* F203, Fig. 2.25, and F234, F235, F249 and F262, Fig. 2.26). One of these, a shallow circular pit (F235, see Fig.

Fig. 2.25 Area B; Phase 3 tanning pit F203.

Fig. 2.26 Area B; photograph illustrating major Phase 3 features and sections.

2.15, S1) was filled with lime. This could have been where quicklime (calcium oxide) was 'slaked' with water to produce hydrated lime (calcium hydroxide), employed in the pre-tanning process. Slaking produces heat and the process must be completed and the lime suspension thoroughly cooled before it is added to the unhairing liquors (pers. comm. Roy Thomson). The fact that pit F235 was full of lime suggests that this process had not yet been attempted in this case. A second feature containing lime was recorded in the southwestern corner of Area B (F200) Fig. 2.27. This wood-lined pit, or possibly a sunken wooden barrel, was located close to the Moat watercourse and had a wooden lid preserved *in situ*. The pottery and clay pipe evidence suggest that this feature went out of use in the third quarter of the 17th century (see Rátkai, Chapter 7). A square pit (F202) and layer 2003 (from which a significant group of pottery was recovered) were located close to pit F200.

Another area within the southern third of the excavation, and which was better preserved in plan, revealed a sequence of slots (F239, F240, F241, F242, F243 and a drain F281) which appeared to channel water, or liquid, from one area of the tannery into a large tanning pit (F275) (Fig. 2.23). Four stake-holes (F271–F274) were cut into the fill of this pit. A small amount of medieval pottery was recovered from tanning pit F275 and slot F241. Drain F281 (also Fig. 2.23), however, contained a good group of post-medieval pottery in its upper fills,

comprising coarseware bowls and jars, blackware drinking vessels and a chafing dish. Three medieval sherds were recorded in the lowest fill.

To the east of the main tanning activity area was a large flat-based pit (F280; see Fig. 2.15, S2) which may have had a clay lining (2217). The lining contained a small amount of redeposited Phase 2 pottery, although the fill material was Phase 3. Large quantities of preserved wood and leather offcuts, including one fragment of a shoe (2219), were found in its backfill. A large sub-circular pit (F261) which contained a concentration of horncores (see Baxter, Chapter 15) and several large pottery vessels, dated to the first half of the 17th century, cut F280 (see Fig. 2.26). Pit F261 was cut by a north-south aligned ditch (F253; see Fig. 2.15, S2) which contained the largest pottery group of this phase, along with large quantities of wood and cattle horncores representing tanning waste or evidence of horn working. Pottery analysis suggests that the ditch fill dates to the mid-17th century at the latest, so providing a close date for the industrial evidence of tanning or horncore working. Several of the sherds from the ditch fill were covered in mortary deposits. In addition, pottery sherds from pit F261 (Fig. 2.15, S2) had limey accretions. There may have been a possible link between ditch F253, pit F261 and the lime pit F200 further to the south, perhaps paralleled by a link in industrial processes.

Two more pits were recorded in this area (F262 and

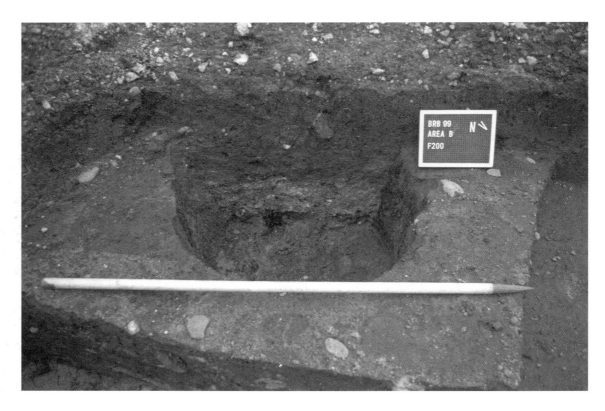

Fig. 2.27 Area B; Phase 3 lime pit F200.

F238; see Fig. 2.26). Pit F262 was heavily truncated by modern disturbance. Pit F238 was sub-circular in plan, with steep sides and a flat base. It was filled with black-brown sand silts (2163, 2164 and 2165). Contexts 2163 and 2164 contained a high percentage of charcoal. A sub-rectangular shallow scoop (F252) which had been filled with tile fragments (2191) was recorded to the south of pit F238.

Later in Phase 3 a number of the tanning pits were backfilled. As with Area A, the episode of backfilling may relate to a change in landownership and reorganisation of the property backplots. Material used for the backfill included thick deposits of leather offcuts which could be offcuts from trimming up the hides or indicate that leather working was being practised close to the tannery itself – possibly in one of the adjacent plots. Drainage appears to have been inserted (F245) and the fill of this feature contained a whetstone (see Bevan and Ixer, Chapter 8 and Fig. 8.12.1, colour).

A cultivation soil (2040), similar to that recorded in Area A, built up. In addition, a series of layers containing generally residual material were excavated across Area B (2006, 2021, 2034, 2040, 2166 and 2175). These are not illustrated.

Area C (Figs 2.17–2.19)
In contrast to earlier phases, Phase 3 saw concentrated activity in Area C with the establishment – or the extension of – a tannery or skinyard (see Figs 2.17, 2.18 colour and 2.19).

The tanning or skin-pits in Area C cut a homogeneous layer of grey charcoal-flecked silt, also referred to here as a 'cultivation soil'. Pottery evidence suggested that this layer was deposited before c.1730 in Areas A and B and marked the cessation of metal working and tanning in these areas respectively. There was little pottery in the backfills of the tan/ skin-pits (see Rátkai, Chapter 7) and what there was seems to date to no later than the first quarter of the 18th century. The clay pipe was of a similar date range. However, some pottery post-dating c.1750 was found in water channel F336, well F305 and pit F345 (Fig. 2.17). The pottery in F336 is perhaps the most significant since it suggests that the water channel was out of use by the late 18th century. It is therefore possible that the disuse of the channel marks another reorganisation of the tan- or skinyard, the date of which would roughly coincide with the establishment of Welch's Skinyard. If this is so, then the industrial activity represented by the features in Area C would seem to run from c.1730–c.1780/90. During this time very little in the way of contemporary refuse was being deposited here, not altogether surprisingly, and most of the pottery found in the area must be residual.

There was extensive survival of a cobble tanning yard (F312 and F329), clinker surfaces (F341 and F342), pits (F300–F304, F309–F311, F315–F317, F320, F323–F326, F328, F330–F331, F333, F334, F338, F343, F344, F346

and F347), a gully (F313), linear features (F336 and F337), two wells (F305 and F327), and building foundations (F353 and F354; see Figs 2.17, 2.18 colour and 2.19). The latter foundations were obscured or truncated by later activity, particularly F353, the base of which was seen beneath pits F323, F324, F325 and F313 (Fig. 2.17). Pottery from F353, which included a substantial section of a dripping tray (Fig. 7.13.294), suggested a deposition date in the first half of the 17th century. The sherd size of the pottery recovered from F353 is more consistent with a destruction rather than a construction deposit.

The pits were laid out in a distinct pattern. The many recuts of the tanning pits relate to frequent emptying and refilling or extensions of their size. A sequence of eight sub-rectangular pits aligned on a north-south axis (from north to south: F338, F301, F300, F304, F309/ F314, F328, F331, F330; see Fig. 2.8, S3–4) were recorded close to the western edge of Area C. All of these pits had similar primary fills of compacted sawdust in different stages of decay (see Ciaraldi, Chapter 12). The north and south edges of pit F338 (Fig. 2.8, S3) were abutted by thin layers of clinker (F341 and F342). A similarly arranged series of wood-lined pits were excavated at Ardee Street, Dublin, dating to the late 18th–19th centuries (Linnane 2004; see Fig. 2.28). They were found to contain lenses of wood chips within the plastic clay backfill. Documentary evidence linked the pits to a tanner. Interestingly, the pits were sited near the River Poddle, in an area of marshy ground prone to flooding not unlike the situation of Area C.

Immediately to the east of this line of pits was a cluster of three east-west aligned sub-rectangular steep-sided pits (F316, F326 and F347) which had multiple recuts relating to their frequent emptying and refilling. Two of the pits (F316 and F326) had similar fills of decomposed ground wood chips and occasional leather fragments. Primary organic deposits recorded in the third pit (F347) were overlaid by cinder or clinker.

The partial skeletons of two perinatal puppies were found in pit F316, whilst a large assemblage of animal bone (cow) was recovered from the area immediately to the south of the east-west aligned pits.

Further east again was a third cluster of pits (F323–F325, F346) which were arranged in a north-south line. All of the pits had primary organic wood fills. A northwest-southeast aligned gully (F353) had a dark green organic fill and was cut by two of the pits (F323 and F324).

A single post-hole (F345) was recorded towards the northern edge of Area C and to the west, a truncated pit F303 was recorded in section only.

The tanning pits in Area B were up to 5m in length, with an average depth of 0.8m. The pits in Area C were smaller, averaging 3–4m in length, with an average depth of 0.3–0.6m. The more elongated pits in Area C were on average 7–9m in length, with depths of 0.25–0.35m. Various early and mid-19th-century textbooks suggest

Fig. 2.28 Tanning pits from Ardee St, Dublin.

tan pit dimensions of 9ft long by 7ft wide by 6ft deep (*c*.2.7m × 2.10m × 1.8m) (pers. comm. Roy Thomson) so both the Area B and Area C pits would appear to be a little larger than this but very much shallower. However, the dimensions of the smaller Area C pits seem to correspond fairly closely in terms of length and surviving depth with the dimension of pits in the Western tannery, dated late 15th–mid-16th century in Northampton (Shaw 1996). The dimensions of the pits in the Eastern Tannery at Northampton (*ibid.*), which was dated to the late 16th–17th centuries, were smaller than those from Areas B and C. The surviving depth of the tan pits is obviously affected by site taphonomy *e.g.* truncation or levelling. It is also true that the timber linings of some of the pits could have extended well above the ground surface. However, illustrations in Diderot (1772, pl. VI: '*Tanneur*', '*Travail des Fosses*'; see Fig. 2.29.3) show a tanner at work in a relatively shallow pit (the furthest left in the illustration), forming spent bark into round cakes (mottes) which were used for fuel (pers. comm. Roy Thomson).

Diderot also illustrates the initial preparation of the hides *e.g.* liming, de-fleshing (1772, pl. III; and Fig. 2.29.1), 'puering' and 'mastering' (treatments with dog and bird dung, see Clarkson 1983, 13, and Diderot 1772, pl. IV, not illustrated here), immersion in tanning liquors of various strengths (Diderot 1772, pl. IV; see Fig. 2.29.2), and the final processing of the hides in tanks known as 'handlers' (Clarkson 1983, 13–14; Diderot 1772, pl. VI; Fig. 2.29.3) where the hides were laid horizontally in tanning liquor, separated by layers of fresh

bark. With the exception of the man making 'mottes' (see above) the tanning processes all seem to involve deep pits and channels and it is the pre-tanning preparation of the hides which seems to involve smaller capacity tanks.

There are two uses for sawdust in skin processing. It can be used to clean furskins. It can also be dampened and used to re-humidify alum or chamois skins prior to softening in the staking process. However, neither of these processes would require the amount of sawdust that seems to have been found (pers. comm. Roy Thomson). This does not rule out skin or hide curing in these pits but might suggest that sawdust was also used to backfill the pits once they had gone out of use. Between Nos 40–58 Edgbaston Street (which includes the excavated sites on Edgbaston Street and an area to the east), in addition to a fellmonger and a skinner, four butchers and one carpenter (the latter two, all likely users or producers of sawdust) were listed in 1770.

By the end of the 18th century, the term 'skinyard' could be used to describe a number of operations. By the end of the 18th century the term skinner had ceased to mean only a furskin processor and a skinyard could simply mean the place were hides and skins were collected together from different butchers and abattoirs, sorted into different sizes, types and qualities, temporarily preserved by salting and then sold on to the tanners. The term skinyard could also refer to a fellmonger's premises. As well as removing wool, fellmongers often made alum or chamois leathers and would require pits to process their skins. Alum or chamois leathers had a variety of uses

Fig. 2.29 Illustrations from Diderot, showing preparation of hides and tanning processes.

including gloves and other items of clothing, corsets, purses and indoor shoes (pers. comm. Roy Thomson). It is tempting to imagine that James Colcomb 'breeches maker' of No. 49 Edgbaston Street (Sketchley's 1770 Directory) may have used such leathers.

The insect fauna recovered from the pits was broadly indicative of settlement waste. The two linears F336 and F337 towards the southeastern section of the site were cut by walls and could be recorded in a limited section only. They appeared to be aligned east-west and were interpreted as water channels and the insect fauna recovered from F337 was indicative of slow-flowing water. Evidence of waterside vegetation corroborated this interpretation.

The building associated with the tanning/ hide curing was probably located along the far eastern side of the site.

A structure which may equate to the tanning building is shown by Westley on his map of 1731 (Fig. 2.2). Heather, which was recorded in the plant macroremains and pollen record, may have been used as animal bedding material or thatch for this building, although the latter is less likely at this date. Later buildings fronting onto Gloucester Street/ Smithfield passage and possibly connected with Welch's Skinyard, which was probably established in the later 18th century, have removed all traces of any previous structure. Welch's skin-pits are shown on Sherrif's map of 1808 (Fig. 2.4) but their alignment is quite different from the ones in Area C and run roughly parallel with the Moat watercourse. Nevertheless Welch's Skinyard provides the final chapter for an industry which seems to have been practised more or less continuously from medieval times in the Edgbaston Street backplots.

Area D (Figs 2.30, colour & 2.31–2.32)
The preparation of animal skins appears to have been carried out on the southern bank of the watercourse for the first time in this phase. A sub-circular lime pit (F419), which was later recut (F421), was recorded in Area D. Pit F419 contained a number of oyster shells and also a group of metal-working finds (see Bevan *et al.*, Chapter 8). These appear to belong to the later 19th century and presumably represent contamination of F419. An apparently associated find was recovered from 2006, a cleaning layer in Area B. As the two areas are on separate sides of the watercourse, this presumably indicates that at the time of the deposition of the metal-working finds the watercourse was no longer a serious barrier.

A band of clinker (4049) to the southeast may represent an attempt to consolidate the wet ground for working on. The use of this material is paralleled in Area C (see above). Two linear gullies (F427 and F429), post-holes (F428, F431, F432), possibly representing further tanning structures set back from the southern bank of watercourse, and pits (F414, F415, F420, F422–F425) signal an increase of activity in Area D (see Figs 2.30, colour – 2.32). This reflects the wider pressure on land within the town centre in this period and the freeing up of land to the south of the Moat watercourse for development after an Act of Parliament in 1766 (see above). The various features in Area D appear on ceramic and clay pipe evidence to have gone out of use in the late 18th or early 19th centuries. If so they were very short-lived.

The wetter ground conditions on the southern side of the watercourse meant that organic material was better preserved here, with one of the gullies (F427) containing wooden 'branches' in its clay-silt fill. The second gully (F429) had been backfilled with demolition debris which included horn fragments – again suggesting the close proximity of a tanning industry.

Transects A–D (Not illustrated)
The watercourse appears to have remained free-flowing and clear of debris during this phase.

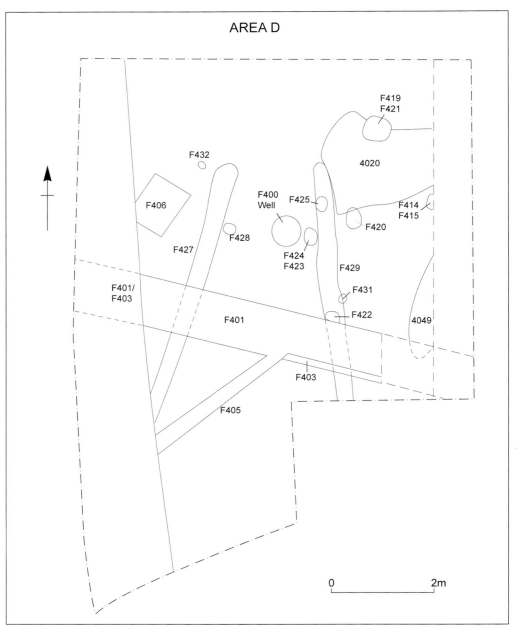

Fig. 2.31 Area D; multi-phase plan.

Phase 4: 19th century

Area A (Figs 2.5, 2.6 colour, 2.7 & 2.8)

Following the backfilling of Phase 3 features, a large north-south aligned service drain (F117) was laid in Area A (see Figs 2.5, 2.6 colour, 2.7 and 2.8). The remains of a small cellar (F102/ F144), complete with a small collection of wine and beer glasses, fragments of oyster shells and a complete cowrie shell, were recorded at the centre of the area. To the northeast, a yard surface (F150) lay adjacent to a well (F111) whose backfill included the remains of glass decanters and oyster shells. Immediately to the south was F104, a well-cut which was abandoned at a depth of 1.14m and backfilled with a single fill of red sand (1009). This feature was cut by a pit (F107). A

roughly cut linear feature (F132) and the remains of a second brick yard surface (F112) lay to the south (see Figs 2.5, 2.6 colour and 2.7).

Area B (Fig. 2.12, Fig. 2.33)

Phase 4 activity survived as a series of drainage features and north-south aligned brick-built walls. The majority of the walls followed earlier medieval property divisions (see Fig. 2.12 and Fig. 2.33).

Area C (Figs 2.17, 2.18 colour & 2.19)

A series of brick-built walls within the eastern third of Area C may have represented the foundations for the Skin House which is illustrated on Sheriff's 1808 map (Fig. 2.4). A discrete brick surface (F318) truncated one

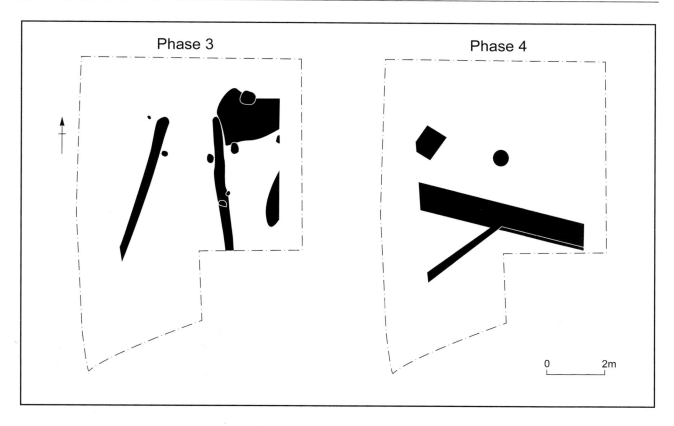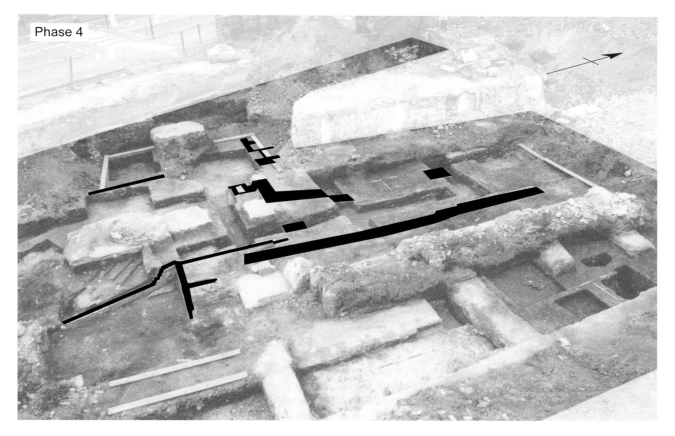

Fig. 2.32 Area D; phase plans.

Fig. 2.33 Area B; photograph of the site showing Phase 4 and 5 structural components.

of the Phase 3 tanning pits (F331) close to Smithfield Passage.

Area D (Fig. 2.31, Fig. 2.30 colour)

The area was dominated by a northwest-southeast aligned drain (F401/ F403) (Fig. 2.31 and Fig. 2.30, colour) which extended across the whole area. A smaller drain (F405) extended southwest from F401. A well (F400) was recorded at the centre of the area, with a small brick surface (F406) at the western edge of Area D. A large quantity of glass bottles was recovered from the backfill (4002) of the well, the date range of which suggests that the well was backfilled sometime around 1895 (Orton 2001).

A series of demolition layers relating to Phase 4 buildings were recorded across the area before being removed by machine. Details of these are contained in the archive.

Transects A–D (Not illustrated)

The drain seen in Area D continued across Transects A–D, with a number of smaller drains leading off to the southwest.

The Moat watercourse began to be less well maintained in this period. Pottery finds suggests that debris was beginning to accumulate from the late 18th century onwards. Watercourse fill 5202 contained a fragment of a glass-making crucible, an 18th-century suede shoe, a horn comb and clay pipe with a suggested deposition date of 1750–1790. Demolition deposits over the redundant watercourse contained large quantities of finds (see Bevan *et al.*, Chapter 8). Demolition deposits in Transect A were dated to the 19th century by leather waste and shoes and by pottery. Transect B demolition was dated to the early 19th century by the pottery and to *c*.1810–1850 by the clay pipe and Transect D demolition deposits were dated to the 18th century by the pottery and to 1750–1850 by the clay pipe. Piggot-Smith's 1824/1825 map shows the layout of the southern side of Edgbaston Street to have been much the same as in the preceding century. However J. R. Jobbin's map of 1838 (dedicated to the Directors of the London and Birmingham Railway Company) shows a very different picture: apart from a narrow line of buildings along Edgbaston Street and a similar narrow line of buildings running along the north of what was to become Smithfield Passage, the backplots to the south of Edgbaston Street are completely devoid of buildings. It seems likely therefore that the destruction and removal of these buildings was the source of the demolition rubble noted across the Transects and Trench 5. The artefactual evidence would seem to support this.

Industrial waste associated with the transects comprised glass-making crucibles from Transect B and glass-blowing moiles, crucibles and cullet from a backfilled well in Transect A. Shell button-making debris was also recovered from the well. The well fills contained pottery of 18th- and early 19th-century date. Clay pipe fragments suggested a broad deposition date of *c*.1780–1880 and fragments of Welsh roof slates suggested later 19th-century material in the well. A brick culvert in Transect

A had a lower fill (5108) dated to *c*.1820–1850 by clay pipe and the upper fill to *c*.1850–1890 by clay pipe and to the post-1830s by the pottery.

Phase 5: 20th century

The majority of Phase 5 features and deposits were removed from all areas by machine to enable investigation of earlier levels. These included the tarmac car park surface and occasional concrete floor slabs. The exceptions were in Trench 1 where extensive cellaring had erased any earlier archaeological deposits relating to Parsonage Moat, in the southern quarter of Area A where terracing had removed traces of earlier activity, and in Area B where substantial concrete pile foundations and wall foundations were left *in situ* to preserve the surviving archaeology around them.

Discussion

Late 19th-century and subsequent construction along the Edgbaston Street frontage, along with terracing of the ground levels further downslope towards the watercourse, had erased all archaeological deposits at the northern end of Area A and in the centre of the site. These areas apart, survival across the Edgbaston Street site was extensive. Phase 4 and 5 construction had a lesser impact on the archaeological record than originally anticipated, with property boundaries following earlier Phase 1 and 2 lines, so preserving the medieval deposits between them. Even where concrete pile foundations had been used in Area B, archaeology survived on all sides.

No prehistoric, Roman or Anglo-Saxon (early medieval, pre-Conquest) features were identified. A single prehistoric scraper was found (see Bevan, Chapter 6), but no artefacts dating to the Roman or early medieval periods were recovered.

It is clear from the excavated record and from the plant macroremains, pollen and insect faunas, that this was originally a wooded landscape that had been partially cleared by the 11th–12th century when the heart of the town was established. Some areas, such as to the south of the watercourse, which linked Parsonage Moat with the Lord of the Manor's Moat, remained partially wooded and subject to flooding up to the 17th or 18th century.

The earliest activity, Phase 1, was dated to the 12th–14th centuries, when domestic occupation, represented by pits, post-holes, and an oven, was recorded in Area A and a tannery was established further back from the street frontage in Area B. Medieval pottery was most plentiful in Areas A and B but small numbers of sherds were also recovered from Areas C and D. Since a good deal of Area A has been truncated, particularly towards the street frontage, and the remaining areas are at the extreme end of the backplots or, in the case of Area D, to the south of them, the comparatively small amount of medieval pottery need not be of any significance. Perhaps of greater significance is the near absence of medieval pottery from the Parsonage-Manor Moat watercourse, suggesting that it was regularly maintained throughout the medieval period. The almost complete absence of charred plant remains may be an indicator of a low level of domestic occupation but, like the pottery evidence above, it may just reflect the poor survival of layers and features where this material is likely to be found. Indeed, the insect fauna was characteristic of human settlement and there are also indicators that this was initially a prestigious place to live, with finds such as a glazed ridge tiles and decorated floor tile pointing to high quality housing fronting onto Edgbaston Street.

The pollen record and insect fauna for the steep-sided square pit in Area A (F123), which had a smaller square-cut at its base (F149), suggest that this feature held water – the lack of slumping and the insect fauna suggest that the sides were lined. This feature may have served as a water cistern or tank.

For a prestigious street to have a tannery sited close by is not so surprising considering the natural resources available here and the proximity of the market providing the necessary materials. Analysis of the mammal assemblage suggests that only the skins were being delivered to the site for tanning. The pollen and insect remains confirm that – as suggested in the earlier desk-based assessment – land close to the watercourse, towards the base of the slope from Edgbaston Street, had been used as pasture, or as a stocking yard. The presence of grassland pollen, which may have come from hay brought in to feed the animals or from the dung they produced whilst being kept on site, is recorded. Bracken, recorded in Area A, may have been used for animal bedding. The recovery of calf remains from Area B and the recording of several breeds of cattle further support the interpretation that livestock was kept here prior to sale at the nearby market.

The tannery was characterised by a series of tanning pits set out in regular lines within a long property which extended from the Parsonage-Manor watercourse to Edgbaston Street. The pits were either clay-lined or wood-lined. The identification of the pits in Areas B and C as tanning features was initially made during excavation on the basis of form, fill and the organised layout of the features within plots, which was comparable to known examples elsewhere in the country *e.g.* in Northampton (Shaw 1996). Plant macroremains, pollen and insect analysis has further confirmed this identification – although in the case of the Phase 3 'tannery' in Area C the identification of sawdust within the pit fills has prompted a reconsideration of the precise function of the pits (see below) and their re-interpretation as hide-curing pits. This would seem to tie in with the documentary evidence (see historical profile above) where skinyards rather than tanneries are mentioned on Edgbaston Street. Thus, although the preparation and preservation of skins and hides seems to have been a mainstay of Edgbaston Street from the medieval period until the 19th century,

the process changed from tanning to curing in the post-medieval period.

The presence of leather offcuts and the high percentage of cattle horncores in the backfill of some of the Phase 1 features suggest that tanning or leather working was being practised near by. Horncores were found, for example, both within disused tanning pits and within a layer sealing them at a late 18th–19th-century tannery in Dublin (Linnane 2004). However, as Baxter discusses (Chapter 15), with the exception of a high percentage of horncores, which are considered waste products, the mammal assemblage is not typical of one associated with tanning.

The Phase 1 tannery is one of the earliest known examples in the West Midlands. Other possible tanneries in the West Midlands were recorded at Hereford (Shoesmith 1985), Warwick (Hurst 2003), Stratford (Palmer 2003), Stafford and Newcastle-under-Lyme (Hunt and Klemperer 2003) and Brewood (Ciaraldi *et al.* 2004). None of these examples are however anything like as extensive or as securely identified as the tannery at Edgbaston Street. At Brewood, for example, the presence of bark sclereids and leather offcuts would certainly seem to indicate that tanning was taking place but there was an absence of anything resembling a tanning pit, although the report authors suggested that wooden barrels, found during excavation, may have served instead. A tanning complex was also found on Sandford Street, Lichfield (Nichol and Rátkai 2004), but this dated from the early post-medieval period and was composed of circular clay-lined pits rather than the rectangular ones found at Edgbaston Street. Perhaps the closest parallel can be found at Northampton (Shaw 1996) although the beginning of the industry at The Green was later, beginning in the later 15th century.

There had been little indication of the existence of tanneries on Edgbaston Street from the available maps and documents. The discovery of 13th- and 14th-century tanning at Edgbaston Street shows that there was a thriving industry and trade in Birmingham well before the 16th-century tanneries at Hartwell Garage (Burrows *et al.* 2000), Floodgate Street (Williams 2001) and the Custard Factory (Mould 2001a) in Digbeth and also well before Walsall's leather-working industry began to expand in the 18th century. The importance of the Edgbaston Street evidence is also enhanced by the scarcity of known medieval tanning sites within the West Midlands as a whole.

Phase 2 activity, dated to the 15th and 16th centuries, was more limited, although the reasons for this are not altogether clear (see Rátkai, Chapter 7). It was concentrated in Area B, with the continuation and expansion of the Phase 1 tannery. The plant macroremains provide conclusive evidence that water from the nearby watercourse was being used to fill the tanning pits and that bark was being imported to the site to aid production of the tanning liquor. Domestic occupation may have declined in this period but it may simply be that the excavations were located in areas where substantial occupation debris was less likely to have accumulated. There is evidence that leather working, and perhaps hemp retting, was being carried out close by. Nevertheless, there is scant archaeological trace of Phase 2 domestic activity in Areas A and C, with none in Area D.

Phase 3, dated to the 17th–18th centuries, marks a resurgence of activity, principally in Areas A, B and C. The pottery evidence (Rátkai, Chapter 7) suggests little domestic occupation after *c*.1730 or perhaps, more correctly, that the backplots were turned over to agricultural use or gardens and/ or rubbish disposed of elsewhere. The clay pipe evidence reinforces this since all of it falls within the 1620–1730 bracket (Higgins, Chapter 9). Likewise, there is an absence of glass wine bottles dating from between the 1720s to the mid- or late 18th century (Orton and Rátkai, Chapter 8). On the Westley map of 1731 (Fig. 2.2), small garden plots are shown to either side of the excavated areas and a large ornamental garden feature appears to lie within the excavated areas. This garden also appears on Bradford's 1750 map (Fig. 1.2) and on Hanson's 1778 map (Fig. 2.3) along with other smaller gardens within the excavated areas. Even on Sherriff's map of 1808 (Fig. 2.4) gardens are still shown to the north of Welch's Skinyard.

In Area A, a series of bell-shaped and sub-rectangular pits were dug. The former, if not the latter, probably had an industrial use, possibly connected with metal working. These pits appear to have been subjected to a single phase of backfilling which was probably associated with a reorganisation of land use. This coincides with documented changes in landownership (see historical profile above). Strangely, in the midst of all this industrial activity, an oven or kiln F114/ F115 was constructed in Area A. The pottery from the kiln fill suggests that it went out of use in the later 17th century.

The tannery in Area B continued and expanded up to the end of this phase, when the pits were backfilled with leather-working waste – presumably from an adjacent industrial site. Concentrations of cattle horncores from pit backfills in Area B and the recovery of small finds from the site suggest that horn, ivory and bone working was being carried out in adjacent plots. Waste from handle making may indicate that there was also some cutlering being practiced, as there was on Park Street (see Burrows *et al.*, Chapter 4).

Tanning now extended into Area C where a well-preserved tannery, or possibly a curing yard, was established, which subsequently became the site of Welch's Skinyard, shown on Sherriff's map of 1808. This is likely to have been a small-scale industry, probably run by a single family. The many recuts of the pits relate to frequent emptying and refilling or extensions of their size. The clinker surfaces are likely to be an attempt to consolidate the wet ground, to act as pathways between the pits for access. The clustering of the pits suggests that

they were located within a single backplot, which extended from the watercourse to Edgbaston Street. On Sherriff's Map of 1808 (Fig. 2.4), Welch's skin-pits are shown on a completely different alignment, roughly parallel to the watercourse. By this date the skinyard was bordered to the east by Gingerbread Court and this period may mark the breakdown of the long medieval backplots into smaller units on differing alignments. Two wells provided an on-site source of water, additional to the nearby Parsonage-Manor watercourse and two smaller watercourses F336 and F337.

The elongated pits (F316, F326 and F347) may have been used to empty the waste material into as the hides were removed from the smaller pits to the west. However the cisterns employed for draining used tanbark before it is pressed into blocks to be burnt (illustrated in Diderot 1772), are very much larger at 8 piés (2.4m) wide by 4 piés (1.2m) deep and 10 toises (60 feet, 18m) long (pers. comm. Roy Thomson). However the relationship of the elongated pits to the smaller tan- or skin-pits certainly suggests that they must be connected in some way.

The Phase 3 evidence demonstrates how tanning (and later skin curing) continued to be a major Birmingham industry into the post-medieval period. By this time, it was more widespread, with other sites along the Digbeth/ Deritend High Street, at Hartwell Garage (Burrows *et al.* 2000) and at the Custard Factory (Mould 2001a). Cartographic analysis suggests additional tanneries and related industries along Upper Dean Street (Litherland and Watt 2000).

Phase 3 marks the first reclamation of land to the south of the Moat watercourse (Area D), which continued to be free-flowing at this time. There are still signs of a heath landscape, but this phase signals the beginning of Birmingham's encroachment onto previously undeveloped land to the south of the town. This ties in with the available historic map evidence which shows that land to the south of the Edgbaston Street site was open up to the granting of an Act of Parliament which allowed the Gooch family to parcel off the land for sale. By the mid-19th century there was no trace of this former wooded landscape – it had been replaced by an industrial streetscape, characterised by industrial units, chimneys and cramped court housing.

Phase 4 is dated to the 19th century. A north-south aligned brick boundary wall which extended from Edgbaston Street remained standing until 1998. The foundations of similarly aligned boundary walls also survived in Area B. The presence of these walls demonstrates that an earlier premise of Dr Nigel Baker, who has carried out extensive historic town-plan analysis for Birmingham – that property boundaries, surveyed in the early 18th century, had probably not moved significantly since the area was first laid out for settlement in the medieval period – is correct.

The watercourse began to fall into disuse probably in the late 18th century. This process was probably accelerated in the early 19th century and the watercourse was backfilled, although the line of its course was followed by Smithfield Passage. Ackerman's 1847 (Fig. 16.8) panoramic view of Birmingham shows the whole block from Edgbaston Street to Bromsgrove Street completely built over and with buildings lining either side of Smithfield Passage. Much of the area, however, is shown as open on Piggot-Smith's map of 1824/25, with what looks like a small stretch of the watercourse still remaining. It therefore seems likely that the watercourse went out of use completely in the late 1820s or 1830s. The wide range of datable artefacts recovered from watercourse infills and demolition deposits over the watercourse, including pottery sherds, leather shoe soles, laces and offcuts, metal shoe rivets, mother-of-pearl buttons and button-blanks, glass wasters, a glass bead and animal bones (see Bevan *et al.*, Chapter 8), tends to confirm the suggested dating. It is possible that the rubble over the line of the watercourse was wholly or in part intended to consolidate what was a rather marshy area prior to development. It is also likely that the large drain F401/ F403 in Area D was constructed to divert what had been the Parsonage-Manor watercourse, which was doubly redundant with the

infilling of the Parsonage and Manor Moats.

In Area C a series of foundations are likely to represent the Skin House marked by Sherriff on his map of 1808. However, at least one other building was represented by foundations F353 and F354. They are the only pre-18th-century building remains recovered at Edgbaston Street. The exact date and function of the building are unknown, although pottery associated with it dated to the first half of the 17th century.

Phase 4 marked the beginning of improvement to the city's sewerage system, represented by the large drains in Transects A–D and in Area D. These drains may well have served more than one function and have carried storm and spring water as well as waste (see above). A well in Area D is likely to have been domestic in nature – serving the court housing which was packed in between the town's expanding industrial plan. The recovery of a large quantity of glass medicinal bottles from the backfill of the well gives some insight into the industrial population's health (Orton 2001).

Phase 5 is dated to the 20th century and was represented by a tarmac carpark surface, concrete slabs, piles and a lift-shaft of former buildings.

3 Moor Street

Bob Burrows, Catharine Patrick and Eleanor Ramsey

with a contribution from Steve Litherland

Background to the excavations

The Moor Street excavations now lie under the iconic Selfridges Store opposite St Martin's Church. Before this part of Bull Ring was built the site was bounded by Bull Ring, Moor Street, Moor Street Station and Park Street (Fig. 3.1). Land use consisted of a mixture of rundown offices, octagonal shopping booths, an unusual public house on concrete stilts called the Ship Ashore, a multi-storey car park and other car parking located on rough ground to the south of Moor Street Terminus Station (see Fig. 3.2, colour). The latter car park once formed the upper storey of an early example of concrete-framed construction called the Moor Street Goods Shed A, built shortly before the First World War, and affectionately known locally as the 'Banana Warehouse'. All the buildings associated with this upper storey of the goods shed were swept away in the 1960s with the exception of an office block adjacent to the Ship Ashore, built in the same early 20th-century Great Western Railway style as the main terminus façade, that would once have overseen the flow of goods in and out of the railway yard.

The archaeological investigations began with a desktop assessment in 1995 (Mould and Litherland 1995a). This identified the potential significance of medieval and later archaeological deposits for understanding the early development of the town – if these had survived the impact of the 20th-century redevelopment. Trial trenching showed that well-preserved medieval deposits and features dating from the 12th century onwards had survived between the concrete stilts of the Ship Ashore, and elsewhere very deep features such as a medieval stone-lined well had survived, albeit in a severely truncated form (Fig. 3.11, colour). Unfortunately, trial trenching confirmed that most of the site had been cleared of archaeology down to the level of the sandstone bedrock. Two areas were opened up for excavation: Area A towards the Moor Street frontage and in the area of the Ship Ashore, and Area B close to the Park Street and Bull Ring frontages (Fig. 3.1). Unfortunately there was no surviving archaeology in Area B.

Historical profile
by Steve Litherland and Catharine Patrick

The development of the street plan of Birmingham may be characterised as that of a simple, essentially rural road pattern transformed by a series of town-planning exercises, including the laying out of the triangular market place in the 12th century. Moor Street followed a contour of the sandstone ridge overlooking the Rea valley, connecting the market place with Dale End Bar. By looking at the development of the town plan in detail it has been proposed that Moor Street was created as an extension to the basic town plan by cutting through the earlier properties fronting the market place (*e.g.* Baker, in Litherland *et al.* 1995, 12). Although the documents are silent about exactly when Moor Street was laid out, it is logical that the land nearest the market and highest up the hill would have been developed first.

This expansion encroached upon the Little or Over Park of the Lord of Birmingham and here, like Edgbaston Street, the properties that were developed along the street were held in diverse ownership as 'burgages' from the lord of the manor. Also like Edgbaston Street, several streams issued from near the fault line here between the water-carrying sandstone and the impermeable Mercia Mudstone. One of these, the Hersumdych or Hersum Ditch, is known from documents dating from the 14th through to the late 17th century (Demidowicz 2003, 144).

In the 1400s and 1500s Moor Street was called Molle or More Street and the side of the market it opened out onto was called the Corn Cheaping, which probably

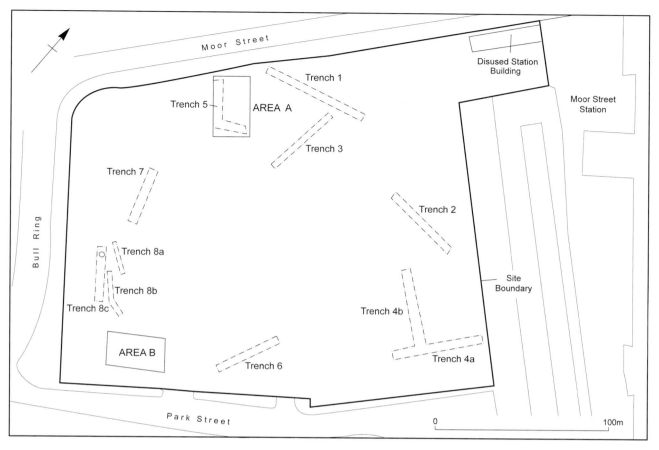

Fig. 3.1 Moor St; location plan showing trenches and excavated areas.

reflects a trade specialisation within this part of the market. Although it is more difficult to locate accurately the positions of buildings and burgages described in the sequence of the three 16th-century surveys of the town than Hill and Bickley's plan, based on the best survey of 1553 and compiled in 1891, may suggest, it seems apparent that Moor Street was more intensively developed than its neighbour, Park Street. Furthermore, it seems probable that those properties nearest the market would be the most attractive, and 'a burgage and other houses in Mollestrete called the Corner House in the tenure of Henry Crosse' is specifically mentioned in the 1553 survey, while an earlier survey also describes a Corner House as being newly built. Other property in Moor Street belonged to the trustees of William Lench and included 'a tenement, cottage, barn and croft in More Street, near the park there', which may indicate that these were on the east side of the street. Other holders in Moor Street included Robert and William Colmore, Henry Russell, and Maria Vernon, a widow. Although we cannot be sure of the exact meaning of the terms that the Elizabethan surveyors used to classify buildings, words such as 'cottages', 'barns', 'crofts' and 'gardens' feature just as frequently as 'tenements' and 'burgages', which probably indicates that the street was not fully developed or

exclusively given over to commercial or industrial functions even by the mid-1500s, particularly towards its northern end away from the market place.

The first detailed representation of the area is provided by Westley's map of 1731 (Fig. 2.2). This clearly shows the primacy of the plots at the market end of the street and there is still a tailing off of occupation towards Dale End. The properties which front onto Corn Cheaping extend back from the street in a dense arrangement of courts. In contrast, those on Moor Street remain fairly compact, with buildings focused on the street frontage, and the backplots occupied by many gardens and orchards with scattered standing structures. Bradford's map of 1750/51 (Figs 1.2 and 16.1, colour) and Hanson's map of 1778 (Fig. 2.3) show that the open areas of the backplots were beginning to be colonised by more and more buildings by the later 18th century, but that this pheno-menon was as yet mainly confined to those plots on Moor Street closest to the market frontage of Corn Cheaping.

This process of infilling continued apace into the next century, and Ackerman's Perspective View of Birming-ham dated 1847 (Fig. 16.8), although not necessarily accurate, does give an impression of the cramped and congested character of this area. These changes should be set against the nine-fold rise in the population of

Birmingham from about 24,000 in 1750 to around 220,000 in 1850. Thus within a generation or two even the houses of relatively prosperous tradesmen were often subdivided internally, and court housing or specialist workshops called 'shoppings' built over the gardens behind. Moreover this process was seen in several districts of the city, for example around Bradford Street and the Colmore estate, as well as Moor Street. However, at Moor Street a distinction is maintained, from the 16th century through to the 19th century, between the old properties fronting the market, the properties on Moor Street closest to the market, and those furthest away. During the later 1800s the properties fronting the market place still retain their general pattern and shape, probably because the commercial pressure on this space bought high rents that tended to militate against plot amalgamation and rationalisation. The plots on Moor Street nearest the market frontage also retain recognisable elements depicted upon the 18th-century maps, albeit with a gradual increase in the density of workshops and courts, whereas the plots near Dale End become very densely built up. These changes may reflect the emergence of distinctive zones of commerce, manufacture, and working-class housing and, as such, represent in microcosm the forces at work that were changing the fabric and identity of many older districts of Birmingham in the 18th and 19th centuries as it emerged as a regional, and then later, a national commercial and industrial centre. However, in spite of all these changes, it is a remarkable feature of the character and development of this area that the main property boundaries remained largely undisturbed and that continuity rather than change was the norm in this respect until the mid-20th century, albeit with a few notable exceptions. For example, the Birmingham Street Commissioners, a forerunner of the town council, tried to stamp their mark on the market place in the early 19th century by clearing away much unplanned development. The construction of the Public Office in Moor Street in 1807, which housed the town courtrooms and prison, was one example of this attempt at town planning. Briefly, in July 1839, the Public Office was besieged when an angry Chartist mob chased a contingent of 60 Metropolitan Police there, who had travelled up especially by train to try to restore public order. Two policemen were stabbed and order was eventually restored by the army. The First Edition 1:2500 Ordnance Survey map, dated 1888, illustrates the prominence of the Public Office building on the Moor Street frontage and there was by then a permanent police station adjacent to it.

The Public Office was swept away by a further large-scale development that bought the Great Western Railway into this side of the city and the markets. Moor Street Station was eventually fully opened in 1913/14, but such a development had been proposed by other smaller railway companies for many years previously. The boundaries of Moor Street Station encompassed approx-imately 17,340 square yards and involved the purchase and demolition of about 34 properties, including the Public Office.

While work on the passenger station was taking place, a further opportunity arose to purchase the site of the former police station and other land that became the site of Goods Sheds A and B, otherwise known as the 'Banana Warehouse'. The design incorporated many advanced features, including a very strong proprietary reinforcing system for ferro-concrete developed by Hennebique in France. It was also a passenger and goods station combined and operated on two levels. Hoists transferred goods wagons between levels and heavy traversers enabled steam engines as large as the 'Castle' class to transfer from one line to another without the need of run-round loops. The station provided a vital link for the city's expanding wholesale food and metal markets and superseded to a large extent the earlier goods yard situated at Bordesley.

Although the construction of the railway station severely affected the plot pattern in part of Moor Street, property boundaries elsewhere remained essentially unchanged. In the years following 1905 this part of the street block enjoyed a period of stability and the Ordnance Survey 1:2500 survey of 1952 depicts remarkably little change. However, several forces were at work to change the character of the area. There had been a certain amount of bomb damage during the war, as the railway lines into Moor Street and New Street provided readily identifiable targets from the air. However, it was urban planners not the Luftwaffe that destroyed the remaining historic character of the area. Herbert Manzoni's vision of a modern city of the motor car included the driving through of the Inner Ring Road in the late 1950s and early 1960s and, following on from this, an office block, NCP car park and the Ship Ashore public house were constructed as part of the broader development of the Bull Ring Shopping Centre. Today, the Inner Ring Road has disappeared and this area has been reintegrated into the markets as part of the new Bullring development. Moor Street Station has also been refurbished and reopened to passenger traffic, and even parts of one of the 'Banana Warehouses' have been saved and now form an imposing entrance to a multi-storey a car park.

Excavation results

Phase 1: 12th–14th centuries

The cut of a large linear ditch (F537, F561 and F568) was aligned northwest-southeast and was excavated, along with its recut, in three sections (Figs 3.3–3.5, 3.7 colour, 3.8–3.9). The recut was numbered F538 in the southernmost section and was identified in the section drawings for the other two excavated sections (Figs 3.6, 3.7 colour, 3.8–3.9). The fills within each excavated section showed significant differences and are likely to

Fig. 3.3 Area A; showing location of ditch sections (southeast facing).

reflect the type of material in the immediate area as the ditch was infilled. There was no evidence for a bank on either side of the ditch or its recut.

The ditch, where it was excavated as F537 (Fig. 3.4, Figs 3.6–3.7, colour), was 1.65m deep and 4.40m wide, with sloping sides to a flat base and two fills of redeposited subsoil. The upper fill (5129) was a light red brown sand, with a lower fill (5195) of much cleaner red sand. The ditch was recut by F538.

The ditch recut (F538, Fig. 3.4 and Fig. 3.6) was approximately 3.80m wide and 1.40–1.60m deep, with sloping sides and a flat base. It had two fills; the lower fill (5130) was a soft grey-brown silty sand that contained fragments of coal and some stones; the upper fill was a more compact red-brown sandy silt that also contained

some stones and fragments of coal (5194). Green-glazed roof tile was found in the lower fill (5130).

The middle section through the ditch (F561) showed a more complicated sequence of deposition (Fig. 3.8). At the base of the ditch there was a 0.20m-thick layer of red redeposited subsoil (5166). Overlying this, against the northeast edge, was another deposit of red-brown redeposited subsoil containing flecks of charcoal and an early 13th-century whiteware fluted jug (5161). The jug (Fig. 7.18.1 colour) linked this section of the ditch with the northernmost section (F568 5186) where sherds of the same jug were found. The earliest fill (5166) was partially overlaid by a thin layer of charcoal-flecked orange-brown clayey silt sand (5160). Against the southwest edge was a layer of redeposited subsoil which

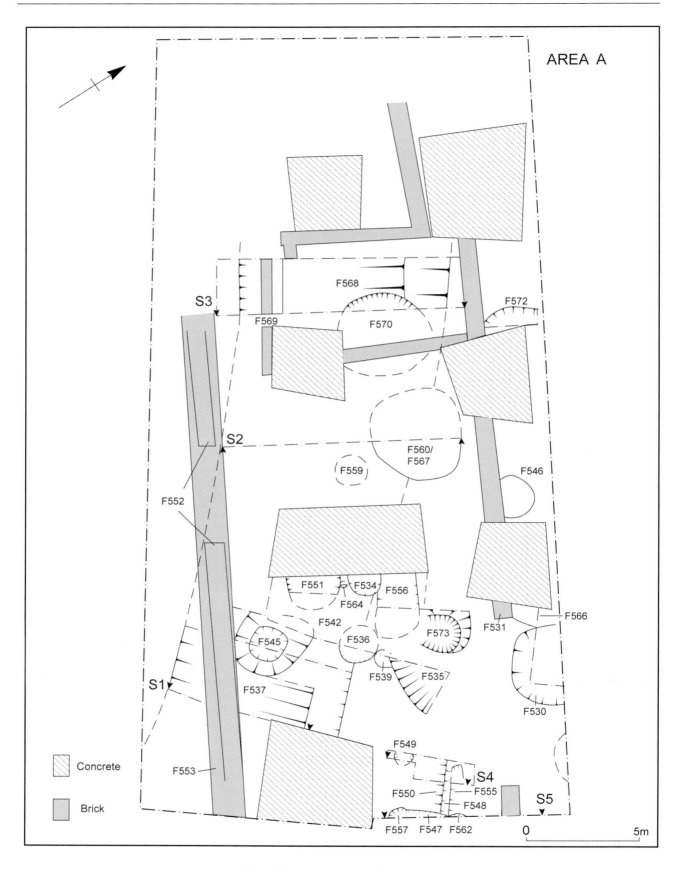

Fig. 3.4 Area A; multi-phase plan.

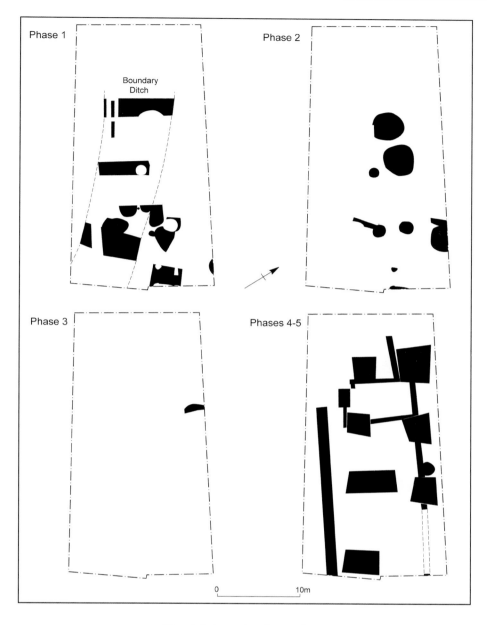

Fig. 3.5 Area A; phase plans.

contained a crucible fragment and a cooking pot with external sooting (5165). A charcoal-flecked red-brown sandy silt (5167) overlay 5160 and 5161.

Ditch F561 was recut and the primary fill of the recut was a brown-grey silty clay, 0.18–40m thick, with some stones, burnt peat, coal, fallow deer remains, a whiteware jug, heavily sooted cooking pots and, most interestingly, a Roman sherd (5158). Over this, there was a series of smaller deposits which included a grey silty clay, 0.34m thick with stones, burnt peat, charcoal, large pieces of coal and an externally sooted Deritend cooking pot (5155); and a brown-red sandy silt, 0.20m thick, with occasional stones, charcoal flecks and externally sooted pottery (5154). The uppermost fill of the recut (5150) contained a jug with partial external sooting and green-

glazed roof tile. Contexts 5151, 5152, 5153, 5156, 5157, 5159, 5162, 5163 and 5164 were identified only in section. A cleaning layer (5171) over the uppermost fill of the recut of ditch F561 contained cooking pots with external sooting and an example of 'rusticated' pottery where the surface had been criss-crossed with horizontal and vertical scoring, and green-glazed roof tile.

The northernmost section through the ditch F568 (Fig. 3.9) also contained a 0.40m-thick layer of red-brown redeposited sand subsoil on the northeast edge (5191). This was overlaid by two deposits of grey-brown sandy silt with stones and charcoal flecking (5190 included a Deritend jug handle; 5189 included an unparalleled base and lower wall of a Deritend jug).

The recut of F568 had some waterlogged wood and

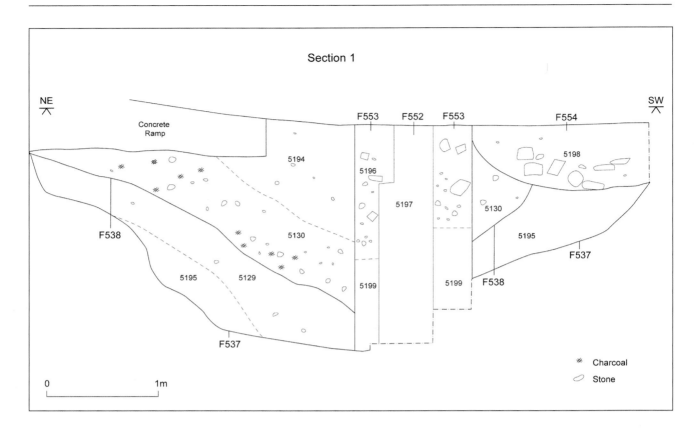

Fig. 3.6 Area A; ditch section, F537.

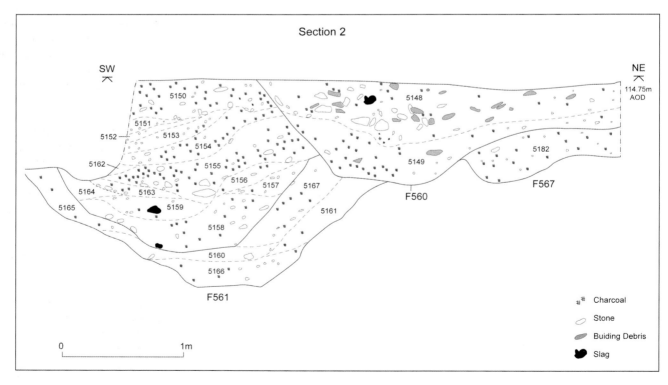

Fig. 3.8 Area A; ditch section, F561.

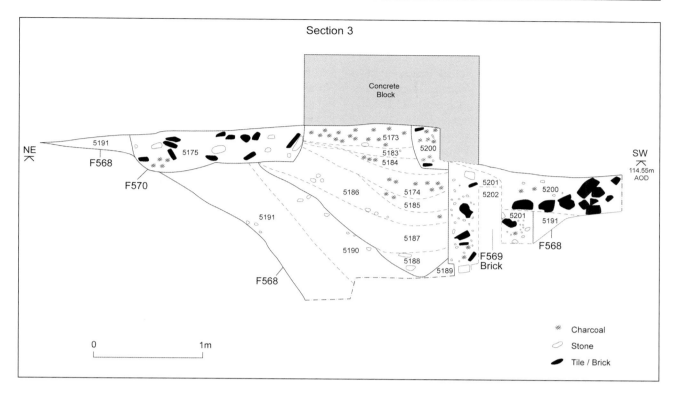

Fig. 3.9 Area A; ditch section, F568.

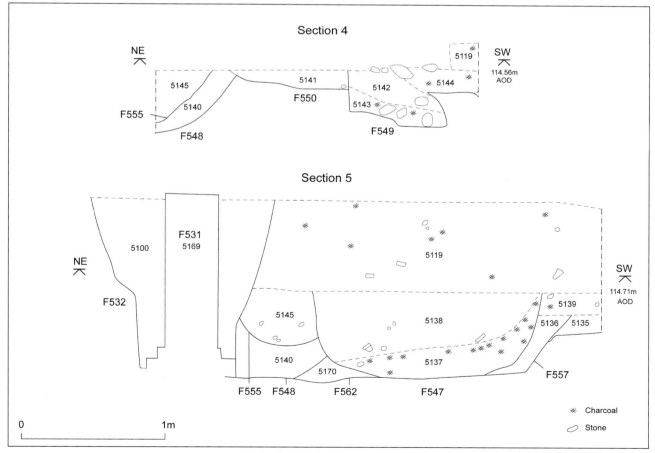

Fig. 3.10 Area A; sections 4 and 5.

well-preserved plant remains at its base (5188), giving information on the surrounding landscape. Above this, 5187 included a Deritend jug, and 5186 contained whiteware sherds from the same jug as those found in ditch section F561. Upper fills comprised a charcoal-flecked pink-brown sand with jug sherds (5185), a charcoal-rich dark grey clay silt containing a Deritend jug handle (5174), a mottled sand silt with charcoal and ash which contained a Deritend jug, charred plant remains and a few waterlogged plant remains (5184), a mottled silt sand (5183), and a brown charcoal-flecked sand (5173).

The plant macroremains and pollen count (5188) suggest that the ditch recut carried water, as the presence of rushes and sedges – which would have grown along the banks of the ditch in a localised damp environment – is noted. The surrounding landscape appears to have been wooded with some grassland in Phase 1. A large cereal assemblage is likely to represent charred fodder, whilst ova from intestinal parasites suggest a small level of sewage contamination (see Ciaraldi, Chapter 12, and Greig, Chapter 13). The environmental evidence is not inconsistent with the ditch being the boundary between the town and the deer park, known as Over Park, but the pottery and other finds indicate that normal backplot waste was also accumulating in the ditch. The importance of the ditch clearly diminished in the 13th century and despite a recut around the middle of the century was out of commission by *c*.1300. An episode of pit digging followed the disuse of the ditch. Other pits (see below) to the east of the ditch may represent early activity in a backplot running back from Moor Street.

A Deritend cooking pot found in the recut of F561 (5155) provides a *terminus post quem* of 1250. Once the recut ditch had been backfilled, a small number of pits and a post-hole were cut. One of the pits (F545, see Fig. 3.4) was 1.80m in diameter, with sloping sides to a depth of 1.10m, then vertical sides for another 0.65m to a flat base 0.80–0.90m in diameter. The fill of the pit was a mid–dark brown silty sand, with redeposited red sand subsoil and occasional coal and charcoal flecks (5128). A Deritend jug with a rod handle and cooking pots were recorded from this context. The fill also contained discrete lenses of white/ yellow mortar and coal in bands, and had a higher clay content towards the base of the feature. The pit F545 was truncated slightly on the southern side by a Phase 4 19th-century wall (F552), and was cut by another Phase 1 pit (F565) to the west. Pit F565 was not clearly visible in plan and was heavily truncated by a modern concrete pillar. In section, the feature had gently curving sides to a round base, and was filled with a dark brown sandy silt with occasional charcoal flecks (5179) to a depth of 0.52m. The fill contained two glazed Deritend ware jug sherds. Pit F565 also cut a layer of reddish brown silty clay sand which was largely made up of redeposited sand subsoil with occasional charcoal flecks (5176, not illustrated) and, in turn, was cut by a sub-

circular pit (F551) which had steeply sloping sides to a flattish base. Pit F551 was 1.10m wide and 0.22m deep and was filled by a medium grey-brown silty clay sand which contained occasional small stones and flecks of coal (5133). It was also heavily truncated by a modern concrete pillar. Truncated by pit F551 and cutting layer 5176 was a post-hole (F564) 0.40m in diameter and 0.14m deep. It was filled with a mid-grey sandy silt with occasional charcoal flecks (5178).

The layer of redeposited sand mentioned above (5176) overlay the upper fill of the ditch recut F538 and was cut by a series of pits, the earliest of which had a charcoal-rich fill (F556, 5122, see Fig. 3.4) and lay just to the east of the main ditch. The fill contained frequent flecks of charcoal, occasional small stones, coal, burnt peat and badly burnt sherds. These sherds appear to be contemporary with the charcoal-rich fill and may represent clearance after a domestic fire. Pit F556 was 1.20m in diameter and 0.64m deep, with steeply sloping sides to a flat base. It was truncated by a Phase 5 concrete pillar to the west and was cut to the south by a Phase 1 pit (F534, Fig. 3.4). Pit F556 cut another pit (F558) (Fig. 3.4). In turn, Pit F558 cut Pit F535 (see below). Pit F558 was sub-circular in plan and was heavily truncated to the northwest by a modern drainage ditch. The edge that was undisturbed showed a steeply sloping side to a flat base, at a depth of 1.08m. Pit F558 contained three fills. The lowest fill (5181) was a dark grey-brown silty clay sand with frequent flecks of charcoal and occasional small stones, and was 0.20m in depth. Over this was a light reddish brown silty clay sand with occasional small stones flecks of charcoal which was largely made up of re-deposited red sand subsoil (5172). The upper fill was a dark grey-brown silty clay sand with occasional small stones and frequent flecks of charcoal (5146), and was 0.60m in depth.

To the south of pit F556, and cutting it slightly, pit F534 was identified cutting through the layer of re-deposited sand (5176). Pit F534 was circular and had quite steeply sloping sides to a slightly rounded base. It was approximately 0.74m wide and 0.50m deep, and contained a single fill, a medium grey-brown silty clay sand with occasional patches of redeposited orange sand, a small amount of stones and charcoal flecks, a roof tile showing the maker's fingerprints and a possible roof tile waster fragment (5107).

A small pit (F539) was cut by a larger pit (F535, Fig. 3.4 – excavated as F500 at evaluation stage). Pit F535 was also cut by pit F558 and a Phase 2 pit F573, see below, which contained the lower part of a jug with white chevron decoration. Sealing the features in this area was a dark grey silty clay sand with a high concentration of charcoal (5132). It was approximately 0.30m deep and was situated directly beneath a grey-brown silty clay sand with frequent flecks of charcoal (5108). To the east were the heavily truncated remains of a small pit (F544).

Next to the eastern edge of the excavation, a layer of

red-brown sandy silt (5135, Fig. 3.10, S5), approximately 0.15m deep, overlay the subsoil (5106). A sequence of intercutting features was investigated within an area approximately 1.5m × 2m (see Fig. 3.4). Due to the intensity of activity in this area most of the earliest features were severely truncated by later ones and were identifiable only as cuts in section (Fig. 3.10, S5). The earliest feature (F562) cut the subsoil (5106) and was cut by a later Phase 1 linear (F548) and a Phase 2 pit (F547). The linear feature F548 had a rounded profile and single sandy fill (5140). It was cut by the Phase 2 pit F547, as well as by Phase 1 pit F550 (Fig. 3.10, S4) and a linear feature (F555). The pit F550 was a shallow sub-circular feature with a brown sandy silt fill containing the remains from a small pony (see Baxter, Chapter 15) and a roof tile with a nail hole (5141). Pit F550 was, in turn, cut by the Phase 2 pits F547 and F549 (Fig. 3.10, S4). The linear feature F555 was aligned northwest-southeast. It had a butt end to the northwest, but continued southeast beyond the excavation area. It had a dark brown sandy silt fill (5145) and was 0.38m deep. This linear was truncated by a Phase 2 pit F547.

In Evaluation Trench 8c, a stone-lined well (F182, Fig. 3.11, colour) was recorded in what would have been a backplot running back from the Bull Ring frontage. It measured 1.50m in diameter and 2.20m in depth and had a thin clay layer over its base. The lining was made up of seven courses of large sandstone blocks (1509), approximately 0.40m by 0.30m in size. The well was backfilled with deposits (1502, 1510) containing Phase 1 pottery and some burnt peat.

Phase 2: 15th–16th centuries

A series of pits characterise Phase 2 activity (see Fig. 3.5). The largest of these pits (F570 and F560) were located within the northern half of Area A.

Circular pit (F570) cut the Phase 1 ditch (F568). This pit was approximately 2m in diameter and 0.40m deep, with steep sides and a flat base. Its fill (5175) contained a large amount of very early brick, roof tile and charcoal (see Fig. 3.9). The upper fills of the Phase 1 ditch were cut by three other Phase 2 pits (F559, F560 and F567, see Fig. 3.8). Pit F559 was a shallow 'U-shaped' feature, approximately 0.50m in diameter and 0.35m deep, with a single fill of red sand and clay containing a fragment of roof tile (5147). To the east was a circular pit (F567; Fig. 3.4), approximately 2m in diameter and 0.50m deep and contained a single fill of grey sandy silt with frequent coal and burnt peat flecks, including a cooking pot with heavy external sooting and a possible roof tile waster (5182). Cutting F567 on the western side, and cutting both the upper fills of the ditch (F561) and the subsoil (5106), was F560 (Fig. 3.4) which contained two fills, the lower fill being a dark grey clay silt containing green-glazed roof tile (5149), the upper fill being a brown sandy silt (5148; Fig. 3.8).

Further to the southeast, a pit (F536 – excavated as

F501 at evaluation stage) cut the upper fill of the Phase 1 ditch (F537; see Fig. 3.4). It was 1m in diameter and 0.90m deep, with vertical sides and a flat base. The lower fill was a light brown sandy silt (5111) and the upper fill was a grey-brown sandy silt with fragments of roof tile and charcoal flecks (5112). The lower fill (5111) contained a large jug base sherd which may have been used as a kiln spacer or it may have been a waster.

Against the northern edge of Area A, pit F556 (Fig. 3.4) was truncated by a later Phase 2 pit, F530 and by a Phase 5 concrete foundation. The fill of F566 was a dark grey-brown silty clay sand with a moderate amount of charcoal flecks (5180). The later sub-circular pit F530 had a dark grey-brown charcoal flecked silty clay sand fill (5103).

Further Phase 2 activity was recorded at the eastern end of Area A (Fig. 3.5). Pits F542, F547, F549 and F557 (Figs 3.4 and Fig. 3.10, Sections 4 and 5) cut earlier Phase 1 features. Fill 5113 of F542 contained a cooking pot and green-glazed roof tile. Pit F549 was a sub-circular feature with an irregular profile (Fig. 3.10, Section 4). It had an eastern edge cut almost vertically and a western edge that was concave with an overhang which suggests that it may originally have been lined or else rapidly backfilled. It contained two fills (5142, 5143), and may relate to an industrial process. Sealing this feature (F549) was a later Phase 2 layer of medium grey-brown sandy silt (5144).

Pit F557 was sealed by a layer of grey brown sandy silt (5139; see Fig. 3.10, Section 5), approximately 0.15m deep. Both were cut by pit F547, whose full extent was unknown, as only its northern edge was visible, but it was at least 1.5m in diameter and 0.5m deep, with near-vertical sides and a flat base. The lower fill was a medium grey-brown sandy silt with a high concentration of charcoal and contained green-glazed roof tile (5137). The upper fill was a dark red-brown sandy silt (5138).

A layer of very dark grey-brown silty clay sand (5119) with a very high concentration of charcoal which may have been the result of industrial activity built up over this area towards the end of Phase 2. A single blackware/ Cistercian ware sherd from this layer suggests that it was deposited or had built up by *c*.1550. This layer contained the remains of a pony (see Baxter, Chapter 15). A charcoal-flecked silt layer (5101) which contained a Roman Severn Valley rim sherd was recorded to the east of 5119.

Phase 3: 17th–early 18th centuries

One feature is dated to Phase 3, a heavily truncated pit (F572) which was shown in section to be 0.90m by 0.50m (Figs 3.4 and 3.5). It contained a single fill, a grey sandy silt with large amounts of roof tile and charcoal (5203). The pottery from within it contained probable 17th-century coarseware sherds and some residual material.

Pit F572, along with the Phase 2 features and layers, was sealed by a Phase 3 grey charcoal-flecked silt, referred to as a backplot or 'cultivation soil' layer (5105), which was removed from the whole of Area A. A single coarseware sherd, which was not closely datable, and a residual Brill sherd were found in (5105).

Phase 4: 19th century

A series of brick-built walls representing Phase 4 structures and boundaries was recorded (Figs 3.4 and 3.5). One of the walls (F552), and its foundation cut F553, followed a similar alignment to the Phase 1 ditch. It cut through the ditch to a depth of 1.80m. The wall was 0.4m wide and constructed from bricks, with footings visible at the base. The foundation trench (F553) was 0.90m wide and was filled with clean red sand (5199) and crumbly black silt with clinker and brick rubble (5196). A second wall (F531) was made up of 15 courses of red bricks (5205) and was visible directly under the modern concrete surface. The cut for this wall (F532) was also visible in section (Fig. 3.10, Section 5) and had a fill that contained building rubble. The pottery from the fill (5100), which included a sherd of Mediterranean maiolica, appeared to be residual (see Rátkai, Chapter 7). A third wall (F569, 5201) cut through the northern section of the Phase 1 ditch (Fig. 3.4). A well (F546) was recorded close to the northern boundary of Area A.

Phase 5: 20th century

Seven concrete foundations for the former Ship Ashore public house were recorded and the Hennebique Building, which was constructed in the early 20th century, demarcated the northern extent of Area A (see Figs 3.4 and 3.5).

Discussion

The evaluation trial-trenches and subsequent area excavation established that surviving medieval deposits at Moor Street were limited to a discrete area along the frontage of Bull Ring and within the footprint of the former Ship Ashore public house where they were well preserved within 1.60–3m of the modern ground level.

No prehistoric, Roman or early medieval features were identified. A single prehistoric unretouched flake and five sherds of pottery dating to the Roman period attest to some activity in the area prior to the medieval settlement.

The first distinct phase, Phase 1, dated to the 12th–14th centuries, when a large southeast-northwest aligned ditch and its recut, representing the boundary between town and deer park in the 12th century, was cut. This ditch, which may have carried water but if not was certainly waterlogged for periods of time, was also recorded during excavation at Park Street to the southeast. The high tree pollen count may indicate that the surrounding landscape was wooded or that woodland products were utilised on the site. Unfortunately, macrofossils from tree species tend not to survive and plant remains from fill (5188), from where the tree pollen came,

suggested only disturbed and some waterlogged ground. Ceramic evidence (Rátkai, Chapter 7) suggests that 5188 dated to c.1250. Pollen of grassland or meadowland species may indicate open grassland in the vicinity or may have derived from animal dung. Cereals, cornfield weeds, flax, bracken and heathers were also present in the pollen record. Some sewage contamination of the ditch was also recorded. Greig (Chapter 13) notes that the pollen assemblage from 5188 is typical of normal domestic waste, crop growing and processing. The grassland species may indicate some stock rearing. Plant remains (see Ciaraldi, Chapter 12) from a later fill of the recut ditch indicate the importance of cereals and grassland species and provide evidence of crop processing, possibly brewing, and stock keeping. In short, the environmental evidence from the recut ditch fills presents a similar picture and suggests a flourishing settlement mainly dependent on livestock and cereals.

Remains of food animals were few. Horncores formed the majority of identifiable cattle body parts and, although it cannot be certain (see Baxter, Chapter 15), are more likely to be associated with tanning or allied trades. Pony remains were noted, and it is possible that these small equids were kept within the deer park enclosure, although by the time of their burial the main ditch was probably redundant and the development of the Moor Street backplots had begun.

The animal bone and environmental evidence produced nothing which could be linked directly to the deer park, apart from one fallow deer antler fragment from ditch F561. By the 1200s the deer park was already under pressure – possibly due to the success of the Bull Ring market – and the ditch was being infilled. There is evidence of housing, settlement waste, and cereal fodder and stocking for animals on, or close to, the site. The distance from the Bull Ring frontage makes it unlikely that this activity was within Bull Ring backplots and may indicate that Moor Street began to be developed quite early. This would suggest that the importance of the deer park was also comparatively short-lived.

The Moor Street section of the ditch was infilled earlier than the Park Street section, but was also recut. The fills within each excavated section of the ditch show significant differences, reflecting the type of material in the immediate area when the ditch was infilled. Analysis of the pottery shows that the ditch was completely filled before c.1250, subsequently recut, and had been backfilled once more by c.1300. The ditch was not backfilled as a single episode of activity, but rather as a succession of smaller actions. The former would have been more consistent with a planned expansion of the town into the deer park. It is clear that this part of Birmingham was developed very early in the medieval period – possibly in association with, or as a result of the success of, the Bull Ring markets. It is tempting to suggest that, instead of a planned episode of urban development (Baker 1995), Moor Street (and Park Street) were instead formalisations of small tracks or lanes which had grown organically as a result of intense demand for land close to the Bull Ring markets. This might explain why both Moor Street and Park Street appear (for example on Hanson's Map of 1778; Fig. 2.3) so narrow at their junction with the Bull Ring and Digbeth and then widen out once beyond their back-plots.

Environmental evidence from the ditch fills suggests a variety of activities in the area, such as broom making, crop processing (cereals and flax), beer making, stock keeping and possibly leather working or tanning. The presence of heather pollen is indicative of roofing material – possibly for stock buildings. Roof tiles suggest more substantial domestic structures. Small amounts of sewage suggest that the ditch became a repository for normal household/ domestic rubbish. Analysis of the pottery from the upper ditch fills suggests that earlier midden material was dumped into the ditch once it had fallen out of use or when its significance had diminished. Some of the ditch fill is suggestive of a domestic clearance following a fire, which ties in with further evidence of a house fire from pit F500.

This demand was not just for domestic housing; the recovery of an unparalleled Deritend ware jug (see Rátkai, Chapter 7) may hint at pottery production in the area. If so, together with the wasters and a fire bar from Park Street, it would suggest that local Deritend pottery production extended from the River Rea up to the town itself in the 13th century.

A crucible fragment from the Moor Street ditch backfill hints at nearby metal working. Another industry was represented by the frequency of shorthorned cattle horncores (Baxter, Chapter 15) and this is in line with the horn working and associated tanning evidence found at the Edgbaston Street, Park Street (both this volume) and Hartwell Garage sites (Burrows *et al.* 2000) and at the post-medieval Custard Factory site (Mould 2001a). The frequent occurrence of burnt fuel, represented by charcoal, coal and charred peat in Phases 1 and 2, along with the presence of hammerscale, further suggests that this land was being used for domestic and industrial purposes.

Phase 2 is dated to the 15th and 16th centuries and is represented by a series of pits, some of which cut the backfill of the Phase 1 ditch. The recovery of roof tile suggests the proximity of housing which would have fronted onto Moor Street. In contrast to the mix of domestic and industrial activity recorded in Phase 1, a period of inactivity or – more likely – a change in land use is suggested by the accumulation of a dark layer of silty-clay-sand with a high concentration of charcoal towards the end of Phase 2. The pottery suggests a continuation of occupation from Phase 1, but at a reduced level.

Domestic activity appears to be non-existent in Phase 3 (dated to the 17th–early 18th century) and only one pit was recorded, along with a deep layer of organic 'cultivation soil'. Similar layers have also been identified at Edgbaston Street and at Park Street. The character and exact date of these layers varies from site to site. The spread of these layers across a high percentage of the excavated 18th-century town can best be seen as evidence of a change in land use, perhaps reflecting a temporary decline in industry and perhaps also a change in landownership. This is discussed in more detail in the overall discussion (Chapter 16).

Phase 4 is dated to the 19th century and is represented by a series of brick-built walls representing structures and boundaries extending back from Moor Street. A well was also recorded cutting through one of the earlier Phase 4 boundary walls. One of the walls roughly followed the alignment of the Phase 1 boundary ditch. This continuity of boundaries from the medieval through to the post-medieval period is characteristic of the Bull Ring area and is also recorded at Edgbaston Street and Park Street.

Phase 5 is dated to the 20th century and is represented by a brick-built wall along the northeastern limit of Area A, which formed part of the Hennebique Building associated with Moor Street station, and by the concrete foundations for the foremer Ship Ashore public house.

4   Park Street

Bob Burrows, Simon Buteux, Helen Martin and Stephanie Rátkai

with a contribution from Steve Litherland

Background to the excavations

The excavations in Park Street, undertaken from February to July 2001, were situated on the east side of the street (Fig. 4.1) at a location which is today opposite the striking Selfridges building and under a multi-storey car park serving Bullring. Before excavations took place, the site was largely open ground devoted to car parking that was sandwiched between Goods Shed B of Moor Street Station to the north, Well Lane to the east, and the rear of a Victorian music hall called the London Museum, and the remains of Corporation stables to the south.

Two generalised archaeological assessments were conducted over larger areas that included the Park Street site within their remit (Litherland *et al.* 1995; Mould 1999), and there was one specific to the development site (OAU 1997). Each assessment identified that this location, in close proximity to the medieval focus of Birmingham, was likely to provide evidence of medieval and post-medieval industry, commerce and settlement. Furthermore, the earlier excavations which had taken place near to Park Street, at Edgbaston Street and Moor Street (this volume), had found evidence for a sequence of activity from the 12th century onwards. This, in addition to the notable lack of 20th-century building activity, indicated that there was good potential for the survival of archaeological deposits and features, albeit possibly as 'islands' between truncation by 19th-century cellars and building foundations.

In order to accommodate the contractors' demolition programme, the archaeological investigations were divided into three areas (A, B and C), which were excavated in turn. In advance of area excavation two sets of evaluation trenches were opened up, two in Area A and two in Area C. The evaluation trenches showed significant survival of deposits dating from the 12th and 13th centuries, at a depth of around 1m below the modern ground surface.

Historical profile

by Steve Litherland and Stephanie Rátkai

The reasons behind the creation of Park Street are likely to have been broadly similar to those described for Moor Street. Both streets were additions to the basic town plan laid out upon the upper part of the Little (or Over) Park. Park Street is about 100m down-slope of Moor Street, and occupies roughly the same contour of the sandstone ridge as Edgbaston Street, entering the market place just below St Martin's Church. This places Park Street very close to the line of the Birmingham Fault, the drift geology here consisting of sands and gravels overlying a horizon of weathered sandstone bedrock. For most of its length, Park Street ran roughly parallel and equidistant to Moor Street, apart from a sharp turn towards Dale End to keep within the old park boundary.

The area of the excavations at Park Street straddled the boundary between the older properties facing the market place and those lining Park Street itself. As the excavations revealed, this boundary was demarcated by a large ditch, although the correlation of this ditch with the 'Hersum Ditch' identified from documentary sources (Demidowicz 2003) is unlikely.

The first mention of Park Street is in a collection of deeds of the Lench Charity and dates from 1331 when it was called Overe Parkstrete (Demidowicz 2003, 145). In 1437 an indenture of the Guild of the Holy Cross granted to John Belle one messuage in Moor Street and one croft of land in Park Street 'between the land of William Stretton, and a small lane leading into the Little Park' for 30 years, and ordered him to maintain the hedges of the croft in good condition (Langford 1868, 24). Robert Rastell held a tenement called the Swan at the head of Little Park Street in 1553, later to be called the George (pers. comm. G. Demidowicz). However, there are far fewer references to property in Park Street in comparison

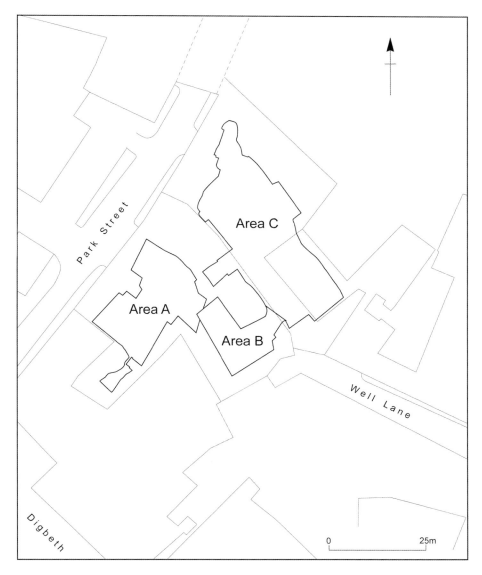

Fig. 4.1 Park St; location plan showing excavated areas.

to Moor Street in the 1553 survey. These properties are recorded as belonging to Thomas Cowper, Richard Smallbroke and William Phillips (Phillippes). The Phillippes' holding included two vivaries (fish stews or ponds) in a parcel of land on Park Street in the tenure of William Hethe, and also land and a pool called a 'pytte' in Park Street in the tenure of Thomas Marshall. Bickley and Hill (1891) place this land in the vicinity of the excavation site, and certainly the excavated evidence for a confluence of watercourses and a pond gives credence to this assertion, which is further backed up by recent unpublished documentary research by George Demidowicz.

Therefore it would appear that over 200 years after it was laid out, with the possibility of a few very localised and undocumented exceptions, the overall development along Park Street lagged behind that of Moor Street and

tended to be concentrated towards the market place, with closes, crofts, ponds and watercourses beyond, particularly on the east side of the street where the excavation site was located.

A substantial ditch, probably water-filled, ran along the back of the crofts and closes fronting onto the east side of Park Street, roughly at a right angle to the main boundary ditch dividing the back of the Digbeth plots from what had been the deer park and was to become Park Street backplots. This ditch (which may be correlated with one identified in the excavations) was probably dug when Park Street was laid out to mark the new boundary of the shrunken park, and fed the ponds and vivaries belonging to William Phillips in 1553. It probably also broadly follows the junction between the sandstone and clay along the Birmingham Fault here, a similar phenomenon being observable in the Parsonage–

Manor watercourse in the Edgbaston Street excavations (see Patrick and Rátkai, Chapter 2). These ponds and watercourses channelled and collected runoff and ground water from higher up the hill, distributing it down towards the thirsty smithies and tanneries concentrating in Digbeth in the 1500s and 1600s, particularly as the north side of Digbeth was not nearly as amply supplied with water as the south side (Fig. 16.2, colour).

Between 1700 and 1750, it has been estimated that the population of Birmingham tripled in size. Most of the new building that took place in Birmingham in the 18th century was on the better-drained land towards the top of the sandstone ridge. This was noticeable even to visitors to the town, one of whom remarked in 1755 that 'the lower part is filled with the workshops and ware-houses of the manufacturers, and consists chiefly of old buildings; the upper part…contains a number of new, regular streets, and a handsome square, all well-built and well-inhabited' (quoted in Buteux 2003, 67). In an early 18th-century context, when several of the major owners of the estates around the town, like Dr Sherlock, Bishop of London, were still reluctant to release land for development (see Litherland and Patrick, Chapter 2), Park Street offered opportunities for expansion, and a large tract of land is shown as marked out for building towards the northern end of the west side of Park Street beyond the Baptist Meeting House on Westley's map of 1731 (Fig. 2.2). This was followed by further northwards expansion at the northern end of Park Street onto land owned by the Jennens family that began with the construction of St Bartholomew's Church in 1749.

In contrast, the development of the eastern side of Park Street remained comparatively stagnant in the 18th century. Two and a half acres of land at the northern end of the street, formerly a series of closes belonging to the Guild of the Holy Cross and later to King Edward's School (pers. comm. G. Demidowicz), was eventually sold to the Street Commissioners in 1807 for an extension to St Martin's, the graveyard being later landscaped into Park Street Gardens. Development on the eastern side of Park Street more or less ceased at its junction with a lane marked Lake Meadow Hill (that entered Park Street roughly where Bordesley Street does today) on Westley's and Bradford's maps. Only one large building is shown to the east of Lake Meadow Hill (Fig. 16.1). Moving back towards Digbeth, a number of properties are shown lining the street, including a yard with what appear to be tenter racks shown (Fig. 2.2) which were probably associated with the drying and processing of textiles or animal hides.

While the general layout of the east side of Park Street did not change much between Bradford's map of 1750/51 (Fig. 1.2) and Hanson's map of 1778 (Fig. 2.3), it is possible to stitch together a more complex picture than this from disparate fragments of evidence such as old photographs of houses and other documents.

For example, Old Park House, a three-storey town house of five bays (with a basement and an attic with dormer windows) set back from the street, is a late 17th- or early 18th-century house (Turner 1994, 35–6) which can be traced on Westley's map of 1731. The house had a chequered history. By the time of Sketchley's Directory of 1770, the property was used by George Humphreys 'factor and merchant' as business premises (he himself lived in Sparkbrook). The anti-Nonconformist riots of 1791 saw Humphreys, a Dissenter, driven from the premises. The riots had a secondary effect on the house, since the Dissenting School on Meeting Lane (Freeman Street on the maps of Westley and Bradford; see Fig. 16.1), which ran off the north side of Park Street, was burnt down and the school moved to Old Park House. The school had a manufactory by 1801, which was used to train the pupils in a useful trade. The house was still recorded as a Dissenting School in the 1820–23 Rate Book but is not mentioned in the 1835 Rate Book, although listed as a Unitarian Charity School in an 1839 Directory. By 1856 Old Park House was a nail factory and subsequently became a brush manufacturer.

Further along Park Street, No. 18 (Turner 1994, 34), a reasonably large town house, was built around 1764 by Sampson Lloyd III, who was part of an important milling and iron-working family in Birmingham. The house was situated at the junction of Park Street and what later became New Vale Court (Goad Insurance Map 1895). By 1801 the house was in the ownership of Theophilus Merac, a French cloth merchant domiciled in London with business premises at 73 Queen Street, Shoreditch. As there is no mention of him or his brother, Moses Le Port Merac, with whom he was in business partnership, in any of the Birmingham trade directories, it seems safe to assume that he bought the several properties he owned on Park Street as a speculative venture. Theophilus Merac's properties are recorded as being in the hands of a sale agent in the 1835 Rate Book. Other entries in the later 18th-century trade directories and rate books suggest that one John Hasluck ('merchant/ gentry') may have owned the property and, later, James and William Reeves ('merchants/ factors'). Thus, although the house may not have survived long as a private residence, its links to the merchant classes were maintained from the 1780s through to the 1820s. By the mid-1820s it had become Henry Shaw's nail manufactory. The house is shown as Nos 16–18 Park Street on the 1895 Goad Insurance Map, by which time it had been bought by the Shaw family and is marked as Henry Shaw and Sons Nail Factory and Walter Shaw and Co H.W.

Neither of the above houses seem to have lasted long as private residences, despite the obvious quality of the buildings, and were turned to industrial or commercial use in as little as a generation in the case of No. 18. This process has been documented elsewhere in Birmingham, for example in the Jewellery Quarter in the later 18th and early 19th centuries, and it would seem that the momentum towards workshop-based industrialisation was very great in Birmingham at this time. Industrialisation was undoubtedly further fuelled in Park Street by the arrival of the canals on the old demesne and parkland to the east held by Thomas Gooch in the late 18th century. Following his securing a Parliamentary Act to enable development in 1766, industrial-led development swallowed up all of the former parkland and beyond in a period of less than 50 years, and it is in the early 1800s that the rest of the eastern side of Park Street began to be seriously developed, with the exception of the burial ground.

Trade directories from this time indicate a broad range of activity taking place in this area, noting shopkeepers and trades such as shoemakers, cutlers, cabinet makers, button makers and other manufacturers of 'Birmingham toys'. Even Birmingham's own poet, John Freeth, is recorded as living on Park Street in the 1767 directory. A list of tradesmen and women associated with Nos 1–10 Park Street is given in Table 4.1. The data were compiled primarily from trade directories but cross-referenced, where possible, to the rate books and house numbers given on the draft Rating Map of *c.*1850. It must be stressed that this list is by no means exhaustive. Clearly not all tradesmen and women lived and worked at the same premises and not all tradesmen owned their work and/ or domestic premises. Some of the smaller industrial concerns may have changed premises frequently. So, for example, Isaac Sargeant appears as owning a shop, probably to the rear of No. 9 Park Street, in the 1785–89 Rate Book. However, in Pye's 1787 Directory Isaac Sargent (surely an uncommon enough name for them to be one and the same man) 'saddlers tool and pinking iron maker' is listed with premises at No. 18 Digbeth and, in 1803, on Moat Row.

The processes at work to create the 19th-century congestion noted in Moor Street and elsewhere around the town were probably felt just as profoundly in Park Street, as most of the tenements near the market were not houses of any particular pretension. Another building, 29 and 30 Park Street, about which we know a little because it was surveyed before demolition in 1987, probably illustrates something of the general changes to the character of Park Street in the 19th century (Molyneux 1984). Built in the 1820s or 1830s, 29/30 Park Street was partly a public house, called the Duke of Cumberland, and partly a tinplate works.

According to the 1851 census, much of the excavated area of Park Street was occupied by newly arrived, impoverished Irish immigrants, which may say something of the quality of the housing at this time. It was during this period that a public house, the Daniel O'Connell, named after the Irish M.P. known as the 'Great Liberator', a fighter for Catholic emancipation and a proponent of Home Rule, was established at No. 9. The disproportionately large numbers of Irish at the southern end of Park Street probably explains why it was a target for the anti-Catholic rioters in 1867 (Fig. 4.31).

Photographic evidence taken to show damage to Nos 6–7 caused by the riots shows Park Street looking from

Digbeth (Twist 2001, 122) (Fig. 4.32). Clearly visible to the right of the picture is the Phoenix Tavern and Livery Stables. Just discernible in the distance is the one-storey shop frontage of Old Park House, a painted advert for William Shaw on a neighbouring house wall, and in the far distance the gables of No. 18 are just visible. The Phoenix Tavern (No. 3, Park Street) also suffered some riot damage (McKenna 2006), although this is not visible on this photograph. At some point in 1871, Nos 4–8 Park Street had all been demolished and were replaced by a school (see Rátkai below).

Both No. 3 and No. 10 Park Street were of vital importance in relating the documentary, cartographic and photographic evidence to the excavated areas (see Rátkai below).

There are further clues in some of the surrounding street-names to one of the more unusual aspects of the history of this area that, again, is directly related to its geological location close to the Birmingham Fault. In the 18th century the upper end of Digbeth High Street was called Well Street, another street called Well Lane was situated just to the east of the excavations, and Well Court is also marked on Bradford's map running off the west side of Park Street, more or less opposite No. 18. Numerous wells had been dug here from the medieval period onwards, excavated into the sandstone, which is relatively easy to cut, as well as being water carrying. However, while today Digbeth hardly springs to mind as a production centre for mineral water, in 1850 the firm of Goffe and Company was situated in Well Lane. They pumped water from a 400ft-deep artesian bore into a large cistern and there was also an underground reservoir some 40 feet long. All of this was found by workers in 1889 and reported in the monthly magazine *Birmingham Faces and Places* on the 1st of March. By this time most of Birmingham's water was piped and the ground water supply was becoming increasingly contaminated. On the Goad Map, adjacent to Goffe and Son, was a second mineral water production site – Job Wragg, Mineral Water Factory.

The arrival of the railways serving New Street Station and Snow Hill Station in the 1850s had a profound effect on Park Street, effectively cutting it in half. The northern half of the street developed industrially while the southern half became even more closely linked to the commercial activity of the markets. Nevertheless, the 1895 Goad Insurance Map reveals that the area behind or adjacent to the excavated areas was a maze of dwellings and industrial premises, with every sort of industry and trade represented from slaughterhouses, metal working, japanning, umbrella manufacture, candle making and confectioners to brush makers and curriers.

The plot fronting onto Digbeth was occupied by a Victorian music hall and public house, shown as the Museum Public House and Concert Hall on the 1850 Rating Map and as the Museum Palace of Varieties on the 1895 Goad Map. This became associated with the 'Peeky Blinders', a group of local hooligans. Behind this,

Date	House No 1850/1895	Directory address	Trader	Trade Description
1770		No 1	Luke Rogers	Sacking Weaver and Potter
1770	3	No 3	William Boman	Publican
1770	4	No 4	Timothy Smith	Brass Founder and Factor
1770	6	No 6	William Abel	Baker
1770	9	No 9	Jesse Harrison	Steel stamper, gun furniture and weavers mail
1770	10	No 10	George Humphreys	Factor and Chapman
1781	4	No 4	Timothy Smith	Brass Founder
1781	10	No 10	George Humphreys	Merchant
1783	4		Timothy Smith	Brass founder
1783	9		Richard Sheldon	Bellows maker
1787	4	No 4	John Hawkins	Locksmith
1787	6	No. 6	John Cooper	Thumb latch maker
1791	4		John Hawkins	Locksmith
1793	3		Thomas Hadley	Victualler
1793	4		John Hawkins	Locksmith
1801	6		Thomas Upton	Whip maker
1803	4	No. 5	John Hawkins	Locksmith
1803	9		Martha Sheldon	Bellows maker and sacking weaver
1803	6		Thomas Upton	Baker and grocer
1803	9		Martha Sheldon	Bellows maker and sacking weaver
1812	9 or 10		John Sheldon	Schoolmaster (possibly associated with the Dissenting School)
1815	court behind No 2?	2ct	James Hassall	Farrier and Blacksmith
1821	*1 to 3**		*Josiah, Ebeneezer and Cornelius Robins*	*Land surveyors, auctioneers, appraisers etc*
1821	3		Benjamin Bailey	Victualler
1821	9		Martha Sheldon	Sacking weaver
1821	Ct No 2 and No. 5		Sarah Shaw	Sword gripe (?) maker
1821	"		John Shaw	Nail ironmonger
1831	court behind No 2?	2ct	Jas Hassall	Smith and farrier
1831	3		Deborah Bailey	Victualler
1831	8	No. 8	Thomas Upton	Dealer in groceries
1839	1	No. 1	R Davenport	House painter
1839	3	No. 3	Thomas Justin (Tustin)	The Old Phoenix Tavern
1839	5	No. 5	W Hassall	Smith
1839	8	No. 8	G Hodgkins	Spade and shovel maker
1839	9	No. 9	John Lowe	Retail brewer
1839	10		The Unitarian Charity School	
1856	2	No. 2	William Baynham	Shoeing Smith
1856	3	No. 2	Thomas Justin (Tustin)	Old Phoenix Inn
1856	6	No. 6	Thomas Butler	Last maker
1856	8	No. 8	Francis Davis	Shopkeeper
1856	9	No. 9	George Taylor	Beer retailer *(The Daniel O Connell)*
1856	10	No. 10	William Shaw	Nail and chain maker

* Information from the Rate Book suggests that these properties were for sale

Table 4.1 Trades recorded for Park Street Nos 1–10 (and associated courts) 1770–1856. (Data derived from Trade Directories and Rate Books).

running partly into Area A, were the Corporation Stables. Stables are attested here from at least the first decade of the 19th century.

The later creation of the Moor Street passenger and goods stations by the Great Western Railway between 1905 and 1914 was the apogee of railway expansion here and, in the opening decades of the 20th century, the subsequent construction of Moor Street Station and its Goods Yard, including Goods Shed B, eradicated the buildings to the east of the excavated area.

With the 1960s redevelopment of the Bull Ring Shopping Centre this area fell into serious decline and, with the exception of the Digbeth frontage plots and the amazing survival of the London Museum, became empty ground awaiting the latest round of redevelopment, now completed.

Excavation method

Initial machine clearance of the modern overburden and levelling deposits was carried out under archaeological supervision. Machining continued down to the level of a 'dark earth' layer which covered the whole site. Three 1m-square sondages were hand-dug in this layer, one in each area, with the aim of ascertaining its composition and to recover any dating evidence. Machining then continued down to the top of the underlying archaeological deposits, with all subsequent work carried out by hand (Figs 4.2, colour and 4.3, colour).

Results

Roman

Four sherds of Romano-British pottery were found residually in later contexts. Two sherds of Roman pottery were recovered from a Phase 1 feature (F746) and two possible Roman sherds from Phase 1 layer 1838 and Phase 3 layer 1797.

Phase 1: 12th–14th century

Boundary ditches

In Area A, a massive ditch (F174/ F201; see Figs 4.4–4.5, 4.6, colour and 4.7, colour) extended across the site on a northwest to southeast alignment. This ditch had steeply sloping sides, stepped on the eastern side, a flat bottom, and measured at least 7m in width by 2m in depth. It was cut into the natural sand (1102) and continued beyond the limits of excavation, probably forming a continuation of the boundary ditch observed in the Moor Street excavations. The ditch is interpreted as marking the boundary between the burgage plots fronting onto Digbeth and the lord of the manor's hunting park, Little (or Over) Park. It would thus be a very early, indeed original, feature of the layout of the town. If this interpretation is correct, in the earliest period of the development of the town the bulk of the Park Street site

– everything to the north of the ditch – would have lain within the park.

A large quantity of pottery, over 880 sherds, was recovered from fills of the first section, excavated through ditch F201 (see Fig. 4.5). Approximately one-third of these sherds came from the middle fill of the ditch (1314) and analysis of the sherds suggested that they predominantly represented kiln waste from the production of Deritend ware vessels (see Rátkai, Chapter 7). Corroborative evidence for this was provided by the recovery of part of a fire-bar from layer 1326, the ditch fill immediately below 1314. This discovery, together with the slighter evidence from the Moor Street excavations, extends the range of the production of Deritend ware from Deritend and Digbeth up into the medieval town centre itself. Overall, the pottery from the ditch indicated that backfilling of the ditch had probably begun before the middle of the 13th century, and that the ditch had been filled in by the 14th century. A very small amount of pottery dating from the 15th to the 17th centuries, present in the upper fill (1252), could be explained as a result of trample.

The disappearance of the ditch as a major feature in the 13th century may be related to the laying out of Park Street, which cuts across it. However, there is evidence that the line of the ditch survived as a significant property boundary down to the 20th century. Visible in the upper fill of the ditch section (F174) was a recut ditch (F234), which produced 17th-century pottery as well as much residual medieval pottery. Then, in the late 19th century, the central line of the ditch was precisely followed by the wall of a building whose foundation (F263) had been dug deep down into the ditch.

A slighter, curvilinear ditch (F195) ran very close to, and parallel with, the southern edge of the massive ditch F174/ F201. One edge of this smaller ditch sloped steeply down to a flat base, but the feature had been heavily truncated to the north by the wall of a late 19th-century building (F212/ F214), thus obscuring the full profile. The ditch measured 1.16m in depth and produced a similar range of pottery to the large ditch, but its relationship to the latter, if one existed, could not be determined.

Seven samples from the fills of both excavated sections of the major boundary ditch (F174 and F201) and from the slighter parallel ditch (F195) were analysed for charred and waterlogged plant remains (see Ciaraldi, Chapter 12). The results provide an indication of the environment and activities in the vicinity of the ditch as well as of the character of the ditch itself in the 13th century. Numerous charred remains of cereals were identified, including bread/ club wheat, barley, oats and rye. Flax and hemp, cultivated for their fibres, seeds and oil, were also present, together with beet, suggesting vegetable gardens, fig and grape.

The range and character of the grassland species present suggested that they may represent charred fodder, indicating the keeping of animals, presumably cattle and

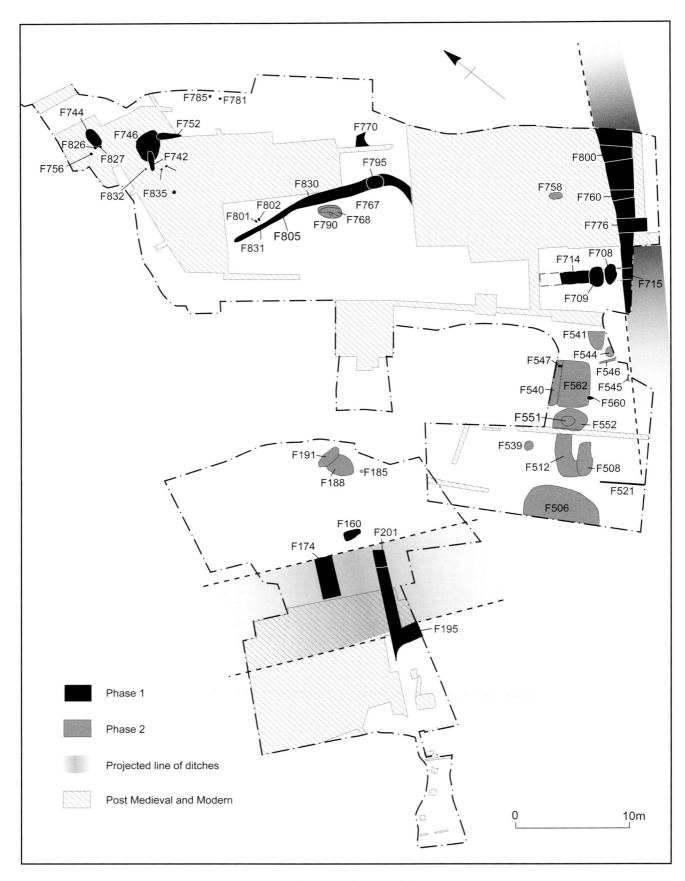

Fig. 4.4 All areas; phases 1–2 features.

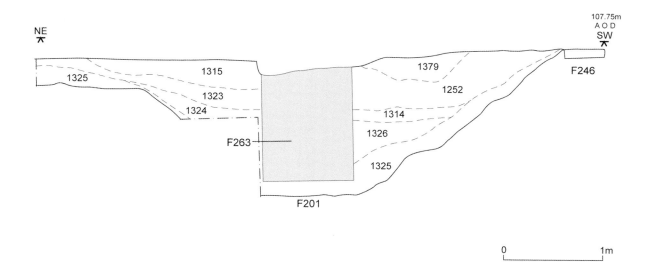

Fig. 4.5 Area A; section through Phase 1 town/ deer park boundary ditch, F201.

horses, in the vicinity. The waterlogged plant assemblage contained a predominance of species typical of disturbed ground, as well as many species typical of wet or damp environments. The remains of caddis fly from the major boundary ditch (F174) indicated that it had been filled with water.

Buds, seeds and cones of trees such as birch, alder and willow were indications of woodland, but this was more strongly represented in three samples from the major ditch (F174) which were examined for pollen and spores (see Greig, Chapter 13). Tree pollen accounted for upwards of 50% of the pollen in these samples, with alder, oak, birch and hazel well represented. Other trees included hawthorn and alder buckthorn, possibly indicative of hedgerows, while poplar and willow suggest damp ground. The other pollen remains generally reinforced the picture from the plant macrofossils, while the presence of diatoms again indicates standing water in the ditch.

That the ditch (F174) was water-filled at least part of the time was confirmed by analysis of the insect remains in its lowest fill (1246). The relatively large insect fauna from this context was dominated by a range of water beetles typical of slow-flowing or standing water, while the range of ground beetles, leaf beetles and weevils indicated weedy wasteland or grassland in the vicinity.

In the areas adjacent to the boundary ditch, the survival of medieval features and deposits was severely limited by intensive industrial activity during the 17th and 18th centuries, and building development in the 18th–20th centuries. The medieval remains were characterised by small islands of archaeology. The natural sand and a layer of redeposited sand were overlain by a grey-brown sandy clay silt layer (1196/ 1212), which produced a

fairly high quantity of pottery dated to the 13th and 14th centuries, as well as roof tile, slag and animal bone. The layer had been truncated by a solitary pit tentatively assigned to Phase 1 (F160, Fig. 4.4). The pit was irregularly shaped, contained pottery from the 13th and 14th centuries as well as slag, and had been partially truncated by a Phase 3 pit (F177).

At the southeastern end of Area C, a short stretch of a second major ditch was identified (F715/ F820/ F821/ F800) (Fig. 4.4, Fig. 4.8, colour and Fig. 4.9, colour), just within the limits of the excavation. The alignment of this ditch, northeast to southwest, is roughly parallel to the alignment of Park Street, and the ditch is interpreted as defining the rear boundary of plots fronting onto Park Street. The digging of the ditch is thus perhaps to be associated with the laying out of Park Street itself. It proved impossible to ascertain the complete profile of the ditch due to modern drainage and wall disturbance (again the indications are that the line of the ditch was preserved as a property boundary down to the 20th century). However, the steep slope of the partially excavated western edge of the ditch indicated that it was probably quite deep. The ditch had been recut along the original alignment, the recut ditch (F760, F799, F776) also continuing beyond the limits of excavation. Along the western edge of the ditch a number of timbers were observed. Two of these were uprights in situ (F777, F778) and others were substantial timbers, also *in situ*, arranged horizontally along the edge of the ditch. These timbers may be the remains of a fence that followed the line of the boundary ditch or part of a revetment lining.

The original ditch produced only eight sherds of pottery, but these were nevertheless indicative of a 14th-century date; the pottery from the recut is also most likely to be of 14th-century date (see Rátkai, Chapter 7). That the infilling of the boundary ditch to the rear of the Park Street plots should have occurred slightly later than the infilling of the boundary ditch to the rear of the Digbeth plots (*i.e.* F174/ F201) is consistent with a scheme whereby Digbeth is part of the original layout of the medieval town and the laying out of Park Street represents a later expansion.

Three samples from the ditch recut (F760, 1811; F799, 1871; F776, 1864) produced waterlogged plant remains (see Ciaraldi, Chapter 12). The assemblage included a wide range of species indicative of disturbed and wet environments, while remains such as watercress and caddis fly cases indicate that the ditch itself was water-filled. Many arboreal species were also present, including the buds, seeds and twigs of willow, birch, poplar and holly. Hemp was present in two of the samples, its presence having already been noted in the other major medieval boundary ditch (F174/ F201). It is possible that retting, the processing of hemp in water to extract the fibres, was undertaken in the water-filled ditch. Two samples from fills of the recut were examined for insect remains but produced only a small assemblage. Amongst the species present, however, were several indicative of aquatic and damp environments.

In both Area C and Area B the area adjacent to the ditch had evidently been liable to flooding, resulting in the accumulation of very dark, humic silty deposits to a depth of around 0.10m to 0.15m. Environmental samples from two of these deposits (1596 and 1652) produced waterlogged plant remains, again indicative of disturbed and wet environments.

Possible tanning pits

A section (F715) across the southeastern boundary ditch (Fig. 4.10) revealed a series of cut features post-dating and adjacent to it. Pit F708, which contained a very dark organic fill and what appeared to be a thin, greyish-white clay lining mixed with lime. The fill (1704) included a repaired child's leather turnshoe (see Macey-Bracken and Mould, Chapter 8). Extension of the section showed that this pit had been cut to the northwest by pit F709, which also contained a very dark organic fill. Pit F709 was notable for an oval hole dug into its base and infilled with redeposited sand. To the northwest lay a large, fairly deep feature, which appeared to be rectilinear in plan with indications of a clay lining (F714). This feature contained a number of distinct fills and produced pottery suggesting a backfill date in the 14th century. The fills also included many pieces of tile, in addition to a small amount of slag, leather, lead and animal bone.

This group of pits may be associated with leather tanning. Two (F708 and F714) appear to have been clay-lined, which suggests they were intended to hold water, while the oval pit F708 also contained lime, which, when slaked, is used in the pre-tanning process to remove hair from the hides. The adjacent pit F709, with the hole dug in its base, is possibly a soakaway, while the size and rectilinear form of the large pit F714 recalls the medieval

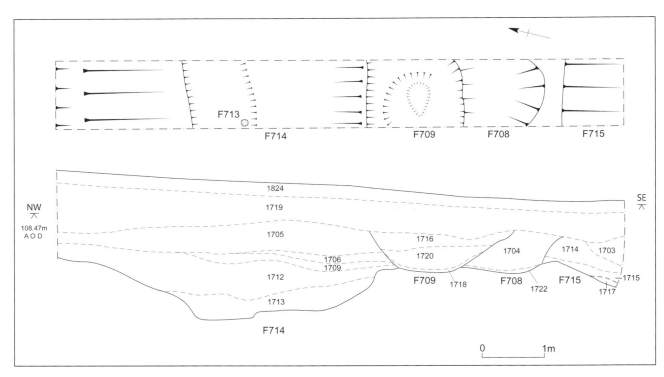

Fig. 4.10 Area C; phases 1–2 plan and section, showing possible industrial features adjacent to southeastern boundary ditch, F715.

tanning pits at Edgbaston Street. The presence of leather offcuts in pit F714, presumably some of the partial shoe remains and offcuts mentioned by Macey-Bracken and Mould (Chapter 8), may well indicate leather working in addition to tanning. Perhaps surprisingly, the manufacture of shoes in the medieval period was an important Birmingham industry and McKenna (2005, 16) notes the strong presence of Birmingham shoemakers in London for most of the 14th century. If this group of pits is correctly associated with tanning, ditch F715 may have been a permanent watercourse, supplying the tanpits. Tanning on Park Street may have begun before the burgage plots were officially laid out or have been one of

the first industries established after the pits had been formed.

Burials

In the northern corner of the site, close to the Park Street frontage in Area A, the preservation of medieval deposits was particularly good and included two human burials (Fig. 4.12). Here a series of layers produced substantial quantities of pottery, dated principally to the 13th century but including some apparently 12th-century fabrics and occasional, probably intrusive, later material. The lowest of these layers (1761/ 1763/ 1877), unlikely to pre-date the 13th century (see Rátkai, Chapter 7), was cut through

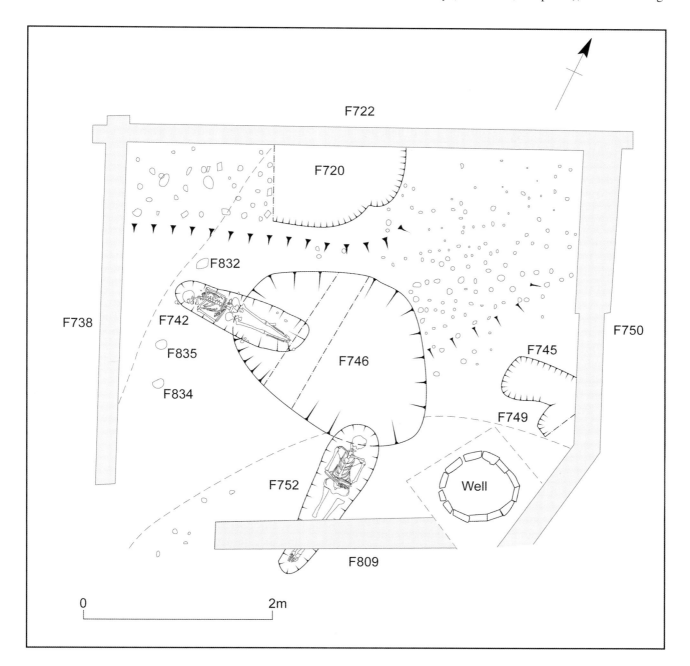

Fig. 4.12 Area C; detailed plan of inhumations.

by a large, sub-circular pit (F746). The lower fill of this pit contained pottery similar in character to the layer into which it was cut but the upper fill contained a larger (98 sherds) and more diverse assemblage, generally indicative of a later 13th-century date but including fabrics which ought to pre-date the mid-12th century, and three post-medieval blackware and yellow ware sherds. Notably, it also contained two Roman Severn Valley ware sherds.

The dating of pit F746 is of particular interest because it was cut by two graves (F742 and F752) which contained well-preserved, fully articulated skeletons. One skeleton (F742; Fig. 4.13, colour) was orientated northeast to southwest, with the head to the southwest. This was identified as a probable female who died in middle age (see Ives, Chapter 11). The other skeleton (F752) was orientated roughly perpendicular to the first, northwest to southeast, with the head to the northwest. It was identified as probably male and in the age range 18–22 years. This skeleton displayed several indications of pathology, including defects to the spine, suggesting a strained back perhaps caused by manual labour, and a shin injury which had become inflamed and had not healed properly, perhaps because of a diet poor in vitamin C. A poor diet was also indicated by the teeth, which were very decayed. Both skeletons had been placed in the graves on their backs, with the arms neatly folded over the stomach; there were no indications of coffins.

The graves contained pottery which, to judge from the average sherd weights, is likely to have been residual and which dated to the mid- and later 13th century (see Rátkai, Chapter 7). Approximately 3m to the northwest of the two graves was a third grave-shaped cut (F744), which, however, contained no bones. The pit (F746), the two graves (F742 and F752) and the grave-shaped cut (F744) were all sealed by a layer (1749/ 1760/ 1841) which contained a pottery assemblage of differing character, pointing in general to a 13th- to 14th-century date, and with sherd weights consistent with a surface accumulation of rubbish (see Rátkai, Chapter 7). However, post-medieval yellow ware, blackware and creamware sherds were also present. The likelihood of disturbance was also suggested by a further layer (1756), stratigraphically earlier than 1760, which contained, in addition to predominantly 13th-century pottery and a medieval lead weight (Fig. 8.6.1, colour), a large sherd from a 19th-century stoneware bottle.

Associated with this group of features was a scatter of post-holes. Two (F826 and F827) may have been cut by the grave-shaped pit (F744), although the presence of a thornapple seed in the fill of F826, a plant not introduced to Europe until the 16th century (see Ciaraldi, Chapter 12), suggests that the post-holes are more likely to have cut F744; a third post-hole (F756) was located in close proximity. A further three small post-holes (F832, F834, F835; Fig. 4.4) were located immediately surrounding one of the graves (F742). Two more isolated post-holes (F785 and F781) were exposed close to the northeastern boundary of the site. It is possible that some of these post-holes could relate to screening around the graves. No pottery was found in the post-holes apart from one 3g sherd (Fabric ip2) in F781.

The interpretation and dating of the graves and associated features present difficulties. The two graves are outside any known burial ground and are not orientated according to Christian practice. It is unlikely at this period that the burials were of non-Christians. Several possibilities remain for the reasons for the interments: from murder victims (although the careful positioning of the bodies and lack of any visible trauma makes this least likely) and suicides to plague victims.

The grave-shaped cut (F744) may have been a grave from which the body had been subsequently removed, and the excavators speculated that the large pit (F746) was possibly also a burial from which the bones had been removed, perhaps at the time the two graves cutting it were dug; a number of nails in the pit could have come from a coffin. A small number of disarticulated hand and foot bones in the layer sealing the graves (1760) might also suggest that the burials were once more numerous. However, the disarticulated bones probably derive from the known skeletons – they represent elements missing from these – and coffins are unlikely to have been used in the medieval period, at least for the burial of those at the lower end of the social spectrum. The evidence that the two burials formed part of a larger group is thus less than compelling.

The date of the burials is also uncertain. The pottery from the contexts cut by and sealing the burials would generally indicate a late 13th- to 14th-century date. However, occasional sherds of yellow ware and blackware were present throughout the sequence. The likelihood is that these were intrusive – there is more than enough post-medieval activity in the area to account for this – but the possibility remains that the burials could date as late as the 17th century.

Possible boundary or drainage gully
Towards the centre of Area C a shallow linear gully (F767/ F805/ F804/ F831), aligned roughly northwest to southeast, was dated to Phase 1. Three post-holes (F801, F802, F830) cut the gully and were situated along its edge. The gully had also been cut by a small pit (F795) containing a markedly compact orange clay fill. The gully may possibly be interpreted as the truncated remains of a boundary, the post-holes representing the remains of a fence line or, alternatively, as a drainage gully.

To the east of F767 was pit F770. The size and nature of this feature had been obscured by the later cutting of post-medieval industrial pit F769, pits F761, F764 and F763, and wall F786 running south from Structure 5. The pit contained 13th-century pottery and an intrusive blackware sherd.

Phase 2: 15th and 16th centuries

The major concentration of features relating to this phase were located in Area B, towards the rear of the Park Street plots, adjacent to the line of the former boundary ditch defining the back end of the plots. This area remained wet, and a series of clay-lined pits or tanks were dug into the dark, humic, silty medieval deposits here, which were attributed to flooding (see above). The function of these pits or tanks, which were probably water-filled, is unclear. Textile processing, dyeing or fulling are possibilities. Alternatively, they may simply be troughs and ponds for the watering of livestock.

Elsewhere on the site, in Areas A and C, features relating to this phase of activity were few and scattered. These included a possible kiln but mainly comprised pits that in form and content presage those associated with various industries, mainly iron smithing, that were to become much more numerous in Phase 3.

As is discussed in more detail in the pottery report, the quantity of 15th- and 16th-century pottery was very low compared with earlier and later periods, accounting for less than 4% of the overall assemblage in Area B and Area A, and less than 3% in Area C. Furthermore, the bulk of the pottery in the Area B features was medieval, with the small amount of Phase 2 pottery, if not in some cases intrusive, providing only a *terminus post quem* for the disuse of the features. The pits assigned to Phase 2 in Area A were sufficiently similar in form and content to the more numerous pits assigned to Phase 3 that their attribution to the earlier phase must be questionable. In general, therefore, Phase 2 is marked by a low level of archaeologically recognisable activity and many features can be attributed to this phase with only limited confidence.

Clay-lined pits and tanks

The largest feature in Area B assigned to Phase 2 was a pond or tank (F506) (Fig. 4.14, colour). The feature appeared to be rectilinear in shape and measured at least 6.5m across, although the full dimensions were obscured by the southwestern limit of excavation. The edges sloped gently to a flattish base and it appeared that the feature had been clay-lined. It was filled with very rich organic deposits (1584, 1511) which contained mainly medieval pottery, animal bone and roof tile. The upper of these two fills (1511) also produced a late iron-poor fabric suggestive of a 15th-century date. The uppermost fill (1519) contained a substantial assemblage of Phase 3 pottery, but this is interpreted as a late dump post-dating the initial infilling of the feature and subsequent settling of the fills. The insect faunas from F506 were indicative of a sometimes wet environment, probably pools of standing water or evidence of periodic flooding. Grassland species and species associated with decaying organic matter were also present (Smith, Chapter 14).

To the north-east of this 'pond' was a series of other pits or tanks, likewise dug into the water-laid silts which had accumulated at the rear of the plots, and likewise apparently clay-lined and intended to hold water.

Adjacent to the 'pond' were two shallow clay-lined pits, F508 and F512, with rich organic fills; one of the fills (1508) of F508 produced the sole of a leather shoe. Plant remains consistent with the feature being water-filled and animal hair were also recovered from F508 (Ciaraldi, Chapter 12). To the northeast of these pits was a large sub-circular pit (F552) measuring 3m across and 0.25m deep. It had been cut by a shallow, sub-circular pit (F551), 1.20m in diameter. These latter two pits contained unquestionable 15th–16th century pottery assemblages (see Rátkai, Chapter 7). The fill of earlier pit (F552) was dated to the 15th century, while the fill of the later pit (F551), which contained no residual pottery, could be dated *c*.1500–1550.

Northeast again was a rectangular pit or tank (F562/F561). It had steeply sloping sides, a flat base, and measured 4.50m by 3.00m by 0.50m deep. The insect faunas were much the same as those from pond or tank F506 (see above) and the plant remains also indicated a wet environment. Three pieces of secondary leather-working waste were found in the pit. The northwestern corner of the feature had been truncated by a shallow, circular pit (F540), which continued to the northwest beyond the edge of excavation.

To the east of this group of pits were further features cut into the medieval silt deposits and, although otherwise lacking in dating evidence, are most likely to be of a similar date. These included two small pits (F545 and F544), a shallow oval pit (F541) and a shallow linear gully (F546).

Possible industrial pits and kiln

Aside from the group of pits just described, only a few other features could be tentatively assigned to Phase 2. These comprised four pits which, from their form and content, appeared to be associated with the industrial activities more fully documented in Phase 3, and a possible kiln.

In Area B a sub-circular pit (F539) was located a little to the northwest of the group of clay-lined pits or tanks. It was dated on ceramic evidence to the mid-16th century and had been heavily truncated by a Phase 3 pit (F504). The pit measured 1.20m wide, 0.40m deep and produced pieces of charcoal and occasional iron.

In Area A a pair of intercutting pits was assigned to Phase 2. A large sub-circular pit (F186/ F188; Fig. 4.4), measuring 3.00m in diameter and 0.76m in depth, was dated to the 15th/ 16th century but also contained a probably intrusive yellow ware sherd. The fill of the pit (1220), a grey-brown sandy silt, produced evidence of industrial activity with iron nails, copper alloy objects, slag, and frequent roof tile, including glazed roof tile and a white slip-decorated floor tile fragment (see Macey-Bracken, Chapter 8), amongst a large amount of pottery and animal bone. The northern edge of this large pit had been truncated by a bowl-shaped pit (F191) measuring 0.80m by 0.50m and 0.52m deep. The fill (1237), also a grey-brown sandy-silt, contained animal bone and pottery and was in turn cut by a Phase 3.1 pit (F187).

Adjacent to this group of pits a small circular pit or post-hole (F185; Fig. 4.4) was uncovered. It measured 0.30m in diameter and was filled with distinctive grey, charcoal-rich sandy silt (1216) containing pottery. The pit had been truncated by a Phase 3 pit (F180).

A more direct indication that high temperature industrial processes had been carried out was provided by the discovery of a possible kiln (F768) towards the centre of Area C (Fig. 4.15, colour). This oval-shaped feature was approximately 2.00m long and 1.20m wide with vertical sides extending down to a flat base. The interior of the feature had been cut into a keyhole shape. It was filled with grey-brown silty clay sand (1829), which contained a moderate amount of pottery and roof tile as well as a small amount of slag and animal bone. A sherd of Tudor Green suggested a 15th–16th-century date. The southwestern edge of the feature had been cut by a shallow post-hole (F790) measuring 0.36m in diameter and packed with many small stones.

Phase 3: Late 16th–early 19th centuries

This phase was characterised principally by a large number of pits, 63 in total, located in clusters across the site (see Fig. 4.16). The pits were associated with the debris from industrial activities, notably metal working (both iron and copper alloy) and bone working. The only other features attributed to this phase were two wood-lined tanks at the southeastern edge of the site, possibly also associated with industrial activities, a robbed-out well and ten post-holes, located individually and in clusters but nowhere forming interpretable patterns.

The most immediately apparent characteristic of the distribution of the pits was that, with one exception (pit F259), they were confined to the northeast of the major medieval boundary ditch F174/ F201. This means that the pits and other features were located in plots fronting onto Park Street rather than Digbeth. As was noted earlier, the boundary ditch appears to have been partially recut (F234) in the late 16th or early 17th century as the recut fill (1166) contained, amongst much residual medieval pottery, ten sherds of this date (see pottery report). The re-establishment of this boundary may thus be associated with the beginning of a phase of intensified activity on the Park Street site.

Sub-phasing

The assemblages from the pits, principally the pottery, together with the stratigraphic relationships of inter-cutting pits, enable the 200-year span of Phase 3 to be subdivided and some chronological and spatial patterning to be discerned. Three sub-phases have been designated:

Phase 3.1: Late 16th–c.1720/30
Phase 3.2: c.1720/30–c.1760
Phase 3.3: c.1760–c.1800/ 1810

Of the 63 pits investigated, 44 could be assigned with reasonable confidence to one of these sub-phases; the remaining 19 pits could not be more closely assigned than 'Phase 3'.

Phase 3.1: Late 16th–early 18th centuries

In Area A, nine pits were assigned to this sub-phase. Running from the Park Street frontage southeastwards towards the rear of the plot, these pits are F134, F155, F141, F144, F172, F162, F187, F182 and F183. Two intercutting pits in Area B, F504 and F527, probably also belong to this group, which is likely to represent pit-digging activity which took place in the backplot of a single property fronting onto Park Street. Of these pits, F134, F182, F187 and F504 contained clay pipe dating to 1660–1680, 1650–1750, 1680–1730 and 1650–1700 respectively.

The pits, sub-circular or oval in shape, are amongst the largest of the whole of Phase 3 at Park Street, about half (five examples) having diameters in excess of 2 metres, with an overall range from 1.15m to 2.70m in diameter. The pits were generally characterised by steep sides and flat bases, with surviving depths ranging from 1.16m to 0.33m.

The material backfilling these pits reflected a range of activities which had taken place on or near the site. General domestic debris is represented by pot sherds, fragments of clay pipe, animal bones, plant remains and the occasional miscellaneous artefact. The sherd size from many of the pits was comparatively large, suggesting primary or near primary deposition, although the number of sherds was never large, with a maximum of 25. It was noteworthy that the pits closest to the frontage, *e.g.* F141 and F144, contained material associated with both domestic and industrial activities while in pits further back from the frontage the emphasis was more strongly on the debris from craft activities. There was also a possible chronological trend, with the pits nearest the frontage dating to the late 16th and early 17th centuries and those further back perhaps somewhat later.

Domestic activity in the late 16th to early 17th century is best represented by the intercutting group of three pits, F141, F144 and F134, closest to the frontage (Fig. 4.16). Pit F141 is the earliest in the sequence and may date wholly to the late 16th century (see pottery report). The large quantity of unworked animal bone from pits F141 and F144 is indicative of domestic waste. A sample from pit F134 was analysed for the plant remains present, as was one from the nearby and contemporary pit F187 (Ciaraldi, Chapter 12). The species identified from these two pits are consistent with domestic activities. Cereals – barley, oats and rye – were all present. The remains of beet, typically grown in vegetable gardens, were present

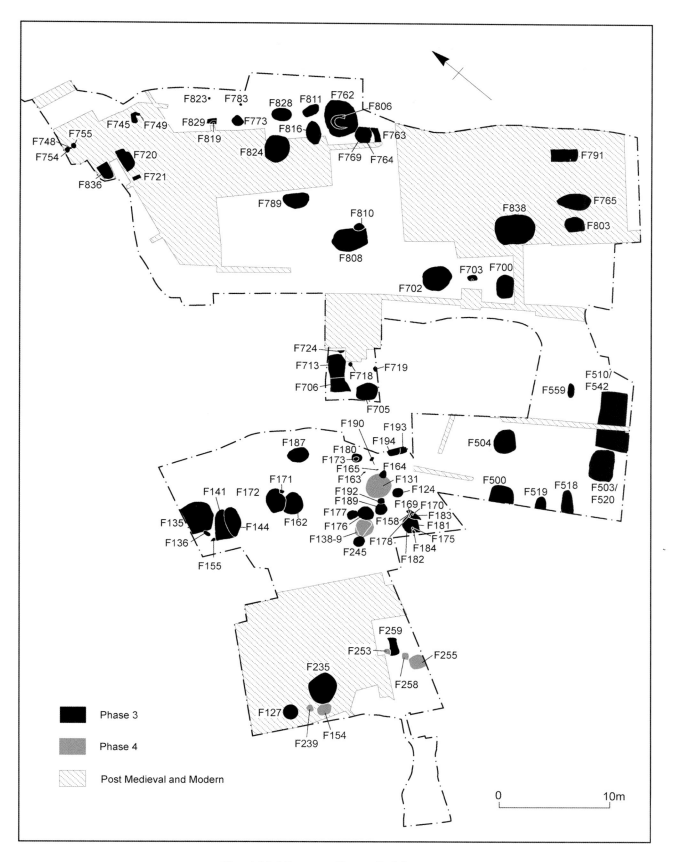

Fig. 4.16 All areas; Phases 3–4 features.

in large quantities in pit F134. The broken, weedy ground one might anticipate in a backplot is evoked by a range of typical weeds including, in substantial quantities, the common nettle, bramble and elder. More exotic, and suggesting a certain sophistication of lifestyle, were the remains of figs (in a substantial quantity), plums and grapes. Pit F134 also produced a copper alloy clothing hook.

Complementary to the evidence for domestic activity is that for development – the debris from demolition and construction. The fill of pit F182, towards the rear of Area A was composed largely of building rubble. Roof tile was present in many of the pits, with numerous pieces found in pit F141 towards the frontage. Such dumps of building debris must represent demolition and building work in the vicinity, presumably along the frontage, from the early 17th century.

Evidence for domestic activity and building work in the backfills of the pits was accompanied by evidence for iron smithing and cutlering. The evidence for smithing took two forms, hammerscale and slag. Hammerscale is produced when the surface of a hot iron object is struck and its presence is generally considered to indicate where smithing actually took place (see Nicholas, Chapter 10). It is interesting, therefore, that all the hammerscale identified at Park Street came from Areas A and B and that it was predominantly found in the nine Phase 3.1 pits currently under consideration. However, the absolute amounts are small, just 146g for the whole of Park Street in all phases, with 54g from the Phase 3.1 pits. It was found in all three of the intercutting group of pits nearest to the frontage (F141, F144 and F134) and in the nearby pit F187, but the largest concentration, 25g, came from Pit F504, at the rear of the group, in Area B.

Curiously, iron-smithing slag was either absent or present in only small quantities in most of the pits containing hammerscale, while it occured in the largest quantities in Area C where hammerscale was absent. This suggests that slag was not generally disposed of in the immediate vicinity of smithing activity (see Nicholas, Chapter 10).

Evidence of ivory- and bone-working was generally slight, with two pieces of debris (wedge-shaped pieces of cut bone) being found in pit F134 near the frontage and one in pit F187 a little further back. However, pit F504 in Area B, near the rear of the plot, produced 76 pieces of handle-making debris, double the amount from the whole of the rest of the site (38 pieces), and a pit cutting it, F527, produced a further ten pieces. One fragment bore traces of a large cut circular hole and one or two pieces were stained green from contact with copper alloy. The waste was more fragmentary and 'splintered' than the bone hafts illustrated by Moore (1999, 272), although this was not inconsistent with it deriving from the manufacture of knife handles.

Pit F504 also produced 25g of hammerscale, as has been noted, and one of the largest assemblages of slag from the site, including a substantial amount of 'hearth bottom', characteristic bowl-shaped pieces of slag that have collected at the base of the smith's hearth. It is

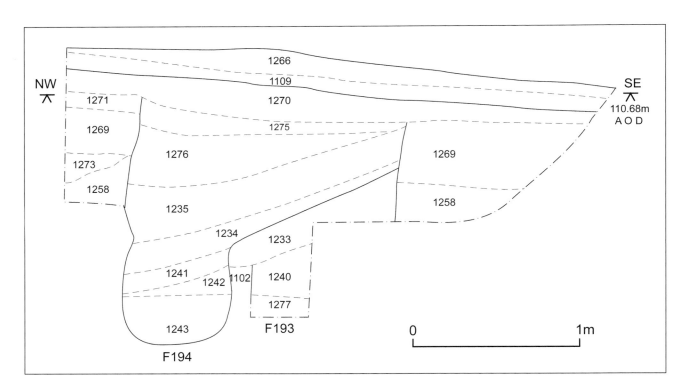

Fig. 4.17 Sections; phase 3.1 pits F162 and F172, phase 3.3 pits F194, F193.

therefore an exception to the general rule at Park Street that hammerscale and slag tend not to be found together. Taken as a whole, the contents of the pit may be interpreted as a primary or near primary dump of mixed industrial waste. The combination of smithing debris with the evidence for knife-handle manufacture is suggestive of the waste from a cutler's workshop. The pottery evidence suggests that the pit was backfilled rather later than those nearer the frontage, perhaps in the late 17th century.

Overall, the group of ten Phase 3.1 pits in Areas A and B conjure up a picture of a tenement plot on Park Street in the late 16th and 17th centuries with combined domestic dwellings and workshops on the street frontage and waste disposal to the rear.

Area C may represent a property distinct from Areas A and B (see Rátkai below); the layout of the 19th-century buildings excavated and Bradford's map of the town in 1750/51 would both seem to indicate this. In this area nine pits were assigned to Phase 3.1, all probably belonging to the 17th century. These are, from northwest to southeast, F829, F773 (Fig. 4.18, S4), F789, F808, F761, F810, F702, F765 and F803. Pits F773, F789 and F808 were the only ones to contain clay pipe, dated 1680–1730, 1650–1750 and 1650–1730 respectively. Also probably to be assigned to this phase is a brick-lined well, F806. A massive pit (F762, Fig. 4.18, S6) had apparently been dug to remove the well, which was reduced to just three courses. The pit contained 60 sherds with a date range of the late 17th to the mid-18th century and clay pipe dating to 1680–1730, so the well itself was probably 17th century in date.

The Phase 3.1 pits in Area C were more varied in shape and size than those identified in Areas A and B but several (F789, F808, F702, F803) were more than two metres across. Insect remains from F803 were similar to those recovered from Phase 2 pond or tank F506 and rectangular pit or tank F561/ F562. The pit fill was notable for the high percentage of tree pollen from within its fill (see Greig, Chapter 13) and for the presence of hemp. Pit F808 (2.0m by 3.0m by 1.2m deep) had a somewhat rectilinear shape. Pit F773 (Fig. 4.18, S4) had an irregular 'concave' profile, that is the profile of the pit 'bellied out', suggesting perhaps that it had once had an organic lining of some sort (otherwise the pit would have collapsed if left open for any period of time), or indeed that the lower parts of the sides of the pit had collapsed prior to backfilling. Concave pits of this general character were also found in Phase 3.2 and the shape may have been linked to a particular industrial function.

All the Phase 3.1 pits in Area C were dated on ceramic grounds to the 17th century, and none contained the large quantities of unworked animal bone, presumed to be indicative of primarily domestic debris, found in some of the pits nearest the Park Street frontage in Area A. This contrast may reflect the fact that the pit group does not run up as close to the frontage as that in Area A. Several of the pits contained substantial quantities of demolition debris, however, particularly those to the rear of the plot (F702, F765 and F803), and most produced general occupation debris such as fragments of clay pipes and ceramic roof tile.

The most notable characteristic of these pits was that all except one contained deposits of slag. The actual amount of slag was often not large (four pits contained less than 100g), but pit F702, which produced a particularly diverse range of finds, produced a massive 42,179g, which is by far the largest assemblage from the whole site. The slag from all the pits was classified as 'non-diagnostic' but is very likely to be iron-smithing slag. The absence of hammerscale and hearth bottoms together with incorporation with building rubble suggests that these are not primary deposits; they seem to be mixed dumps of material from activity elsewhere, perhaps workshops/ residences on the street frontage.

In addition to smithing, bone- and ivory-working was also represented in the pit fills, although absolute quantities of bone-working debris were small – three pits produced one piece of bone-working debris and one pit produced two pieces. Evidence for smithing and bone working represents the same combination of industrial activities identified in Areas A and B. Single sherds of crucible from pits F789 and F810, weighing 11g and 27g respectively, represent evidence for a new activity, the manufacture of objects from copper alloys. However, crucible fragments are much more common in later contexts, mainly of 18th-century date, with the site as a whole producing 130 crucible fragments. It is quite possible, therefore, that these two fragments from 17th-century contexts are intrusive. Analysis has shown that the crucibles were used for the melting of copper alloys (see Nicholas, Chapter 10).

Other finds of significance were generally sparse and include a copper alloy stud from pit F808 and a decorated leather strap with pewter studs from pit F765. Analysis of environmental samples from two pits towards the rear of the plot, F765 and F803, adjacent to the former medieval ditch defining the back of the plot, produced traces of figs, plums and nuts, as well as hemp, turnip and parsnip and many weeds indicative of broken ground, notably common nettle (see Ciaraldi, Chapter 12). There was also a high percentage of tree pollen from the pit (see Greig, Chapter 13). Remains of duckweed and waterflea indicated waterlogging of the pits.

A pit worthy of particular mention amongst this group is F702, which, as already noted, produced a huge quantity of slag (43,179g). The pit also produced, in addition to a piece of handle-making debris, a small double-sided ivory comb, a gaming token carved in the shape of a fish, a hoop-shaped copper alloy earring and a copper alloy pin.

If Areas A and B, on the one hand, and Area C, on the other, represent two separate properties, the nature of the activities carried out in the two properties was nevertheless very similar. Indirectly, we have evidence for

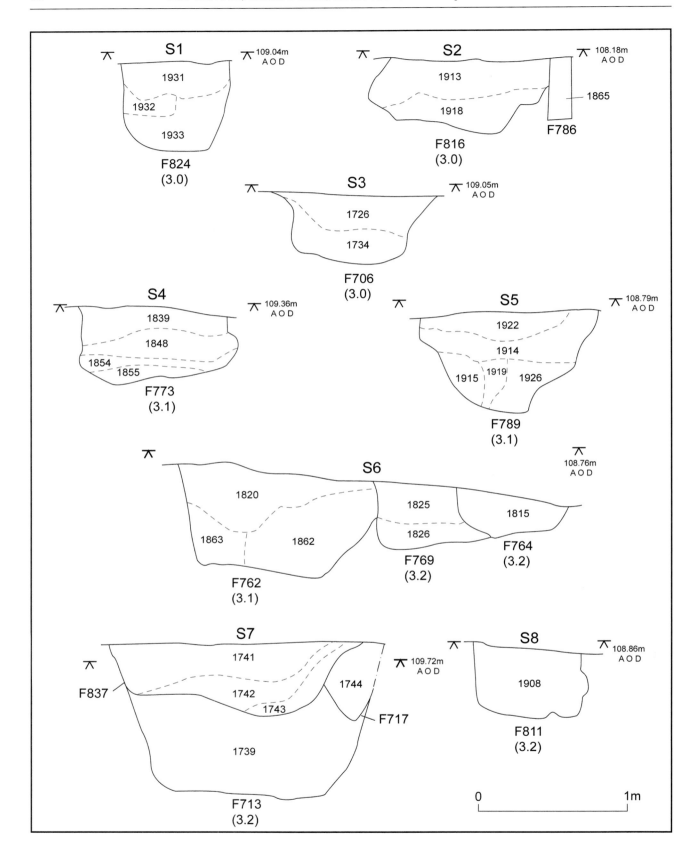

Fig. 4.18 Sections; pits F773, F824, F811, F815, F762–F769–F764, F789, F706, F713.

building activity and residences, probably along the Park Street frontage, where workshops for smithing and bone- and ivory-working may also have been situated. To the rear of the frontage we have evidence for weedy, broken ground, tending towards waterlogging at the back of the plots, where pit digging, waste disposal and perhaps gardening took place.

Phase 3.2: Early to mid-18th century

In the 18th century, although the theme of combined residential and industrial activities continues, there is evidence for a change in the emphasis of the industrial activities. The evidence again comes almost exclusively from pit fills. The Phase 3.2 pits tended to be smaller than the Phase 3.1 pits, typically in the range of 0.5m to 1.5m in diameter, whereas the earlier pits were often large, in the region of 2.0m to 2.5m in diameter. There is also a difference in the distribution of the pits. Whereas the Phase 3.1 pits were widespread, the Phase 3.2 pits tend to be found neither towards the frontage of the plots nor at the rear, but are concentrated in a band running roughly southwest to northeast across the centre of the plots.

In Areas A, B and C combined, 16 pits are assigned to this sub-phase. These are, from southwest to northeast, F259, F253, F133/ 245, F173 and F180 in Area A (see Fig. 4.16); F500 and F559 in Area B; and F713, F700, F763, F769, F764, F762, F811, F828 and F745 in Area C. Pits F173 and F180 contained clay pipe dating to 1720–1740 and 1720–1780 respectively. From the clay pipe evidence pits F707, F713 and F828 dated to the second or third quarter of the 18th century.

While, due to the range and quantity of material it contained, pit F133/ F245 in Area A cannot be described as typical, it illustrates most of the key features of the early to mid-18th-century pits and may usefully be described in some detail. The pit was circular, 1.30m in diameter and 1.05m deep, and had been cut into the infill of the major medieval boundary ditch F174/ F201. The upper fill of the pit (1125) contained large quantities of slag and pottery, as well as glass, clay pipe, roof tile, and many fragments of crucible. The pottery from the pit, totalling 215 sherds, indicated a date range c.1725–1750, and included a crude hand-made vessel which, although unsooted, must have been intended for some industrial purpose. The clay pipe from the pit suggested a somewhat later date, c.1760–80, and combining the two lines of evidence a mid-18th-century date is most likely for its infilling. Other finds included a one-piece trapeziodal copper alloy buckle, 29 facetted glass beads, a wine bottle base, and a fragment of a wine glass. Analysis of an environmental sample revealed hazelnut, fig, plum, grape, hemp, turnip, beet, and a wide range of weeds, an assemblage similar in character to those from the 17th century. Of particular interest, though, is the presence of rose, cypress and poplar, which may suggest ornamental gardens in the vicinity.

The chief interest of pit F133/ F245, however, lies in the quantity and range of metal-working debris recovered from its fill. This included a large quantity (763g) of hearth bottom, evidence of iron smithing, and a very large quantity (3,115g) of non-diagnostic slag, also probably deriving from iron smithing. The pit also produced a small amount of hammerscale (3g), the only Phase 3.2 pit to do so. It is especially noteworthy that, in addition to the evidence for iron working, the pit also produced extensive evidence for the working of copper alloy. This comprised a comparatively large amount of copper alloy slag (320g) and no less than 45 crucible fragments. Analysis of the copper alloy slag showed the presence of zinc, showing that brass was being melted, while analysis of seven crucible fragments also indicated that most had been used to melt brass (see Nicholas, Chapter 10). However, one crucible contained the residue of the melting of gunmetal, an alloy of copper that contains both zinc and tin.

Pit F133/ F245 shows unequivocally, therefore, that brass working was added to iron working amongst the industries pursued at Park Street in the 18th century. However, other pits of this sub-phase producing crucible fragments were comparatively few. There were no others in Area A, none in Area B and only two pits in Area C, F769 (Fig. 4.18) producing just one fragment and F700 producing ten. Pit F700 produced a substantial assemblage of pottery (85 sherds) and is dated on the ceramic evidence to c.1700; as the ten crucible fragments are unlikely all to be intrusive, this suggests that the working of copper alloy began on the site no later than the beginning of the 18th century.

Iron-smithing slag continues to be a significant feature in the fills of pits in Phase 3.2, occurring in just over half of the pits (nine out of 16). The largest quantities were found in the pits of Area C, where the primary fill (1826) of pit F769 was composed almost entirely of large lumps of slag (7,487g) mixed with considerable amounts of charcoal and clinker. Here and elsewhere at Park Street, however, fragments of coal embedded in the slag indicates that coal, not charcoal, was the fuel used for smithing (see Nicholas, Chapter 10). Pit F769 formed part of a pit complex with pits F763 and F764. Clay pipe from their fills and from neighbouring pit F762 (see above) dated to 1680–1730. The paucity of yellow ware within the fills suggests a deposition date probably at the beginning of the second quarter of the 18th century. The activity represented by these pits is thus on the cusp of Phases 3.1 and 3.2.

If the evidence suggests that iron working continued unabated from the 17th century into the 18th century on Park Street, there are slight indications that handle-making tailed off in the later period. No bone-working debris was recovered from pits of Phase 3.2 in Area A. In Area B pit F500 produced a possible ivory handle in three fragments (Fig. 8.11.4); and in Area C just two Phase 3.2 pits produced ivory-working debris (four pieces in all). Pit F500 did produce a fairly large group of 18th century pottery and clay pipe dating to 1720–1820.

The shape of three of the Phase 3.2 pits in Area C (F769, F713 and F811: Fig. 4.18) may be described as 'concave' in that the profile of the pit displayed a more or less distinct 'bellying out'. As noted above, this was a characteristic of one of the Phase 3.1 pits also and may suggest that the pits were at one stage lined for an unknown but presumably industrial function, or that the steep sides of the pits had partially collapsed prior to backfilling. Three further pits in Area C, F824, F816 and F706 (Fig. 4.18, S1–3), assigned to Phase 3 but not more closely dated, displayed this characteristic, together with a Phase 3.3 pit (F194) in Area A (Fig. 4.17). Pit F824 (Fig. 4.18, S1) had been disturbed by the construction of Structure 5 and only the uppermost fill 1931 contained pottery, the 19th-century elements of which are likely to be intrusive. Thus eight pits in total can be assigned to the category of 'concave' pits.

Whether the concave pits form a coherent group is debatable. They do occur in a rough band running from southwest to northeast across the middle of the plots but this is a general characteristic of the Phase 3.2 and 3.3 pits. All of the pits except one produced slag, often in quantities well above the average, and three contained crucible fragments, which perhaps suggest an association with metal working (or at least the fact that these pits were open when the slag was deposited). The fills are also notable for the presence of substantial quantities of charcoal and ash. However, the considerable variation in shape and size of these pits, together with their wide date range, from the 17th century through to the late 18th century, argues against a uniform function.

Post-hole F823 was also assigned to this phase and contained 16 sherds and clay pipe. The clay pipe dated to 1620–1720. The pottery was largely in agreement with this date, apart from a tiny 1g sherd of white salt-glazed stoneware and a small refined body ware sherd which would suggest a date later than 1720, although the sherds could, of course, be intrusive.

In Phase 3.2, as in Phase 3.1, evidence of 'domestic' activities and building/ demolition activity forms a background to the evidence for industrial activities. Pottery and clay pipe fragments were a regular component of the fills, although unworked animal bone occurred somewhat less frequently than in the Phase 3.1 pits. Miscellaneous 'domestic' finds from the pits were infrequent and included vessel glass and various functional items in iron (including nails and a staple), copper alloy and bone (including a bone finial or pinhead). Roof tile and, to a lesser extent, building rubble was noted in a significant number of the pits.

Phase 3.3: Later 18th century/ early 19th century

A cluster of five pits in Area A is dated to the later 18th century or early 19th century and, both spatially and in their character, these form a continuation of activity

documented by the Phase 3.2 pits here. The pits are F176, F177, F163, F194 and F193 (Fig 4.17). With the exception of pit F176 the clay pipe evidence suggested a backfilling date before 1800. The pits, like those of Phase 3.2, tended to be relatively small, less than 1.5m in diameter. Slag was present in three of the five pits, although not in large quantities, and crucible fragments in two of them, one fragment in F194 (a 'concave' pit: Fig. 4.17) and three fragments in F176. Bone- and ivory-working debris was absent from the pits and only small quantities of unworked animal bone were recovered. Other than fragments of sheet metal vessels from pit F194 there were no small finds of note. Perhaps the principal value of this group of pits is to indicate that the metal-working activity characteristic of the 18th century seems to have continued in this part of the site up to the major transformation which occurred in the 19th century.

The most intriguing features from Phase 3 at Park Street were two large wood-lined tanks (F503/ F520, F510/ F542, Figs 4.19, 4.20, Figs 4.21–4.26, colour) situated side by side at the southeastern end of the Area A/B plot, adjacent to the filled-in medieval boundary ditch. The larger of the two tanks, F510/ F520, measured around 4m northeast to southwest by 2m northwest to southeast, with a surviving maximum depth of 0.5m. It had a flat bottom, vertical sides and had been lined with a series of wooden planks (1695) held in place by timber uprights, many still *in situ*. Numerous post-holes around the edges of the base of the tank marked the position of similar uprights that had been removed. The lower (1635, 1634) and upper (1621) fills of the tank produced very considerable quantities of brick, post-medieval pottery, glass and slag. The slag included both hearth bottom (1,027g) and non-diagnostic slag (2,272g) and eight crucible fragments were also recovered. Amongst the other finds were two copper alloy buttons, a plain leather strap, a glass bottle neck dating to *c*.1750–1800 and ivory handle-making debris. A layer midway up the infilling of the tank (1622) was notable for being very organic, with large amounts of plant remains and twigs present, as well as a cylindrical fragment of Millstone Grit. A 19th-century drain (F502) cut across the tank.

Tank F503/ F542 was again a large, vertically sided, rectilinear pit, approximately 3m by 2m and surviving to a maximum depth of *c*.0.45m. Thirteen post-holes, some quite deep and shaped to take pointed timbers, were located at fairly regular intervals around the edges at the bottom of the pit. These presumably had held posts which once retained a plank lining similar to that which partially survived *in situ* in tank F510/ F520. In the base of the pit were found the well-preserved remains of a wooden chair, dated on stylistic grounds to the mid-17th-century but found associated with a deposit (1580) containing late 18th-century pottery, suggesting that the chair may have been more than a century old when it was discarded. A wicker sheet (1532) overlay the chair (Fig. 4.23), which might conceivably once have formed part of a canopy

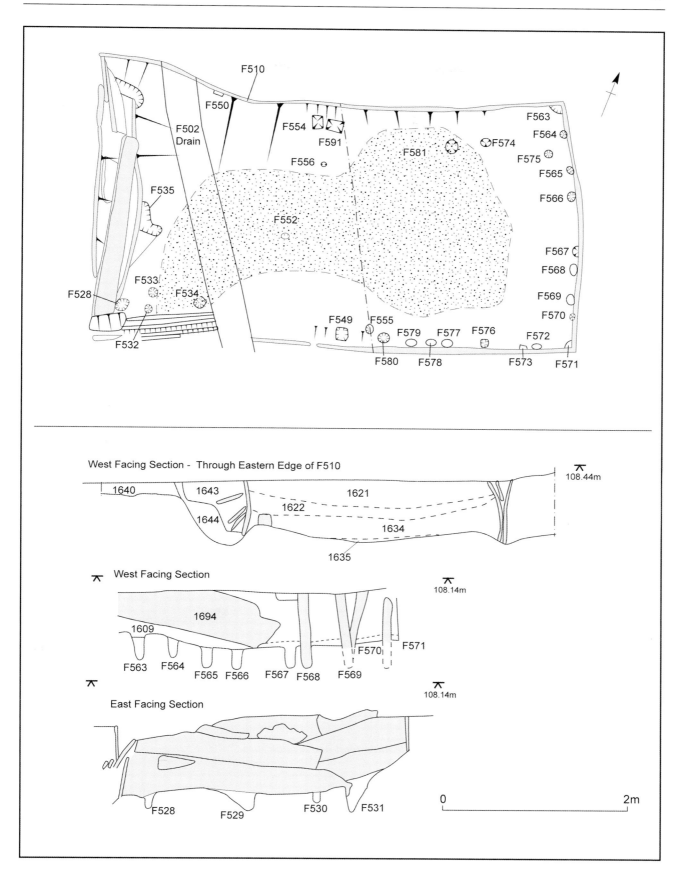

Fig. 4.19 Area B; detailed plan and section tank F510/ F542.

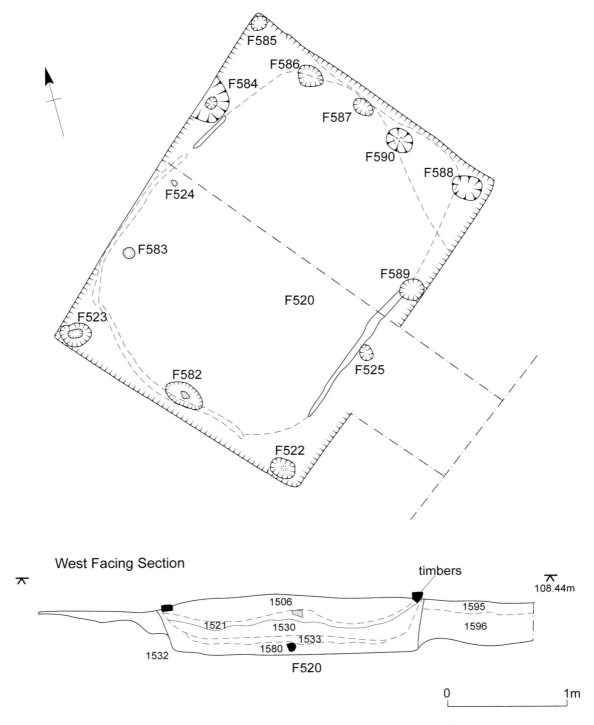

Fig. 4.20 Area B; detailed plan and section tank F503/ F520.

over the pit. Above this, forming a layer in the middle filling of the pit as in tank F510/ 520, was an organic deposit (1521, 1533) which contained twigs, bark and matted, straw-like material. The final layers infilling the pit contained a substantial quantity of pottery dating predominantly to the late 18th century.

The large collection of pottery found in the backfills of the two tanks is considered in detail in the pottery report. It contained a very small quantity of residual medieval material (*c.*1%) and the majority of the assemblage from both the lower and upper fills of the tanks appeared to be more-or-less contemporary, dating to the late 1770s or early 1780s; the tanks were presumably filled in a few years after this. The low level of residuality, the large size of the assemblage, the fact that it forms a fairly tight chronological group, the fact that it is found distributed throughout the fillings of the tanks, and the character of the vessels all suggest that the pottery was dumped in a single episode, perhaps relating to a house clearance.

If the date of the disuse and infilling of the two tanks presents few difficulties, the date of the construction and use of the tanks, and the question of their function are more problematical. The tanks were cut through a sand layer (1609) which contained two medieval sherds, a blackware drinking vessel sherd and a flower-pot base. Assuming the tanks were not maintained scrupulously clean throughout their use, a mid- to late 18th-century date seems most likely, although an earlier date is certainly possible. The tanks were presumably designed to hold water, but water is a component of such a wide range of industrial and other processes that this does little to narrow the focus. An environmental sample from the bottom of tank F503/ F520 (1580, associated with the chair) produced fig, hemp (in small quantities), weeds and willow. However, as this assemblage is not associated with the primary use of the tank and differs little from the assemblages found in Phase 3 pits in general, it is of little assistance. In the absence of corroborative evidence, tanning can probably be excluded. Dyeing and textile processing are possibilities, but one might question how many diverse crafts are likely to have been practiced contemporaneously with metal working on what seems to be a single plot of land. Unfortunately, the 18th-century trade directories shed no light on what possible industry could be represented by these tanks, unless they are in some way connected with Luke Rogers, sacking weaver (and potter), recorded at No. 1 Park Street in Sketchley's 1770 Directory.

The wood-lined tanks add a further dimension to the range of industrial features and – possibly – activities carried out in the plot represented by Area A (to the northeast of the major medieval boundary ditch) and Area B of the archaeological excavations. If the dumps of pottery in the two tanks, as well as a contemporaneous dump in the upper fill of the Phase 2 'pond' F506, are correctly interpreted as relating to a house clearance (the house in question presumably stood on the frontage), then these dumps and the disuse of the features which contained them signify a break with a pattern of usage of the plot that had its beginnings in the late 16th century.

Other features

One pit, F791, could belong to Phase 3.2 or Phase 3.3. It lay towards the back of the plot and had been cut by the construction of the modern building Structure 8. The fill contained clay pipe dating to 1720–1820. Clay pipe and ceramic evidence suggest that pit F749, which was cut by wall F750 of Structure 2, dated to the end of Phase 3.3. Pit F124 (Fig. 4.27, colour) in Area A contained 18th-century pottery and clay pipe with a suggested deposition date of 1680–1750 indicating that the pit is either late Phase 3.1 or Phase 3.2. However, due to the absence of pottery or other chronologically diagnostic finds, useful stratigraphic relationships with other pits or recording problems, there was a residue of pits that could not be assigned to any of the sub-phases of Phase 3. On the basis of their character and/ or relationships to deposits of Phases 2 and 4, they can however be assigned to Phase 3 with reasonable confidence. These pits are F136, F189, F192, F158, F171, F164, F190 and F169 in Area A; F518 and F519 in Area B; and F824, F816, F706, F783, F724, F703, F838, F754 and F755 in Area C. Many of these pits were small or highly truncated and devoid of finds. Others, with the exception of reasonable dating evidence, reflected the range of pit types and pit contents already discussed.

Ten Phase 3 post-holes were also identified, five in Area A and five in Area C. A cluster in Area A (F178, F184, F175 and F170) had been truncated by pits F158 and F183; an isolated post-hole (F165) was near by. The post-holes in Area C (F748, F819, F718 and F719) were more scattered. Post-hole F819 cut Phase 3.1 pit F829. No interpretation may be offered for these post-holes.

'Dark earth' and buildings

An apparent horizon encountered early in the excavation was a number of layers of dark earth (1108, 1168, 1520, 1797 and 1824), ranging from 0.2m to 0.7m in depth, found extending across the site. The research priorities of the excavation focused on the medieval and earlier post-medieval deposits, so neither the 'dark earth' deposits nor the structural remains were investigated in detail. Three hand-dug 1m-square pits were dug though the dark earth to obtain some idea of composition and date but the remainder of the layer was removed by machine. This limited understanding of the deposits (1108, 1168, 1520, 1797, 1824) precluded the collection of fully representative samples of pottery and other material from the deposits. The dark earths were initially interpreted as representing a single event, taken to signify a major hiatus in the development of the site, comparable to the 'dark earth' layers also recognised at Edgbaston Street and Moor Street, with the buildings constructed following the deposition of the layer representing a radical transformation in the nature of the activity carried out on the site. Closer study of the nature of the layers and the finds from within them suggests that this was not the case and that it is more likely that they represent a series of deposits of differing character and dates, which accumulated from the 17th century through to the early 19th century (see Rátkai, Chapter 7). On the pottery evidence, only one of these deposits, 1797 in Area C, could be considered a cultivation layer, possibly dating to the 17th century, although most of the pottery found within it was of medieval date. This layer was of particular interest since it also contained a post-medieval rock crystal swivel seal (Fig. 8.3.12). Layer 1520 in Area B, on the other hand, contained large amounts of roof tile and brick, suggesting a demolition deposit, together with

18th-century pottery and clay pipe with a suggested deposition date of 1690–1750. Clay pipe, which dated to 1680–1730, was also found in 1108, whilst layer 1168 contained no clay pipe but a ladle and a knife (see Bevan *et al.*, Chapter 8). Obviously, the deposits, *e.g.* 1505 sealing the two tanks (F503/ F520 and F510/ F542) in Area B (see Barker and Rátkai, Chapter 7), must post-date their infilling towards the end of the 18th century.

Combining this evidence with the dating of the infilling of the Phase 3 pits, a scheme may be proposed whereby there is a general, but by no means uniform, trend for the pits nearest the frontage to be infilled first, followed possibly by episodes of cultivation. The area to the rear of the plots, notably Area B, stayed open longer, to be finally sealed and built up with demolition deposits at the end of the 18th century.

It is likely that the pattern of building which followed the deposition of the 'dark earth' reflects this scheme, with the earliest buildings being constructed nearest the frontage with later infilling of the rear portions of the plots. In Area C, the building foundations are on different alignments. Structure 2 (see below) seems to be aligned with the Park Street frontage and wall F722 may be the backwall of the properties along the frontage. Both Structure 1 and 2 had less substantial walls and were constructed of smaller, less regular bricks than the buildings further back from the frontage. It is possible that these buildings, perhaps combining both domestic and workshop elements, were at least in part contemporary with the metal working and other craft activity associated with the Phase 3 pits.

Cartographic and documentary evidence for the Phase 3–5 Structures
by Stephanie Rátkai

Before analysis of the structural remains from Park Street, it is necessary to look briefly at the history of the burgage plots running south from Park Street and their topography. For the purposes of the following, Park Street has been taken to run north–south, with St Martin's Church at the southern end and St Bartholomew's at the northern end. The excavated area of Park Street is therefore the eastern side of Park Street.

The area of excavation covered part of the end of the backplot running back from Digbeth (part of Area A) and part of two backplots running back from Park Street, one comprising part of Area A and Area B and the other Area C. There were two major boundaries: the first a large ditch running more or less parallel with Digbeth High Street, which formerly marked the edge of urban development and formed the boundary to Over Park, and a second running more or less at right angles to this boundary and forming the back edge of the Park Street plots.

Examination of the cartographic evidence for the area of the Park Street backplots reveals two anomalies in their layout. The first is represented by a bulge in Park Street itself. This is clear on Bradford's map of 1750/51 (Fig. 1.2) and on subsequent maps but is less marked on the earlier Westley map (Fig. 2.2), although evidence tends to suggest that this map is the least accurate of any. The second feature is a distortion in the shape of the backplots running back from the 'bulge' in Park Street. Here the plots begin more or less perpendicular to the street but veer off to the southeast towards Digbeth High Street. As Park Street represents a development of the medieval town on virgin parkland, distortions of both the street and plot layout must have been influenced by existing geographic features. Closer examination of the 18th-century maps reveals a possible cause for this. On the Bradford map (Fig. 16.4) what at first appears to be a field boundary runs back from the far edge of the Park Street bulge in a southeasterly direction; beyond this point the Park Street burgage plots run parallel to each other and perpendicular to the street. The Bradford 'field boundary' is also shown on the Westley map although here its course is rather more serpentine, suggesting that this is either a watercourse or follows the line of one. On both the Westley and Bradford maps this stream appears to feed into the major boundary separating the Digbeth plots from what was originally Over Park. The line of this suggested watercourse has been noted by Demidowicz (2002) and equated with Hersum Ditch, a landscape feature which was still extant in the 16th and 17th centuries. However, Demidowicz is mistaken in the siting of the sections of archaeologically excavated ditch, which he places too far to the north. The longevity of this watercourse as opposed to the park/ town boundary ditch, which appears to have been backfilled by the early 14th century (see above and Rátkai, Chapter 7), would explain why the distortion of the plot layouts was still manifest in the 18th- and 19th-century development of Park Street. Water in Hersum Ditch, as it flowed southeast, may also have fed the Park Street backplot boundary ditch F715 etc.

On the Goad map of 1895 (Fig. 4.30) and the draft Rating Map of *c.*1850 (Fig. 4.29), the 'kinks' in the plot layouts are clearly visible and it can be seen that a long section of wall F710/ F725 (see Fig. 4.33) follows this alignment and almost certainly represents a boundary of some antiquity and significance. The main boundary ditch at the back of the Digbeth plots seems to have been respected by a 19th-century building in Area A, Structure 9, whose back wall ran along its centre. Likewise, the back wall of Structures 7 and 8 in Area C ran along the line of the ditch defining the back edge of the Park Street plots. The interesting thing about all these examples is how once boundaries were established (by man or nature) they were perpetuated even though ditches had long since been filled or watercourses culverted.

Working from the 1895 Goad Map and the draft Rating Map of *c.*1850 it is possible to establish the house numbers of the properties and relate these both to the rate books and census returns (Dodds and Rátkai in prep).

Fig. 4.28 Cartographic evidence for the development of Park Street backplots from the mid-eighteenth to the late-nineteenth centuries.

Cartographic and documentary evidence show that the excavated areas lay for the most part behind houses numbered 1–8 and within Courts 1–3. The westernmost end of the excavated area (western part of Area A) lay within backplots running back from Digbeth. The rest of Area A and Area B lay in a yard area associated with house No. 3 which became the Phoenix Inn or Tavern and the Phoenix Brewery. From the rate book of 1832 it is clear that Court No. 1 was also in this area, although it is not marked as such on the Rating Map. Area C was

behind houses numbered 4–8 and included Courts 2–3 (Fig. 4.29). This was the area which later became the site of St Martin's National School (see Fig. 4.30).

The following discussion uses two fixed points to cross-reference the Park Street house numbers, their owners and occupiers and the possible trades associated with them. The first is No. 3 Park Street recorded as a public house in 1767, even then known as the Phoenix Tavern, with William Steen listed as maltster and publican (see Figs 4.29 and 4.30). McKenna (2006) notes that the

Bob Burrows, Simon Buteux, Helen Martin and Stephanie Rátkai

Fig. 4.29 Area C: location of structures in relation to mid-nineteenth century buildings (based on Draft Rating Map c.1850).

Fig. 4.30 Area C; location of structures in relation to late-nineteenth century buildings (based on Goad Insurance Map 1895).

Phoenix Tavern dates back to 1720 and so should be on both Westley's and Bradford's maps. The tavern was rebuilt in the early 19th century and engravings and photographs from 1867 (Twist 2001, 122) and 1965 (Moxam 2002, 19) show a simple three-storey building (Fig. 4.3, colour). The latter photograph is also of interest in that it shows, albeit somewhat obliquely, some of the buildings to the rear of the Phoenix and to the rear of adjacent properties. A section of particularly high wall is visible, which must be located in the backplots of Nos 4–5.

The second point of reference is No. 10 Park Street (see Figs 4.29 and 4.30). A late 19th- or early 20th-century photograph of No. 10 (Turner 1994, 35–6) which by this time was a brush manufacturers, shows a rather fine Queen Ann style house. The house was used by George Humphreys, merchant, as business premises (he was resident in Sparkbrook) until the anti-Nonconformist riots of 1791. Shortly after, the house became a Protestant Dissenting School, replacing the one which had been burnt down in the same riots, situated on nearby Meeting Lane. In the first two decades of the 19th century the school is listed as 'school and manufactory' in the rate books.

The house numbers are usually consistent but there are occasions where the school appears as No. 9 or No. 11 in the rate books. The Phoenix appears to be No. 3 (once as No. 4 and once as No. 2). The ground plan and location of No. 10 is sufficiently different from its neighbours to be easily identifiable on all the maps, as to a certain extent is No. 3. Their respective uses as public house and school also help in their identification.

From the cartographic evidence, it seems likely that the medieval boundaries suggested by Bickley and Hill (1891) existed well into the post-medieval period (see above and Fig. 4.28) and it is suggested that the three plot boundaries were reflected in the line of wall F710/F725 (Fig. 4.33) marking the eastern extent of the first plot and the wall running between the later St Martin's School and No. 9 (Fig. 4.30), marking the eastern extent of the second plot. The third plot, incorporating Nos 9–10, was marked by a similarly orientated boundary to the east of that visible on the other two plots, which may have been following the line of a watercourse, possibly Hersum Ditch. If this scheme is correct then each plot may well have had one house per plot, i.e. No. 3 for plot 1, No. 10 for plot 3 and No. 6/7 for plot 2. The shape of the western wall of No. 4 and the wall between Nos 8 and 9 suggest that the buildings are later infill. The changes in the numbering of No. 10 are consistent with continued development and change along the frontage of Nos 4–9. However, even on the Westley Map of 1731 a continuous run of buildings is shown along the frontage from No. 3 to No. 10, so if there ever was a single house in plot 2 it was quickly surrounded by or replaced by smaller infill properties. However, what is not so clear on the early maps is the additional boundary shown between properties Nos 5–6 on the c.1850 Rating Map.

The Rate Book of 1801–2 shows that two courts, between Nos 3 and 4 and between Nos 7 and 8, were already in existence. A third court between Nos 5 and 6 is recorded in the 1810–13 Rate Book. In 1801 Nos 5–8 and the court between No. 7 and No. 8 was in the ownership of Dickens. The court is later referred to as 'Dickens Court No. 3' and as Dickens does not appear as a property owner on Park Street in the 1794–1801 Rate Book it may suggest that Dickens was responsible for the speculative development of the court which later bore his name.

Exactly when the courts mentioned in the 1801–2 Rate book were first constructed is difficult to determine from the documents. The 1785–89 Rate Book lists eleven property owners, up to what would have been No. 10, one of whom (Isaac Sargeant, 'saddlers tool and pinking iron maker') appears to have owned a workshop to the rear of No. 9, although he is listed in the 1787 Directory with premises at No. 18 Digbeth and in 1803 at Moat Row. In 1784–89 only seven or eight property owners are listed and in 1794–1801 No. 9 (No. 10) is listed as a Dissenting School with only five property owners listed for the preceding properties. In the 1801–2 Rate Book, Jones is listed as owner of the court between Nos 3 and 4, possibly a development to the rear of No. 3, as well as properties Nos 1–2. Jones is also listed first for Park Street in the rate books of 1785–89, 1789–94 and 1794–1801 so presumably he owned Nos 1 and 2 then and could have built the court at any point in the later 18th century. By c.1840 the court was in the ownership of Thomas Justin (or sometimes Tustin) and described as a 'warehouse'. By c.1850, judging from the draft Rating Map (Fig. 4.29), the court was redundant. Likewise the buildings in Court No. 2 (between Nos 4 and 5) were described in the 1845 Rate Book as 'dilapidated'.

Evidence from the various Birmingham Directories is illuminating. In Sketchley's 1767 and 1770 Directories, No. 4 Park Street was occupied by Timothy Smith, brass founder and factor. He is listed again in 1781 and 1785. By 1787, Pye's Directory lists John Hawkins, locksmith, at No. 4, where he remained until at least 1803. The same directory lists John Cooper, thumb latch maker, at No. 6. Both these men are listed as owning property on this section of Park Street in the 1780s and 1790s. In the third decade of the 19th century, metal working was still in evidence, with Jas. Hassall, blacksmith and farrier, at Court No. 2 in 1831 and W. Hassall, smith, at No. 5 Park Street in 1839. Hassall was owner of Nos 4 and 5 and part of Court No. 2 in 1810–13. Finally Thomas Justin appears as the publican of 'The Old Phoenix Tavern' in Robson's 1839 Directory and as owner of Nos 1–3 in the 1837 Rate Book. Something of a decline sets in and Nos 1–2 seem to disappear, although R. Davenport, house painter, is listed at No. 2 in Robson's 1839 Directory but by the time of the 1845 Rate Book, Justin owns a smith's shop and premises in the area formerly occupied by Nos 1–2 and Court No. 1.

Thomas Upton was resident at No. 5 in 1801–2, at No. 9 in 1813–16 and owned a number of the houses and Court No. 3 in the 1820–23 Rate Book. He is listed as a whip maker in Chapman's 1801 Directory, a baker and grocer on Park Street in 1812 and a dealer in groceries at No. 8 Park Street in 1831. Two of the properties, Nos 5 and 6, are listed as a house and a bakehouse in the 1801–2 Rate Book and Sketchley's 1770 Directory lists William Abel, baker, at No. 6 Park Street. Finally, Sketchley's 1770 Directory lists a Luke Rogers as sacking weaver and potter (which seems a rather odd combination) at No. 1 Park Street.

The above information suggests that the stretch of Park Street under consideration was industrialised in the 18th century. The presence of buildings to the rear of the plots shown on the Westley map in 1731 and linear development along the backplots shown on the maps of Bradford, and Hanson and Piggott-Smith (Fig. 4.28) is consistent with industry being established from the second quarter of the 18th century and continuing well into the 19th century. The linear development behind No. 4 or 4/5 shown on the Bradford map looks rather court-like, as does the facing development, and this may have been the original of the later Court No. 2 shown on the *c*.1850 draft Rating Map. Whatever the precise construction and date of these backplot developments, there clearly has been a long history of development against which the excavated structural remains have to be set.

The construction of courts behind the main street frontage housing led to the backplots becoming steadily infilled. Ackerman's 1847 panoramic view of Birmingham (Fig. 16.8) suggests very little in the way of open space at the western end of Park Street and the Goad Insurance map of 1895 shows close-knit buildings where factories and stables, warehouses and court housing nestle cheek by jowl, in what must have become a rather insalubrious area. Something of the nature of the area in the mid-19th century can be gained from the 1851 census where poor Irish immigrants, including an entire family of beggars at No. 6 Park Street, seemed to have occupied a disproportionately large number of dwellings at the St Martin's end of the street. Occupations listed for the Irish immigrants, *e.g.* 'agricultural labourer' and 'washerwoman', suggest that they were unlikely to be engaged in self-employed skilled work of the type which had traditionally been carried on along this stretch of Park Street in the houses and courts and were more likely to have earned a living as labourers or factory workers.

The change in the type of occupant of Park Street marries quite well with the documentary evidence, in that Court No. 1 seems to have been defunct by this date, the area probably being used primarily for brewing for the Phoenix Tavern, and Court No. 2 had already been described as dilapidated. The 1856 Post Office Directory of Birmingham lists only a shoeing smith at No. 2 Park Street, presumably kept in work by the nearby Corporation stables, the only other tradesmen listed being

a last maker at No. 5, a shopkeeper at No. 8, and the publicans at No. 3 and No. 9.

The 1867 photograph of Park Street after the anti-Catholic riots shows damage to the roofs of Nos 6 and 7, which may have quickly led to their demolition (see Figs 4.31 and 4.32 for a depiction of the riots and the post-riot damage). The 1871 Rate Book records Nos 4 and 5, perhaps also damaged during rioting, as having been 'taken down'. Sometime in the same year Nos 4–8 Park Street had been replaced by a school, marked as St Martin's National School on the Goad Map (see Fig. 4.30). This school, which replaced one on nearby Allison Street, was however short-lived and was closed by *c*.1891, although the property was still in the ownership of the School Board in the 1896 Rate Book. The site was subsequently taken over by manufacturing concerns. A revision of the Goad map dating to *c*.1937 shows the site of the school and the erstwhile backplots completely built over.

Phase 3/4 features

In the following section the term 'Structure' has been used to describe a related group of walls but which may not belong to a single building phase.

Along the southwestern edge of Area C a northwest to southeast aligned wall (F710/ F725), together with the walls of Structures 1 and 6, may respect a property boundary of considerable antiquity (see above), separating an 'Area C' Park Street plot from an 'Area A/B' plot (Figs 4.33 and 4.34). The latter was in turn divided from the Digbeth plots by the ancient boundary originally marked out by the massive medieval ditch F174/ F201 (see Fig. 4.4) and apparently respected by the 19th-century wall F214/ F211 (Fig. 4.33).

In the northeastern half of Area A and Area B the principal structural features of this phase was a series of brick-lined drains (F166, F502, F505, F507 and F146; Fig 4.33) that reflect the improvements in sanitation and water supply which occurred as the 19th century progressed. In the southwestern part of Area A, an irregular grid of walls (F214, F153 *etc*.), Structure 9, represent the infilling with buildings of the rear end of the plots fronting onto Digbeth. Some of these walls, *e.g.* F213, F219, F220, can be closely matched with those shown on the 1895 Goad Insurance Map and the draft Rating Map of *c*.1850. Wall F212/ F218 appears to follow the line of the old Corporation stables. Associated with these buildings was a brick-lined well (F127), partially excavated to a depth of 2m. The pottery in well F127 seemed to be predominantly 18th century in date although some 19th-century pottery was recorded. Clay pipe recovered from the fill dated to 1760–1820. The well may be associated with the George Inn, which ran back from the top of Digbeth in the area later to become the London Museum public house and the Museum Palace of Varieties (see Fig. 4.35, colour).

The building activity in Area A was also represented

Fig. 4.31 Engraving showing an impression of 'Murphy's riots' as they hit Park St, 1867.

Fig. 4.32 Photograph of the Park Street buildings, post-riot in 1867. Taken by Joseph William Pickering as a narrative of the riots (Source; McKenna 1979).

Fig. 4.33 All areas; building remains Phases 3–4.

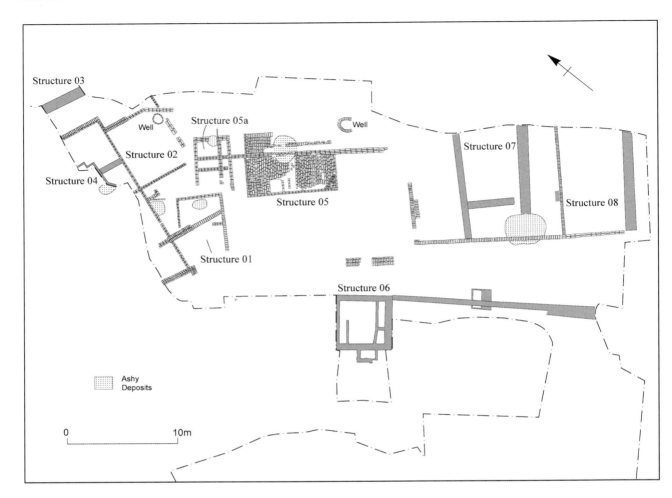

Fig. 4.34 Area C; structures, Phases 3–5.

by a cluster of pits (F154, F235, F239, F253, F255, F258), mainly containing building debris. The pits varied greatly in size and shape, from more than 3.0m across (F235) to less than 0.8m. Once the general character of the pits was established many were only partially excavated. No datable finds were recovered from F239, F253, F255 and F258. Pit F154 was noteworthy for containing a large quantity of 'hearth bottom' slag and four crucible fragments, as well as a fragment of bone-working debris and clay pipe, with a suggested deposition date of 1820–1860. The pit appears to have been dug in a yard area to the north of the stables. It is possible that it was connected with the shoeing smith, William Baynham, recorded at No. 2 Park Street in the 1856 Post Office Directory, or possibly Thomas Justin's smith's shop and premises recorded in the 1845 Rate Book. An 1867 view of the area just after the Murphy riots (Fig. 4.32) shows a gated entrance to livery stables in what would be excavated Area A/B.

In the northeastern part of Area A, three further pits (F138, F139, F131) were also assigned to Phase 4. These pits were located in an area that also contained a dense cluster of Phase 3 pits (mainly of sub-phases 3.2 and 3.3), into which they were partially cut, and both spatially and chronologically are best seen as a continuation into the 19th century of the activities represented by the earlier pits. This is reflected in the form and contents of the pits, which contained pottery, roof tile, clay pipe, copper alloy, glass, iron nails, slag, animal bone, and leather. Two intercutting pits (F139 and F138/ F159) lay in what was probably a small open area in Court No. 1, behind the Phoenix Tavern. The pottery from the pits consisted of a mix of medieval, post-medieval and 19th-century sherds. A copper alloy button and a bone 'button-back' found in the pits may indicate that button manufacture was carried on for a while in this area, especially since a further button back was found in pit F137 and a second copper alloy button in F131. The two pits also produced one of the largest collections of crucible fragments from the site as a whole. The earlier of the two (F139) produced 14 fragments of crucible, while the later pit (F138/ F159) produced 13 fragments. A solidified copper alloy droplet was also found (see Bevan *et al.*, Chapter 8). Clay pipe from F138 and F139 suggested deposition dates of 1820–

1880 and 1750–1850 respectively. Brass founders on Park Street become increasingly difficult to detect in the directories from the end of the 18th century, although five were listed in Sketchley's 1767 Directory and it is difficult to tell whether the crucible fragments were residual in the pits or represent a late flourishing of that industry.

Area C falls almost exclusively (with the exception of Structure 6) within the backplots of Nos 4–8 Park Street (see Rátkai above). The documentary and cartographic evidence indicates that there had been much building and industrial activity here and the sequence and interpretation of the structures is not always clear. Where brick sizes were recorded, the majority of structures had bricks consistent with a date before the Brick Tax of 1780 (pers. comm. Malcolm Hislop). However the likely nature of the buildings in the backplots, sheds, workshops and court housing would favour the reuse of bricks and, indeed, the primary record notes that some of the walls (F736, F737, F741, Structure 4) appear to have been made up of badly chipped and marked bricks consistent with reuse. Further evidence of reuse is provided by wall foundation F779 which contained a variety of bricks ranging from 5cm in thickness to 8.5cm. Unfortunately the continued history of construction in the backplots, culminating with the building of a school in c.1870 over the entire area, provided ideal conditions for disturbance and contamination, especially of the ceramic and clay pipe evidence, leaving the dating of some features open to doubt. However, the building of the school effectively marked the end of any domestic occupation in this area and it is therefore safe to assume that all the buildings in the backplots of Nos 4–8 pre-date 1870.

Towards the street frontage were the remains of Structure 1 (F812). The remains of Structure 1 were not very well preserved and it was impossible to retrieve the entire ground plan or define construction deposits (see Fig. 4.34). It was stratigraphically earlier than Structure 2 which cut through it in part. Structure 1 appears to be aligned along boundary wall F710/ F725 (see above). The dimensions of the bricks used in its construction were 22 × 10.5 × 5.5cm, which represent some of the smallest brick sizes found at Park Street. The brick size strongly suggests that the building pre-dates the intro-duction of the Brick Tax of 1780. The building was over medieval layer 1841 and cut dark earth 1824 (see above). Buildings certainly seem to be in this location on the Hanson map of 1778 and possibly also on the Bradford map of 1750/51 and it is possible that Structure 1 is associated with Timothy Smith, brass founder, who was resident here until the end of the 18th century. Ash and clinker were associated with the interior of the building. A small section of wall F813, with bricks of the same size as those from Structure 1, was noted in the northeastern baulk and was possibly part of the boundary wall to No. 9 Park Street.

Structure 2, which cut Structure 1, was built of slightly thicker bricks (c.6.25cm) but was still probably earlier than the 1780 Brick Tax. The alignment of this structure is quite different from Structure 1 and, indeed, of all the structures in Area C and Area A, with the exception of cellar wall F747 (Structure 3) at the northernmost edge of excavation. However both structures seem to follow the alignment of a neighbouring building, marked HW on the 1895 map and previously shown as the Daniel O'Connell public house c.1850. Wall F722 and parallel wall F809, although apparently on a rather odd alignment to Structure 1, do seem to follow the alignment of Nos 5–8 shown on the c.1850 Rating Map and it is possible that F722 forms the back wall of properties fronting onto Park Street. A patch of ash and clinker lay against wall F722 but this may have been associated with a possible extension to Structure 1. A cut feature F720, running up to Wall F722, was originally interpreted as a construction cut for the wall. However an excavated depth of 111cm and width of 114cm seems unusually large for a con-struction trench. Finds from within the lower fill (1757) of F720, a thin layer with abundant coal fragments, comprised clay pipe with a probable deposition date of 1720–1820 and 19th-century pottery. Upper fill 1752, a considerably thicker layer making up most of the backfill, contained 19th-century pottery, pins and a thimble.

A second cut, F721, identified as a construction trench, lay a little to the south of F720 at the intersection of walls F738 and F722. The fill (1755) produced pottery probably deposited in the 1770s or 1780s, clay pipe with a deposition date of 1750–1800, a bone knife handle (Fig. 8.10.5, colour), and a key.

Wall F750 cut pit F749 which in turn cut F745. Assuming that the pottery and clay pipe (dated 1720–1820) in F749 were not intrusive, there is a strong possibility that wall F750 dates to the very early 19th century. Wall F825, offset at about 45 degrees from wall F750 and which appears to cut F809, seems to reflect the kink in the property boundaries noted above. A sondage cut to the north of the intersection of walls F825 and F809 contained early 19th-century pottery and clay pipe dated 1750–1850 and may indicate that F825 and, possibly, wall F750 were late additions to Structure 2. A well appears to cut the back wall, F809, of Structure 2.

The history of Structure 2 is clearly quite complicated and several phases of activity seem to be indicated – there are, for example, several rather ephemeral traces of walls, including a corner of a structure to the west which overlies F722. The identification of F720 as part of a construction trench seems unlikely, although the feature is similar to F836 (below), also with an uncertain interpretation. There is a strong possibility, however, that F720 and F836 are more or less contemporary. The evidence, as it stands, that all or part of Structure 2 dates to the 19th century, is far from conclusive. However, the structural remains do tend to suggest that this area of the site is something of a palimpsest with successive building, addition, modification and destruction, an interpretation that the documentary and cartographic evidence would tend to support.

A fourth structure (Structure 4) was just visible at the edge of excavation. It too had an off-set wall F737, but the exact nature of this structure and its relationship to Structure 2 remain unclear. Brick sizes were broadly similar to those in Structure 2, albeit slightly thinner at 6cm. Information regarding the construction of Structure 4 was almost totally removed by the digging of a large pit F836 and hazardous working conditions meant that further excavation in this area had to be abandoned. The fills of pit F836 (1768, 1769, 1770, 1771 and 1772) contained the largest group of non-ceramic finds from the site, including cobbling waste (see Bevan *et al.*, Chapter 8), and also included a good group of pipes dated 1850–1870 (see Higgins, Chapter 9). The clay pipe evidence would seem to suggest that Structure 4 pre-dates the 1850s; this is corroborated by the brick sizes. A discrete dump of ash and clinker was recorded in plan to the north of Wall F736.

Further south lay Structure 5, a well-laid brick yard or floor surface. It too lay under the area later occupied by the school. It was provisionally dated to the late 18th or early 19th centuries and overlay pit F826. A wall F786 ran through the surface and continued northwest through Structure 5a, possibly joining originally with wall F738. If so, this may be another angled boundary wall running from the back of property No. 6/7. Wall F786 also continued southwest from the brick surface cutting Phase 3.1–3.2 pit complex F769, F761, F763 and F764 (Fig. 4.18). The wall could conceivably have formed the boundary between properties Nos 5 and 6. In the second and third decades of the 19th century, Nos 5 and 6 always had different owners (it may be true of the 1801–2 Rate Book entry also but the evidence is less clear), and it is possible that a boundary marker was found necessary. The boundary may not have been a standing wall as such, since Cattell *et al.* (2002, 73 fig. 81) illustrate a division between two yards visible in the brick paving, which looks very similar to 'wall' F786. A small stretch of wall (unnumbered) ran parallel with F786 in the area of the brick surface, cutting pits F824 and F816 (Fig. 4.18). Both pits contain some 19th-century pottery but the chances of it being intrusive are high. Whether this stretch of wall was contemporary with F786 or was a forerunner of it is not clear.

Structure 5a may or may not be associated with Structure 5. Its alignment is the same as both Structure 5 and Structure 1 and it appears to abut Structure 1. A small section of construction trench F782 was excavated along one of the walls of Structure 5a. It contained a coarseware base sherd and clay pipe with a likely deposition date of 1680–1730. Destruction rubble (1827) from within the building contained a small amount of pottery comprising blackware, coarseware, white salt-glazed stoneware, creamware and some (unspecified) 19th-century pottery. A clay pipe bowl dating to 1740–

1790 (Fig. 9.3.35), and a second dating to 1840–1900 (Fig. 9.8.143), were also found in the rubble and Higgins (Chapter 9) suggests that the likely deposition of the clay pipe was in the second half of the 19th century. It is difficult to say whether the evidence points to the demolition of the building in advance of the building of St Martin's School or whether the construction of the school resulted in contamination of pre-existing demolition deposits. Ephemeral traces of walls running east from Structure 5a were also recorded but their exact nature was never clear. Another ashy dump was recorded by the easternmost wall of Structure 5a.

To the north of Structures 5 and 5a (see Fig. 4.34), at the baulk edge, was a possible construction trench F784 or beam slot. This is possibly an early feature, the fill of which was a sandy silt containing small stones and charcoal. The pottery suggested a date in the 17th century for its backfill. Clay pipe from the fill dated to 1650–1750. The most likely date for the backfill of the feature is therefore *c.*1650–1700.

It is noticeable that the pitting in Area C is concentrated away from Structures 1–4, the exceptions being Phase 4 pits F836 and F749 and Phase 3.3 pit F745. The distribution of the remaining pits is strongly suggestive of the northern section of the site, running back from the street frontages, having been built over or having otherwise remained inaccessible for pit digging until the late 18th and 19th centuries. This again would tend to support an earlier rather than later date for Structures 1–4.

Moving south is Structure 6. This is the only structure which can be accurately matched to the map evidence. It is a small roughly square building with a brick floor and a drain. The brick size (23 × 11 × 7.5cm), which is consistent for both walls and floors, suggests that it dates from the 19th century. This structure seems to match exactly a small brewery building within the Phoenix brewery and public house shown on the 1895 Goad Insurance map (Fig. 4.30). It forms part of a set of small buildings running back from the public house and finishing with a stable block. On the 1888 Ordnance Survey map a similar arrangement is shown, although the brick structure has yet to be formed from the division of a larger building. It would seem likely that the structure therefore dates from between 1888 and 1895. The small drain in floor F731 and the brick floors within the structure are consistent with a brewhouse.

To the east of this structure, small patches of a brick yard surface were revealed. Unfortunately it was too disturbed to determine its original size or relationship to other structures. Further south another small structure F701 is likely to be a fairly modern drain, possibly connected with the school.

Structure 7 comprised a series of rubble-filled wall foundations (F814a–d) towards the back of the site, which marked out a rectangular building with at least one internal partition. A rubble-filled construction trench

F799, which was cut into the medieval boundary ditch F715 etc and followed its alignment, may have formed the back wall of Structure 7. The rubble fill of the construction trench F779 contained a mix of bricks with sizes ranging from 20cm × 12cm × 5cm to 24cm × 12cm × 8.5cm, some degraded, others in good condition. Structure 7 had been partly cut by a large, rubble-filled pit F838 which contained no datable finds and is presumably associated with the destruction of the building. The pit and its fill are similar in character to pits F239, F253 etc found in Area A (see above).

Beneath the building were pits F765 and F803 which were backfilled in the 17th century, possibly quite early in that century, and pit F791 which contained a rather mixed fill of medieval and post-medieval pottery together with a clay pipe stem dated 1720–1820. A large structure similar to Structure 7 is not present on Piggott-Smith's 1824/25 map, or on the Rating Map or Goad map. Something broadly similar can be seen on the 1937 (revised, second edition) Goad map, and the remains, as uncovered by excavation, must represent a building constructed after the closure of the school in the 1890s. However, apparently early bricks were noted amongst the fill of F799. Westley and Hanson seem to show buildings standing towards the rear of the backplots and it may be that bricks from these demolished buildings have become incorporated into the fill of F799. A very high wall is shown in this area on a photograph taken in 1965 (see also the photograph of 1867, Fig. 4.32), which could be one of the walls of Structure 7.

Overlying Structure 7 were the remains of Structure 8, comprising four brick walls, F815, F815a, F771 and F757. Wall F815 abutted F771, a modern wall on concrete foundations. At right angles to this junction, running eastwards, was wall F757 which also had a concrete foundation. This modern building, vacated by a car hire firm, was demolished during the course of the excavation but, despite the building's substantial foundations, the deeper archaeological deposits had not been disturbed. It was observed that the back wall of the building appeared to respect the line of the large boundary ditch (F715 *etc.*) which ran across the bottom of the site. The continuity of a medieval boundary into the 20th century is noteworthy.

Discussion
by Simon Buteux and Stephanie Rátkai

The sherds of Roman pottery, found residually in later contexts (see Rátkai, Chapter 7, 147), may be taken together with the four or five sherds from the Moor Street excavations to indicate a low level of Roman-period activity in the vicinity of what is now Birmingham city centre. It is likely that such sherds derive from Romano-British farmsteads, assumed to have been widely scattered across the Birmingham plateau, rather than from any nucleated settlement.

Medieval Park Street

The clearly definable absence of Anglo-Saxon ceramics at Park Street and the other Bull Ring sites is noteworthy and there is indeed no evidence of medieval activity at Park Street that need be dated earlier than 1166, the year when Peter de Birmingham obtained a charter for a market at Birmingham. That there was a small settlement at Birmingham at the time of the Domesday Survey is beyond dispute, but the excavations have provided no support for the supposition that such a settlement was located at, or in the immediate vicinity of, the triangular market place which was to form the heart of the medieval town from the 12th century onwards.

The core of the medieval town, established in 1166 if not before, is believed to comprise the triangular market place and the three principle streets radiating out from the corners of the triangle – Digbeth, High Street and Edgbaston Street on Hanson's Map (Fig. 2.3). The original burgage plots would have been laid out perpendicular to the market place and to these streets, the basic pattern of these plots surviving down to the 18th century (when the first detailed maps of the town were produced) and beyond. The rear end of these plots would have been defined by a substantial 'town ditch' (or, in the case of Edgbaston Street, use was made of the pre-existing watercourse connecting the Parsonage Moat with the Manorial Moat), separating the town from surrounding farm and park land. The properties to the southwest of the excavated area fronting Digbeth (Nos 136–140) retain their burgage plot boundaries – an unusual and very important survival in Birmingham city centre (pers. comm. M. Hodder).

The massive ditch F174/ F201, at least 7m wide and 2m deep, uncovered in Area A of the Park Street excavations, is almost certainly a stretch of this town ditch. Another stretch of what is very probably the same ditch was uncovered at the Moor Street site. At both Moor Street and Park Street, the ditch marked the boundary between the town and one of the two hunting parks belonging to the de Birmingham family, Little (or Over) Park. Incidentally, Little Park Street was an early name for Park Street.

There is no direct evidence for the date at which this boundary ditch was dug but, given the foregoing analysis, a mid- 12th-century date is probable. The pottery from the backfilling of the ditch suggested that the infilling of the ditch had probably begun before the middle of the 13th century and that the process was complete by the 14th century. The artefactual, plant and insect remains from the ditch therefore provide a valuable record of activities in this part of the town in the first century or so of its existence, together with a picture of the broader environmental setting of the early town.

The most significant artefactual evidence is provided by a group of about 300 sherds from the ditch interpreted as kiln waste from the production of Deritend ware vessels. Corroborative evidence for pottery manufacture is provided by the discovery of part of a fire-bar, while some evidence for pottery production was also found at the Moor Street site. The evidence for pottery production at Park Street and Moor Street extends the range of locations at which pottery was being made in medieval Birmingham from Deritend (where evidence was first uncovered in the 1950s) and Digbeth up into the centre of the town, suggesting that the industry was widespread and substantial despite the lack of any documentary references to potters in the (scant) historical records for medieval Birmingham.

The charred plant remains from the ditch fills revealed a typical range of the cereals cultivated in the medieval period – bread/ club wheat, barley, oats and rye. Also present were flax and hemp, widely cultivated in the medieval period for their fibres (hemp is used to make ropes and canvas, flax for linen), seeds and oil. The range and character of the grassland remains present indicated they may have derived from charred fodder, suggesting the keeping of stock near by. Tree pollen was strongly represented in the samples, suggesting considerable stands of woodland in the vicinity.

The insect remains from the lowest fills of the ditch strongly indicated that the ditch itself was water-filled at least part of the time, with the assemblage dominated by a range of water beetles typical of slow-flowing or standing water. This impression was reinforced by the waterlogged plant assemblage, with many species typical of wet or damp environments.

The evidence for standing or slow-flowing water in the partially backfilled ditch is important because it suggests that when the ditch was kept open, as it presumably was in the early decades, it would have provided a useful supply of running water. This suggestion is supported by the topography of the ditch and from what can be deduced of Birmingham's early water supply from the cartographic evidence (see Patrick, Introduction). The ditch could have provided a source of water for watering animals (tying in with the evidence for charred fodder), as well as for a variety of light industrial functions. Indeed, the presence of such a water-filled ditch running along the rear of the plots may have made these 'watered plots' particularly valuable, especially to the town's butchers.

The infilling of this major boundary ditch must be related to the expansion of the town and the laying out of Park Street, which cuts across it. It is not clear, however, exactly how or when this process took place. From even a cursory inspection of the plan of Birmingham, Moor Street and Park Street look like secondary additions to the town plan, with the laying out of Moor Street logically preceding that of Park Street. Furthermore, both streets encroached substantially on Little Park and this development could not have taken place without the permission of the lord of the manor, if indeed it was not the de Birmingham family who directly initiated the scheme.

If the date of the backfilling of the former 'town ditch' is taken as indicating the date at which Park Street was laid out, then this cannot have occurred until the late 13th century. However, the ceramic evidence, notably from the sequence of deposits in the northern corner of Area C, suggests activity outside the ditch earlier than this, with an admittedly small quantity of pottery pointing to activity as early as the 12th century. This apparent contradiction can be resolved if informal encroachment onto this land – a result, perhaps, of the early success of the town – occurred prior to the formal laying out of Park Street. Perhaps, as has been suggested for Moor Street (see Burrows *et al.*, Chapter 3), Park Street started out as an informal track – the way both Park Street and Moor Street sinuously follow the natural contours might provide some support for this proposal.

The formal laying out of Park Street is probably to be associated with the digging of a second major boundary ditch (F715 *etc.*), this time delineating the back end of a series of plots fronting onto Park Street itself. No direct evidence bearing on the date at which this second boundary ditch was dug was forthcoming but it had fallen into disuse and had been backfilled by the 14th century. The line of the boundary, however, was preserved by a fence, some of the waterlogged timbers of which were uncovered along the northern edge of the ditch. This boundary marked the eastern limit of the developed area of Birmingham here until the end of the 18th century.

The environmental evidence from this second boundary ditch suggests that in the medieval period it too held water. Indeed, the back end of the Park Street plots was clearly wet and liable to localised flooding, as was indicated by water-laid humic, silty deposits of medieval date found in a band adjacent to the ditch. These wet conditions were exploited, from medieval times down to the 18th century, for the digging of various clay-lined or – later – timber-lined pits or tanks, the precise function of which could not be determined but which were clearly intended to hold water. The earliest of these date to the medieval period and comprise a group of three pits possibly associated with hide preparation (F708, F709 and F714). This boundary ditch may have been fed by water from 'Hersum Ditch' (see Rátkai above).

The absence of any evidence of structures is of interest. It could be argued that subsequent land use has obliterated what few traces there may have been or that any buildings were closer to the street frontage and hence beyond the scope of the excavation. However, there is the possibility that the area lying between the town/ park boundary ditch and 'Hersum Ditch' was never properly developed until the post-medieval period. It is clear that the land here was often wet and boggy and the curvature of Hersum Ditch would have made the laying out of regular burgage plots awkward. In effect, the area would have been waste ground. However, the land would have been well suited to the production of pottery for which plentiful and easily accessible water would have been a necessity. The pottery production waste may then derive from the area to the northeast of the town/ park boundary ditch rather than from within the Digbeth backplots, the kilns lying just outside the excavated area in what was later to become Nos 9 and 10 Park Street.

The only other medieval features of note on the Park Street site were the two graves, one identified as that of a young man and the other as that of a middle-aged woman, found near the Park Street frontage in Area A. These burials are frankly mysterious, most likely representing either murder victims, social outcasts or victims of plague. While the balance of the evidence favours a late 13th- or 14th-century date for the burials (thus also admitting the possibility that they are associated with the Black Death of 1348/9), a 17th-century date is also possible (thus permitting an association with the Civil War 'Battle of Birmingham' of 1643).

The two burials are a useful reminder of the dual character of the Park Street site. On the one hand the massive 'town ditch' is an early – quite possibly original – feature of the medieval town associated with its historic core around the Bull Ring market place. On the other hand, the bulk of the site, lying outside this ditch, is on the periphery of the town, and it is clear from the map evidence that many of the plots on the east side of Park Street were never fully developed until the 19th century. This peripheral location is where one might anticipate activities such as pottery production, other industrial processes, or the stocking of animals prior to butchery or sale in the market.

Tudor and Stuart Park Street

Birmingham's economic fate cannot be detached from that of the wider region, and indeed the nation. Regionally and nationally – indeed on a European scale – the 12th and 13th centuries were a period of growth. The early success and physical expansion of Birmingham, represented by the laying out of Moor Street and Park Street, belongs to this period. However, on the regional and national scale, the 14th century was a period of crisis and decline. It is not appropriate to attempt to analyse the historical factors in detail here, but in the opening decades of the century a series of crop failures and sheep and cattle murrains led to widespread famine. Then in 1348 the Black Death struck. The overall result was population decline and a complex web of economic and social changes.

England's market towns were badly affected by the crisis, with the number of market towns in Warwickshire declining from about 34 in 1300 to about half that number by 1500. Even the market towns that survived, such as Birmingham, would have experienced contraction and recovery during the 15th and 16th centuries was slow and uneven.

This broad pattern seems to be reflected in developments at the Park Street site which, situated on the periphery of the medieval town, might be envisaged as a particularly sensitive barometer of the town's general fortunes. Overall it is striking that very little pottery from the site is assigned specifically to the 14th century. Of course, to a certain extent this may be an artefact of the uncertainties of dating the pottery, and patterns of pottery usage and discard, but nevertheless it seems reasonable to interpret the scarcity of 14th-century ceramics largely at face value: at Park Street there was a marked decline in activity in the 14th century. Indeed, the only event that can be attributed with some confidence to the 14th century is the silting up of the boundary ditch (F715 *etc.*) which defined the rear ends of the plots.

Likewise, the pottery report (Rátkai, Chapter 7) emphasises how little pottery is assignable to the 15th and 16th centuries and how few features can be dated with confidence to this period. The main features assigned to Phase 2 comprise the 'pond' (F506) and group of clay-lined pits dug into the damp ground at the rear of the plots in Area B; the tight clustering of these features suggests that they may have been confined to the rear of a single property. We know nothing about the function of these features other than that they probably held water and were probably intended to do so. While it is tempting to assign an industrial function to these pits – perhaps dyeing, tanning or tawyering – they may as well have been dug simply for the watering of animals (certainly this interpretation seems most likely for the 'pond' with its shallow, sloping sides) or may be connected with the fish ponds which Bickley and Hill (1891) place in a parcel of land immediately to the east of the excavation site.

Both the slight amount of 15th- and 16th-century pottery and the 'water features' accord with the documentary evidence (see Litherland and Rátkai, above), which strongly suggest that that the plots in this part of Park Street were largely undeveloped at this time and had a decidedly 'rural' character.

The post-medieval recut of the ditch poses the question about the status of the plots and their use in the later medieval period. Clearly the ditch marked an important boundary in the early history of Birmingham's development. The evidence from both Moor Street and Park Street suggests that the ditch had been backfilled by the 14th century. What then took its place? If the boundary was redundant then it is hard to explain the recut F234 and the alignment of the 19th-century buildings. But why was it necessary to recut the ditch at all? It is almost as if there was so little activity in this area in the 15th and 16th centuries (confirmed to a certain extent by the paucity of ceramics and other finds of this date) that it was not worth maintaining the ditch. Renewed and more extensive activity in the 17th century may therefore have been the stimulus to reasserting old boundaries. In this we can perhaps detect some sort of decline or shrinkage in the later Middle Ages on Park Street. This may well have been reversed at the same time that the industry associated with pits F134, F141, F144 in Area A and pit F504 in Area B was begun.

Park Street in the 17th and 18th centuries

'The ancient and modern state of Birmingham must divide at the restoration of Charles the Second (1660)', wrote William Hutton, Birmingham's first and most colourful historian, in 1781. Up until then, Hutton believed, smiths were Birmingham's 'chief inhabitants' and 'the chief if not the only manufactory…was in iron'; after the Restoration, 'many of the curious manufactures began to blossom'. By 'curious manufactures' Hutton meant 'toys' in the sense of small articles, often of brass, such as utensils, household fittings, buckles, buttons, snuff boxes, and trinkets and knick-knacks of all kinds.

Judging from the archaeology of Park Street, Hutton was correct. Phase 3 at Park Street is characterised by a large number of pits, 63 in total, located in clusters across the site. The contents of these pits includes both domestic debris (pottery, animal bones, charred plant remains) and the debris from various industrial processes (slag from iron smithing, offcuts from bone and ivory working, crucible fragments from copper alloy melting, button backs possibly associated with button manufacture), together with building debris (rubble, bricks and roof tile). Together, the pits chart a story that sees a revival of industrial activity in the plots from the end of the 16th century, with small-scale iron working as the dominant theme, to be accompanied by the working of copper alloys – brass and gunmetal – from the end of the 17th century.

Another industry represented is bone and ivory working, the debris suggesting that a particular product may have been knife handles. Pit F504 contained what appeared to be debris from cutlering. The pottery assemblage itself (see Rátkai, Chapter 7) was not particularly noteworthy but was important in giving a late 17th-century date to the rest of the finds from the pit. Most notable among these was a large quantity of ivory offcuts. The waste was more fragmentary and 'splintered' than bone hafts illustrated by Moore (1999, 272) but not inconsistent with it deriving from the manufacture of knife handles. The fill of F504 also contained smithing hearth bottoms, slag and the second largest quantity of hammerscale (25g) from the entire Park Street site. Knife hafter and iron worker were normally two separate and distinct occupations. A combination of the two skills might suggest embryonic or low-scale industry, or the type of minor industry which occurred in the suburbs or back streets away from the settlement centre as at Cutler Street, London (pers. comm. Geoff Egan).

If the debris from the pit does represent cutlery manufacture it may indicate the beginnings of the post-Restoration surge in industry mentioned by Hutton (see above) and the expansion of metal-working trades from the Rea Valley into other parts of the town. The cutlery trade was important in Birmingham even at the time of Leland (McKenna 2005, 18) and Birmingham was second only to Sheffield in the manufacture of cutlery in the post-medieval period.

Leather working is likewise hinted at by leather offcuts and there is the possibility that the two tanks in Area B were associated with tanning or tawyering but there is nothing to suggest an industry of any scale on Park Street, unlike Edgbaston Street.

By about 1650 Birmingham was supplying 'all or most of the London ironmongers' with their products (McKenna 2005, 22) and the Great Fire opened up London to metalware such as tools for construction and building fitments from Birmingham (*ibid.*). The boom in Birmingham's economy led to speculative building, resulting in the infilling of plots and the turning of houses into tenements from the mid–late 17th century (*ibid.*, 23). We should not be surprised, therefore, to see what appear to be long linear developments, which look suspiciously like embryonic courts, to the rear of the Park Street plots on Bradford's map of 1750/51 (Fig. 1.2 and Fig. 4.28).

Maps, such as those of Westley (1731) and Bradford (1750/51), also show the far end of the excavated backplots to have had gardens. Through time, the buildings encroached deeper into the plots. This pattern is reflected in the archaeology, with building debris from the pits acting as a proxy for the buildings themselves and plant remains indicating gardens and broken ground. Large quantities of beet from one of the pits suggest a vegetable garden. Subtle differences in the distribution, chronology and contents of the pits hint that the site contained distinct properties. Perhaps in the latter half of the 18th century the two large wood-lined tanks were constructed at the rear of the Area A/B plot, while Structures 1 and 2 towards the front of the Area C may belong to this period.

The pace of change quickened in the late 18th and early 19th centuries. Park Street, in common with other areas around Birmingham's centre, experienced development pressure and social down-grading as the more wealthy sought to move to the new squares that were being laid out, and then to the suburbs. It is perhaps in this context that the apparent 'house clearance' dump of pottery dating to the 1780s, found in the filling of the two tanks and adjacent 'pond', is to be interpreted. The obvious source for this pottery is No. 3 Park Street which, it was suggested above, may have been a house of quality. However, as No. 3 was recorded as a public house from at least 1720, a clearance by departing 'gentry' residents in the 1780s seems rather less compelling. The last resident of Park Street listed as 'gentry' was one John Hasluck who appears in Pye's 1791 Directory and lived somewhere in the vicinity of Nos 16–18 Park Street. A Revd ?N. Taylor, a Dissenting Minister, was resident, probably at No. 10 Park Street, in the late 1780s but, as far as it is possible to tell, the remaining residents in the excavated area of Park Street were 'in trade', although that is not of course to say that they were not men (or women) of means.

19th- and 20th-century Park Street

The map and documentary evidence shows further infilling of the Park Street plots during the 19th century. On the site of the excavations, the Park Street plots came first to be mainly occupied by court housing, workshops, sheds, stables and warehouses, a process that had probably begun in the previous century. By the early 1870s a large proportion of Area C was occupied by a school, which at its demise in the early 1890s was turned into yet another factory. Effectively, from the 1890s this area was completely built over. The structural evidence for this dense infilling is rather difficult to gauge from the excavations but good groups of 19th-century finds were recovered, *e.g.* from pit F836 (see above and Bevan *et al.*, Chapter 8). By the beginning of this period metal-working industries seem to have largely disappeared from the excavated area of Park Street and, although some may have lingered on, the archaeological evidence for their existence is lacking. Overall, though, the character of this part of Park Street changed (see Litherland and Rátkai above) and the latter half of the 20th century saw the area sink into further decline until its fortunes were revived by the construction of Bullring at the opening of the 21st century.

5   The Row Watching Brief

Chris Patrick

An archaeological watching brief, which was carried out during the construction of The Row, identified a substantial ditch that represented the northern edge of the medieval moat that once surrounded Birmingham's manorial site. Pottery recovered from the lower fills of the moat was dated to the 12th or 13th centuries exclusively. Samples of the fills were taken for water-logged plant and pollen analysis. These have added to our understanding of the evolution of the environment that once surrounded the site and have provided interesting comparative material for an assessment on another part of the moated site carried out twenty years earlier.

Historical background of the Manorial Moat

Maps from the 18th and 19th centuries show the location of the Manorial Moat (Figs 2.2, 2.3) and present-day street-names like Moat Lane perpetuate its memory. Birmingham's Manorial Moat, along with its neighbour, Parsonage Moat, were two of thousands of similar earthworks constructed throughout England.

As outlined above, the first tenant of Birmingham's Manorial Moat was William de Birmingham and the town's market charter was granted to his son Peter. The de Birmingham family had a long association with the manor and the moat remained in their possession until it was forfeited to the Crown in 1536. John Dudley, Viscount Lisle, acquired the moat along with several other local properties sometime between 1543–1545, before it was sold to Thomas Marrow in 1557. The moat then stayed in possession of the Marrow family until 1746.

The earliest description of the site comes from the 1529 survey of the town and it is portrayed as being in a dilapidated state. The moat is described as being overgrown with weeds and filled with rubbish, and bridged by a drawbridge, while the manor house itself is said to be so ruinous that no man has been prepared to rent it. The exact date of the removal of the medieval buildings is unclear but is thought to be during the 16th century when a member of the Francis family built a mansion on the moat platform. The earliest illustration of the complex is William Westley's map of 1731 (Fig. 2.2). The map shows the close relationship between the Birmingham Manorial Moat and the Parsonage Moat that lay to the west with the watercourse between them. The watercourse forms the southern boundary to the town with plots running south off Edgbaston Street terminating there. The Birmingham Moat appears to have a bridged entrance onto Moat Lane with a gate on the inner edge replacing the drawbridge mentioned above. The larger of the buildings is assumed to have been the manor house, flanked to the north and south by outbuildings and with a circular dovecote to the rear. None of the buildings shown appears to be medieval in origin but the illustration may only be representative. The next view of the moat is a map by Bradford in 1750/51 (Fig. 1.2). The location of the moat and the buildings contained within it differ on Westley's and Bradford's maps. The latter seems to show the moat to be further down Moat Lane, away from the church. The buildings inside the moat are on a different alignment from that suggested by Westley. The alignments shown on the Bradford map are repeated in 1778 (Fig. 2.3). By 1767 Thomas Abney, a thread maker, was a tenant at the moat and the area had become a centre for small-scale industrial production. An advert placed in the *Aris Gazette* after Thomas Abney's death in that year advertised the property for lease for 21 years and describes the Moat House as:

Containing four rooms to a floor and being three stories high, with a large back kitchen thereto adjoining, and convenient warehouses, shopping and other buildings thereto, situated in the Moat yard. The premises are moated all around and are very fit and convenient for carrying on large manufactory, there being buildings which at small expense may be converted to work-shops capable of employing 300 workmen.

Between 1769 and 1799 nails, coffin nails, ironwork, wire and various wooden products were produced on the moat site. The town also began to expand southwards and by 1778 the moat was surrounded by a triangle of streets consisting of Moat Row, Moat Lane and Jamaica Row.

In 1781 Birmingham historian William Hutton visited the moat and recorded some details of the site: 'In one of the outbuildings is shown the apartment where the ancient lords kept their court leet'; this was held 'in what we should think a large and shabby room'; 'another outbuilding which stands to the east was the work of Edmund, Lord Ferrers'. This stood on the northeastern side of the moat and bore the Ferrers' arms in the timbers of the ceiling.

This description seems to confirm the survival of some medieval structures late into the 18th century. This is further supported by William Hamper's drawing of 1814 (Fig. 5.1), which shows the moat from the east. Hamper shows a timber-framed house on the northeastern side of the moat, to the right of the 'rebuilt' manor house. He also noted that the timbers of the structure had apparently been used in an earlier building. The moat itself still contained water at this time although Mr John Parker commented on 14 October 1805 that 'The moat was in such a muddy condition, it would not be correct to call it a water mark'.

The end of the Birmingham moat came in 1815 when the land was sold to the Town of Birmingham for the construction of the new Smithfield Market. A sale document dated to 1815 includes a detailed inventory and valuation of the property within the moat prior to the demolition of the moat and island. The main house was demolished in May 1816 and the moat was infilled around the same time. Following this destruction, Moat Lane and Moat Row encroached upon the circuit of the ditch, and the remainder of the island was contained within the market buildings of the later 19th century. The new market was officially opened on the 5th April 1817 and can be seen in Ackerman's 1847 Panoramic View of Birmingham (Fig. 16.8). The curve in Moat Row clearly demonstrates the outline of the former moat's southern edge.

Results

The location of the northern edge of the former Birmingham Manorial Moat was recorded during The Row watching brief. The location of the moat appears to be broadly correct when compared to the map sources from the 18th century, although one notable aspect is that the moat's location now appears to be slightly further north towards the church than was previously thought. If so, it may suggest that the location given by the Westley map of 1731 is correct rather than the later, neater and presumed more accurate map by Bradford in 1750/51. If the moat was closer to St Martin's Church, it may explain the crowded nature of the backplots shown by Westley. Watt had previously commented that the extent and width of the moat did not appear to line up with Westley's depiction (Watt 1980).

The only dating evidence for the moat fills comes from the pottery and the assumption that it is con-

Fig. 5.1 The Birmingham Moat and Manor House, Hamper's watercolour of 1814 (Source; Dent 1894).

temporary with any silting. The earliest material comes from the base of the moat, and is dated to the 12th–13th century exclusively. There is no later material. The moat appears to have been regularly cleaned during the medieval period, preventing any later silting-up and leaving only pockets of earlier material.

The 1975 watching brief also demonstrated the poor survival of medieval deposits in the moat. Of the 166 foundation bases examined by Lorna Watts, only five contained deposits that could definitely be described as being medieval in date. The stratigraphy that was recorded in March 2000 was very similar to that observed in 1975. Contexts 1010, 1011, 1003 and 1005 correspond with Watts' Master Level 2 representing the medieval phase of the moat. Context 1012 and 1013 correspond with Master Level 3, post-medieval; while 1014 and 1015 correspond with Master Level 4 representing the final period of the moat.

Most of the moat fills were post-medieval in date, with pottery dating to the 18th and 19th centuries. These represent deliberate backfilling either late in the moat's existence or at the time of the documented backfilling episode in 1816.

The results of the 1975 watching brief are strati-graphically very similar to the results of the 2000 project and the environmental results are broadly similar, although the later samples were more nitrogen-rich. This contrast may reflect local differences between the western and southern areas of the moat exposed during 1975 and the northern side exposed in March 2000. The pollen results confirm that trees were close by, but the lack of seeds suggests that they were not directly over the northern edge of the moat. The presence of hemp in both the 1975 and 2000 samples is of particular interest (see Hodder *et al.*, Chapter 16).

The source of water supply to the moat is still not understood. It is not known if the water was flowing through the northern part of the moat or whether it was still. The presence of caddis flies in 1010 show that the moat was certainly close to a source of water and was clean. This is confirmed by the lack of sewage present in the moat. The Bradford map of 1750/51 (Fig. 1.2) seems to show a stream entering the moat on its western side and then exiting under Moat Lane and flowing into the mill pool. It may be that the water flowed around either the northern or southern side of the moat, but not both. This would explain the differences between the samples taken in 1975 and those taken in 2000.

6 Prehistoric Worked Flint

Lynne Bevan

Four items of prehistoric worked flint were recovered during the Birmingham excavations, comprising a scraper, a retouched flake and two unretouched flakes. The small, chronologically undiagnostic side scraper with substantial remnant cortex was recovered from the Edgbaston Street site (2216), and was made from a light grey-brown flint with the thin, compacted cortex typical of flint from secondary deposits.

The retouched flint flake was recovered from a burial at St Martin's Cemetery (1605). Its triangular shape was strongly suggestive of a preform for an Early Bronze Age barbed and tanged arrowhead. The material used was a light grey flint, again with the thin, compacted cortex typical of flint from secondary deposits. However, it is possible that this item may have been a gunflint (de Lotbiniere 1977) in view of the general dating of the other finds and Birmingham's connection with the gun-making industry, but its shape and light brown colour argue against this.

Two unretouched flakes were recovered, to which only a broadly post-Palaeolithic date can be attributed. The first, from Edgbaston Street, was of a light brown translucent flint (1197) and the second, from Moor Street, was of a partly burnt, opaque grey flint (5155).

In all cases, the raw material used was entirely in keeping with the flint sources exploited throughout prehistory in the British Midlands where primary flint from mines was unavailable. While these isolated implements attest to prehistoric activity in the vicinity of the excavated sites, further chronological resolution is not possible. Moreover, despite the disturbed nature of these urban sites, based upon the present evidence, this small number of flint artefacts does not denote settlement of any intensity or duration.

Catalogue

Side scraper, light grey-brown flint. Length: 25mm, width: 17mm, thickness: 4mm. Edgbaston Street, 2216.

Retouched flint flake, triangular in shape and possibly a preform for an Early Bronze Age barbed and tanged arrowhead. Light grey flint. Length: 21mm, width: 19mm, thickness: 3mm. St Martin's, SF9, 1605.

Flint flake, light brown translucent flint. Length: 12mm, width: 13mm, thickness: 2mm. Edgbaston Street, SF 16, 1197.

Flint flake, partly burnt, opaque grey flint. Length: 26mm, width: 17mm, thickness: 3mm. Moor Street, 5155.

7   The Pottery

Stephanie Rátkai

Introduction

All the medieval pottery was examined under ×20 magnification and divided into fabric types. The post-medieval pottery was divided macroscopically into ware groups. The ware groups were subdivided depending on obvious differences in fabric, *e.g.* 'iron-poor', 'iron-rich', and these subdivisions are recorded on the database but are not used within the report where generic ware types are used, *e.g.* 'yellow ware', 'coarseware', 'mottled ware', etc.

The pottery was quantified by sherd count and weight, minimum rim count (and rim percentage (eves) for Phases 1 and 2). The late 18th-century refined wares from the Park Street tank fills were quantified by sherd count and weight and minimum rim/ base count. The quantified pottery assemblage by site and phase is shown in Table 7.1. Details of form, decoration, surface treatment, glaze, sooting and abrasion were recorded.

Lengthy descriptions of fabric and form have, where possible, been kept to a minimum. Known fabric types are not described and the reader referred to the appropriate source(s). Forms are not described individually since most forms have been illustrated in the form series.

The term 'Bull Ring sites' has been used in the text to denote Edgbaston Street, Park Street and Moor Street together.

The pottery fabrics

Deritend ware, Reduced Deritend ware and Deritend cooking pots

Deritend ware was first described by Sherlock (1957), when wasters were found in Deritend on the High Street, in the area between Chapel House Street and Alcester Street. This area lies across the road from Gibb Street

		Sherd count	Sherd weight	Rim count	eves
Edgbaston Street	Phase 1	532	9641	60	398
	Phase 2	316	8066	45	488
	Phase 3	1294	63299	205	
	Total	2142	81006	310	886
Moor Street	Phase 1	370	7348	36	462
	Phase 2	64	1249	10	75
	Phase 3	28	2048	7	
	Total	462	10645	53	537
Park Street	Phase 1	1702	22676	176	1152
	Phase 2	288	3633	67	168
	Phase 3	2496	67668	401	
	Total	4486	93977	644	1320
All sites	Total	7090	185628	1007	

Table 7.1 Quantification of pottery from all the Bull Ring sites by Phase, by Site (sherd count and weight, min vess and eves Phases 1 and 2).

and Heath Mill Lane, the Custard Factory and the Old Crown. At the latter site, a waster pit was found in 1994 (Litherland *et al.* 1994; Rátkai 1994c). Excavations at the Custard Factory (Mould 2001a) revealed large clay pits, thought to be post-medieval, and small islands of medieval deposits which also seemed to contain possible wastered material. Further west along the High Street, at Hartwell's Garage, excavation revealed yet more possible pottery waste (Rátkai 2000a; Rátkai 2000b). Finally, a site on Floodgate Street/ High Street, excavated in 2002, produced post-medieval coarseware and flower-pot wasters, probably dating to the 18th century (Rátkai 2002a) and a saggar was found from excavation on the High Street, Bordesley (Cook and Rátkai 1995). When the evidence of pottery production at Park Street (and possibly Moor Street) is added to the existing knowledge, it is apparent that pottery production in the medieval period must have extended from Alcester Street in the east to at least Park Street, a distance of about half a mile, and lay to either side of the River Rea and within two parishes. The presence of post-medieval wasters may indicate that there was an unbroken tradition of pottery production along the High Street, but as yet there is no hard and fast evidence for this.

Sherlock (1957) divided Deritend ware into two types: an unglazed gritty reduced ware and a red ware, either decorated with white slip or with an overall white slip coating (sometimes on both the internal and external surfaces). Sherlock deduced that the reduced ware pre-dated the red ware, although the evidence was somewhat circumstantial.

The term 'Deritend ware' has tended in recent literature to be used to describe the red ware jugs decorated with white slip. The fabric is micaceous and varies from very fine to moderately sandy. The quartz grains are rounded and rarely larger than *c.*0.25mm. There seemed to be little difference in form or decoration between the fine and the sandy fabrics, although it is just possible that the very fine fabric was the earliest (see Edgbaston Street Phase 1, below). A range of moderately to coarsely sandy fabrics was found in the waster pit behind the Old Crown, and the differences probably represent first and foremost varying degrees of clay preparation. The jug forms are illustrated in Fig. 7.1.1–7.1.11. Decorated sherds were often quite small and mainly unsuitable for illustration but a sample is shown in Fig. 7.15, colour. The decoration fell into seven groups: a) vertical white slip bands, lattices and curvilinear designs which were brushed onto the surface of the pot (Fig. 7.1.11; Fig. 7.15.4, 7, colour); b) thicker applied or trailed white slip lines (Fig. 7.15.1, 3, 5, colour); c) roller stamped white slip bands (Fig. 7.15.2, colour); d) applied white slip scales (Fig. 7.15.1, colour); e) deep horizontal bands of roller stamping; f) deep bands of horizontal combing on the shoulder (often above white slip lattice decoration) (Fig. 7.15.6–8, colour); and g) wide spaced single incised horizontal lines (Fig. 7.15.9, colour). A

small number of sherds had a completely white slipped surface but these were so small that it was impossible to tell what the overall effect would have been. Other sherds had white slip over the rim and on the interior of the neck (Fig. 7.14). This more liberal use of slip may have been intended to disguise the body colour of the vessel and imitate whiteware vessels (see Moor Street Phase 1, below). If this is so, then it argues for a post-AD 1250 date for these vessels, since whitewares seem to have been first manufactured in the second half of the 13th century.

There was a diversity of glaze colour from thin and clear to a thick opaque tan. There was some correlation between glaze type and decoration. Type (f) decoration was associated with a tan glaze, type (e) with a dark olive glaze, type (g) with a thin clear glaze, and the remaining decorative schemes with a thin olive or yellowish olive glaze.

Both rod handles and strap handles were present, the latter being most common. Rod handles were either plain (Fig. 7.1.7) or had a single vertical row of circular piercings. Strap handles were slashed (Fig. 7.1.1, 2, 10) or ?thumbnail impressed producing a 'ladder' pattern (Fig. 7.1.3). The 'ladder' pattern was the most frequent design and is one of the characteristics of Deritend ware jugs.

Other vessel types were also produced in Deritend ware. Sherlock (1957, fig. 2.7) illustrated a single oxidised cooking pot, the form of which is paralleled by Fig. 7.2.31 from a fill (1314) of the major boundary ditch at Park Street. The cooking pot fabric begins at the sandier end of the jug fabric range, *i.e.* moderately sandy, and continues to a very sandy fabric with rounded quartz grains up to 0.5mm. Petrological analysis (see Williams, Appendix 7.1) of three cooking pot sherds (probably production waste) from Park Street ditch fill 1314 and of a wastered, white slip-decorated Deritend jug (Fig. 7.1.11) from Park Street ditch fill 1198 confirmed the similarity of the fabrics.

The cooking pot forms are illustrated (Figs 7.1 and 7.2.19–34) and consist of both round-bodied and straight-sided forms, sometimes with applied thumbed strips. The round-bodied forms were more common. The forms illustrated in Fig. 7.1.24 and Fig. 7.2.27 and 31 were the most common vessel forms in the Park Street ditch fills. One of the most characteristic aspects of the cooking pots are the heavily modelled rim forms, many of which appear designed to take a lid (Figs 7.1 and 7.2: 19, 24, 27, 29–31, 34). These are paralleled by pottery from Weoley Castle (Oswald 1962, fig. 9.29–30) in the lowest fill of the moat, *i.e.* Period V dated *c.*1280–1320. These were found with what looks like reduced Deritend ware jugs and an oxidised roller stamped jug, which may also be Deritend ware. However, there was clearly a residual element in the lowest moat fill since the spouted pitcher form (Oswald *ibid.*, fig. 9.34) cannot possibly belong in the Period V date range. A similar spouted pitcher

(Oswald *ibid.*, fig. 7.13) was found on a Period II floor surface, dated 1200–1230. Both these vessels look and sound from their descriptions as though they were Stamford Ware (cf. Kilmurry 1980, fig. 3.5, fig. 4.8). If so, then both spouted vessels are earlier than *c.*1200 and in all probability date to the earliest occupation of Weoley Castle.

Heavily modelled rims are found in Warwick in 13th-century contexts (Rátkai 1990, fig. 15.63–64; Rátkai 1992a, fig. 6.34, 45) but in rather coarser fabrics than Deritend ware. These types of rims appear to be unknown in Coventry (see Redknap 1996) and Staffordshire (see Ford 1995). They appear to be a distinctive Warwickshire rim form which must have had a special functional merit since their manufacture, especially rims like Fig. 7.1.19 and Fig. 7.2.30, would have required additional and time-consuming labour.

The cooking pot illustrated by Sherlock (1957) had a cream interior slip. None of the Deritend cooking pots from the Bull Ring sites were slipped and the only example of a vessel with the heavy slipping mentioned by Sherlock was the lower portion of a jug found at Moor Street (see below).

There was a single example of the 'squared angular' rim type on a cooking pot or possibly pipkin (Fig. 7.1.16) in the finer Deritend jug fabric. This bridges the gap between the oxidised and reduced ware forms (see below). Other forms occurred in Deritend ware but were never common. These were sloping sided bowls (Fig. 7.2.35–36), pipkins (Fig. 7.1.13, 15, 17), and dripping trays (Fig. 7.1.14). The latter two forms tended to be in the finer fabric used for the jugs. A possible lid was also found in the finer jug fabric (Fig. 7.1.18). A small diameter base (*c.*8cm) may have come from a bottle. It can therefore be seen that a fairly full range of forms was being produced by the Birmingham potters in the oxidised Deritend ware. The greatest number of these occurred at Park Street.

The reduced Deritend ware ('DeritendR' in this report) was also well represented. The reduced wares had originally been divided into ten subgroups (RS01, RSa–RSd, RSf–RSi). However, in the light of the petrological report this seems excessive. Fabric RS01 was directly paralleled by pottery found elsewhere in Warwickshire and the code RS01 was taken from the County Type Series (Rátkai and Soden 1998). Petrological thin sections revealed that the fabric was much the same as the oxidised Deritend ware jug and the fabric of a Fabric RSc cooking pot sherd. Under ×20 magnification Fabric RSb closely resembled, but was somewhat sandier than, Fabric RS01. These three fabrics have therefore been re-categorised as DeritendR. There were two important macroscopic differences between RS01 and RSb, and RSc. RS01 and RSb consistently had black, slightly lustrous surfaces and a brown core, whereas RSc was grey throughout. In addition, Fabrics RSd, RSg and RSh were included in the DeritendR category, since the vessel forms were

essentially the same and the small differences in fabric could be ascribed to slightly different clay preparation or firing. There appeared to be no chronological significance in the fabric variations. Cooking pots were generally round bodied with squared angular, often undercut, rims (Fig. 7.3.44–53). This form/ fabric combination is well attested in Warwickshire, for example in Warwick (Rátkai 1990; Rátkai 1992a), Alcester (Rátkai 1994b; Rátkai 1996; Rátkai 2001b) and Stratford-upon-Avon (Rátkai 1992b; Rátkai 1994a). A second cooking pot form has a more sinuous profile and undercut rim (Fig. 7.3.54–57). These two forms made up the bulk of the cooking pots and are paralleled in Sherlock (1957, fig. 2.2–5). One of these cooking pots had traces of an applied thumbed strip but this type of decoration was more common on the oxidised Deritend cooking pots. Some of the cooking pots had quite distinctive surface treatment. One of these was a sort of 'rilling', *i.e.* close-spaced shallow horizontal grooves (cf. Sherlock 1957, fig. 2.1). This looked to have been done by applying a tool to the exterior of the vessel and rotating the vessel. A rare version of this produced an almost faceted appearance (cf. *ibid.*, fig. 2.6), with broader horizontal bands. There were two examples of a type of rustication where the surface had been deliberately roughened and a third where the surface had been criss-crossed with horizontal and vertical scoring (from a cleaning layer (5171) at Moor Street). A second example of this was found at Edgbaston Street in pit F224. This sherd is likely to have come from a jug since there was a trace of external glaze. A similar effect to the latter was described and illustrated by Oswald (1962, 74 and fig. 8.23) on an unglazed reduced ware jug. He considered this an imitation of slip decoration but this sounds rather implausible considering that the greyware jugs were coeval with the white slip decorated Deritend ware. A small number of cooking pots were decorated with incised horizontal or wavy lines.

There was a small group of cooking pots with a more barrel-shaped profile (Fig. 7.2.38, 39, 40; Fig. 7.3.43), although the rims were still quite angular. It may be significant that these forms only occurred at Moor Street and Park Street. The form looks earlier than the other more common types. Vessel Fig. 7.2.40 had a thumbed rim and was one of the very few examples of this rim treatment. The thumbing also suggests that this was an early type and that this is most likely to be a 12th-century vessel. On the interior, the neck-shoulder junction was worn, perhaps from the use of a lid. The vessel was found residually in F153, fill 1310, a sub-rectangular pit recorded in Evaluation Trench 9 at Moor Street.

Vessel Fig. 7.2.37 was the only example of a straight-sided cooking pot or bowl. There was part of a drilled hole in the vessel but there was insufficient evidence to indicate whether this had been part of a repair or had served some other function.

Nearly every cooking pot/ jar sherd was sooted, often heavily, suggesting that the vessels had been used mainly for cooking over an open fire. Some of the rim forms were slightly dished (*e.g.* Fig. 7.3.47, 49, 51) suggesting that they could also have been designed to take lids.

Jugs were the second best represented form after cooking pots/ jars. The DeritendR jugs are very distinctive. They are large globular vessels with broad strap handles springing from the rim or occasionally just below the rim (Figs 7.3 and 7.4.66–85). The handles were decorated with the 'ladder' pattern (Fig. 7.4.72, 85) seen on the oxidised jugs, oblique slashing (Fig. 7.3.67; Fig. 7.4.68, 69, 71, 82), stabbing (Fig. 7.4.83) and thumbing (Fig. 7.4.80–81). The handle (Fig. 7.4.80) from the large ditch F568 at Moor Street was very similar in both fabric and form to Thetford ware. However, the absence of any other Saxo-Norman pottery from the Bull Ring sites, with the possible exception of the socketed bowl (Fig. 7.6.136) from the large pit F746 at Park Street, suggests that the similarity may be fortuitous. It could, however, be seen as another small piece of evidence for the local production of reduced wares in the first half of the 12th century. Parallels for the other jug handles are to be found in Sherlock (1957, fig. 2.9, 17).

The jugs were unglazed (with the one exception described above). The fabric of the jugs and the 'ladder' decoration are points of connection with the oxidised Deritend jugs, as is the use of 'rilling'. One of the jugs from Moor Street (Fig. 7.4.72) was obviously valued enough to be repaired (see below), which is unexpected since the jugs have no special aesthetic merit. Perhaps it is to be inferred from this that they had a functional merit, now unknown to us.

One pipkin or skillet was represented by a tapering 'pan' handle with fingernail impressions (Fig. 7.3.65). This fabric/ form combination was not recorded by Sherlock. Three forms, represented by single vessels, looked surprisingly early. The first of these (unfortunately too small for illustration) was a tiny rim fragment from a small diameter (15cm) curved everted rim jar, which looked unnervingly like a late Anglo-Saxon or Roman form. The sherd came from a Phase 1 layer (1042) at Edgbaston Street. The second was a cooking pot/ jar with an expanded flattened rim (Fig. 7.3.63), with a diameter of 15cm, which looked even more unnervingly like an early–middle Saxon form. This vessel came from a Phase 1 layer (1763) at Park Street. However, Oswald (1964, fig. 47.8) mentions the similarity of one of the Period I (1200–1230) reduced ware sherds to pagan Anglo-Saxon vessels and the general look of Fig. 7.3.63 is not dissimilar to, although much smaller than, one illustrated by Oswald (1962, fig. 6.2), dated to the second half of the 12th century. Apart from this sherd, layer 1763 at Park Street contained other Deritend reduced wares, oxidised Deritend ware, an iron-poor sherd and an ?intrusive blackware sherd. The third rather odd sherd came from Edgbaston Street (2160, the fill of tanning pit F237). It was a bevelled rim sherd from a curving-sided form with a small diameter of 11cm (Fig. 7.3.64). This form, an

incurved rim bowl, is paralleled at Weoley Castle in a context dated 1250–70 (Oswald 1964).

The dating of Deritend ware and DeritendR ware is problematical. On the face of it, it would be strange if two very different and distinct types of pottery were being manufactured contemporaneously in the Deritend/ Digbeth area of Birmingham. Both Sherlock and Oswald were hampered by the infancy of medieval pottery studies and were heavily reliant on parallels, most usually provided by Dunning or Jope, from well outside the West Midlands. In addition the pottery is described in general terms such as 'fine light grey ware' making it difficult to equate with pottery from later excavations. Finally, the pottery is not quantified. The dating evidence, once parallels from outside the West Midlands are removed, can be summarised as follows. Sherlock argues for reduced ware production first, followed by, and overlapping for a time with, the oxidised Deritend ware. This is based on three pit fills, one of which contained mainly reduced Deritend ware and one or two oxidised jug sherds and the other two of which contained only oxidised Deritend ware. However, as the pottery in the fills was partly kiln waste, the relative proportions of the wares within the pit fills need only reflect different firings not, necessarily, different dates. Obviously, when faced with red-bodied decorated glazed wares and grey, rather functional looking, unglazed wares it is tempting to modern sensibilities to place the latter class as a forerunner to the former. The end result is that Sherlock suggested that reduced Deritend ware was made *c.*1250–1280 and oxidised Deritend ware *c.*1280–1320.

This dating was modified by Oswald in view of the excavations at Weoley Castle. This provided a stratigraphic sequence dated by coin evidence, but Oswald also made use of documentary sources and some rather far-flung pottery parallels. The interim report appeared in 1962. Working without a substantial body of local evidence, some of the dating now looks open to question. For example what must be a DeritendR cooking pot (Oswald 1962, fig. 6.4) occurs in Period 1 dated 1150–1200. This was found with other reduced wares which sound and look as if they are related to the putative early reduced wares (Fabric RSi) from Moor Street. Period II, dated 1200–1230, contained what looks like a whiteware pipkin, which throws some doubt on the date of the period since both fabric and form would be unparalleled at this early date. Likewise the green-glazed whiteware jug (*ibid.*, fig. 8.22) from Period III suggests a date after 1250. However, Oswald notes that greyware which 'appears to be the same ware as that found at Deritend' (*ibid.*, 75) nearly all occurred in Periods II and III. Periods II–III are dated to 1210–1270.

A second, more detailed report on a timber building at Weoley Castle was also published by Oswald (1964). Here 'hard grey wares' were associated with Period I (12th century) and were less frequent in Period II (1200–1230). The illustrated pottery from Period I does not closely resemble that from the Bull Ring sites. However, a DeritendR jug (Oswald 1964, fig. 49.21) came from Floor 4 (1240–50) but the text records that similar glazed handles (*i.e.* those with 'ladder' decoration) were also found 'in this level and above'. A DeritendR skillet handle was found in Floor 6 (1250–70). No oxidised Deritend ware associated with the building is illustrated although one highly decorated jug (fig. 50.35), unrecognised as Deritend ware (see discussion below, Park Street Phase 1), is illustrated and dated to 1264–80. In the discussion of this vessel, Oswald states that this type of jug is 'firmly dated 1250–80' at Weoley Castle, although there is little corroborative evidence for this.

It is now very difficult to test the validity of the Weoley Castle dating. It rests on the evidence of two coins, one of King John, from a layer outside but abutting the building on the north side and equated with Floor 2, and the other of Henry III found in the top floor level of the stone building. The second piece of dating evidence is the licence to crenellate granted in 1264, which may have led to the destruction of the stone and timber buildings that were sealed with a thick clay layer, possibly derived from the construction of a new moat. The first pillar of the argument is that the wooden and stone buildings were intimately connected with each other, so that the coin evidence can be used to date both buildings. Secondly, there is an implicit assumption that none of the pottery or other artefacts were residual, redeposited or intrusive. This is brought into question by the waterlogged nature of the site in the area of the wooden building and by the numerous cross-joins from between the building's floors and layers outside the building. Oswald notes that there was little pottery from the floor surfaces but assumes that what pottery there was related to its use in the building. It is, of course, just as possible that the pottery came into the building from outside as part of levelling material for the six floor surfaces which were laid, in which case the sequence would be somewhat less reliable.

Outside Birmingham, DeritendR has been found in Warwick at numerous sites. The most useful of these as far as sequencing the pottery is concerned are Bridge End (Rátkai 1990) and Park House (Rátkai forthcoming a). These were adjacent sites in the medieval suburb, situated across the river from Warwick Castle. At both sites DeritendR occurs most abundantly with the advent of pottery of the second half of the 13th century, *e.g.* whitewares and decorated glazed wares such as Boarstall-Brill. More recent work on the Park House assemblage has made a reassessment of the Bridge End pottery possible and suggests that the dates for the phasing should be pushed back by about 25–50 years. This would give a *terminus ante quem* of 1325 for the end of DeritendR. The date of the arrival of DeritendR is still insecure, although there was some stratigraphic evidence at Park House to suggest that there was some DeritendR before the advent of whitewares, *i.e.* before *c.*1250.

At Bridge End (Rátkai 1990) oxidised Deritend ware jugs first occur in Phase 2, suggesting that reduced wares pre-date them. With the modified phase dating suggested by the Park House assemblage (see above) this would suggest that oxidised Deritend ware jugs could have appeared at Bridge End *c.*1250–75.

The oxidised Deritend jugs, like the reduced ware cooking pots with the angular rims, are unique in the region. They are very distinctive and bear no relation to pottery produced in the surrounding counties. The closest parallels for the oxidised jugs are to be found in London-type ware (cf. Pearce *et al.* 1985) and Mill Green Ware (Pearce *et al.* 1982), in terms of overall form, white slip decoration and glaze, although the handle types – with the exception of the rod handle – are different. Simple slip decoration and rounded forms are paralleled by Pearce *et al.* (1985, pl. 1 and figs 14–15, examples dated to the late 12th century). More complex white slip decoration is paralleled by the North French/ Highly Decorated styles dating to the second half of the 13th century and early 14th century. Within this group were anthropomorphic and zoomorphic decorations. There was one possible anthropomorphic decorative element, a 1mm diameter rod 'handle' from Park Street (1517). However, face masks and a ram's horn were found among the Old Crown wasters, and part of a crude hand and arm, with a tan glaze, was found at Knowle Hall, Warwickshire (pers. inspection by author). The parallels with London-type ware therefore suggest a possible date range of *c.*1200–1325 for the oxidised Deritend ware jugs, although there is no corroborating evidence for such an early start date, which on the face of it seems unlikely. Mill Green Ware is dated later 13th–early 14th centuries. Vince (1983) suggests that the use of white slip around the inside of the neck of a redware jug dates to the early–mid-13th century, based on examples from Worcester and Hereford, and that all-over white slip was in use in London in the early 13th century.

There is no doubt that Deritend oxidised glazed jugs were made by the mid-13th century. The stratigraphic information from the Bull Ring sites suggests that both the oxidised and reduced Deritend ware pre-date the whitewares, giving a *terminus ante quem* of *c.*1250. Certain decorative elements were shared by both the reduced and oxidised Deritend ware vessels, *e.g.* the 'ladder' handle and 'rilling', which would seem to indicate that there was some overlap in the production of the two wares, yet the oxidised and reduced cooking pot forms have nothing in common.

In addition there are a few tantalising pieces of evidence that suggest that some DeritendR ware was made in the 12th century but there is insufficient evidence to build up a complete picture. Suffice it to say that it is not these putative early forms that are found outside Birmingham.

The more unusual decorative elements on the oxidised jugs were only found at Park Street. These can be summarised as roller stamping on applied white strips from the large pit F746 and a layer that sealed it (1841), applied white clay scales from pit F746 and grave F742, and interior white slip on the neck and/ or over the rim from a layer sealing the graves (1760), the major boundary ditch F174 and pond F506. Underglaze slip was found on a sherd from pit F746 and interior and exterior white slip on sherds from grave F742, and from the major ditch F568 at Moor Street. From this it is apparent that most of these sherds came from the area of the two graves in Area C at Park Street. The roller stamp decoration on white slip and the use of applied scales is likely to date to the last quarter of the 13th century or first quarter of the 14th century. The use of overall white slip and interior white slip could, on the analogy of Worcester jugs, date to the early–mid-13th century, but given that these sherds tend to occur alongside those with later styles of decoration, perhaps they too date to the post-1250 period. Certainly, roller stamped sherds and sherds with white slip on the interior of the neck were found together in the waster pit behind the Old Crown, Deritend (Rátkai 1994c), which suggests that these decorative elements were contemporary.

Coventry-type cooking pots; Coventry and Coventry-type glazed wares

See Redknap (1985 and 1996) for a discussion of Coventry wares' fabrics and forms.

There were no diagnostic sherds in the cooking pot fabric. An unglazed plain strap handle from Park Street (1842) was closer to the cooking pot fabric than the glazed ware. A similar handle/ fabric combination was seen at Burton Dassett, southeastern Warwickshire (Rátkai forthcoming a). The fabric is WCTS Sq20.2 and noted as a possible Coventry A ware type. Coventry cooking pots are conventionally dated c.1150–1250 (see Redknap 1985; 1996). The glazed fabrics are the equivalent of Bridge End Fabric 110 (Rátkai 1990), which is WCTS Fabric Sq21.1 and was identified as a Coventry ware by Mark Redknap (cf. Redknap 1985), and WCTS Fabric Sq21, Coventry tripod pitcher ware (Coventry D ware). One sherd from Park Street (1245) was from a Coventry glazed tripod pitcher (WCTS Fabric Sq21) with incised wavy line decoration and a thin green splash glaze. A second pitcher sherd came from a Phase 1 tanning pit at Edgbaston Street (F229, 2080). The glazed sherds are likely to date to c.1150–1225. A pitcher rim and the splash-glazed base of a large jug or pitcher (Fig. 7.4.86–7) came from a fill (1325) of the major medieval boundary ditch at Park Street (F174/ F201) and the fill (1831) of the Phase 1 pit F770 respectively.

One tiny sherd from 1326, the middle fill of ditch F174/ F201 at Park Street, appeared to have a complex roller stamp design. This would be rather unusual for Coventry-type glazed ware. The sherd was in WCTS Fabric Sq21.1 (Fig. 7.18.4, colour). However, a similar roller stamped sherd was found at Kings Norton (Rátkai

2001a, fig. 5.25) in a similar sounding fabric, but described as a Coal Measure Clay ware. It is therefore possible that this sherd from Park Street has been assigned to the wrong fabric group.

Boarstall-Brill ware

For fabric description *etc.*, see Mellor (1994).

This too was not a well-represented fabric. Three highly decorated sherds came from Area B at Edgbaston Street, and consisted of anthropomorphic decoration (Fig. 7.16.1, colour; cf. Mellor 1994, fig. 57.2, dated 1250–1300), part of a jug with roller stamped red slip and incised 'leaf' pattern (Fig. 7.16.2, colour; cf. *ibid.*, fig. 51.23, dated 1250–1300) and a sherd from a 'triple-decker' jug with a type of polychrome decoration comprising two red clay stripes with copper-mottled glaze between them, to the side of which is an area with thin yellowish olive glaze and applied, self clay, scales (Fig. 7.16.3, colour; for the decorative scheme (see Mellor *ibid.*, fig. 56.1, dated c.1250–1300). The decoration on the latter sherd is very similar to that found on the later oxidised Deritend jugs from Park Street and from the Old Crown, Deritend. Three vessels were represented from Park Street, a baluster jug base, an indeterminate jug sherd and a bowl sherd. The latter two sherds were associated with the two graves in Area C. The baluster base was from 1811, a fill of the recut boundary ditch F760. Three jugs were represented from Moor Street, from Phase 1 pit F556 (Fig. 7.16.4, colour; see below), ditch F561 and residually in a Phase 3 layer.

There was a small number of probable late Boarstall-Brill (or possibly Nettlebed) sherds. The sherds had an external bright green, copper-coloured glaze and an interior pale yellow glaze. Vessel forms represented were cups, and a possible lobed vessel (from Moor Street). This fabric was only found on Moor Street and Area A, Park Street.

Worcester-type glazed ware

This fabric was not well represented and only occurred at Park Street in the upper fill (1252) of boundary ditch F174/ F201, in Area A, and residually in F775, Area C. The sherd from 1252 had a splash of white slip on the interior, placing the sherd in the early–mid-13th-century date range.

Chilvers Coton C fabric

See Mayes and Scott (1984).

Only one sherd from the entire Bull Ring assemblage was sourced to the Chilvers Coton kilns (WCTS Fabric SQ30). The sherd was from fill 1323 of the boundary ditch F174/ F201. The fabric dates from the end of the 13th century through to the 15th century. It is perhaps surprising that such a large production centre as Chilvers Coton failed to have any real impact on Birmingham.

Glazed wares or unglazed jug fabrics

Fabric Medg2
Moderate to abundant rounded quartz 0.25–2.5mm, with ill-sorted grains up to 2mm, sparse rounded iron ore up to 0.5mm, rare rounded mudstone/ siltstone *c.*0.5mm, sparse angular fine grained sandstone *c.*0.5mm, sparse organics, and mica flecks visible on the surface. Quite hackly fracture. Surfaces orange/ brown with grey or brown margins and grey core.

This fabric is very poorly represented but the two form sherds, both from strap handles (Fig. 7.4.88–89), were found at Edgbaston Street in a Phase 1 tanning pit (F228, 2070) and residually in a Phase 3 gully (F240, 2181). The handles, with an applied central thumbed strip, look like pitcher handles and typologically should date to *c.*1150–1225. Body sherds were found at Park Street in the major boundary ditch (F174/ F201, 1213) and residually in a Phase 3 layer in Area A (1368), and presumably represent occupation in the 12th or early 13th centuries along Digbeth.

Fabric Medg3
Moderate well-sorted rounded pink, white and grey quartz 0.2–0.5mm, sparse iron ore up to 0.5mm, rare rounded siltstone/ mudstone fragments <0.25mm. Orange-brown fabric.

This fabric was represented by two sherds, an undiagnostic body sherd with traces of external glaze or possibly fuel ash slag and a slashed strap handle with yellowish olive glaze (Fig. 7.4.90).

Fabric Medg4
Sparse rounded quartz <0.25mm, sparse rounded mudstone/ siltstone, <0.25mm. Orange external surface and margin, light grey core, internal margin and surface. Spots of yellowish glaze.

One sherd only, from Area A Park Street.

Fabric Medg6
Hard-fired, fine, wheel-thrown fabric. Moderate fine quartz <0.25mm. Glossy olive glaze, orange internal surface and core, remainder of sherd mid-grey.

Date: ?mid-13th–14th centuries. From Moor Street, fill 5154 of ditch F561.

Fabric Mudst
Moderate sub-angular and rounded quartz <0.25mm, sparse sub-angular siltstone/ mudstone up to 0.5mm, sparse iron ore flecks, 0.5mm. Orange-brown external surface and margin, remainder of sherd grey-brown.

This fabric is the same as Fabric cpj13. Jug sherd with complex roller stamping (Fig. 7.18, colour) from 2233, F268 (Phase 1 pit), Edgbaston Street.

Fabric Mudstg (similar to WCTS Fabric Sq212)
Moderate ill-sorted rounded quartz up to 1mm, sparse-moderate, rounded mudstone/ siltstone up to 1mm.

One sherd with two bands of rectangular roller stamping and thin applied thumbed strip (Fig. 7.18.2,

colour). Trace of thin, decayed or poorly fluxed glaze. This rather crude hand-made sherd looks to have come from a pitcher with a date of *c.*1150–1200/ 1225. The sherd came from Area A, Edgbaston Street, fill 1075, F147 (Phase 1 pit).

Light-bodied (iron-poor) wares

Fabric ww1
Moderate–abundant, ill-sorted, rounded quartz *c.*0.25–0.75mm.

This fabric was the same as one found at Wishaw (WISMD01), in northern Warwickshire (Rátkai 2002b). ?Wheel-thrown. Body colour white or cream. Vessels were mainly made up of green-glazed jugs (Fig. 7.4.91–93; Fig. 7.5.94) or bowls with an internal green glaze. The combed decoration found on Fig. 7.5.94 is commonly found on whiteware jugs in the region and is paralleled by Ford (1995, fig. 15.103–105) in Staffordshire.

Fabric ww2
Sparse ill-sorted, iron-stained, sub-angular quartz 0.25–1mm, sparse iron oxide, sparse organics, rare sub-angular off-white inclusions up to *c.*0.5mm.

Wheel-thrown. The surfaces of the sherds are very smooth. Glazes range from mottled apple-green, to copper-green coloured to dull olive-brown. This is quite a distinctive fabric and has been recognised at Minworth Greaves (Rátkai 2001c), where it was a favoured fabric for bowls. Body colour cream sometimes with a pinkish tone. There were few diagnostic sherds but forms represented comprised green-glazed bowls and jugs.

Fabric ww3
Moderate sub-rounded quartz *c.*0.25mm, sparse–moderate iron oxide up to 1mm.

Body colour white or cream. Glazes vary from bright green, to yellowish olive to dull brownish green. Wheel-thrown. There were few diagnostic sherds. Jugs with combed decorations were represented.

Fabric ww4
Abundant rounded quartz *c.*0.25mm, moderately frequent flecks of iron oxide in the clay matrix with occasional larger lumps up to 0.5mm.

Body colour white or cream. Wheel-thrown. This fabric was paralleled at Minworth Greaves (Rátkai 2001c), where it occurred with red painted decoration. Glazes were apple-green or olive. Vessel forms comprised jugs (Fig. 7.5.95) and bowls. Jugs were decorated with combing and/ or comb impressions (*e.g.* Fig. 7.5.97), applied and combed decoration (Fig. 7.5.96) or lines of triangular roller stamping.

Fabric ww5
Moderate quartz up to 0.1mm, sparse iron oxide flecks, 0.25mm.

A very fine wheel-thrown fabric with a cream or pale grey body, sometimes with a grey core, external surface pale brown. Glazes pale, thin grey-green, thin olive spots and splashes. Jugs with thumbed bases. Similar fabric known from Dudley Castle (personal inspection by author).

Fabric ip1

This is in essence a variation of Fabric ww3. It is slightly coarser but has been fired in such a way that large sections of the sherd are salmon pink coloured, the remainder being cream. External surfaces tend to be a pale orange; the internal surfaces are most often cream. Glazes are olive, often with copper speckles. The glaze can be very 'dribbly' and there is a thin reddish 'shadow' at the edges of the glaze or where the glaze is very thin. This suggests that the glaze has been applied to the pot in a thin liquid medium. Fairly plain ware. Jugs and at least one bottle base from Edgbaston Street context 2004 (a cleaning layer).

Fabric ip2

Moderate–abundant, sub-angular quartz *c*.0.25mm, sparse iron oxide (red or black depending on firing) flecks, 0.25mm, sparse organics.

Wheel-thrown. Clay colour varies from yellowish buff, to pale orange to pale grey. Inner surfaces tend to be buff. External surfaces are usually pale brown or pinkish orange. The latter is most common on glazed sherds and suggests that something may have volatilised from the glaze or glaze medium affecting the external surface colour. Glazes are yellowish olive with copper speckles. There is a large base sherd from a jug in this fabric from a Phase 2 pit at Moor Street (F536, 5111). It is made up of three, slightly burnt, joining sherds. There are splashes of glaze on the exterior, one of which continues over the break onto the interior surface. The positioning of the glaze splashes and the surface coloration suggests this sherd may have been used as a kiln spacer. There are tiny fragments of clay body stuck in the glaze which appear to be from an iron-rich fine sandy fabric, possibly Deritend ware. This sherd is important in that it suggests that pottery production in the medieval period may have extended as far as Moor Street. If the sherd has been used as a spacer then Fabric ip2 was contemporary with Deritend ware. If the sherd is itself a waster then this would be evidence for the production of more than just Deritend ware in the medieval period in Birmingham.

Forms represented were jugs (Fig. 7.5.98–100) with thumbed bases (Fig. 7.5.101) and bowls (Fig. 7.5.102). Decoration consisted of incised horizontal lines either singly or in groups, and bands of rectangular roller stamping.

Fabric ip4

Sparse sub-angular quartz generally less than 0.25mm, sparse–moderate iron ore (generally rounded but some quite angular pieces) red or black depending on firing, flecks up to 1mm.

A fine wheel-thrown fabric generally buff or pale grey in colour. Pale-dark olive glazes. Forms represented were jugs (Fig. 7.5.103), some decorated with incised horizontal lines.

Fabric ip6

Very fine sandy matrix with abundant quartz <0.1mm, sparse larger sub-rounded quartz grains up to 0.25mm, sparse iron ore, mainly flecks in the clay body, rare larger lumps up to 0.5mm. Very smooth, slightly powdery surface feel.

Buff surfaces and external margin, remaining body pale orange-brown colour. Vessel forms consisted of a jug with a knife trimmed base, with heavy sooting on base and just over base angle; the lower part of a cup with internal and external olive glaze, and an olive-glazed oval-sectioned handle with central groove. The handle was largely reduced.

Fabric ip7

Sparse ill-sorted sub-rounded quartz (iron stained), up to 0.25mm, sparse iron ore flecks, 1.0mm, rare sub-rounded red sandstone up to 0.25 mm.

Wheel-thrown. Cream to pale pink fabric, surfaces sometimes darker and more orange toned.

Fabric ip8

Rare rounded quartz <0.25mm, sparse organics, sparse iron oxide, sparse subangular white inclusions – ?gypsum (powdery when scratched with a metal point, no reaction with HCl).

Wheel-thrown. Buff to pale brown fabric, sometimes with pale grey core or internal margin. Olive or tan glazes. This was possibly a later medieval fabric (Fig. 7.5.104).

Fabric ip9

Moderate–abundant sub-angular quartz *c*.0.25mm.

Evenly fired yellowish to buff fabric. Only three sherds were ascribed to this fabric. All were small and it is possible that they represent more than one fabric. One sherd came from F123 (1011), a Phase 1 square pit in Area A at Edgbaston Street. It was from a pitcher with a thin, virtually clear glaze and decorated with a row of square roller stamping and an applied, thin vertical-thumbed strip. The glaze and decoration suggest a date of *c*.1150–1200. Within the fabric of this sherd there was a single clay pellet and an angular piece of white micaceous ?siltstone. The second sherd, from a Phase 1 pit in Area A at Park Street (F160, 1177), was un-decorated but bore traces of a decayed splash glaze. The third sherd, from a Phase 2 pit or tank in Area B at Park Street (F562, 1661), was a plain body sherd, somewhat less sandy than the other two sherds.

Fabric ip10

Sparse sub-rounded quartz *c*.0.25mm, sparse organics, sparse iron oxide 0.25–0.5mm, very rare red sandstone 0.25mm.

Pale orange fabric. There were only two sherds, both from layer 1841, which sealed the graves in Area C, at

Park Street. One had a tan glaze with olive mottles and horizontal combing, the other had a similar glaze but partly decayed and was decorated with an applied vertical strip and a trace of horizontal combing. The decoration and glaze suggest that these sherds date in the later 12th–mid-13th centuries.

Reduced wares

Fabric RSf
Sparse rounded quartz 0.25–0.5mm, sparse–moderate rounded mudstone/ siltstone 1.0–5.0mm, sparse burnt out organics.

A grey ware with a fine sandy (quartz 0.01mm) micaceous matrix. Vessels are hand-made and thick bodied. Only body sherds were represented, which appeared to have come from cooking pots.

Fabric Rsi
Ill-sorted sub-rounded quartz grains 0.25–1mm, sparse iron oxide 0.25–2mm, sparse rounded mudstone/ siltstone 1–3mm.

Hand-formed, wheel-finished? Hard grey ware with slightly hackly fracture. Only body sherds and one base sherd were present. One sherd has a light surface rilling, a second has incised wavy line decoration, and a third incised horizontal lines.

Iron-rich cooking pot fabrics

Fabric cpj1
Moderate–abundant, rounded quartz c.0.25–0.5mm, rare silver mica flecks visible on the surfaces.

Fabric usually brown with a grey core. Many of the vessel forms closely resemble Deritend ware cooking pots and Fabric cpj1 could be a variant of Deritend ware, although vessels Fig. 7.5.105 and 107 look like rather earlier forms than the standard Deritend cooking pots (Fig. 7.5.105–117).

Fabric cpj2
Sparse–moderate well-sorted sub-angular quartz c.0.25mm.

Orange-brown external surface and margin, remainder of sherd reduced dark grey, sometimes internal surface is orange-brown (Fig. 7.6.118).

Fabric cpj5 (Deritend cpf)
See above for discussion of this ware.

Fabric cpj6
Moderate sub-angular quartz, some iron-stained, 0.25–0.5mm.
Oxidised orange throughout (Fig. 7.6.119, 120).

Fabric cpj7
Fine sandy 'granular' matrix. Sparse–moderate ill-sorted sub-rounded quartz 0.1–0.5mm, sparse organics, sparse sub-rounded mudstone up to 0.5mm.
Surface and margins orange or brown, core light–mid-grey (Fig. 7.6.121–125).

Fabric cpj9
Moderate-fine rounded quartz c.0.1mm, rare rounded grains up to 0.25mm.
Hand-formed. Dense, fine black fabric, sherds very thin-walled. One sherd has an almost burnished appearance. Sherd with flat-topped expanded rim is possibly from a jug, although there was very little curvature on the rim.

Fabric cpj10
Sparse, rounded quartz 0.25–0.5mm, sub-angular granular rock (?igneous), sparse rounded mudstone, sparse sub-angular ?quartzite, rare sub-angular dark glassy inclusion, sparse organics, scattering of fine golden mica visible on surfaces.
Hand-formed. Black, 'paste-like' fabric. The sherd has an internal sooty deposit. Certain elements of the one sherd in this fabric closely resemble early–middle Anglo-Saxon pottery. This sherd, found residually in a Phase 3 pit at Park Street (F162, 1179), is very different from the rest of the assemblage and, if not Anglo-Saxon, must be early.

Fabric cpj11
Moderate–abundant rounded quartz (occasional sub-angular grains) 0.5–1mm, sparse sub-angular quartzite 1.0–2.0mm, fine-grained angular sandstone c.0.5–1.0mm.
Brown fabric with grey core. The fabric seems to be the same as WCTS Fabric Sq11 (Warwick, Bridge End Fabric 113). The fabric occurred in Phase 1 at Bridge End, Warwick, suggesting a later 12th–13th-century date. This dating is confirmed by a residual spout from a spouted pitcher (an early form) from an oven fill at Brook Street, Warwick (Rátkai 1992a). In Birmingham, this fabric was only found at Moor Street.

Fabric cpj12
Sparse rounded, ill-sorted, sub-angular quartz, 0.25–4.0mm, sparse–moderate mudstone 0.5–5.0 mm, sparse burnt out organics, rare igneous inclusions.
This fabric is the same as WCTS Fabric Sq22 (Warwick, Bridge End Fabric 125). A sherd in a coarse version of this fabric, from a fill (5158) of the boundary ditch (F561) at Moor Street, was examined petrologically by Dr David Williams (Appendix 7.1 this volume) who suggests that the fabric may derive from the boulder clays. Brown or greyish brown fabric. Hand-formed (Fig. 7.6.126–128).

Fabric cpj13
Sparse ill-sorted sub-angular and sub-rounded quartz c.0.2–5.0 mm, sparse mudstone c.0.5–1mm, sparse organics, rare sandstone c.0.5mm, rare iron oxide up to 0.5mm, flecks of golden mica visible on the surfaces.
Hand-formed. The surfaces are smooth although larger quartz grains are visible in most fractures. Sherds generally have brown surfaces and margins and a grey core (Fig. 7.6.129–132).

Fabric cpj14

Moderate ill-sorted rounded quartz grains 0.25–1.0mm, rare larger sub-angular grains 1–3mm, sparse mudstone/ siltstone 0.5–2.0mm, sparse organics, rare sandstone *c*.0.5–0.75 mm, mica flecks visible on the surfaces.

This is essentially a brown fabric, sometimes reduced grey or black. There is no consistency in the final fired colour of the clay nor in the sorting of the inclusions within the clay. The fabric may well be a variant of Fabric cpj13. It is unfortunate that very few vessel profiles survived. The two most complete vessels were straight-sided cooking pot/jars (Fig. 7.6.133, 135). At least seven other rim forms were identified. All of them had broken at the rim-body junction so it was not possible to say with any degree of certainty whether the remainder of the vessel would have been straight-sided or rounded, although the former seemed more likely.

Fabric cpj15

Moderate–abundant rounded and sub-rounded quartz *c*.0.25–0.5mm, sparse clay pellets up to 3mm, sparse organics.

There was only one sherd in this fabric, from a spouted bowl (Fig. 7.6.136). The sherd colour is buff, with thin, pink margins. There is a small amount of smoke blackening and soot on one side of the spout. The fabric is similar to Oxford ware OXY (Mellor 1994) and to WCTS Fabric Sq26. A spouted bowl in OXY is illustrated by Mellor (1994, fig. 20.5), which is dated to the late 12th–early 13th centuries. Similar vessels are also known from the early timber phase of Stafford Castle (Rátkai 2007). The form is also known from the late Anglo-Saxon period. The vessel was found in Area C, Park Street in the fill of the large pit F746, which was cut by the graves, where it was clearly residual. Unfortunately, it is not possible to say with any accuracy what date the vessel might be, other than that it is most likely to pre-date 1200.

Late wheel-thrown iron-rich oxidised wares

The following fabrics mark the transition, in the 15th and 16th centuries, from the medieval repertoire to that of the post-medieval period. It is during this transitional period that the boundaries between fabrics and between fabrics and forms become blurred. For example, some of the late oxidised wares under different firing conditions would be classed as Midlands Purple ware (this has also been noted by Ford 1995). Some of the jar forms, although in late oxidised fabrics, prefigure the later coarseware jars, *e.g.* Fig. 7.7.152. Some of the finer late oxidised wares are used for what would normally be considered Cistercian ware forms. However, there are certain features which set the late oxidised wares apart from both the medieval and post-medieval traditions. The vessel forms are dominated by jars/cisterns and bowls, with cooking pots and jugs less well represented. A small number of more specialised forms are present, such as chafing dishes

and salts. This is also the period in which Cistercian ware and blackware cups first make their appearance. In general the vessels are very functional with little decoration (the cistern illustrated in Fig. 7.7.149 is unusual in this respect) and with rather cursory glazing. Glazes range from glossy olives and tans through to mid-brown, often reddish toned, and purple-browns. As the glaze colour testifies, the use of underglaze slip is not usually practised. However, a very small number of the sherds do have an iron-rich slip or wash, a surface treatment which was to come into prominence in the later coarsewares and yellow wares. Many of the late oxidised ware, Midlands Purple ware and Cistercian ware forms can be paralleled by material recovered from Oakeswell Hall (Hodder and Glazebrook 1987), much of which is thought to have been made in Wednesbury, where a pottery industry is attested in the later Middle Ages and post-medieval period.

In the following section the fabrics of Cistercian ware and Midlands Purple ware have not been described since they are well-known types regionally.

Fabric lox1

Sparse rounded quartz up to 0.25mm, rare iron oxide <0.25mm.

Buff or orange fabric. Wheel-thrown. Often knife trimming around lower parts of vessels. Olive brown glazes (Fig. 7.6.137–142).

Fabric lox2

Very fine fabric with rare rounded quartz <0.25mm, sparse organics.

Wheel-thrown. Clay colour orange to weak red. Sherds are usually uniformly oxidised, although external surfaces can be pale brown. Knife trimming evident on lower sections of vessels. Two ?jar sherds have an external coating of purplish red slip, linking this fabric to the later coarsewares. Bowl with internal tan glaze, jug/jar/cisterns with external purple, purple-brown, dark olive or copper-speckled tan glazes. One cistern had been decorated with a segmented stamp (Fig. 7.7.149). This vessel is directly paralleled by material from Oakeswell Hall (Hodder and Glazebrook 1987, fig. 4).

Fabric lox3

Abundant sub-angular quartz, up to 0.25mm, rare sub-angular, fine-grained sandstone up to 5.0mm.

Sandy orange fabric, often with grey core. Wheel-thrown. Olive-brown or tan glazes. Forms represented were bowls with internal glaze, bifid-rim jars and a dripping tray (Fig. 7.7.154–155).

Fabric lox5

Moderate rounded quartz *c*.25–0.5mm, sparse iron oxide 0.25–0.5mm.

Wheel-thrown. Orange fabric, sometimes buff–pale orange surfaces and margins. Two sherds from the same vessel from Moor Street have white clay streaks within the body. This foreshadows some of the later iron-poor coarsewares. Surfaces are sometimes purplish where the glaze is thin or has burnt off. Forms represented were a possible jar (Fig. 7.7.156), bowls with internal tan glaze (Fig. 7.7.157–158) and a chafing dish or possibly a strainer (Fig. 7.7.159).

Fabric lox8
Moderate–abundant fine rounded quartz generally <0.25mm.

The fabric is hard fired and is almost a Midlands Purple. Orange or red fabric. Purplish, red or grey-brown surfaces. Purple-green, dark green or olive glazes.

Fabric lox9
Abundant rounded quartz 0.1–0.25mm (mostly *c*.0.1mm), rare sandstone up to 0.5mm, very rare chert. Fabric weak red or grey, surfaces orange, brown or purplish. Dull olive glazes. This fabric, like Fabric lox8 above, would, with a slightly different firing, be Midlands Purple. Forms are made up of jugs, jars or cisterns.

Fabric lox10
Sparse iron oxide 0.5–5.0mm, sparse rounded quartz *c*.0.25mm, rare sandstone *c*.0.5mm.

Orange to weak red fabric, patchy grey core. The clay matrix has some lighter clay streaks. Unglazed jar/ cistern with purplish brown exterior surface and jar/ cistern with internal dark brown, slightly metallic glaze. There were only two vessels represented in this fabric, from contexts 2062 a fill of a Phase 2 tanning pit F223 and 2139 the fill of Phase 2 tanning pit F214 at Edgbaston Street. This fabric is transitional between the late oxidised iron-rich fabrics and the iron-rich coarsewares of the 17th and 18th centuries.

Gritty ware
Abundant sub-rounded quartz *c*.0.5mm, sparse angular sandstone with loosely cemented grains *c*.0–1mm.

Body colour varies from buff to orange. The fabric is very coarse and vessels are thick walled. Few forms were represented. Two jar forms were recorded, one with a plain everted rim, and a second with an everted slightly dished rim. There was one possible bowl base. The bowl and some of the jars had an interior olive-brown glaze. The fabric was not well represented and occurred mainly on Area B, Edgbaston Street and Area A, Park Street. The fabric first appears in Phase 2 but is most common in Phase 3.

Midlands Purple ware
Forms represented were largely unglazed jars (Fig. 7.7.160–165) with one jug (not illustrated) and one cistern (Fig. 7.7.166).

Cistercian ware
Vessel forms consisted of two-handled cups (Fig. 7.7.167–168), three-handled cups (Fig. 7.8.170) and the base of a candlestick or salt (Fig. 7.8.173). A small number of sherds were decorated with applied white pads or more complex designs in white clay (Fig. 7.8.170–71).

A similar type of decoration to the latter is recorded on a candlestick base from the Austin Friars, Leicester (Woodland 1981, fig. 42.233).

Cistercian ware/ blackware
Sherds were put into this category if they were too small for accurate identification or if the vessel form contained elements of both the Cistercian and blackware traditions. The most frequent vessel type was a 'funnel'-mouthed mug (Fig. 7.8.174–175, 177–178) or with a carination below the rim (Fig. 7.8.176). Both these forms are paralleled at Stafford Castle (Rátkai 2007) and Oakeswell Hall (Hodder and Glazebrook 1987). The carination is also a feature of blackware but it tends to occur lower down the vessel and be surmounted by a gently everted rim (*e.g.* Fig. 7.8.184). Mugs (Fig. 7.8.180–181) have the rounded profiles associated with Cistercian ware but the lightly turned bands are more commonly found on blackware. Parallels for the latter form occurred on the motte at Dudley Castle. A frilled base (Fig. 7.8.182) from a Phase 2 tanning pit (F208, 2008) at Edgbaston Street may be an imitation of a German stoneware form (cf. Gaimster 1997, fig. 3–48.272).

Other late medieval/ early post-medieval wares

Tudor Green and Tudor Green-type ware
A small number of mainly undiagnostic sherds were present. At least one cup, one bowl and one lobed cup were represented.

Late Boarstall-Brill ware
See above under Boarstall-Brill.

Post-medieval wares
Many of the blackwares, yellow wares and coarsewares can be paralleled by material from Oakeswell Hall (Hodder and Glazebrook 1987) and Dudley Castle (Rátkai 1987). In addition, recent work at Floodgate Street (Rátkai 2002a) has demonstrated some pottery production in the post-medieval period in Birmingham. It therefore seems safe to assume that most of the post-medieval pottery was from local sources. The exceptions to this were probably the trailed, embossed and jewelled slipwares, much of which probably came from the Potteries, and the 18th-century refined wares (see Barker and Rátkai below).

Blackware
The blackware forms were dominated by drinking vessels, particularly corrugated mugs (Fig. 7.8.185–186, 199, 201–202). At least one vessel (Fig. 7.8.191) appeared to imitate 16th-century German stoneware. The blackware tradition appears to have begun in the second quarter of the 16th century, since blackware was present along with Cistercian ware at the Whitefriars, Coventry in deposits associated with Hales School dated 1540–1570 (Woodfield 1981; Rátkai 2005). Other evidence for at least a mid-16th-century date for the production of blackware is provided by the small but consistent number

of imitations of German stoneware forms of this date. There seems to have been an overlap in the use of Cistercian ware and blackware, resulting in some hybrid forms (see above). In the later 16th–mid-17th centuries the 'corrugated' cylindrical mug seems to have been one of the most popular forms. By the later 17th century, finer bodied cylindrical mugs, sometimes with a recessed turned base (Fig. 7.8.196, 203–204), replaced the corrugated form and continued in use into the 18th century. One blackware sherd from F133, a Phase 3.1 pit in Area A at Park Street, was decorated with an applied festoon or scroll (see Barker 1986, fig. 6), a form of decoration which dates to the later 17th and early 18th centuries. Vessel Fig. 7.8.192 was worn around the rim, perhaps suggesting that it had once had a metal mount. Vessel forms such as the latter and Fig. 7.8.194–196 are late 17th–18th-century forms. Earlier blackwares tend to have 'dribbly' glazes which are less in evidence in the later 17th century and have disappeared by the 18th century.

A small number of other forms were represented, *e.g.* a ?candlestick (Fig. 7.8.207), a jug (Fig. 7.8.208), a stool pot (Fig. 7.8.209), a handled bowl (Fig. 7.8.210), a lid (Fig. 7.8.211), and a large hook-rim jar (Fig. 7.9.213). The stool pot form was paralleled amongst Civil War debris at Dudley Castle. The hook rim jar is clearly a late form and falls somewhere between a blackware and a slip-coated ware.

Yellow ware

Yellow wares were first discussed as a group by Woodfield (1966) and most of the forms from the Bull Ring sites are paralleled in his typology. Four fabrics were identified, one white (YW1), one yellowish buff (YW2), one orange (YW3) and one red (YW4). The latter two fabrics had an underglaze white slip, but perhaps somewhat surprisingly the unglazed exterior surfaces had a red or purplish red slip. There seemed to be no particular preference for particular form and fabric combinations so that tablewares, *e.g.* cups and dishes, were as likely to have iron-rich bodies as iron-poor bodies. Likewise vessel forms overall were the same regardless of fabric. Forms represented were bowls and dishes (Fig. 7.9.214–229), jars (Fig. 7.9.230; Fig. 7.10.231–233), cups and mugs (Fig. 7.10.234–236), candlesticks and salts (Fig. 7.10.237–238), a lid or salt (Fig. 7.10.239), small jars, ointment pots or albarelli (Fig. 7.10.242–44), part of a chafing dish (Fig. 7.10.241), and the lower half of a strainer or colander. Another lid (not illustrated) was found at Edgbaston Street. By far the best represented forms were bowls and dishes.

Coarsewares

Coarseware is a rather general term for a range of black- or brown-glazed utilitarian forms, which were in use from the later 16th century through to the 18th and 19th centuries. They are generally large, thick-bodied vessels, whose forms consist of jars, bowls and flower-pots. The coarseware tradition seems to have derived from the late wheel-thrown iron-rich oxidised wares of the 15th and 16th centuries but the coarsewares tend to be less well made with coarser less well-prepared clay bodies.

The fabric colour of the coarsewares varies from brick red and orange through to cream. The coarsewares were therefore divided into those with iron-rich bodies and those with iron-poor bodies. Generally, the coarsewares were slipped, usually internally and externally. On the iron-rich coarsewares it is not always clear if a slip has been applied or a thin wash, or whether the surface has just been wiped. By the later 17th and 18th centuries the slip is thicker and more obvious. It is at this point that it is sometimes difficult to distinguish between coarsewares and slip-coated wares (see below), particularly in the case of small body sherds.

The development of the iron-rich coarsewares out of the late medieval tradition are exemplified by Fig. 7.10.245, which was in a fabric somewhere between a coarseware and a Midlands Purple ware, and by Fig. 7.10.246 and Fig. 7.10.247, whose fabrics are quite fine and more closely resemble the late oxidised wares. The rim forms of several of the vessels (*i.e.* Fig. 7.10.246–250, 252) appear to have been designed to take a lid. The jars were glazed on the interior. Jars of the 17th century tend to have 'dribbled' glazes, whilst those of the following centuries are glazed more neatly (*e.g.* Fig. 7.10.258). This chronological distinction in the glazing also applies to the bowls. Bowls were usually splay-sided, with a variety of rim forms. The clubbed rim (Fig. 7.11.270–271) is a later form and seems to have been used in the later 17th and 18th centuries. There were one or two examples of smaller straight-sided bowls (*e.g.* Fig. 7.11.269) and bowls with horizontal handles (Fig. 7.12.272–274). Large capacity hollow wares (*e.g.* Fig. 7.12.275) are a feature of the later 18th century, since these vessels were only found in the fills of tanks F510/ F542 and F503/ F520 at Park Street. Likewise the bowl/ jar with a collar rim (Fig. 7.12.277) is also a late form. A small fragment of a strainer or colander (not illustrated) was found in a pit (F791, 1876) at Park Street.

In addition to kitchen wares, flower-pots were also made in a red coarseware. The flower-pots were concentrated in Area B at Park Street. The pots had a central perforation in the base but also three regularly spaced perforations in the wall of the vessel, c.2cm above the base. This form is known from Floodgate Street, Birmingham (Rátkai 2002a), where flower-pot wasters were discovered together with 18th-century black-glazed coarsewares.

The iron-poor coarsewares are broadly similar in form to the iron-rich coarsewares. However, there were fewer examples of jars with lid-seated rims and rather less variation in the rim forms of the bowls. Some forms were unique to the iron-poor coarsewares, *e.g.* the rounded bowl Fig. 7.13.291 and the straight-sided bowl/ jar with horizontal handle Fig. 7.13.292. Both of these vessels were from Park Street and appear to date to the 18th century. The shallow dish with the horizontal handle (Fig. 7.13.293) was an unusual form. The vessel came from Park Street Area A, from the fills of Phase 3.1 pits F181 and F182. It was unglazed and highly abraded both internally and externally. The remaining pottery from the pit fills suggests that the vessel must date to the 17th century. Dripping trays (*e.g.* Fig. 7.13.294) were also only found in the iron-poor fabric. The illustrated vessel was glazed internally and had a shallow channel or groove running part way along the base towards the pouring lip. A similar feature can be seen on the dripping tray in Fabric lox3 (Fig. 7.7.155). The dripping tray was abraded on the external base and base-angle, and sooted along the opposite side to the handle, demonstrating that the vessel was indeed used as a dripping tray. Other pottery found with the dripping tray in F353 (3166), a Phase 3 foundation trench at Edgbaston Street, suggests that it dates to the 17th century. A second fragmentary and highly abraded dripping tray was found at Edgbaston Street in the fill of a 17th-century pit, F334 (3075). A small fragment from a chafing dish (not illustrated), with patches of an almost metallic, purplish slip, was also found at Edgbaston Street in drain F281. Both the slip and form are paralleled at Stafford Castle and Dudley Castle in early–mid-17th-century contexts.

Tin-glazed earthenwares

A small amount of tin-glazed earthenware was recovered from Edgbaston Street and Park Street. These consisted of undecorated or blue-striped albarelli (Fig. 7.19.1, colour), a probable tea bowl (Fig. 7.19.2, colour), an undecorated hook rim bowl, decorated bowls (Fig. 7.19.3–8), plates (Fig. 7.19. 9–11, colour) and a teabowl (Fig. 7.19.12, colour). The footring bowls (Fig. 7.19.7, 8, colour) from Edgbaston Street, in the fill of a Phase 3 pit in Area D (F425, 4060), and from Park Street, in the fill of a Phase 3.2 pit (F828, 1938), probably date to the early 18th century and are paralleled at Norwich (Jennings 1981, fig. 95.1497). The two bowl sherds (Fig. 7.19.6, colour) were from Edgbaston Street, from a Phase 4 cleaning layer (2002). Both bowls had a clear lead glaze on the exterior and probably date to the 17th century. The tin-glazed earthenwares mainly occurred in 18th-century contexts or residually in 19th-century contexts. There was one exception to this, Fig. 7.19.2, colour, which was found in a 17th-century pit (F702, 1721) at Park Street.

Slipwares

A variety of slipware (*i.e.* slip-decorated) types were found. The earliest of these was light-on-dark trailed slipware flange rim bowls or dishes, *e.g.* Fig. 7.21.2, colour. Elsewhere, this type of slipware is known from deposits sealed by Civil War destruction rubble and can therefore be securely dated to the 1640s, although more

typically it is found in the late 17th and early 18th centuries (pers. comm. David Barker). The trailed slipware dish (Fig. 7.21.1 colour) is unusual and may well date to the 18th century, particularly since it was found within the fill of the 18th-century tank F510/ F542 at Park Street.

Slipware types which begin in the later 17th century, such as embossed slipwares (Fig. 7.22, colour), feathered slipware (Fig. 7.23, colour), dark-on-light slipware (Fig. 7.21.3, colour), and multi-coloured or three-colour slipware (Fig. 7.20, colour) were all found on the Bull Ring sites. The feathered and multi-coloured slip decorations are mainly found on large mould-formed shallow dishes or platters, with pie crust rims. There were, however, also examples of wheel-thrown flange rim dishes with multi-coloured slip decoration (Fig. 7.20.3–4, colour).

Slipwares occurred mainly as flatwares. There was a feathered slipware cup from a Phase 3 pit in Area C at Edgbaston Street (F326, 3061) and a cup from a Phase 3 drainage feature (F245, 2179) in Area B of the same site, with horizontal bands of slip (three bands, alternating tan, dark brown and tan) on a yellow ground. Both of these vessels seem to date to the late 17th or early 18th centuries.

Mottled ware

The Bull Ring sites were striking for the paucity of mottled wares. The usually ubiquitous cylindrical mugs were represented by only a handful of sherds. In fact, there were very few diagnostic sherds at all. There were some hook-rim hollow wares and straight-sided bowls (*e.g.* Fig. 7.13.296) and one albarello (Fig. 7.13.297). The curvature on some sherds suggested that there may have been one or two porringers amongst the mottled wares. The shortage of mottled wares might have been explained by chronological factors were it not for the fact that other wares of the later 17th–mid- 18th centuries were well represented. It therefore seems as if there was a bias against mottled ware vessels which operated in favour of blackware and to a lesser extent slip-coated ware. This could be seen as an example of consumer preference but the evidence from Floodgate Street of late pottery production may indicate that blackwares were produced in Birmingham in the late 17th and early 18th centuries and this may have provided a barrier against the purchase and use of mottled wares.

Slip-coated wares

Slip-coated wares were first produced in the later 17th century. In Birmingham and elsewhere in the Midlands they seem to be a consistent and important part of the 18th-century groups. The most common forms are dishes with flange or everted rims (Fig. 7.13.298–302). A smaller number of dishes had pie-crust rims (Fig. 7.13.304). Bowls with flange or everted rims were also represented (Fig. 7.13.303). Dishes and bowls were particularly common in the fills of the Park Street tanks F503/ F520 and F510/ F542, and within the fills of the Phase 3 pits F133, F194 and F700 and F713 (these pits are assigned to sub-phases 3.2 and 3.3, which span the 18th century). A smaller number of hollow wares with hooked or simple everted rims were present (Fig. 7.13.305–308) and a collar-rim jar (Fig. 7.14.309).

The bowls and dishes had a thick internal underglaze slip which extended over the rim of the vessel and sometimes part way down the exterior (*e.g.* Fig. 7.13.300). Sometimes the exterior surface had splashes of slip (*e.g.* Fig. 7.13.303). Glazes were very dark brown or black. Hollow wares were usually glazed internally and externally, although there were exceptions (*e.g.* Fig. 7.13.306).

Brown salt-glazed stoneware

Brown salt-glazed stoneware was another poorly represented fabric, with few diagnostic sherds. It was found more commonly at Park Street than Edgbaston Street. In Area B at Park Street it was only found in the tanks F503/ F520 and F510/ F542 (Fig. 7.14.310–313) and the upper fill of the 'pond' F506. The vessel forms from the tank are discussed by Barker and Rátkai (below). The vessels from the rest of the Park Street site consisted mainly of mugs with a small number of bowls or dishes. Only four brown stoneware sherds were found at Edgbaston Street, in Area C. They represented a bowl and a mug.

White salt-glazed stoneware, creamware, pearlware and other refined body earthenwares.

These wares came primarily from the tank fills in Area B at Park Street and are discussed in more detail by Barker and Rátkai (below). They are illustrated in Fig. 7.14.314–324 and in colour in Figs 7.24–7.27, colour.

Imported continental pottery

The largest class of imported wares was made up of Rhenish stonewares of the 16th–18th centuries. The earliest of these comprised undiagnostic Siegburg body sherds and Cologne and Frechen plain, undecorated drinking jugs (*e.g.* Fig. 7.14.327–328). Five bartmänner (*e.g.* Fig. 7.14.329) of late 16th- or 17th-century date came from Edgbaston Street (four from Area B and one from Area A). These were the only occurrences of this form. Westerwald stoneware mugs were represented by five sherds from Edgbaston Street Area C (two sherds) and Park Street Areas A and C (two and one sherd respectively).

Another import was a Spanish olive jar found within the tank fills in Area B, Park Street (see Barker and Rátkai, below, and Williams, Appendix 7.1). The third group of imports was represented by two bowl sherds. One, decorated with concentric circles of manganese purple and turquoise and with a clear lead glaze on the exterior (Fig. 7.19.13, colour), was from the fill of a

19th-century construction trench (F532, 5100) at Moor Street. The second, a small fragment of a burnt flange rim bowl or dish with a thin turquoise band on the rim and a thin purple band just below the rim, came from a late 17th- or early 18th-century pit fill (F347, 3131) in Area C, Edgbaston Street. The sherd from Moor Street is not Spanish (pers. comm. Alejandra Gutierrez) but the style of decoration and the colours used, particularly the turquoise, set both sherds apart from the usual Anglo-Dutch tin-glazed earthenwares. A Mediterranean source is therefore likely for both sherds.

Two Martincamp flask (Type III) sherds came from Area B, Edgbaston Street. One was unstratified and the second came from the fill of Phase 3 pit F234.

Phase 1

Edgbaston Street (see Table 7.2)

Area A

A small number of features contained pottery of medieval date (F105, F109, F121, F123, F134, F135, F143, F147 and F149, and layers 1042 and 1074). Generally the features contained only one or two sherds, making interpretation uncertain. However, pit F105 contained 143 sherds, including a virtually complete straight-sided cooking pot (Fig. 7.1.19). F105 was a recut of pit F123 (see Table 7.3). The high average sherd weight for the fills of F105, even when adjusted by the removal of the large cooking pot (just under 19g for 1010 and just under 18g for 1011), suggests that the sherds were deposited soon after breakage. The large straight-sided cooking pot may not have been a discard as such but may have been placed deliberately in the pit for an unknown function. Before deposition the vessel had obviously been used and was heavily sooted on the exterior, with occasional traces of dribbles through the soot where the vessel contents had overflowed during heating.

The fills of F105 contained quite small amounts of Deritend ware. Fill 1011 contained larger sherds than the later fill 1010 and no whiteware, whereas 1010 contained more and larger whiteware sherds than Deritend sherds. However, the bottom fill 1012 contained an early cpj12 cooking pot sherd and a whiteware jug sherd. It is possible that the latter represents contamination. There were three iron-poor sherds, a thumbed jug base with partial olive glaze and two sherds from a further jug, all from 1010. Amongst the whitewares was a red-painted whiteware handle and a flaring base from a baluster type jug with a green copper-coloured glaze. An unglazed reduced Deritend ware jug was also found in this context (Fig. 7.4.73). Sherds consisted mainly of cooking pot/ jars, some with applied thumbed strips. One of the reduced Deritend ware sherds had a light external rilling over the surface. The cooking pot/ jar sherds were almost all sooted, some very heavily. There was an internal carbonised deposit on a Fabric

Fabric	Area A				Area B				Area C			
	Sherd count	Sherd weight	Rim count	eves	Sherd count	Sherd weight	Rim count	eves	Sherd count	Sherd weight	Rim count	eves
Boarstall-Brill												
Coventry type	2	20										
Coventry type glazed	1	19			3	37						
cpj1	109	1928	9	53	48	731	11	29	14	126	3	13
cpj2	2	12			2	38			1	18		
cpj6					5	41	1	10				
cpj7					5	65	2					
cpj8					3	12						
cpj9					1	5						
cpj12	3	93	1	6	1	6						
cpj13					7	69	1					
cpj14	3	52			22	279	6		2	16	1	7
Deritend	11	93			17	315			2	48		
Deritend cpj	39	2234	6	124	10	184	2	11	3	40		
DeritendR	57	388	3	33	69	1169	10	81	18	252	1	22
ip1	5	78			2	39						
ip2	1	28			6	93			2	9		
ip4	2	3			1	24						
ip8	2	4										
ip9	1	1										
mudst					1	6						
mudstg	1	27										
RSf	2	13			1	33						
ww1	12	398	1	1	7	140	1	10	1	8		
ww2	2	14										
ww3	1	3			3	273						
ww4	2	33			7	62						
ww5					2	12						
intrusive	3	7			5	33	1	8				
Total	261	5448	20	217	228	3666	35	149	43	517	5	42

Table 7.2 Edgbaston Street; Phase 1 pottery.

cpj1 cooking pot sherd and an internal white-brown deposit on a Deritend cpj sherd. In fill 1011, one Fabric cpj1 sherd had iron staining. One Deritend cpj sherd had been shaped into a counter. There was, however, no striking evidence that the pottery was put to any use other than the normally domestic.

The whitewares, especially the red-painted whiteware handle and possible baluster base, suggest a date of post-1250 for 1010. However, the near absence of glazed wares and/ or jugs, and the straight-sided form of Fig. 7.1.19, makes it unlikely that the fill is later than the second half of the 13th century, although the straight-sided vessel could have been in use in the pit for some time before F105 was finally backfilled, making a pre-1250 date a possibility.

Layer 1042, into which various features including F123, were cut, contained sherds with a much lower average sherd weight than one would expect (8.36g) and demonstrates the effect that different depositional processes are likely to have on sherd size. There was a

Fabric	Sherd count	Sherd weight	Sherd count	Sherd weight	Sherd count	Sherd weight	Sherd count	Sherd weight	Sherd count	Sherd weight
Coventry-type glazed	1	19								
cpj1	77	1494	12	249						
cpj2	1	3								
cpj12					1	20				
cpj14	1	21					1	12		
Deritend	2	23	2	33						
Deritend cpj	32	2027								
DeritendR	20	219	4	42						
ip1	1	54								
ip2	1	28								
ip9			1	7						
RSf			1	8						
ww1	5	318							1	3
ww2					1	11				
ww4	1	30								
Total	142	4236	20	339	2	31	1	12	1	3

Table 7.3 Edbaston Street; pottery from Pit F105/ F123/ F149 Phase 1.

higher percentage of glazed sherds and reduced wares, and there was also a whiteware bowl.

The fill (1075) of pit F147 may well be early. There was an absence of glazed Deritend ware and whiteware. The fill contained Coventry-type ware cooking pot, glazed mudstone-tempered ware (Fig. 7.18.2, colour), Deritend R, Deritend cooking pot and Fabric cpj1. There was one small (4g) Fabric lox2 sherd, which was almost certainly intrusive. The average sherd weight was less than 10g, so there could well be some residuality. Nevertheless, a late 12th-century date for the pit fill is not unfeasible, although a date in the first half of the 13th century is perhaps more likely.

Although there was some medieval pottery which occured residually in Area A, mainly in 17th-century and later contexts, it was not plentiful.

Area B

A series of tanning pits (F218, F224, F226, F227, F228, F229, F233 and F237), pits (F266 and F268) and watercourse F256 contained only medieval pottery in their fills. A significant number of layers, predominantly silty and often containing organic and/ or carbonised material, dated to the 13th–15th centuries. In addition, unlike Area A, there was a relatively high frequency of residual medieval pottery in later phases.

The feature fills each contained fewer than 20 sherds, and of these most contained fewer than ten sherds,

making detailed interpretation of the fills, and particularly the possible chronology of the features, difficult. The average sherd weight overall was 15.2g. When the average sherd weight for each context was calculated, it was apparent that the features with more than one fill had the greatest number of contexts with average sherd weights above the mean (c.64%). This may indicate that these feature fills were primary. As would be expected, the average sherd weight for c.67% of the layers was below the mean, and single fill features were more-or-less equally divided between above and below the mean.

Tanning pits

Tanning pit F218 contained several large sherds (e.g. Fig. 7.5.107) in a mixture of cooking pot fabrics, reduced wares and iron-poor wares. The sherd size and lack of abrasion suggests that the sherds were not residual and that the fill material ought to date to the second half of the 13th or to the 14th century. Tanning pit F228 contained 17 sherds from two cooking pots, one in Fabric cpj1 and the other in reduced Deritend ware. Both vessels had very heavy external sooting and the latter had traces of an applied thumbed strip on the external body. The lowest fill (2080) of tanning pit F229 was similar to the previous tanning pits and contained a mixture of Deritend, reduced ware and whiteware sherds, including a Fabric ww5 sherd (see below) linking it to the watercourse. There was also a Coventry glazed ware sherd in the fill. This fabric is paralleled by F110/ 115 from Warwick (Rátkai 1990). Pit F266 contained only three sherds, two in Fabric cpj1 and one in Fabric cpj13. Two of the sherds were heavily abraded, probably indicating that the fill of the pit was residual.

The pottery was consistent with normal domestic use and rubbish disposal, with the exception of one DeritendR cooking pot sherd which had a metallic sheen on its surfaces. This may have been caused by contact with cess or the tanning process. The proportion of cooking pots was slightly higher, at 75%, than in the watercourse below but provides further evidence of a 13th-century date for the disuse of the tanning pits.

The water channel F213/ F255/ F256

This is a small water channel which may have fed into the larger Smithfield Passage watercourse. Ceramics were recovered from Area B contexts 2017, 2018, 2036 and 2202. A total of 43 sherds were recovered from these fills, weighing 543g. This gives an average sherd weight of 12.6g, which is more-or-less consistent with normal backplot detritus. Roughly two-thirds of the sherds were from cooking pot/ jars (*e.g.* Fig. 7.3.51, 61), which is consistent with a pre-14th-century date. The remaining sherds were made up of jugs, with only one bowl, in Fabric cpj7 (Fig. 7.6.121), being represented.

Contexts 2036 and 2202 contained no whitewares or iron-poor wares, whereas 2017 and 2018 contained six whiteware sherds. Interestingly, 2018 contained Fabric ww5, a very uncommon fabric (also found in Park Street layer 1841), as did 2080, the fill of tanning pit F229. Both sherds were small and it was not possible to say if they were from the same vessel, but there is a strong possibility that they were, thus providing a tangible link between the watercourse and the Phase 1 tanning pits. The quantity of whitewares suggests that the watercourse may have been redundant in the late 13th or early 14th century. This is consistent with the greater number of whitewares in proportion to Deritend ware (6:3 sherds) and the functional breakdown outlined above. There was nothing in the pottery which suggested that it had been part of or had come into contact with any industrial process. The pottery from those features associated with tanning, *i.e.* the pits and watercourse, showed no sign of having been waterlogged or in prolonged contact with cessy material apart from the Deritend sherd mentioned above.

Tanning pits F233 and F237 also appear to have had primary fills. The lower fill (2129) of F233 contained DeritendR, cpj1, cpj14, and Deritend ware; the upper fill contained the same range but with the addition of whiteware jug sherds (*e.g.* Fig. 7.4.92) with copper-green glazes and combed decoration. This fill also contained a Coventry glazed ware sherd similar to the one from 2080, F229.

The fills of pit F237 contained a similar range of pottery to F233. The lowest fill (2165) contained cpj2, cpj7, cpj14 and DeritendR. The middle fill contained an ip2 pitcher decorated with incised horizontal lines, Fabric cpj1, DeritendR and a ww4 sherd. The latest fill contained cpj1, cpj6, cpj13 and cpj14, Deritend, DeritendR and one ww1 sherd. There were some unusual sherds in this fill, including a cpj13 rim (Fig. 7.6.129), the fabric of which was paralleled by 12th-century material from Warwick (Rátkai 1990), a DeritendR bowl (Fig. 7.3.64) and a 'rusticated' DeritendR sherd. The middle and upper fills therefore seemed to be a mix of later 13th-century fabrics, like ww1 and ww4, and 12th-century material.

Area C

A few features containing medieval ceramics survived in Area C, *i.e.* pits F306 and F351, and gully F350, together with medieval layer 3025. Only fill 3020 of pit F306 contained a reasonable amount of pottery, totalling 31 sherds. The remaining medieval features contained 13 sherds in all. Of the phase group, one sherd was from a whiteware ?cooking pot/ jar (F350) and two sherds were from an iron-poor glazed ware decorated with oblique roller-stamping (F306). Despite the group being small, the paucity of whitewares and iron-poor wares suggest that the medieval activity in Area C probably dates primarily to the first half of the 13th century.

About 10% of the Area C assemblage for all phases was made up of medieval pottery, and even then the residual component consisted of only one further iron-poor sherd. It is clear from this that there never was much whiteware, iron-poor ware or Deritend ware, and that the total proportion of glazed medieval wares was never very large. This could reflect a functional bias in the use of Area C but seems more likely to be chronological. If this group is early then the coarse Deritend fabric must also be early.

The average sherd weight in Phase 1 was *c.*12g, but this drops to under 10g when one large cooking pot sherd in DeritendR fabric from 3025 (Fig. 7.3.53) is removed from the equation.

Area D

Other than a single tree bole, there were no Phase 1 features in Area D but there were 22 sherds of residual medieval pottery (19% of the area group). The residual pottery consisted mainly of Deritend cpj and DeritendR fabrics. There were three Deritend sherds and no whiteware sherds.

Discussion

Glazed wares were infrequent on all areas and were no better represented residually, so that the whitewares, iron-poor wares and Deritend ware were scarce. Deritend ware was found together with whitewares but also as the only glazed ware in a group. Deritend ware was always found with DeritendR sherds but the DeritendR sherds were also found without any glazed wares. This could perhaps indicate that DeritendR was first manufactured before Deritend ware and the iron-poor and whiteware glazed wares. This chronological relationship between the DeritendR and Deritend ware was first suggested by Sherlock (1957).

There were differences between the area assemblages in Phase 1. In Areas A, B and C the most common cooking pot fabric was Fabric cpj1, which was about four times more common than Deritend cpj (the most common fabric at Park Street). In Areas B and C there were roughly equal amounts of the oxidised cooking pot/ jar fabrics and DeritendR fabric, with Fabric RSb being the most frequent DeritendR sub-group. In Area A there were over twice as many cpj fabrics as reduced wares, with Fabrics RS01 and RSd being the most frequent variants of DeritendR. There were roughly equal amounts of whiteware and Deritend ware from Areas B and C, but in Area A there was roughly twice the amount of whiteware to Deritend ware.

These variations may suggest that Fabric cpj1 is earlier than Deritend cpj. The higher amount of whitewares in Area A probably indicates that activity in this area is later than the other two areas, in which case DeritendR fabric variants RS01 and RSd may be later than variant RSb.

Moor Street

The principal feature on the Moor Street site was a major boundary ditch (see Table 7.4) which accounted for all but 35 sherds from this phase. Three sections were taken across the ditch (Figs 3.6, 3.8–3.9), designated, from south to north, F537, F561 and F568. The feature numbers relate to the primary ditch cut. However, the ditch was subsequently recut. The recut of F537 was numbered F538 but the recuts in sections F561 and F568 were not given a separate feature number but are clearly visible in the section drawings. The sequence then is F537, primary fills 5195 and 5129, F561, primary fills 5166, 5161 and 5165 and F568, primary fills 5190 and 5189.

The primary fills of the ditch were characterised by the absence of whitewares and iron-poor wares which strongly suggests that the original ditch was filled before *c*.1250. There was one exception to this, which was fill 5161 of ditch section F561, but in this case there was a cross-join between the whiteware sherds and a sherd from 5186 ditch section F568 (see below) which suggests that there might have been some contamination (although other interpretations are possible). The earlier ditch fills contained siltstone tempered cooking pots (Fabrics cpj12 and cpj13) and other cooking pot wares, Deritend wares and Coventry-type wares. The siltstone tempered cooking pot fabrics were not common at the Bull Ring and appear to be early. The Coventry-type cooking pot would also favour a date before 1250. A Coventry glazed ware sherd came from a jug with a thumbed base and, because of this, probably dates no earlier than the first half of the

13th century. The average sherd weights of the pottery from the early fills suggest that they represent primary deposition and the proposed chronology and relative chronology should be reasonably secure. The early fills also contained very little pottery, *e.g.* F537, 13 sherds; F561 fills 5166, 5161 and 5165, twelve sherds; and F568 fills 5190 and 5189, 30 sherds. This is in contrast to the later fills, particularly of the recut of F561 where reasonably large pottery groups were present.

The comparative dating of whiteware, Deritend ware and reduced Deritend ware may be elucidated by the study of their occurrences in the fills of the Moor Street ditch and its recuts. Most of the whiteware sherds occur in the later fills of F561 and F568 and recut F538. The primary fills of F537 and F568 and the greater proportion of fills overall did not contain whitewares. Given the poor showing of whitewares in the ditch fills and at Moor Street in general there is a case to be made for the recuts of the ditch having been re-filled by *c*.1300. The occurrence of other iron-poor wares mirrors the whiteware distribution. Deritend wares were, by contrast, spread more evenly and consistently through the ditch and other feature fills and layers.

At Moor Street there was a high proportion of DeritendR in Phase 1. This is most clearly manifested in the fills of the ditch and particularly in the fills of ditch section F561. In chronological order, F561 recut fills 5158, 5155 and 5150 contained 68.9%, 40.0% and 28.6% DeritendR respectively. There was a concomitant increase in whitewares and iron-poor wares through time.

The fills of recut ditch section F568 contained only two whiteware jug sherds (Fig. 7.18.1, colour), which came from fill 5186. One of these was part of a vessel, two sherds of which were also found in fill 5161, one of the lower fills of ditch section F561. These three sherds were themselves atypical. The sherds, although classed as Fabric ww4, were largely reduced to a dark grey colour with only a thin white margin below the glaze. The glaze was an opaque, dull olive with an 'orange peel' texture. The firing and glaze suggest that these sherds are early. The form too was unusual. It was a large hand-formed jug or pitcher with a sagging base and body sherds with a marked undulating profile. The author knows of no parallels for this form but feels it is so far removed from the normal whiteware cannon that it is most likely to be early (especially when coupled with the details of manufacture, firing and glazing) and suggests a date in the early 13th century. The second whiteware sherd from 5186 had an olive-tan glaze with copper speckles. The partially oxidised glaze was also slightly unusual for a whiteware and may be an accident of firing or perhaps a pointer to an earlier manufacture date than the *terminus post quem* of mid-13th century normally ascribed to whitewares. A Coventry glazed ware jug sherd with wavy combing and opaque olive glaze of mid-12th- to early 13th-century date was also present in fill 5186 of F568 and provides further evidence of some early fill material.

Fabric	537 5195	537 5129	538 5130	538 5194	561 5166	561 5161	561 5165	561 5158	561 5155	561 5154	561 5153	561 5150	561 5171	568 5190	568 5189	568 5188	568 5187	568 5186	568 5185	568 5174	568 5184	Total
?									2			1										3
brill									1													1
covt	2																					2
covtg		1	1															1				3
cpj1		1					3	6	8			5					1		1			25
cpj11																	3					3
cpj12								2	1													3
cpj13	1						1		2				2									6
cpj14									2													2
cpj2									1													1
cpj7	1											3										4
cpj9								1														1
cwip													2									2
Deritend	3		4	1					9	1	1	7	2	1	8		1		2	3	1	44
Deritend cpj								1	9		1	2		2			1		1	1		18
DeritendR	1	2	20		1	4		29	28	3		10	3	17		1	4	2	5	2	1	133
fired clay																				1		1
ip						1																1
ip1																				1		1
ip2								5	1	1		1							1			9
ip7												1										1
ip8												3	3									6
lox2													1									1
lox3												1	1									2
medg3																	1					1
medg6										1												1
mp												1										1
nettlebed																	1					1
Roman								2				1										3
Roman?								1														1
RSf								1														1
RSg			1					1	2			3						1				8

																		Total
RSi	1	1				11		1		2		1				2		19
ww1																		4
ww2						3		2										4
ww3						1	2	1										4
ww4			2	2		3	3	3	1									14
Total count	8	5	29	7	4	61	75	49	15	22	8	13	8	1	10	8	2	335
Total weight	157	174	468	160	260	976	1066	735	333	608	510	321	151	84	164	126	78	6480
asw*	19.6	34.8	16.1	22.9	65	16	14.2	15	22.2	27.6	63.8	24.7	18.9	84	16.4	15.8	39	19.34

*average sherd weight

Table 7.4 Moor Street; pottery from Boundary ditch Phase 1.

The two iron poor sherds from F568 were from jugs, one (from 5185) with an applied thumbed strip and yellow glaze with copper speckles, and the other (from 5174) undecorated but with an olive glaze.

When the first occurrence of whiteware is plotted on the fill sequences for ditch sections F537/ F538, F568 and F561, it would appear that the infilling of the ditch was not a more-or-less contemporaneous action (a fact which the environmental evidence would seem to support). Ditch F537 seems to have begun to fill earliest since no whiteware appears until 5130, the fill of the ditch recut F538. The two sherds from this fill form just 6.9% of the pottery group, which was otherwise dominated by reduced Deritend ware sherds. Likewise, whiteware only appears in a middle fill (5186) of the northern recut section of F568, whereas whiteware was present in the second lowest fill (5161) of middle recut section F561. However there were cross-joining sherds (see above) from 5186 and 5161, suggesting that these fills could have been near contemporary. Fill 5186 occurs between two environmental samples (5188 and 5184) which suggest that the beginning of the use of whiteware is roughly coeval with a change of land use manifested in the change from a waterlogged plant assemblage in 5188, probably occurring naturally in the ditch, and evidence of crop processing/ brewing/ animal husbandry in 5184. Fill 5188 was the lowest fill in the proposed recut of ditch section F568.

This could be interpreted in two different, but not mutually exclusive, ways. First, the paucity of pottery in the lower fills of all the ditch sections, coupled with the environmental evidence from 5188, suggests that the ditch was still an important enough boundary to be kept relatively clean and free of domestic waste. The larger groups of pottery do not occur until after the 'whiteware horizon'. This suggests, firstly, that the ditch began to lose its significance at some point after *c*.1250 and, secondly, that at roughly the same date there was a change in land use or increased activity/ occupation in the area, resulting in the evidence of crop processing etc found in the environmental samples from 5184. Indeed, Greig's suggestion (Chapter 13) that some of the heather pollen might have come from material used for roofing could perhaps reflect the construction of new buildings in the area, possibly for stock.

However, the recutting of the ditch suggests a more complex history and chronology. The original was probably cut in the 12th century, associated with the expansion of Birmingham. The original ditch appears to have been filled before the introduction of whitewares, *i.e.* before *c*.1250, and was then recut. The recut may have been associated with renewed or greater activity in the area. The recut however, does appear to have been relatively short-lived since on the evidence of the whitewares and iron-poor wares it was itself refilled by *c*.1300.

Vessel forms from within the fills of section F561

were also distinctive. There were several examples of shouldered and cylindrical cooking pot/ jars in Fabric cpj1 and in DeritendR (Fig. 7.2.38 and 39; Fig. 7.5.108). Most of these vessels appeared to have been coil-made but finished on a slow wheel. The vessel form and manufacture is consistent with a late 12th- to early 13th-century date. There are no exact parallels for these forms from Weoley Castle, although reduced ware cylindrical cooking pots (*e.g.* Oswald 1964, fig. 47.10–11) came from a floor surface of a timber building and were dated to 1230–40. The presence of unglazed DeritendR jugs (Fig. 7.3.67; Fig. 7.4.79, 80, 82) in both F561 and F568 would also seem to fit in with this date. At Weoley Castle several vessels belong to this tradition (Oswald 1962, fig. 9.33; fig. 10.38 and 47) but are found in Period V and later groups, *i.e.* after 1280, but there is a strong likelihood that they are residual since they were found in construction layers, possibly associated with a licence to crenellate granted in 1264. At Kings Norton, parallel reduced ware jugs (Rátkai 2001a, fig. 4.13 and 17) were found in Phase 1 (13th-century) contexts.

In one of the lower fills (5189) of section F568 was an unparalleled vessel, the slightly sagging base and lower wall of a sandy Deritend ware jug. This had been completely covered inside and out with white slip that had clearly been brushed on, rather than the vessel being dipped in slip. This seems to defy all logical explanation. Does it represent some sort of biscuit-firing technique, where the vessel has broken before the second firing? From the sherds that survive there is nothing obviously wrong with the vessel. There was not a single trace of glaze on the pot, which to some extent supports the biscuit-firing theory. If this is the case, then presumably pottery manufacture extended beyond Park Street (see below) and up to Moor Street, but there was no other real evidence for the industry in Moor Street apart from a possible kiln spacer and a Deritend jug sherd from pit F500 of the evaluation (equivalent to Phase 1 pit F535 of the excavation). This may have had applied decoration, but apart from a small area of dark green glaze the surface was covered with a thick, white, cratered, ?burnt glaze. It is impossible to say if this was an accident of firing or whether the vessel had been in a house fire or similar. The nature of the glaze is strongly reminiscent of pottery from a pit at Deansway, Worcester, interpreted as clearance debris from a house fire (pers. comm. Victoria Bryant). The second question is why were all the surfaces covered with white slip, including the underside of the base? The use of slip on the interior of the rim and neck is known on Deritend ware. Is the white slip being used to mask the actual colour of the clay body and, if so, does this indicate a consumer preference for white-bodied jugs (or the concomitant bright green glazes) in the second half of the 13th century? If this is an attempt to imitate whitewares then this has repercussions for the dating of the ditch fill since it would suggest that 5189 post-dates the mid-13th century. The all-over white slip hints at an

attempt at deception with respect to the true colour of the jug, but in the final analysis does the jug just represent an experiment which went horribly wrong?

Other dating evidence for the ditch backfilling is provided by a yellow-glazed Boarstall-Brill sherd from 5155, a middle fill of the recut of ditch section F561, which suggests a *terminus post quem* for this fill of 1250. Environmental evidence from the ditch fills (Ciaraldi, Chapter 12; Greig, Chapter 13) suggests a variety of activities in the area, for example broom making, crop processing (cereals and flax), beer making and stock keeping. This, together with small amounts of sewage, suggests that the ditch became the repository for normal household/ domestic rubbish. Where small amounts of pottery came from the fills, jug sherds mostly made up between a third and a half of the group. There were one or two exceptions, *e.g.* 5189 and 5184, which consisted entirely of jug sherds. By contrast, fills 5191, a primary fill of F568, and 5187, the fill of the recut section F568, contained only 9% and 13% jugs respectively. Roughly one-third of one of the larger groups (5150), which occurred at the very end of the fill sequence for the recut of F561, was made up of jugs, the sort of proportion one would expect in deposits of the late 13th and 14th centuries. However, this fill also contained two 15th–16th-century sherds (Fabrics lox3 and mp) which most probably represent contamination, possibly trample, into 5150. Further evidence of the possibility of contamination is provided by the presence of a clay pipe stem, dated 1620–1720 from fill 5130 of ditch section F538.

However, the larger groups, *e.g.* 5155 and 5158, the earliest fills of the recut of ditch section F561, were different. Fill 5158 was the earlier of the two and contained 10% jug sherds, whilst the later 5158 contained 24% jug sherds. This chronological progression with increasing proportions of jugs sherds is consistent with vessel function figures from many West Midlands sites. The figures suggest that the recut of F561 began to be backfilled in the third quarter of the 13th century. A cup sherd with an internal yellow and external copper-green glaze, possibly Nettlebed ware, was found in 5187, a lower fill of the recut of F568. This sherd should date to the 15th–16th centuries also but its presence in 5187 must surely represent intrusion caused by features cut into the southwestern side of the ditch.

Once the major boundary ditch had become infilled, a series of pits were dug. Many of these pits were cut into the backfilled ditch.

One pit, F545, was cut into the upper fill of ditch section F538. The fill of this pit (5128) must post-date 1250 since it is later than ditch fill 5130, which contained whiteware sherds. The pit contained only 17 sherds but these weighed 632g, suggesting primary deposition. Four jugs were represented: a DeritendR ware jug with a strap handle with 'ladder' decoration (Fig. 7.4.72), a second DeritendR jug (Fig. 7.4.76), a Deritend ware rim and rod handle (Fig. 7.1.7) and an iron-poor stabbed strap handle

(Fig. 7.5.100). Fig. 7.4.72 was of particular interest since it had several drilled holes for repair to the vessel. This suggests that the jug may already have been quite old when discarded. A second DeritendR sherd in this group also had traces of a drilled hole. There were two Fabric cpj7 cooking pots (Fig. 7.6.122–123), with the remainder of the group being made up of cooking pot body sherds in DeritendR and Deritend cpj.

A second pit fill with a relatively high average sherd weight (36g) was 5000, the fill of pit F500, first identified during the evaluation of the site (the pit was designated F535 in the subsequent excavation). This contained an intrusive blackware mug or tankard of late 17th- or early 18th-century date, three Deritend jug sherds and a straight-sided cooking pot (Fig. 7.6.133) in a fabric with igneous temper. The latter had a sooting pattern of heavy external soot and partial heavy internal soot, probably indicating that the vessel had served a specialised (?non-culinary) function.

A third pit of interest was F556, which had a charcoal-rich fill (5122). The fill contained nine sherds. Among these were four sherds from a Boarstall-Brill biconical jug (Fig. 7.16.4, colour; see also Mellor 1994, fig. 60.2–4) with alternate red clay and self clay vertical strip decoration, and a Deritend ware jug sherd. Both the Deritend ware and the Boarstall Brill sherds were badly burnt suggesting that they were contemporary with the charcoal-rich fill. It is possible that the fill represents part of a clearance after a domestic fire. This would be a second possible indication of a house fire at Moor Street (see above F500) and, although fires were relatively common in medieval towns, there is a documentary reference to a large fire in Birmingham in the late 13th or early 14th centuries (Razi 1978) to which the burnt sherds may be related. The other sherds were from cooking pots in Fabric cpj2, Deritend cpj and DeritendR. The latter was heavily sooted on the exterior but this seems to have been connected with its use and the three cooking pot sherds have no obvious connection to the burning evidenced in the fill. The burning of the Deritend and Boarstall-Brill sherds indicates that they were subjected to the same event and in all probability were in contemporary use. The Boarstall-Brill jug dates from the late 13th–early 14th centuries.

Park Street (see Table 7.5)

Area A

The large boundary ditch first identified at Moor Street continued southeast from Moor Street and was picked up again in Area A, Park Street. Here, the ditch was sectioned in two places, F174 and F201. F201 was subsequently cut by a curvilinear ditch, F195. The fills of the large boundary ditch contained over 880 sherds, just over a third of which came from 1314, the middle fill of ditch section F201. The fills of the large ditch at Park Street contained completely different proportions of pottery from those at Moor Street. The cooking pot

fabrics, in particular the oxidised Deritend cooking pot fabric (Fabric cpj5), made up *c*.89% of the assemblage from ditch section F201 and 67% of that from ditch section F174. Deritend ware, whiteware and iron-poor wares formed an insignificant amount of the pottery from the fills of F201 but formed *c*.13.5% of the pottery from F174.

All but four of the 309 sherds in fill 1314 of ditch section F201 were in Deritend cpj fabric. This fabric, as noted above, appears to be a sandier version of glazed Deritend ware. The Deritend cpj sherds from 1314 weighed 4665g, and contained rim sherds from a minimum of 36 vessels, 242% eves, although only three bases were represented. Rim diameters ranged from 25–36cm, with some slight clustering around the 29–30cm mark. There were several unusual features about the Deritend cpj sherds from 1314. A large proportion of the sherds had patchy surface coloration, varying from bright orange to blue-grey and buff, suggesting poor control over the firing conditions. A few sherds with similar patchy surface colour were noted at Edgbaston Street and Moor Street but were never common. Many of the sherds had cracked surfaces, and chipping and flaking along the rim edges was common. Watts (1980) noted that some of the cooking pot sherds from Birmingham Moat were cracked, which she ascribed to poor clay preparation. A high proportion of the sherds from 1314 were spalled. Many of the rim sherds had broken at the shoulder junction. Most surprisingly of all, only seven sherds were sooted (cooking pot Fig. 7.2.30 and bowl Fig. 7.2.35, two further rim sherds and three body sherds). All the evidence taken together suggests that most of the pottery from 1314 represented kiln waste or mis-fires. Corroborating evidence for this interpretation was found in fill 1326, another middle fill of ditch section F204, which contained a number of Deritend cpj sherds similar to those from 1314 and part of a fire-bar. Among this group was a DeritendR jug with a slashed handle (Fig. 7.4.71) with a very patchy surface colour, perhaps suggesting that this too was a mis-fire. Some comparative dating evidence for this group may be provided by a Coventry-type glazed ware jug/ pitcher sherd with complex roller stamping and olive-orange patchy glaze (Fig. 7.18.4, colour). Unfortunately this sherd was very small but it is unlikely to be later than the mid-13th century. It could of course be residual but the paucity of any other material in the fills of F201 (with the exception of upper fill 1252, which had clearly been disturbed) suggests that backfilling of the ditch had probably begun before the mid-13th century. An over-fired, distorted Deritend jug with white slip lattice decoration (Fig. 7.1.11) was found in fill 1195 of ditch section F174, providing yet more evidence of pottery production in the vicinity.

When the distribution of wasters, mis-fires and kiln furniture was plotted over the whole of the Park Street site, it was clear that virtually all this material was found

Fabric	Area A				Area B				Area C			
	Sherd count	sherd weight	Rim count	eves	Sherd count	sherd weight	Rim count	eves	Sherd count	sherd weight	Rim count	eves
Roman/?Roman	1	5							3	13		
Boarstall-Brill		6							3	26		
Chilvers Coton C?	1	6										
Coventry type	10	431							1	3		
Coventry type glazed	2	11							7	352		
cpj1	19	430	2	28	3	11			60	601	6	30
cpj2					1	10			11	127	1	10
cpj6	1	2			3	2			7	31		
cpj7					2	13			21	316	1	9
cpj9									3	26		
cpj12	25	537	3	21	2	22			13	177	1	7
cpj13	1	74	1	8	3	31			15	176	2	7
cpj14									12	163	1	8
cpj15									1	42	1	5
Deritend	41	1078	2	25	1	18			99	199	12	104
Deritend cpj	756	10465	94	547	5	26			107	1083	18	91
DeritendR	85	1915	5	51	13	106	2	14	219	2057	15	111
ip1	6	165										
ip2	10	237	1	17					14	230		
ip4	1	10							1	25		
ip6									5	45		
ip9	1	7										
ip10									2	11		
medg2	2	40										
medg3	1	52										
medg4	1	7										
RSf									2	5		
ww1	5	113							11	119		
ww2	1	4	1	6	2	14			7	77	2	11
ww3	1	3							5	50		
ww4	15	378			5	18			8	61		
ww5									1	16		
fire bar	1	60										
waster									1	9	1	6
intrusive post-med	2	25							34	404	4	36
Total	989	16061	109	703	40	271	2	14	673	6444	65	435

Table 7.5 Park Street; Phase 1 pottery.

within the boundary ditch fills or adjacent layers. This in itself may be unsurprising but the relative paucity of identifiable pottery production waste to the north of the ditch may indicate that pottery production was taking place on the burbage plots running back from Digbeth. If the kilns were situated in the Digbeth series backplots, all evidence of them has probably been removed by 18th- and 19th-century development. Bradford's map of 1750 already shows most of the backplots as built over. However, the northern area of the Park Street site is precisely where the greatest amount of disturbance was caused by later buildings and this may account for the apparent lack of pottery production waste. In many respects, this area of Park Street would have been an ideal location for pottery production, being a marginal, probably boggy area outside the town. The situation of kilns here would have reduced the fire risk and smoke pollution to the Digbeth properties.

Wasters and mis-fires have been found further down Digbeth at Hartwells Garage (Rátkai 2000a; Rátkai 2000b), at the Old Crown (Litherland *et al.* 1994; Rátkai 1994c), and adjacent to and opposite the Old Crown (Mould 2001a; Sherlock 1957), so there is a reasonable case to be made for pockets of pottery production stretching along Deritend and Digbeth. If this industry were largely sited in the burgage backplots, it would explain the lack of kiln evidence, since these are the very areas which over the years have suffered the heaviest redevelopment, much of it before anyone would have had an antiquarian or archaeological interest in Birmingham's past. However, there is also the possibility that this area of Park Street was not properly developed in the medieval period and may have been little better than waste ground, where pottery kilns could be sited close to but outside the town (see Rátkai, Chapter 4).

The curvilinear ditch F195 contained a small number of medieval sherds, which were much the same as those in the lower two fills of the main ditch F201. The upper fill (1245) contained further medieval pottery including a Coventry glazed ware pitcher sherd decorated with incised wavy lines. The fill also contained a late oxidised ware sherd, two Midland Purple ware sherds, a Nettlebed sherd of 15th–16th-century date, and a brown salt-glazed stoneware sherd. This latter material is most likely to be intrusive or trample into the upper fill of F195.

The only other feature assigned to Phase 1 in Area A was pit F160 which contained only four sherds probably dating to the mid-13th century.

Overall, Area A was dominated by Deritend ware jugs and cooking pots, with DeritendR forming the second largest group. The assemblage make-up, however, merely reflects the fills of the large ditch F174/ F201 and as such is unlikely to represent the range of pottery in use by individual households.

Area B

Only a small amount of medieval pottery was recovered from this area. Roughly equal amounts of the oxidised cooking pot fabrics and DeritendR cooking pots were recovered. There was approximately twice the amount of whitewares and iron-poor wares (20% of the area group) to Deritend glazed wares (8.5% of the group). This suggests 13th- and 14th-century occupation in this area. The average sherd weight of 7.6g indicates that there is likely to be a high degree of residuality. The small sherd size is consistent with normal backplot accumulations of rubbish.

Area C

The date and nature of the development of Park Street is complicated by two graves in Area C, F742 and F752, which were cut into a large pit (F746) and, together with the pit, into a medieval layer or layers (1761/ 1763/ 1877). The whole was overlain by a layer or series of layers (1749/ 1760/ 1841), in turn cut by various features of Phase 3 and later. Layer 1761 contained cooking pot/ jar sherds in DeritendR, Deritend cpj, Fabrics cpj1, cpj2 and cpj14 and one Deritend ware jug handle (Fig. 7.1.10). This layer was equated with 1763, which contained mainly DeritendR cooking pot sherds (*e.g.* Fig. 7.3.63), a single cpj1 sherd, a Deritend ware jug, a tiny (1g) iron-poor sherd and an intrusive 17th-century blackware sherd. Another layer which overlay the natural was 1877, which contained a possible Deritend ware variant jug rim sherd with white-slipped interior surfaces. This is unlikely to pre-date the 13th century. The earliest material would therefore seem to comprise cooking pot sherds, particularly in DeritendR, and the fine Deritend ware. The lower fill (1785) of pit F746 contained the same material as that from the layer 1761/ 1763 into which it was cut, and this group may just represent disturbed and redeposited material from the layer. However, the upper fill (1784) of the pit contained a much larger assemblage (98 sherds), of a rather mixed nature. The presence of two whiteware sherds and six iron-poor sherds indicates that the fill post-dates the mid-13th century, but there are anomalies. The first of these are two Roman sherds (Severn Valley ware with organic temper). Two other possible Roman oxidised ware sherds were found in Phase 1 layer 1838 and Phase 3 layer 1797. Secondly, the only example of a sandy fabric containing clay pellets, Fabric cpj15, came from this fill. The sherd (Fig. 7.6.136) is from a socketed bowl. The fabric and the form may link this vessel to the Oxford region. Mellor (1994) has an example dated to the late 12th or early 13th centuries. Other fabrics such as the siltstone tempered wares (Fabrics cpj12 and cpj13) and Fabric cpj9, which ought to pre-date the mid-12th century, were also found in the fill. At the other end of the chronology, two blackware sherds and one yellow ware sherd were recovered from within the fill. The likelihood is that these are intrusive, but their presence highlights the fact that there may be more intrusive material in the fill which is not so easily recognised. The uncertainty about these layers is not helped by layer 1756, which underlies 1760 and overlies 1761, and which shares many of the ceramic characteristics of 1761 but also contains a medieval lead weight (Fig. 8.6.1, colour, see Bevan *et al.*, Chapter 8) and a large sherd from a 19th-century stoneware bottle. The average sherd weight of just under 10g suggests that 1784, the upper fill of pit F746, is far from a primary deposition. The fill of grave F752 contained only eight sherds. The grave appears to have only partly cut through the pit F746, and the pottery was largely the same as that from the underlying layer (1761) with the addition of a whiteware sherd, suggesting a post-1250 deposition. Grave F742, on the other hand, which cut pit F746 much more completely, contained a much greater amount of pottery but this comprised mainly DeritendR, small quantities of oxidised cooking pot fabrics and Deritend fabrics, *i.e.* no pottery which need be later than the mid-13th century. The average sherd weights in both grave fills (just over 4g in F752 and just over 9g in F742) are typical of residual material. However, grave F742 did contain a large proportion of a DeritendR jug which had been wrongly fired, giving a sickly yellowish buff cast to the surfaces. Sealing all the above was layer 1749/ 1760/ 1841. This contained a substantial amount of pottery (377 sherds). Although doubts about intrusion and disturbance still remain (there were, for example, yellow ware, blackware and creamware sherds in 1749 and 1760), there is nevertheless a marked difference between this layer and the preceding fills and layers. In general, this is manifested by increased amounts of iron-poor wares and whitewares, increased amounts of Deritend cpj fabric in relation to the DeritendR sherds, and by the appearance of sandier versions of Deritend ware. The average sherd weights obtained from 1749, 1760 and 1841 were 13.5g, 8.3g and 10.8g respectively. This is within the usual range one would expect to find for surface accumulations of rubbish in tenement plots and indicates that a certain amount of contamination is likely.

Disturbance to the pottery sequence in the area of the graves is further suggested by two examples of cross-joining sherds. One cross-join simply linked the lower (1785) and upper (1784) fills of the large pit F746. The other linked the upper fill of the pit (1784) with the fill (1780) of one of the graves (F742) which cut it.

One interesting feature about Area C is that it is the only one in which Deritend sherds were found which could be matched to the pottery from waster pits behind the Old Crown, Deritend (Litherland *et al.* 1994; Rátkai 1994c). The Old Crown pottery consisted almost entirely of Deritend jug sherds. Several decorative elements stood out as unusual. These comprised narrow, roller stamped bands of white slip, applied white clay scales and applied face masks below the rim (and other elements of anthropomorphic or zoomorphic design). The two former motifs were found in pit fill 1784 and layer 1841. A rim sherd with a face mask was found residually in the fill of F700, a Phase 3 pit. The use of white slip on the interior

surface of the rims was also noted at the Old Crown and was again found only in Area C. These elements of decoration were presumably short-lived and only ever formed a small portion of the potters' output. However, they were represented at Weoley Castle (*e.g.* Oswald 1964, fig. 50.35, dated 1254–80, and Oswald 1962, fig. 8.25, dated 1276–80), although not recognised as Deritend ware and described as a 'fine red ware', presumably on account of the strangeness of the decoration.

The history of the 'frontage' zone of Park Street Area C, with its two graves, is therefore complex. None of the deposition of the pottery is likely to be primary. It does however suggest occupation from possibly the late 12th century and into the 14th century. The graves remain a puzzle. If they were cut after Park Street was laid out they would have been very close to the street frontage, an odd location for nefarious burials. To some extent, illicit burials before the laying out of Park Street, when the area was still parkland, would make more sense but the evidence simply cannot support this. However, there is also a question mark over the date of the burials. Is it possible that the intrusive blackwares and yellow wares are contemporary with the burials? There are a number of post-holes in the area of the graves, only one of which F781 contains pottery: a single sherd of an iron-poor jug. Perhaps they are the remnants of a fence or partition which may have screened the burials from view? However, the post-holes could just as easily be a later disturbance of the area, also evidenced by the yellow ware and blackware sherds associated with the graves. In some respects the 17th century might be a more understandable period in which the clandestine disposal of bodies was carried out since it could be linked indirectly to the Civil War and Prince Rupert's burning of part of the town. It may be significant in this context that posthole F819, which cut pit F829, had a charcoal-rich fill. Pit F829 contained the base of a 17th-century blackware mug.

A second focus of documented activity at Park Street Area C in Phase 1 is at the southeast end of the area. Here another substantial boundary ditch (F715/ F820/ F821/ F800) was excavated, running roughly perpendicular to the boundary ditch (F174/ 201) uncovered in Area A and roughly parallel to Park Street itself. This ditch appeared to define the back end of the burgage plots fronting onto Park Street, and is therefore interpreted as being dug at the same time that the street and its burgage plots were laid out. Only one side of the ditch lay within the excavation area, so that the ditch could only be partially investigated.

Only eight sherds were recovered from the fills of the ditch. The presence of part of a red-painted whiteware jug (Fabric ?ww3) and a second whiteware sherd (Fabric ww2) with an internal and external copper-coloured glaze, together with the absence of any Deritend jug sherds, perhaps indicates a 14th-century date for the infilling of the ditch. However, there was a large, heavily scored pipkin handle (Fig. 7.1.15) in the fine Deritend fabric from one of the ditch sections (F800). The form but not the fabric of this handle is paralleled by a Phase 1 (13th-century) pipkin from Kings Norton (Rátkai 2001a).

The ditch was recut by a second ditch (F760/ F799/ F776). The recut contained small sherds for the most part, including whiteware jugs sherds and a single Deritend jug sherd. There was also a small fragment from the base of a Boarstall-Brill baluster jug. The largest sherd (52g) came from a Fabric ip2 jug, decorated with three bands of two-tooth combing and a pale olive glaze. This is most likely to date to the 14th century. This date is consistent with the paucity of Deritend ware jugs and greater quantities of whiteware in the fills. The fill (1869) of ditch section F799 was disturbed and contained blackware, yellow ware and coarseware sherds dating to the 17th century, and a late oxidised ware sherd (Fabric lox6) dating to the 15th–16th centuries.

Adjacent to the ditch, possible tanpit F708, contained a whiteware jug sherd, a coarse Deritend-type cooking pot sherd (Fabric cpj5c) and a wastered (*i.e.* burnt and spalled) rim sherd in a fabric resembling the fine Deritend jug fabrics. The pit had a clay lining mixed with lime, and was associated with two further features, a ?soakaway (F709) and a large ?rectilinear pit with indications of a clay lining (F714). The presence of features designed to hold liquids, together with the presence of lime, could indicate tanning in this area. The sherds from the fill of F714 were generally large; the average sherd weight was *c.*17g. Fabrics which were well below the mean were Deritend ware and DeritendR wares, suggesting that these sherds were residual. However, a large body sherd (weighing 102g) decorated with intersecting wavy lines in Deritend cpj fabric is paralleled by pottery from the 13th-century wooden building at Weoley Castle (Oswald 1964, fig. 48.18), dated 1230–40. A second sherd in the same fabric was decorated with applied thumbed strips and is also paralleled by Oswald (*op. cit.*). Nevertheless, a very heavily abraded whiteware baluster jug with apple-green glaze and two whiteware bowls seem more likely to date to the 14th century. There was one sherd of 15th–16th century date, a lox3 bowl with external knife trimming and with internal ?limescale, which is assumed to be intrusive.

The area adjacent to the boundary ditch was liable to flooding, leading to the accumulation of very dark, humic silty deposits (*e.g.* 1588, 1640 and 1816), which ran along the southern edge of Areas B and C. Only six sherds were recovered from these deposits, but these suggested that the silts had accumulated from the medieval period until the 15th or 16th centuries, since one Midlands Purple sherd was found in 1816. The generally waterlogged conditions in this area would have led to greater than usual trampling and mixing of deposits, which perhaps explains the mixed nature of the ceramics in the pits in

this area, for example in F714 discussed above, and in the pits attributed to Phase 2, discussed below.

Phase 2

Edgbaston Street (see Table 7.6)

There was little Phase 2 activity and comparatively little 15th–16th-century pottery from Edgbaston Street. Phase 2 features were recorded in Area B and C and only one in Areas A, which did not contain pottery, and none in Area D. Area B had the best Phase 2 group where *c.*40% of the pottery was of 15th–16th-century date, the remainder being mostly composed of residual medieval sherds. Phase 2 pottery occurred residually in Areas A and C and odd 15th–16th-century sherds were present in Area D. The overall impression is that there was much less intensity of occupation in the 15th and 16th centuries in Area A, although a minimum of *c.*15% (blackwares are not included in this figure since they could date from the mid-16th century through to the 18th century) of the Phase 3 group was made up of pottery of this date. It is therefore possible that this decline is illusory and merely reflects the absence of Phase 2 layers and features which could have lain towards the front of the plot and hence have been mostly scoured away. Phase 2 pottery formed *c.*5% of the Phase 3 group in Area C which was roughly the same as the Phase 2 pottery from Phase 3 in Area B. However the paucity of Phase 1 and Phase 2 pottery in Area C, overall, possibly suggests that, along with Area D, there had been little or no occupation until the post-medieval period.

In Edgbaston Street Area B, the pottery came primarily from the backfill of tanning pits F214, F223 and F229. Tanning pits F214 and F223 contained good groups of late medieval/ early post-medieval pottery, with only one or two residual medieval sherds. The make-up of both groups was broadly similar, with a mix of blackware or some Cistercian ware, early coarsewares with clean sandy orange-red fabrics, late oxidised wares, and a small amount of Midlands Purple. Evidence from the White-friars Coventry (Woodfield 1981; Rátkai 2005) has demonstrated that both blackwares and coarsewares were in use from the mid-16th century. This, together with the absence from the tanning pits of yellow wares, which most probably were first made in the last quarter of the 16th century, would tend to suggest a date of *c.*1550–1575 for the backfilling of the pits. There is some evidence from the Austin Friars, Leicester (Woodland 1981), that yellow wares occur in pre-Dissolution contexts (a small lid in the fill of the drain, Phase 9A, Area IV) but in the absence of other examples of yellow wares being found in levels of this date the evidence should perhaps be treated with caution. In addition, at the Austin Friars, yellow wares occurred more frequently in Phases 10C and 10B, but the presence of a blackware form (*ibid.* fig. 43.261) and a Westerwald mug with cobalt decora-

	Area B				Area C			
Fabric	Sherd count	sherd weight	rim count	eves	Sherd count	sherd weight	rim count	eves
residual cpj1-14	35	508	5	26	1	16	1	5
residual Deritend wares	48	567	4	36	1	32		
residual medieval glazed wares	3	124						
residual whitewares	17	363						
?residual iron-poor wares	20	350						
lox1	13	251	4	35	1	78	1	35
lox2	28	1069	6	68				
lox3	5	170						
lox5	2	17	3	36				
lox8	1	88						
lox10	2	156						
Midlands purple	3	134						
gritty ware	3	293	1	14				
Rhenish stoneware	1	5						
blackware	39	563	2	16				
blackware/cistercian ware	21	233	5	50				
cistercian ware	9	103	2	14				
coarseware/Midlands purple	1	33						
coarseware (iron-rich)	60	2906	11	153				
intrusive	2	7						
Total	313	7940	43	448	3	126	2	40

Table 7.6 Edgbaston Street; Phase 2 pottery.

tion, which is extremely unlikely to be earlier than *c.*1600, suggest that there must have been some post-Dissolution occupation and that therefore the yellow wares need not be earlier than the later 16th century.

Tanning pit F229 contained mainly mixed medieval pottery with a small number of 15th- to 16th-century sherds (Midlands Purple) or 16th-century sherds (blackware and Siegburg stoneware). The Siegburg stoneware was salt-glazed and most likely belongs to the first half of the 16th century. Siegburg stoneware is less commonly found than other stonewares in the West Midlands, although a small number of such sherds were found sealed below a plaster floor of *c.*1530 in the keep at Dudley Castle (personal inspection by the author). A vessel such as that found in F229 may well have been valued and hence had a long period of curation before disposal.

Although all three tanning pits are likely to have gone out of use at roughly the same time, the source of the backfill material in F229 is clearly different from that in the other two tanning pits.

The vessel forms represented in F214 were primarily drinking vessels or jars (*e.g.* Fig. 7.8.178, 7.10.250). Some of the latter may have been bung-hole jars (cisterns). Only one jug was definitely represented (Fig. 7.7.145), in Fabric lox2, and one bowl in a red coarseware fabric. A similar range and proportion of forms was observed in F223, with two bowls represented in Fabrics lox3 and lox5, similar in form to Fig. 7.7.154, jars similar to Fig. 7.10.249 in red coarseware, a corrugated black-ware mug and a blackware/ Cistercian ware drinking vessel with a marked carination below the rim (Fig. 7.8.179). There was little or no sign of sooting or abrasion on the sherds, suggesting that they were normal domestic rubbish, and the sherds were generally large, suggesting primary deposition. The sherds from tanning pit F229, in contrast, were much smaller (with an average sherd weight of 12.7g), as would be expected in a largely residual group. Perhaps the most interesting aspect of the residual material is that it includes one of the earliest sherds from the site, a pitcher handle (Fig. 7.4.88) with traces of an external glaze and internal olive-brown glaze runs. The handle form and glaze suggest that this sherd dates to the later 12th or early 13th centuries.

A number of layers were dated to Phase 2. Of these, 2042, 2043, 2143, 2149 and 2168 contained small numbers of sherds, but much the same in character as those found in the tanning pits F214 and F223. Vessel forms were made up of drinking vessels for the most part, but examples of jars, cisterns and bowls were also present. A late oxidised ware chafing dish or possibly a strainer (Fig. 7.7.159) was present in 2168. It had slipped surfaces and an internal, slightly metallic-looking brown glaze. Layer 2035, which sealed tanning pit F214, contained a Fabric lox1 jug (Fig. 7.6.140) and a Fabric lox2 small conical jug with a faceted base (Fig. 7.7.148). These jugs may have been used as drinking vessels. There is a resemblance between their form (albeit larger and cruder) and that of stoneware schnelle of the 16th century. Also present in 2035 was a gritty ware jar sherd and an intrusive dark-on-light slipware flatware, probably dating to the late 17th or early 18th centuries. Layers 2044 and 2167 contained residual material apart from a red coarseware sherd and blackware or Cistercian ware sherd respectively. Layer 2075 contained residual medieval pottery and one intrusive mottled ware sherd but was placed in Phase 2 because of its stratigraphic relationship. Another interesting group of pottery came from layer 2023/ 2025. The group contained a blackware mug handle, an iron-rich coarseware jar similar to Fig. 7.10.245, and iron-poor coarseware bowl similar to Fig. 7.12.284, a Fabric lox1 jug and a Fabric lox2 cistern (Fig. 7.7.149) and four residual Deritend jug sherds. This group was unusual in that there was only one sherd from a drinking vessel, the rest of the sherds being associated with storage or food preparation. The coarseware jar and bowl have fairly simple forms and are probably early in the sequence of coarsewares. The cistern (or bung-hole jar) would have had two handles but only the scar of one of them remains. Around the neck was a clay cordon which had been decorated with a 'wheel' stamp. This stamp has been found on a cistern handle from Dudley Castle (personal inspection by author) and at Oakeswell Hall (Hodder and Glazebrook 1987). The latter examples are thought to have been made at Wednesbury in the later 15th or 16th centuries (Hodder1992; Hodder and Glazebrook 1987). The form of the coarsewares and the stamped cistern suggest a date in the mid–late 16th century.

Analysis of sherd weights from the layers produced some interesting results. The average sherd weight for most of the contexts is high, suggesting that the layers had not been subject to prolonged exposure or trample. There are exceptions. The lowest average sherd weights, of 8g and 4.5g, occur in 2044 and 2075 respectively. This is in keeping with the large residual component in these two groups. However, 2168, which contained only Phase 2 pottery, had an average sherd weight of 12g, and 2042,

comprising mixed Phase 1 and Phase 2 material, had a slightly higher average sherd weight of 12.5g. The remaining layers had average sherd weights ranging from 16g to 35.5g.

Average sherd weights in the tanning pits F214, F223 and F229 showed a similar patterning to that in the layers. Pit F229, which contained mainly residual medieval pottery, had an overall fill average of 10g, which compares well with the averages for layers containing predominantly residual pottery. The contents of pits F214 and F223, which contained primary dumps of material, had overall average sherd weights of just under 72g and 19.25g respectively. It may not be coincidental that the highest average sherd weight (35.5g) among the layers came from 2035, which sealed pit F214. It is therefore possible that the backfilling of F214 and the accumulation of 2035 were contemporary or near contemporary, and may mark a major reorganisation of the site and partial abandonment of this area.

The pottery from tanning pit F230 had an overall average sherd weight of 14g. The greater part of the pottery was made up of residual material. The three late medieval/ early post-medieval sherds, in gritty ware and Fabric lox2, comprised a jar with internal and external wash/ slip, a lid like Fig. 7.7.151 and a jug/ jar/ cistern. The lid diameter of 18cm would suggest that it was for use with either a jar or cistern (see Fig. 7.7.151–152).

Moor Street (see Table 7.7)

Only 23 sherds of late medieval/ early post-medieval date (15th–16th centuries) were recovered from Moor Street, the majority of these in late oxidised wares. A number of sherds of this date came from the fills of pits cut into the backfilled boundary ditch or were from the ditch recut itself. The residual medieval pottery largely reflected the Phase 1 assemblage, although some of the iron-poor sherds, in particular those in Fabric ip4, could date to the 14th or 15th centuries. An unlikely find in 5111, the lower fill of Phase 2 pit F536, were three joining Fabric ip2 sherds from a ?wastered base, with glaze running from the centre of the sherd out and over a section of the break. There is no very rational explanation for this since the fabric is unlikely to be very local. It is possible that the sherd had been used as a spacer in a kiln. A late iron-poor fabric (ip8) found in pit F501/ F536 came from either a jar or cistern and would seem to date to the 15th or, possibly, the 16th century. Apart from a single sherd of blackware/ Cistercian ware from layer 5119, there was an absence of Cistercian ware, which may indicate that most of the pottery was deposited before c.1500 but could equally reflect the overall shortage of pottery on the site, presumably due to abandonment or change of land use. A clay pipe fragment, presumably intrusive, dating to 1680–1730, was also present in 5119. A second clay pipe fragment dated 1650–1750 was found with a 15th–16th-century sherd (Fabric lox1) in 5030, the fill of pit F530. The presence of Tudor Green ware and a sherd of a lobed

	sherd count	sherd weight	rim count	eves
Fabric				
residual Roman	1	33	1	11
residual cpj1-14	3	163	2	18
residual Deritend wares	14	252	2	9
residual whitewares	2	15		
?residual iron-poor wares	21	350		
blackware/cistercian ware	1	9	1	10
lox1	2	16	1	14
lox2	3	61		
lox3	2	29	2	9
lox5	8	143		
lox8	1	88		
lox9	4	65		
late Brill/Nettlebed	1	23	1	4
Tudor green	1	2		
Total	64	1249	10	75

Table 7.7 Moor Street; Phase 2 pottery.

late Brill ?cup, together with the blackware/ Cistercian sherd, would seem to suggest that the standard of living on Moor Street was still reasonable even though the evidence was sparse. Most of the 15th- to 16th-century sherds were from indeterminate jug/ jar/ cistern forms, often knife-trimmed around the base-angle and lower body, with only one or two bowls represented (*e.g.* Fabric lox3, Fig. 7.7.154). A small sherd, in what appeared to be a coarse Deritend-type fabric with tan glaze, looked to have come from a mortar. Ceramic mortars are not common but similar ones are known from Park House, Warwick (Rátkai forthcoming b), Lichfield (Nichol and Rátkai 2004) and Knowle Hall (personal inspection by author). The small fragment from Moor Street was almost certainly residual.

A charcoal-flecked silt layer (5101) contained a single sherd. However, this was unusual in that it was a Roman Severn Valley rim sherd from a wide-mouthed jar. The sherd was in good condition with no sign of abrasion. This sherd brings the number of Roman sherds or possible Roman sherds from Moor Street to five. The other sherds came from 5150 and 5158, fills of Ditch F561. All the sherds were from oxidised wares and included two rim sherds from Severn Valley ware tankards. The significance of these finds should not be underestimated (see Hodder *et al.*, chapter 16) especially when combined with the evidence from Park Street where two Severn Valley sherds, two oxidised Roman sherds and a grey ware sherd were found.

Park Street (see Table 7.8)

The principal features at Park Street assigned to Phase 2 were clustered in Area B. These comprised a group of pits of various shapes and sizes, including a largish 'pond' (F506). There were traces of clay lining in several of these pits, suggesting that they were intended to hold water, and they had been cut into silt 'flood' deposits in what was evidently a frequently waterlogged part of the site, adjacent to the projected line of the boundary ditch that defined the rear end of the plots fronting onto Park Street. Although an industrial function is possible for these pits, there is no compelling evidence for such and it is perhaps more likely that they were intended for the watering of animals. As was noted above, the conditions in this part of the site are likely to have given rise to more mixing of pottery than would generally occur in drier conditions, and if the pits are related to the watering of animals much muddy trampling should be anticipated, leading to both mixing and fragmentation of pottery.

The absolute number of sherds from Area B datable to the 15th and 16th centuries is very small (36 sherds) and is greatly outweighed by the amount of residual or probably residual pottery (104 sherds), the majority of which (65 sherds) were Deritend wares.

The 'pond' (F506) and adjacent clay-lined pits (F508 and F512) in Area B contained very little pottery (eight, three and eleven sherds respectively). There was a Phase 3 fill (1519) to F506, which contained 67 sherds but this must be part of a general backfilling (?and change of use) which appears to have occurred on the site in the late 18th century. As noted, the Phase 2 pits contained mainly

Fabric	Area A				Area B				Area C			
	sherd count	sherd weight	rim count	eves	sherd count	sherd weight	rim count	eves	sherd count	sherd weight	rim count	eves
residual Roman					1	2						
residual cpj1-14	13	83	2	7	22	232	3	20	6	30	1	2
residual Deritend wares	61	634	5	25	65	644	9	46	9	109	1	9
residual reduced wares (RSf-RSi)	1	11										
residual medieval glazed wares	5	59										
residual whitewares	2	1	1	1	3	34	1	10	2	24		
?residual iron-poor wares	10	122	1	10	13	105	1	7	2	11		
? late medieval (burnt)					4	35						
lox1	1	27			1	6			1	6		
lox2	4	129			8	334						
lox3	5	96	1	5	1	29	1	5	1	8	1	5
lox5					14	192	1	5				
late Brill/?Nettlebed	1	23										
Tudor green	2	2							1	2		
Midlands purple	5	80	1	10	8	213	1	6				
gritty ware	2	92							1	4		
blackware	1	8			1	3			1	2		
blackware/cistercian ware												
cistercian ware	1	2			2	26	1	5				
coarseware/Midlands purple					1	27						
coarseware (iron-poor)	3											
coarseware (iron-rich)	1	28							1	106		
intrusive	2	54			3	29						
Total	120	1451	11	58	143	1880	53	104	25	302	3	16

Table 7.8 Park Street; Phase 2 pottery.

residual medieval material and the phasing of these features depends on a late iron-poor fabric (Fabric ip8) from fill 1511 of 'pond' F506, a Fabric lox2 sherd from fill 1508 of pit F508, and a very small, 16th- or 17th-century blackware sherd from fill 1524 of pit F512. Fill 1524 also contained a fragment of bone-working debris, which might favour a 17th-century date for the fill, although a Phase 2 charcoal-rich layer (1625) also contained some bone-working debris. The lower fill (1584) of 'pond' F506 contained only Deritend wares (both oxidised and reduced). Fill 1525 of pit F512 was very similar, but in addition had a Fabric ip2 sherd which could have been contemporary with or later than the Deritend wares. The average sherd weight from these fills was less than 10g, apart from fill 1511 of 'pond' F506, which contained a 43g Fabric ip8 sherd. The

general impression is that the features were backfilled with material which contained a background scatter of pottery. If this is so, then there was clearly very little 15th- to 16th-century pottery dumped in this area. The ceramic evidence, such as it is, does not prove that any of these features dates to the 15th–16th centuries but merely give a *terminus post quem* for their disuse.

The rectangular pit or tank F562/ F561 presented a similar picture to the above. Most of the pottery from the fills was medieval. Sherd size was more varied than in features F506 etc, and ranged from 4g to 40g. This large feature was dug in two sections, designated F562 and F561. The primary fill (1661) of F562 contained a Fabric ip9 sherd, which was probably early medieval in date. The second fill (1660) contained Fabrics lox1, lox2, lox3 and lox5, together with a greater quantity of residual medieval pottery. The upper fill (1659) contained a Fabric lox5 sherd and residual medieval pottery. The evidence from F562 is therefore consistent with the feature being backfilled in the 15th or 16th centuries. However, the other section cut through the same feature (F561), contained no pottery in fill 1656, only medieval pottery in 1657 (reduced and oxidised Deritend wares), whilst the uppermost fill (1655) contained a Fabric lox2 sherd and a slip-coated ware sherd. The latter dates to the later 17th or 18th centuries but is probably intrusive. Pit F562/F561 was cut by circular pit F540, which contained a single Fabric ip2 sherd of mid-13th- to 15th-century date. The absence of any other material, particularly late material, in this pit tends to support the idea that the slip-coated sherd was intrusive, particularly since F562/F561 was also cut by a Phase 3 pit (F559), which contained 18th-century pottery.

Pits F551 and F552 contained rather more convincing 15th- to 16th-century assemblages. Pit F551 produced a Cistercian ware cup sherd and several Fabric lox2 sherds, which appeared to have come from (?bunghole) jars or jugs. For once, there was no residual material and the fill must date to c.1500–1550. Pit F551 cut pit F552. The latter did contain some residual medieval pottery but the greater part of the group was made up of Midlands Purple ware, including a jug/ cistern (Fig. 7.7.166). This fill must date to the 15th century. Most of the other possible Phase 2 features in this area contained no pottery. Pit F541, however, contained two ?residual medieval sherds. Pit F539 was small and stood somewhat apart from the main group. It contained, once more, mainly residual material and was phased on the strength of the presence of a Cistercian ware cup, two Midlands Purple ware sherds and a coarseware/ Midlands Purple sherd. These four sherds would seem to give a date of the mid-16th century. Pit F504, which truncated F539, contained a convincing later 17th-century group with no Midlands Purple ware or Cistercian ware, which suggests that the sherds in F539 were unlikely to be intrusive.

In Area A a similar pattern of predominantly residual material in feature fills was observable. The total amount of pottery from the area datable to the 15th and 16th centuries comprised only 36 sherds, and only two intercutting pits (F188/ F186 and F191) were assigned to Phase 2. Pit F188/ F186 contained an iron-poor gritty ware sherd, Fabrics lox2 and lox3, Midlands Purple ware, Tudor Green and yellow ware. With the exception of the latter, this gave a general date range of 15th–16th centuries. These sherds accounted for only seven sherds out of a total of 64 sherds from the fill. The yellow ware sherd is presumably intrusive. No pottery was recorded from pit F191, which cut F188/ F186. However, pit F191 was in turn cut by a Phase 3.1 pit (F187), which was the latest in the sequence and contained blackware, coarseware and slip-coated ware (amidst mainly residual material), together with 17th-century clay pipe, giving a *terminus ante quem* for F191 of the late 17th–early 18th century. It is therefore also possible for pit F191 to be assigned to Phase 3.

Area C produced only six sherds dated to the 15th and 16th centuries, and only one feature in the area, a kiln of uncertain function (F768), was assigned to Phase 2. The kiln contained only eleven sherds of pottery, including a Tudor Green sherd of 15th- to 16th-century date. Two sherds, probably late oxidised wares, were too burnt for identification. One, however, was a plain strap handle, which also suggests a 15th–16th-century date. Clearly, with the possible exception of the latter two sherds, the pottery had no association with the kiln and its use.

The Phase 2 pottery is disappointing and not easy to interpret. However, it is clear that any activity in the 15th or 16th centuries was concentrated in Area B, with lesser activity in Area A. It is difficult to mesh these activities together. Clearly the late medieval or early post-medieval pottery is not connected in any way with the function of the various features and must represent general ground scatter detritus which had become incorporated into the fills. The one exception to this may be F551 which is the most likely example of primary waste disposal in this phase on the site. The functional component of this admittedly small group *i.e.* a drinking vessel and jugs, jars or cisterns, is typical of ordinary domestic urban assemblages of this period (see, for example, Sandford Street, Lichfield: Nichol and Rátkai 2004).

Secondly, there was clearly a massive reduction in the amount of pottery dating to the 15th and 16th centuries, even allowing for the fact that there was medieval kiln waste in Phase 1. Cistercian ware, late oxidised wares, Tudor Green and Midlands Purple ware account for less than 4% of the overall assemblage total in Area B and in Area A and less than 3% in Area C. However, what 15th–16th-century pottery there was, was of a normal domestic kind. Drinking vessels were found in Cistercian ware, Tudor Green, Cologne and Frechen stoneware, and late Boarstall-Brill ware. Otherwise, the late oxidised wares and Midlands Purple ware was made up of jugs/ jars/ cisterns (storage vessels), bowls (food preparation) and cooking pots. Some of the bowls had been sooted externally, sometimes heavily, suggesting that they had been used for cooking.

The three areas did not produce the same 15th–16th-century assemblages. Area A contained the largest quantity of Cistercian ware cups (24 sherds) and almost equal quantities of jugs/ jars/ cisterns and bowls. A higher proportion of all kitchenware vessels were sooted. Areas B and C, in contrast, had assemblages that consisted of tablewares (drinking vessels) and storage vessels. Very few bowl sherds were present and sherds were generally unsooted.

The 15th–16th-century pottery is not without other features of interest. The presence of Rhenish stonewares, Tudor Green and a late Boarstall-Brill cup suggest occupants of at least middling affluence (although other vessels which seem to form the *sine qua non* of bourgeois existence in this period, *e.g.* the chafing dish and the salt, are absent). The importance of these wares in the west Midlands tends to be overlooked since they can be commonplace in other areas of the country, particularly on southern sites and coastal sites or ports. However, neither Rhenish stoneware nor Tudor Green are generally well represented in the west Midlands, even in an urban setting.

The 15th–16th-century pottery, to sum up, appears to indicate a period of abandonment or alternative land use in the 15th and 16th centuries. There seems to have been little or no ordinary domestic occupation in this area of Park Street in Phase 2. However, what pottery is present represents detritus from occupation of quite high status. How is it possible to equate what would seem like the semi-desertion of the area and the absence of domestic structures with a small amount of occupation debris? Some occupation must have centred on the burgage plots

running back from Digbeth High Street, which would account for the pottery in Area A. The remaining pottery presumably represents overspill from an adjacent Park Street plot or may also have originated in Digbeth.

Phase 3

Edgbaston Street (see Tables 7.9–7.11)

The Phase 3 pottery from Edgbaston Street is discussed as single phase groups rather than by feature since most fill groups are too small for meaningful data to be extracted. There are a small number of exceptions, *e.g.* in Area B layer 2003 with 40 sherds, tanning pit F234 (2138) with 44 sherds, ditch F253 (2197) with 85 sherds, and pit F261 (2198) with 44 sherds; and in Area C pit F334 (3075) with 283 sherds and water channel F337 (3108) with 59 sherds.

	Area A			Area B			Area C			Area D		
Fabric/Ware	sherd count	sherd weight	rim count	sherd count	sherd weight	rim count	sherd count	sherd weight	rim count	sherd count	sherd weight	rim count
residual Phase 1 pottery	20	374	4	35	571	4	16	201	1	1	13	
residual Phase 2 pottery	43	474	5	61	2629	10	39	1102	5	2	26	1
Martincamp Type III				1	9							
blackware	75	1315	8	78	1768	8	43	652	6	7	62	1
brown salt-glazed stoneware	1	21					1	5	1			
coarseware/Midlands purple	2	48		5	210		26	1523	2	1	9	
coarseware (iron-poor)	48	1258	3	74	11111	6	6	8071	13	8	147	
coarseware (iron-rich)	57	3010	7	117	8741	25	275	14429	46	4	85	
creamware	1	3	1				4	24		6	9	
mottled ware				1	1		2	9	1			
slipware	1	8		10	61	3	1	1				
slipware (feathered)	3	24		2	4		3	17	1			
slipware (embossed)	1	17		5	69	2	1	13				
slpware (trailed)	2	9	1	8	53	2	3	23				
slipware (three colour)				3	173	1	1	35	1			
slip-coated ware	2	40								3	49	1
tin-glazed earthenware	1	13				3	1	7	1	2	15	
Westerwald stoneware							1	5				
white salt-glazed ware										2	16	
yellow ware	66	743	9	82	3311	16	25	579	6			
waster?							1	52				
intrusive	1	38					3	14				
	324	7395	38	482	28711	80	452	26762	84	36	431	3

Table 7.9 Edgbaston Street; Phase 3 pottery.

Area A

The pottery from Area A was derived, in the main, from
the fills of a series of sub-rectangular and bell-shaped
pits. The pits seem to have been backfilled in a single
episode and the reorganisation of the area was followed
by the accumulation of a black 'cultivation soil' (1005
and 1076). The range of pottery from the fills was broadly
similar and is in keeping with the suggested single
backfilling. The assemblage largely comprised blackware,
coarseware and yellow ware, which in the West Midlands
typifies the 17th century. There was an absence of mottled
ware but the presence of feathered and multi-coloured

Ware	Area A	Area B	Area C
Blackware	23.0	17.1	6.7
Yellow ware	20.3	18.3	3.9
Slipware	2.2	3.2	1.7
Coarseware (iron-poor)	13.5	16.7	24.4
Coarseware (iron-rich)	16.6	22.8	47.1

*Table 7.10 Edgbaston St; quantification of major wares
in Phase 3.*

slipwares, and a stoneware Bartmann jug, place the
assemblage in the later 17th century or early 18th century.
Pit F106 contained two feathered slipware sherds along
with clay pipe dating from *c*.1650–1700, which suggests
that most of the backfilling might have occurred by the
early years of the 18th century at the latest. There was a
single intrusive 19th-century utilitarian whiteware sherd
in fill 1021 of F106. The later 'cultivation soil' (1005)
contained only twelve sherds, in keeping with the nature
of the layer. A single creamware sherd and glass bottles
of mid- to late 18th-century date were recovered from
layer 1005, suggesting that the cultivation soil was still
in existence in the later 18th century. That there was
reasonably prosperous mid- to late 18th-century occupation in the vicinity is attested by the presence of at least
nine queen edge (Fig. 7.24.1, colour) and hexagonal (Fig.
7.24.2, colour) creamware plates found in the backfill of
the Phase 4 well, F104. In fact, the discard of these plates,
some of which were clearly complete when thrown into
the well, may have been associated with another stage of
development of the area and represent part of a house
clearance/ demolition.

Vessel Form	Area A		Area B		Area C	
	Sherd count	Rim count	Sherd count	Rim count	Sherd count	Rim count
Drinking vessel	64	11	90	16	26	5
Bowl	31	11	64	32	80	34
Pancheon	4	2				
Dish	10	6	6	4	3	
Flatware			5	1	1	
Platter			1		2	1
Strainer					1	
Jar	5	3	74	15	112	29
Cistern			4			
Jug/jar/cistern	3		1		2	
Jug	13	1	17	1	7	1
Bottle					1	1
Flask			1			
Dripping tray					17	2
Chafing dish			2		2	1
Salt			2			
Chamber pot	1		1	1		
Crucible			1			
Flowerpot					1	1
Lid					1	1
Total assignable to form	131	34	269	70	256	76

Table 7.11 Edgbaston St; vessel form by area Phase 3.

Just under half the sherds could be assigned to form. Drinking vessels were the best represented form, at just under 42%. These occurred in blackware (67%) and yellow ware (15%), the remainder occurring in Cistercian ware and Tudor Green ware. Bowls were next best represented (*c*.20%), and dishes formed *c*.5%. Pancheons were not common, nor jars, although the latter are probably under-represented since some of the sherds in the miscellaneous hollow ware category may well have come from jars. There was a single coarseware chamber pot. Such a high incidence of drinking vessels is unusual. The Phase 4 fills (1006, 1007) of cellar F102 and the fill (1009) of well F104 contained mixed pottery, the latest of which post-dates the 1840s. The cellar fills also contained clay pipe, dating somewhat earlier than the latest pottery. Fill 1006 contained clay pipe dating to 1720–1820 and 1007 clay pipe dating to 1760–1810. Only two other contexts produced clay pipe which could possibly be of 19th-century date – namely 1026 with clay pipe dating to 1780–1810 and 1030 the fill of post-hole F116, with clay pipe dating to 1750–1850. In the latter case the presence of blackware, coarseware, slip-coated ware and yellow ware suggest a date in the 18th century for the backfilling of the post-hole.

Area B

The tanning pits and associated drainage features contained only small amounts of pottery in their fills. The fills contained varying amounts of yellow ware, blackware and coarseware, which would suggest a 17th-century date. This could be further refined by the presence of trailed slipware, suggesting a date in the second half of the 17th century, and feathered slipware, embossed slipware and three-colour slipware, suggesting a date range of late 17th–early 18th century. Tanning pit F275 contained only residual medieval material in the fill. No feature had only late medieval/ early post-medieval pottery in its fill. The latest closely datable pottery in drain F281 was a single light-on-dark trailed slipware sherd (*c*.1645–1700). The pottery evidence seems to suggest that tanning had stopped in Area B by the early 18th century at the latest, but if drain F281 was pivotal in the tanning process then tanning may have ceased before 1700. The clay pipe evidence is in complete agreement with activity in this area being concentrated in the period *c*.1650–1725.

Layers 2006, 2021, 2034, 2040, 2166 and 2175 generally contained some residual material, as would be expected. Layer 2021 was the only layer to produce clay pipe which was dated 1620–1700. Cultivation soil 2040 produced a single mottled ware sherd, the only layer to do so, giving a *terminus ante quem* of *c*.1750 but the majority of the post-medieval pottery looked to pre-date *c*.1725.

The largest pottery group (85 sherds) came from 2197, the fill of ditch F253. Over half the group (54%) consisted of coarseware, whilst blackware and yellow ware made up 21% and 14% respectively. The remaining pottery consisted of residual medieval and late medieval/ early post-medieval material, including two Cologne/ Frechen drinking vessels dating to the ?second half of the 16th century. The absence of any clearly later 17th-century types in this group suggests that the ditch fill may date to the mid-17th century at the latest. The pottery from the ditch fill differed from the rest, since several sherds were covered in mortary deposits. These deposits and limey accretions found on pottery from pit F261 (see below) may link both these features to the lime pit F200. Pit F200 contained clay pipe dating to 1650–1670 but the pottery in the fill was mostly residual the latest sherd being from an embossed slipware dish. This together with the clay pipe evidence suggests a date of *c*.1670 for the disuse of the pit or possibly *c*.1650 if the slipware sherd is intrusive. Pit F261 also did not contain any pottery datable to the later 17th century. The largest number of sherds assignable to form came from drinking vessels, most of which occurred in blackware. Bowls were the second largest category, with roughly equal amounts occurring in coarseware and yellow ware. One of the coarseware bowls had a horizontal handle (Fig. 7.12.272), a less common form. Jars were the third best represented. There was only a single flatware sherd, in yellow ware. Ditch fill 2197 is also of interest because of the accumulation of horncores from mediumhorned cattle (see Baxter, Chapter 15). Baxter suggests that the horncores in the ditch could represent tanning waste or evidence of horn working. If this is so, then it may be the only feature fill which can be said to tie in industrial evidence with a relatively closely dated ceramic group. In addition it is also possible to tie a group of industrial workers with the pottery they are likely to have used. As such, the relatively high proportion of table wares and, in particular, the presence of two Rhenish stoneware vessels, probably 'curated' rather than residual, is of interest.

Pit F261 contained the second largest group of sherds, including a blackware chamber pot with heavy internal scale and a substantial amount of a coarseware jar, which was partly burnt on the exterior and covered in limey accretions. The large number of jar sherds form a disproportionate amount of the group, the other forms represented being two drinking vessels (blackware and yellow ware) and two bowls (coarseware and yellow ware).

Area C

This area is the one for which there is good documentary evidence for tanning, skin curing and leather dressing. Residual medieval or late medieval/ early post-medieval pottery accounted for *c*.4.5% of the phase group; in Areas A and B the figure was 10% and 11.5% respectively. This may indicate that Area C was relatively under-utilised in the medieval period.

There was a smaller amount of more closely datable pottery from this area, since slipwares were less common.

There were single examples of dark-on-light slipware from gully F313 (3113), and three-colour slipware from pit F343 (3117); two sherds each of embossed slipware from pit F309 (3042) and water channel F337 (3109); and three examples of feathered slipware from pit F326 (3061) and water channel F336 (3106). This suggests that these feature fills belong to the later 17th–early 18th centuries. Clay pipe was found in F313, F326 and F336, the dating of which is consistent with the proposed pottery dating. Two sherds of light-on-dark slipware were recovered from pits F328 (3073) and F344 (3139), and it is possible that these two fills could be slightly earlier than the preceding ones although the clay pipe evidence suggests a similar date to these. Glass bottles from pit F338 were also dated to the late 17th–early 18th centuries. The hide-curing pits to the west of the site did not contain much pottery. Only pits F300, F301, F304, F328 and F338 contained pottery, which suggested a date of later 17th–early 18th century. Clay pipes from F328 and F338 were dated 1680–1730 and 1680–1720 respectively. The pits which abutted the hide-curing pits were dated by the pottery to the later 17th or early 18th centuries, a dating which was reinforced by the clay pipe from F326 (1680–1730) and F347 (1680–1730). Further pits associated with hide curing, F323, F324, F325 and F346, to the east of the site, did not contain any slipwares and appeared initially to be the earliest. However, the pits F233 and F324 cut gully F313, which did have a dark-on-light slipware sherd in its fill and clay pipe dated to 1710–1800. This would tend to suggest that these pits could have been backfilled later than the others.

The construction cut F353 (for a building pre-dating the late 18th- or early 19th-century skinhouse) contained a mix of residual 13th- to ?early 14th-century medieval sherds and post-medieval coarseware sherds. The coarseware formed an interesting collection. The majority of the sherds were from a large dripping tray with a horizontal handle (Fig. 7.13.294). The interior base was marked by a series of shallow channels, presumably to help fat and liquids drain towards the pouring lip. The same arrangement was seen in a Fabric lox3 dripping tray (Fig. 7.7.155) from fill 3093 of well F327. This vessel was sooted on the exterior and heavily abraded on the exterior base. As one would expect, Fig. 7.13.294 was sooted along one side, *i.e.* where the side was placed closest to the fire or hearth. The tray had evidently seen a lot of use, since both the base and base-angle were abraded. This perhaps suggests that it had been used on a stone-flagged floor. It is quite a substantial vessel, at 2266g, to have been found in a construction trench. Other coarsewares found in F353 comprised a bowl and a jar of the type found in Civil War destruction deposits at Dudley Castle (Rátkai 1987, fig. 3.5). There was also a burnt late oxidised ware jug or cistern sherd from the construction trench. There is nothing to suggest that the fill of the construction trench need be later than the mid-17th century and the use of a large ceramic dripping tray is

perhaps more consistent with the first half of the 17th century than post-Civil War. The dumping of the dripping tray into the construction trench may indicate a primary deposition (but see below) giving a construction date for the building of c.1600–1650. The absence of clay pipe from the construction trench may also favour an early construction date.

A large group, the largest Phase 3 group from Edgbaston Street, came from 3075, the fill of pit F334. As only a small section of the pit, which lay on southwestern edge of the excavation, was excavated, the original fill must have contained a sizable dump of pottery. The excavated pottery comprised mainly coarsewares but with a small group of Midlands Purple ware, three sherds of yellow ware and four sherds from a Cologne stoneware drinking mug (Fig. 7.14.327) dating to the second half of the 16th century. The absence of blackware sherds is unusual in this group. The average sherd weight for the group is very high at 49g and the fill must represent a primary or near primary dump. At least 25 vessels were represented by rim count (eves 334%). The vessel count broke down as follows: Cologne stoneware – one drinking vessel; yellow ware – two unidentifiable hollow ware sherds; Midlands Purple – two jars (Fig. 7.7.162, 164); coarseware – eleven jars, ten bowls and one dripping tray which was heavily abraded externally. Abrasion was rare, occurring on one bowl with internal wear (?perhaps from mixing something abrasive) and on three jars, one with wear on the base and another with wear on the base and base-angle, presumably caused by rotating the jars on a hard surface during use, and the third jar with generalised wear over internal and external surfaces (Fig. 7.10.249). As a large proportion of Fig. 7.10.249 survived, the wear may well be associated with its use rather than being a secondary, post-breakage feature.

Iron-poor coarseware was the least well represented, with a jar, a bowl (Fig. 7.11.268) and a dripping tray (not illustrated). Iron-rich coarsewares were dominant (*e.g.* Fig. 7.10.249, 252–3), with a hard-fired, smooth-fractured coarseware, somewhere between a coarseware and a Midlands Purple, forming a small sub-set (Fig. 7.10.245).

The fill of pit F334 was clearly derived from a kitchen/pantry area since nearly all the vessel forms were associated with storage, food preparation or, in the case of the dripping tray, cooking. There were only seven sherds which were exceptions to this – the four Rhenish stoneware sherds and the three yellow ware sherds. The beginnings of the coarseware tradition can be seen in the late red wares of the 15th and 16th centuries, and several examples of fabrics which lay somewhere between the late red wares and the coarsewares were noted from the Bull Ring sites (*e.g.* Fig. 7.10.246–47). There is a strong suggestion, therefore, that the earliest coarsewares had iron-rich fabrics. The preponderance of iron-rich coarseware, together with Midlands Purple ware and the

German stoneware, seems to suggest a date in the first half of the 17th century. It is possible that pottery from this pit and from the construction trench F353 was derived from the same place although the features are some distance from each other, and it is notable that neither the construction trench nor pit F334 contained reduplicated clay pipe. At any rate, both these feature fills would seem to be earlier than the backfilling of the tanning pits.

There was a small amount of information from cross-joining sherds. These were found between 3062, the fill of well F327, and 3106, the fill of water channel F336; and between 3074 and 3009, the fills of hide-curing pits F328 and F304 respectively. This evidence may suggest that, like the bell-shaped pits in Area A, the hide-curing pits were backfilled in a single action, which both the clay pipe and pottery evidence shows to have been in the late 17th or early 18th century. Whether this was in preparation for the construction of Welch's Skinyard shown on Sheriff's map of 1808, or marks a relocation of tanning and/ or hide curing within the backplot, or marks a cessation of industrial activity and a temporary reversion to gardens, is difficult to say. The 18th-century maps certainly seem to show buildings always in this location although there were gardens to the north of the excavated area.

Fill 3062 of well F327 produced clay pipe dating to 1680–1720, although a second fill (3093) of F327 contained clay pipe dating to 1750–1850. This may indicate that the well was one of the last features to be backfilled and its disuse may be unconnected to the backfilling of the tanning pits. The two cross-joins recorded between the well F327 and the water channel F336 came from an iron-poor coarseware jar (Fig. 7.12.279) and a handled bowl in an iron-rich coarseware fabric (Fig. 7.12.273). Pottery from the water channel F336 was rather more mixed than from other feature fills, since it contained medieval material and sherds post-dating 1750. This, of course would tie in with the later dated clay pipe from F327. The later pottery from the water channel comprised a creamware sherd, a tortoise-shell ware footring base and a 19th-century utilitarian whiteware sherd which was probably intrusive. Other post-1750 pottery was found in 3125, the fill of post-hole F345 (a creamware sherd and a bone china or porcelain sherd), and 3038, the fill of well F305 (a late 18th-century pale bodied creamware sherd and an industrial slipware sherd dating to the early 19th century).

Area D
Only a small amount of pottery (36 sherds, weighing 431g) was recovered from five pits: F415, F419, F420, F422 and F425. All except F419 contained 18th-century pottery, *e.g.* tin-glazed earthenware (see Fig. 7.19.7, colour), creamware or white salt-glazed stoneware, and an admixture of residual pottery. Clay pipe from Area D was consistent with an 18th- or early 19th-century date

(although clay pipe from F425 and F415 could have been deposited as late as the mid-19th century). The remaining features contained a probable 17th-century coarseware sherd and residual material including a gritty ware jar, possibly for industrial use.

Discussion
The environmental evidence did not add any information which might help with the interpretation of the Phase 3 ceramics other than to confirm the presence of settlement waste. A comparison across Areas A–C produces some interesting results. There is little evidence to separate the three areas chronologically, since all of the assemblages seem to contain 17th- and possibly early 18th-century pottery in the feature backfills. However, there are marked differences in the proportions of the major ware types (see Table 7.10). It seems most likely that these represent the different functional compositions of the groups (see Table 7.11). Very few sherds were sooted and some of the sooting was post-breakage. Areas A and C had only a handful of sooted or burnt sherds. Area B had by far the greatest number at 27 sherds.

In the following section comparisons are made using quantification by sherd count. When the phase groups are quantified by minimum rim count there are some differences between the ratio of bowls to drinking vessels but the overall trends remain the same.

The Area A assemblage was dominated by 'table wares', such as drinking vessels and dishes. Utilitarian (*i.e.* kitchen and storage) wares were poorly represented and, of these, bowls were the most common. Area C was at the opposite end of the spectrum, with a preponderance of utilitarian wares, the greater part of which were composed of jars. Other utilitarian wares were represented by sherds from two dripping trays and a yellow ware strainer. The chafing dish sherds could be interpreted as either utilitarian or table wares. One of the chafing dish sherds was in yellow ware, the other in an iron-poor coarseware fabric. The latter type, often quite crude, with a thick purplish brown external slip, which sometimes has a metallic sheen, is known from other sites in the West Midlands, *e.g.* Dudley Castle and Stafford Castle. These rather crude chafing dishes may have been used in the kitchen for the gentle heating of food rather than at table as food warmers. The predominance of utilitarian wares from Area C may add some weight to this conjecture. One unusual form from Area C was a yellow ware terminal possibly from a money box or lid (Fig. 7.10.240). Area B had a similar number of form types to Area C. Drinking vessels were the best represented class but were outnumbered by the utilitarian wares. Of these, the dominant class was the storage jar, since just under half the bowls were in yellow ware or trailed slipware and, as such, were more likely to be table wares. However, 13 of the yellow ware and two of the slipware sherds were sooted, raising some questions about the exact definition of table wares and utilitarian wares. In general, bowls or undifferentiated hollow wares were most likely to be sooted amongst the yellow wares, although a yellow ware cup (Fig. 7.10.234) from pit F261 (2198) was sooted on the base and lower body. It is tempting to see this as evidence of the preparation of a posset, *i.e.* a gently heated mixture of eggs, cream, sugar and spices, a confection popular in the early post-medieval period. Sooting was also found in Area B on the exterior of an embossed slipware platter from the lime pit F200 (2029), and heavy sooting was present on the interior of a dark-on-light slipware bowl from layer 2034 and on the exterior of a light-on-dark slipware flange-rim bowl from drain F281 (2176).

The two chafing dish sherds were in an iron-poor and an iron-rich coarseware fabric. The (blackware) chamber pot, more properly a stool pot in this case, was paralleled by blackware vessels from Civil War destruction debris at Dudley Castle. The vessel from pit F261 had heavy internal scale, attesting to its use. There was a greater similarity between Area B and Area A, however, since when the vessel classes are calculated taking note of the ware type, *e.g.* yellow ware, blackware etc, the two groups were heavily biased in favour of table wares. This bias is reflected in the presence of two salts (or possibly candlesticks) from Area B. One, in Cistercian ware, (Fig. 7.8.173) came from the lime pit F200, the other (Fig. 7.10.237), in yellow ware, came from layer 2166.

The average sherd weights for Phase 3 across the three areas were variable, at 22.65g (Area A), 63.71g (Area B) and 45.05g (Area C). All of these are quite high for backplots, even allowing for the bulky nature of much post-medieval pottery. Normally, this would be interpreted as evidence of primary or near primary deposition. A number of feature fills had exceptionally high average sherd weights: Area A pit fill 1066 (F139), 1138g; Area B pit fill 2008 (F208), 80.8g, drain fill 2176 (F281), 123.29g, pit fill 2198 (F261), 224.8g; Area C water channel fill 3108 (F337) 74.6g, and construction trench fill 3166 (F353), 96.59g. Environmental evidence (Smith, Chapter 14) from water channel F337 indicated settlement waste was present in the fill. There is unfortunately no common link between the features with high average sherd weights and no obvious explanation except stochastic.

Moor Street (see Table 7.12)

There was very little information regarding Moor Street in Phase 3. Pottery of this date came almost exclusively from coarsewares. The majority of the pottery was made up of residual medieval and late medieval/ early post-medieval pottery. There was one unusual sherd, a tin-glazed earthenware sherd decorated on the interior with narrow concentric bands in turquoise and purple (Fig. 7.19.13, colour). The exterior was covered with a clear lead glaze. The vessel is not Spanish (pers. comm. Alejandra Gutierrez) but the decoration and the use of turquoise suggest that this may be a Mediterranean

Fabric	count	weight	mv
residual Phase 1 pottery	14	271	4
residual Phase 2 pottery	3	93	
blackware	1	1366	
coarseware (iron-poor)	4	119	2
coarseware (iron-rich)	5	196	1
tin glazed earthenware	1	3	
Total	28	2048	7

Table 7.12 Moor St; Phase 3 pottery.

maiolica. It was found in a Phase 4 construction trench (F532) together with the base of a 17th-century blackware drinking vessel (a 'corrugated' tankard), an iron-poor coarseware jar and an iron-rich coarseware bowl with a simple everted, slightly dished rim similar to Fig. 7.12.272. Most of this material seems to date to the 17th century but the maiolica could be earlier. Layer 5200 which contained a coarseware jar sherd and a DeritendR sherd also had one clay pipe fragment dating to 1750–1850.

Park Street (see Tables 7.13–7.26)

Phase 3 at Park Street was principally characterised by 65 pits located in clusters across the three areas of the site. Many of the pits were associated with debris from metal working but other activities were also represented, including bone working. The pottery from these pits, and occasionally other datable artefacts (notably clay pipe), enabled the 200-year period represented by Phase 3 to be subdivided into three sub-phases:

Phase 3.1: Late 16th to early 18th century
Phase 3.2: Early to mid-18th century
Phase 3.3: Later 18th/ early 19th century

Of the 65 pits investigated, 46 could be assigned with reasonable confidence to one of these sub-phases. In addition to the pits there were two other features of particular interest, two large wood-lined tanks in Area B.

Phase 3.1

The earliest series of pits, and also the cluster closest to the Park Street frontage, was made up of intercutting pits F141, F144 and F134 (in stratigraphic order). Pit F141 contained eleven sherds, one of which was medieval. The remainder comprised two Cistercian ware sherds (Fig. 7.8.172), three blackware sherds and five coarseware sherds. Three of the latter were in a clean well-prepared red clay, which marks them out as comparatively early (see above under fabric discussions). The medieval sherd was small at 4g but the later pottery weighed 324g, giving an average sherd weight of 32.4g, which suggests primary or near primary deposition. The early type of coarseware,

Phase	3			3.1			3.2			3.3		
	count	weight	mv	count	weight	mv	count	weight	mv	count	weight	mv
Fabric/Ware												
Residual Phase 1 pottery	68	794	9	11	93	1	20	149	4			
Residual Phase 2 pottery	16	405		14	190	5	2	41	1			
blackware	44	984	5	16	272	1	59	2480	3	8	199	
blue shell edge plate	1	6	1									
brown salt-glazed stoneware	3	37					11	48	1	4	17	1
creamware	3	54	1							5	22	
coarseware/blackware							1	35	1			
coarseware (iron-poor)	19	1055	4	7	365	1	50	3196	14	8	315	1
coarseware/midlands purple				1	6							
coarseware (iron-rich)	34	2311	6	9	355	1	24	1886	6	7	248	1
mocha ware										1	1	
mottled ware	11	191	3	1	14		10	222	1	4	164	1
pearlware										3	5	
porcelain										1	4	
slip-coated ware	13	462	2	1	4		38	1532	10	11	286	1
slipware (feathered)	6	171					25	479	4			
slipware (embossed)							1	50				
slipware (three-colour)							1	53				
slipware (trailed)	2	10					4	86	3	1	32	
tin-glazed earthenware	1	2					1	20				
westerwald stoneware							1	4		1	11	1
white salt-glazed stoneware	1	4					2	28	1			
yellow ware	7	43	1	11	127	3	1	1	1			
Total	229	6529	32	71	1426	12	251	10310	51	54	1303	6

Table 7.13 Park St; Area A, Phase 3 pottery.

with its purplish brown almost metallic slip and glaze, and the absence of yellow ware, probably indicate that the pit fill dates to the late 16th century. Pits F144 and F134 contained similar fill material. Pit F144 had a mix of blackware and Cistercian ware, early coarseware and yellow ware. The fill produced nine sherds in total, weighing 107g. Pit F134 contained two residual medieval sherds, seven blackware sherds, one blackware/ Cistercian ware sherd, three coarseware sherds (two of which were iron-poor), a Midlands Purple ware sherd and eight yellow ware sherds. The presence of yellow ware in F134 and F144 suggests that the fills date to the 17th century. The absence of pottery normally associated with the 1670s and later such as slipwares suggests a *terminus ante quem* for the deposition of the group. Clay pipe from F134 was given a suggested deposition date of 1660–1680 by Higgins (this volume). The backfill date of the latest pit F134 probably dates to *c*.1660–1670. It is worth noting that the average sherd size of the fills of F134 and F144 were 11.8g and 11.3g respectively,

roughly a third of the average sherd weight from the earliest pit F141.

Located slightly further back from the frontage in Area A was a pair of intercutting pits, F162 and F172 (in stratigraphic order). There was only a single medieval sherd in F172, and four sherds, comprising residual medieval ware, Midlands Purple ware, blackware and iron-poor coarseware, in F162. The four sherds from F162 weighed 212g, *i.e.* an average sherd weight of 53g, which suggests that they represent primary or near primary deposition. On the evidence of the ceramics this is unlikely to be later than *c*.1650, an earlier 17th-century date perhaps confirmed by the absence of clay pipe from the pit fills.

Close to this pair of pits was a further cluster of three intercutting pits, F188/ F186, F191 and F187. Pit F188/ F186 probably belongs to Phase 2. No pottery was recorded from pit F191, which cut F188/ F186 and could therefore belong to Phase 2 or Phase 3. Pit F191 was in turn cut by pit F187, which was the latest in the sequence

Phase	3.1			3.2			3.3		
	count	weight	mv	count	weight	mv	count	weight	mv
Fabric/Ware									
Roman?							1	2	
Residual Phase 1 pottery							24	262	5
Resiidual Phase 2 pottery							1	7	
blackware	6	33	1	14	267	3	1	4	
brown salt-glazed stoneware							1	6	
creamware							7	46	1
coarseware (iron-poor)				18	597	2	1	10	
coarseware (iron-rich)	18	299	2	3	78		8	215	1
industrial slipware				1	6				
mottled ware	1	3		20	560	3	1	5	
refined body wares				2	3				
slip-coated ware				17	424	2	33	31	
slipware (feathered)				18	572	1			
slipware (embossed)				1	10				
tin-glazed earthenware	1	8		5	28	2			
white salt-glazed stoneware	1	2		8	200	2	2	9	
yellow ware	1	12							
Total	28	357	3	107	2745	15	80	597	7

Table 7.14 Park St; Area B, Phase 3 pottery excluding tank fills.

and contained blackware, coarseware and slip-coated ware (amidst mainly residual material), together with clay pipe with a suggested deposition date of 1680–1730. A final pair of intercutting pits in Area A, located a few metres further back again from the Park Street frontage, belonged to Phase 3.1. Pit F182 contained clay pipe with a deposition date of 1650–1750, a sherd from a yellow ware albarello and three sherds from a handled coarseware vessel (Fig 7.13.293), another piece of which was found in pit F181. Pit F183 contained four sherds also, comprising two blackware sherds and single sherds of yellow ware and coarseware, and clay pipe with a suggested deposition date of 1680–1720. One of the blackware sherds, probably from a tankard, may have been a waster since there was glaze over one of the breaks. The clay pipe from both pits comprised only four sherds in poor condition.

In Area B, pit F504 was possibly a part of this group of Phase 3.1 pits. It contained only 25 sherds, with a single mottled ware sherd which dated the pit fill to the later 17th century, a date which is reinforced by the dating of the clay pipe fragments to 1650–1700. The pottery assemblage itself (see Table 7.19) was not particularly noteworthy but was important in giving a date to the rest of the finds from the pit. Most notable among these was a large quantity of worked ivory (see Bevan *et al.*, Chapter 8, and Hodder *et al.*, Chapter 16), which was found

together with smithing hearth bottoms, slag and the second largest quantity of hammerscale (25g) from the entire Park Street site. The pottery from the pit contained one burnt blackware sherd and the lower part of a coarseware jar with overfired adhesions etc on the base. Both of these may have been occasioned by a high temperature industrial process. The possibility that the debris from this pit represents the waste from both the manufacture of knife blades and the hafting of knives is explored in Chapter 4.

The Phase 3.1 pits in Areas A and B were all contained within a single burgage plot running back from the Park Street frontage. The southwest side of this plot abutted the rear of the plots fronting onto Digbeth. The major medieval boundary ditch F174/ F201, which defined the rear of the Digbeth plots but had been infilled since at least the 14th century (see Park Street Phase 1 above), appears to have been recut around the time the pits were dug. A substantial amount of pottery was found within the fill (1166) of the recut (F234). Most of the pottery was residual medieval, presumably derived from the original ditch fills. The dating of F234 depends on the presence of three blackware sherds, four iron-rich coarseware sherds, three late oxidised sherds (Fabrics lox1 and lox3), a Tudor Green sherd, and two yellow ware sherds. The coarseware appeared to be of 17th-century type. The blackware could be dated to the later

Phase	3			3.1			3.2			3.3		
	count	weight	mv	count	weight	mv	count	weight	mv	count	weight	mv
Fabric/Ware												
Roman?	2	5	1									
Residual Phase 1 pottery	28	360	3	72	700	7	21	384	6	10	107	2
Residual Phase 2 pottery	2	3		7	39	1	9	267	1	1	21	
blackware	10	91	1	26	266	2	72	1385	8	19	184	1
blackware/Midlands Purple							1	9		1	22	
creamware	1	2	1							3	50	1
coarseware (iron-poor)	6	291		8	213	1	89	4589	19	18	706	
coarseware/Midlands Purple							4	93	1			
coarseware (iron-rich)	4	126		12	608	2	34	2660	5	22	1398	4
flowerpot										1	9	
industrial slipware							1	7				
mottled ware							22	396	2	12	85	4
mottled ware?							1	5	1			
19th-century glazed wares	3	25								1	2	
pearlware							3	64	1	1	1	
refined body wares							2	10				
slip-coated ware				1	22		22	371	4	10	83	1
slipware										3	14	
slipware (feathered)							9	121	2			
slipware (embossed)							1	9	1			
slipware (three-colour)							2	51				
slipware (trailed)	1	6	1	1	28	1	4	91				
brown salt-glazed stoneware	2	15					8	89	1	4	61	
tin-glazed earthenware							4	25		4	6	
white salt-glazed stoneware							2	7	1	3	30	
yellow ware	3	8		19	153	2	10	161	3	6	43	3
Total	62	932	7	146	2029	16	321	10794	56	119	2822	16

Table 7.15 Park St; Area C, Phase 3 pottery.

16th–17th centuries. The fill 1166 therefore seemed to consist of late medieval or early post-medieval wares and residual medieval pottery and gives a *terminus ante quem* for the digging of F234 of the 17th century, assuming, of course, that the post-medieval pottery did not represent 'trample' into the fill. The absence of clay pipe in the fill may be significant.

Area C represents a distinct Park Street burgage plot from that represented by Areas A and B (see Rátkai, Chapter 4). This area also contained a series of pits dated ceramically to the 17th century (Phase 3.1) and thus broadly contemporary with the series described above from Areas A and B. However, in contrast to Area A, no pit fills were identified which could be dated wholly to the 16th century, so the pit sequence in Area C may have started somewhat later than that in Area A.

The pits in Area C assigned to Phase 3.1 were, from northwest to southeast, F829, F773, F789, F808, F761,

F765 and F803. Of these pits, only F773, F789 and F803 produced relatively substantial groups of pottery, 30, 35 and 38 sherds respectively. This was further enhanced by clay pipe deposition dates of 1680–1730 for F773 and 1650–1750 for F789 The other pits produced only between two and 13 sherds each.

Pit F829 is shown on the plans as cut by pit F819. The latter contained no pottery. Pit F829 contained three sherds from a blackware mug of 17th-century date and two residual medieval sherds. Pits F761, F765 and F803 also did not contain clay pipe. Pit F761 contained a rim sherd from a coarseware pancheon and a blackware mug or cup handle. Pit F765 was dated to the 17th century by four blackware sherds, although there were also six residual medieval and one 15th–16th-century late oxidised ware sherd (lox02). Pit F803 contained a substantial amount of residual medieval pottery together with sherds from a number of blackware drinking vessels

Fabric/Ware	count	weight	mv	Vessel form by rim count							
				bowl	cpj*	dish	drv*	hw*	jar	pancheon	platter
residual Phase 1 pottery	19	144	4		4						
residual Phase 2 pottery	1	36	1						1		
Blackware	50	2003	2				1	1			
brown salt-glazed stoneware	6	25									
Coarseware (iron-poor)	50	3196	14	10					3	1	
Coarseware (iron-rich)	19	1641	5	4					1		
Mottled ware	7	206	1					1			
Slip-coated ware	32	1440	9	5		3	1				
slipware (feathered)	22	443	3								3
slipware (embossed)	1	50									
slipware (three colour)	1	53									
slipware (trailed)	3	82	2			1					1
Tin-glazed earthenware	1	20									
Westerwald stoneware	1	4									
Total	213	9343	41	19	4	4	2	2	5	1	4

Table 7.16 Park St; pottery from F133/ F245, Phase 3.1.

Fabric/Ware	count	weight	mv	Vessel form by rim count							
				bowl	chpot*	dish	drv*	jar	platter	plate	?
Residual Phase 1 pottery	1	5									
blackware	15	214	1		1						
brown salt-glazed stoneware	5	43	1				1				
coarseware (iron-poor)	30	1375	10	4		1		3			1
coarseware (iron-rich)	14	741	1	1							
industrial slipware	1	7									
mottled ware	9	140									
pearlware	3	64	1							1	
refined body ware	1	5									
slip-coated ware	8	171	2				1		1		
slipware (feathered)	6	63	1						1		
slipware (three-colour)	1	42									
slipware (trailed)	1	42									
white salt-glazed stoneware	1	6									
yellow ware	4	26									
Total	100	2997	17	5	1	1	2	3	2	1	1

Table 7.17 Park St; pottery from Pit F713, Phase 3.2.

(e.g. Fig. 7.8.185 and 188) a yellow ware hollow ware (Fig. 7.10.231) and a toffee brown-glazed coarseware. The latter may have been part of a cross-join with a sherd from the fill of pit F763. The final pit in this group F808 contained clay pipe with a deposition date of 1650–1730, four coarseware sherds, a small yellow ware sherd and residual medieval sherds.

Although no pottery was recorded from it (although a slipware sherd and a tin-glazed earthenware sherd were noted in the assessment), pit F702 was added to this

Fabric/ Ware	count	weight	mv	bottle?	bowl	dish	drv*	hw*	platter	teabowl	?
				Vessel form by rim count							
blackware	10	220	2	1				1			
coarseware (iron-poor)	18	597	2		2						
coarseware (iron-rich)	3	78									
industrial slipware	1	6									
mottled ware	16	395	3				1	2			
slip-coated ware	17	424	2			1					1
slipware (feathered)	18	572	1						1		
slipware (embossed)	1	10									
tin-glazed earthenware	4	20	1							1	
white salt-glazed stoneware	6	197	2		1	1					
Total	94	2519	13	1	3	2	1	3	1	1	1

Table 7.18 Park St; pottery from Pit F500, Phase 3.2.

Fabric/Ware	count	%	weight	%
Residual Phase 1 pottery	29	2.8	394	1.4
Residual Phase 2 pottery	12	1.2	185	<1.0
Agate ware	4	<1.0	10	<1.0
Blackware	199	19.4	2474	8.9
Blue underglaze painted pearlware	2	<1.0	10	<1.0
Bone China	1	<1.0	22	<1.0
Brown salt-glazed stoneware	41	4.0	590	2.1
Cane ware	7	<1.0	65	<1.0
Coarseware (iron-poor)	111	10.8	6302	22.7
Coarseware (iron-rich)	124	16.5	8626	31.0
Coarseware/Midlands purple ware	2	<1.0	91	<1.0
Creamware	170	16.5	1946	7.0
Grey salt-glazed stoneware	1	<1.0	23	<1.0
Grey stoneware	1	<1.0	15	<1.0
Industrial slipware	3	<1.0	47	<1.0
Miscellaneous	1	<1.0	5	<1.0
Mottled ware	40	3.9	663	2.4
Porcelain	1	<1.0	35	<1.0
Redware	1	<1.0	20	<1.0
Scratch blue	3	<1.0	13	<1.0
Slip-coated ware	124	16.5	2810	10.1
Slipware (feathered)	31	3.0	1727	6.2
Slipware (three-colour)	8	<1.0	292	1.0
Slipware (trailed)	7	<1.0	135	<1.0
Soft paste porcelain	2	<1.0	18	<1.0
Spanish olive jar	3	<1.0	121	<1.0
Sponged ware	1	<1.0	10	<1.0
Tin-glazed earthenware	12	1.2	112	<1.0
White salt-glazed stoneware	68	6.6	834	3.0
Yellow ware	19	1.9	229	<1.0
Total	1028	100.0	27824	100.0

Table 7.19 Park St; quantification of pottery from tank fills, Phase 3.3.

	Ceamware	White salt-glaze	Redware	Pearlware	Soft-paste porcelain	Porcelain	Brown salt-glazed stoneware	Grey salt-glazed stoneware	Agate ware	Grey stoneware	Whiteware	Yellow ware (cane ware)	Bone china	Miscellaneous	Total
plate/platter	1	2													3
soup plate	1														1
plate (10-inch)	13	4									4			1	22
plate (8-inch)		3													3
bowl	4	2		1		1	3		1		2				14
large bowl/basin	1	1													2
mug	4	1		1			1	1	1		1				10
jug	3	1	1	1			1					1			8
dish	1	4					2		2			2			11
undiagnostic											1	1			2
bottle/jar										1					1
teapot		1													1
teabowl	5	2													7
saucer	6	2			1								1		10
basket				1											1
salad dish	1														1
chamber pot	1														1
unknown							1								1
bellarmine							1								1
Total	41	23	1	4	1	1	9	1	4	1	8	4	1	1	100

(Quantification by rim/ base count)

Table 7.20 Park St; refined ware vessels from tanks and sealing layer 1505 by function, Phase 3.3.

group on the basis of the presence of clay pipe dating 1680–1730. The pit also contained an 18th-century bone gaming token, a comb (datable to the 17th or 18th century) and an earring (see Bevan *et al.*, Chapter 8, Fig. 8.4.1). As such, the pit would seem to date from the very end of Phase 3.1.

Pit F810 produced only medieval pottery but, due to its relationship with pit F808 and the presence of a fragment of crucible, was also assigned to the group.

Phase 3.2
The distribution of pits assigned to this sub-phase, the early and middle 18th century, contrasted with that of the pits assigned to Phase 3.1. They were mainly found in a broad band – with occasional outliers – aligned roughly parallel to Park Street but set back from the frontage and running through the middle of the plots. The pits also

tended to be somewhat smaller than those of the 17th century and, significantly, several contained fragments of crucible in addition to quantities of slag, the latter being a frequent component of the pit fills throughout Phase 3 (see Burrows *et al.*, Chapter 4).

There were two main clusters of Phase 3.2 pits, one in Area A and one in Area C. The Area A cluster comprised pits F259, F253, F133/ F245, F173 and F180, which appears from the plans to have been cut by F173. Pit F259 is anomalous in that it was the only pit that lay to the southwest (*i.e.* on the 'Digbeth side') of the F174/ F201/ F234 boundary ditch. Coincidentally, it was the only pit in this group not to contain clay pipe and the only one to contain sherds from 'formal dining wares'. Pit F133/ F245 is the most interesting in this group. The pit cut the edge of the Phase 1 ditch F174 etc, which

	Blackware	Coarseware (ron-poor)	Coarseware (iron-rich)	Mottled ware	Slipware (feathered)	Slipware (embossed)	Slipware (three colour)	Slip-coated ware	Tin glazed earthenware	Olive jar	Yellow ware	Total
Albarello									1			1
Bowl		15	8				1	3	1		1	28
Bowl/Dish		1						1				2
Dish								7				7
Drinking vessel	18		1					1				20
Flower pot		6										6
Hollow ware	13	1	1	4				2			1	21
Jar		1	4					1		1		7
Pancheon		1										1
Platter					2	4	1	2				9
unknown	1	5	1	3				2				
Total	32	23	21	8	2	4	2	19	2	1	2	102

Table 7.21 Park St; coarseware vessels from tanks by function, Phase 3.3.

presumably indicates that at least by the period 1700–1750 the ditch was completely backfilled. However, the presence of a 19th-century building, one of whose walls ran along the midline of the ditch, suggested that the boundary or division first represented by the ditch was respected into the modern period. Pit F133/ F245 contained industrial debris, including slag and crucibles. A crude hand-made vessel in a coarse orange fabric (Fig. 7.14.326) also came from the pit. It was unsooted but must have been used or intended for some industrial process. The pit contained a large pottery assemblage, which probably dated to *c*.1725–1750 and a variety of other artefacts including clay pipe, 17th-century bottles, an 18th-century buckle, wine glass fragments and 29 facetted glass stones. However, the clay pipe has a possible date range of 1620–1850 (Higgins, Chapter 9) and although some of the pipe is of the 17th century and first half of the 18th century in date, these fragments are in a poor condition, suggesting residuality. This is rather at variance with the pottery which was made up of large unabraded sherds. In addition, some of the better preserved clay pipe dated to the mid-18th century, which is not incompatible with the pottery, but a late 18th-century pipe bowl, in good condition, must surely be intrusive.

Another point of interest with the fill of F133/ F245 is that no 'formal dining wares' (see discussion below) were present. By the time of the backfill of the pit, white salt-

glazed stonewares would have been available for the best part of 30 years and creamware was first made in the 1750s. However, the Ravenscroft-style wine glass fragment (Fig. 8.3.7; see Orton and Rátkai, Chapter 8) is indicative of an affluent household of the sort which might be expected to use formal dining wares. There is therefore something of a lingering doubt about the nature of this fill.

Pit F259 contained a white salt-glazed stoneware plate and a small unidentifiable fragment, together with a slip-coated ware dish. Pit 173 contained a mix of pottery broadly similar to that from F133/ F245, as did pit F180. Pits F173 and F180 had suggested clay pipe deposition dates of 1720–1780 and 1710–1740 respectively; like pit F133/ F245, neither contained any formal dining wares, unlike pit F259.

In Area C the pits assigned to Phase 3.2 were F713, F700, F763, F769, F764, F762, F811, F828 and F745.

Clay pipe evidence suggests fill dates of 1680–1730 for F763, F769, F764, F762. With the exception of F763, which contained only a mottled ware sherd and a residual medieval sherd, the pottery from the other pits was dominated by blackware drinking vessels and iron-poor coarseware bowls or pancheons. Odd slipware, mottled ware and yellow ware sherds were also found in these pits. Further links between these pits was evidenced by a number of cross-joins.

Pit F713 produced 100 sherds and appeared to date to

	Blackware	Brownsalt-glazed stoneware	Coarseware (iron-poor)	Coarseware (iron-rich)	Mottled ware	Slipware (feathered)	Slipware (embossed)	Slipware (trailed)	Slip-coated ware	Yellow ware	German stoneware	White salt-glazed stoneware	Creamware	Blue shell edge pearlware	Total
Bowl		1	21	16					7	2					47
Handled bowl			1												1
Chafing dish	1														1
Dish	1		1					2	6	1					11
Drinking vessel	29	1			1				4			1			36
Hollow ware	18	1	3	6	7				6	2					43
Jar			9	4	1										14
Pancheon			2	1											3
Plate											1	1			2
Platter						5	1		3						9
Flatware									1						1
Porringer									2						2
albarello										1					1
unidentified	3	1		2	2				1				3	1	13
Total	52	4	37	29	11	5	1	2	29	7	1	2	3	1	184

Table 7.22 Park St; vessel function Area A Park St, Phase 3.

c.1725–50. However, included amongst the pit group were three pearlware sherds and an industrial slipware sherd. The absence of any creamware sherds, suggests that the industrial slipware and the pearlware sherds were probably intrusive. Clay pipe within the fill is consistent with a fill date of 1680–1730 but with a small intrusive late 18th- or early 19th-century component, consistent with the pottery evidence. The situation of F713, adjacent to a Phase 4 building and a pit (F706) dated to the 19th century, makes intrusion not implausible. Blackwares were not so well represented in the fill as in the other Phase 3.2 pits described above but iron-poor coarsewares were still very well represented. A single white salt-glazed handle was found in this group.

Pit F700 produced a similarly large assemblage of 85 sherds. Unlike most of the Phase 3 pits there was a marked residual component in this group dating from the medieval to the early post-medieval period, including sherds from a large Cologne stoneware jug. The clay pipe evidence also attests to a residual component but a number of bowl fragments suggest that the pit was backfilled in the period 1740–70. The much smaller group of pottery from F769 (15 sherds) suggested a date of c.1700. Pits F762, F763 and F811 were dated to the later 17th–early/mid-18th centuries, as was pit F745 close to the frontage. However, the latter was somewhat anomalous. Clay pipe evidence indicated a residual component dating to 1660–1680 which was not particularly recognisable in the admittedly small group of pottery. The remaining clay pipe was dated to the 18th–early 19th centuries. Pit F762 was a large pit evidently dug to remove a brick-lined well, F806. The well contained pottery indicating a similar date range, but is assigned to Phase 3.1 in the narrative by virtue of the fact that it is likely to have been constructed in this earlier period. Pits F764 and F828 probably dated to the 18th century. The latter was dated to 1710–1740 on clay pipe evidence.

There were only two pits in Area B assigned to Phase 3.2. Pit F500 contained a substantial assemblage of pottery (94 sherds) indicating an infilling date of c.1725–50. The pottery from this pit is quantified in Table 7.17. The fill contained no pottery which need be later than c.1750, the white salt-glazed stoneware representing the latest pottery in the group. The pit also contained a bone handle and a wine bottle dated to 1700–1740. The pit fill is notable for having the greatest concentration of clay

	Blackware	Brown salt-glazed stoneware	Coarseware (iron-poor)	Coarseware (iron-rich)	Mottled ware	Slipware (feathered)	Slip-coated ware	Tin glazed earthenware	White salt-glazed stoneware	Creamware	Total
Albarello								1			1
Bottle?	1										1
Bowl			2	1				1	1		5
Dish							1				1
Drinking vessel	4				2						6
Hollow ware	1	1	4	1	2						9
Hollow ware (handled)			2								2
Jar				1							1
Pancheon				1							1
Plate										1	1
Platter						1					1
Strainer					1						1
Teabowl									1		1
Total	6	1	8	4	5	1	1	3	1	1	31

Table 7.23 Park St; vessel function Area B excluding tank fills, Phase 3.

pipes (227 fragments) from anywhere on Park Street, which probably suggest a deposition date of the mid–late 18th century. An early 19th-century industrial slipware sherd, weighing only 4g, was found in this group and must be intrusive, the proximity of the baulk edge to this feature making contamination a real possibility. The second Phase 3.2 pit in Area B contained sherds from two blackware vessels, one a mug, four mottled ware sherds, three from a strainer, two small white salt-glazed stoneware sherds, two small, undiagnostic, refined body sherds and a tin-glazed earthenware bowl sherd. The tin-glazed earthenware bowl had been ground along the upper edge. This presumably represents an attempt to repair, or make usable, a vessel whose rim had become chipped or damaged in some way. Surprisingly, in view of the care and time spent on the repair, the bowl was undecorated. A suggested deposition date of 1740–1780 for the fill, given by the clay pipe, would seem to be about right, with c.1740–1760 being perhaps the more likely.

Phase 3.3
'Industrial' pits apparently dating to the later 18th century/ early 19th century were only identified in Area A, where six pits were uncovered which, both spatially and in their character, appear to form a continuation of

activity documented by the Phase 3.2 pits here. The pits in question are F176, F177, F163, F194 and F193.

Three of these pits, F176, F177 and F163, had creamware and/ or pearlware in their fills, indicating a late 18th-century date. Clay pipe from these pits corroborates this dating. The fills of pit F194 contained comparatively little pottery, a total of eleven sherds, but with an average sherd weight of just over 29g suggesting near primary deposition. The lower fills (1242) and (1234) contained what appeared to be early 18th-century pottery, comprising slip-coated wares, coarseware, brown stoneware and trailed slipware (a dark-on-light slipware platter). Fill 1234 contained clay pipe with a suggested deposition date of 1680–1730, although Higgins (Chapter 9) notes that one fragment could be as late as 1750. The uppermost fill (1235), however, produced two creamware sherds and an iron-poor coarseware sherd and clay pipe dating to 1720–1780. The creamware dates the fill to the second half of the 18th century. In addition, pit F194 cut pit F193, which had an early 19th-century mocha ware sherd in its otherwise 18th-century fill, which included a Westerwald stoneware sherd. It is therefore difficult to escape from the conclusion that F193 and F194 were backfilled quite late in the site's history. It is, of course,

	Blackware	Brown salt-glazed stoneware	Coarseware (irin-poor)	Coarseware (iron-rich)	Coarseware/Midlands purple ware	Mottled ware	Slipware (feathered)	Slipware (embossed)	Slipware (three-colour)	Slipware (trailed)	Slip-coated ware	Tin glazed earthenware	Yellow ware	Creamware	Pearlware	Total
Albarello												1	1			2
Bowl	1	1	17	9		4			1	1	1		4	1		40
Chamber pot	1															1
Dish				1						1		1	1			4
Drinking vessel	25	3				3					2		1			34
Hollow ware	2					6					1		2			11
Jar			6	2	2						1					11
Pancheon			6	3												9
Plate														1	1	2
Platter							2	1		1	1					5
Strainer			1													1
Total	29	4	30	15	2	13	2	1	1	3	6	2	9	2	1	120

(quantification by minimum rim/ base count)

Table 7.24 Park St; vessel function Area C, Phase 3.

always possible that later pottery represents intrusion or trample into the pit fills. The proximity of pit F194 to the baulk makes contamination with later pottery a distinct possibility. There was also a cross-join between fill 1234 of pit F194 and fill 1125 of pit F133/ F245, the latter pit dated to the middle decades of the 18th century (see Phase 3.2 above).

Unfortunately, due to the excavation priorities, many of the late deposits were not studied in detail and it was assumed that the various buildings all dated to the 19th century. This now seems unlikely (see Rátkai, Chapter 4). Towards the Park Street frontage in Area C were two 19th-century pits F720 and F836 which post-dated Structures 2 and 4 respectively, and construction trenches F782 for Structure 5a and robbed out construction trench F784. A possible construction trench (fill 1755) for wall F738 of Structure 2 contained 25 sherds, all but two of post-medieval date. The group was made up mainly of large coarseware sherds. However there were also three creamware sherds in the group, probably dating to the 1760s or 1770s: one possibly from a large oval Queen's edge serving plate and a second from an over-glaze painted bowl (Fig. 7.25.5, colour). The third creamware sherd was too small to assign to vessel form. The creamware sherds are one of the few examples of 'formal dining wares' found outside the Area B tank fills.

Finds from F720 and F836 (see Bevan et al., Chapter 8, and Higgins, Chapter 9) dated the pit fills securely to the 19th century; however, both contained residual 17th–18th-century pottery. Construction trench F784 contained five sherds, the largest of these (42g) from a coarseware cistern; the remaining sherds comprised a yellow ware and coarseware sherd and two residual medieval sherds, together weighing only 13g. A date in the first half of the 17th century seems likely for the fill of F784. However, clay pipe evidence indicates that the backfilling more probably belongs to the second half of the 17th century. Construction trench F782 contained a coarseware base sherd and clay pipe with a likely deposition date of 1680–1730. A fuller description of the ceramic and artefactual evidence associated with the structures and their possible date is given in Chapter 4.

As will be seen below, the large assemblage of late 18th-century pottery from the two wood-lined tanks and pond in Area B suggests a house clearance towards the end of the century. The obvious building from which the pottery may have come is No. 3 Park Street recorded as the Phoenix Inn (see Rátkai, Chapter 4), although there

Context	1108			1520			1797		
	count	weight	mv	count	weight	mv	count	weight	mv
Fabric/Ware									
Roman							2	5	1
Residual Phase 1 pottery	4	37					9	84	3
Residual Phase 2 pottery	4	82					1	7	
Rhenish stoneware	1	5							
blackware	6	204	1	2	17	1			
blue shell edge	1	6	1						
brown salt-glazed stoneware	1	3							
coarseware (iron-poor)	2	252	1						
coarseware (iron-rich)				6	195	1	3	62	
creamware				4	51				
mottled ware	1	34	1	1	8	1			
slipware (embossed)				1	132	1			
slipware (feathered)	3	67							
slip-coated ware	2	49		3	84				
tin-glazed earthenware				1	7				
Total	25	679	4	18	494	4	15	158	4
Average sherd weight		27.16g			27.44g			10.53g	

Table 7.25 Park St; pottery from the 'Dark Earth' layers, Phase 3.

Fabric	brb A	brb B	brb C	msb	psb A	psb B	psb C
Deritend	4.6	7.4	4.7	13.5	4	2.2	14.7
Deritend cpj	7.9	4.3	7	6.5	76.4	10.9	16
DeritendR	19.5	28.1	41.9	38.3	8.4	24	28
cpj1	45.2	20.8	30.6	7.8	2	6.5	8.9
whitewares (ww1-4)	7	7.4	2.3	7.8	2.2	15.2	4.8

(quantification by percentage sherd count)

Table 7.26 Comparison of main pottery types from Edgbaston Street, Moor Street and Park Street in Phase 1.

are some difficulties with this conjecture. The Phoenix appears to have been in existence from *c*.1720 (McKenna 2006) but was rebuilt in the early 19th century. There is the possibility that the rebuilding and the pottery from the tanks are associated, although the pottery would have been around 40 years old when disposed of and possibly of rather too good a quality to be associated with an inn or tavern. Whatever the source of the pottery, it is certainly different from the early 19th-century pottery recovered from elsewhere on the site, which appears to be predominantly low-status or 'artisanal' in character. This is entirely in keeping with the court housing, which documentary and cartographic evidence show to have been built in the Park Street backplots (see Rátkai *ibid.*). In Area B only a small number of features or feature fills were assigned to Phase 3.3. The largest assemblage, a

more or less contemporary dump of material, came from the fill of tanks F503/ F520 and F542/ F510. This assemblage is discussed in detail below. The only other large group came from 1519, the upper fill of 'pond' F506. This could be dated to *c*.1760–1780. A single pipe stem of 18th- or early 19th-century date was found in the upper fill of F506 which also contained quite a high proportion of residual medieval material, but this presumably reflects the earlier backfilling of the feature. The fill is similar to the pottery from the backfilled tanks F503/ F520 and F542/ F510. It is possible that after the first backfilling of F506, attributed to Phase 2 (see above), there was some settling or slumping of the fills and that this was remedied by a further episode of backfilling in the later 18th century, probably at the same time that the tanks were backfilled.

The Park St tanks (F503/ F520 and F510/ F542)

by David Barker and Stephanie Rátkai

A large collection of pottery was found within the fills of the tanks (see Tables 7.19–7.21). The large sherd size and cross-joining sherds across the fills indicated that the pottery group probably represented a single dump of material. The consistency of the refined ceramics throughout all of the contexts also suggests strongly that these contexts were formed at more or less the same time. The impression is very much of the tanks having been filled in a short-lived, single deposition episode. In order to try to date this event accurately, and to assess the socio-economic significance of the group, the refined wares were examined in detail. This work was undertaken by David Barker of the Potteries Museum, Stoke-on-Trent.

Tank F510/ F542 was half sectioned. Section F542 had a sequence of fills – 1694, 1635, 1634, 1622 and 1621 in ascending order. Section F510 was removed as a single spit (1531). Tank F503/ F520 was also half sectioned and there were two fill sequences: 1532, 1521 and 1506 for F503; and 1680, 1580, 1533 and 1530 for F520 (in ascending order). The tanks were overlain by an extensive 19th-century sealing layer (1505), containing ceramics mainly dating to the 1830s–60s. A mid-17th-century chair (see Bevan *et al.*, Chapter 8) was found in the bottom of tank F503/ F520.

Clay pipes from the fills produced date ranges of 1680–1730 and 1760–1840 for tank F503/ F520. All the clay pipe was fragmentary and worn suggesting long exposure before burial. The latest bowl was, according to Higgins (Chapter 9), either late 18th century or possibly early 19th century. Tank F542/ F510 had a wider variety of clay pipe types, the earliest of which dated to 1690–1730, the remainder all dating to the 18th century. The pottery and clay pipe evidence together would therefore seem to suggest a deposition date before 1800.

Most fills contained *c.*1% residual medieval or late medieval/ early post-medieval transitional sherds. The exceptions to this were fills 1533 and 1622, which contained no pottery pre-dating the 17th century. Two tank fills, 1694 (F542) and 1680 (F520), contained only single medieval sherds in Fabrics ip3 and cpj5 respectively. Both these fills were bottommost in the tanks but it is unlikely that they date the disuse of the features since the tanks cut through a sand layer (1609) which contained two medieval sherds, a blackware drinking vessel sherd and a flower-pot base.

This assemblage contains 100 refined ware vessels and is dominated by three main 18th-century ware types – creamware (41 vessels), white salt-glazed stoneware (23 vessels), and brown salt-glazed stoneware including one late 17th-century Bellarmine or bartmann-type bottle (nine vessels). In addition, there are four agate ware vessels, two of pearlware, and one each of grey salt-glazed stoneware, redware, soft-paste porcelain, oriental

porcelain, and an unusual lead-glazed earthenware type which is not precisely identified. There are also some 19th-century vessels from layers 1505, which sealed the tanks, including two of pearlware, eight of whiteware, one of bone china, four of yellow ware (cane ware) and one of Bristol-glazed grey stoneware (vessels are listed by minimum vessel equivalent). These counts are based primarily upon different rims; bases have only been used when they are clearly distinct vessels, whose inclusion does not interfere with the rim counts). In order to make the function figures for the refined wares and coarsewares comparable, a combined minimum rim/ base count has been used for all the Phase 3 pottery from Park Street.

The remainder of the group was made up of iron-rich and iron-poor coarseware, slip-coated ware, blackware, yellow ware, feathered, trailed and embossed slipware, tin-glazed earthenware, mottled ware, a Spanish olive jar and flower-pot, together with the medieval and late medieval/ early post-medieval wares.

In addition to the small amounts of residual medieval and late medieval/ early post-medieval transitional material, the fills also contained a small amount of 17th-century pottery, mainly blackware drinking vessels (similar to Fig. 7.8.186, 193), the base of a small cup from fill 1580, and a blackware vessel with an applied 'festoon'. The yellow ware is also likely to be predominantly 17th century. However, it is difficult to date with any accuracy small blackware, yellow ware and coarseware body sherds. Secondly, some of the post-medieval wares span the later 17th to early/ mid-18th centuries. It is therefore very difficult to say how much pottery, if any, dates to the same period as the chair found abandoned in tank F503/ F520. However, the greater part of the assemblage appears to be of 18th-century date and under the circumstances it seems most sensible, in this context, to ascribe an 18th-century date to wares dating to the later 17th–18th centuries, such as mottled wares, feathered slipwares, *etc.*

Tank F503/ F520 contained fewer rim and base sherds than F510/ F542. Bowls, jars and platters were the best represented forms. An iron-poor coarseware jar (similar to Fig. 7.12.278), possibly of 17th-century date, and two iron-rich coarseware large capacity vessels, sometimes known as 'pans' (Fig. 7.12.275), of 18th-century date were found in F503/ F520. The coarseware bowls had flange rims and were similar in form to Fig. 7.13.286. Most of the remaining coarseware sherds could not be ascribed to form with any certainty, although at least one of the vessels had a horizontal handle.

Despite the paucity of rim and base sherds, blackware body sherds represented at least seven drinking vessels, including a small cup base, and at least a further eight drinking vessels were represented in mottled ware. A hook rim bowl (Fig. 7.13.305) was found in slip-coated ware and body sherds represented a dish, a bowl or dish and possibly a platter. Two sherds may have been from a drinking vessel. Pie-crust edge platters were represented in feathered slipware (Fig. 7.23.1, colour), in three-colour (yellow, tan and dark brown) slipware and by body sherds in trailed slipware.

In the second tank (F510/ F542) blackware vessels were rather better represented. They comprised a 17th-century mug from fill 1621 and two drinking vessel rim fragments. From the fabric, glaze and overall finish, one appeared to be 17th century, from fill 1635, the other 18th century, from fill 1634. A minimum of 20 drinking vessels (16 by minimum rim/ base count) were represented from all the fills. One mug was decorated with a festoon. There were a number of 'rebated' blackware tankard bases (*e.g.* Fig. 7.8.204) and several vessels resembling Fig. 7.8.196 from fill 1622 (F542). Both forms are almost certainly of 18th-century date. Another 18th-century blackware drinking vessel, a rounded cup (Fig. 7.8.194) was found in the fill of a pipe trench (F505) cutting the tank. A more barrel-shaped mug (Fig. 7.8.190), possibly slightly earlier in date, was the only example of this form from the tanks. Two sherds may have come from a jug, which is more likely to have been a 17th-century form.

Iron-rich coarsewares were represented by a bowl with a horizontal handle (Fig. 7.12.274), a sloping sided bowl (Fig. 7.11.266), an undiagnostic hollow ware sherd and six large flower-pots similar to ones manufactured at Floodgate Street, Digbeth, in the 18th century (see Rátkai 2002a). An iron-poor 'splay-rimmed' dish or bowl (similar to Fig. 7.13.287) may have been either a slip-coated ware or an iron-poor coarseware. In total, ten iron-poor coarseware bowls were represented. Most of the remaining sherds were not assignable to form, the exception being a possible jar sherd and two very thick-bodied sherds with an internal black glaze, presumably from large storage jars. Slip-coated wares were better represented in this tank. Forms consisted of shallow bowls or dishes (Fig. 7.13.298, 299), a pie-crust rim bowl (Fig. 7.13.304), a hook rim bowl (Fig. 7.13.306), a hook rim hollow ware (Fig. 7.13.307), a plain everted rim hollow ware (Fig. 7.13.308), and a collar-rim hollow ware (Fig. 7.14.309). At least five further shallow bowls or dishes like those illustrated were represented by body sherds, and two further vessels like Fig. 7.13.307. Four more hook rim hollow wares, a jug handle and a strainer were present.

Rims from two slip-decorated platters with pie-crust rims came from the tank (Fig. 7.20.2, colour, Fig. 7.23.1, colour) and the rim of a flange rim bowl (Fig. 7.21.1, colour), which was decorated with trailed and feathered slip. A dark-on-light slip trailed bowl was also found in the tanks (Fig. 7.21.4, colour). The decorative treatment of the rim is somewhat unusual and this, coupled with the dark brown glaze, makes a date in the first half of the 18th century more likely. The remaining rim sherds were from a tin-glazed earthenware albarello and bowl, both undecorated, from a yellow ware splay-sided bowl (similar to Fig. 7.9.216) and from an undiagnostic yellow ware hollow ware.

The functional composition (Tables 7.20–21) of the tank fills has been analysed as a single group since there is evidence to suggest that the fills represent a single dump of material.

The coarseware group (Table 7.21) was dominated by bowls, platters and dishes. The bowls could be broadly divided into two groups. The first comprised basic utilitarian coarseware vessels associated with the preparation of food. The second group was made up of slip-coated ware bowls which were thinner walled and either splay-sided with a flange rim or rounded with a hook rim. These were more likely to have been kitchen wares than table wares and could have been associated with both the preparation and consumption of food in an 'informal' setting. Two further bowls were represented in tin-glazed earthenware and light-on-dark trailed slipware. These were more likely to be table wares associated with the serving or consumption of food, as were the slipware and slip-coated ware platters (although see below). Other kitchen or utilitarian wares were represented by, sometimes very large, storage vessels such as the coarseware jars. A slip-coated ware body sherd from a strainer was also recorded. Some of the slip-coated ware hollow wares may have come from jars also but the number would be insufficient to redress the predominance of utilitarian vessels for food preparation rather than food storage. A third class of vessel, for liquid consumption, was mainly represented by blackware mugs.

Throughout the 18th century, mugs, bowls and dishes would probably have been used at the table for the consumption of food and drink, in conjunction with vessels of pewter, wood and horn, by most households. They should not, however, be seen as 'table wares' in the sense of the mid-18th-century and later matching sets of plates, dishes, etc, which suggest a more formal approach to dining. A role in food preparation is equally possible for vessels such as bowls and dishes, three of which from the tanks show signs of burning or sooting. A slip-coated ware platter was burnt, but this could have been post-discard. A further slip-coated ware ?platter and a feathered slipware platter were sooted externally. A blackware mug also had heavy external sooting below the glaze, suggesting the heating of its contents. The above shows that the perceived function of vessels is not always borne out by the archaeological evidence.

Perhaps the most surprising vessel from the tanks was a possible olive jar (found in fills 1531 and 1622 of F510/ F542). The sherds were sent for petrological analysis (Williams, Appendix 7.1) and the metamorphic rocks present in the specimens were found to be consistent with an Andalucian source, although not the Guadalquivir Valley. Very little of the vessel survived but it was presumably post-medieval in date.

Typically, the refined wares occur as table wares, tea wares, toilet wares, and as other drinking vessels. The table wares occur as creamwares and white salt-glazed stonewares (see Fig. 7.14.314–24 and Figs 7.24–7.27, colour). In the latter are both 10-inch and 8-inch plates (three examples of each) with plain circular or moulded edge patterns. Barleycorn, basketwork, star/ diaper and other moulded edge designs, well known in white salt-glazed stoneware, are represented here. There are two rim sherds of larger plates or platters. The creamware plates have 'royal', 'queen's', feather, scalloped and fleurs-de-lys, or concave edges, and there are two sherds of a circular plate with an unusual single shallow groove or line around its edge. There is at least one oval platter with a royal edge and a probable soup plate, also with a royal edge. A creamware lobed salad dish and two round-bodied bowls or dishes with rolled rims are also table wares, as are four white salt-glazed stoneware dishes. There are no further obvious table wares, such as tureens, sauce boats or vegetable dishes, in these two types, although a single sherd of a basket form in under-glaze blue-painted pearlware would probably have been used at the table, perhaps for serving fruit.

Tea wares are well represented. The creamwares include five teabowls with plain (three) and beaded rouletted (one) rims, and a single example with a moulded narrow-ribbed exterior. There are six saucers, one of which has internal moulded fluted decoration. Hemispherical bowls are likely to have been used as slop bowls in tea drinking, and at least one of three creamware jugs is probably a milk jug. There are two teabowls and two saucers in white salt-glazed stoneware, as well as three hemispherical bowls which are likely to have been slop bowls. The only probable teapot in the assemblage is in white salt-glazed stoneware; it is round-bodied with moulded trailing vine leaves and stems, and would have stood on three lion's mask and paw feet, one of which survives (Fig. 7.27.4, colour). Moulded teapot forms in white salt-glazed stoneware are well known in today's museum and private collections, but no parallel for this can be cited. One redware jug is of a size to have been a large milk jug, but the only other vessel definitely associated with tea drinking is a soft-paste porcelain saucer with under-glaze blue-painted floral decoration.

Other creamware forms include four cylindrical mugs, a possible basin or large bowl and a chamber pot handle (Fig. 7.14.314, 316, 322).

Mugs are also found in brown salt-glazed stoneware (one example, Fig. 7.14.313), as are bowls (three examples, Fig. 7.14.311), dishes (two examples, Fig. 7.14.312), a jug, and a globular-bodied vessel with a rolled rim whose precise function is not known (Fig. 7.14.310). It is doubtful if the brown salt-glazed stoneware bowls were related to tea drinking, as any other tea wares are extremely rare in this type during the 18th century. They are more likely to relate to food preparation activities. The use to which a small, crudely made oriental porcelain bowl was put cannot be known.

Other vessels likely to be connected to food consumption are two dishes and one bowl (the last with slip decoration) in agate ware (Fig. 7.27.5–6, colour). A further mug, also with slip decoration, is in agate ware, while another is in a grey salt-glazed stoneware with a thin brown iron wash to the exterior.

The majority of the assemblage dates to the 1760s to 1780s, with most falling within the 1770s. The presence of just two pearlware vessels (*e.g.* Fig. 7.27.3, colour) suggests that the deposition of the assemblage took place before this type of ware became common in the late 1770s and 1780s. (Another pearlware vessel is later, dating to *c.*1820; a fourth is probably later still and is arguably better described as a whiteware.) Pearlware is known to have been introduced around 1775 (Miller 1987, 85–90) and is present in very large quantities in the pre-1782 phase of the excavated waster dump of William Greatbatch, potter, of Fenton, Stoke-on-Trent (Barker 1991, 165, 198–203).

The white salt-glazed stonewares are difficult to date precisely, having been in production over a period of 70 to 80 years, from *c.*1720 to *c.*1790 or later. Their association here with creamwares is significant, the smaller proportion present showing that by the time of deposition creamwares were the dominant ceramic type. The same is true of the brown salt-glazed stonewares, whose forms and decoration seem to change little over the course of the 18th century.

A small number of the creamwares are of the darker cream colour which seems to be more characteristic of the 1760s (Barker 1991, 176), but the majority are lighter in colour. The change to lighter-coloured creamwares, involving improvements in both glazes and bodies, occurred around 1770, although domestic assemblages typically contain examples of the darker ware as late as the early 19th century (Barker and Barker 1984, 88).

The feather moulding occurring here on creamware plates was very commonly used throughout the 1760s and 1770s (Fig. 7.14.324 and Fig. 7.24.4, colour); the 'queen's' edge is more typical of the 1760s (Fig. 7.24.1, colour), but was still made into the 1770s. The 'royal' edge, by contrast, does not seem to appear until *c.*1770, but then it remains common into the 19th century. The scalloped edge with fleurs-de-lys moulding (Fig. 7.24.3, colour) had a much shorter life, first appearing in the late 1760s in a darker cream colour, but being more typically produced in the lighter ware, although apparently not much beyond 1780. This is one of the most common edge patterns found on the creamwares of Phase 3 of William Greatbatch's Fenton waster dump, dating to *c.*1770–1782 (Barker 1991, 179–80), but it was absent in the earlier dumping phases. Examples in the darker cream colour were recovered from the wreck of the Ledbury, which sank off the coast of Florida in 1769 (Barker 1991, 179).

The turned, banded decoration found on the creamwares is very common during the 1770s phase (Phase 3) of dumping on the Greatbatch site, although they were by no means absent earlier (Barker 1991, 18–187). Also relatively common in the 1770s on the Greatbatch site were creamwares with under-glaze painted decoration in alternating stripes and spots in browns, yellows and other colours; this type may have had a short life beyond 1780, and a single teapot so decorated was recovered in a c.1810 domestic rubbish pit group at Haregate Hall in Leek, Staffordshire (Barker and Barker 1984, 103, fig. 8.1).

One other diagnostic feature identified amongst the creamware sherds is an impressed maker's mark on a plate base from sealing layer 1505. This reads 'TURNER' and is the mark used by John Turner of Lane End (modern Longton), Stoke-on-Trent, during the 1770s and 1780s (Godden 1964, 626). This is the only maker's mark in the assemblage.

The agate wares are at the coarser end of the quality spectrum; they are not uncommon in collections or in excavated assemblages, but their precise dating is uncertain at present. Suffice to say here that they are probably of the period 1760–1800.

The soft-paste porcelain teabowl is in a style which was common during the 1760s and 1770s, but beyond this it is not possible to be more precise.

Most of the 19th-century wares are from layer 1505, which sealed the tanks, although a pearl/ whiteware bowl with blue sponged decoration, which should date to the 1830s, is from 1634, a fill of tank F510/ F542. The later wares from layer 1505 include a pearlware slip-decorated mug of c.1820; whitewares, most with printed patterns, belonging to the 1820s to mid-19th century; and four yellow ware (or Derbyshire caneware) vessels, which date to roughly the same period. A Bristol-glazed grey stoneware vessel (?jar or bottle) is also from layer 1505. Bristol glaze, introduced in 1831, does not become common until after 1835 (Green 1999, 159), after which date it is ubiquitous on sites of all types.

A number of whitewares, yellow wares and a grey stoneware sherd in 1505 are clearly later in date than the rest of the assemblage and have been introduced as a result of later activity on the site.

Unlike the ceramics which survive in modern collections, most of the wares produced during the mid- to late 18th century were undecorated. This is clearly seen in the Park Street assemblage, in which only a handful of the creamwares have over-glaze decoration. There are just two creamware sherds (from 1621) with decoration, one a saucer (Fig. 7.25.4, colour), the other a hollow ware of indeterminate form; the saucer has a painted edge pattern of running arcs in red, together with a floral pattern in red and olive green, while the other sherd has a stylised floral pattern in red and black. A similar sherd was found in F738 (Fig. 7.25.5 colour).

Under-glaze painted decoration is found on a single creamware saucer (Fig. 7.25.1, colour) and a pearlware jug or similar. The forms comprise crudely painted stripes and dots in light brown, dark brown and green, while the pearlware bears the remains of an oriental landscape pattern in blue. A later pearlware mug has banded slip decoration in brown, combined with three different roulette patterns. A creamware mug has marbled slip

decoration in dark brown, light brown and white. One other vessel with traces of slip decoration is a yellow ware jug, or similar, of the 1830s to 1840s. These slip-decorated wares were consistently the cheapest decorated wares of their day until, that is, the introduction of sponge-decorated wares; one sponged pearl- or whiteware bowl sherd was found in fill 1634 of tank F510/ F542. A few creamwares have green glaze applied patchily as a decorative effect.

Lathe-turned decoration, taking the form of horizontal lines of varying widths, is found on the creamwares, including a mug, a possible jug, a chamber pot and a bowl. A variation of this is turned and diced decoration which uses a dicing lathe. Two of the agate wares, a bowl and a mug, each have an external white slip coat which has been diced and also, in the case of the mug, is rouletted to reveal the colour of the agate clay body beneath. Rouletting is used on a range of creamwares including, in this group, a bowl rim, a bowl base, a mug rim and a teabowl rim; it also occurs on some of the brown salt-glazed stonewares.

None of the salt-glazed stonewares have over-glaze painted decoration – this is not unusual – but there are three vessels with scratch blue decoration (Fig. 7.27.1, colour), whereby a pattern is incised or scratched into the unfired clay body of a vessel and is then coloured with a cobalt-rich mixture, probably painted on as a slip; the excess is removed from around the scratched design and the vessel is then fired and salt-glazed.

The 19th-century whitewares from sealing layer 1505 display the tendency of ceramics of this date to be preferred with decoration. In this case it is mostly printed decoration, including plates with 'willow' in blue and 'sea leaf' in green.

The refined wares are, for the most part, typical of the wares produced in north Staffordshire, but this does not rule out the possibility that some of the Park Street wares originated at other ceramic manufacturing centres. Similar creamwares, white salt-glazed stonewares and redwares were being produced at other manufacturing centres in the country. In the Midlands, the main competitor to the growing north Staffordshire industry was at Derby, and there the limited evidence available suggests that identical wares were produced during the 1750s to 1770s. Certainly, there is nothing in the assemblage to suggest that the creamwares and white salt-glazed stonewares were made anywhere other than Stoke-on-Trent and, indeed, the presence of a north Staffordshire maker's mark supports this conclusion. The single redware vessel is likely to be a Staffordshire product. Even the majority of the refined 19th-century whitewares and the bone china saucer are likely to be Staffordshire products.

For other wares, the situation is different. The 19th-century yellow wares, or canewares as they were often referred to in their day, are most likely to have originated in south Derbyshire, where the main centre for the production of these distinctive buff-bodied, yellow-glazed wares was the town of Swadlincote and its immediate environs. Other potteries in Derbyshire or perhaps Nottingham/ Nottinghamshire were the source of the brown salt-glazed stonewares, while a grey salt-glazed stoneware mug was from London or Bristol.

The agate wares, with or without slip, cannot be precisely sourced; they were made in Staffordshire and, it seems, other centres. The single Bristol-glazed grey stoneware vessel is also difficult to source.

Of the two porcelain vessels, one – the soft paste saucer – is English; it was probably made at Liverpool. The other is a crude hard-paste porcelain which is a Chinese provincial product (Fig. 7.14.325). Its presence in this assemblage is a surprise.

The composition of the Park Street assemblage is as one would expect for the late 1770s or early 1780s. A similar range of wares can be seen in a large domestic pit group excavated in St Mary's Grove, Stafford (Kershaw 1987), which is slightly earlier in date. It, too, contains a range of contemporary ceramic types, comparatively few of which are decorated. A date of *c*.1770 to 1775 has been suggested for this group on account of the greater proportion of white salt-glazed stonewares to creamwares, and the darker cream colour of most of the creamwares. Moreover, there are no pearlwares in the Stafford assemblage. The other fine wares include brown salt-glazed stonewares, soft-paste and oriental porcelains, and blackwares.

The tank assemblage reflects the growing popularity and availability of ceramics in the years after *c*.1760. At this time it was creamware which marked the way forward. With creamware, pottery manufacturers were able to produce an affordable ceramic type which was of a sufficiently good quality to have widespread appeal. Josiah Wedgwood's well-known promotion of his own creamware, marketed as 'Queensware', brought lead-glazed earthenwares into the homes of the gentry and middle classes in a way that had not been previously possible. The increased production of creamware plates noted by Barker (1991, 178) represents the increased consumption of ceramic table wares, probably at the expense of pewter, from the late 1760s or early 1770s. The St Mary's Grove, Stafford, group does not obviously reflect this as its plates are predominantly of white salt-glazed stoneware, although it may indicate a household's upgrade of old-fashioned table wares. The Park Street table wares, by contrast, are predominantly of creamware (at least 15 vessels compared to nine in white salt-glazed stoneware). Tea drinking at Park Street was also dominated by creamware (eleven vessels to five in white salt-glazed stoneware). Current trends in ceramic consumption were clearly being followed.

The presence of vessels in brown salt-glazed stoneware, blackware and slip-coated ware reflects the need for a range of utilitarian domestic vessels which were unlikely to be used at the tea or dinner tables, rather than competition between ceramic types or ceramic manufacturing centres. Creamwares or white salt-glazed stonewares and brown stonewares, blackwares and slip-coated wares were used together in the later 18th-century house, but in different ways. Domestic activities extended beyond the more formal 'front-of-house' activities of dining and tea drinking, to 'backstage' activities of food preparation and food storage, not to mention the regular consumption of beverages other than tea, as probably represented by the presence here of cylindrical mugs in both brown salt-glazed stoneware, creamware and drinking vessels in slip-coated ware and blackware.

The combination of refined-bodied wares and utilitarian or coarseware vessels is germane to the possible source of the vessels in the tank fills. Clearly the greater part of the pottery is more or less contemporary and dates to the 1770s–1780s. This suggests that the slipwares were either contemporary, or may have been residual, or had been curated. The curation could take the form of preservation for the intrinsic value or aesthetic appeal of the pottery, or mark the transfer of a ware seen as 'table ware' earlier in the century to a kitchen use when no longer seen as fashionable. Clearly, there were also elements within the tank groups which were residual. Some of this material must have been derived from stray, ground-scatter sherds in the Park Street backplot. The presence of the mid-17th-century chair in tank F503/ F520 suggests an act of clearance and dumping. The chair could have been damaged or could have been a victim of fashion. Could the disposal of the pottery within the tank fills similarly reflect the disposal of pottery which was no longer in style? This seems unlikely in view of the utilitarian and coarseware component in the group, unless of course the refined-bodied wares were also out of fashion and had been relegated to low-status use. In the latter case, this would make the backfilling of the tanks rather later than the date of the ceramics themselves, although presumably before the 1830s, based on the evidence of the sealing layer 1505. There is no evidence that the chair was deposited in the tank in the 17th century, although the presence of 17th-century clay pipe and the small amount of 17th-century pottery may indicate that there was a dump of material more or less contemporary with the chair. This could, for example, have accumulated in a cellar and have all been cleared out together. The differing dates of the pottery could then reflect contemporary clearances but from different parts of the same building. Documentary and photographic evidence suggests that the No. 3 Park Street (the Phoenix Tavern), behind which the tanks were situated, was rebuilt in the early 19th century and such a clearance might then be associated with this, although the evidence is equivocal.

Park St; Functional analysis of the Phase 3 pottery (Tables 7.20–7.24)

The following functional analysis is quantified by minimum rim/ base count of vessels.

Functional analysis of the Phase 3 pottery from Park Street is dominated by the assemblage from Area B, and in particular by the group from the tank fills (see discussion above). However, the remainder of the pottery comes almost exclusively from pits, and the absolute quantity of pottery from these in each area occurs in rough proportion to the number of pits, *i.e.* Areas A and C dominate over Area B.

Just under a third of the Phase 3 assemblage in Area A was made up of utilitarian coarsewares (Table 7.13) the greater number of which were composed of bowls or pancheons (Table 7.22). A similar pattern was seen in Area C (Table 7.15, Table 7.24), although jars were even less well represented. Coarsewares formed about a quarter of both the group from the tanks and from the remaining Area B contexts but bowls and pancheons were still better represented than jars. Thus in all areas the coarseware vessels seem to have been primarily associated with food preparation rather than storage. In Area A and in Area C a small number of the coarseware sherds, both bowls and jars, were sooted. It is just possible that the coarsewares were somehow used in, or were essential to, some of the industrial processes, although this is not very convincing. It was, however, more common for the coarsewares to be abraded, often quite heavily. This abrasion could be on the interior and/ or exterior of the vessels. The most common type of wear pattern was found on the exterior of bowl bases. This consisted of a narrow band around the circumference of the base, which had been worn smooth. This indicates that there had been vigorous mixing of substances within the bowl, causing friction between the base edge and the work surface. This wear pattern is seen, although less frequently, on coarsewares from normal domestic assemblages and need not represent anything other than normal kitchen use.

In Area A, at least 20% of vessels were associated with food consumption *e.g.* dishes, platters and bowls. This percentage figure excludes bowls and dishes made in coarseware and also assumes that remaining bowls and dishes were not used as kitchen wares for cooking or baking. Around 20% of vessels were associated with liquid consumption. Evidence for formal dining wares was negligible consisting as it did of a single white salt-glazed stoneware plate rim, a creamware bowl rim and a blue feather-edge pearlware plate. Area A was the only area to produce sherds from a chafing dish and a dripping tray, both of which were 17th century in date.

In Area C, vessels for liquid consumption were much better represented, at just under 30% of the group. Roughly 17% of vessels were associated with food consumption. As with Area A, formal dining wares were poorly represented and consisted of the rim from a creamware plate. This paucity was also represented in the overall sherd count for white salt-glazed stoneware and creamware from these areas (Table 7.15). In contrast, formal dining wares and tea wares were better represented in the Area B contexts other than the tank fills (Tables 7.14, 7.23). Drinking vessels comprised over 20% but vessels for 'ordinary' food consumption were not as well represented as in other areas. When the entire Area B rim/ base count figures are combined, formal dining and tea wares form about a third of the group. This sets Area B apart from the other two areas.

The near absence of white-bodied table and tea wares from Areas A and C is striking, and is in marked contrast to the Area B assemblage. In the latter, ordinary drinking vessels such as blackware mugs form less than 10% of the group by rim/ base count. There is a possibility that some, perhaps many, of the drinking vessels found in Areas A and C may have been used by labourers. 'Hot' industrial processes such as glass blowing and foundry work are well known for generating thirst, and glass blowers, for example, were given a beer allowance for consumption during the working day. At the post-medieval glassworks in Rugeley, most of the pottery found there was from drinking vessels (pers. comm. Chris Welch). Other artefactual evidence from Park Street, *e.g.* crucibles, hammerscale and slag, attests to hot industrial processes on or close by the site. Hartley discusses 'trade cooking' and notes that 'Iron workers, by reason of the furnace heat, learnt much about light beers and strengthening ales and liquors' (1985, 232–4). One can well imagine that, in this case, learning must have occasioned a certain amount of pleasure. If the drinking vessels were primarily used by labourers it is not impossible that some of the other vessels, for example the dishes, were also used by them. There is little solid evidence for how ordinary working people behaved in the course of a working day. They must have eaten but what form the food would have taken and where it was consumed are matters for conjecture. Would it have been bread and cold meat or cheese, or something more substantial? At the end of the 18th century, Colonel Byng (Adamson 1996, 359) noted what seems to be a rather modern-sounding provision of a lunch hour for the pottery workers at Wedgwood's Etruria manufactory but further details are absent. Oral history and personal reminiscences indicate that in the last century children were often despatched to the works with a covered plate containing 'father's dinner'. Could a similar system have operated in the 18th century? Documentary evidence suggests that in the 18th century there were probably some court buildings in what would be Area C, and in the second half of the century metal working, amongst other trades, was taking place in the backplots (see Rátkai, Chapter 4). Some craftsmen were clearly living and working in one and the same place but others were not. Any middle-class or gentry component seems to have long since vanished from the excavated area of Park

Street, at least by the 1760s, so whatever the ceramics represent in terms of working and eating/ drinking practices, they must represent the sort of ceramics in daily use by craftsmen and artisans.

Hartley also notes that 'The modern thermos flask and "works canteens" have put an end to much of the unofficial cooking that went on around the old factory-heating stoves' (1985, 233). If we substitute furnace for factory heaters we have a situation not dissimilar to the one which may have been in place at Park Street. Finally, Hartley also makes the point that the size and shape of the pots and pans could also reflect the owner's job and the associated 'trade cooking'.

The presence of large 18th-century flower-pots in the tank fills is also worthy of note. Flower-pot sherds were concentrated in Area B, with only one or two examples being found in the other two areas. Only two chamber pots were identified: one in blackware from Area C and the other in creamware from the tank fills in Area B. Three albarelli were identified, two from Area C and one from Area B. Otherwise the range of utilitarian and ordinary domestic pottery for the preparation, consumption and storage of food and drink was much the same.

Although the pottery was more fragmentary and not easily assignable to form, a similar range of fabrics was found in the upper fill of 'pond' F506 to that from the tanks and it looks very much as if the fill material from the tanks and the pond derived from the same source. This source is unlikely to have been the same for the fills of other Phase 3 features, although an overglaze painted creamware ?bowl sherd (Fig. 7.25.5, colour) was found associated with Structure 2 in the northwestern area of Area C with other pottery similar to that recovered from the tanks and pond. The tank fills were the only other place where painted creamwares were found, apart from one lid (Fig. 7.25.6, colour), which was found residually in a 19th-century pit F138. The pottery from these four features is typical of urban 'bourgeois' consumption in the second half of the 18th century and is in marked contrast to the range of more utilitarian pottery of consumption, typified by the slip-coated and mottled wares found elsewhere on site. However, even 'bourgeois' households would have used large quantities of these wares (pers. comm. David Barker) and the differences in spatial distribution between the lower and higher status ceramics may say more about the sources of rubbish or the reasons for its disposal (*e.g.* house clearances) than be directly related to the status of the users of the pottery.

However, despite the chronological differences evident between the tank and pond fills, and the 17th–mid-18th-century pit groups, these different phases of activity do not altogether explain the apparent status difference in the groups. For example, white-bodied formal dining wares were available in the form of white salt-glazed stonewares from the 1720s onwards. These were not well represented in either Area A or Area C. They were, for example, completely absent from the large pit group from F133, deposited some time around the mid-18th century (Table 7.16). Secondly, tea wares in porcelain or tin-glazed earthenware were also absent in Areas A and C. In fact there was only one example of a tin-glazed earthenware tea bowl which came from the Phase 3.2 pit F500 in Area B (Table 7.18). Over all, tin-glazed earthenware was very poorly represented. If the pit fills were derived from groups of middling or high status, it would not be unreasonable to expect a greater amount of tin-glazed earthenware in them. In short, there was little in the way of a 'gentry element' in the Phase 3.1 and 3.2 pit fills. The presence, therefore, of a Ravenscroft-style wine glass (Orton and Rátkai, Chapter 8), a high-status find, from pit F133, is in stark contrast to the ceramics with which it was found.

The contrast between the higher and lower status groups may be evidence of 'dual purpose' land use in this part of Park Street and may suggest a combination of middle-class domestic occupation, probably towards the front of the plot, with industrial workshops or working areas and, probably, court housing to the rear. This combination of domestic and working life was the norm throughout the Middle Ages and well into the post-medieval period, with perhaps the best example of this system in the later post-medieval/ early modern period being provided by the Jewellery Quarter, in Birmingham (Cattell *et al.* 2002). However, as noted above, any 'gentry' element on the excavated stretch of Park Street had probably mostly, if not completely, gone by the mid-18th century and the 'formal dining' and tea wares must have belonged to those 'in trade', such as Timothy Smith, factor and brass founder or have derived from the Phoenix Tavern (see Rátkai, Chapter 4). Documentary and map evidence also indicates gardens to the rear of Park Street and this would tie in quite nicely with the flower-pots in Area B and the environmental evidence of garden plants (see Ciaraldi, Chapter 12).

Park St; pottery from the 'dark earth layer' (Table 7.25)

When the excavators mechanically stripped the modern overburden from the site, a 'dark earth layer' was encountered. This layer, described as extending across the whole of the site, sealed the pits, ditches and other features relating to the Phase 3 and ealier activity on the site, but pre-dated the majority of the 19th- and 20th-century structures and deposits assigned to Phases 4 and 5. Given the excavation priorities, only three small test-pits, each 1m square, were excavated by hand into the 'dark earth layer', one in each of the three excavation areas (A, B and C). The remainder of the layer was removed by machine. This strategy necessarily severely restricts the conclusions which can be drawn from the small, and quite possibly unrepresentative, assemblages of pottery recovered from the 'dark earth layer' (see Table 7.25). Nevertheless, the material recovered was sufficiently diverse to call into question any assumption that the 'dark earth layer' represented a uniform phenomenon of a single date, or that it corresponded in any simple fashion to the 'cultivation soil' identified on the Edgbaston Street site.

In Area C, the sample of material from the 'dark earth layer', context 1797, contained no clay pipe and predominantly medieval pottery, the latest material being three iron-rich coarseware sherds, probably of 17th-century date. The average sherd weight is small, which confirms that the pottery is largely residual, but the absence of clay pipe is puzzling, unless 1797 consists primarily of redeposited medieval layers. A rock crystal seal (Fig. 8.3.12) was also recovered from this context. The pottery from contexts 1108 (Area A) and 1520 (Area B) has virtually the same average sherd weight, over two and a half times greater than in 1797. The average sherd weights of the former do not sit very happily with either of the layers being interpreted as a cultivation soil. Both contexts contained clay pipe, although the quantity is hardly impressive and its paucity is unusual in later post-medieval layers.

Context 1108 (Area A) contained some residual medieval and early post-medieval material. Other pottery was consistent with a late 17th- to early/ mid-18th-century date. The clay pipe is described by Higgins as a small but coherent group dating to 1680–1730. There was, however, one small fragment from a blue shell edge plate of early 19th-century date, which is perhaps best seen as intrusive. Context 1520 (Area B) differed from 1108 in not having any residual medieval pottery. It also contained 119 fragments of roof tile and 29 fragments of brick, and hence more closely resembles a destruction layer than a cultivation soil. Most of the pottery within it could date to the late 17th–early/ mid-18th centuries, with the exception of the four creamware sherds, which are unlikely to be earlier than *c*.1760/ 1770. Higgins (Chapter 9), however, suggests that the clay pipe is likely to have been deposited before 1750.

The material from the layer 1505, which sealed the two tanks (F503/ F520 and F510/ F542), was different again. As would be expected, given the date of the assemblage filling the tanks, this pottery was totally consistent with a post-1780 deposition date. Here, the clay pipe (27 fragments) was dated 1760–1800 and there was a considerable quantity of late 18th- and 19th-century pottery. The group comprised 110 sherds, weighing 2,375g. Creamware formed 10.9% of the group and 19th-century pottery 18.2%.

To sum up, the pottery evidence from the various layers does not suggest that that they were different manifestations of the same layer across the site, although they may each reflect periods of abandonment, levelling or change of use in different areas of the site. With the possible exception of 1797 in Area C, the pottery does not seem consistent with an agricultural or garden use, since the sherds are for the most part large, although the documentary evidence, the environmental evidence (see Ciaraldi, Chapter 12), and the presence of flower-pot fragments in F176, F503, F506, F510, F542 and 1609, does suggest that there must have been gardens somewhere in the vicinity. The evidence from these layers is not the same as that retrieved from late 17th–early 18th-century 'abandonment layers' at Edgbaston Street and it would be quite wrong to infer that there was a general simultaneous period of change at Edgbaston Street and Park Street.

General discussion

The three sites, Edgbaston Street, Moor Street and Park Street, have given valuable insights into the archaeology of Birmingham. It is possible to compare the sites both in terms of the chronology of pottery supply and early urban development, and also to compare pottery use on areas with clearly different industries in the medieval and post-medieval periods.

There was no great quantity of pottery which definitely pre-dated the 13th century. The earliest pottery comprised four or five Roman sherds from Moor Street and a minimum of three and maximum of eight Roman sherds from Park Street. Under certain circumstances such a small amount of Roman pottery would be seen as risible. However, recent excavation and fieldwalking along the line of the Birmingham Northern Relief Road have highlighted the paucity of Roman ceramics on Romano-British rural settlements in the area. The Wroxeter Hinterland Survey (Gaffney *et al.* forthcoming) and information from other counties in the west Midlands seems to indicate a very limited usage of Roman ceramics outside the urban, military or villa environment. There are strong indications that areas of Britain were never fully Romanised (pers. comm. Dr Jerry Evans) and the use of Roman ceramics is correspondingly low. As Hodder notes 'concentrations of Roman pottery in small quantities which would be interpreted elsewhere as evidence for manuring...through extensive field survey... can be recognised as significant local concentrations' (2004, 69–70). In this situation the presence of a few Roman sherds at Moor Street and Park Street is worthy of note. It may also be significant that no Roman sherds were found at Edgbaston Street, which may in this period have been too boggy to be utilised in any way.

Pottery which dated wholly or in part to the 12th century comprised the Coventry type wares, Fabric cpj9, Fabric cpj15, reduced Fabric RSi, Worcester glazed ware and the mudstone-tempered fabrics (mudst and mudstg). Although both Worcester glazed ware and Coventry type wares were also made in the first half of the 13th century, it is tempting to see their presence in Birmingham to a large extent as pre-dating the establishment of the Deritend ware industry. It is possible that the reduced Deritend ware was first made towards the end of the 12th century but this is far from certain. Some or all of these putative 12th-century fabrics appear on all three sites. Some 12th-century material should be expected in view of the date of Birmingham's market charter, granted in 1166. Some of this early material, albeit in small quantities, was found in Area C at Park Street, well away from the backplots extending east from Digbeth. This suggests that some encroachment onto Over Park, before the formal laying out of Park Street and Moor Street, took place early in the life of the town.

Pottery supply to Birmingham in the Middle Ages seems to have been dominated by local products. Sources for the iron-poor wares and whitewares lie outside Birmingham, probably in south Staffordshire and north Warwickshire. The whiteware industries and the location and extent of their production in the West Midlands are imperfectly understood. There is one known kiln site at Chilvers Coton (Mayes and Scott 1984), which seems to have supplied the Coventry market in the second half of the 13th century, but many of the whitewares found to the west and southwest of Coventry seem to have come from a different source or sources in northern Warwickshire and southern Staffordshire. It is certainly plausible to link most of the non-local pottery in Birmingham to this area especially since this would reflect the known commercial exchanges between Birmingham and the iron and coal producers to her north. This area is probably also the source for the white clays used for the slip decoration of Deritend ware (pers. comm. Mike Hodder).

Some of the non-local pottery, *e.g.* Boarstall-Brill ware, which was made in Buckinghamshire, demonstrates links between Birmingham and the south Midlands. Again, the underlying reasons for the distribution pattern of Borstall-Brill ware in the west Midlands are not fully understood. Some of it may be linked to the salt trade from Droitwich (Rátkai 2003) but this would not explain the presence of Boarstall-Brill ware in Warwick (Rátkai 1990; 1992a) or Birmingham or, in contrast, the paucity of the ware in Coventry. Deritend ware jugs and the reduced cooking pots and jugs, on the other hand, seem to be fairly widely distributed in the west Midlands, even if not in very great quantities. The oxidised jugs, for example, are known from Stafford Castle, Dudley Castle, Kenilworth Castle, Lichfield, Worcester, Warwick, Alcester, Stratford-upon-Avon and Burton Dassett, and various rural and manorial sites in Warwickshire.

The question of the distribution of non-local wares into Birmingham, and the 'export' of Birmingham-produced wares to its hinterland and beyond, is germane to the understanding of Birmingham's trade and commercial contacts and the wider issues of the relationship of pottery distribution to underlying socio-economic factors. Pottery can be distributed in three different ways. The first is by direct purchase from a market at or close to the site of production. The second is through movement of high-status households as they progress from estate to estate taking their baggage, which included pottery, with them. The third method is 'indirect', *i.e.* when there is

trade in some commodity, not preserved in the archaeological record. For example, salt production in Droitwich led to the establishment of salt ways and salt rights. Some of the salt ways ran southeast from Droitwich through Stratford-upon-Avon, across southern Warwickshire and into Buckinghamshire (see Hurst 1992). The salt would have been transported by cart. On the outward journey from Buckinghamshire the cart would have been empty. Entrepreneurial spirit being what it is, it would make sense to fill the cart with goods which could be sold en route and one possibility was pottery from Boarstall-Brill, since the transport cost which would normally limit the extent of the market would be subsumed in the cost of transporting salt. This would account quite nicely for the small (*c*.5%) but consistent presence of Boarstall-Brill products in southern Warwickshire, Worcester and Droitwich. In this model the presence of non-local pottery represents the removal of goods or commodities from the area in which the non-local pottery is found. This would perhaps explain why there is comparatively little non-local pottery in Birmingham but a comparatively widespread distribution of Deritend wares. This would suggest bulky goods, such as iron and coal, agricultural produce and livestock, coming into Birmingham and small items of metal, pottery and leather making the return journey. Certainly, by the early 14th century, items, probably of metal, known as 'Birmingham pieces', are recorded as far away as London (Gooder 1988; I am grateful to Dr Mike Hodder for drawing my attention to Gooder's note).

This pattern of trade and exchange could have had quite early origins. It is difficult to understand why Birmingham's market charter is the earliest in Warwickshire unless a thriving but 'unofficial' market already existed. The origins of this may have lain in the droving of cattle from the west since, if nothing else, Birmingham had an abundance of streams and springs, ideal for the watering of livestock. In such a situation it is easy to see how Birmingham could have become a 'service point' for drovers and their needs, providing not only refreshment but also small goods necessary to long journeys. The provision of such services could have been the germ from which a regular market was developed.

Comparisons between the Bull Ring sites in the medieval period show that the components of the three assemblages are different (see Table 7.26). At Edgbaston Street, Fabric cpj1 consistently occurs in greater quantities than at Moor Street and Park Street. The data from Park Street are, of course, skewed by the presence of kiln waste from Area A but this should not apply to Areas B and C where Deritend wares are still the major component. The data could perhaps suggest a sequence wherein Fabric cpj1 is the earliest cooking pot fabric, followed by DeritendR and then Deritend cpj, but the evidence is not conclusive. If it were so, then Edgbaston Street would have the heaviest early occupation, followed by Moor Street and then Park Street. However, there is a certain amount of overlap between the cooking pot forms in Fabrics cpj1 and Deritend cpj. Some Fabric cpj1 forms (like Fig. 7.5.107 and 108) look early but others (such as Fig. 7.5.106 and 112) are much the same as some Deritend cpj forms.

There was comparatively little clearly 14th-century material from any of the sites. The whitewares are unlikely to be Chilvers Coton products, which are dated to *c.*1250–1300, and are more likely to follow the rather more expanded date range of *c.*1250–1400 given to whitewares in Staffordshire (Ford 1995). Likewise, the iron-poor wares seem to have a broad date range of *c.*1250–1500. Even allowing for this, there is still not much material which can belong to the 14th century. This could of course be fortuitous but it may mark a decline in Birmingham's fortunes in the 14th century.

By Phase 2 some variation across the sites is apparent. Area B at Edgbaston Street seems to have been flourishing, Area A less so, although late oxidised wares and Cistercian ware occurring residually in Phase 3 indicate that there must have been some occupation in the vicinity even if there were virtually no archaeological features which could be put in this phase. Area D contained hardly any 15th- to 16th-century pottery, likewise Area C. At Moor Street, Phase 2 was less well represented than Phase 1 but there were sufficient amounts of 15th- and 16th-century pottery to suggest continuous occupation from the preceding phase, even if at a reduced level. At Park Street, the greatest amount of 15th- to 16th-century pottery was found in Area B. There appears to have been less activity at Park Street than in Area B at Edgbaston Street but more than in Areas A, C and D, and Moor Street.

By Phase 3, pottery consumption seems, in general, to have increased again and some areas, such as Area D at Edgbaston Street, seem from the ceramic evidence to have been first utilised in this period. Domestic activity on Moor Street seems to have been virtually non-existent and although residual Phase 3 pottery, *e.g.* a Mediterranean maiolica sherd (Fig. 7.19.13, colour) in construction trench fill 5100, indicates that there must have been some. It is clear from Table 7.10 that 17th-century activity was most concentrated in Areas A and B at Edgbaston Street since these are the two areas with the highest percentages of yellow ware. Other wares which begin in the later 17th century but are common in the 18th century, such as mottled ware, brown stoneware, feathered slipware and slip-coated ware, are poorly represented, if at all. Of the remaining slipwares, the best represented are trailed slipware, which dates from *c.*1640–1700 (although is perhaps more common in the later 17th century), and embossed slipware dating to the later 17th–early 18th centuries. There is a complete absence of white salt-glazed stoneware, which has a floruit of *c.*1720–1760, although there are indications that there was some continued production into the 1770s and 1780s (pers. comm. David Barker). In short, there is nothing in these two areas which need post-date 1700 or 1725 at the latest,

the one creamware sherd from Area B being the exception. Area C may date to the same period, or possibly slightly later, since there is proportionally less yellow ware to blackware. However, there is clearly a major functional difference between Areas A and B, on the one hand, and Area C, on the other. The latter is dominated by utilitarian coarsewares, whereas the former have a much higher component of table wares. Area D, in contrast, has a later assemblage, which belongs primarily to the 18th century, probably *c.*1725/ 1750–1780. This is a small group but the absence of yellow ware, slipware and mottled ware is striking. They do not even occur residually in any quantity apart from two yellow ware sherds and one jewelled slipware sherd. Area D more closely resembles the assemblage from Park Street and in particular the group from Area B.

At Park Street some evidence of 17th-century activity is provided by the presence of yellow ware and trailed slipware and by some of the blackware forms, *e.g.* Fig. 7.8.182, Fig. 7.8.183 and Fig. 7.8.188 and the bases of 'corrugated' mugs like Fig. 7.8.199, Fig. 7.8.200, *etc.* However, the relative frequency of mottled ware, slip-coated ware and brown stoneware is indicative of a strong 18th-century component. This is reinforced by the presence of white salt-glazed stoneware and creamware. Looking at the relative proportions of the wares, Area C seems to have had more 17th-century occupation. Area A seems to have been used less in the 17th century (Phase 3.1) (although there was clearly a discrete group of pits of this date) but to have continued into the second half of the 18th century. Area B has the latest assemblage with little 17th-century material but a comparatively large component dating to the second half of the 18th century (Phase 3.3). The pottery from the fills of Phase 3 features marks, of course, their abandonment. Nevertheless, it is possible to see a shift in the focus of industry over the site through time. By the same token, at Edgbaston Street there seems to have been a gradual shift from Areas A and B to Area C and then Area D.

A comparison of the post-medieval pottery used on Edgbaston Street and Park Street reveals both similarities and differences. In general, bowls were much better represented than jars. The exception to this was Area C, Edgbaston Street, where there was a greater number of jar sherds but slightly fewer jars to bowls by rim count. Drinking vessels were well represented on both sites. The similarity in vessel function across the sites is interesting, not least because the chronology of the sites is different, with Edgbaston Street having a greater 17th-century component and Park Street having more 18th-century material. In the earlier period, flange-rim bowls and dishes were found in yellow ware. In the 18th century similar forms were made in slip-coated ware. This shows a functional continuity in the post-medieval period even though the wares change. This, in turn, demonstrates that pottery usage was not associated with the industries taking place on the two sites, although there are one or two cases where this can be argued. There was also no particular difference discernable in the status of the occupants of Park Street and Edgbaston Street, with the exception of the high-status later 18th-century group from the tank fills on Park Street. The post-medieval pottery seems to reflect moderately prosperous urban living in the town centre in the 17th and 18th centuries. Although the 19th-century ceramics were only scanned (apart from layer 1505, Park Street) it is possible to say that the nature of the ceramics did change. The 19th-century pottery from Park Street is overwhelmingly artisanal in character, with a range of 'cheap but cheerful' ceramics such as sponged ware, painted ware, Mocha ware and transfer printed wares. This ties in perfectly with the increasing development of court housing and workshops to the rear of Park Street and Edgbaston Street, and the general social downgrading of the historic heart of the town, that is attested by the cartographic and documentary evidence.

Illustration catalogue

Fig. 7.1 Medieval pottery, nos 1–24

1   Jug, Deritend ware (fine fabric), trace of white slip decoration, olive glaze
    Edgbaston Street (2115)
2   Jug, Deritend ware (fine fabric), ext. white slip splash, olive glaze
    Moor Street (5187) F568
3   Jug, Deritend ware (fine fabric), olive glaze
    Park Street (1158)
4   Jug, Deritend ware (sandy fabric), applied face mask, int. white slip, olive glaze
    Park Street (1708) F700
5   Jug, Deritend ware (fine fabric), trace of ext. white slip
    Park Street (1756)
6   Jug, Deritend ware (fine fabric)
    Park Street (1584) F506
7   Jug with rod handle, Deritend ware (fine fabric), ext. tan glaze with cu. flecks
    Moor Street (5128) F545
8   ?Jug, Deritend ware (fine fabric), ext. tan glaze spots, ext. soot, int. band of soot
    Park Street (1784) F746
9   Jug, Deritend ware (sandy fabric), blackened int.
    Park Street (1818) F765
10 Jug handle, olive glaze
    Park Street (1761)
11 Wastered jug base, Deritend ware (sandy fabric), white slip decoration, dark olive glaze
    Park Street (1195) F174
12 ?Jug, Deritend ware (fine fabric), ext. soot
    Park Street (1784)
13 Pipkin, Deritend ware (sandy fabric) trace of thin int. glaze
    Park Street (1863) F762
14 Dripping tray, Deritend ware (fine fabric), stabbed socketed handle, int. patchy, opaque, pale olive glaze
    Park Street (1841)
15 Pipkin handle, Deritend ware (fine fabric), int. yellowish

olive glaze, ext. glaze spots, partially blackened
    Park Street F800
16 Cooking pot, Deritend ware (fine fabric)
    Park Street (1526) F512
17 Pipkin, Deritend ware (fine fabric), ext. soot
    Park Street (1888) F810
18 Lid Deritend ware (fine fabric), heavy ext. soot
    Park Street (1760)
19 Cooking pot, Deritend cpj, heavy ext. soot with clear dribbles through the soot where the contents have boiled over. (See also Fig 2.9, colour)
    Edgbaston Street (1010) F105
20 Cooking pot, Deritend cpj, heavy ext. abrasion
    Edgbaston Street (2115)
21 Cooking pot, Deritend cpj, ext. soot
    Edgbaston Street (1010) F105
22 Cooking pot, Deritend cpj, ext. soot
    Edgbaston Street F704
23 Cooking pot, Deritend cpj
    Edgbaston Street (3106) F336
24 Cooking pot, Deritend cpj, distorted rim, applied thumbed strip
    Park Street (1212) F174

Fig. 7.2 Medieval pottery, nos 25–42

25 Cooking pot, Deritend cpj
    Park Street (1165) F174
26 Cooking pot, Deritend cpj
    Park Street (1213)
27 Cooking pot, Deritend cpj, patchy ext. colour, some spalling
    Park Street (1239) and (1247)
28 Cooking pot, Deritend cpj (organics in fabric) patchy surface colour
    Park Street (1314) F201
29 Cooking pot, Deritend cpj, patchy surface colour
    Park Street (1314) F201
30 Cooking pot, Deritend cpj, very heavy ext. soot, int. soot, abrasion on int. rim suggests use of lid
    Park Street (1314) F201
31 Cooking pot, Deritend cpj, patchy surface colour, applied thumbed strip
    Park Street (1314) F201
32 Cooking pot, Deritend cpj
    Park Street (1314) F201
33 Cooking pot, Deritend cpj
    Park Street (1314) F201
34 Cooking pot, Deritend cpj
    Park Street (1314) F201
35 Bowl, Deritend cpj, very heavy ext. soot, int. smoke blackened
    Park Street (1314) F201
36 Bowl, Deritend cpj, combed rim, drilled hole, abraded int. and ext.
    Park Street (1314) F201
37 Bowl, DeritendR (fabric RS01), drilled hole
    Park Street (1820) F762
38 Cooking pot, DeritendR (fabric RSd), heavy ext. soot
    Moor Street (5158) F561
39 Cooking pot, DeritendR (fabric RSc) ?coil made, wheel finished, heavy ext. soot
    Moor Street (5158) F561

40 Cooking pot, DeritendR (fabric RSc), finger impressed rim, abrasion on int. rim-shoulder junction, ?from use of lid
Moor Street evaluation (1310) F153

41 Cooking pot, DeritendR (fabric RSc)
Park Street (1784) F746

42 Cooking pot, DeritendR (fabric RSc)
Moor Street (5200)

Fig. 7.3 Medieval pottery, nos 43–67

43 Cooking pot, DeritendR (fabric RS01), heavy ext. soot
Park Street (1756)

44 Cooking pot, DeritendR (fabric RSh)
Park Street (1625)

45 Cooking pot, DeritendR (fabric RSb) abraded
Edgbaston Street (2104) F224

46 Cooking pot, DeritendR (fabric RSb)
Edgbaston Street (7009)

47 Cooking pot, DeritendR (fabric RSa), patchy ext. colour
Edgbaston Street (2045)

48 Cooking pot, DeritendR (fabric RS01)
Park Street (1312) F195

49 Cooking pot, DeritendR (fabric RSc)
Edgbaston Street (2057) F229

50 Cooking pot, DeritendR (fabric RSb)
Park Street (1756)

51 Cooking pot, DeritendR (fabricRSa)
Edgbaston Street (2017)

52 Cooking pot, DeritendR (fabric RSb) heavy ext. soot on rim and neck
Edgbaston Street (2044)

53 Cooking pot, DeritendR (fabric RSa), stained with iron oxide
Edgbaston Street (3025)

54 Cooking pot, DeritendR (fabric RSc), ext. soot
Moor Street (5155) F561

55 Cooking pot, DeritendR (fabric RSb) trace of ext. soot
Park Street (1749)

56 Cooking pot, DeritendR (fabric RS01), int. shiny, burnt deposit
Park Street (1841)

57 Cooking pot, DeritendR (fabric RSc), patchy ext. soot
Park Street (1760)

58 Cooking pot, DeritendR (fabric RSd)
Park Street (1220) F188

59 Cooking pot, DeritendR (fabric RSb) ext. soil adhesions
Moor Street (5158) F561

60 Cooking pot, DeritendR (fabricRSd) ext. soot, int. abrasion
Park Street (1841)

61 Cooking pot, DeritendR (fabric RSb)
Edgbaston Street (2017)

62 Cooking pot, DeritendR (fabric RSc)
Park Street (1220) F188

63 Cooking pot, DeritendR (fabric RS01)
Park Street (1763)

64 Bowl, DeritendR (fabric RSb)
Edgbaston Street (2160) F237

65 Tapering handle, DeritendR (fabric RSb)
Park Street (1841)

66 Jug, DeritendR (fabricRSc)
Park Street (1660)

67 Jug, DeritendR (fabric RSc)
Moor Street (5184) F568

Fig. 7.4 Medieval pottery, nos 68–93

68 Jug, DeritendR (fabric RSb)
Park Street (1196)

69 Jug, DeritendR (fabric RSc)
Park Street (1756)

70 Jug, DeritendR (fabric RS01), distorted, possibly a waster
Park Street (1835) F803

71 Jug, DeritendR (fabric RSb)
Park Street (1325) F201

72 Jug, DeritendR (fabric RSc), drilled holes for repair
Moor Street (5128) F545

73 Jug, DeritendR (fabric RSg)
Edgbaston Street (1010) F105

74 Jug, DeritendR (fabric RS01)
Park Street (1220) F188

75 Jug, DeritendR (fabric RSc)
Park Street (1652)

76 Jug, DeritendR (fabric RSc)
Moor Street (5128) F545

77 Jug, DeritendR (fabric RSb)
Park Street (1780) F742

78 Jug, DeritendR (fabric RSb)
Park Street (1310) F233

79 Jug, DeritendR (fabric RSb)
Moor Street (5155) F561

80 Jug handle, DeritendR (fabric RSc)
Moor Street (5190) F568

81 Jug handle, DeritendR (fabric RSb)
Park Street (1165) F174

82 Jug handle, DeritendR (fabric RSc)
Moor Street (5174) F568

83 Jug handle, DeritendR (fabric RSc)
Park Street (1198) F174

84 Jug handle, DeritendR (fabric RS01)
Park Street (1841)

85 Jug handle, DeritendR (fabric RSb)
Edgbaston Street (2107) F224

86 Large jug/pitcher rim, Coventry-type glazed ware, partial olive glaze
Park Street (1325) F201

87 Large jug/pitcher base, Coventry-type glazed ware, patchy ext. olive splash glaze and incised horizontal lines
Park Street (1831) F770

88 Pitcher handle, fabric medg2, trace of ext. glaze
Edgbaston Street (2070) F229

89 Pitcher handle, fabric medg2, trace of yellowish olive glaze, int. glaze streaks
Edgbaston Street (2181) F240

90 Jug handle, fabric medg3, opaque yellowish glaze
Park Street (1119)

91 Jug, Whiteware (fabric ww1), ext. olive glaze, partly flaked away from body
Edgbaston Street (1010) F105

92 Jug, Whiteware (fabric ww1), int. and ext. green (copper-coloured) glaze
Edgbaston Street (2079)

93 Jug, Whiteware (fabric ww1), ext. green (copper-coloured) glaze, ext. abrasion
Edgbaston Street (1010 F105)

Fig 7.5 Medieval pottery, nos 94–117

94 Jug, Whiteware (fabric ww1), combed decoration ext. green (copper-coloured) glaze
    Park Street (1315) F201

95 Jug, Whiteware (fabric ww4), ext. olive glaze
    Moor Street (5158) F561

96 Jug, Whiteware (fabric ww4) applied and combed decoration ext. apple green glaze
    Park Street (1835)

97 Jug, Whiteware (fabric ww4), pendant triangle filled with comb impressions, ext. olive glaze with green (copper-coloured) streaks
    Park Street (1213) F174

98 Jug/Pitcher, fabric ip2, tan splash glaze
    Park Street, (1197) F174

99 Jug, fabric ip2, ext. thin mottled olive glaze, ext. abrasion
    Park Street (1680) F520

100 Jug, fabric ip2
    Moor Street (5128) F545

101 Jug, fabric ip2, ext. olive glaze with (copper) green speckles
    Park Street (1831)

102 Jug, fabric ip2, heavy ext. soot
    Edgbaston Street (1008) F103

103 Jug, fabric ip2, ext. tan glaze
    Edgbaston Street (2006)

104 Jug, fabric ip8, partial ext. olive glaze
    Moor Street (5150) F561

105 Cooking pot, fabric cpj1, ext. soot
    Edgbaston Street (2115)

106 Cooking pot, fabric cpj1, trace of applied strip
    Edgbaston Street (1010) F105

107 Cooking pot, fabric cpj1, patchy surface colour, int. and ext. abrasion
    Edgbaston Street (2087) F218

108 Cooking pot, fabric cpj1, thin applied strip, ext. soot
    Moor Street (5165) F561

109 Cooking pot, fabric cpj1, ext. soot
    Moor Street (5158) F561

110 Cooking pot, fabric cpj1, ext. soot
    Moor Street (5158) F561

111 Cooking pot, fabric cpj1, drilled hole, int. and ext. abrasion
    Park Street (1198) F174

112 Cooking pot, fabric cpj1, ext. soot, soot on int. rim, applied strip, stabbed decoration on int. rim
    Park Street (1326) F201

113 Cooking pot, fabric cpj1, faint abrasion on rim
    Edgbaston Street (2167)

114 Cooking pot, fabric cpj1
    Edgbaston Street (1010) F105

115 Cooking pot, fabric cpj1, ext. soot
    Edgbaston Street (3020) F306

116 Cooking pot, fabric cpj1, int. and ext. abrasion
    Edgbaston Street (3099)

117 Cooking pot, fabric cpj1, patchy int. soot, patchy oxidised surfaces
    Edgbaston Street (1010) F105

Fig. 7.6 Medieval pottery, nos 118–142

118 Cooking pot, fabric cpj2, patchy ext. soot
    Park Street (1841)

119 Cooking pot, fabric cpj6, patchy ext. colour

120 Cooking pot, fabric cpj6, some abrasion
    Edgbaston Street (2160) F237

121 Bowl, fabric cpj7, trace of int. glaze
    Edgbaston Street (2018)

122 Cooking pot, fabric cpj7
    Moor Street (5128) F545

123 Cooking pot, fabric cpj7
    Moor Street (5128) F545

124 Cooking pot, fabric cpj7, notched rim, heavy ext. soot
    Moor Street (5182) F567

125 Cooking pot, fabric cpj7, ext. soot
    Moor Street (5150) F561

126 Cooking pot, fabric cpj12, heavy ext. soot
    Edgbaston Street (1035) F121

127 Cooking pot, fabric cpj12
    Park Street (1625)

128 Cooking pot, fabric cpj12, ext. soot, int. abrasion on rim
    Park Street (1784) F746

129 Cooking pot, fabric cpj13
    Edgbaston Street (2160) F237

130 Cooking pot, fabric cpj13, ext. soot, patchy ext. surface colour
    Moor Street (5171) F561

131 Cooking pot, fabric cpj13, ext. soot
    Moor Street (5171) F561

132 Cooking pot, fabric cpj13, heavy ext. soot, int. abrasion
    Park Street (1213) F174

133 Cooking pot, fabric cpj14, heavy ext. soot, partial heavy int. soot
    Moor Street (5000) F501

134 Cooking pot, cpj14, ext. soot
    Moor Street (5155) F561

135 Cooking pot, cpj14, heavy ext. soot
    Park Street (1195) and (1197) F174

136 Socketed bowl, fabric cpj15
    Park Street (1784) F746

137 Flange rim bowl, fabric lox1,
    Edgbaston Street (2010) F208

138 Bowl, fabric lox1
    Edgbaston Street (2029) F200

138 Bowl, fabric lox1, ext. soot
    Park Street (1664) F553

140 Jug, fabric lox1
    Edgbaston Street (2035)

141 Jug, fabric lox1
    Edgbaston Street (1010) F105

142 Jar, fabric lox1
    Edgbaston Street (2244) F279

Fig. 7.7 Medieval and early post-medieval pottery, nos 143–168

143 Bowl, fabric lox2
    Edgbaston Street (2010) F208

144 Jar, fabric lox2
    Edgbaston Street (2166)

145 Jug, fabric lox2, partial dark green glaze
    Edgbaston Street (2100) F214

146 Jug, fabric lox2
    Park Street (1514) F502

147 Jug, fabric lox2, trace of thin ext. glaze
    Edgbaston Street (3099)

148 Jug, fabric lox2, facetted base
Edgbaston Street (2035)
149 Cistern, fabric lox2, partial ext. olive glaze, stamped
decoration, trace of handle
Edgbaston Street (2023)
150 Cistern, fabric lox2, int. partial dark olive glaze, heavy
ext. knife trimming
Edgbaston Street (2003) F202
151 Lid, fabric lox2
Edgbaston Street (2010) F208
152 Jar, fabric lox2
Edgbaston Street (1047) F131
153 ?Jug, fabric lox2, partial tan glaze, applied stamped white
clay pad
Edgbaston Street (2004)
154 Bowl, fabric lox3
Edgbaston Street (2074)
155 Dripping tray, fabric lox3, int. olive glaze, int. groove on
base
Edgbaston Street (3093) F327
156 ?Jar, fabric lox5
Edgbaston Street (2216) F261
157 Bowl, fabric lox5, int. slip or wash
Edgbaston Street (2010) F208
158 Bowl, fabric lox5, int. olive glaze
Edgbaston Street (1021) F108
159 Chafing dish or strainer, fabric lox5, patches of int. tan
glaze
Edgbaston Street (2168)
160 Jar, Midlands Purple
Edgbaston Street (3108) F337
161 Jar, Midlands Purple, int. dribbles of black glaze
Edgbaston Street (2176)
162 Jar, Midlands Purple
Edgbaston Street (3075) F334
163 Jar, Midlands Purple, int. and ext. purplish 'metallic'
glaze
Park Street (1150)
164 Jar, Midlands Purple
Edgbaston Street (3075) F334
165 Jar, Midlands Purple
Park Street (1220) F188
166 Jug/Cistern, Midlands Purple, ext. patches purple glaze
Park Street (1642) F552
167 Two-handled cup, cistercian ware
Edgbaston Street (2008) F208
168 Two-handled cup, cistercian ware
Park Street (1127) F135

Fig. 7.8 Post-medieval pottery, nos 169–212

169 Cup, cistercian ware
Edgbaston Street (1021) F108
170 Three handled cup, cistercian ware, applied white clay
pads
Park Street (1108)
171 ?Mug base, cistercian ware, trailed white slip decoration
Edgbaston Street (2197) F253
172 Cup base, cistercian ware
Park Street (1141) F141
173 Base of salt or candlestick, cistercian ware
Edgbaston Street (2031) F200
174 Cup, cistercian ware/blackware

Edgbaston Street (2144)
175 Cup, cistercian ware/blackware
Edgbaston Street (2164) F238
176 Cup, cistercian ware/blackware, shallow impressions on
carination
Park Street (1834) F803
177 Cup, cistercian ware/blackware
Edgbaston Street (2007) F208
178 Cup, cistercian ware/blackware, 'metallic' black glaze
Edgbaston Street (2088) F214
179 Cup, cistercian ware/blackware
Edgbaston Street (2060) F223
180 Cup, cistercian ware/blackware
Edgbaston Street (2197) F253
181 Cup, cistercian ware/blackware
Edgbaston Street (2197) F253
182 Frilled base, drinking vessel, cistercian ware/blackware,
?imitation German stoneware form
Edgbaston Street (2008) F208
183 Mug, blackware
Edgbaston Street (1005)
184 Mug, blackware
Park Street (1749)
185 'Corrugated' mug, blackware
Park Street (1834) F803
186 'Corrugated' mug, blackware
Edgbaston Street (2138) F234
187 Mug, blackware
Edgbaston Street (1058) F137
188 Tall, three-handled mug, blackware
Park Street (1834) F803
189 Mug, blackware
Edgbaston Street (3109) F337
190 Mug, blackware
Park Street (1632) F542
191 ?Mug, blackware
Edgbaston Street (4057) F422
192 Mug, blackware, wear on rim from ?metal mount
Park Street (1820) F762
193 Two-handled mug, blackware
Edgbaston Street (1049) F130
194 Mug, blackware
Park Street fill of pipe trench F505
195 Mug, blackware
Park Street (1820) F762
196 Mug, blackware
Park Street (1632) F542
197 Three-handled mug base, blackware
Edgbaston Street (2002)
198 ?Mug base, blackware
Park Street (1820) F762
199 'Corrugated' mug base, blackware
Edgbaston Street (2176) F281
200 Two-handled mug base, blackware
Edgbaston Street (2005)
201 Two-handled, 'corrugated' mug base, blackware
Park Street (1179) F162
202 'Corrugated' mug base, blackware
Park Street (1157) F148
203 Base of cylindrical mug, blackware, rebated base
Edgbaston Street (3037)
204 Base of cylindrical mug, blackware, rebated base

Park Street (1621) F542
205 Two-handled cup base, blackware
Edgbaston Street (2192) F252
206 Three-handled cup base, blackware
Park Street (1820) F762
207 Candlestick/Salt base, blackware
Park Street (1108)
208 ?Jug, blackware
Edgbaston Street (3061) F326
209 Stool pot, blackware
Edgbaston Street (2198) F261
210 Handled bowl, blackware
Park Street (1820) F762
211 Lid, blackware
Edgbaston Street (3037)
212 ?Form, blackware
Park Street (1512) F500

Fig. 7.9 Post-medieval pottery, nos 213–230
213 Large hook-rim jar, blackware
Edgbaston Street (1009) F104
214 Bowl, yellow ware
Edgbaston Street (2219)
215 Bowl, yellow ware
Edgbaston Street (2164) F238
216 Bowl, yellow ware
Edgbaston Street (2004)
217 Bowl, yellow ware
Park Street (1820) F762
218 Bowl yellow ware, patches of int. wear
Edgbaston Street (3127)
219 Bowl, yellow ware, heavy ext. soot, int. wear
Edgbaston Street (2138) F234
220 Bowl, yellow ware, ext. base sooted
Edgbaston Street (2197) F253
221 Bowl, yellow ware, sooted on int. and ext. rim
Edgbaston Street (2179) F245
222 ?Dish, yellow ware
Edgbaston Street (2005)
223 Bowl/Dish, yellow ware, notched rim with incised wavy
line, ext. soot
Edgbaston Street (2197) F253
224 Dish, yellow ware, heavy ext. soot
Edgbaston Street (2004)
225 Dish, yellow ware
Edgbaston Street (2198) F261
226 ?Dish, yellow ware, very heavy ext. soot
Park Street (1138)
227 Dish, yellow ware
Edgbaston Street (2003) F202
228 Dish, yellow ware
Edgbaston Street (2177) F247
229 Dish, yellow ware
Edgbaston Street (1050) F131
230 Handled jar, yellow ware
Edgbaston Street (2197) F253

Fig. 7.10 Post-medieval pottery, nos 231–258
231 Jar, yellow ware, very heavy int. and ext. soot
Park Street (1834) F803
232 Jar, yellow ware
Edgbaston Street (4019)

233 Jar, yellow ware, ext. soot
Edgbaston Street (3024)
234 Cup, yellow ware, sooted base
Edgbaston Street, (2196)
235 Cup, yellow ware
Edgbaston Street (3108) F337
236 ?Mug base, yellow ware, ext. soot
Edgbaston Street
237 Salt or candlestick base, yellow ware
Edgbaston Street (2166)
238 Candlestick base, yellow ware
Edgbaston Street (2034)
239 Lid or salt, yellow ware
Edgbaston Street (2164) F238
240 Terminal from ?money box or ?lid, yellow ware
Edgbaston Street (3069) F365
241 Knob from chafing dish, yellow ware
Edgbaston Street (3009) F304
242 Base of small jar or albarello, yellow ware
Park Street (1739) F713
243 Small jar or albarello, yellow ware
Park Street (1204) F182
244 Small jar, yellow ware
Edgbaston Street (2021)
245 Jar, coarseware/Midlands Purple ware, int. black glaze
Edgbaston Street (3075) F334
246 Jar, iron-rich coarseware, ext. 'metallic' bloom, int.
'metallic' brown glaze spots
Edgbaston Street (2063) F223
247 Jar, iron-rich coarseware, unslipped, int. mid brown glaze
spots
Edgbaston Street (2063) F223
248 Jar, iron-rich coarseware, int. black glaze
Edgbaston Street (3108) F337
249 Jar, iron-rich coarseware, int. mid brown glaze, int. and
ext. abrasion
Edgbaston Street (3075) F334
250 Jar, iron-rich coarseware, int. and ext. ?wash, int. brown
glaze, heavy int. and ext. abrasion
Edgbaston Street (2088) F214
251 Jar, iron-rich coarseware, int. black glaze
Edgbaston Street (3073) F328
252 Jar, iron-rich coarseware, int. dark brown glaze
Edgbaston Street (3075) F334
253 Jar, iron-rich coarseware, int. black glaze
Edgbaston Street (3075) F334
254 Jar, iron-rich coarseware, patch of int. brown glaze
Edgbaston Street (2197) F253
255 Jar, iron-rich coarseware, int. and ext. slip, int. dark brown
glaze, grooved ext., ext. abrasion
Edgbaston Street (3166) F353
256 Jar, iron-rich coarseware, int. and ext. ?wash, ext. glaze
dribble
Edgbaston Street (3062) F327
257 Jar, iron-rich coarseware, int. brown glaze
Edgbaston Street (3037)
258 Jar, iron-rich coarseware, int. dark brown glaze
Park Street (1755) F738

Fig. 7.11 Post-medieval pottery, nos 259–271
259 Bowl, iron-rich coarseware, int. and ext. wash, int. patchy
tan glaze

Edgbaston Street (2164) F238
260 Bowl, iron-rich coarseware, int. and ext. slip, glaze flaked away from int. surface
    Edgbaston Street (2216) F261
261 Bowl, iron-rich coarseware, int. and ext. streaky brown-tan glaze
    Edgbaston Street (2003) F202
261 Bowl, iron-rich coarseware, int. and ext. 'metallic' slip, int. brown glaze
    Edgbaston Street (2143)
263 Bowl, iron-rich coarseware, patchy int. and ext. soot
    Edgbaston Street (2034)
264 Pancheon, iron-rich coarseware, int. and ext. brown glaze streaks
    Edgbaston Street (1066) F139
265 Bowl, iron-rich coarseware, int. dark brown glaze
    Edgbaston Street (3075) F334
266 Bowl, iron-rich coarseware, int. slip, int. dark brown glaze, int. soot
    Park Street (1621) F542
267 Bowl, iron-rich coarseware, int. and ext. slip, int. dark brown glaze, int. wear
    Edgbaston Street (2197) F253
268 Bowl, iron-rich coarseware, int. dark brown glaze
    Edgbaston Street (3075) F334
269 ?Bowl, iron-rich coarseware, int. and ext. mid-brown glaze
    Edgbaston Street (1050) F131
270 Bowl, iron-rich coarseware, int. slip, int. black glaze
    Park Street (1505)
271 Bowl, iron-rich coarseware, wear on ext. base edge, under-glaze slip, ext. wash, int. dark brown glaze
    Park Street (1104)

Fig. 7.12 Post-medieval pottery, nos 272–285
272 Handled bowl, iron-rich coarseware, int. and ext. brown glaze splashes
    Edgbaston Street (2197) F253
273 Handled bowl, iron-rich coarseware
    Edgbaston Street (3062) F327 and (3106) F336
274 Handled bowl, iron-rich coarseware
    Park Street (1634) F542
275 Large 'pan', iron-rich coarseware/slip-coated ware, int. black glaze, int. slip
    Park Street (1530) F520
276 Bowl, iron-rich coarseware, int. mid-brown glaze, ext. wear, ext. iron stained adhesions
    Edgbaston Street (3074) F328
277 Bowl, iron-rich coarseware/slip-coated ware, int. black glaze, int. slip
    Park Street (1205) F180
278 Jar, iron-poor coarseware, int. black glaze
    Edgbaston Street (3108) F337
279 Jar, iron-poor coarseware, int. dark brown glaze, ext. glaze streak
    Edgbaston Street (3062) F327 and (3106) F336
280 Jar, iron-poor coarseware, int. black glaze, ext. glaze streak
    Edgbaston Street (3118) F344
281 Jar, iron-poor coarseware, int. and ext. wash, int. and ext. glaze spots, ext. iron stained adhesions
    Edgbaston Street (2164) F238
282 Jar, iron-poor coarseware, int. black glaze

Edgbaston Street (3075) F334
283 Jar, iron-poor coarseware, int. black glaze, very heavy ext. soot, ext. and heavy int. wear
    Park Street (1104)
284 Bowl, iron-poor coarseware,
    Park Street (1820) F762
285 Bowl, iron-poor coarseware,
    Park Street (1739) F713

Fig. 7.13 Post-medieval pottery, nos 286–308
286 Bowl, iron-poor coarseware
    Park Street (1530) F520
287 Bowl, iron-poor coarseware, int. dark brown glaze
    Edgbaston Street (3054) F305
288 Bowl, iron-poor coarseware, ext. and int. slip, int. dark brown glaze
    Edgbaston Street (2138) F234
289 Bowl, iron-poor coarseware, int. dark brown, crazed glaze
    Edgbaston Street (3054) F305
290 Bowl, iron-poor coarseware
    Park Street (1505)
291 Bowl, iron-poor coarseware
    Park Street (1505)
292 Handled ?bowl, iron-poor coarseware
    Park Street (1820) F762
293 Handled dish, iron poor coarseware, heavy int. abrasion, very heavy ext. abrasion
    Park Street (1206) F181 and (1204) F182
294 Dripping tray, iron-poor coarseware, int. brown glaze, int. and ext. slip, ext. abrasion on base-base angle, sooted along opposite edge from handle
    Edgbaston Street (3166) F353
295 Lid, iron-poor coarseware, ext. dark brown glaze
    Park Street (1512) F500
296 Bowl, mottled ware
    Park Street (1512) F500
297 Albarello, mottled ware
    Park Street (1132) F138
298 Dish, slip-coated ware, int. black glaze
    Park Street (1621) F542
299 Dish, slip-coated ware, int. black glaze
    Park Street (1621) F542
300 Dish, slip-coated ware, int. black glaze
    Park Street (1512) F500
301 Dish, slip-coated ware, int. black glaze
    Edgbaston Street (2005)
302 Dish, slip-coated ware, int. black glaze
    Edgbaston Street (2005)
303 Bowl, slip-coated ware, int. black glaze
    Park Street (1402) F259
304 Pie-crust rim dish, slip-coated ware, int. black glaze, burnt
    Park Street (1634) F542
305 Hook-rim bowl, slip-coated ware, int. and ext. black glaze
    Park Street (1530) F520
306 Hook-rim bowl, slip-coated ware, int. and ext. black glaze
    Park Street (1621) F542
307 Hook-rim hollow ware, slip-coated ware, int. and ext. black glaze
    Park Street (1621) F542
308 Hollow ware, slip-coated ware, int. and ext. black glaze
    Park Street (1621) F542

Fig. 7.14 Post-medieval pottery, nos 309–329

309 Collar-rim hollow ware, slip-coated ware, int. and ext. black glaze
Park Street (1621) F542

310 Bowl, brown salt-glazed stoneware
Park Street (1621) F542

311 Bowl rim, brown salt-glazed stoneware
Park Street (1506)

312 Everted-rim dish, brown salt-glazed stoneware
Park Street (1621) F542

313 Mug, brown salt-glazed stoneware
Park Street (1621) F542

314 Cylindrical mug, turned decoration, creamware
Park Street (1621) F542

315 Small milk jug/mustard pot, creamware
Park Street (1621) F542

316 Bowl with rounded/rolled rim, white salt-glazed stoneware
Park Street (1634) F542

317 Bowl with rounded/rolled rim, creamware
Park Street (1531)

318 Salad dish, creamware
Park Street (1634) F542

319 Tea bowl, moulded ribbed decoration, creamware
Park Street (1622) F542

320 Bowl base, moulded flutes and beaded decoration, creamware
Park Street (1621) F542

321 Jug base, with turned decoration and twisted rope handles with flower terminals, creamware
Park Street (1621) F542

322 Chamber pot handle, creamware
(1621) F542

323 Royal edge, soup plate, creamware
Park Street (1621) F542

324 Moulded edge plate, creamware
Park Street (1621) F542

325 Foot-ring base sherd, oriental porcelain
Park Street (1531) F510

326 ?Industrial vessel, sandy brick-like fabric
Park Street (1125) F133

327 Drinking jug, Cologne stoneware
Edgbaston Street (3075) F334

328 Drinking jug, Cologne/Frechen stoneware
Edgbaston Street (2197) F253

329 Bartmann, Frechen stoneware
Edgbaston Street (evaluation 'pit next to sewer')

Fig. 7.15 colour, Deritend Ware (13th–early 14th centuries), nos 1–9

1 PSB (1784) F746 Jug, white slip and applied scale decoration

2 PSB (1784) F746 Jug, roller-stamped white slip decoration

3 MSB (5000) F500 Lower part of jug, white chevron decoration

4 BRB (2070) Jug, trailed white slip bands

5 BRB (2051) Jug, brushed white slip band

6 PSB (1197) F174 Jug, ?combed decoration, ?fuel ash slag adhesions

7 BRB (2103) Jug, horizontal combing on shoulder above white slip lattice

8 BRB (2136) Jug, combing on shoulder

9 BRB (2103) Jug, wide-spaced, shallow, incised horizontal lines

Fig. 7.16 colour, Boarstall-Brill ware, nos 1–4

1 BRB (2045) Anthropomorphic jug fragment, mid-13th–early 14th century

2 BRB (2004) Jug, incised decoration and trace of roller stamped red strip, late 13th–early14th century

3 BRB (2088) Jug, applied scale and red slip decoration, late 13th–early 14th century

4 MSB (5122) Burnt triple-decker jug, applied vertical slip lines, late 13th–early 14th century

Fig. 7.17 colour, Decorated iron-poor ware (fabric ip2), nos 1–6

1 MSB (5158) F561 Jug, square, roller stamped decoration

2 BRB (3020) Jug, square roller stamped decoration
BRB (2115) and (2166) Jug, oblique roller stamped decoration

3 BRB (2070) Jug, anthropomorphic/zoomorphic decoration

4 BRB (2088) Jug, applied notched strip and comb impressions

5 PSB (1652) Jug, applied notched strip, incised wavy lines

6 BRB (2072) Jug, applied crimped strip, brushed with iron-oxide

Fig. 7.18, colour Miscellaneous glazed wares, nos 1–4

1 MSB (5161) F561 'Fluted' jug (fabric ?ww4) ?early 13th century

2 BRB (1075) Jug/pitcher sherd, applied strip and roller stamped decoration (fabric mudstg), mid–late 12th–early 13th century

3 PSB (1326) F201 Jug/pitcher sherd, complex roller stamp decoration (fabric mudst), late 12th–early 13th century

4 PSB (1326) F201 Jug/pitcher, complex roller stamp decoration (fabric ?Coventry type glazed ware), late 12th–early 13th century

Fig. 7.19 colour, Tin-glazed earthenwares, nos 1–13

1 PSB (1115) F127 *Albarello* fragments, 17th–18th centuries

2 PSB (1721) F702 *Albarello* base, 17th–18th centuries

3 PSB (1193) Bowl, external blue decoration, ?18th century

4 PSB (1115) F127 Bowl, external multi-coloured floral decoration, 18th century

5 PSB (1115) F127 Bowl, external blue decoration, trace of internal blue decoration

6 BRB (2002) Bowls: sherd with internal blue decoration, clear external lead glaze, ?17th century; sherd with internal green and blue decoration, external clear lead glaze, ?17th century.

7 BRB (4060) Bowl, internal blue decoration (cf Jennings 1980, fig. 95, 1497), English, early 18th century

8 PSB (1938) F828 Footring bowl similar to (7), early 18th century

9 BRB (5200) Plate, internal blue floral decoration 18th century

10 PSB (1115) F127 Flatwares, internal blue decoration, 18th century

11 PSB (1876) F791 Flatware, internal blue decoration, 18th century

12   PSB (1512) F500 Tea bowl, external blue decoration, 18th century
13   MSB (5100) F532 Flatware, Mediterranean maiolica, internal purple and turquoise concentric bands

Fig. 7.20 colour, Slipware, nos 1–4
1   PSB (1505) Platter, three-colour slipware, 18th century
2   PSB (1621) F542 Platter, three-colour slipware, 18th century
     PSB (1635) F542 As above
3   BRB (3117) F343 Dish, brown and tan slip trellis design on rim, late 17th–early 18th century
4   BRB (2138) Base of dish, internal slip decoration, late 17th–early 18th century

Fig. 7.21 colour, Slipware, nos 1–4
1   PSB (1621) F542 Flange rim bowl, trailed and feathered slip decoration, first half of 18th century
2   PSB (1839) F773 Light-on-dark trailed slipware flange rim bowl, c.1640–1700
3   BRB (2005) Dark-on-light trailed slipware, flange rim dish, late 17th–early 18th century
4   PSB (1621) F542 Trailed slipware platter, 18th century

Fig. 7.22, colour Slipware, nos 1–3
1   PSB (1520) F505 Embossed slipware dish, heraldic design, late 17th–early 18th century
2   BRB (2138) F234 Embossed slipware dish, late 17th–early 18th century
3   BRB (3042) F309 Embossed slipware dish, part of human head, late 17th–early 18th century

Fig. 7.23 colour, Slipware, nos 1–2
1   PSB (1530) F520 Trailed/feathered slipware dish, first half of 18th century
2   PSB (1512) F500 Feathered slipware dish, late 17th–early 18th century

Fig. 7.24 colour, Creamware (c.1760–1780), nos 1–4
1   BRB (1009) F104 Queen's edge plate
2   BRB (1009) F104 Octagonal plate
3   PSB (1621) F542 Plate with scalloped edge and moulded fleur-de-lys design
4   PSB (1621) and (1622) F542 Creamware plate edges

Fig. 7.25 colour, Decorated creamware (1750s–70s), nos 1–6
1   PSB (1622) F542 Saucer, internal green brown and ochre decoration
2   PSB (1634) F542 Fluted saucer, internal green glaze stripes
3   PSB (1531) F510 Totoiseshell mug rim, sprigged decoration
4   PSB (1621) F542 Saucer rim and body sherd, overglaze painted decoration
5   PSB (1755) F738 Overglaze painted creamware
6   PSB (1139) F138 Lid, underglaze painted decoration

Fig. 7.26 colour, White salt-glazed stoneware (c.1720–1760), nos 1–3
1   PSB (1621) F542 Plain circular 8-inch plate
2   PSB (1621) F542 Plate, moulded chevron and basketwork pattern
3   PSB F542 and F503 Various plate rims, moulded basketwork pattern, barley corn and basket and barley corn pattern, weave and star/diaper pattern, plain circular 10-inch plate

Fig. 7.27 colour, Miscellaneous post-medieval glazed wares, nos 1–6
1   PSB (1621) F542 White salt glaze, scratch blue bowl rim sherd c.1740s–60s
     PSB (1621) F542 Two small white salt-glazed, scratch blue body sherds.
2A PSB (1621) F542 Saucer, soft paste porcelain, internal blue decoration
2B PSB (1530) F542 Saucer, soft paste porcelain, internal blue decoration
3   PSB (1622) F542 Pearlware, external blue underglaze painted decoration
4   PSB (1621) F542 ?Teapot, lion's mask and paw foot, moulded white salt-glazed ware
5   PSB (1621) F542 Mug rim, agate ware
6   PSB (1632) F542 Bowl rim, agate ware

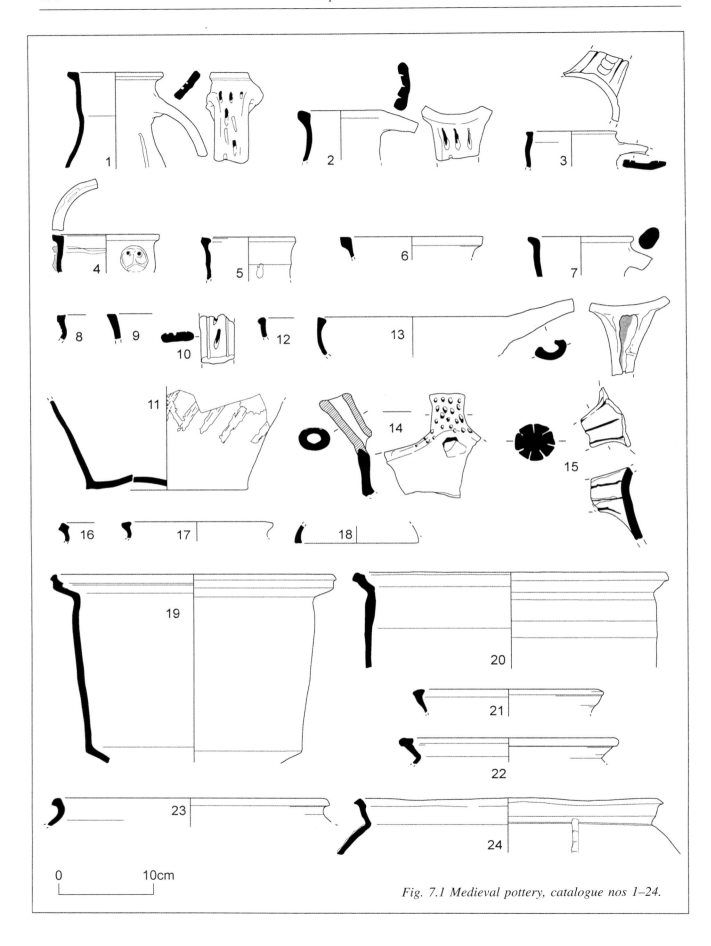

Fig. 7.1 Medieval pottery, catalogue nos 1–24.

0   10cm

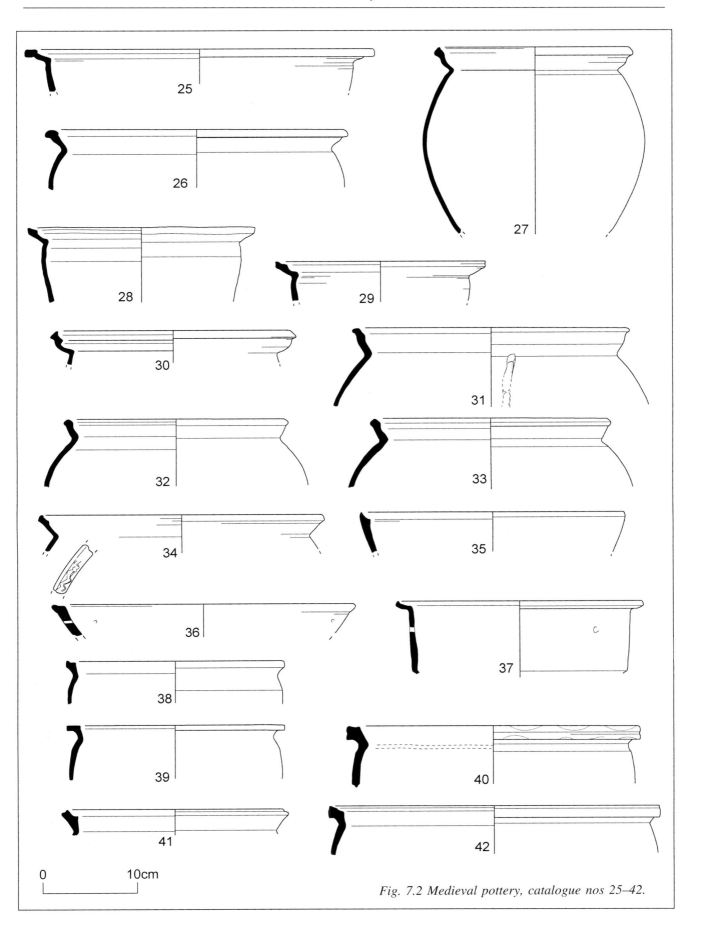

Fig. 7.2 Medieval pottery, catalogue nos 25–42.

0   10cm

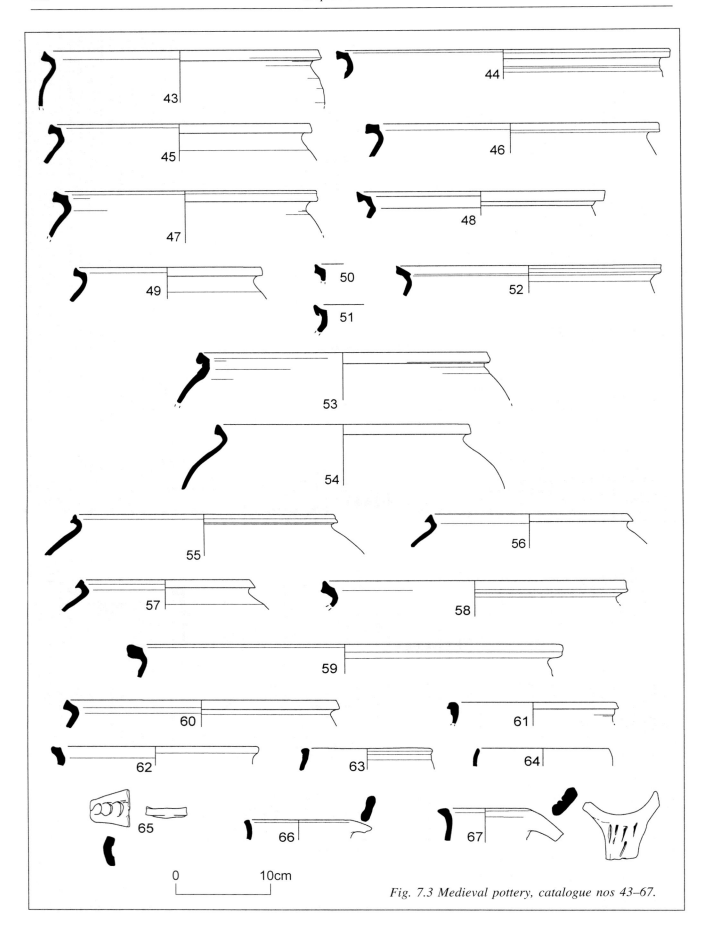

0   10cm

Fig. 7.3 Medieval pottery, catalogue nos 43–67.

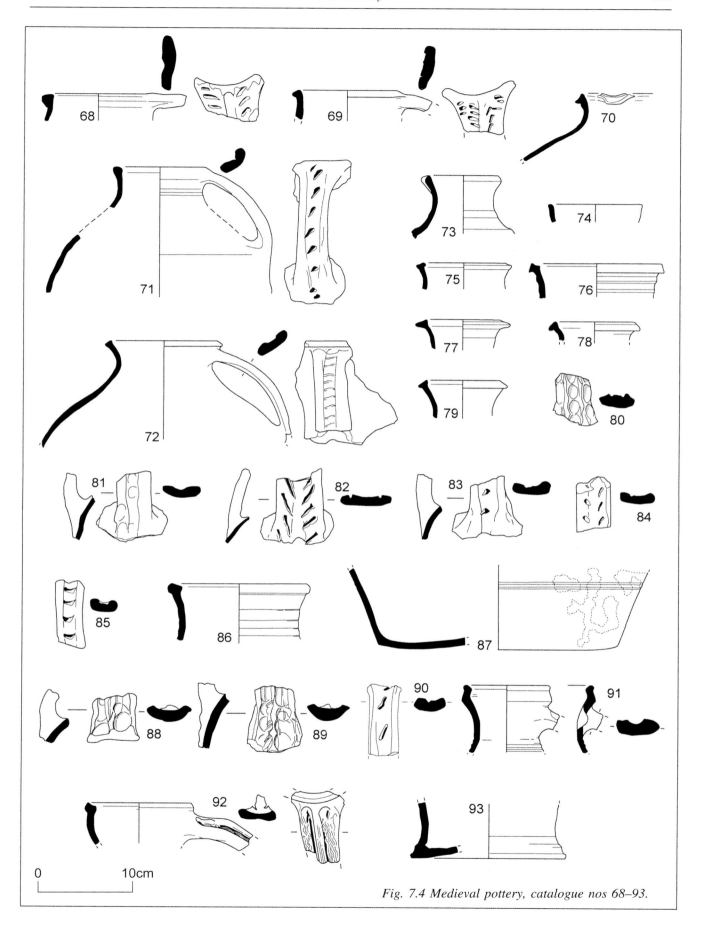

Fig. 7.4 Medieval pottery, catalogue nos 68–93.

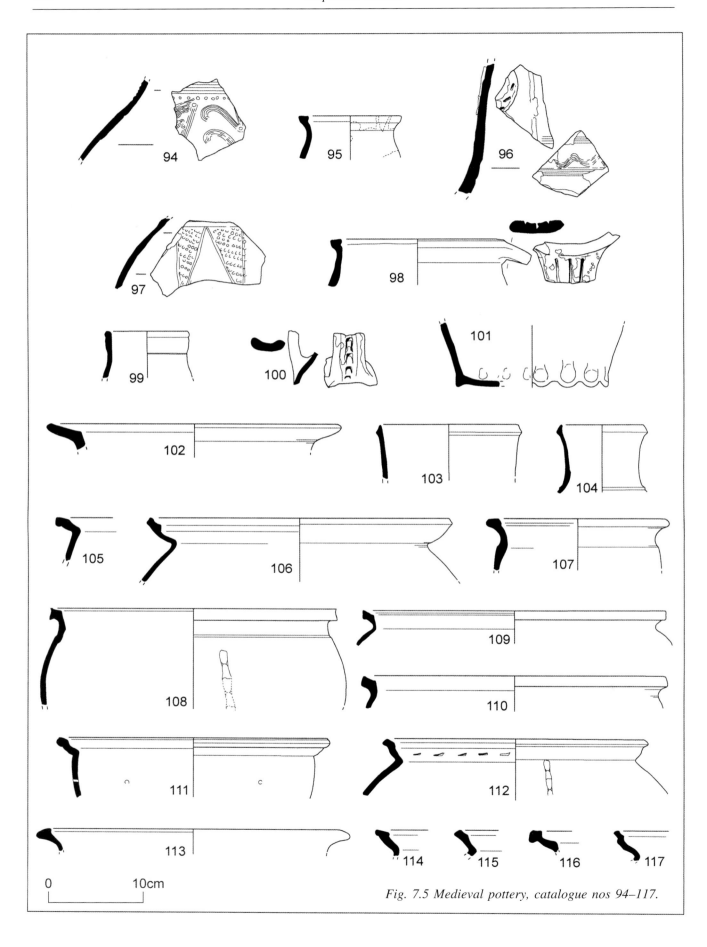

Fig. 7.5 Medieval pottery, catalogue nos 94–117.

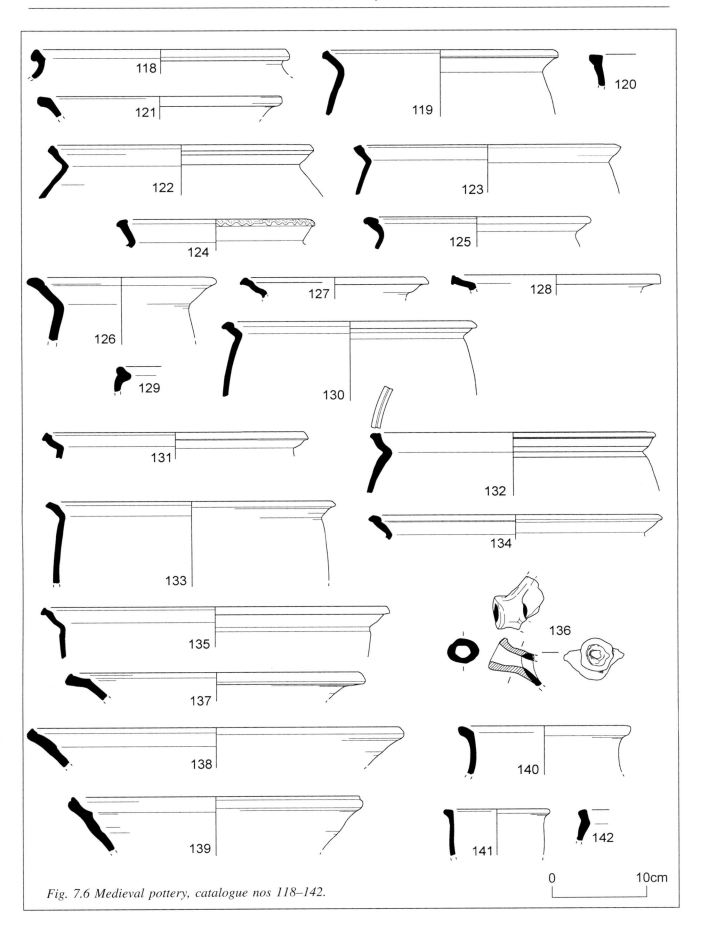

Fig. 7.6 Medieval pottery, catalogue nos 118–142.

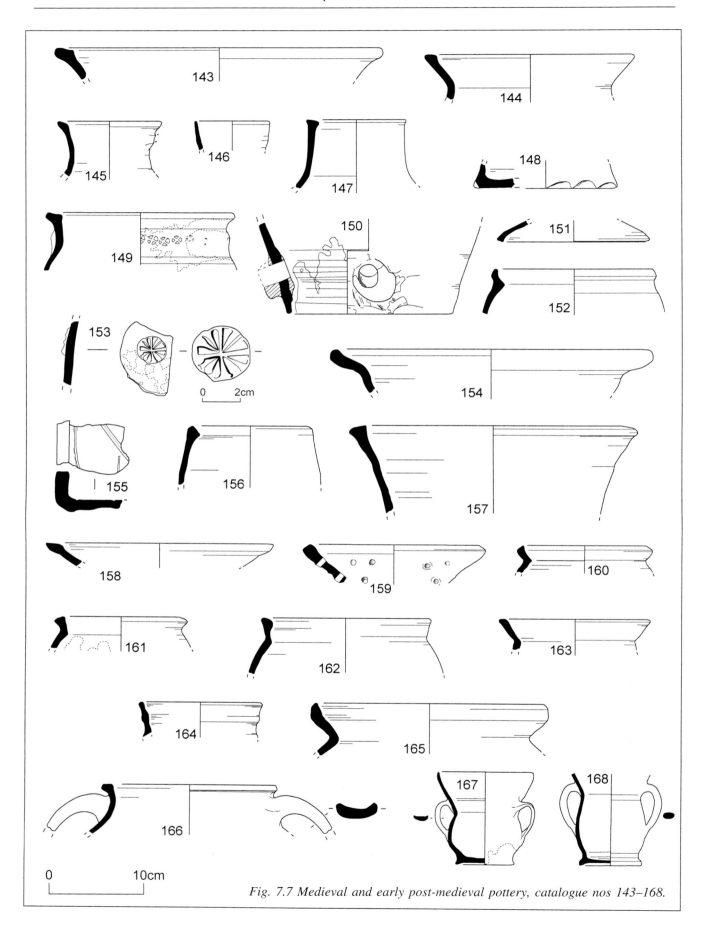

Fig. 7.7 Medieval and early post-medieval pottery, catalogue nos 143–168.

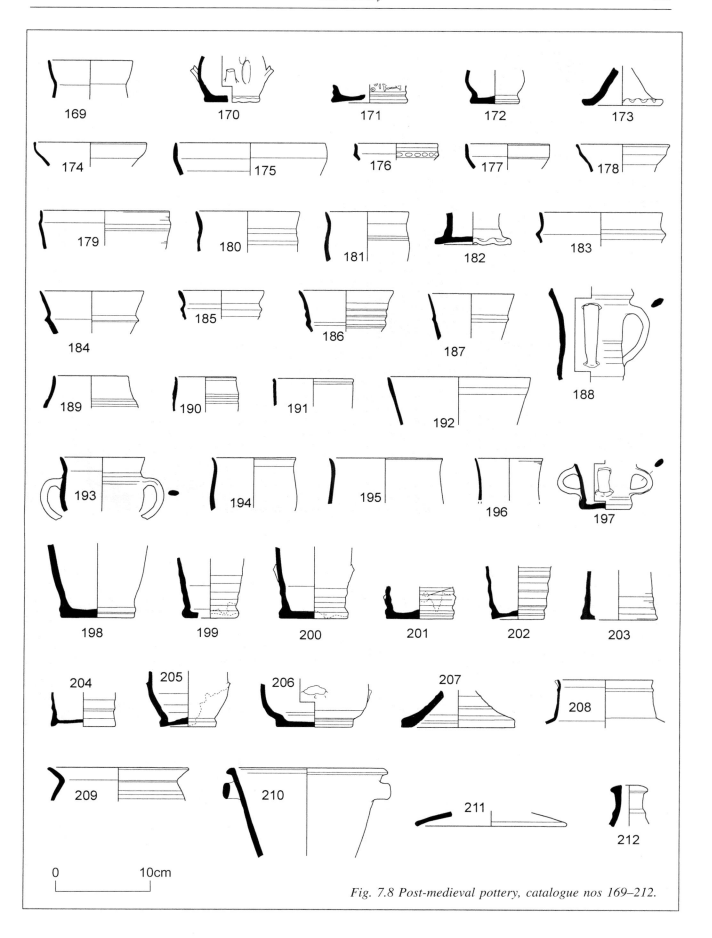

Fig. 7.8 Post-medieval pottery, catalogue nos 169–212.

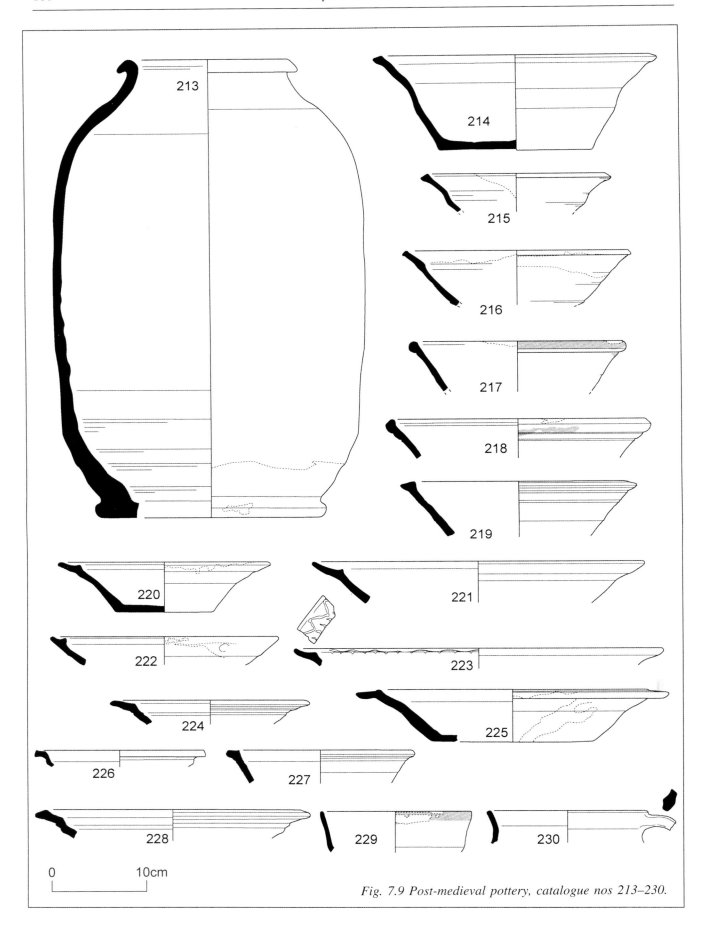

0 10cm

Fig. 7.9 Post-medieval pottery, catalogue nos 213–230.

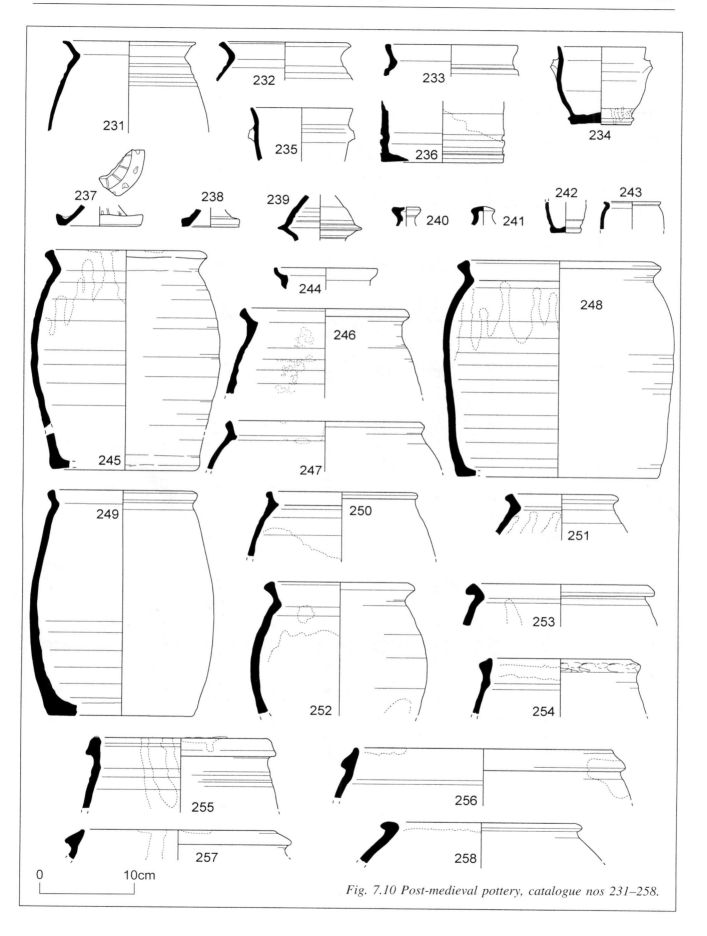

Fig. 7.10 Post-medieval pottery, catalogue nos 231–258.

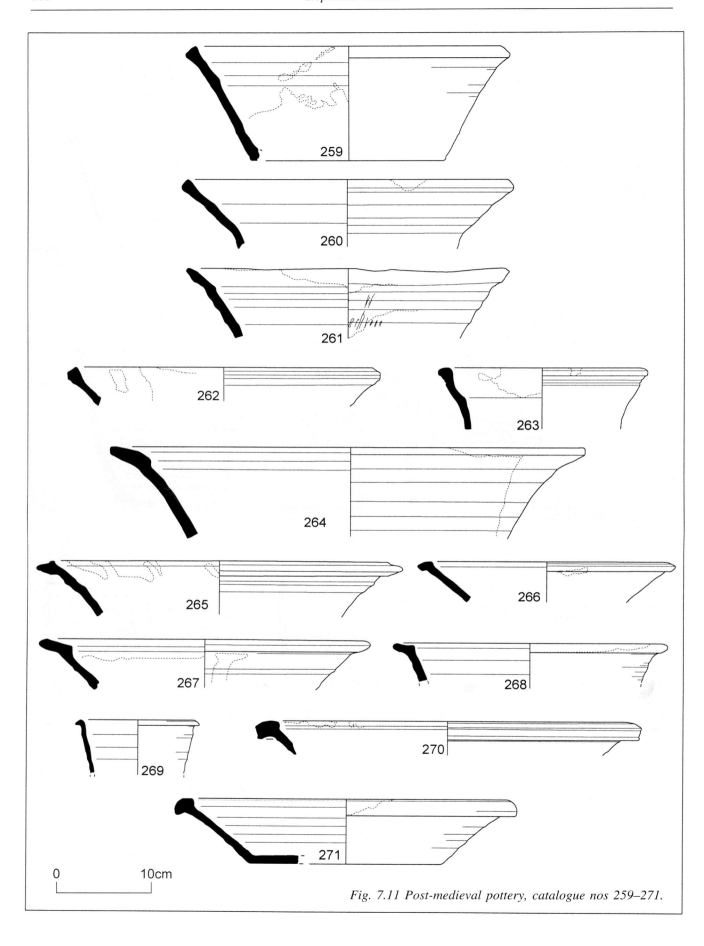

Fig. 7.11 Post-medieval pottery, catalogue nos 259–271.

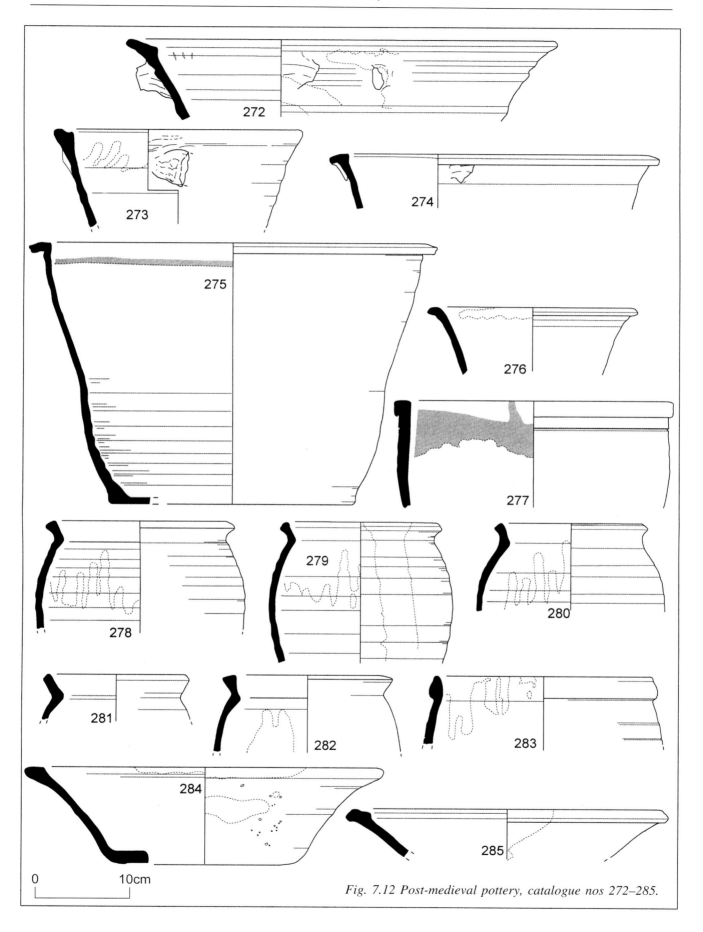

Fig. 7.12 Post-medieval pottery, catalogue nos 272–285.

0   10cm

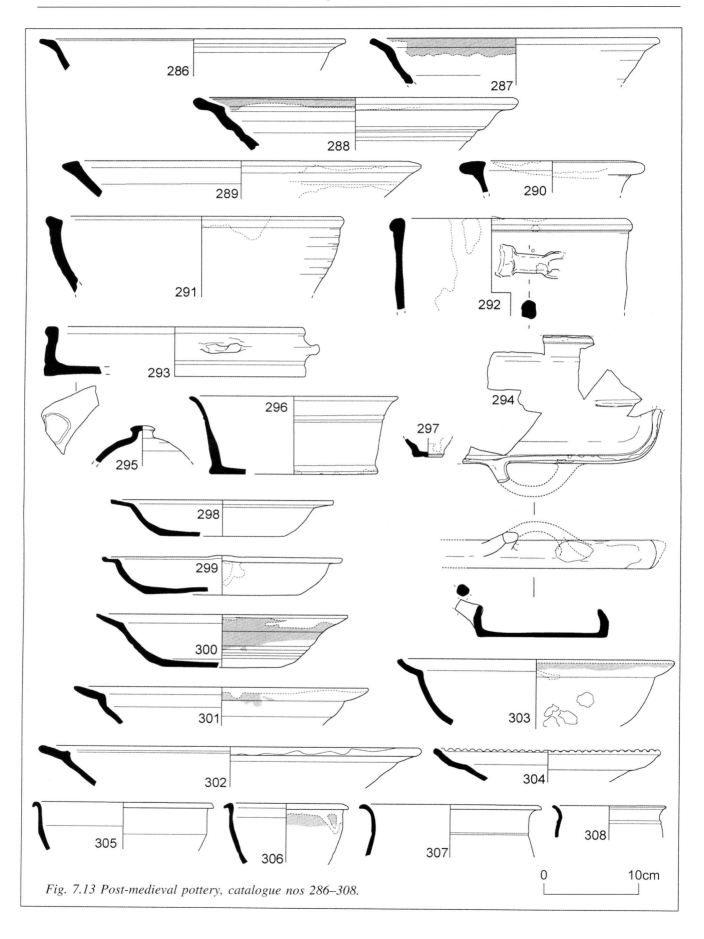

Fig. 7.13 Post-medieval pottery, catalogue nos 286–308.

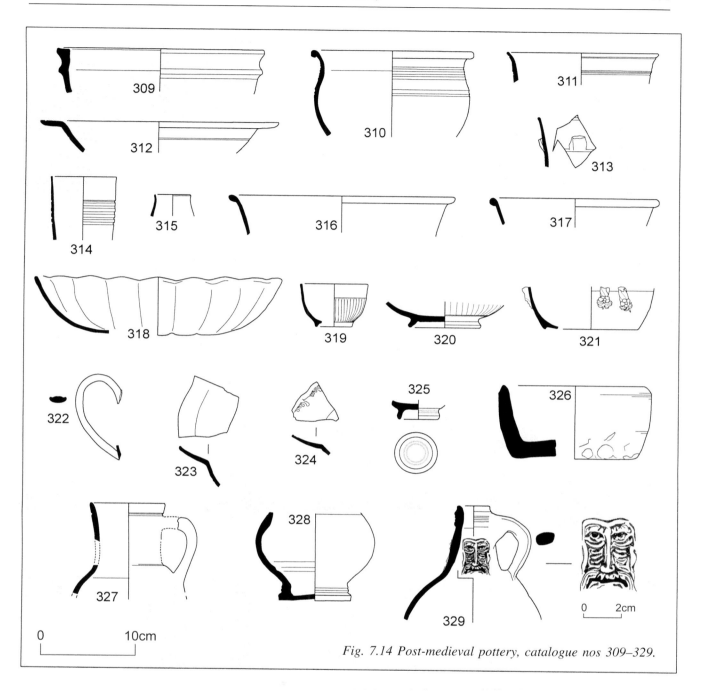

Fig. 7.14 Post-medieval pottery, catalogue nos 309–329.

8 The Medieval and Post-Medieval Small Finds

Lynne Bevan, Quita Mould and Stephanie Rátkai

with contributions by Sheila Hamilton-Dyer, Rob Ixer, Erica Macey-Bracken and David Orton

Overview
by Stephanie Rátkai and Lynne Bevan

Introduction

Prior to the Bull Ring excavations, the only assemblage of small finds from the city centre was that recovered during salvage recording on the site of the Birmingham Moat in the 1970s (Watts 1980). The small finds assemblages from Edgbaston Street, Moor Street and Park Street therefore form an invaluable body of evidence for both every-day life and for the numerous crafts and industries practised in Birmingham from the medieval period through to the 19th century. A limitation of the evidence from the small finds is the large quantity of material that was residual, mostly found in the backfills of pits and ditches.

Certain material groups discussed in detail below, including the bone, ivory and horn finds, the glass vessels and waste material, and the evidence for shell working and leather working, are of considerable importance in terms of reconstructing past industrial and commercial activities in the historic centre of Birmingham. Even with the benefit of trade directories detailing the location of various crafts in the city and the names of the craftsmen who practised them (*e.g.* Wrightson 1818), very little information is available regarding the organisation of the crafts and the kinds of artefacts and waste material they produced. This is exactly the kind of information provided by these excavated assemblages. Such small-scale craft industries are known to have been an important aspect of Birmingham's economy in the 18th and 19th centuries and the evidence presented here demonstrates that certain craft and industrial activities, including the cutlery trade, were present in the earlier post-medieval period and possibly in the medieval period.

Range of medieval and post-medieval artefacts

A wide range of artefacts was recovered, of both medieval and post-medieval date, the majority of which were photographed in order to provide a visual record of the finds. The standard of preservation was particularly high among the organic materials such as bone, horn and shell, and wood. One of the more complete were the remains of an oak chair dated to the mid-17th century preserved in the backfill of a wood-lined tank on the Park Street site (Fig. 8.1 and 8.2, colour). Metals tended to be more fragmentary and generally less chronologically diagnostic.

Many of the artefacts discovered were connected with various trades and industries; others were of a more personal nature, often commonplace. However, the presence of early vessel glass (Orton and Rátkai below), albeit in small quantities, the crested ridge and glazed roof tiles from Edgbaston Street, together with a decorated floor tile fragment – a rare find in Birmingham – (Macey-Bracken below), suggest buildings and occupation of some status in the late medieval period.

Three groups of finds stood out from the rest because of the quantity of material in them. The first of these came from Phase 4 pit F836 (fills 1768, 1769, 1770, 1771 and 1773) which lay adjacent to Structure 4 on the northwestern edge of Area C Park Street. Deposit 1771 was the earliest in the sequence. Notable among the finds were lace ends, thimbles, an eyelet, a belt slider and pins, together with leather shoe parts, including a Victorian laced leather boot and a large quantity of probably 19th-century leather offcuts. Taken together, these finds would seem to indicate a dump of cobbler's waste. Copper alloy wire and buttons found in the fills may also have been connected with this trade. Other finds included a brush (Fig. 8.10.7, colour) fragments from an iron bucket and a sheet metal box, and a padlock. The deposit was clearly quite late and produced a good group of clay pipe dated 1850–1870. A third deposit (1769), which lay above 1770, produced large amounts of slag and charcoal (see Nicholas, Chapter 10). The clay pipe suggested a deposition date of 1790–1840 for this fill. The function of F836, which is bordered on three sides by walls F736, F737 and F741, is unclear (see Chapter 4) but it seems most likely that it was dug and backfilled before the construction of St Martin's National School in *c*.1871.

The second group, also from Park Street came from a cleaning layer (1738) after the removal of the overburden in the area of Structures 2 and 4. This too contained shoe parts and a Victorian boot but the variety of other finds suggested that they had not derived from one particular craft or trade. Finds included various metal fittings, window sash stays and furniture castors, metal-working tools, a whetstone, bone and copper alloy-working waste, a bone spoon, a copper alloy buckle, a piece of possibly early window glass and a possible pipe tamper. The suggested deposition date for the clay pipe was 1800–1880, although most of the clay pipe belonged to the period 1680–1740. The pottery too contained 19th-century wares but also residual medieval and post-medieval sherds.

Finally there was another group from Park Street (1101), which was a cleaning layer like 1738. This contained the largest group of clay pipe from the Bull Ring, with a suggested deposition date of 1820–1840. As with 1738, bone-working waste and leather shoe parts were present. Metal waste for recycling was noted, together with copper alloy buttons, a scabbard chape and a finial. An iron knife, wine bottles and window glass were also present.

Although the latter two groups were very mixed they do present a snapshot of the wide variety of trades that had been carried on in Park Street. In the 18th and 19th centuries it was not uncommon to have single-cell workshops, sometimes multi-storey, in the courts of back-to-back and blind-back housing. Small-scale, one-man trades, such as bicycle-spoke maker, would utilise such premises (pers. comm. Margaret Bonham). Such working practices probably offer an explanation for the amalgamation of different kinds of trade debris at Park Street. However, it is very difficult, if not impossible, to tie in industrial processes with excavated features and artefactual material (pers. comm. Geoff Egan) and it may never be possible to know exactly what industries were taking place on Park Street nor their exact location, at least from archaeological evidence alone.

Evidence for craft activity

Evidence for various industries and crafts was recovered, including bone-working, possible horn-working, ivory-working, leather-working, glass-making and shell-working. The bone- and ivory-working industries at both Edgbaston Street and Park Street produced distinctive waste products (Figs 8.11.7, colour). There was also

evidence for the production of knife handles and toothbrushes at Park Street (Fig. 8.10.10, colour and Fig. 8.11, colour), where bone- and ivory-working were practised from the 17th–19th centuries, although probably not continuously. Bone-working appears to have been a very long-lived craft in central Birmingham, probably dating from the beginning of the city's history and continuing into the Victorian period, when ivory turning became part of the craftsman's repertoire (Wrightson 1818). As ivory offcuts, including part of an elephant tusk (see Hamilton-Dyer below), were found in Phase 3 contexts at both Edgbaston Street and Park Street, the working of ivory appears to have begun well before the Victorian period.

Tanning, leather-working and cobbling waste was found at Edgbaston Street and Park Street from the medieval period onwards. There is good evidence for leather-working at Edgbaston Street (see Macey-Bracken and Mould, below), where a dump of shoe-making waste was found in a 19th-century demolition deposit. Further shoe-making waste of a similar date was found at Park Street.

Shell working was conducted on an apparently small scale at Edgbaston Street for the production of pearl shell buttons, probably mainly in the early years of the 19th century. Here, a fragment of waste shell was recovered with hand-cut circular perforations from which button blanks had been removed (Fig. 8.7, colour), along with other shell-working debris. Similar evidence has been recovered from the excavations at the nearby Custard Factory (Mould 2001a), Floodgate Street, Digbeth (Williams 2002), and from Tameside Park, Perry Barr (Halsted 2006). Despite Birmingham's pre-eminence in this trade, shell button waste was also found at a site in Bilston, near Wolverhampton (Jones 1993).

The location of this evidence for shell button manufacture is of particular interest since it was outside the main focus of button-making, in the area bounded by Colmore Row, Snow Hill, Mount Street and Congreve Street, during the peak of the industry in the mid–late 19th century (White 1977, 75–6). In the earliest days of the craft, prior to mechanisation, it appears that shell button making was carried out on a small scale from workshops near the Bull Ring. This area appears to have been a focus for other crafts such as bone-, and possibly horn-working, as well as being associated with tanning, leather-working and metal-working. Evidence for small-scale glass-working and possibly recycling has also been documented (see Orton and Rátkai this volume).

Evidence for metal-working (apart from the crucibles discussed in Chapter 10) comprised copper alloy scrap for recycling, solidified lead droplets and a button with casting sprue attached.

The small finds

Wooden objects

Park Street

A broken, but still partially articulated, wooden chair was discovered in the backfill of a probable wood-lined tank (F503/F520) on the Park Street site, together with a dump of pottery, possibly associated with a house clearance of the late 18th century (Phase 3.3). Part of the back of the chair was missing at the time of its deposition and only a small segment of the leather chair seat and back, and some traces of organic stuffing, probably horse hair or wool, had survived (see Figs 8.1 and 8.2, colour). Despite degradation, it was possible to reconstruct the original form of the chair. It was a heavy, solid style of chair, probably made of oak, with bobbin-turned front legs and stretcher, and would originally have had a studded leather seat. A number of similar copper alloy upholstery studs were found elsewhere on Park Street (see below). Such chairs, usually made of oak, were popular during the mid-17th century (*e.g.* Edwards 1951, fig. 23; Yarwood 1979, 95: 172). The chair was probably over a hundred years old when it was disposed of in the tank.

Colour illustration Fig. 8.2 gives an impression of how the chair may have originally looked.

Catalogue

– Remains of a wooden chair, comprising two front legs and a stretcher with bobbin-turned decoration, one rear leg and part of chair back and seat with fragments of leather attached. Surviving length of rear chair leg: 720mm, width: 70mm. Surviving length of front chair legs: 380mm, width: 50mm. Area B, F503/F520 (tank), 1506/ 1521, Phase 3.3. Figs 8.1 and 8.2, colour.

Copper alloy objects

Edgbaston Street

This small assemblage was poorly preserved, fragmentary and not chronologically diagnostic; the majority came from Phase 4 (19th-century) contexts. It comprised wire (5024), a worn penny (1007), a token, and a Victorian penny (4002), another possible coin (1005), two broken nails (5100, 7005), a circular domed object, possibly a nailhead or rivet (3017), a curved strip (2105), a nail with fragment of cloth attached, (2062 Phase 2 tanning pit F223), a curved fragment from a large ring (2069), two fragments of plate (5107), copper alloy sheet (2002), and pins and collars of thin sheet (5100). An unfinished button of a white metal with the casting sprue still attached was found unstratified.

Moor Street

A very small quantity of material from the manufacturing of small copper alloy items was found at Moor Street in evaluation contexts of uncertain date, and comprised slag fragments along with a possible nail/ pin (1316), wire (4004), and an unstratified sheet fragment.

Fig. 8.1 Surviving parts of wooden chair in situ.

Park Street

This copper alloy assemblage was likewise poorly preserved and largely fragmentary but not without interest. Two small dress accessories, a small decorative double-lobed bar mount for leather found in context 1108, one of the post-medieval 'dark earths' discussed in Chapter 4, and the possible head from a spherical button from context 1678, a Phase 3 pit fill, may be of medieval date but residual in their contexts. Other items of personal dress included three lace ends or aiglets with the textile lace preserved within (*e.g.* Fig. 8.3.1, 1141, 1770, 1771, the latter with the entire lace present). The lace end from 1141, the fill of Phase 3.1 pit F141, is of probable early post-medieval date (Egan and Pritchard 1991, 281) and not residual in its context. The lace end from 1771 was found with a laced Victorian boot, shoe parts and leather offcuts (amongst other things) and may therefore be the lace end from a 19th-century shoe-lace. A scabbard chape was found in 1101 (Fig. 8.3.2). Similar chapes made from folded sheet have been recovered from late 15th- to mid-16th-century contexts at Winchester (Hinton 1990, fig. 368; 4033, 4034, 1083). Buckles were found in three contexts (1158, 1738, 1798), two of which from Phase 3 layer 1158, were shoe buckles.

A hook for clothing (SF13/1126, Fig. 8.4.2, colour) was recovered from a Phase 3.1 pit F134. Buttons were recorded from 19th-century contexts 1101 Phase 4/5, 1122 F131, 1133 F139 and 1771 F836 Phase 4, from a 17th-century context 1678 (see above), and two came from Phase 3.3 tank fill 1634. A domed button inlaid with blue-green glass (Fig. 8.4.4, colour), probably of late 18th-century date, was found unstratified in Area C. A hoop-shaped earring (SF23/1728, Fig. 8.4.1, colour) was found in a pit F702.

There were several items of haberdashery in the assemblage, including three thimbles from late contexts

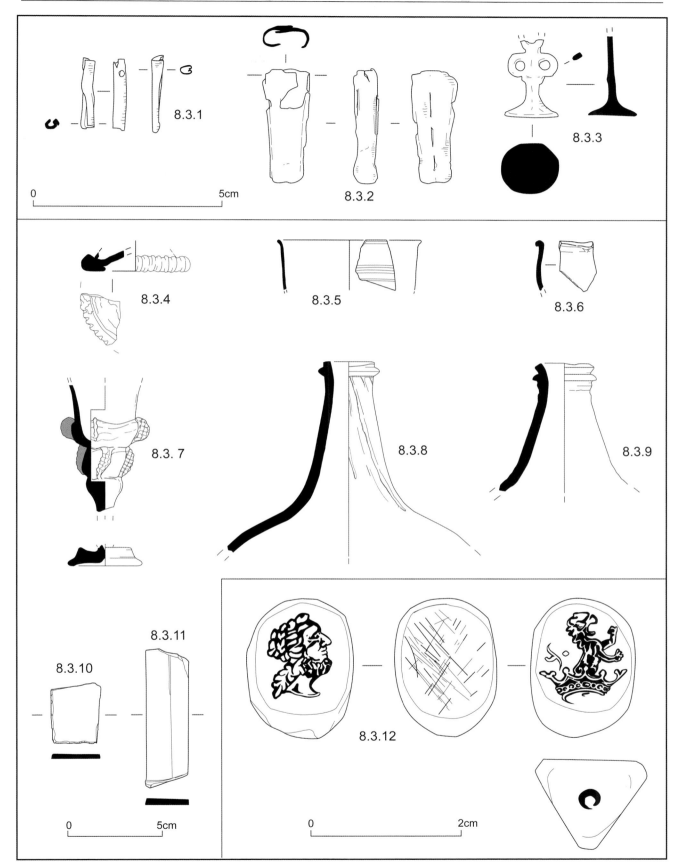

Fig. 8.3 Cu Alloy, glass and crystal objects; 8.3.1 Cu alloy lace end, 8.3.2 Cu alloy chape, 8.3.3 Cu alloy pipe tamper, 8.3.4 beaker base, 8.3.5 ?goblet rim, 8.3.6 glass ?bowl rim, 8.3.7 Ravenscroft-style lead glass wine glass stem, 8.3.8 wine bottle, 8.3.9 wine bottle, 8.3.10 window glass, 8.3.11 window glass, 8.3.12 rock crystal swivel seal.

(SF 27/1770 F836, SF5/1752, SF 28/1771) and one from (SF 4), unstratified. A late 19th- to early 20th-century date is likely for the complete thimble (1770 F836), which is machine-made with a series of regularly spaced concentric circles radiating from a wide register of plain banding at the base. This typological dating accords with the Phase 4 (19th-century) context of the find.

Brass pins with wire-wound heads were found in 1752, fill of Phase 4 pit F720, 1768 and 1770, fills of Phase 4 pit F836, 1842, fill of Phase 3 pit F775, 1806 cleaning layer Phase 4/5. Examples with upset heads, products of automated manufacture introduced in the middle of the 19th century, were noted in 1728, 1771 and 1806. An eyelet and a looped strip (possibly a belt slider or other fitting) were also found in 1771.

Other identifiable objects included a small decorative finial with a screw thread (1101, Fig. 8.4.3, colour), and a token or head from a flat button, now totally degraded (1101). A ferrule was found in a 19th-century context 1167 F154. A probable pipe tamper (Fig. 8.3.3), originally identified as a seal, was recovered from 1738.

A piece of loop-in-loop chain was seen from 1220, the fill of Phase 2 pit F188. Loop-in-loop chain was used from at least the Roman period onwards, so it is not independently datable. The fill of the pit contained predominantly medieval pottery (see Rátkai, Chapter 7) and the absence of occupation evidence in Phase 2 of the Park Street backplots may suggest that the chain was medieval and residual in the pit fill. The chain was probably from an item of jewellery or from a trinket.

Domestic fittings included the arm from a small hinge (1144 F141 Phase 3.1), studs with domed heads (1125 F133 Phase 3.2, 1678 Phase 3, 1917 F808 Phase 3.1), probably from upholstery, a tap head from layer 1505 sealing the tanks in Area B, and a key hole escutcheon with openwork decoration (1798 F749).

There was evidence for the working of copper alloy. Small pieces of copper alloy slag were found in five contexts (1102 × 2, 1708 F700 Phase 3.2 × 2, 1721, 1738 and 1798). A solidified droplet (1133 F139 Phase 4, 1842 F775 Phase 3), a partly made item (1172), offcuts of copper alloy sheet (1176 F159 Phase 3, 1917 F808, Phase 3.1), small fragments of sheet folded ready for re-cycling (1101, 1738×2), and wire fragments (1103 Phase 4/5, 1770 and 1771 Phase 4 pit F836). Other fragments of broken copper alloy sheet were also found (1219 F186 Phase 2, 1708 F700 Phase 3.2, 1908 F811 Phase 3.3, 1101, 1738, 1107 and 1110 Phase 4/5).

Catalogue
– Aiglet or lace end (with fibres preserved). Length: 18mm and 19mm, width: 3mm, thickness: 2mm. Area A, 1141 F141 Phase 3.1, Fig. 8.3.1.
– Hoop earring for pierced ear. Length: 22mm, thickness: 2mm. Area C, F702 (pit), 1728 (SF23), Phase 3.1. Fig. 8.4.1, colour.
– Clothing hook. Length: 17mm, width: 15mm, thickness: 1.5mm. Area A, F134 (pit), 1126 (SF13), Phase 3.1. Fig.

8.4.2, colour.
– Scabbard chape, of sheet form, very degraded. Length: 60mm, width: 24mm, thickness: 1mm. Area A, 1101 (SF6), Phase 4/5. Fig. 8.3.2.
– Ornamental fitting or finial, possibly from furniture, with a bun-shaped head with concentric ring decoration, collar and a screw thread shank. Possibly 19th/ 20th century in date. Diameter of head: 7mm. Length: 29mm. Area A, 1101, Phase 4/5. Fig. 8.4.3, colour.
– ?Pipe tamper, broken at terminal. Area C, 1738, Phase 4/5. Fig. 8.3.3.
– Ornamental button, inlaid with pale blue-green glass, with milled decoration around the metal edge. Probably late 18th or early 19th century. Diameter: 13mm, thickness: 5mm. Area C, 1738, Phase 4/5. Fig. 8.4.4, colour.

Iron objects

Edgbaston Street

Over a hundred iron finds were recovered, just over half of which consisted of nails. Further research was precluded in many cases by the generally poor condition of the objects, their high degree of corrosion and fragmentation and, in several cases, their relatively recent appearance. With one exception, a fragment of plate from a Phase 1 pit (F105, 1010), all the iron finds are of post-medieval or modern date and were all found in late contexts.

Of interest in the iron assemblage was a damaged, but largely complete, cauldron which originally had a tripod base (Fig. 8.5). The cauldron was recovered from 5039, a layer in the watercourse, during the evaluation. Cauldrons were used in down hearth cooking and were still in use in the south of the country as late as the 1930s (Butler and Green 2003, 17). This makes dating the cauldron morphologically very difficult, although its context (5039) suggests a 19th-century date. Fragments of sheet metal vessels were also present in 5041 a late clinker layer and 5107 the upper fill of a brick culvert. Other household items of iron included a candleholder (5107), a possible key (1009), a knife (1006), and a possible knife from (1056) the fill of a Phase 1 post-hole or pit F135.

Structural ironwork included a large bolt and washer (5119), two wall ties (1009, 1026), and a large ring-headed pin (1026).

Evidence for metal working was present, including small fragments of slag (5039, 5112) and small snippets of sheet metal (5012). Context 2006, a Phase 3/4 cleaning layer, and (4054) the fill of a Phase 3 lime pit F419, produced an interesting group of finds associated with the working of sheet metal. A series of flat discs of sheet, the largest with a diameter of 120mm (4054), three measuring 100mm in diameter and a further four of 61mm, were found along with a small disc tag stamped with the number 23 and four metal punches used to punch such numbers into metal. The punches were of square cross section and measured 60mm, 64mm, 66mm and 72mm in length. The better preserved example could be seen to have the number 23 on the head and it is possible that it had been used to punch the numbers onto the identification tag found with it. This same context also contained two tanged rasps, a large broken twist bit for a drill, and two lengths of bar iron covered in soot. This collection of tools is clearly much later than the pottery found in both contexts which was no later than the 18th century.

Catalogue
– Cauldron with tripod base, only two legs of which remain *in situ*. Surviving diameter: *c*.200mm, height: 220mm, average thickness: 5mm. 5039 (recovered from backfill of watercourse during evaluation). Fig. 8.5.

Moor Street
Seven iron nails were recovered, three from the Phase 1 ditch and a pit (5130, 5153, 5128) and four from later contexts (5105, 5112, 5119, 6000).

Park Street
Iron objects were in a generally poor state of preservation, with a high incidence of corrosion. Identifiable items included two buckles (1125, 1053), a plier punch, a small file, a small scriber and three decorative fittings (1738), a range of household items, and 213 iron nails. The plier punch or punch pliers (1738) was a small hand tool used to punch a hole by various leather trades including boot and shoe making, saddle and harness making (Salaman 1986, 165). The pliers had sprung handles to hold the jaws apart.

One of the buckles (1053) was a harness strap buckle of mid-19th–early 20th-century date (Cuddeford 1994, 10, 14), and the other was a one-piece trapezoidal buckle of probable 18th-century date (1125) recovered from Phase 3.2 pit F133.

Much of the ironwork comprised domestic implements

and household fittings, the largest group being found in context 1738, a Phase 4/5 cleaning layer. Domestic items included knives (1101, 1168, 1680 Phase 3.3 tank fill), a spoon (1752), a possible ladle (1168), a large key (from the construction trench fill 1755 of wall F738), Structure 2 Phase 3), a shield-shaped padlock (1770 F836), furniture castors (1738, 1793 associated with cellar F747, Structure 3, Phase 4) and box fittings (1738). With the exception of the key and the knife, all these finds were from 19th-century contexts.

A number of sheet metal vessels with rolled rims could be identified (1122 F131 Phase 3, 1739 F713 Phase 3.2, 1235 and 1241 F194 Phase 3.3, 1770 and 1771 F836 Phase 4), though now badly decayed; while most were buckets, at least two sheet metal boxes (1235, 1771) were represented. Most of the sheet metal vessels are likely to date to the 19th century. Household fittings such as window and sash stays (1517 F539 Phase 2 but disturbed by later Phase 3 pits F504 and F527, layer 1753 Phase 3/4, 1738 Phase 4/5) were also recorded.

Three unidentified iron rod fragments were found in a Phase 1 layer 1763 and a fourth in 1815, the fill of Phase 3.2 pit F764. Much of the remaining iron was fragmentary and largely unidentifiable. A full archive listing of the nails and corroded and fragmentary items has been compiled by context.

Lead and lead alloy objects

Edgbaston Street
Lead finds comprised an unstratified dome-shaped solidified droplet, a partly melted object with pelleted decoration (1034 pit F120 Phase 3), likely to be a buckle, two domed stud heads of lead alloy (3009/3010 pit F304 Phase 3), and a fragment of strip (1007).

Moor Street
A fragment of folded lead sheet from fill (5122) of a charcoal-rich Phase 1 pit F556, a small piece of piping from a Phase 4 well (5134), and a solidified droplet (unstratified) were recovered.

Park Street
An ovoid lead weight with a perforation for suspension (Fig. 8.6.1, colour) was recovered from a probable medieval layer (1756) in the vicinity of the graves in Area C. The weight is comparable with a 'pendant weight' from London (Egan 1998b, fig. 231, 310–311) which was probably used for industrial purposes (*ibid*. 311), the exact nature of which is not specified.

Other lead finds included a spatulate object with a circular-sectioned stem (1706), possibly a spoon, and a fragment of offcut sheet (1705); both these items are from the fill of a Phase 1 tank or pond (F714) and may represent scrap for recycling. Small quantities of window leading (trimmings from window cames) were recovered from 18th-century pits in Area C (1739 F713 Phase 3.2, 1752 pit F720 Phase 4). A possible buckle of pewter was found in 1758.

Fig. 8.5 Reconstruction drawing of the cauldron.

Catalogue
- Ovoid weight, with a diamond-shaped section and a perforation for suspension. Length: 61mm, maximum width: 20mm, weight: 80 grams. Area C, SF 9/1756, Phase 1. Fig. 8.6.1, colour.

Glass
by David Orton and Stephanie Rátkai

A large collection of vessel glass was found on all three sites, although that from Moor Street was too fragmentary for detailed analysis. Most of the vessel glass was made up of 19th-century bottles. A full report on all the later glass by David Orton can be found in the archive (Orton 2001).

Edgbaston Street
Vessel glass
The earliest fragment of a drinking vessel is from the base of a mid-green, now opaque, Forest Glass beaker with a crimped or rigaree-patterned foot (1048, Fig. 8.3.4). The form is paralleled in Willmott (2002, 111, fig. 149). The beakers have a floruit of c.1550–1650 but are most common in the first half of the 17th century. The rigaree-patterned foot disappeared during the middle of the 17th century (Willmott 2002, 36–7). The fragment was recovered from a Phase 3 pit (F129) in Area A. The pottery from this pit was dated to the first half of the 17th century.

Nine fragments from at least five clear glass decanters were recovered from the infilling of a Phase 4 well (F111), all of which appear to date from the late 18th to early 19th century.

Catalogue
- Base fragment from a mid-green, now opaque, beaker. Diameter: 60mm, thickness: 4–6mm. Area A, F129 (pit), 1048, Phase 3. Fig. 8.3.4.

Wine bottles
Glass wine bottles were introduced in the early 17th century (Hedges 1996, 7). While it would appear that the earliest wine bottles, consisting of globe body with a long neck, are not present in the Edgbaston Street assemblage, two examples of the more globular, shorter-necked bottles produced from the late 17th to the early 18th century were present, one found in the fill of the Phase 3 pit F301, the other in the fill of Phase 3 pit F338. Both of these pits are part of the regularly laid-out series of tanning or tawyering pits in Area C (see Patrick and Rátkai, Chapter 2). However, there is an absence of bottles from the 1720s to c.1750s in the Edgbaston Street assemblage, when the globe shape evolved into a narrower bottle with a longer neck. The absence of wine bottles of this date reflects the pottery and clay pipe data and seems to provide further evidence of a change in use of the backplots, interpreted as their use as gardens (see Patrick and Rátkai, Chapter 2). The next period represented is the mid- to late 18th century, with the remains of at least 20 wine bottles from this period recovered. One was found

in the backfill of Phase 3 well F327. The remainder were either unstratified in Areas B, C and D (a minimum of six bottles) or came from Phase 4 wells F104, where they were found with part of a creamware dinner service (see Rátkai, Chapter 7 and Fig. 7.24.1–2) and F111 in Area A and Phase 4 well F400 in Area D.

Glass manufacture
Evidence for glass production is also present in the Edgbaston Street glass assemblage, in the form of two clear moiles from glass blowing (5112), two almost-complete ceramic crucibles (unstratified) and broken fragments from several other examples (5112, 5202, 5207, 5221, 5222), some of which had green vitreous deposits. The Edgbaston Street site included or adjoined the site of Hawkers glassworks which was built in 1777–8. The glassworks had gone by 1786–7, although Glasshouse Court is marked on Sheriff's map of 1808. The contexts in which this debris was found, relate to the 19th-century backfill of a well (5112) in Transect A, watercourse infills (5202) and (5222) and brick culverts (5207) and (5221), all situated in Transect B, lying to the south of the eastern part of Area B. Fill (5202) was dated ceramically to the late 18th–early 19th century. Cullett was also found in well backfill (5112).

Park Street
Vessel glass
A small irregular-shaped fragment from the rim of a small vessel (Area C, unstratified) may be of medieval or early post-medieval date (Fig. 8.3.6). This fragment might have originated from a similar vessel to a green glass vessel from Winchester Castle dated to the mid-14th century (Charleston 1990, fig. 291: 3289, 941–2). Further potentially early fragments of glass were also present in the assemblage, including a rim fragment possibly from a goblet probably of 17th-century date (Fig. 8.3.5). A wine glass fragment in clear glass decorated with applied 'raspberry' prunts, grid-stamped glass trails and plain glass trails was found in the fill of pit F133, fill (1125), together with a foot fragment (Fig. 8.3.7 and 8.6.2, colour). The fragment is heavy and has a solid stem and knop. There is very little decay on the glass apart from a very fine layer of iridescence. The weight would suggest that the glass is lead glass; if so, the absence of 'crizzling' would suggest a date towards the end of the 17th century. However the decoration is similar to that found on *façon de Venise* vessels e.g. Willmott (2002, fig. 73) and the solid rod stem can also be paralleled (*ibid.*, fig. 84) although the foot fragment is unlike anything found in *façon de Venise*. The glass appears very similar to vessels produced by George Ravenscroft in London (see Elville 1961, 160, pls 226 and 228) in the last quarter of the 17th century. The vessel may be a Ravenscroft vessel or a more local imitation in the Ravenscroft style. In either case it is a rare archaeological find and would have been highly prized in its heyday. Contents of pit F133 suggest a

deposition date of *c*.1750, although some of the pottery could have been quite old by the time of its deposition (see Rátkai, Chapter 7) and a good-quality piece of glassware is likely to have been curated and have been of some age before it was discarded.

Other finds consisted of 29 facetted stones in green, blue and clear glass (SF3/1125), also from pit F133, which contained a rich assemblage of finds and metal-working debris, and an opaque square-shaped stone with a faceted top (SF1/1133) from a Phase 4 context.

Catalogue
- Rim fragment from a light green ?goblet with air bubbles and scratched surface. Height: 77mm, diameter: 52mm thickness: 3mm. Area B, F500 (pit), 1512, Phase 3.2. Fig. 8.3.5.
- Vessel fragment with irregular-shaped, folded rim, slightly bulbous. The fragment is too small to estimate vessel diameter. Translucent green glass. Height: 28mm, width: 20mm, thickness: 1.5mm. Unstratified. Fig. 8.3.6.
- Wine glass fragment with applied 'raspberry prunts' and grid-stamped glass trails running obliquely across the knop and foot fragment possibly from the same vessel. Clear ?lead glass with some fine iridescent decay on the surfaces. Surviving length 170mm, diameter *c*.35mm. Fig. 8.3.7 and Fig. 8.6.2, colour.

Wine bottles
Most of the glass consisted of wine and beer bottles fragments of 17th–20th-century date, most of which were too small and undiagnostic for dating purposes. However, some distinctive rim and neck fragments from wine bottles were broadly datable. The earliest bottle (Fig. 8.3.9) in the collection was found residually in 1725 pit F705, disturbed by a late drain cut F711 and between pit F702 and Structure 7. Clay pipe evidence suggests a date of *c*.1750–1790 for F705. Only the broad neck and 'string rim' of the bottle survives, the shape of which is similar to the globular wine bottles of the late 17th century. This fragment is contemporary with the earliest glass bottle fragment from Edgbaston Street (Orton 2001, fig. 2, 5–6 and Orton and Rátkai, above). Other datable fragments include the 'string rim', neck, and shoulder from a globular wine bottle (1512, Fig. 8.3.8) which dates to *c*.1700–1740 (Blakeman 2000, 29) and was found in a Phase 3.2 pit (F500), and the rim and short neck fragment of a bottle (1621, not illustrated) which dates to *c*.1750–1800 (Blakeman 2000, 29) and was found in the infilling of the Phase 3.3 wood-lined tank F510/ F542. In addition, several broad bases from earlier wine bottles potentially dating to the 17th century were found residually in 1125 the fill of Phase 3.2 pit F133 and in 1101 Phase 4/5 and 1167 F154. Most of the surviving bottle bases, however, were narrower in size and more suggestive of a late 18th/ 19th-century, and, occasionally, 20th-century date.

Catalogue
- 18th-century wine bottle rim-shoulder, heavily decayed, 1512 F500 Phase 3.2. Fig. 8.3.8.

- Late 17th-century wine bottle rim-neck 1725 Pit F705 Phase 3.3. Fig. 8.3.9.

Window glass
The potentially earliest glass fragments were five small window panels with grozed edges (Figs 8.3.10–8.3.11), which may be of medieval date, although all were found residually (1101, 1103, 1139, 1143, 1738).

Catalogue
- Rectangular-shaped window quarry with two grozed edges, opaque green glass. Length: 33mm, width: 25mm, thickness: 2mm. Area A, F138 (pit), 1139, Phase 4. Fig. 8.3.10.
- Rectangular-shaped window quarry with grozed ends, opaque green glass. Length: 76mm, width: 22mm, thickness: 3mm. 1738, Phase 4/5. Fig. 8.3.11.

Worked shell

Edgbaston Street
Several items of worked mother-of-pearl were recovered, including six circular discs and two fragments, one with circular indentations and the other with circular cut marks where discs had been removed (Fig. 8.7, colour). This debris provides clear evidence for the small-scale manufacture of mother-of-pearl buttons. The debris was recovered from contexts 5112 and 5117 associated with the backfilling of a well in Transect A to the south of Smithfield Passage. From ceramic evidence, the well seems to have gone out of use in the early 19th century. The well backfills also contained evidence of glass making and metal working in the form of copper alloy offcuts for re-melting. In addition, the site produced 45 complete oyster shells (see Fig. 8.8, colour), 37 of which came from 5004, a yard surface extending over most of Trench 5A. These may represent raw material intended for the manufacture of buttons but could equally be food remains, oysters being a cheap and popular food until the latter part of the 19th century (Hope 1990, 116). The remainder of the complete shells came from a range of contexts of varying dates (1026 × 2, 3037, 4054 × 4) as did the fragments of 15 other shells (1006 × 4, 1009 × 3, 1020, 2101, 2123, 3037, 3063 × 2, 5202, 5039). These contexts range from Phase 2 tanning pits to the 19th-century backfills of a cellar and well, and are more likely to represent the debris from oyster consumption. Other shells included a large cowrie shell (Fig. 8.8, colour), recovered from the 19th-century infilling of a cellar (F102, 1006).

Shells were used to produce buttons and other ornaments from the 18th to the earlier 20th century, when mother-of-pearl jewellery and inlay was popular. Buttons made from a variety of mollusc shells were being made in Birmingham as early as 1767 (Sketchley 1767, 13) and mass-produced from the beginning of the 19th century (Peacock 1996, 62). Mother-of-pearl buttons were predominantly a Birmingham product, for which vast quantities of shells were imported from as far away as the

East Indies, the Philippines, the Red Sea and Persian Gulf (White 1977, 71). There were three main processes involved in shell button manufacture, firstly the cutting of blanks with a tubular saw (White 1977, pl. XXII, 71). The second process was through-drilling the blank or fitting it with a shank and split pin, followed by the skilled task of decorating the button with engraving or facet-cutting and polishing it with soap or rottenstone (*ibid.*, 71).

In the early days of manufacture, only the fine white centres of shells were used and the rest was discarded, leading to the accumulation of tons of waste shell on tips around Birmingham (White 1977, 71). By 1866 the Birmingham trade employed approximately 2,000 people and approximately 22 tons of different shells were consumed in Birmingham each week (Turner 1866, 441). The American Civil War of 1861–1865 effectively closed the American market for shell buttons and, although this revived slightly after the war, by then there was competition from the Continent (White 1977, 72). The craft declined further with the introduction of cheaper buttons made from corozo nuts, a form of vegetable ivory from Venezuela, in the 1860s, and shell buttons were eventually replaced by plastics by the turn of the 20th century (White 1977, 72).

The debris from button manufacture at Edgbaston Street is of particular interest since shell working has not been widely researched or published and the archaeological evidence substantially augments the documentary evidence in terms of the distribution of the industry. Similar debris consisting of shell fragments from which blanks have been cut have been recorded at other sites in Birmingham (see above). In addition, all the evidence seems to point to the button-working debris pre-dating the introduction of mechanisation and may reflect, therefore, an early phase of the industry towards the end of the 18th century or very early 19th century. This may help explain why the Edgbaston Street button production was situated away from the areas which were later to become the hub of shell button making (see below).

The main focus of mechanised button making in Birmingham, which peaked between 1860 and 1875, was in the area bounded by Colmore Row, Snow Hill, Mount Street and Congreve Street (White 1977, 75–6). However, it is known that, due to the low level of mechanisation in the shell button branch of the industry, so-called 'garret-masters' operated from their own small premises, producing small quantities of buttons of various materials and selling them for a good profit (White 1977, 72). Such a small workshop may provide a context for the Edgbaston Street finds.

Catalogue
– Shell button-making debris. Well fill, 5117, Phase 4. Fig. 8.7, colour.
– Large cowrie shell and two oyster shells 1006 cellar, F102, Area A, Phase 4. Fig. 8.8, colour.

Worked bone, ivory and horn
Edgbaston Street
A broken bone handle from a tanged implement such as a knife was recovered from 2002, a cleaning layer containing predominantly 17th- or 18th-century pottery (Fig. 8.9.5, colour). Part of the iron tang and a possible copper alloy collar were present. A second modern knife handle probably dating to the later 19th century was found in 5107, which was dated by clay pipe to the 1850s or 1860s. Evidence of the possible manufacture of knife plates, in the form of bone-working offcuts, was found in contexts 1020 F106 Phase 3, 1028 oven F109 Phase 1, 1034 F120 Phase 3, 1050 F131 Phase 3, 2005 cleaning layer with predominantly 17th- or early 18th-century ceramics, 2016 cleaning layer similar to 2005, 3000 cleaning layer, 3066 (cut from a rib) F324 Phase 3, 3071 (cut from a rib) F325 Phase 3, 3073 F328 Phase 3, 3093 well F327 Phase 3, and U/S. The bone-working debris consisted of a total of 30 bone offcuts, mainly of triangular section, but including some of rectangular section. The average size of the fragments, a selection of which are shown in Fig. 8.9.7, colour, was *c*.80mm long by 10–20mm wide. Although a couple of fragments of bone-working debris were found in a fill of Phase 1 oven (F109, 1028) in Area A, most of the debris came from Phase 3 pits in Areas A and C and cleaning layers in Area B, the latter containing almost exclusively 17th- and early 18th-century pottery, suggesting that the layers represent detritus of that period. The bone working thus appears to be a predominantly 17th- to early 18th-century phenomenon. Similar debris was also recovered from the excavations at Park Street, dating to the 17th century, and the interpretation of this is discussed in more detail below.

A piece of sawn ivory from 2138 F234 Phase 3 and a segment of elephant tusk 8.11.5 (see Hamilton-Dyer below) from the same context are further examples of manufacturing waste (Fig. 8.9.1, colour).

Other bone objects comprised a scoop/ apple corer (2005 cleaning layer, see above), two double-sided combs (2004 cleaning layer, see above, 5202 watercourse infill dated ceramically to the late 18th or early 19th century) and a hairbrush (1031).

The apple corer or cheese scoop (Fig. 8.9.3, colour) is almost certainly of post-medieval date (cf. Margeson 1993, fig. 85: 758, 759, 120). While early examples do exist, most datable examples belong to the 18th century and they are certainly not common until the post-medieval period (MacGregor 1984, 180).

The comb fragment (Fig. 8.9.4, colour), possibly made from ivory rather than bone, has broadly spaced teeth on one side and narrowly spaced teeth on the other. The form is known from the 17th century and several examples of this kind have been found at Norwich (Margeson 1993, figs 35–36, 66–68). A double-sided ?horn comb in a badly degraded condition was found in

5202. Despite 17th-century parallels, the combs could just as easily date to the 18th century or even 19th century (Megaw 1984, 82). The form of the hairbrush (Fig. 8.9.6, colour) is suggestive of a later date than the combs, possibly the 19th century.

Catalogue
- Ovoid section of elephant tusk sawn at both sides, Dimensions: 103mm x 83mm, thickness: 32mm, average width: 12mm. SF4, Area B, F218/ F232 (tanning pit), 2138 (SF4), Phase 3. Fig. 8.9.1, colour.
- Tapered, rectangular, highly polished handle, probably from a knife. Length: 96mm, width: 17mm, thickness: 7mm. 5107, upper fill of brick culvert, Transect A Phase 4. Fig. 8.9.2, colour.
- Comb, probably horn, with narrowly spaced teeth, very poorly preserved. Length: 45mm, height: 33mm, thickness: 1mm. Watercourse, 5202, Phase 4. Not illustrated.
- Hairbrush. Length: 147mm, width: 20mm, thickness: 4mm. 1031, Phase 4/5. Fig. 8.9.6, colour.
- Apple corer or cheese scoop, made from a sheep metapodial, the interior of which has been hollowed. Length: 78mm, width: 25mm, thickness: 15mm. 2005, unstratified. Fig. 8.9.3, colour.
- Comb fragment, with broadly spaced teeth on one side and narrowly spaced teeth on the other. Height: 62mm, surviving width: 22mm, thickness: 3mm. 2004, unstratified. Fig. 8.9.4, colour.
- Bone handle fragment with iron tang with copper alloy collar. Length: 52mm, width: 28mm, thickness: 22mm. Area B, 2002, unstratified. Fig. 8.9.5, colour.
- Hairbrush. Length: 147mm, width: 20mm, thickness: 4mm. 1031, Phase 4/5. Fig. 8.9.6, colour.
- Bone handle-working debris (various contexts). Fig. 8.9.7, colour.

Note on ivory offcut (Fig. 8.9.1, colour)
by Sheila Hamilton-Dyer
The ivory item submitted for identification was recovered from 17th-century deposits (F234 context 2138 item 4) and preliminarily identified as possibly an ivory offcut.

The item is an ovoid slice of 108 × 83mm maximum external and 84 × 63mm maximum internal dimensions. Outer depth of the section varies from 10–33mm. The thickness from the external to internal surface is 10–12mm.

The preservation is good and the item has only very minor cracks; it is of a light brown colour. While smooth, it is not highly polished. The outer surface has broad longitudinal ridges while the inner surface has fine lines and has a mottled, rougher surface texture with some small cracks.

Clear saw marks are visible on both surfaces of the cut section. The lines run across the narrow part of the oval and on the best preserved surface a tang has been left on the deepest section showing that, in this case at least, the piece was sawn from the narrowest point of the ovoid.

The item was sawn by hand not by machine, as the saw marks, although all running in one direction, are not exactly parallel.

The sawn surfaces reveal intersecting light and dark lines, particularly clear at some angles of view. These decussating lines, often described as resembling machine turning, are known as Schreger lines and are definitive for ivory from the Proboscidea, the elephants and mammoths. Other types of ivory, *e.g.* from walrus, hippo or narwhal, do not have these. The angle of intersection of the lines is different in the living members of the elephant family in comparison with the extinct mammoth. In mammoth these angles are acute while in the African and Asian elephants they are obtuse (for example, see Eapinoza and Mann 1991). The angles in this specimen vary slightly but are always clearly obtuse and it is therefore elephant. It has been suggested that it is possible to distinguish the Asian from African by colour, hardness and translucence in fresh ivory (Penniman 1952) but not in archaeological specimens. Recent work on distinguishing the species has included SEM, X-ray diffraction and Transform Fourier Raman spectroscopy (*e.g.* Edwards *et al.* 1998, Singh in prep). These techniques and others in progress such as DNA analysis may be able to reveal which of the species this specimen is from.

Elephant ivory is the specialised upper incisor and is formed of dentine. The presence of a large pulp cavity in this specimen implies that this section is taken from near the origin of the tooth, even within the maxilla itself, rather than towards the tip where the tooth is solid. There are no visible lines of Owen (growth lines) probably implying that this was a tusk of a young animal; this is consistent with the rather small size of the ovoid.

Park Street
This was one of the more interesting finds assemblages from the Bull Ring sites, both artefactually and in terms of evidence for an on-site bone- and ivory-working industry. The objects were in a good state of preservation and many of the items were complete, and identifiable.

Three handles were found in Area C 1753, 1820 and 1870 and a fourth in Area B. The latter was an ivory knife handle and was found in 1512 F500 Phase 3.1. The handles from Area C comprised a pistol grip knife handle with three iron rivets from (1755), the fill of the construction cut for wall F738 of Structure 2, Phase 3 (Fig. 8.10.5, colour), a faceted handle possibly unfinished and broken during manufacture, 1820 F762 Phase 3.2, and a handle with incised bands (Fig. 8.10.1, colour). The latter handle is interesting because it derives from a Phase 1 recut of the medieval boundary ditch which defined the rear end of the Park Street plots. Thus the handle could be of medieval date. However, pottery from fill 1869 of F799 indicates 17th-century disturbance to the Phase 1 feature and the handle could date from this disturbance. The pistol-grip scale-tang knife handle, which retains part of the tang *in situ* between the two scales (Fig. 8.10.5, colour), is probably of an 18th- or 19th-century date. Clay pipe and ceramic evidence from the construction trench in which it was found, suggest a date *c.*1750–1800.

A marrow or condiment spoon (Fig. 8.10.9, colour), with a decorated handle, was found in a late cleaning layer but is likely to be of post-medieval date. Marrow spoons of metal were produced from the 17th century onward and marrow eating became increasing popular in the 18th century.

A narrow-bladed implement (Fig. 8.10.6, colour), which has one broad, curved end and one smaller, tapering end, may be a small paper knife or may have been used to clean the finger nails as part of a manicure set (1768). A set of bone 'toilet implements' in a bone case was found in a mid-17th-century context at Dudley Castle (pers comm. S Rátkai) but such items have a long history and there is no reason why the Park Street example could not be later.

Other finds included a double-sided ivory comb with curved ends and some breakage to the teeth (1728 F702 Phase 3.1 Fig. 8.10.3, colour). The comb may be a nit comb, since both sides have narrowly spaced teeth. The form is paralleled by 17th-century examples (Egan and Henig 1984, fig. 39: 31, 229–230) but as with the Edgbaston Street combs (see above) there is no reason why the comb could not be later.

Two brushes (Figs 8.10.7, colour and 8.10.10, colour) were also found. One of the brushes (Fig. 8.10.7, colour) is probably of early to mid-19th-century date, based upon its general morphology and the grooves for copper wires that held the bristles in place (Egan and Henig 1984, fig. 39:16, 229–230); this dating accords with its discovery in a Phase 4 pit F836. The other brush (Fig. 8.10.10, colour), which is a toothbrush, is unfinished and was abandoned during manufacture due to the first two perforations of the third row going through the outer edge of the head, near the tip. The brush was then discarded before completion, attesting to the on-site manufacture of brushes, as well as knife handles (see below). A published brush of similar shape from Exeter dates to c.1690–1720 (Megaw 1984, fig. 195: 30, 350–351) and another similar brush, but double-headed, described as 'possibly a toothbrush', from Aldgate High Street has been dated to 1750–70 (Grew 1984, fig. 63: 115, 127 and 120). Unfortunately the Park Street brush is from a Phase 4/5 cleaning layer. However, it does attest to some 18th- or 19th-century bone working on site in addition to that recovered from the 17th-century deposits (see below). The 1895 Goad Insurance Map (see Chapter 4) shows a brush manufacturer situated a little to the east of the excavated area, at No. 10 Park Street, and late 18th-century directories (see Chapter 4) list one John Boswell, 'brush manufacturer', at No. 16 Park Street.

Several Birmingham sites have produced 18th- and 19th-century bone button blanks and waste, *e.g.* the Soho Manufactory and Deritend (Hodder 2004, 140), and Edgbaston Mill (Mitchell forthcoming). Although shell button making was carried out in the area of Edgbaston Street (see below) definite evidence for bone button manufacture on any of the Bull Ring sites is absent.

However, four bone buttons from Park Street could conceivably represent button manufacture (Pye's Trade Directory for 1791 lists one William Pring, button maker, at No. 13 Park Street). They comprised two buttons with a single central perforation, likely to be button backs from decoratively covered buttons (1131 F137 and 1176 F159/ 138 Phase 4: Fig. 8.10.4 and 8.10.8, colour) F137 and two with four holes (1757 F720 Phase 4, 1798 F749 Phase 3 not illustrated). Pit F749 was cut by the construction of wall F750, part of Structure 2 and 1757 a fill of Phase 4 pit F720.

The most aesthetically pleasing item was a carved fish with incised detail, the tail of which is missing (Fig. 8.10.2, colour). The bone fish is a gaming token, used as a token of account when playing card games in the 18th century. A very similar fish-shaped gaming token from Winchester, with ring-dot eyes but without defined gills, was found occurring residually in a 19th–20th-century context (Brown 1990, 697, fig. 196: 2241, 705). The Birmingham example comes from a pit (F702) assigned to Phase 3.1 on ceramic and clay pipe evidence. This evidence is consistent with a date in the first three decades of the 18th century for the gaming token.

Catalogue

– Handle, decorated with incised or turned bands. Length: 66mm, diameter: 18mm, thickness: 2mm. Area C, F799 (ditch recut), 1870, Phase 1. Fig. 8.10.1, colour.
– Carved fish. Length: 47mm, width: 11mm, thickness: 2mm. Fig. 8.10.2, colour.
– Comb, double-sided, with some breakage to the teeth. Length: 51mm, width: 37mm, thickness: 1–1.5mm. Area C, F702, 1728, Phase 3.1. Fig. 8.10.3, colour.
– Circular button, with single perforation. Diameter: 15mm, thickness: 1mm. Area A, F137, 1131, Phase 3. Fig. 8.10.4, colour.
– Pistol-grip knife handle, with three iron rivets. Length: 86mm, width: 26mm, thickness: 13–22mm. Area C, F721, 1755, Phase 3. Fig. 8.10.5, colour.
– Implement with pointed rectangular sectioned handle and narrow, gently curving blade. The surface is shiny with wear. Length: 111mm, width at widest end: 8mm, thickness: 1–4mm. Area C, 1768, F836 Phase 4. Fig. 8.10.6, colour.
– Brush, with three rows of circular perforations for bristles. Length: 105mm, width: 11mm, thickness: 5mm. Area C, F836, 1770, Phase 4. Fig. 8.10.7, colour.
– Circular button, with single perforation. Diameter: 10mm, thickness: 1mm. SF23, Area A, F159/ F138 (pit), 1176 (SF23), Phase 4. Fig. 8.10.8, colour.
– Spoon, with incised decoration on edges of handle and some damage to the bowl. Length: 109mm, width of bowl: 15mm, thickness: 1–5mm. Area C, 1738, Phase 4/5. Fig. 8.10.9, colour.
– Brush, with two rows of circular perforations and the beginning of a third row, which was started too near the outer edge. The item appears to have been abandoned before completion. Length: 120mm, width: 8mm, thickness: 4mm. Area C, 1738, Phase 4/5. Fig. 8.10.10, colour.

With the exception of an unfinished handle terminal (Fig. 8.11.2, colour), the remaining items (114 fragments) were either offcuts from cutlery handle manufacture, Fig. 8.11.7 or unfinished handles. One curved fragment is likely to have been an unfinished side from a handle, probably from a knife (Fig. 8.11.6, colour). One wedge-shaped piece had incised cross-hatched decoration at one end (Fig. 8.11.3, colour) and a flattened fragment with a curved upper face was possibly an unfinished knife handle (Fig. 8.11.5, colour). Three fragments had split from the exterior of a partially hollowed, polished bone handle (Fig. 8.11.4, colour). With the exception of the first of these fragments, which was unstratified, the others came from Phase 3.2 pits and one of the Phase 3.3 wood-lined tanks (F510/ F542).

The vast majority of the fragments, a total of 76 pieces, probably ivory (Fig. 8.11.7, colour), came from context 1515, the fill of a pit (F504) assigned to Phase 3.1. A further ten pieces came from context 1516, the fill of a Phase 3.2 pit (F527) which cut pit F504. The other 21 pieces came from the following contexts: Phase 2 pit (1524); Phase 3.1 pits (1126 × 2 probably ivory, 1219, 1721 possibly horn, 1728 F702, 1819 × 2, 1839); Phase 3.2 pits (1708 × 2, 1814, 1938); Phase 3.3 tank (F510/ F542: 1621 × 2 probably ivory, 1634); Phase 4 pits (1139 F138, 1167 F154); unstratified (1101 × 3, 1625, 1738). There is a quite a strong trend, therefore, for the bone-working debris to be found in pits assigned to Phase 3.1, the late 16th and 17th centuries, with comparatively little dated to before or after that period. It is also noteworthy that the pits containing bone-working waste were found towards the rear of the Park Street plots, in Areas B and C.

The majority of the fragments appear to be in the region of 75mm long, with an average thickness of 5–8mm. A number of very similar pieces were also recovered from the Edgbaston Street site (see above). The pieces appear in the main to be offcuts from ivory-working, consistent with the manufacture of scales for knife and fork handles. Documentary evidence from Birmingham demonstrates the existence of various bone- and ivory-working workshops in the area of the site during the early 19th century, including Joseph Horton, a hard wood, bone and ivory turner, in Park Street and Samuel Butler, an ivory and hard wood turner, in the Bull Ring (Wrightson 1818).

The contextual dating at both Edgbaston Street and Area B Park Street suggests a floruit of production during the 17th century. In Area B Park Street the production of these handles was also associated with possible evidence of blade making in pit F504 (see Chapter 4). By the 18th century, the manufacture of bone handles seems to be associated with Area C at Park Street. The discarded toothbrush (see above) also from Area C could be seen as a continuation of the bone-working trade.

Catalogue

– Tapering bone handle fragment. Length: 81mm, maximum width: 24mm, thickness: 4mm at one end and 11mm at the other. Area C, F761 (pit), 1819, Phase 3.1. Fig. 8.11.1, colour.

– Unfinished handle terminal. Length: 22mm, diameter: 11mm. Area C, F762 (pit), 1820, Phase 3.2. Fig. 8.11.2, colour.

– Handle fragment, with incised cross-hatch decoration. Length: 56mm, width: 14mm, thickness: 5mm. Area C, F828 (pit), 1938, Phase 3.2. Fig. 8.11.3, colour.

– Handle, split along the longitudinal axis. Dimensions of largest piece: Length: 72mm, width: 20mm, thickness: 8mm. Area B, F500 (pit), 1512, Phase 3.2. Fig. 8.11.4, colour.

– Tapering piece of ivory, possibly an unfinished handle. Length: 73mm, maximum width: 24mm, thickness: 6mm. Area B, F510/ F542 (tank), 1621, Phase 3.3. Fig. 8.11.5, colour.

– Unfinished handle, with curved outer face. Length: 86mm, width: 26mm, thickness: 5mm. 1101, cleaning layer, Phase 4/5. Fig. 8.11.6, colour.

– Debris from the manufacture of ivory handles (1515) F504 Phase 3.1. Fig. 8.11.7, colour.

Worked stone
by Lynne Bevan and Rob Ixer

Edgbaston Street

The most significant finds were a whetstone and two whetstones or rubbing stones. The earliest, a whetstone or rubbing stone of micaceous sandstone (Fig. 8.12.1, colour), was recovered from a Phase 1 pit (F308) in Area C.

A whetstone of blue phyllite (Fig. 8.12.2, colour) was the most attractive item in the collection. A 15th-century date is possible for this artefact, based upon a similar item of Eidsborg schist with a partially grooved, broken terminal from Winchester (Ellis and Moore 1990, fig. 264: 3049, 871, 878). Although the pit F208 from which it came was probably constructed in Phase 2, the fill, dating its disuse, belongs to early Phase 3. If the whetstone is indeed of 15th-century date, it is residual in F208.

A possible whetstone or rubbing stone of fine-grained psammite (Fig. 8.12.3, colour) was recovered from a Phase 3 drainage feature (F245) in Area B. It bore one smoothed, slightly dished surface carrying a gloss, possibly the result of being rubbed against an organic substance. The one smoothed and worn surface suggest that it was used to sharpen blades. The gloss may be from sharpening tools used to cut vegetation such as scythes and billhooks. The whetstones may be more evidence for the cutlery or blade making industries (see above).

The other worked stone items in the collection included part of a stone roof tile or flagstone (1011) found in the fill of a Phase 1 pit (F123) in Area A. Two fragments (168mm × 84mm × 18mm and 110mm x 118mm × 18mm) of dark-coloured marble with irregular calcite streaks, possibly facing stones or floor tiles, were found in fill (1021) of Phase 3 pit (F108), which lay towards the street frontage in Area A. Each had one polished surface. The pottery from the fill of the pit was of 17th- or possibly early 18th-century date but there was also one probably intrusive 19th-century sherd. The use of marble architecturally, either as flooring, facing or within fireplaces, would be associated with stone-built houses of some status, although there was no excavated structural evidence for such a building.

The remaining items comprised a fragment from the base of a round mortar (5039), a rectangular stone block of oolitic limestone, found within well backfill (5118), and four fragments from slate roof tiles (5112 × 2, 5117 × 2). All these contexts date to the 19th century.

Catalogue
– Whetstone or rubbing stone. Fine-grained, pale-coloured micaceous sandstone. Length: 73mm, width: 32mm, thickness: 27mm. Area C, F308 (pit), 3026, Phase 1. Fig. 8.12.1, colour.
– Whetstone, with a carved, decorative terminal The other end is broken with a transverse fracture. Blue phyllite. Length: 82mm, width: 9mm, thickness: 7mm. Area B, F208 (pit), 2010, Phase 3. Fig. 8.12.2, colour.
– Possible whetstone or rubbing stone, with one smoothed, slightly dished surface carrying a gloss. Fine-grained psammite. Length: 235mm, width: 35mm, thickness: 26mm. Area B, F245, 2179, Phase 3. Fig. 8.12.3, colour.

Moor Street
A stone roof tile fragment in a fine-grained, thinly bedded pale yellow Mesozoic sandstone, similar to Cotswolds stone, with a roughly rectangular nail hole, was recovered from the Phase 2 pit F559. The nail hole has been drilled from two different directions. Its dimensions were 120mm × 97mm, thickness 15mm.

Park Street
The worked stone included three grindstones and fragments from two others with square holes for machine-driven shafts. They are of fine-grained micaceous sandstone, one of the many lithologies in the Millstone Grit, from which they are likely to derive. Pelham (1950) notes that the finer types of sandstone were used for knives, scissors and razors. The grindstones had diameters of 330mm, 350–360mm, 420–430mm and 520mm. They were unstratified apart from one fragment from the backfilling of one of the wood-lined tanks (F510/F542) in Area B; the ceramic evidence dates this backfilling to the end of the 18th century. Mortar traces on one side of one of the stones are likely to have resulted from subsequent reuse. Late wall F212/ F214 at Park Street had possible drive-shaft holes through them and it is not impossible that they were related to the use of the excavated grindstones. Two similar stones had been used to support a coffin in a vault with a *terminus post quem* of 1808 at St Martin's Cemetery (Bevan 2006).

Other late stone finds found in Phase 4 contexts comprised a dark green-brown marble base, possibly from a flower vase, from a grave of probable Victorian date, a cylindrical corundum whetstone (1738), and two fragments of Welsh roofing slate (1738 and 1931).

The swivel seal
by Stephanie Rátkai

The most intriguing find was a three-sided swivel seal (Fig. 8.3.12). The seal was originally recorded as clear glass but the absence of any air bubbles or other impurities, and the fact that the surface could be easily scratched with a metal point, makes it more likely that it was rock crystal.

Either end of the seal had been drilled to take a metal attachment. One face was carved with a classical-style head. The second depicted a lion 'sejant erect' emerging from a crown. The crown is shown with nine pearls which, in heraldic terms, indicate a viscount (pers. comm. Glennys Wilde). The third face, which was plain, was usually for some other family device or motto. The undecorated face was very scratched, which would at first suggest that this face originally rested against something. However, this is difficult to equate with its use as a swivel seal.

Swivel seals were made from c.1760–1820, and were particularly in vogue in the early 19th century. They were pierced for fitting into a fob for attachment to a gentleman's watch chain and were mostly associated with merchants or minor aristocracy (pers. comm. Glennys Wilde). As such, the presence of a swivel seal on Park Street in 'dark earth' layer (1797) is not easily explained. A watch-chain maker appears in the 1781 Directory at No. 12, Park Street (Pearson and Rollason 1781), and two jewellers are noted on Park Street in 18th-century directories (Sketchley 1767; Bailey 1783) but unfortunately no house numbers are given for the latter, so it is not possible to say whether the seal derived from their premises. Up to the time of the Nonconformist riots, a wealthy merchant had premises at No. 10 Park Street, slightly to the north of our excavated area, and No. 4 Park Street (within the excavated area) was the premises of Timothy Smith, 'brass-founder and factor', presumably a reasonably well-off character. Either of these could be candidates for ownership of the seal although if so, neither of them had any claim to the heraldic device of a viscount!

Catalogue
– A three-sided rock crystal seal, the plain surface of which is very scratched. The other two surfaces bear carved decoration in the form of a lion sejant erect emerging from a crown and a Classical style male head (SF 30/1797). Length: 18mm, width: 14mm, thickness: 14mm. Area C, 1797, Phase 3. Fig. 8.3.12.

Leather

by Erica Macey-Bracken and Quita Mould

Edgbaston Street

There is evidence for leather tanning on the Edgbaston Street site from Phase 1, although the industry seems to have become more prolific in the late medieval and post-medieval periods. A hide edge of cow hide (2065) and fragments of a turnshoe (2087) were recovered from Phase 1 tanning pits F217 and F218 respectively. The Phase 2 tanning pit F214, dated to the 15th–16th century, produced a fragment of seam and a layer (2035) sealing this pit produced a small offcut. A large quantity of leather offcuts was recovered from the backfills of Phase 3 tanning pits in Area B (see Patrick and Rátkai, Chapter 2). A shoe fragment was also found in 2219 the fill of Phase 3 pit F280.

Tanning seems to have been replaced by skinyards in the 18th century. This continued into the 19th century with the establishment of Welch's Skinyard probably in the late 18th century. A group of leather offcuts, over 2kg in weight when wet, were recovered from context 5100, a deep layer of demolition debris post-dating the disuse of the Moat Watercourse and dated by ceramics to the 19th century. The shape of the offcuts indicated they were waste leather from the manufacture of shoes.

The remains of four welted shoes were recovered from the site, two from infill 5105 of the watercourse, one from 5202, also a watercourse infill, and the fourth from 5100, a demolition deposit over the infilled watercourse in Transect A. One shoe of suede leather (5202), buckled over the instep, dates to the 18th century; the others were of late 18th- or 19th-century date. Context 5202 contained 18th–early 19th-century pottery; the other two contexts contained only 19th-century pottery. The shoes appeared to be well worn, suggesting that they had been discarded at the end of their useful life and hence are domestic detritus rather than evidence of any craft or industry.

In the area around the Bull Ring, there were many workshops of cobblers, saddlers, and the like, and significant quantities of leather offcuts from the same period were also recovered at the Park Street site (see below). The leather-working debris from Edgbaston Street can be set alongside the debris from the manufacture of glass and shell buttons as evidence for numerous small workshops plying diverse trades in this area in the 18th and 19th centuries.

Park Street

A total of 292 pieces of leather, which appeared to date predominantly to the 19th century, were recovered from the site. The majority of these came from 1771, the fill of F836, a 19th-century pit (see above). Fragments of textile, initially taken to be leather, were found in 1917, the fill of Phase 3.1 pit F808, 1621 a fill of Phase 3.3 tank F510/ F542, and 1770 and 1771 fills of pit F836. The most interesting items in the assemblage were two complete shoe soles (Fig. 8.13.1, 1704 pit F708 Phase 1 and 1508

pit F508 Phase 2, not illustrated), from medieval and early post-medieval contexts respectively; two leather straps (Fig. 8.13.2, 1822 pit F765 Phase 3.1 and 1634 a fill of Phase 3.3 tank F510/ F542, not illustrated) and a section of a leather belt (unstratified, not illustrated). The remainder of the assemblage consisted of partial shoe remains and offcuts, which were not studied in detail.

The remains of a turnshoe, of child size 4 (1508) pit F508 Phase 2 and a repaired turnshoe sole of child size 6 (1704) pit F708 Phase 1 were found; both date to the medieval period, 13th–15th century. Shoe parts of post-medieval date were found in six contexts (1521 tank 503/ 520, 1634, tank F510/ F542 Phase 3.3, 1771 and 1773, fills of F836 Phase 4, and Phase 4/5 cleaning layers 1101 and 1738). The post-medieval shoes were of welted construction, with the exception of one shoe (1773) of 19th-century date that was of nailed construction with brass tacks holding the upper to the sole. The remains of a welted shoe with a wooden 'louis' heel of 17th- or early 18th-century date was found in 1521, a fill of tank F503/ F520, while two Victorian boots lacing up the instep through a series of lace holes with copper alloy eyelets were found in 1738 and 1771.

The turnshoe sole (Fig. 8.13.1) was from a left shoe and was found in the backfill (1704) of a lime-rich Phase 1 pit (F708) tentatively associated with tanning. The shoe had been repaired at the tread and seat. The other turnshoe (1508, 135mm long × 48mm wide at widest point, not illustrated), had parts of the vamp and quarters present and was from a right shoe. It was found in one of the cluster of Phase 2 clay-lined pits (F508) in Area B.

A very small quantity of late medieval or early post-medieval waste leather was found. It does indicate leather working but in much too small a quantity to be of significance here. The waste leather was from:

- 1508 (pit F508 Phase 2) 3 trimmings (secondary waste from cutting out pattern pieces)
- 1529 (Phase 2/3) below dark earth (1520) one piece secondary waste
- 1642 (pit F552 Phase 2) one piece primary waste (a hide edge of cow hide)
- 1655 (pit F562/ F561 Phase 2) secondary waste (two of calfskin, one of sheep/ goatskin)
- 1822 (pit F765 Phase 3.1) one trimming, three other pieces of secondary waste and one piece primary waste (an udder).

In addition, a 19th-century pit F836 (1771) produced large quantities of offcuts, indicating leather working. The 1851 Census Returns for Park Street indicate several shoemakers and other leather workers living on Park Street but not in the houses associated with the Park Street excavation. However, Thomas Butler, a last maker, is listed at No. 6 Park Street in the 1856 Post Office Directory. Leather offcuts provide similar substantial evidence for 19th-century leather working at the Edgbaston Street site (see above).

Two stratified straps were recovered from the site (Fig.

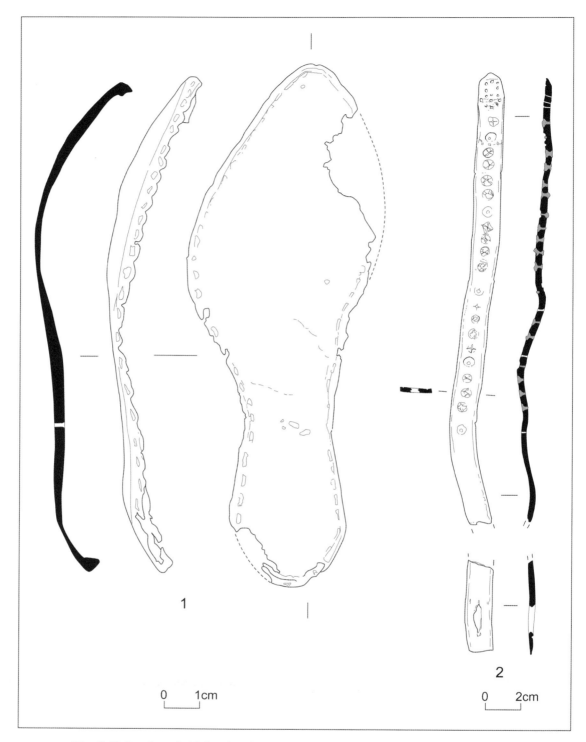

1

2

0   1cm

0   2cm

Fig. 8.13 Leather; 8.13.1 sole of child's turnshoe, 8.13.2 strap with pewter studs.

8.13.2, 1822 pit F765 Phase 3.1 and 1634, a fill of Phase 3.3 tank F510/ F542, not illustrated). The former was a long, narrow strap, 15mm in width, decorated with a series of 22 dome-headed mounts probably of pewter; medieval girdles, horse harness and spur leathers are all decorated in this way. Pit F765 is part of a pit complex disturbed by Structure 5. There was a strong residual medieval element to the pottery and there is no reason why the strap could not also be residual and medieval in date. The second strap (1634 Phase 3.3) was 37mm in width with a line of grain/ flesh stitching along each edge. A third unstratified strap was 36mm wide with six buckle holes and a line of grain/ flesh stitching along each edge and one along the centre. The two latter straps are probably from harnesses and not independently datable.

Catalogue

– Sole of child's turnshoe, to fit left foot. 151mm long × 51mm wide at widest point. Area C, F708 (pit), 1704, Phase 1. Fig. 8.13.1.
– Strap. Dimensions: 310mm long, broken into three sections a. 48mm b. 203mm c. 60mm, width:15mm. Pewter studs along first 200mm of longest piece. Area C, F765 (pit), 1822, Phase 3.1. Fig. 8.13.2.

Ceramic tile
by Erica Macey-Bracken with petrology by Rob Ixer

Quantities of roof tile were recovered from all three sites and a small sample retained (Fig. 8.14, colour). The samples were quantified by count and weight and examined macroscopically for the purposes of fabric identification. A full list of tile by site and context is provided in the site archive. Most of the roof tile was recovered from Park Street, where four distinct roof tile fabrics (Fabrics T1–T4) were identified. The same roof tile fabrics occurred in the Edgbaston Street assemblage but an additional roof tile fabric (T5) was identified at Moor Street. Roof tile fabric 1 (T1) predominated on all three sites. The presence of light-coloured fine-grained sandstone in Roof Tile Fabrics T1 and T4 almost certainly indicates that these fabrics were made in the centre of Birmingham, since similar light-coloured sandstone inclusions were present, albeit rarely, in both the reduced and oxidised Deritend wares (pers. comm. S Rátkai). Given the overall similarity of the tile fabrics, it seems safe to assume that all of them were made in the city centre.

Ceramic roof tile was clearly in use in the medieval period at all three sites and may indicate at least one high-status building on or near Edgbaston Street. Ceramic roofing tile was available by the beginning of the 13th century and became increasingly popular (Salzman 1952, 229). Several sites have produced evidence of tiled roofs in Birmingham (see Hodder 2004, 120–1) and it seems probable that roof tiles were made in the centre of Birmingham, where they would have formed an adjunct to pottery production. The preference, probably by the 13th century, for ceramic tiles, as opposed to wooden shingles or thatch, may indicate the prevalence of fire-based industrial processes, with their attendant fire risks, in the centre of Birmingham from an early date. However, there is also possible evidence for the use of heather thatch at Moor Street (see Ciaraldi, Chapter 12; Greig, Chapter 13) and perhaps less convincingly at Edgbaston Street (see Patrick and Rátkai, Chapter 2). Rye, an important crop in the West Midlands, was found at Moor Street and Park Street (*ibid.*) and in addition to being a food source was also used for thatching.

Fabric Descriptions
Fabric T1
Very hard-fired and evenly mixed fabric, with abundant fine-grained rounded quartz grains up to 2mm in diameter and rare, rounded, pale-coloured quartz/ quartzite clasts up to 1.2cm, together with clasts of fine-grained, pale-coloured sandstone up to 1.5cm in size. Usually moderate reddish orange in colour (10R 5/6 on the G.S.A. rock-colour chart) although some examples have a dark grey core and orange margins. The differences in colour across the tiles of this fabric are attributed to variations during the firing process.

Fabric T2
Similar to T1, but with a softer appearance and not so well levigated. Core is light grey in colour.

Fabric T3
Pale pink sandy fabric, very hard fired.

Fabric T4
Most examples are a moderate reddish brown (10R 5/6 on the G.S.A. rock-colour chart), although some are much lighter in colour. The fired clay carries abundant, fine-grained 1–2mm diameter rounded to subangular, milky white quartz/ quartzite grains. Subangular, pale yellowish orange (10YR 7/6), fine-grained ?sandstone clasts are rare.

Fabric T5
Poorly levigated fabric; some examples with grey margins and surfaces and others with moderate reddish brown surfaces and core. Very hard fired clay, which is quite clean, but does carry very fine-grained quartz quartzite grains and rare larger rounded quartz/ quartzite clasts, both of which belong naturally to the clay. Present at Moor Street only.

Edgbaston Street
The site at Edgbaston Street produced 25.85kg of flat roof tile. The assemblage displayed a high incidence of fragmentation, but individual pieces were generally unabraded. No complete tiles were recovered.

Examination of the assemblage noted four distinct fabrics (Roof Tile Fabrics T1–T4), although the physical appearance of the tile varied little across the fabrics. The tile was always flat, with a uniform thickness of between 15mm and 17mm and with one rough face and one much smoother, finished face. Fabric T1 dominated the assemblage, with only a few examples of the other fabrics occurring. Two examples of broken glazed crested ridge tiles, of Fabric T1, were also recovered.

Roof tile, which was not closely datable, appears in all phases of the site. The glazed crested ridge tiles are of medieval date. The presence of one of the crested ridge tiles in a Phase 2 layer (2196) together with 16th-century pottery suggests that it must date at least to the 15th century if not earlier (Fig. 8.14.4, colour). The second glazed ridge tile fragment was recovered residually from a Phase 3 pit (F139, 1066) (Fig. 8.14.5). The presence of the crested ridge tiles suggests that there may have been a building or buildings of quite high status in the vicinity.

Catalogue
- Partially complete ridge tile. 103 × 115 × 17mm. Area B, 2196 (layer), Phase 2. Fig. 8.14.4, colour.
- Partially complete ridge tile. 112 × 80 × 20mm. Area A, F139 (pit), 1066, Phase 3. Fig. 8.14.5, colour.

Moor Street
A small assemblage of 344 fragments of ceramic roof tile, weighing 31.18kg, was recovered. The assemblage was largely unabraded, despite its fragmentary condition, with no complete tiles represented. Roof tile occurred in all phases of the site.

Macroscopic analysis of the assemblage noted only two distinct fabric types, Roof Tile Fabric T1 and Roof Tile Fabric T5, the latter only present at Moor Street. As at Edgbaston Street, Roof Tile Fabric T1 dominated the assemblage, with Fabric T5 appearing only sporadically. Both fabrics present in the Moor Street assemblage appear to have been used to make flat roof tiles. A nail hole was noted in one example from a Phase 1 pit (F550, 5141). Two possible waster fragments came from a Phase 1 pit (F534, 5107) and a Phase 2 pit (F567, 5182), the latter cut into the Phase 1 boundary ditch. One fragment of minor interest from a Phase 1 pit (F534, 5107) bore the maker's fingerprints.

A small quantity of green-glazed roof tile of possible 13th-century date (van Lemmen 2000, 20) was also noted. Some of the fragments came from fills of the Phase 1 medieval boundary ditch, 5130 F538 (Fig. 8.14.3, colour) 5150 F561 and 5175 F568. The bulk of the remainder came from the Phase 2 pits (5137 F547, 5113 F542, 5149 F560) one of which, F560, was cut into the Phase 1 ditch. Other examples were from a Phase 4 wall cut (5201) and a cleaning context (5171). All of the glazed fragments were made from Fabric T1.

The presence of roof tile in the boundary ditch fills and other Phase 1 features, indicates that roof tile was being used in the 13th and 14th centuries. The glazed roof tiles would suggest a good-quality building in the vicinity of the site although no evidence of medieval structures, with which they might have been associated, was recovered. The presence of two possible wasters may, however, be evidence that some or all the medieval roof tile could have derived from production waste rather than demolition debris.

Catalogue
- Fragment of green-glazed medieval roof tile 80 × 52 × 15mm. F538 (ditch), 5130, Phase 1. Fig. 8.14.3, colour.

Park Street
In total, 2,406 fragments of ceramic roof tile, weighing

177.78kg, were recovered. This included eight fragments of glazed medieval roof tile. No complete examples were noted, although individual fragments were largely unabraded. The four distinct fabrics (Roof Tile Fabrics T1–T4) recognised at Edgbaston Street were noted and, once again, Fabric T1 dominated the assemblage, although the physical appearance of the tile varied little across the fabrics. The roof tile was flat, and in thickness and other characteristics corresponded to the Edgbaston Street assemblage.

All of the fabrics occurred in both the medieval and post-medieval phases of the site. Fabric T1 was evenly distributed across all areas of the site, with no significant groups or clusters being noted. None of the other fabrics occurred sufficiently frequently to detect any significant distribution patterns.

The presence of such a large assemblage of roof tile points to the probable existence of at least one tiled building in the vicinity, although the fact that the same kind of roof tile appears in both medieval and post-medieval contexts points to both high levels of residuality and possible reuse of the material. The reuse of building materials such as tile and brick was very common (Cowell 1993, 168), and renders exact dating of the assemblage impossible. Secondly, pottery wasters and a kiln-bar were found at Park Street and it is possible that some of the roof tile may have been used to form a temporary roof over the pottery kilns which must have been in the vicinity, not to mention the Phase 2 kiln F768 in Area C.

Single fragments of green-glazed roof tile of probable medieval date were also recovered from 1809 F758 Phase 2, 1829 kiln F768 Phase 2, 1643 F558 Phase 3.1, 1519 pond F506 Phase 3.3, 1103 Phase 4/5, 1131, F137 and two fragments from 1707, the fill of rectilinear pit F714 Phase 1. As with the bulk of the unglazed assemblage, all the glazed roof tile was of Fabric T1. Unfortunately the assemblage was too small and too fragmentary for further analysis.

Other fragments of note included a small fragment of medieval floor tile of probable 14th-century date which was recovered from a Phase 2 pit (F186/ F188, 1220) in Area A. This fragment had the remains of a white slip decoration (Fig. 8.14.2, colour). A fragment of an unglazed, possibly line-impressed floor tile, dated tentatively to the 14th–15th century, was also recovered from a Phase 2 context in Area B (Fig. 8.14.1, colour).

Catalogue
- Fragment of medieval floor tile, with white slip decoration. 42 × 29 × 18mm. Area A, F186/ F188 (pit), 1220, Phase 2. Fig. 8.14.2, colour.
- Fragment of medieval floor tile, with possible incised pattern. 40 × 43 × 17mm. Area B, F501, 1513, Phase 2. Fig. 8.14.1, colour.

9   The Clay Tobacco Pipes

David A. Higgins

Introduction

The clay pipe assemblage provides an important corpus for the city. It contains the largest group of marked pipes to have been recovered from excavations in Birmingham, as well as valuable information on manufacturing techniques and their evolution. The pipe forms and marks are of regional and national significance. This work has not only established a framework for the evolution of bowl forms, particularly for the 17th and early 18th centuries, but also produced a number of previously unrecorded makers' marks. In addition, there is further evidence relating to known Birmingham pipe makers as well as to a number who were previously unrecorded. The detailed recording and analysis of this material, which forms the subject of this report, was carried out during 2004 and 2005.

Although, overall, local manufacturers seem to have dominated the market, there is strong evidence for the importance of clay pipes made in Much Wenlock and Broseley from the middle of the 17th century onwards, although this influence appears to have waned in the second half of the 18th century. The presence of these Shropshire pipes seems to reflect trade between Birmingham and this area, which were linked by their industrial use of coal, by metal-working trades and by engineering. Other pipes indicate trading contacts, although on a rather more limited scale, with pipe makers in places such as Coventry and Chester.

Methodology

The pipe fragments have been individually examined and details of each fragment logged on an Excel worksheet. The layout of the worksheet has been based on a draft clay tobacco pipe recording system that has been developed at the University of Liverpool (Higgins and Davey 1994, Appendix 9.1). A context summary has also been prepared as a similar Excel worksheet and this is included below as Appendix 9.2. This gives the overall numbers of fragments and the likely deposition date for the pipes from each context. Digital copies of the worksheets and the draft recording system have been provided for the site archive.

In order to identify the individual bowl fragments where there is more than one piece in the same context, letters have been allocated to the duplicated fragments so that they can be cross-referred to the computerised record. These individual fragment letters (A, B, C, *etc.*) have been pencilled onto the bowls following the context number and they are given in the full catalogue (below) as well as in the captions accompanying the figures. An assessment of the likely date of the stem fragments has also been provided in the catalogue. The stem dates should, however, be used with caution since they are much more general and less reliable than the dates that can be determined from bowl fragments. A large number of stamped makers' marks were present within the excavated material, details of which have been added to the national catalogue of pipe stamps that is being compiled by the author.

The pipes, by site

The excavations produced a total of 2,168 pieces of pipe, comprising 458 bowl, 1,643 stem and 67 mouthpiece fragments. The pipes were recovered from four different seasons of excavation on three different sites, as shown in Table 9.1. The excavations at Edgbaston Street produced a reasonable group of pipes (354 fragments in total) while only a small assemblage was recovered from Moor Street (59 fragments). By far the largest group of material was recovered from Park Street, where 1,755 fragments were recovered. The material from these three sites will be considered first, followed by a discussion of the pipes as a whole. In particular, the marked pipes are discussed in detail since they provide an important body of evidence of regional significance.

Site	Code	Bowl	Stem	Mouthpiece	Total
Edgbaston Street Evaluation	BRB 97	10	62	2	74
Edgbaston Street Full Excavation	BRB 99	67	199	14	280
Moor Street	MSB 00	10	49	0	59
Park Street	PSB 01	371	1333	51	1755
Total		458	1643	67	2168

Table 9.1 Clay pipes; overall numbers of pipe fragments recovered.

Edgbaston Street

The two seasons of excavation at Edgbaston Street (the Bull Ring site) produced 354 fragments of pipe from 81 different contexts, plus three groups of unprovenanced material. Most of the context groups are small with only eight groups containing more than ten pieces of pipe. Seven of these groups contained between ten and 20 fragments of pipe while the largest (BRB99 1026 the fill of well F111) contained 48. Although the pipe fragments provide useful dating evidence for the contexts in which they occur, the small size of many of the assemblages limits how much reliance can be placed on these individual groups. Furthermore, some of the larger groups are clearly of mixed date and some contained only stems, which do not provide such good dating evidence as the more diagnostic bowl fragments.

The earliest two bowl fragments from this site, one of which is shown in Fig. 9.5.71, both date from *c.*1620–40, a period when smoking had already become fairly well established in the country as a whole. The majority of the bowl fragments, however, date from between about 1640 and 1730. This shows that not only had smoking become a popular habit in Birmingham but also that there was plenty of activity and/ or waste deposition on this site during this period. There are far fewer 18th-century pipe fragments dating from after about 1730 but this may be partially due to the thinner bowls of this period, which crushed more easily, making them less likely to be recovered archaeologically. At the same time snuff taking became popular, leading to a decline in smoking, and so it is normal to observe a decline in pipe deposition during this period. However, the paucity of 18th-century clay pipe dating to after *c.*1730 is mirrored both by the pottery and other artefactual evidence and seems to represent a real hiatus on Edgbaston Street (see Chapter 2). Similarly, there are relatively few 19th-century pipes, although this was a period that saw a resurgence in pipe production and consumption. This low incidence of 19th-century material is also commonly observed on archaeological sites. This phenomenon may be partly due to a tendency to strip off more recent layers and partly due to changes in municipal waste disposal, with a much higher proportion of rubbish being collected and taken away from towns.

Although many of the groups are too small for detailed analysis, there are a number of contexts that seem to have produced good, coherent groups of pipes. Contexts 2002, 2005 and 2016, all cleaning layers, produced groups that were primarily of late 17th-century date while 3000 appears to contain a good group of *c.*1680–1730. The largest group from these excavations, 1026, the fill of Phase 4 well F111, not only represents one of the few groups of later material from the site but also one of the most consistent looking groups. The fragments recovered are all relatively large and 'fresh' looking, and the thin-walled bowls are largely intact. Both of these characteristics suggest a primary deposit of material that has not been subsequently disturbed, which is consistent with the context, which was the fill of Phase 4 well F111. The bowl fragments from this deposit are all plain and make up five almost complete examples, all of which are spur types. Four of the bowls were made in the same mould, with a pointed spur (Fig. 9.8.126), while the fifth has a slightly longer, blunt-ended spur (Fig. 9.8.125). The associated stem fragments make it clear that these were all long-stemmed pipes with stems in the order of about 16" (40cm) in length. This is shorter than the minimum length of about 19" (48cm) noted for an inn clearance group of *c.*1800 from Eccleshall in Staffordshire (Boothroyd and Higgins 2005, 200). The surviving fragments suggest that these pipes had gently curving stems and almost all of the nine surviving mouthpieces show traces of some sort of finish. In most cases this takes the form of a degraded red coating, probably paint or wax, sealing about the last 30mm of the stem. In one case, however, a green glaze coats the stem for 45mm from its tip. There are also some other stem fragments with splashes of green glaze on them. Given that four bowls were from one mould and the fifth from another, it is tempting to suggest that the duplicate bowls were the ones associated with the red tips and that the fifth may have had a green-glazed tip. Complete pipes of this period are extremely rare, especially with the associated tip finish, and so it is unfortunate that no complete pipes could be reassembled from this deposit. The presence of such large, fresh fragments and multiple examples of one bowl type all suggest that this is a discreet deposit of pipes, representing a very short-lived period of disposal from a single household. Pipes of this period are not well represented in the archaeological record and so the dating of these bowl forms is still rather poor. The only mark with this group is part of a single line stem stamp, which would probably have read 'BROSLEY' (Fig. 9.5.73). This style of mark was current from *c*.1770–1840 while curved stems and the use of green-glazed tips are thought to have come in around 1800 (although see the Park Street tank fills, discussed below). The well fill included fragments of several decanters dating to the late 18th or early 19th centuries and patent bottles made by Ricketts of Bristol (see Orton and Rátkai, Chapter 8), which date from after *c*.1821, and so the suggested date for this well deposit is around 1820–1840. This group is important in helping to refine the dating for these large spur forms, which are not often securely associated with their stem marks and which are still poorly fixed in the regional bowl form typologies.

The latest group of any note was recovered during the evaluation works (5107) from the upper fill of a brick culvert in the area of the Moat watercourse. This group also contains some large fragments, especially long stems, suggesting that it was a discreet and undisturbed deposit. Most of the fragments are from long-stemmed pipes, for example Figs 9.3.44 and 45, but there is one nipple mouthpiece that would have come from a shorter 'cutty' pipe, of a style that only became popular from the middle of the 19th century. The group also contains a stem fragment from an imported short-stemmed French pipe made at the well-known Fiolet factory (Fig. 9.2.25). The presence of only two short-stemmed pipes as opposed to around 17 fragments from long-stemmed pipes suggests that this group dates from around the 1850s or 1860s, after which time a much larger proportion of these types would be expected. The group also includes a good fragment from a local pipe made by one of the Reynolds family, who are recorded in Birmingham from the 1850s to 1890s (Fig. 9.3.44).

When all of the pipes from this site are considered, it is noticeable that there is a wide range of material represented. The marked pipes (see below for details) include local 17th-century wheel and initial stamps, for example WT and EW, as well as 'imported' types from the Broseley area of Shropshire, such as MD and WILL SAVAG. The same is true of the 18th-century bowl and stem marks. This mix of products and styles is evident on the Park Street site as well (see below) and shows that this diversity is truly representative of the pipes circulating in Birmingham rather than being a product of a biased sample coming from one particular household or excavation area.

Moor Street

The Moor Street excavation produced the smallest assemblage of pipes with only ten bowl and 49 stem fragments being recovered from 13 contexts (plus one unstratified fragment). The majority of the pipes came from a single evaluation context (6000), which produced 34 of the pieces, representing nearly 58% of all the fragments from this site. This group of fragments are rather broken and mixed in nature, suggesting that they are not from a well-sealed deposit, although most of them date from the late 17th to early 18th century. No marked or decorated pipes were recovered from this site and the only piece worth illustrating is an unstratified heel bowl dating from *c*.1660–1690 (Fig. 9.6.92).

Park Street

By far the largest assemblage of pipes from the three excavation areas was recovered from Park Street, which produced a total of 1,755 fragments of pipe from some 135 different contexts, plus three unstratified groups. This site produced quite a lot of good-sized pipe groups as well as a large number of marked examples. In general terms it is interesting to note that no bowl forms dating to before *c*.1640 were identified and only five of the bowls have date ranges that start before *c*.1660 (just 1.3% of the bowls from the site). This is in marked contrast with the Edgbaston Street group that, although smaller, produced a couple of pieces dating from the 1620s or 1630s and nearly a quarter of all the fragments were allocated a date range starting before 1660. This clearly demonstrates that there was a much higher level of deposition during the second quarter of the 17th century at Edgbaston Street and that virtually no pipes were being discarded at Park Street before the Restoration period.

Once pipe deposition had started, however, it rose sharply so that nearly two-thirds of all the Park Street bowls were dated to within the 1660–1730 period. Just under one-third of the bowls were dated to *c*.1700–1800, but quite a number of these are poorly datable fragments and some would also fall within the earlier range anyway. Just under 10% of the bowl fragments were allocated a 19th-century date. This shows that, on this particular site, most of the pipe-bearing deposits were laid down during the late 17th to early 18th century and that much smaller levels of deposition took place thereafter.

Although this site produced a large number of pipe fragments it is noticeable that many of the context groups contain rather abraded, fragmentary material or are of mixed date. Both of these characteristics suggest that the material derives from very disturbed and/ or redeposited contexts. Furthermore, despite the fact that the majority of the finds date from *c*.1660–1730, it is noticeable that there are not many good context groups containing material of just this date. The clear impression is that this site has been intensively used and redeveloped since the late 17th century, resulting in the pipes becoming quite mixed between contexts. Having said that, there are still some good context groups and the quantity of surviving material clearly shows there was a lot of depositional activity taking place on the site.

The bulk of the pipes date from *c*.1660–1730, a period when the forms being used in Birmingham were strongly influenced by the styles being set in the Much Wenlock/

Broseley area of Shropshire (Higgins 1987a). Imports from that area were mixing freely with more local products, many of which were produced in Shropshire styles. The presence of these locally produced forms can be seen, for example, in 1126, the fill of Phase 3.1 pit F134, which produced nine bowl and 18 stem fragments with a likely deposition date of c.1660–1680. This group includes several bowls with Shropshire characteristics, such as large heels and burnished surfaces, but neither the marks (Fig. 9.5.76 and 81) nor the specific bowl forms, fabrics and finish (for example, Fig. 9.6.99) are typical of Shropshire products. These differences suggest a more local origin for most, if not all, of this group.

Other groups of a similar date include both local and imported pieces. Evaluation context 1015 produced a large group (16 bowl, 77 stem and eleven mouthpiece fragments) that appears to form a consistent group of c.1680–1720. The marked pipes include both local and Shropshire products, which perhaps provides a better indication of the nature of the assemblages at this period. Not all of the bowls are marked but the fabric and manufacturing details can often provide a clue as to the origin of the pieces, such as the spur pipe (Fig. 9.7.110), which is probably a Shropshire piece.

The 18th-century groups from this site are more problematic, both because many of the groups appear to contain material of mixed date and because bowls of this period are particularly difficult to date accurately. One pit group that is of special interest, because of the pottery and metal-working debris that it contained, is 1125, the fill of pit F133, Phase 3.2. Large sherds of pottery from this group date from c.1725–1750 (see Rátkai, Chapter 7), suggesting that the fill itself dates from around 1750–60. The pit produced 48 pieces of pipe comprising ten bowl fragments, 18 stem fragments, and a mouthpiece from the main fill and six small bowl fragments and 13 stem fragments from a sieved sample. At least four of the bowl fragments are from Shropshire style bowls with tailed heels, which were most popular from c.1680–1730. Most of these pieces are small and abraded, and so could be residual, but one complete bowl survives. This complete bowl is the only piece with a heel stamp surviving and it has an inverted 'IOHN/ IAMS' mark on it, for John James, who worked in the Broseley area of Shropshire. The bowl form is fairly thin-walled and it has quite a thin stem and stem bore. These are all late characteristics for this form and, if it is contemporary with the pottery, may suggest that some examples of this form were being produced into the 1730s or 1740s (although the use of milling this late would be very unusual). There are also at least four spur bowls represented in the group. There is one complete bowl of c.1700–1740 (Fig. 9.7.114) and a damaged example that is harder to date, but probably of somewhere between 1710 and 1770 (Fig. 9.7.115). This pipe has quite a thin stem and narrow bore, arguing for a later date within this range. The final piece is rather fragmentary, but is from a large burnished bowl with quite thin walls of mid- to late 18th-century date (Fig. 9.7.116). The most problematic piece is an early 19th-century-looking bowl, very similar to an unstratified example from the BRB 97 excavations (Fig. 9.8.127). The rim is sharply cut and the spur has not been trimmed, both of which are clearly later features than those found in the rest of the group. This bowl appears to have been freshly damaged in two places, and so may be intrusive in this context. The only other mark from the group is an HH stamp on a burnished bowl fragment of c.1730–80 (Fig. 9.2.28). A few of the plain stem fragments are certainly 17th century but most of the larger pieces are generally thin and cylindrical with relatively narrow bores, which would fit with a mid-18th-century group. Some of the pieces may even be slightly curved, which would suggest a late 18th-century date. Overall the pipes are hard to pin down to a narrow period of deposition and the other finds are equally ambiguous, making it hard to refine the bowl dates at all. This context certainly contains a significant number of 17th- or early 18th-century pipe fragments, but many of these are rather small and abraded, suggesting that they are residual. The majority of the pipe bowls would fit within a c.1720–1760 date range without any problem but there is one bowl, and possibly some of the stems, that appear to be later, suggesting a degree of contamination or intrusive material within this group.

One of the most interesting groups of pipes from this site was recovered from the fill of two Phase 3.3 features, Tank 1 F503/ 520 and Tank 2 F510/ F542. These tanks produced good assemblages of pottery, which suggested that they had both been filled during the late 1770s or early 1780s (see Barker and Rátkai, Chapter 7). Pipes of this period are poorly understood for two reasons. First, complete bowl forms of this period are rarely found during excavations because, being very large and thin, they were easily crushed after being discarded. Second, even where bowl forms are recovered they are rarely marked, making it hard to establish a typology for late 18th-century forms. The material from this pit is, therefore, significant in that it provides a reasonably well-dated sample of bowl forms from this period.

Unfortunately, the pit fills also contained a lot of residual pipe fragments dating from the 17th and earlier 18th centuries, which means that the deposition group of c.1780 has to be extracted from a rather mixed assemblage. In most cases the final fill group can be separated with confidence but there are one or two pieces where the interpretation is a little more doubtful. In broad terms, however, it is evident that there are a number of 17th- and 18th-century fragments that have become incorporated into the fill. Most of these are rather fragmentary and abraded, in contrast to the generally 'fresher looking' and more complete bowls of c.1780. These clearly residual pieces will not be considered in detail. Where 18th-century fragments that may or may not be residual occur, they will be discussed in more detail. There was also a mixed Phase 4 layer of material overlying the two tanks (1505), which contained 19th-century material. Most of the finds from this context were rather broken and abraded but there was one quite fresh-looking complete spur bowl with an IS stamp that could have come from the top of one of the tank fills (Fig. 9.3.50). If this is the case, then this form and mark may belong with the c.1780 deposition group as well.

The first tank F503/ F520 produced 29 pieces of pipe (six bowl and 23 stem fragments) from four different contexts (1506, 1521, 1530 and 1580). This group includes three stamped marks. Two of these are clearly residual, since they occur on tailed heel fragments dating from c.1680–1730 (TA and MB). The other one is a bowl stamp on a spur bowl comprising the crowned initials IB (Fig. 9.1.6), which is slightly more difficult to date. This piece is also fragmentary but probably dates from the first half of the 18th century and it would be very surprising if this style of mark were still in use as late as c.1780. The same is true of an almost complete spur bowl from 1521 (Fig. 9.7.113). In fact, the only diagnostic piece from this tank that would fit with the c.1780 infilling of the tank is a damaged bowl from 1506 (Fig. 9.7.124).

The second tank F510/ F542 produced a rather larger pipe assemblage, comprising 76 pieces (16 bowl, 59 stem and one mouthpiece) from five different contexts (1531, 1621, 1622, 1634 and 1635), plus another bowl from a cleaning layer over 1621. Once again, the fill includes some residual fragments, including two stamped heels (a wheel mark, Fig. 9.5.75, plus a 'IOHN/ IAMS' heel) and an IB bowl mark that probably pre-dates the main deposit. There is also the larger part of a spur bowl, the milling on which shows that it dates from the early 18th century (Fig. 9.7.109). This piece has a thicker stem junction than the later group of spur bowls from the tank. It is worth noting that this particular bowl may well have come from the same pipe as a stem from the same context decorated with a spiral pattern of incised lines (of the same type as that shown in Fig. 9.5.83). This context (1634) also produced a stem with a lion oval on it, which is also thicker than the stems associated with the c.1780 bowls (Fig. 9.5.84).

Some slightly more problematic stem marks from Tank 2 are represented by a IOHN PHIPSON mark (Fig. 9.3.42) and two examples with lattice decoration on (Fig. 9.5.85 and 87). The Phipson mark is a little thicker than the stems associated with the surviving bowls of c.1780 and so it could be a slightly earlier residual fragment. On the other hand, the St Mary's Grove pit from Stafford of c.1775 included one or two pipes with slightly thicker stems that appeared to be part of the contemporary range being produced at the time (Higgins 1987b, figs 142 and 145). Either way, thinner stems from elsewhere on this site (see below) suggest that Phipson was working at some point between c.1740 and c.1800 and there are no surviving bowl forms from the tank with thick enough

stems to have been associated with this mark. The same problem arises with the lattice-decorated stems, two of which were recovered from this tank. One of these is on a thick stem that probably dates from before c.1750 and so must be residual in this context (Fig. 9.5.85). The other example, however, occurs on a much thinner stem, which is probably contemporary with the c.1780 deposit (Fig. 9.5.87). It seems most likely that this style of border was used locally for much of the 18th century with some examples still being used as late as c.1780.

Having looked at the material that is probably residual or doubtful, there is finally a group of bowls that are of late 18th-century form and which can confidently be attributed to the filling of this tank in c.1780. By far the best group of bowls and stem fragments of this date was recovered from 1621, which includes the remains of five or six large bowls and a number of long, thin stem fragments of contemporary type. One of these had been freshly broken during the excavation and joins a fragment from 1622, showing that there was some mixing between contexts during the excavation itself. These two fragments are of interest since they make up a stem section 106mm long that appears to be slightly curved. Prior to the late 18th century all pipes had straight stems, as did all the pipes from the St Mary's Grove pit, which dates from the 1770s (Higgins 1987b). If this fragment represents a pipe with a deliberately curved stem, then it is one of the earliest examples known and provides a date of c.1780 for the introduction of this new style, which was to become standard from the late 18th century onwards.

The bowls themselves are all spur types and can be matched by other examples from (1622) and (1634) and the cleaning layer over 1621. These bowls (Fig. 9.7.120–123) are characterised by their large, forward leaning forms, with their thin walls. One particular characteristic of these forms is a tendency for the underside of the bowl to continue almost in line with the stem for a short way before turning up towards the rim. This particular feature is not evident amongst the earlier or later forms and may well provide useful as a means of identifying the pipes of this period. The rims are either cut roughly parallel to the stem or tilting back slightly towards it and most of the rims have been internally knife-trimmed to give a uniform (and internally bevelled) finish. The stems are relatively thin and frequently slightly oval in section, especially where they join the bowl. The stem bores are usually 5/64" or, occasionally, 4/64" in diameter. With regard to finishing techniques, the bases of the spurs have usually been trimmed, although in one instance this is not so (Fig. 9.7.121). This un-trimmed example possibly heralds the end of this technique, which was generally abandoned by around 1800. Likewise only about one-third of the bowl fragments from this group are burnished (three out of eight fragments, or 37.5%). These three bowls are all neatly burnished, the finish being of average or a little above average quality. The low number of burnished bowls, however, contrasts with the material of the St Mary's Grove group from Stafford, which is probably a few years earlier in date, where most of the bowls were burnished (Higgins 1987b, Fig. 9.1.13 and 14). Burnishing became far less common from the late 18th century onwards and, although these two groups are too small to make a definitive statement, the indications are that the incidence of burnished bowls dropped markedly between about 1770 and 1780. The final piece of note is a mouthpiece fragment recovered from 1631, which has a degraded red wax or paint coating extending 18mm from the tip. The use of red tip coatings only seems to start at the end of the 18th century and, if this is a securely stratified piece, it represents one of the earliest known examples. The doubt as to how securely stratified this piece is arises because almost all of the other pipe fragments from both tanks are quite badly iron-stained, giving the pipes a mottled light brown surface. This piece, however, is very clean and white looking in comparison, suggesting that it may be intrusive from another context. Unfortunately no other mouthpieces were recovered from either tank, making it impossible to look at the mouthpiece finish on comparative examples from this group.

Although these tanks contain a lot of residual material, as well as some possibly intrusive finds, there is still a useful group of pipes that can be attributed to the c.1780 filling of the tanks. These not only show the styles of pipe that were being produced at this date but also shed light on the manufacturing techniques and their evolution that was taking place. The thin-walled bowls typically have the base of the bowl projecting in line with the underside of the stem and thin, slightly oval stems with stem bores of 5/64" or 4/64". The rims are usually internally trimmed and around one-third of the bowls were still being burnished, although this technique appears to have been in rapid decline. Likewise the ends of the spurs were still usually trimmed, although the first evidence of untrimmed spurs was noted. The pipes were all long-stemmed forms, some of which probably had lattice decoration or makers' marks stamped across the stem. Some of the earliest evidence for curved stems and, possibly, the use of red mouthpiece coatings was noted. Taken together, these characteristics form a distinctive and very useful set of indicators that can be used to identify other late 18th-century assemblages of pipes. By around 1800 many parts of the country show a marked decline in the quality of pipes being produced. Time-consuming finishing techniques such as internal trimming of the bowl, trimming the bowl seams and base of the heel or spur, and burnishing the surface of the pipe were all largely abandoned in favour of more cheaply produced pipes of lower quality. The late 18th-century group from Park Street represents a last flourishing of the 18th-century styles before the fundamental changes in design and finish that took place during the early 19th century.

Very little 19th-century material was recovered from the excavations, making it difficult to chart the evolution of pipe usage during this century. The best group is undoubtedly from 1771, a fill of pit F836, which produced a large number of finds (See Chapter 8) and which produced a consistent-looking group comprising 15 bowl, 27 stem and four mouthpiece fragments. There are one or two pieces of residual stem but all of the bowl fragments are of 19th-century types, with the most likely date for this group being c.1850–1870. There is one plain spur bowl that would have come from a long-stemmed or 'churchwarden' pipe, of the type that is characteristic of Broseley (Fig. 9.8.134). Where the form is evident, all of the other pieces are from spurless pipes, many of which would have been from short-stemmed or 'cutty' pipes. Three or four plain bowls of this type are represented, for example, Figs 9.8.136 and 137. The most common decorated forms had raised beaded ribs on the seams. There is one fragmentary example with single beaded rib on the mould seam (not illustrated) and then six fragments belonging to pipes made in two different moulds. There are two identical bowls with thick stems (Fig. 9.8.138) and four fragments from at least three different pipes with a thinner stem (Fig. 9.8.139, which shows a composite drawing from two of these fragments). There is one fragment from a bowl decorated in the form of a man's head, with elements of his hair, beard and left ear surviving (Fig. 9.8.142). This fairly crudely modelled type of figural bowl appears to have been made in small numbers across many parts of England during the early to mid-19th century. Other contemporary decorative designs are represented by a stem with traces of a fluted bowl surviving and part of a bowl with a basket-weave pattern on it. This may well have come from the same pipe as a stem fragment with beaded decoration on either side, surrounding a raised area (Fig. 9.8.140). No marked fragments were recovered, although part of a stem with a beaded name border on it was found (Fig. 9.8.135). Four mouthpieces were collected, two with simple cut ends and two with nipple ends on them. The two nipple types have both been trimmed at the end, an unusual feature on English pipes and perhaps characteristic of the local Birmingham area industry at this period, or perhaps even an individual manufacturer. The final point of interest with regard to this group is the evidence for reuse of the pipes. Despite the fact that many of these pipes already had short stems, there are at least two instances where the pipes appear to have been reused with broken stems. In one instance, a stem already opening out into a flattened mouthpiece has been rubbed against something quite coarse to smooth and shape it into a series of facets (Fig. 9.8.141). In another instance, a broken stem end is just very slightly rounded at the broken edges but there are also scuffed areas where it has been clenched between the smoker's teeth, which make it clear that the broken pipe was reused (Fig. 9.8.140). The reuse of broken pipes was much more common during the 19th century than it had been at earlier periods, probably because short-stemmed pipes were in fashion anyway. This type of reuse is, however, more likely to have been associated with the lower end of the socio-economic scale and with the cheaper 'cutties', rather than the thin-stemmed 'straws' or the long-stemmed 'churchwardens'. This lower status is reinforced by the types of 19th-century pottery from the site.

The pipes themselves

As well as providing useful archaeological information about the excavated sites and deposits, the pipe remains also provide a lot of new evidence about the local pipe industries themselves and the styles of pipe that were marketed in Birmingham. The styles of bowl being used are represented both by the marked pipes, which are presented in alphabetical order in Figs 9.1–9.5.1–88 and by the unmarked examples, which are presented in roughly chronological order in Figs 9.6–9.8, 89–144. Taken together, these illustrations provide not only the first significant overview of pipes from the city but also a corpus of forms and marks that is of regional and national significance. In the following sections, some of the individual characteristics of the pipes will be discussed, followed by a detailed description of the marked pipes.

Internal bowl marks

Internal bowl marks are occasionally found on pipes of 18th-century or later date. These generally occur on the flat internal base of the bowl and are deliberately formed by marks on the metal stopper used to form the bowl cavity during the moulding process. These marks are not the same as the 'roughing up' marks on the stopper, which were randomly applied nicks in the stopper, made to assist with its release from the bowl when being withdrawn.

Only three pipes with internal bowl marks were noted amongst the excavated material. The first occurs in a spur bowl of *c.*1740–80. This example (Fig. 9.3.50) has a small flat internal base but adjacent to it, on the side away from the smoker, a small grid made up of four lines has been cut, appearing as a relief moulded mark within the bowl. This is an unusual form of mark and one which has not been previously noted from anywhere in the Midlands. The second occurs inside a slightly later spur bowl of *c.*1750–90. This example has a large flat internal base that has a single tapering rib running half-way across it. The final example is later in date and occurs inside a spur bowl from the well fill of *c.*1820–40. This example is particularly interesting since it has a combination of marks on it. The whole of the end of the stopper has been 'roughed up', probably with a file, and then five irregularly spaced and positioned cuts have been made running roughly along the length of the stopper. The marks formed by these cuts run more than half-way up the bowl interior, creating long, thin, raised ribs running at odd angles and for various distances up the inside of

the bowl. The base of the interior itself comes to a rounded point, without any flat internal base. The bowl form is shown in Fig. 9.8.125 but the marks are not shown as they run up the inside surface of the bowl rather than occurring on a flat internal base.

The precise reason for these ribs or the marks noted on the other examples is not known. What is interesting is that these marks are different from those normally found in other areas of the country. In most other areas internal bowl marks typically consist of a cross, arranged either in line with (+) or at 45 degrees to the long axis of the pipe (x). This sample is too small to draw any firm conclusions, but it may be that, for whatever reason, different styles of internal bowl mark were adopted in the west Midlands.

Decorated pipes

Early pipes were rarely decorated, other than with the band of milling that was applied around the rim of the bowl. Occasionally bands of milling were employed decoratively elsewhere on the pipe, most frequently on the stem, where it was often used to disguise repairs made during the manufacturing process. One example of a milled stem attached to a Michael Browne bowl was found (PSB01 U/S). This is a bowl with a tailed heel, similar to Fig. 9.1.13, but with traces of a milled band at the broken stem end, about 23mm from the bowl junction. Not enough survives to be sure of the form or extent of this stem milling. Other than this single example, there were no examples of decorated 17th- or 18th-century pipes from the excavations.

In general terms, moulded decoration did not become common in the Midlands until around 1800 but too small a sample was recovered from the excavations to see this change in any detail. Finds recovered from elsewhere in the area suggest that quite a wide range of mould-decorated pipes developed in Birmingham during the early 19th century, but these decorative styles have not been properly defined or studied as yet. One particularly interesting element that has been noted, however, is a distinctive series of political union pipes that were produced at Birmingham during the 1830s (Melton 1990; Hammond 1991).

The excavations did not produce any late 18th-century or early 19th-century decorated fragments, despite the fact that some groups of this period were recovered. The *c.*1780 tank fills (see F503/ 520 and F510/ F542 above) contained only plain bowls, as did the Edgbaston Street well group of *c.*1820–1840 from 1026. In other parts of the country fluted bowls were extremely popular at this period but these were never common in Shropshire and they appear to have been equally rare around Birmingham too, with plain forms continuing to dominate the market. By the second quarter of the century bowls with leaf-decorated seams were being produced (*e.g.* Fig. 9.8.130), sometimes in association with other motifs (*e.g.* Fig. 9.8.128 and 129). The earlier leaves tend to be crudely modelled (as in Fig. 9.8.130) with later examples often having more detail, including veins and serrated edges (*e.g.* Fig. 9.3.44). Some of this decoration picks up on national themes found across the country during this period, such as the rose, thistle and shamrock motifs (representing different areas of the British Isles) used on Fig. 9.8.131, while other designs, such as the ears of wheat on Fig. 9.8.129, appear to be more local. It is probable that a wide range of local decorative motifs were developed during the early 19th century and that, after around 1850, imported pipes from London, France and Scotland would have circulated in the city along with regionally produced products.

In total, there were only about 25 fragments of mould-decorated pipe recovered from the excavations, and nearly half of these (twelve examples) came from PSB01 1771, F836, a good group dating from the third quarter of the 19th century. By this time, many of the bowl forms were without a spur or heel and nipple mouthpieces show that many of these pipes were of the short-stemmed 'cutty' type. Bold moulded decoration was frequently employed to decorate this style of pipe. This context group includes fragments with raised ribs and leaves on the seams (Fig. 9.8.138 and 139), a basket-weave motif and part of a bowl crudely decorated in the form of a man's head of a type that was widely if thinly distributed across the country (Fig. 9.8.142). There is also one plain spur bowl from a long-stemmed pipe (possibly from Broseley), which shows that some traditional forms continued to be used amongst the short, decorative new styles.

During the third quarter of the century the spurless bowls with raised ribs on the seams seem to have been very popular, with fragments from several different versions being represented, including both long-stemmed (Fig. 9.8.143) and short-stemmed varieties (Fig. 9.8.139). As well as the English style figural bowl (Fig. 9.8.142), there is a fragment of French stem, which hints that the more elaborate continental European counterparts would also have been available (Fig. 9.2.25). Other common English motifs include bowls with basket-weave decoration (Fig. 9.8.144) and there is no doubt that many other decorative designs would have been available during the later 19th century.

There is no doubt that a much wider and more elaborate range of decorated pipes would have been produced and used in Birmingham from the late 18th or early 19th century onwards, since there was a national trend in favour of this type of pipe, but the excavations did not produce very much evidence from these periods. Future work should focus on recovering a good range of 19th-century deposits from the city so that these styles can be defined and the evolution of pipe production and consumption in this area explored.

Reused pipes

The final comments in this section relate to the evidence for the reuse of pipes. There does not seem to have been very much reuse of 17th- and 18th-century pipes, especially where they were in plentiful supply. Only three fragments of this date were noted where broken stem ends had been ground smooth, or had become rounded. One of these is of interest since the stem taper clearly shows that it is the thicker, or bowl end, that has been rounded (Fig. 9.6.108). This clearly shows that the smoothing cannot have been so that the pipe could be smoked in a broken state. Stems sometimes became rounded when they were used for drawing with, like a stick of chalk, when they were reused as hair curlers, or as the result of idle doodling.

There are two later examples, both of which occur in a context that probably dates from the third quarter of the 19th century. By this date short-stemmed 'cutty' pipes were popular and it became much more common practice to smoke these even in a shortened, broken state. In one instance a chipped mouthpiece has been ground and reshaped (Fig. 9.8.141) while in the other a stem fragment has a rounded break and clear tooth marks where it has been clenched between the smoker's teeth (Fig. 9.8.140). These two examples represent a much higher percentage of the few 19th-century pipe stems recovered than the three earlier ones do of all the 17th- and 18th-century fragments recovered. These contrasting frequencies clearly show how smoking habits changed over time.

The marked pipes

The excavations produced a very large number of marked pipes, which are important for a three main reasons: first, they can generally be dated more accurately than plain pipes; second, they can be used to source the pipes that were arriving at the site; and, third, they provide the largest group of marked pipes ever to have been recovered from the city. Despite the fact that for many years Adrian Oswald, the founding father of modern pipe studies, was Keeper of Archaeology at Birmingham City Museum, there has been comparatively little study of the local pipe industry. This may in part be due to the fact that comparatively little material has been available for study. This group provides an excellent opportunity to redress this balance so the marked pipes have been studied in particular detail.

The excavations produced a total of 170 fragments with some sort of mark on them. The majority of these, 166 fragments, date from the 17th or 18th centuries and have stamped marks on them. A stamped mark is one that has been applied to the pipe after it has been shaped in a metal mould and trimmed but before the clay had become completely dry. These marks were created using specially-made dies that were individually hand-pressed into the partially dried clay. In contrast, only four moulded marks were recovered, all of which date from the 19th century or later. This type of mark formed part of the mould in which the pipes were actually made, so that each example was automatically marked in the same way each time a pipe was pressed. Taken together, the marks recovered represent around 30 different manufacturers.

In the following discussion of the stamped marks, 'Die Numbers' are often referred to. These are the unique identification numbers that are being allocated to each different pipe maker's mark in a national catalogue that is being compiled by the author. Although this is as yet unpublished, the intention is that each different die type that can be recorded from its impression will be illustrated at twice life size and allocated a unique number. The die number not only allows individual dies to be recognised and described but it also provides a means of referring to specific die types in any discussion of the marks. Furthermore, the establishment of a standardised numbering system will save having to describe and illustrate the same mark each time it is encountered on different excavations and it will facilitate the recognition of trade and distribution patterns if a standard nomenclature is used in all excavation reports. As the catalogue is not yet available in a published form, all of the different marks recovered are illustrated in this report. In one or two instances the excavated dies are not as clear as examples already drawn for the national catalogue. When this is the case, die details from the national catalogue have been used and a note of this made in the accompanying text.

All of the marks recovered will first be described and discussed according to their type and position on the pipe. The stamped marks are described first and these are broken into three sections: marks stamped onto the base of the heel or spur, marks stamped onto the bowl facing the smoker, and marks stamped onto or around the stem of the pipe. There is then a short section describing the four moulded marks that were recovered, followed by a discussion of the marked pipes as a whole. All of the different marks recovered are illustrated in alphabetical order in Figs 9.1–9.5, 1–88 and a table providing a summary of the marked pipes is given as Appendix 9.3.

Stamped marks

The stamped marks have been divided into three main sections according to their location on the pipe, *i.e.* heel or spur marks, bowl marks and stem marks. Within each of these sections the marks are presented in alphabetical order with incomplete marks and symbol marks appearing at the end of each list. The stamped marks described were applied to the pipe by the pipe maker after it had been moulded but before it was fully dry. The stamps were impressed using individual dies and it is the impressions created by these dies that are described below. Each die could be applied any number of times on each individual pipe (although it is normally only once on each) and to any number of pipes made in different moulds. The individual moulds in which the pipes were pressed can often be identified from small surface defects

that are reproduced on each pipe. The dies and moulds are quite separate and should not be confused.

A total of 166 fragments with stamped marks were recovered from the excavations. Ten of these marks were too similar, damaged or poorly impressed to allow detailed identification but the remaining 156 examples have been identified to individual die type. Amongst these 156 examples there are 71 different die types, many of which are only represented by a single example. This clearly shows that a much larger sample size will be needed before a realistic assessment of the number of marks being used or traded to Birmingham can be made. Despite this, the 71 different types described below provide a good corpus for the city against which new material can be compared.

Stamped heel or spur marks

A total of some 124 stamped heel or spur marks were recovered, of which 114 could be identified to individual die type, as listed below:

TA Three examples of this mark were found, all made using the same die and all occurring on pipes made in the same mould (Die 2001; Fig. 9.1.11; two examples from PSB01 1739, F713 Phase 3.2 and one from PSB01 1530 F503/ F520 Phase 3.3). These pipes are of a distinctive Shropshire style with a tailed heel, which was popular from c.1680–1730, and all are neatly produced with a good finish. The mark is not known from Shropshire, nor is the distinctive motif above and below the initials. This motif was, however, used in Coventry where TA marks are also found, although the known examples occur on bowls of Warwickshire rather than Shropshire style (Muldoon 1979, figs 12–13). One of the Coventry marks has a similar 'scroll' above and below the initials (*ibid.*, fig. 12c) and may be the same as the Birmingham examples. Muldoon attributes the Coventry marks to the Warwick maker, Tim Averne, who was working in 1718. While this is a possibility, it seems unlikely that a Warwickshire maker would have been producing such good-quality copies of Shropshire forms. Furthermore, a 1714 survey of the Manor of Wenlock includes John Andrews and 'Thomas his brother of Coventry, pipemaker'. The Birmingham pipes date from c.1680– 1730 and so would fit perfectly with this maker. It is suggested that these TA pipes can be attributed to Thomas Andrews, who was working in Coventry in 1714 and who may also have worked in Much Wenlock at some point during his career. This would explain the fusion of Shropshire bowl form with a Coventry style of mark. It also raises the possibility that the other Coventry TA marks were also made by this maker, using a purely local style of bowl form.

EB One example of this neatly cut mark (Die 136; Fig. 9.1.2) was found on a tailed heel fragment of Shropshire style dating from c.1680–1730. Thursfield (1907, fig. 16) recorded this mark and examples have also been noted from Church Stretton (two examples) and Broseley Wood (Higgins 1987a, figs 33.23 and 33.24). There is also an unprovenanced example in Rowley's House Museum, Shrewsbury (*ibid.*, fig. 51.5). The use of initials flanking a hand or gauntlet mark was particularly favoured by the Much Wenlock makers and this piece may well represent an as yet undocumented maker from that area.

MB/MICHAEL BROWN By far the most common marked pipes recovered from the excavations were those stamped either MB or with various forms of the name Michael Brown. All of these marks can be attributed to the Much Wenlock maker of this name, who must have been a prominent maker since his pipes are relatively common, with a wide range of different marks and mould types being represented. Furthermore, his products were marketed over a wide area with examples having been found at other Midlands towns, such as Stafford (Higgins 1986, fig. 4.5).

Despite the number of known examples of his pipes, very little is known about Michael Brown himself or his working life. There was a Much Wenlock pipe maker called Samuel Brown who died in 1668 but, in his will, he left almost all his estate to 'his brother' John Hughes, another Wenlock pipe maker, with no mention of any Michael. A list of Broseley area pipe makers notes that Michael baptised a daughter Jane at Much Wenlock in 1681 (Oswald and James 1955, 222), but a search of the Internet version of the IGI did not relocate this reference and it only gave two references to a Michael Brown at Much Wenlock. These are 7 May 1681 when a Michael Brown married an Anna Ridley, and 11 January 1684, when they baptised a son, also called Michael. Nothing else is known of Michael's life or career, although one of his pipe stamps appears to be dated 1688 and was subsequently altered (see below), suggesting that he was active during the 1680s and 1690s.

The excavations produced 37 examples of pipes stamped with one of Michael Brown's marks, of which 35 were clear enough to be identified to individual die type. A total of eight different die types are represented, six of which are full-name marks and two of which have initials only. These initial marks are not only of a distinctive Wenlock style but they are also well known from the town, as are the full-name marks. Given the stylistic and distributional similarities, it seems reasonable to attribute all of these pipes to the same maker. The eight die types recovered from these excavations do not include all of the types that this maker is known to have used. Furthermore, several of the die types recovered are previously unidentified, showing that an even greater range of Michael Brown marks is likely to be discovered as more examples are collected.

The various die types represented amongst the excavated material are listed below. All of these marks occur on distinctive Shropshire style bowls with tailed heels dating from *c.*1680–1730 with the exception of the 'MICH/ BROUN' mark, which occurs on a round-heeled form of *c.*1670–1690. The documentary sources clearly suggest that Brown was working throughout the 1680s while the number and range of his pipes suggests a long working life, most likely spanning the period *c.*1680–1730. Two of the marks represented amongst the excavated material were too poorly impressed or damaged to attribute to particular die types but the remainder could be divided into eight distinct die types as follows:

MICH/ BROUN (Die 2018; Fig. 9.1.11). A single example of this previously unrecorded die type was found during the excavations. It is the only Brown mark from the excavations to occur on a pipe with a large round heel which, stylistically, dates from *c.*1670–90. This places it early in the sequence of this maker's marks and suggests that he may have started his business using these relatively small, two line marks. A very similar mark but with a slightly wider frame and slight differences in the lettering is also known from an example in the Bragge Collection at the British Museum (Higgins 1987a, fig. 32.2; Die 249). Although the Bragge example occurs on a form with a tailed heel, the bowl is very small, suggesting that it, too, dates from early in this maker's career.

MICH/ BRO /WN / 1688? (Die 251; Fig. 9.1.12). Two examples of this unusual four-line mark were recovered from the excavations. Other examples of this mark have been previously recorded, for example, from excavations at Stafford (Higgins 1986, fig. 4.5). The final numeral of the date always seems to be poorly formed but one of the newly excavated examples suggests that it is most likely to have been 1688. At least twelve different Shropshire style makers' marks with dates ranging from 1687–1718 are known (Melton 1997, 213). Melton argues that the various dates found reflect significant events for Nonconformists, particularly Quakers, and that these dated pipes were made either for or by the dissenting community. Unfortunately, if the suggested reading of 1688 is correct, this represents a new date within this range and not one that Melton has linked with a significant Nonconformist event. This particular mark is also of interest because the die was later altered to remove the date – see Die 2019 below.

MICH/ BRO/ WN (Die 2019; Fig. 9.1.13). Seven examples of this die type were found. This mark is particularly interesting since it appears to have been cut down from the dated example discussed above. The style and spacing of the lettering on this three-line die matches exactly with the dated example and, in particular, there are three distinctive reference points between the two versions. First, the sloping members of the letter 'M' overrun to form a small cross within the centre of this letter. Second, a serif has been cut across the top centre of the 'W' but this has been placed too low, so that a small inverted 'v' projects above it. Thirdly, when the die was cut down, the horizontal dividing line between the 'WN' and '1688' was left in place and this is clearly evident running across the bottom of the mark. In some impressions the top of the '1' is even visible where it comes up to touch this dividing line.

MICH/ BRO/ WN (Die 2020; Fig. 9.1.16). Five examples of this die type were found. This mark has the same arrangement of letters as Die 2019 above, but the three distinctive characteristics are absent and the overall spacing and proportions of the lettering on the die differs slightly. This example is a little more squat and nearly square, as opposed to Die 2019, which is a slightly more like an upright rectangle in outline.

MICH/ BRO/ WNE (Die 250; Fig. 9.1.14). This was the most common type of Brown recovered, with 13 examples being represented. This type is similar to the above two, but has the name spelt with an 'E' at the end. Slight variations in the form and spacing of the individual letters suggest that at least two actual dies of this type were in use, but the differences are not sufficient to adequately separate this group into more closely defined die types. This die type has simply been defined on the basis of the lettering being on three lines and with an 'E' at the end.

MICH/ EALL/ BROWN (Die 871; Fig. 9.1.15). Only one example of this type was found, which is characterised by the use of a full, rather than an abbreviated Christian name.

MB (Die 2017; Fig. 9.1.9). Three examples of this mark were recovered, which comprises the initials MB flanking a hand or gauntlet with dots above and below the letters. The upper dots appear to have been cut over a small cross, the very tips of which project beyond the margins of the dots. The surname letter is poorly formed or impressed in all three examples, making it look rather like an 'E' or 'P' rather than a 'B'. However, this die type is stylistically very similar to the MB mark described below (Die 248) and it clearly represents a previously unrecorded die variant of this type. Two of the three examples are on the same mould type, which is illustrated as Fig. 9.1.9. The third example of this mark, from PSB01 1915 F789 Phase 3.1, has been used with a different mould, which has an almost identical profile. All three of these examples have quite large, thin-walled bowls with quite a forward leaning and streamlined form, which is generally considered to occur later during the currency of this tailed-heel form. This suggests that these initial marks (Dies 2017 and 248, below) come at the end of the sequence of Michael Brown marks, perhaps being introduced to replace the full-name marks during the early 18th century. If this is the case, it goes against the usual trend, which was from initial marks to full-name marks.

MB (Die 248; Fig. 9.1.10). Three examples of this mark were recovered, which comprises the initials MB flanking a hand or gauntlet with three stars above. The type example of this die type from Much Wenlock (shown as the 2:1 detail) has a series of small raised nicks on the left-hand edge of the die, suggesting some type of decorative edging. These marks, however, are not visible on any of the Birmingham examples, or on many of the others examples recorded from elsewhere. Either the die was altered slightly at some point or more than one working copy must have been made from a common master. All of the Birmingham examples occur on different mould types, only one of which has most of the bowl surviving (Fig. 9.1.10). This piece has quite a large and relatively thin-walled bowl, suggesting that it comes fairly late in the sequence of Michael Brown marks.

TC Six pipes with TC marks were found with at least five different dies being represented (Dies 2021–2025; Fig. 9.2.17–21). There is also a seventh damaged mark that may well be another TC example (see 'illegible' below). Three of the identifiable marks are certainly different and occur on pipes with large round heels, dating from c.1670–90 (Dies 2021–2023; Fig. 9.2.17–19). The other three occur on pipes of c.1680–1730 style with tailed heels and at least two further dies are represented (one example of Die 2024; Fig. 9.2.21; and probably two of Die 2025; Fig. 9.2.20). TC marks on pipes ranging in date from c.1660–1730 are well known from the Broseley area, where they

are usually attributed to Thomas Clark. Clark is only known as a pipe maker from full-name marks that occur on pipes of c.1680–1730 from the same area. Several individuals of this name are recorded in the local parish registers but none have their occupation given. It is possible that these marks belong to an otherwise unrecorded maker with these initials but, in any event, they were almost certainly produced somewhere in the Broseley or Benthall area of Shropshire. The use of initial marks tended to die out around the start of the 18th century and so, although the bowl forms continued in use until later, this prolific maker is most likely to have been operating around 1660–1710. The pipes made by this maker tend to be a little variable in quality and the marks are often either completely inverted or placed at an odd orientation on the heel, for example, Fig. 9.2.18 and 20.

WC One example of a WC mark was found on a Much Wenlock/ Broseley area style bowl with a tailed heel dating from c.1680–1730 (Die 2026; Fig. 9.2.22). The bowl is of a reasonable form but the milling is unevenly applied, the burnish is very poor and the mark has been applied upside down. This mark does not appear to have been previously recorded and the small six-arm star with a central dot is not a typical motif for the Broseley area. This pipe may well represent a local maker copying a Shropshire style of pipe.

MD One example of an MD mark on a bowl of c.1670–90 with a large, round heel, typical of the Much Wenlock/ Broseley area, was found (Die 268; Fig. 9.2.23). This mark is common in that area and is usually attributed to Morris Deacon, who is recorded as a pipe maker from pipe stamps. Many different varieties of MD mark are known with a wide distribution, extending as far as north Warwickshire (Melton 1997, 97). An individual named Morris Deacon is documented at Broseley from the 1680s–1720s (Higgins 1987a, 461–2) and he may have been the pipe maker responsible for producing these pipes.

WE Two examples of this mark were found, both of which occurred on pipes with large round heels, dating from c.1670–1700 (Die 564; Fig. 9.2.24). Marks of this type have been found in Cheshire as far north as Chester (Rutter and Davey 1980, 112), so they clearly had a wide distribution. They may have been made by William Evans of Wellington (died 1694) or his son, also called William, who was working in 1694 and who presumably took over the family business following his father's death.

WF One example of an inverted WF heel mark was found (Die 2027; Fig. 9.2.26). Although the c.1680–1720 bowl is influenced by Shropshire styles, the exact form is not typical of that county and the fabric, although 'local', is not of a characteristic Shropshire type. Furthermore, the crude mark, applied upside down, looks like a local copy rather than a Shropshire product. This mark does not appear to have been previously recorded and probably represents a local maker from somewhere in the West Midlands.

IH One example of an IH heel stamp on a Broseley style bowl of c.1670–1720 was found (Die 324; Fig. 9.2.29). IH marks are very common in the Broseley area, where there are known to have been various makers with these initials, for example, John Harper, James Hartshorne and John Hartshorne. While it is not possible to attribute these initial marks with any certainly, it is clear that they were widely marketed across the Midlands, with examples reaching as far as northern Warwickshire (Melton 1997, 97). The die recovered from these excavations is characterised by a marked wedge-shape to the upper left serif of the 'H', extending up from which is a small die flaw. Another example from the same die has been recovered from excavations at Dudley Castle (Higgins 1987a, 596).

II   Three examples of Broseley style spur bowls of *c*.1690–1720 stamped with the initials II were found (Figs 9.2.30–32). II marks are also very common in the Broseley area, where there were at least two makers with these initials, John James (see below) and John Jones. As with the IH marks discussed above, the II marks appear to have been widely marketed but, unless good kiln groups can be found, it is unlikely that they will ever be attributed to a particular maker with any certainty. The three marks from these excavations were all made using different dies. One is poorly impressed and similar to a previously recorded type (Die 988) but the other two appear to be different. One has rather taller and quite thin initials without serifs (Die 2028) while the other is distinctive in that it has a star between the initials (Die 2029). The example with tall, thin initials occurs on a bowl that has either been pushed in slightly during manufacture or has squatted slightly during firing. This piece does not show signs of having been smoked.

IOHN IAMS   Two or three pipes stamped 'IOHN IAMS' for the Broseley area maker John James were found (one is uncertain, being damaged). At least five individuals named John James occur in the Broseley and Benthall parish registers, making it impossible to be sure which one(s) made these pipes. The two complete examples both occurred on pipes of *c*.1680–1730 with tailed heels that were almost certainly produced in the same mould, characterised by distinctive flaws on the right-hand side of the heel. The bowl style suggests that it may well date from fairly late in the series with tailed heels, perhaps more likely dating from the early 18th century rather than the late 17th. Both examples have a rather matt, unburnished surface and the illustrated example (Fig. 9.2.34) has a long section of its rather waney stem surviving. These bowls are not of the usual quality for the Broseley area and suggest that this maker was operating at the bottom end of the market. The two complete stamped marks associated with these bowls are of interest too, since they both appear to be different. One example has a bar below the lettering (Die 2030; Fig. 9.2.34) while the other, which has been impressed upside down on the pipe, has a bar above (Die 2031; Fig. 9.2. 33). These bars appear to be part of the die rather than having been formed accidentally by double stamping the mark. Otherwise the size, spacing and detail of the lettering are so close that they could well have been formed from the same die. It is known that pipe makers sometimes made a number of working dies by taking impressions from a common master and these two examples may well represent another example of this practice.

In addition to the two fully legible examples, there is also a damaged mark from PSB 01 1621 F510/ F542 Phase 3.3 (A) that is probably also a 'IOHN/ IAMS' stamp. This mark is certainly from a different die and, on this impression, the 'I' appears to be missing from the first line, although it is not completely clear whether it is actually missing or simply that it has not come out on this example. What is clear is that the 'O' is quite large and with distinctive straight sections internally, which should allow it to be easily matched with other examples. The second line of the mark is almost completely missing but the surviving serifs would suggest the surname was 'IAMS'. Several different 'IOHN/ IAMS' dies are known to have been in use and so it should eventually be possible to positively identify this die when a good comparative example can be found.

GeORG/ POVeL   One example of a tailed heel dating from *c*.1680–1730 stamped 'GeORG/ POVeL' for George Powell was recovered (Die 595; Fig. 9.3.38). The large tailed heel is made of a Coal Measure clay and has been burnished – all characteristics of pipes from the Much Wenlock/ Broseley area of Shropshire. This maker has not been traced from documents yet, but other members of the Powell family are known to have worked in Much Wenlock. A George Powell married Margaret Preece at Much Wenlock on 17 June 1690 (IGI) and he may well have been the individual responsible for making this pipe. Other examples of this mark have been recorded from the Broseley area (Higgins 1987a, fig. 46.6) and Chester (Rutter and Davey 1980, 122, fig. 81).

IP   One example of an IP mark dating from *c*.1660–90 was found, stamped at a right angle to the normal orientation on the heel (Die 2032; Fig. 9.3.39). The mark is rather faintly impressed but it appears to have rather simply formed initials and a lightly engraved border of dots. A wide variety of different IP dies are found in the Midlands, the majority of which can be attributed to John Pottifer of Coventry. This particular die type, however, has not been previously recorded and it occurs on a Shropshire style bowl rather than a Coventry type. Another group of IP marks, including five different dies, one of which is similar to (but different from) the excavated example, have been found at Foxcote Farm, near Stourbridge (Fearn Collection). The Stourbridge examples occur on heel fragments of *c*.1680–1730, including one with a Shropshire style tailed heel. This cluster of marks with stylistic links to Shropshire rather than Coventry seems most likely to belong to a local maker working somewhere in the Stourbridge area. The Phipsons are thought to have worked in this area (see the John Phipson stem stamps below) and so this family may well have produced these IP marks.

IS   Two heel stamps with the initials IS were found during the excavations, both of which date from *c*.1680–1730 (Fig. 9.3.47 and 48). Although superficially appearing very similar, these two marks were made using different dies, Die 2033 (Fig. 9.3.47) and Die 2034 (Fig. 9.3.48), and they occur on different mould types – one with a tailed heel and the other round. Neither of these pipes is burnished, which would be typical of Shropshire products, and the round-heeled form suggests a Midlands origin for these pieces, perhaps Joseph Simmons, who is recorded from 18th-century stem marks. See also the IS bowl marks and IOS/ SIM/ ONS stem marks below for further details of this maker.

WS One bowl of *c.*1660–80 stamped WS was recovered (Die 2035; Fig. 9.3.53). The die itself is quite crudely executed with quite poorly defined decorative motifs above and below the initials, which have poorly defined edges to them. The bowl form is of a typical Much Wenlock/ Broseley area style and finish and this piece is almost certainly from that area. This particular die does not appear to have been recorded before but numerous similar examples are known. William Savage (I) of Much Wenlock, who took an apprentice in 1660 and who died in 1686, is the most likely candidate to have made these pipes. See also the 'WILL SAVAG' mark below.

WILL SAVAG One Shropshire style bowl with a tailed heel stamped 'WILL SAVAG' was recovered (Die 1296; Fig. 9.3.52). This bowl form dates from *c.*1680–1730 and can be attributed to William Savage of Much Wenlock. This piece is probably too late for the William Savage who died in 1686 but it may well have been produced by his son, also called William, who was recorded as a pipe maker in 1660. See also the WS mark above.

WT Pipes marked WT form one of the largest and most interesting groups from the excavations with a total of 14 examples being recovered. This is a very diverse group with nine different die types represented, ranging from circular and heart-shaped marks to rectangular ones. The earliest examples occur on two bowls of *c.*1670–90 with round heels (Fig. 9.4.54–55) but the remainder are all on tailed-heel types of *c.*1680–1730 (Fig. 9.4.56–62). Although both of these bowl styles are based on Much Wenlock/ Broseley area types, the fabric is rather finer than would be expected in Shropshire and the overall finish is not quite as good. The Birmingham examples tend to have only average to poor burnishing, with some pieces being completely unburnished, while the rims are often only half milled (and sometimes not at all). Furthermore, the bowl types with tailed heels tend to have subtly different forms to those found in Shropshire. All of these features would suggest local production for these pipes, quite apart from the fact that other examples of these marks, including other die types, have been previously recorded from Birmingham, Stourbridge, Sandwell and Dudley (*e.g.* Higgins 1996). The maker of these pipes remains unknown, but he clearly worked locally.

Before describing the nine different marks in detail there are some useful observations that can be made about the dies used by this manufacturer. First, the marks used are often quite weakly cut and/ or poorly impressed. This frequently makes them hard to read and it is only by comparing clearer examples that positive identifications can be made. For this reason, some of the die details shown are taken from the National Catalogue being compiled by the author, so as to show the form of the marks more clearly, rather than using poor examples from this site. Second, the marks are often applied upside down to the normal orientation used, perhaps indicating poor literacy or control over journeymen in the workshop. Where multiple examples of individual dies have been recovered they appear to be consistently one way up or the other. A larger sample is required to see how regular this pattern is, but it may indicate that some workers habitually used their stamp upside down. Thirdly, some of the dies

are very crudely cut so that it is hard to make out the intended letters. The worst case is Die 2039, which is so crudely cut that the 'W' looks more convincing when viewed upside down. This is particularly unfortunate since both examples of this mark have actually been applied upside down, making the 'T' look more like an 'L'. This means that the mark can not only be convincingly read as 'LW' but it was also used in an orientation where this would be the expected reading of the initials. Given the poor quality of the dies, it is quite possible that the two TW marks recovered from the excavations (see below) could also have been used by this maker, the initials having been reversed in cutting the dies.

Some observations about the mould types and finishing techniques can also be made. As would be expected with so many different stamp types, there are also quite a number of different mould types represented. One of the tailed-heel types is particularly distinctive since it has a clear mould flaw consisting of a raised lump at the junction of the heel and tail on the left-hand side. There are six examples from this mould, three marked with Die 870, one marked with Die 2038 and two with Die 2039. This association of the three marks not only shows that all three dies were used in the same workshop but also confirms the reading of the crudely cut and inverted Die 2039, which might otherwise have been read as 'LW' (see above). This mould group also shows that different marks were used with a single mould, so that there was not necessarily a one-to-one relationship between mould and die. In the same way, five of these examples have a distinctive coarse milling at the rim, while the sixth has a much finer band. This shows that different finishing tools were also used with this mould. These six examples may have been made over a period of years but, during this time, different marks and finishing tools were used with it. This shows that there was not a specific set of tools and marks that was always employed with a single mould.

The final point to note is that, with two exceptions, all of the tailed-heel forms where the bowl survives are burnished. The two unburnished examples are the two marked with Die 869 suggesting that this mark was being used on a pipe of different quality, most obviously represented by its surface finish but perhaps with a different stem length as well. None of the other pipes with burnished bowls had burnishing on the stem as well. This suggests that only the minimum amount of burnishing was employed since many of the contemporary Shropshire products would have had burnished stems as well.

Overall, the impression is that the WT maker was copying Shropshire styles from the Much Wenlock/ Broseley area but that he was not able to achieve the same quality. The bowls are less finely finished and the rims less fully milled. Above all, the marks are not so professionally cut and they are often applied upside down. While he was clearly operating a successful workshop, the WT maker was simply copying fashions from elsewhere rather than setting them himself. The nine different WT marks recovered from the excavations are as follows. With the exception of the first two examples, all of the marks occur on Much Wenlock/ Broseley style pipes with tailed heels that were in vogue from *c.*1680–1730.

Fig. 9.4.54 (Die 2037). A circular mark placed upside down on a bowl of c.1670–90 with a large round heel, which is from a different mould to Fig. 9.4.55 below. The burnish on this bowl is only of average quality but it is one of the best burnished of all the WT pipes, perhaps indicating that the quality of finish declined with the later styles. This die has an indistinct decorative motif above the lettering and fine dashes around its edge. It is very similar to another WT die type (Die 898, not found at this site) but that example appears to have bolder dashes around its edge. A similar mark (inverted) has also been recorded from Foxcote Farm, near Stourbridge (Fearn Collection), but this example does not appear to have any dashes around its edge at all.

Fig. 9.4.55 (Die 466). A heart-shaped mark on an unburnished bowl of c.1670–90, with a large round heel, which was made in a different mould to Fig. 9.4.54 above. The Park Street heel is slightly chipped but the complete form of the mark has been illustrated from an identical example found at Dudley Castle.

Fig. 9.4.56 (Die 2038). Two examples of this previously unrecorded heart-shaped mark were found on pipes with tailed heels that, stylistically, were current from c.1680–1730. They have been placed on pipes produced in different moulds and both are correctly orientated on the heel. The top of the 'T' in this particular die is very short, making the second initial look rather like an 'I'. Despite this, it can be shown that it was intended to be a 'T' because one of these examples occurs on a mould type with a distinctive lump on the left-hand side of the heel, which was also used with two other types of WT mark (Dies 870 and 2039 below). The use of heart-shaped marks was rather 'old fashioned' in the Much Wenlock/ Broseley area by the time that the tailed-heel form was introduced. Its use here may reflect the WT maker lagging behind the latest Shropshire styles. It might also suggest that these were early products with tailed heels, overlapping in date with the round-heel forms, but earlier than the bulk of the WT pipes with their rectangular marks. If this is the case, a date of c.1680–1700 could be suggested for this particular mark.

Fig. 9.4.57 (Die 868). One example of this die type was found inverted on the heel of a damaged bowl. The mark is poorly impressed but is characterised by three small 'x' motifs above the initials. It can be matched with an example found at Sandwell, which was also stamped inverted.

Fig. 9.4.58 (Die 947). One example of this simple rectangular mark was found inverted on a pipe with an unusually small tailed heel. The small heel and relatively large bowl with thin walls all suggest that this is probably quite a late mark in the sequence. There is a parallel in Birmingham Museum that had been stamped the correct way up on the heel, showing that this mark was not always used inverted.

Fig. 9.4.59 (Die 869). Two examples of this die type were found, both of which have been stamped inverted and both of which are very faintly impressed. The die is characterised by three small sexfoils above the lettering and the die detail is taken from a better example found at Sandwell. It is not possible to determine whether the two Park Street examples were impressed on pipes made in the same mould but it is noticeable that neither of these

examples is burnished. This might indicate a particular workman or period of production, or a different (cheaper) style of pipe.

Fig. 9.4.60 (Die 870). Three examples of this die were found, all of which occur on a distinctive mould type with a lump on the left-hand side of its heel. This particular mould was also used with two of the other stamp types recovered from the excavations (Dies 2038 and 2039). Two of the examples marked with Die 870 have coarse milling around their rims. The three examples of this particular mark have all left rather faint impressions, suggesting that the die was never very crisp or deeply cut in the first place. The mark is characterised by three small '+' motifs above the lettering. All of these examples are stamped the correct way up on the heel.

Fig. 9.4.61 (Die 2039). Two examples of this mark were found, both of which are inverted and both of which occur on a distinctive mould type with a lump on the left-hand side of its heel. This particular mould type was also used with Dies 870 and 2038 (see above). Die 2039 is very crudely cut and, upside down, looks as if it reads 'LW' although the fact that Dies 870 and 2038 were used on the same mould type makes it clear that this was intended to be a WT mark. Both of the Die 2039 examples are poorly burnished and both have coarse milling at the rim.

Fig. 9.4.62 (Die 2040). One example of this previously unrecorded mark was found. It has been stamped the correct way up on a large tailed heel but, unfortunately, the bowl itself is missing. This mark is the only one to employ a horizontal dividing bar, which was commonly used in Shropshire at this period to divide the lines of full-name marks. In this instance, however, there is merely a decorative pattern of dots in the upper section, which mirrors the dies with crosses and sexfoils in this position (Die Nos 868, 869 and 870).

AW Two bowls of c.1660–80 stamped AW were recovered (Fig. 9.4.63 and 64). Both of the stamps were made using different dies (902 and 2037), one of which is a previously unrecorded type (Die 2037; Fig. 9.4.63). Both of the mould types are also different, too, showing that this maker was established enough to be using a range of moulds and marks in his workshop. The bowls forms are typical of those produced in south Shropshire and in the west Midlands but not of the Much Wenlock/ Broseley area. Other examples of Die 902 have been previously recorded, primarily from the Birmingham area but also from Foxcote Farm, near Stourbridge (Fearn Collection). No documented maker with these initials is currently known but it seems likely that he was based in or around Birmingham, perhaps part of a family of pipe makers with the surname initial W (see EW and TW below).

EW Ten bowls of various styles, ranging in date from c.1670–1710, were found with the initials EW stamped on the heel (Figs 9.4.65–67). This group is interesting for a number of reasons, not least of which is that all of the impressions appear to have been made using the same die (Die 900). This is a heart-shaped mark characterised by a small mark projecting inwards from the outside edge of the die just below the letter E. The number of examples recovered, together with the range of bowl forms, suggests that these came from a well-established and prolific workshop. As such, it is extremely unusual for just one stamp type to be represented since there would normally be a number of journeymen working at different presses in a workshop of this type. It may well be that a number of working dies were produced from a single master but that these are so similar that they cannot easily be differentiated. The bowls forms are also of interest since they form a distinctive stylistic group. They are characterised by a finer fabric than the Shropshire pipes but are still a 'local' type, firing to a slightly off-white colour, and giving an 'eggshell' finish to the pipes. Nine of the pipes are unburnished but one has a finely burnished finish, showing that this technique was also occasionally employed. In form and finish these pipes are very similar to the AW pipes described above. As with the AW pipes, no documented maker is known but the distribution clearly suggests local manufacture, perhaps in Birmingham itself. See also the TW pipes below, perhaps another member of the same family.

IW One tailed heel of *c*.1680–1730 was recovered with a heart-shaped IW mark on it (Die 957; Fig. 9.4.68). This bowl is not burnished, as is typical of Shropshire products, and the fabric is finer than normal for pipes from there. In addition, there is a parallel for this mark in Birmingham Museum. All of these factors point to this being a locally manufactured (*i.e.* Birmingham area) product, from an as yet unidentified maker. Various IW marks have been found in Warwickshire (Muldoon 1979, 277; Gault 1997, 106) but these do not seem to occur on styles with tailed heels and so may represent a different mid-17th-century IW maker from the Coventry area.

TW Two different examples of TW dies were recovered, both previously unrecorded and both applied to pipes with tailed heels, a style popular from *c*.1680–1730. Only one of the bowls is complete (Die 2041; Fig. 9.4.69) and the form of this suggests that it may well be early within the overall range for this bowl style, most likely *c*.1680–1710. The other die is slightly damaged but appears to have a date beneath the lettering (Fig. 9.4.70). This seems to start '169' and the last numeral may be an '0', making it 1690. This reading is confirmed by another fragmentary example from the Smithfield Market area of Birmingham (Krawiec Collection from SP 0753 8639), which was too fragmentary to identify by itself but which now allows the die to be largely reconstructed (Die 2042; Fig. 9.4.70). The date of this die fits well with the suggested range of *c*.1680–1710 for the other bowl form. Melton has listed the dated dies used by various makers from the Midlands and suggested a connection with significant dates relating to the Quaker community (Melton 1997, 213). The date 1690, however, does not appear to be one of these significant dates and this connection with Quakers remains to be proven. The date and style of these TW marks are similar to those of the WT marks discussed above and there is a possibility that all of these marks were produced by one maker, with one set of initials being cut in the wrong order, most likely the much more scarce TW marks. Either way, the TW marks are not quite right for Shropshire products and are likely to have been produced locally. Other marks reading AW and EW also appear to represent local manufacturers and so, if the TW reading does represent a distinct maker, they are perhaps all members of the same pipemaking family.

Illegible

Six examples with marks that are so damaged that they are illegible were recovered. These include part of two circular marks; one on a bowl form of *c*.1620–40 where the first initial appears to be an 'I' (Fig. 9.5.71) and one of *c*.1660–1700 with what is most likely part of a TC mark. The other pieces are all on tailed heels of *c*.1680–1730 and there are two circular and two square marks. One of the circular marks is so damaged that none of the lettering survives but the other clearly has the letter 'H' on it (Fig. 9.5.72). Unfortunately this stamp has been applied at nearly 90 degrees to the normal orientation so that it is not clear whether it is a Christian or surname initial. The other two pieces just have the very edge of square marks surviving but none of the lettering.

Wheel Marks

As well as the initial marks a total of 22 symbol marks were recovered from the excavations. Four of these are hand or gauntlet marks (discussed below) but by far the most common type, with 18 examples, are the wheel or star marks (Figs 9.5.74–80). This type of mark is one of the most widespread and long-lived of any found on pipes. Some of the earliest pipes, dating from around 1600, were marked in this way and the style continued in use until well into the 18th century. Examples are found all over the country and in various positions on the bowl and stem. The mark was clearly used in many different production centres and by many different manufacturers, although it was clearly more popular in some areas and periods than in others. The popularity of this mark is hardly surprising since it is one of the easiest symbol stamps to create. Any cylindrical object that could cut with a knife or other sharp implement could be used to create a visually pleasing stamp of this type and the design has been used by potters from the prehistoric period onwards. In a period when a stamped mark was part of the expected style and finish of a pipe, a wheel mark could be quickly and easily created without the expense of having a professionally cut die prepared.

While the use of these marks may be easy to understand, the dozens of very similar dies that were used makes them very hard to separate into individual types, let alone to identify the makers who used them. In general terms, however, all of the Birmingham examples were produced between about 1640 and 1730 and they are all found on bowls forms that are typical of Shropshire/ Herefordshire/ Worcestershire/ West Midlands types. In other words, they all appear to represent either locally produced products or pipes imported from adjoining areas to the west rather than from elsewhere in the country. Although many of the examples recovered are not diagnostic enough to identify and source without a great deal of work, it has been possible to identify some of the more distinctive types. The two general types of wheel mark are discussed below, including details of those marks that can readily be identified to individual die type.

Wheels without dots

The largest group of wheel marks comprises those without dots, of which there are 14 examples. These are about equally split between bowls with round heels, ranging from *c.*1640–1680 in date (*e.g.* Figs 9.5.74–77), and those with tailed heels, which range from *c.*1680–1730 (*e.g.* Fig. 9.5.80). The round heel forms are generally unburnished while the tailed types are generally burnished. The marks are very diverse in size and character and there are nearly as many different marks as there are examples. They range from small and very crudely executed marks about 6–7mm across (Fig. 9.5.74) to large and professionally cut dies of about 8–9mm in size (Fig. 9.5.80). These marks generally have around eight to twelve spokes to them and sometimes as many as about 17 or 18. There is a mix of types with just simple radiating spokes (Fig. 9.5.74) and those with simple spokes alternating with short spikes extending into the triangles created by the spokes from the edge of the die (Fig. 9.5.76, 77 and 80). With one exception, these types are very difficult to identify to individual die type without having a good range of duplicate reference material with which to compare them. The one exception is a distinctive type that has ten alternating straight and wavy spokes (Fig. 9.5.75; Die 960). The early London makers used this distinctive form but at this site it occurs on a local bowl form. This particular die can be exactly matched by an example in the Birmingham Museum (CP 888), which was found at Corley Rocks, near Nuneaton, supporting the suggestion of a local origin for this pipe.

Wheels with dots

The second and smaller group of wheel marks comprises those with dots between the spokes as part of their decorative design, of which there are four examples, all of which appear to be on different mould types. This type of wheel mark is less common nationally and these four examples all occur on bowls with tailed heels, none of which is burnished. The bowls are clearly copying Shropshire styles but this type of mark is not common there and this style of pipes would usually be burnished in Shropshire. All of these characteristics suggest local manufacture somewhere in the West Midlands and it is quite possible that the same maker produced all four of these pipes. The marks can be divided into two die types. The first has a small spike and, with one exception, a single dot within each segment created by an eight-spoke wheel (Die 889; Fig. 9.5.78). There is one definite example of this type from the excavations and one probable example, which is uncertain as the die has been poorly impressed. An example of this die type has also been recovered from Deritend Church in Sandy Lane, Birmingham (Birmingham City Museum). The second type (Die 1154) also has eight spokes but it lacks the spikes at the edge of each segment and the number of dots is variable, with either one or three in each section (Fig. 9.5.79). There are two examples of this die type

from these excavations and another from excavations at Wood Farm, Grindley near Uttoxeter, in The Potteries Museum, Stoke-on-Trent.

Hand or gauntlet marks

The final type of symbol mark is represented by four examples where a hand or gauntlet forms the principal motif. There are two different dies represented, the first of which is represented by three identical examples, all of which occur on pipes of *c.*1660–90 with a large round heel that were made in the same mould (Die 961; Fig. 9.5.81). Only one bowl survives, which is burnished, as opposed to the two heel fragments with stems surviving, which are both unburnished. This suggests that this maker usually only burnished the bowls of his pipes. The mould type is identified by two faint ridges on the left-hand side of the heel, running parallel with its base. The mark is very neatly executed and comprises a well-formed hand flanked on either side by a spray of foliage. Although hand or gauntlet devices were used in the Much Wenlock/ Broseley area both the marks and bowl forms used there were slightly different in character. This fact, combined with the number of examples and the relatively fine fabric used to produce them, all point to a West Midlands area origin for these pieces. An example of this mark has been previously recorded from Deritend (Birmingham City Museum, CP 961).

The second type is previously unrecorded and is represented by a single example on a bowl with a tailed heel dating from *c.*1680–1730 (Die 2043; Fig. 9.5.82). The bowl is well made and finished but the fabric is rather finer than is typical of Shropshire products. Also, the stamp is rather crudely cut so that the hand or gauntlet is rather indistinct, particularly the fingers. The stamp impression has also been slightly damaged but it looks as if it consists of four dots flanking the hand rather than dots and initials, as is the case with the Michael Brown mark from Much Wenlock (Die 2017). The Much Wenlock makers favoured the hand motif and a number of them used it in their marks. At the same time, this device was also used by some of the Newcastle-under-Lyme makers (Barker 1985), although the tailed-heel form does not seem to have been produced there. The attribution of this piece is problematic since the form, finish and style of mark would all fit with a Much Wenlock area type while the quality of the die and fabric might suggest production elsewhere. The overall style, however, firmly places it as coming from somewhere in the mid-Shropshire/ west Midlands area.

Stamped bowl marks

A total of 16 bowls with stamped marks facing the smoker were found, all of which range in date from between *c.*1710 and *c.*1780. Bowl stamps were occasionally used in the Shropshire/ Herefordshire/ Worcestershire area during the 17th century and, given the number of pipes imported from these areas, it is perhaps surprising that none of these earlier types was found. In contrast, during the 18th century, the areas to the west of Birmingham (especially the Broseley area) did not tend to use bowl stamps, whereas this style is clearly well represented amongst the excavated finds, suggesting that the examples recovered were produced locally.

Excluding the transitional forms of c.1680–1730, there were only around 120 bowls recovered that are likely to date from c.1710–80 of which the 16 stamped examples represent some 13%. This shows that bowl stamping was relatively common in the Birmingham area during the 18th century. The earlier marks of c.1710–40 appear to have been in relief while the use of unbordered incuse marks seems likely to have been prevalent from c.1730–80. The earlier marks are rather more common, suggesting that the use of bowl stamping declined during the second half of the century. The marks recovered are described in alphabetical order below.

IB A total of five IB marks were recovered, all of which occur on the bowl facing the smoker in a Midlands style and all of which are likely to date from c.1710–1740. There are four different dies represented amongst the five marks recovered (Dies 959, 2002, 2003 and 2016; Fig. 9.1.3–6), suggesting a prolific local manufacturer. Only one of these bowls is substantially complete and there is one much more fragmentary example (Fig. 9.1.3 and 4). The other three marks occur on more fragmentary bowls, at least two of which (Dies 2002 and 2003) occurred on burnished spur bowls of a similar form to those illustrated. The only mark type for which the bowl form is unclear is Die 2016 (Fig. 9.1.5). A wide range of IB marks has been noted at Coventry (Muldoon 1979, figs 14–14j), where they occur as both heel and bowl stamps, in one instance associated with moulded initials on the sides of the heel as well. There is also a full-name John Bowlds stem stamp from Coventry (ibid., fig. 16), an otherwise undocumented maker, but who could have been responsible for these IB marks. Alternatively, there were various members of the Britten family working in the Wednesbury area from the late 17th century onwards and for whom many marked stems are known (see stem section below). Given that IB bowl marks are commonly found right across northern Warwickshire (Melton 1997, 98) and into the Birmingham area, it is perhaps more likely that these were produced by the well-known Britten family, rather than John Bowlds, who is only known from a single isolated mark.

HH One bowl fragment with an HH stamp was recovered from the excavations (Die 2044; Fig. 9.2.28). This mark does not appear to have been previously recorded but it is of a typical local Midlands style. The fragment has quite thin walls and a rim that has just been cut and wiped, both features suggesting a mid-18th-century or later date (the suggested range is c.1730–80). The bowl has been burnished and at the bottom it is starting to open into the stem, which shows that it was of an unusually short form. Two HH stem stamps were also recovered from the excavations (see below) and the same maker may well have produced these as well.

IP Two damaged 18th-century bowls stamped with the incuse initials IP were recovered from the Park Street excavations. Both pieces have been badly burnt and discoloured in a similar way, suggesting that they probably came from the same deposit originally, even though they were recovered from different excavation contexts and different areas: (1139) a fill of pit F138 Phase 4 and (1512) F500 Phase 3.2. The bowl forms are a little hard to date but they would probably have been produced around 1730–80. Both of the marks are either incompletely impressed or damaged making it impossible to be sure whether they are from the same die or not, although the presumption has been that they are (Die 2045; Fig. 9.3.40). A wide range of IP bowl marks is known from north Warwickshire but these are all in relief and usually attributed to John Pottifer of Coventry, who took an apprentice in 1710 (Melton 1997). These incuse marks do not appear to have been previously recorded and, stylistically, they are a little later in date than the relief types. The differences in form, distribution and dating for these pieces all point towards a different source for these incuse bowl marks although, from their form, they are clearly Midlands products and comparable in style and date with the incuse IS mark, which was probably produced at Wilnecote in northern Warwickshire (see IS below). A possible candidate for the IP bowl marks is John Phipson, who is known from stem marks and who may have worked in the Kingswinford/ Stourbridge area (see the Phipson stem marks below).

IS This was by far the most common set of initials represented amongst the bowl stamps, with eight examples being recovered. These marks can be divided into two distinct types, the first of which is by far the most common with seven examples. These seven are all relief marks that occur on bowls dating from c.1710–40 (Fig. 9.3.49). The marks are often incompletely impressed but, so far as can be determined, they are all so similar that they can be treated as a single die type (Die 882). Likewise, the bowl forms on which they occur are all so similar in form and finish that individual mould types cannot be determined. Given the number of examples, it is probable that more than one die and mould were actually in use but they are so uniform that they cannot be realistically differentiated. The bowls are all made of quite a fine clay but one that gives a somewhat granular fracture. They are all burnished, usually with a good finish, and all of the rims appear to have been internally trimmed and bottered, i.e. smoothed with a special tool after having been trimmed. None of the rims is milled. The style of both the bowl and mark, together with the number of examples, all indicate a local production centre for these pipes. This mark has not been noted in northern Warwickshire (Melton 1997, 104), but other examples have been found in Birmingham: for example, there are five examples from the Smithfield Market area (SP 0735 8639; Private Collection). The Smithfield Market examples were found in association with 18th-century 'IOS/ SIM/ ONS' stem marks, suggesting that this individual may have been responsible for making the bowls stamped IS as well. The Joseph Simmons pipes were almost certainly produced at Wilnecote, in northern Warwickshire, where at least four and probably five makers of this name have been documented (Melton 1997, 255–6).

The second die type occurs on a later style of bowl, dating from *c*.1740–1780 and consists of the unbordered incuse letters IS (Die 880; Fig. 9.3.50). This could equally be another Joseph Simmons product, but dating from a later period of production. The bowl form is completely different, having much thinner walls and a more elegant form and spur. The finishing is also different since it is unburnished and it has a cut and internally trimmed rim. Likewise, the change to incuse lettering appears to be a stylistically later feature in this area. This particular example was recovered from a Phase 4 layer (1505) sealing two Phase 3.3 tank fills, which were filled in *c*.1780 (see Barker and Rátkai, Chapter 7 for more detailed discussion of these features). This piece may have been disturbed from the upper fill of one of these tanks, in which case it may well date from the *c*.1780 filling of these features. Four similar marks have been found in the Smithfield Market area of Birmingham (SP 0735 8639; Krawiec Collection). See also the IS heel marks, described above.

Stamped stem marks

A total of 27 stems with stamped marks or decoration on them were found. In most cases each stem is just marked with a single stamp but, occasionally, two different stamps have been used on a single fragment. These marks are quite diverse in origin but most date from the 18th century with only odd examples of earlier and later date. With one exception, all of the marks are either stamped across the stem or right around it (roll-stamped) to form a decorative border. The one exception is the '…BROSLEY' stamp, which has been applied along the top of a stem. The initial and name marks are described alphabetically first, followed by the symbol marks and decorative borders.

…BRITTEN One burnished stem with a damaged stamp across it including the surname 'Britten' was recovered (Fig. 9.1.8). The Christian name is almost entirely missing but could possibly have been Thomas. This is a previously unrecorded mark but one that clearly belongs to the Britten family of pipe makers, a prolific family who were active in the Birmingham area from the late 17th century right through to the 19th (Higgins 1988; Melton 1991). Heel marks of *c*.1680–1730 reading 'THO/ BRIT/ TIN' have been found in Birmingham and these were almost certainly produced by the Thomas Brittain/ Brittin who baptised a son at Wednesbury in 1699 and buried another in 1704 (Melton 1991, 2). The new stem mark probably dates from *c*.1710–60 and could well have been made by the same maker as the heel marks.

IOHN BRITTEN One damaged example of a John Britten stem stamp was recovered. This particular roll-stamp has the lettering flanked by a border of foliage, flowers and zig-zags. Four examples of this same mark have previously been recorded from Lichfield and three from Oakeswell Hall. Taken together, these eight examples allow a fairly complete reconstruction of the whole mark to be made (Die 246; Fig. 9.1.7). The example from these excavations occurs on an unburnished stem that was found in a deposit that probably dates to before *c*.1760 and the mark itself is

of a style that was probably used from *c*.1720–1770. The Britten family may well have been operating at Wednesbury during this period since a Joseph was buried there in 1790 and a John Brittin was working at Monway Field, Wednesbury in 1818 (Melton 1991, 2).

L. Fiolet/ à St. Omer/ Déposé One example of a burnished stem stamped with the mark of this well known French manufacturer was recovered (Die 2013; Fig. 9.2.25). Louis Fiolet founded his business at St Omer in the Pas-de-Calais in 1765 where it operated until its closure in 1921 (Raphaël 1991, 104–8). This style of mark was registered in this country in 1876, when it had already been in use for 43 years, *i.e.* since 1833 (Hammond 1988, 87). Large numbers of these pipes were imported from 1850–1920, which is the most likely date for this piece.

HH Two stems dating from *c*.1710–1760 with relief stamps reading HH below a stylised fleur-de-lys were found. The form of this fleur-de-lys is typical of other examples produced in the Much Wenlock/ Broseley area although this mark does not appear to have been previously recorded in that area and the only other known example is from Foxcote Farm, near Stourbridge (Fearn Collection). There is also a Midlands style bowl stamped HH from the excavations (see above) so these marks could well represent the same local maker rather than a Shropshire import. In one instance the mark has been applied upside down about 48mm from the bowl junction (Die 2046; Fig. 9.2.27). Neither of the excavated stems has been burnished.

THOS/ LEGG/ BROSE/ LEY One example of a four-line stamp produced by Thomas Legg of Broseley was found (Die 2047; Fig. 9.3.35). The style of this mark dates it to *c*.1740–90 and there is a small lion at the end, a symbol used by the Legg family on their stamps. The mark is very well executed and it was clearly professionally cut. Although almost identical examples have been previously recorded (Die 49), the lion on the previously noted examples faces to the right, whereas in this example it faces to the left. This particular die is also characterised by a rather large 'O' followed by a much smaller 'S' in the word 'BROSELEY'. The fact that this maker clearly had at least two nicely engraved (and presumably quite expensive) dies made suggests that he was operating a well-established and successful workshop.

ELIAS MASSEY One example of a decorated stem from Chester, dating from *c*.1690–1715, was found. The well-known maker Elias Massey produced this piece, which has one of his lozenge-shaped marks (Die 1967; Fig. 9.3.36) across the stem, flanked by two decorative 'dot and pinnacle' borders (Die 1975; Fig. 9.3.36). Elias took his freedom in 1688 but appears to have been dead by 1715 (Rutter and Davey 1980, 248). The late 17th-century and 18th-century Chester makers specialised in producing pipes with finely decorated stems and their products were extensively exported. Having said that, Chester pipes are not particularly common across the Midlands and this is the only example from the excavations. It does, however, show that at least some trade with the North West was reaching Birmingham by the end of the 17th century.

IOHN/ PHIP/ SON Six stems stamped with the full-name relief mark of John Phipson were found, four of them in a badly burnt and encrusted condition, most likely from having been discarded into a fire (1512). At least four of the marks (and probably five) were all made using the same die, which is characterised by three distinctive flaws (Die 885; Fig. 9.3.41). First, there is a small flaw to the right of the lower serif of the first 'I', which almost links it to the following 'O'. Second, the top serif of the second 'I' extends to the right so that it just touches the 'P'. Third, there is a small vertical mark at the top end of the 'S', perhaps a serif for it, which joins it to the horizontal dividing bar. All of these marks were recovered from (1512) F500 Phase 3.2, which probably dates to no later than c.1760. In contrast, the sixth example is marked using a different die that has much smaller but very neatly formed lettering with good serifs (Die 2048; Fig. 9.3.42). This example occurs on a slightly thicker stem than the other examples and so it is probably earlier in date, although it is still not as thick as would be expected for an early 18th-century stem. This particular example comes from (1531), a fill of a tank F503/ F510 dating from c.1780 although the stem may even be residual within this fill. This smaller mark can, therefore, be dated to the mid-18th century and it was certainly in use before c.1780. The other stems are thinner suggesting a mid- to late 18th-century date and it seems likely that this maker was operating during the period c.1740–1780. None of the stems appears to have been burnished and one of them is sufficiently complete to show that one of the marks (Die 885) was placed 60mm from the bowl junction. A stem produced by this maker has been previously recorded from the Smithfield Market area of Birmingham (Die 885; Krawiec Collection) and examples of both the larger and smaller die types have been found at Foxcote Farm, near Stourbridge (Fearn Collection). These stem marks clearly represent a Birmingham area maker who has yet to be located in the documentary sources. Although the IGI coverage is dependent on the registers that have been transcribed, it is interesting to note that no John Phipsons of the right date are listed in either the Staffordshire or Warwickshire lists. There are, however, a number of individuals of this name listed during the 18th century in the Kingswinford, Old Swinford and Stourbridge area of Worcestershire. Furthermore, there is a THO/ PHIP/ SON stem stamp from Foxcote Farm, near Stourbridge (Fearn Collection), which not only supports the suggestion that these marks come from this area but also shows that more than one member of the family was involved in pipemaking. This being the case, the IP bowl and stem marks (above) and the SP stem stamp (below) could all have been produced be members of this family.

SP Two unburnished stems with the initials SP flanking a fleur-de-lys were found (Die 2049; Fig. 9.3.43). The style of the fleur-de-lys is typical of examples produced in the Much Wenlock/ Broseley area but the mark is previously unrecorded there and the only other known example comes from Foxcote Farm, near Stourbridge (Fearn Collection). All the recorded examples occur on stems that are relatively thick, which, together with the large and relatively crude fleur-de-lys, suggests a date of c.1690–1740 for these marks. The maker remains unknown, but an earlier member of the Phipson family is a possibility, particularly given the finding of a stem near Stourbridge, the area in which the Phipson family are thought to have

worked (see John Phipson above).

SAM/ RO*/ DEN One unburnished stem from the Broseley area with a Samuel Roden mark on it was found (Die 920; Fig. 9.3.46). This maker used a large number of very similar dies that can be quite difficult to distinguish without direct comparison of die detail. This example has an eight-arm star at the end of the second line and some of the letters have distinctive fine serrations at their edges (visible with a lens), especially the O, D and N. The style of the mark and stem suggests a date of c.1750–90 for this piece. Other Samuel Roden marks have been found in the Midlands: for example there are two examples from Foxcote Farm, near Stourbridge (Fearn Collection), and so it is clear that this manufacturer marketed his products quite widely.

IOS/ SIM/ ONS One Joseph Simons stem mark was found (Die 884; Fig. 9.3.51). This mark is characterised by the odd shape of the upper portion and occurred on a poorly burnished stem of c.1720–1780. An example of this mark has previously been recorded from the Smithfield Market area of Birmingham (private collection), where IS bowl marks were also recovered, most likely produced by the same maker (see above). Many members of the Simmons family worked as pipe makers at various places in Warwickshire during the 18th and 19th centuries but the Joseph Simons marks were almost certainly produced at Wilnecote, where at least four and probably five generations with this name worked as pipe makers. The first of these, who is not specifically listed as a pipe maker, died in 1742, and the others are recorded working from at least 1769–1855 (Melton 1997, 255–6).

...OSLEY One stem was found with a fragmentary relief stamped mark along the stem ending in '...OSLEY', being part of the place-name Broseley (Fig. 9.5.73). The Broseley pipe makers changed from marks across the stem to marks along the stem towards the end of the 18th century and this piece probably dates from c.1770–1820. What is unusual about this piece, however, is that it is a single-line mark whereas all of the known marks of this type from the Broseley area are in two or three lines, the place-name being preceded by the maker's name. Single-line marks with both the maker's name and place-name were being used at this date in various other production centres from Worcester in the south, through Staffordshire and up into Lancashire, especially Liverpool. The only close parallel for this mark is a complete stamp on a stem from Dudley Castle that just reads 'BROSLEY' (Higgins 1987a, 596, fig. 8) but, unlike the Birmingham example, this has a finely serrated border. Being damaged, it is impossible to tell whether the Birmingham example is another place-name only mark or whether it is a long, single-line mark with the maker's name as well. Either way, it is highly unusual and not typical of Broseley products. If, as is perhaps most likely, it is another place-name only mark, then it particularly interesting as the second example from the Birmingham area of a type of mark unknown in Broseley itself. This leads to the suspicion that these marks might have been applied to pipes produced elsewhere so as to 'pass them off' as genuine Broseley products. Further examples are clearly needed to help establish the origin and significance of these marks.

PINNACLE AND DOT BORDER One example of a pinnacle and dot border from Chester, dating from *c*.1690–1715, was found (Die 1975; Fig. 9.3.36). This was used to flank a lozenge mark of the well-known maker Elias Massey (Die 1967; Fig. 9.3.36). See the entry for his stem mark (above) for more details of this piece.

LATTICE AND DOT BORDER Four examples of stems decorated with lattice and dot borders were recovered from the excavations. Although generally similar stem borders are known from Chester (Rutter and Davey 1980, figs 58.27–29), the Birmingham examples tend to be rather wider and with a simple, boldly executed design. These stylistic differences, together with the fact that three different dies are represented, clearly suggest that they are local products rather than being imports from the North West. Unfortunately none of the Birmingham examples is attached to a bowl, making dating difficult. However, three of the four examples are on stems of medium thickness that are likely to date from around 1690–1750. Two of these have the same previously unrecorded border on them (Die 2011; Fig. 9.5.85) with quite an elongated lattice and large dots. The other example is a previously recorded type (Die 987; Fig. 9.5.86), which has a squarer lattice and slightly smaller dots. This second stamp type is also characterised by dog-tooth projections along its edges. An example of this type has also been found in the Smithfield Market area of Birmingham (Krawiec Collection), reinforcing the suggestion of a local origin for these pieces. The third stamp type is of the same general style but occurs on a thinner, and possibly slightly curved, stem, suggesting a date in the second half of the 18th century (Fig. 9.5.87). This lattice is elongated, like the first type, but with a rather finer, more regular grid and dots. The impression on the excavated example is slightly blurred and so it has not been illustrated in detail, but this may be typical of this type, since later 18th-century borders were often less crisp and more lightly impressed than earlier examples. Taken together, these borders clearly suggest a distinctive local form that was probably being produced for most of the 18th century.

SPIRAL BORDER Another distinctive and almost certainly local form of mark is represented by two 'spiral borders', dating from *c*.1690–1740 (Die 2012; Fig. 9.5.83). This border type also dates from the 18th century and is reminiscent of the contemporary stem twists that were being produced in Shropshire and Chester. In contrast to these types, however, the Birmingham examples are made of parallel diagonal lines, impressed into the surface of the stem so as to still leave it smooth and cylindrical in form. These lines are finely engraved and create a distinctive spiral pattern on the stem. Another example has previously been recorded from Birmingham (Krawiec Collection) but they are not known from elsewhere, clearly suggesting that they were of local manufacture. What is particularly interesting about the excavated examples, however, is that one of them is also associated with a decorative stem oval, probably representing a griffin (see following entry).

GRIFFIN One of the distinctive spiral borders (above) was associated with an oval stem stamp of *c*.1690–1740. Although too damaged to allocate a unique die number, this appears to have depicted a griffin and it was clearly

finely engraved (Fig. 9.5.83). A series of decorative ovals were being produced in Chester at this period, but the examples from that centre usually have a plain or beaded border around the central motif (Rutter and Davey 1980, figs 54 and 55). Likewise, ovals (including griffins) were being used in Nottingham, where they are usually associated with a roll-stamp bearing the maker's name (Alvey, Laxton and Paeschter 1979, fig. 1). This example from Birmingham appears to be a local type, suggesting that finely decorated stems were being produced in this area as well (see also the rampant lion stamp below).

RAMPANT LION One stem with a poorly impressed decorative oval dating from *c*.1690–1740 was found (Fig. 9.5.84). Although only part of the design has come out, this oval appears to depict a well-executed rampant lion. Similar high quality ovals were being produced in Chester at this period, but the examples from that centre usually have a plain or beaded border around the lion. Given that good-quality stem stamps were clearly being produced in this area (see the griffin above), it seems likely that this is another local product. This example is not clear enough to be allocated a unique die number.

Moulded marks

Only four pipes with moulded marks were recovered from the excavations. This style of marking was rarely used in the Midlands before the 19th century and the low number of examples simply reflects the low incidence of later pipes amongst the excavated assemblage. The four examples comprise two marked spurs and two named stems, which are described below:

TR One spur bowl with the relief moulded initials TR was found (Fig. 9.3.45). This is a very delicate product with a large, thin-walled bowl and the remains of a long and gently curved stem. Stylistically the bowl is likely to date from *c*.1820–60 and it represents a nice quality product of this period. The most likely manufacturer for this piece is Thomas Reynolds, who was working in Birmingham from around 1856 until about 1892 (Gault 1979, 403), although the pipe looks fairly early for this maker. Having said that, the bowl form is typical of pipes produced in the London area and this maker had previously worked at Leighton Buzzard from *c*.1848–55, so it could have been an older style mould that he had brought with him. Also, these long-stemmed 'churchwarden' type pipes were a traditional style that may have been produced, long after fashionable styles had moved on, for a small conservative market. The only other known maker in Birmingham at this period is Thomas Richards, but he is only recorded there in 1851 (*ibid.*), and he may not even have been a master pipe maker.

REYNOLDS.BIRMINGHAM A fragmentary bowl with part of a long stem marked REYNOLDS.BIRMINGHAM was recovered (Fig. 9.3.44). The lettering is moulded in incuse, sans-serif script and, unusually, the pipe is only marked on the left-hand side of the stem. The surviving section of bowl shows that it had leaf-decorated seams and, stylistically, the lettering suggests a date for *c*.1850 or later for this piece. Unfortunately, there were three known pipe makers in Birmingham named Reynolds at this time: J G Reynolds and Sons, recorded in 1864, Thomas

Reynolds, recorded from *c*.1856–92, and William Reynolds, recorded in 1871 (Gault 1979). William is only recorded from a census entry and so may not have been a master manufacturer himself. This being the case, it seems more likely that it was one of the former two who made the marked pipe. The fragment itself clearly comes from a long-stemmed or 'churchwarden' type of pipe that has been burnt after being broken, leaving it a grey colour. Some of the lettering, however, looks rather odd because it is still white. This suggests that the pipe was well used during its life and that grime had built up in the lettering. When the fragment was burnt, its surface was discoloured but the grime protected the incuse lettering so that, now it has been cleaned out, it still looks white.

…L/ G… A mouthpiece fragment with the very ends of an incuse moulded stem mark with serif lettering was found (Fig. 9.3.37). This piece has up to 25mm of translucent orange/ brown glaze on the mouthpiece and can almost certainly be identified as a product from the McDougall factory in Glasgow. This was one of the largest and most prolific of the Scottish factories and operated from 1846–1967 (Anon 1987, 345). The fact that this stem has a lead-glazed mouthpiece and serif lettering suggests that it dates to before *c*.1910 and most likely *c*.1850–1900.

Shields? The final moulded mark occurs on the spur of a plain bowl dating from *c*.1840–1900 (Fig. 9.5.88). In this instance the mark consists of an identical relief moulded symbol on either side of the spur. This is a raised 'egg-shaped' area, divided into six sections by an incuse grid. Sometimes small shield symbols are found in this position, or other motifs, such as dots, stars or even simple leaves. This is not a specific maker's mark, but rather a generic symbol, placed where initials had traditionally occurred but now simply representing a part of the pipe's design. The bowl is rather poorly made and would probably have come from a long-stemmed pipe.

Discussion of the marked pipes

The individual marks recovered have been grouped by type and described above. While this facilitates searching for a particular type of bowl or stem mark, it sometimes splits up similar marks that may have been used by the same maker. A good example is provided by the IS stamps, different varieties of which are found on both bowls and heels, and the IOS SIMMONS stem marks, since all three of these mark types might have been produced by same maker. For this reason a summary of the marked pipes has been prepared that not only places all of the different styles of mark in alphabetical order but also allows the dating and likely origin of each type to be easily compared (Appendix 9.3).

The marks by origin

From the summary of the marked pipes (Appendix 9.3) it can be seen that there was a fairly even split between those pipes produced locally to the Birmingham area and those 'imported' from elsewhere, particularly Shropshire. The local makers appear to have been using symbol marks, especially wheel marks and hands, during the

17th century. From around the 1670s through to about 1730, initial marks are particularly common and then, during the early 18th century, full-name marks in the Much Wenlock/ Broseley style appear. This style, however, did not last and later 18th-century pipes produced locally are marked either with initials across the stem or on the bowl, or with roll-stamped stem marks incorporating the maker's name. Neither of these two styles (bowl stamps or roll-stamped stems) was used by the Shropshire makers, with the use of incuse bowl marks being characteristic of the Midlands (and Bristol) and the roll-stamped stems being a Midlands and northern style. In this sense, Birmingham can be seen as something of a crossroads with styles from several different parts of the country being taken up and used locally.

In terms of the local makers themselves, it is clear that a lot more documentary work is needed since most cannot be identified. The IB marks may well have been produced by the Britten family, and the roll-stamped stems certainly were, but this family is currently poorly documented during the 18th century. The WT marks are particularly common and must represent an as yet undocumented local maker, while the AW/ EW/ IW/ TW marks may well represent a complete family of pipe makers who are also waiting to be discovered. Even when the full name is known, as with the John Phipson and Joseph Simmons marks, these individuals still need to be located in the archives.

Turning to the 'imported' pipes, it appears that various other local production centres were finding a market in Birmingham, for example the TA pipes from Coventry, as well as occasional pieces from further afield, for example the Elias Massey stem from Chester. The most significant area for imports, however, was clearly Shropshire and, in particular, the important pipemaking industry that grew up in the Much Wenlock/ Broseley area (Higgins 1987a). Although Broseley is usually thought of as the principal pipemaking centre this may well be because it is where the industry became centred from the mid-18th century onwards. Many of the earlier makers, however, were based in Much Wenlock and this may have been the main production centre during the early to mid-17th century as the industry was becoming established.

Several Much Wenlock makers are represented amongst the Birmingham assemblage, but it is the products of Michael Brown that stand out in particular, since nearly a third of all the heel marks recovered belong to this one maker. Although Michael Brown is documented in Much Wenlock, he is not particularly prominent in the records and it is perhaps surprising that so many of his pipes occur in Birmingham. This is particularly the case when it is considered that there were other Much Wenlock makers who appear to be more prominent in the records and whose products are known to have been widely marketed, for example the Deacon family, whose pipes occur across the Midlands and as far north as the Mersey. No Deacon marks were found in the excavated sample, which raises the question as to why such an overwhelmingly large proportion of the marks came from Brown's workshop. Either he had a special trading connection with Birmingham or perhaps he moved and actually worked in the area, as did other Shropshire makers, for example Thomas Andrews in Coventry or John and Jane Mats in Stoneydelph (Melton 1997).

Although the marked pipes reveal a lot about the number of workshops and trading connections with Birmingham, they only represent a proportion of all the pipes recovered. It is hard to be exact because of the various degrees of fragmentation represented amongst the excavated bowls, but in total there were around 460 bowl fragments of which around 330 were complete enough to have stem bores. A fragment with a stem bore is likely to include at least part of the heel or bowl facing the smoker, the most commonly marked areas of a pipe. The fact that only about 140 stamped heels or bowls were found shows that only around a third to a half of the pipes were actually marked. If the incidence of marking was the same in all areas, then this would not be significant. But it is known that most of the pipes produced in the Much Wenlock/ Broseley area were marked while those from the Midlands were marked much less frequently. Just over a third of the recovered marks are likely to be of Shropshire origin but this is likely to represent only around one-sixth of the total number of pipes represented. So, although the Shropshire marks are highly visible in the assemblage, because they were usually marked, they do not represent as large a proportion of the total as might be first thought.

Although it is important not to overemphasise the Shropshire link, there is no doubt that this formed a very important source of pipes for Birmingham. Pipes did not normally travel more than about 10–15 miles from their place of manufacture, probably because it was easier to transport the clay to a local workshop rather than transport the fragile finished pipes any distance. The Much Wenlock/ Broseley area is unusual nationally because of the market area that it was able to achieve. The local pipe makers made use of extensive waterborne trade on the river to transport their wares throughout the Severn Valley and down into South Wales. They also established a market across into the Midlands and as far north as the Mersey. The high proportion of Shropshire pipes being used in Birmingham must reflect regular trade between the two areas, which is all the more significant given the industrial links provided by the coal, metal-working and engineering traditions of these two areas. Although most of the artefactual evidence from these excavations is for trade in 17th- and early 18th-century pipes, it is clear that these links continued well into the 18th century. This evidence comes from two newspaper adverts that provide a wealth of evidence about not only the pipemaking families in Broseley and their

organisation but also the use of stamped marks and the trade with Birmingham. The first advert was repeated twice in *Aris's Birmingham Gazette*, on the 6th and 13th of March 1758:

> This is to acquaint Gentlemen and others that Margaret Bradley, widow of John Bradley, late of Benthall…deceased, intends following the business of tobacco-pipe making, in all the different branches as heretofore in her late husband's life time; and to prevent counterfeite (*sic*), doth intend putting the name of John Bradley upon the pipes as usual; and all such as please to favour her with their orders, may depend on being served with the utmost care and diligence, by their most obliged servant MARGARET BRADLEY.

Benthall is a small parish adjoining Broseley, and pipemaking was concentrated in an industrial area that developed straddling the two parishes. This advert clearly shows that a widow was able to continue running a business after her husband's death and that the pipes were specifically marked with his name so as to identify that particular manufactory. At this date these would have been stamped marks across the stem, the marks of John Bradley being well known from examples found elsewhere. The fact that Margaret Bradley felt it necessary to advertise in Birmingham shows that the city must have been an important destination for her wares. The second advert appeared in *Aris's Birmingham Gazette* on 10th May 1763:

> Whereas Margaret Bradley, of the Parish of Benthall, near Broseley, in the county of Salop, widow, tobacco-pipe maker, is lately deceased; this is to give notice, that the business of pipemaking will be carried on by me George Bradley, at Benthall aforesaid, being one of the sons of the deceased; and all Gentlemen and others as please to favour me with their orders, shall be served with as good pipes of all sorts, and at the same price as heretofore, and their favours gratefully acknowledged, by their humble servant GEORGE BRADLEY.

This second advert shows how the business was passed on through the family, with a continuing interest in the trade to Birmingham. As noted above, this trade in pipes is not only reflected in actual Shropshire products found in Birmingham but also by the adoption of Shropshire style full-name stem marks by local makers such as Phipson and Simmons. In contrast, there is very little evidence of either trade with, or stylistic influence from, centres to the north and east of Birmingham. The 17th-century pipes found in Leicester, for example, are almost exclusively a distinctive Midlands style of spur pipe, which does not occur at Birmingham, and almost none of the pipes produced in Leicester were marked, showing that they belong to a completely different stylistic complex (Higgins 1985).

The marks by period

The evolution of pipe styles and supply sources at Birmingham can also be examined by considering the marked pipes chronologically and comparing them with the unmarked pipes found at the same period. The 2,168 pipe fragments recovered from these excavations (458 bowl, 1,643 stem and 1,678 mouthpieces) are not evenly distributed chronologically. Both the number and type of fragments recovered and their date will influence the degree to which they provide a good reflection of the pipes in use at any given time. Many of the bowls are very fragmentary, making it hard to quantify the ratio of marked to unmarked examples, but an attempt has been made to give an overview in the general summary of this disparate evidence, which follows.

There are too few fragments dating from before c.1640 to give any idea of the styles of pipe and mark that were in use before the Civil War. There are around a dozen mid-17th-century bowls of which four (about 33%) are stamped on the heel with wheel marks. All of these pipes, both plain and marked, are likely to be local products, suggesting that there was not any significant trade in pipes at this period. After the Restoration in 1660, pipes become much more common on the site and around 50 bowls dating from c.1660–90 are represented. These show two differences from the preceding period. First, over 20 of the pipes are stamped (40%), mostly with initial marks. This suggests that not only was marking becoming more common but also that it was changing in nature towards initial rather than symbol marks. Second, and perhaps more significantly, nearly half of these marks are likely to have come from Shropshire, showing that the trade in pipes with that area had started. The Shropshire marks are all initial or full-name types (MICH BROUN, TC, MD, WE, IP and WS) and probably represent makers from Much Wenlock, Broseley and Wellington. In all, these represent around a sixth of all the pipes recovered and show that a general trade with east Shropshire had emerged, rather than the market being dominated by any one maker. In contrast, the local makers were still using symbols for about half of their marked pipes (hand and wheel marks) although some makers had changed to initials (AW, EW and WT).

During the period from c.1680–1730, barrel-shaped bowl forms with milled rims were still very popular and some 180 examples of this type were found. This is a good-sized sample, about half of which are marked, showing that, once again, there is a slight increase in the incidence of marking over the preceding period. In the same way, the proportion of Shropshire marks also increases with around 50 of the 90 marked pipes coming from the east of the county, which now represents over a quarter of all pipes in use in Birmingham. Although some eight or nine different Shropshire makers are represented (EB, MB/ MICH BROWN, TC, WE, II, IOHN IAMS, GeORG POVeL and WILL SAVAG) it is the products of Michael Brown that dominate this period, with 36 examples out of the 50 coming from his workshop. Despite the competition from Shropshire it is clear that the local makers maintained the lion's share of

the market. Half of these more local pipes are still unmarked and, of those that are, about a quarter are still marked with wheel marks. Despite this, a growing number of other local makers are represented by initial marks (TA, WC, WF, IS, WT, EW, IW and TW), perhaps influenced by the Shropshire tradition of 'branding' pipes by using the maker's initials.

From around 1690, new styles of pipe appear with larger, more upright bowls, usually with spurs, and these gradually replace the older styles until they come to dominate the market from the 1740s onwards. These essentially 18th-century forms are represented by around 130 examples from the excavations and these show very marked differences from the previous groups. The most radical change is in the style and placing of the marks. Without large heels to act as a vehicle for stamps, the marks had to be applied elsewhere. In east Shropshire the full-name mark was simply transferred from the heel to be placed across the stem. Despite the almost universal adoption of this style by the Broseley area makers, and the documented evidence for their trade with Birmingham (above), only two of these Shropshire stem marks were found (Thomas Legg and Samuel Roden). Some of the 18th-century bowl forms are very hard to date and so it is uncertain exactly how many later 18th-century (after c.1740) pipes are represented in this group. But the very small number of Broseley stem marks certainly suggests a marked decline in the proportion of the market that they held after the old heel styles went out of production. In contrast to the decline of Broseley influence, there is plenty of evidence for a development of the local industry during this period. Distinctive roll-stamped stems appear, quite unlike anything produced in the Broseley area, including decorative borders (lattice designs), named stamps (John Britten) and composite schemes involving both roll-stamps and decorative ovals (spiral motifs and animal ovals). Another break with Broseley styles is seen in the adoption of incuse bowl stamps. The overall level of marking is lower amongst these 18th-century forms, around a quarter, but the proportion of local marks is very much higher, with 34 of the 36 stamps being local types. This figure is somewhat exaggerated by the fact that some of these forms overlap with the older style heel marks, which have been excluded, but the general pattern is clear. The makers who were adopting and developing these new styles are IB/ IOHN BRITTEN, ?THOMAS BRITTEN, HH, IP/ IOHN PHIPSON, SP and IS/ IOS SIMONS.

There are around 50 19th-century pipes represented, only six of which have maker's marks on them. This is too small a sample to make a definitive statement, but the evidence suggests a sharp decline in the use of marking during this period and there is also a change in its nature. Only two of the 19th-century marks are stamped, the remainder being moulded on either the heel or stem of the pipe. There is a very low level of evidence for Shropshire pipes, with only one Broseley stamp being recovered. The other stamped mark is from the firm of Fiolet in France. This firm became a major exporter to the UK during the second half of the 19th century, so the occurrence of this piece is not atypical. Likewise the moulded McDougall mark from Glasgow represents another major producer of the period who marketed very widely. The improved transport facilities afforded by the railways certainly opened up the market in pipes, but the other moulded marks are probably all local (TR, REYNOLDS.BIRMINGHAM, shields) and show that local makers maintained a good share of the market.

Overall, this analysis suggests that local production always provided the majority of the pipes consumed in Birmingham. From the mid-17th century, east Shropshire rapidly grew to become a major supplier, influencing local styles of both bowl and mark. The number of Shropshire imports and the proportion of marked pipes in the assemblage as a whole both grew steadily during the 17th century, peaking around 1700 when the Shropshire manufacturers were supplying about a quarter of the market in Birmingham. From the 1730s, Broseley influence seems to have declined, which is surprising given the documentary evidence for trade later in the 18th century and the fact that Broseley pipes were certainly being widely exported to other centres at this time. The lack of evidence for Broseley pipes from these excavations is interesting and further groups are needed from Birmingham to see if this is a phenomenon peculiar to these sites or part of a general trend for the city as a whole. As the Broseley influence peaked, local manufacturers started developing their own distinctive local styles, including the production of decorated stems and the use of incuse bowl marks. During the 19th century, imports from France and Scotland competed in the market, but local industry remained strong.

Catalogue

Each illustrated example is given a suggested date together with details of it appearance and attributes. Each entry ends with the site and year code, the excavation area, the context and feature number, phase and any reference letter(s) (in brackets) allocated to identify the specific fragment within the context group.

9.1.1. Fragment of *c.*1680–1730 with a good burnish and a stem bore of 7/64". The rim has been bottered and fully milled. The relief stamped mark reads TA (Die 2001). There is another identical mark from the same context, which was stamped on a pipe made from the same mould (B). The illustrated example is Park St. PSB01 1739 F713 Phase 3.2 (A).

9.1.2. Fragment of *c.*1680–1730 with a good burnish and a stem bore of 5/64". The relief stamped mark reads EB (Die 136). Park St. PSB01 1101 cleaning Phase 4/5 (T).

9.1.3. Fragment of *c.*1710–1740 with a good burnish and a stem bore of 5/64". The rim has been bottered and milled. The relief stamped mark reads IB (Die 959). Park St. PSB01 1738 cleaning Phase 4/5 (K).

9.1.4. Fragment of *c.*1710–1740 with an average burnish and a stem bore of 5/64". The relief stamped mark reads IB (Die 2003). Park St. PSB01 A U/S (A).

9.1.5. Fragment of *c.*1710–1740 with an unburnished surface; the stem bore is unmeasureable. The rim has possibly been wiped. The relief stamped mark reads IB (Die 2016). PSB01 Eval. Tr. 3 1015.

9.1.6. Fragment of *c.*1710–1740 with an average burnish and a stem bore of 5/64". The relief stamped mark reads IB (Die 2002). Park St. PSB01 1506 F503/ F520 Phase 3.3 (B).

9.1.7. Fragment of *c.*1720–1770 with an unburnished surface and a stem bore of 6/64". The relief stamped mark reads IOHN BRITTEN (Die 246). The excavated example is damaged but the drawing has been completed using known examples from elsewhere. The Park Street example was recovered from a deposit that may well date to before *c.*1760. Park St. PSB01 1512 F500 Phase 3.2.

9.1.8. Fragment of *c.*1710–1760 with a good burnish and a stem bore of 6/64". The relief stamped mark reads …BRITTEN. The Christian name has been broken away but the few surviving serifs suggest that this could have been been Thomas. Park St. PSB01 1101 cleaning Phase 4/5.

9.1.9. Fragment of *c.*1680–1730 with a good burnish and a stem bore of 6/64". The rim has been bottered and fully milled. The relief stamped mark reads MB (Die 2017). Park St. PSB01 1167 F154 Phase 4 (A).

9.1.10. Fragment of *c.*1680–1730 with an average burnish and a stem bore of 6/64". The rim has been internally trimmed, bottered and milled. The relief stamped mark reads MB (Die 248). The die detail is from the National Catalogue of marks, not from the actual excavated example. Park St. PSB01 1708 F700 Phase 3.2 (D).

9.1.11. Fragment of *c.*1670–1690 with a good burnish and a stem bore of 8/64". The rim has been bottered and fully milled. The relief stamped mark reads MICH BROUN (Die 2018). Park St. PSB01 1101 cleaning Phase 4/5 (K).

9.1.12. Fragment of *c.*1680–1730 with an average burnish and a stem bore of 7/64". The rim has been bottered and milled. The relief stamped mark reads MICH BROWN 1688? (Die 251). The last digit of the date is unclear but other examples suggest that it should be 1688 (although the last digit always appears to be indistinct). Park St. PSB01 1219 F187 Phase 3.1.

9.1.13. Fragment of *c.*1680–1730 with an average burnish and a stem bore of 6/64". The rim has been bottered and three-quarters milled. The relief stamped mark reads MICH BROWN (Die 2019). Edgbaston St. BRB99 C 3000 cleaning Phase 3/4 (I).

9.1.14. Fragment of *c.*1680–1730 with an average burnish and a stem bore of 6/64". The rim has been bottered and half milled. The relief stamped mark reads MICH BROWNE (Die 250). Park St. PSB01 C U/S (A).

9.1.15. Fragment of *c.*1680–1730 with an average burnish and a stem bore of 6/64". The rim has been bottered and fully milled. The relief stamped mark reads MICHEALL BROWN (Die 871). Park St. PSB01 1738 unstratified (D).

9.1.16. Fragment of *c.*1680–1730 with an average burnish and a stem bore of 7/64". The rim has been bottered and three-quarters milled. The relief stamped mark reads MICH BROWN (Die 2020). Park St. PSB01 1839 F773 Phase 3.1.

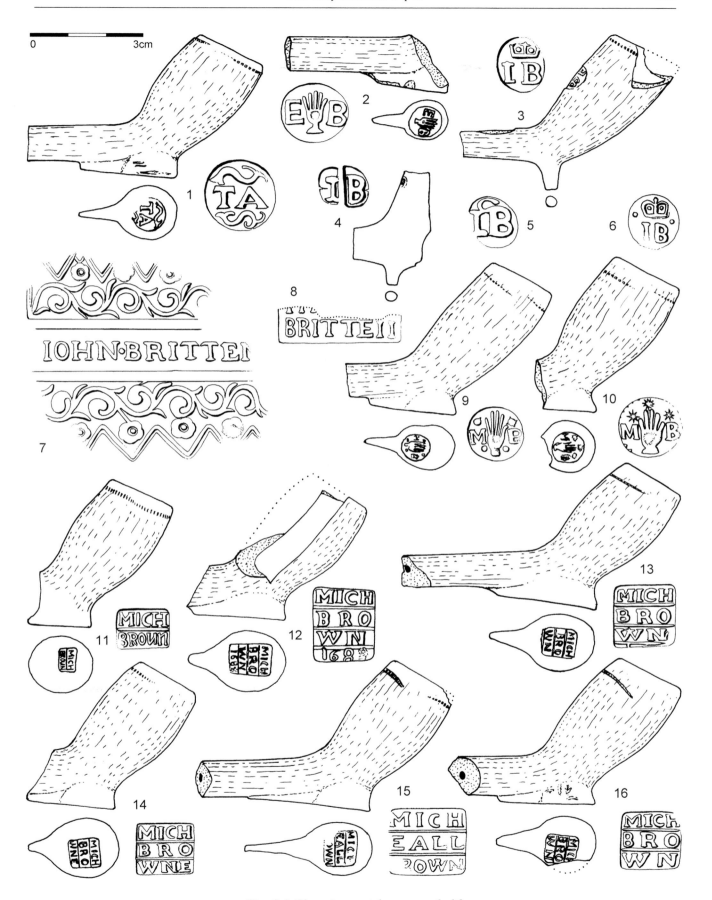

Fig. 9.1 Clay pipe, catalogue nos 1–16.

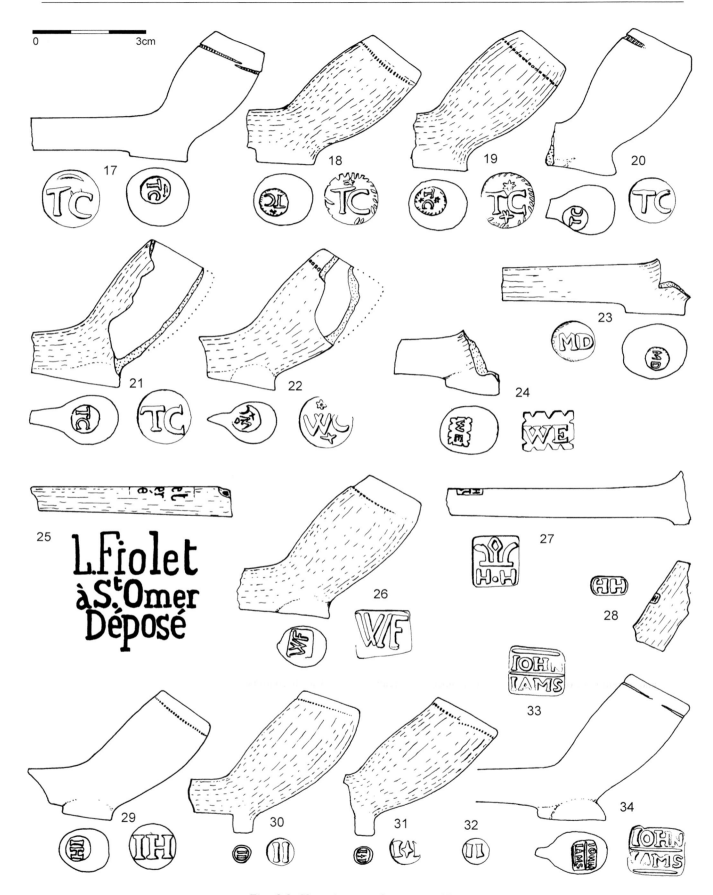

Fig. 9.2 Clay pipe, catalogue nos 17–34.

9.2.17. Fragment of *c*.1670–1690 with an unburnished surface and a stem bore of 7/64". The rim has been bottered and fully milled. The relief stamped mark reads TC (Die 2023). Park St. PSB01 1101 cleaning Phase 4/5 (B).

9.2.18. Fragment of *c*.1670–1690 with a good burnish and a stem bore of 7/64". The rim has been bottered and fully milled. The relief stamped mark, which has been placed at 90 degrees to the stem, reads TC (Die 2021). Park St. PSB01 1738 cleaning Phase 4/5 (A).

9.2.19. Fragment of *c*.1670–1690 with a good burnish and a stem bore of 6/64". The rim has been bottered and fully milled. The relief stamped mark reads TC (Die 2022). Park St. PSB01 1752 pit F720, Phase 4 (A).

9.2.20. Fragment of *c*.1680–1730 with a burnt surface (so uncertain if it was burnished) and a stem bore of 6/64". The rim has been bottered and three-quarters milled. The inverted relief stamped mark reads TC (Die 2025). Park St. PSB01708 F700 Phase 3.2 (O).

9.2.21. Fragment of *c*.1680–1730 with an average burnish and a stem bore of 5/64". The rim has been internally trimmed and bottered. The relief stamped mark reads TC (Die 2024). Damaged bowl but with quite a large, 'sleek' form, suggesting that it may be late within the date range for this bowl type. Park St. PSB01 Eval. Tr. 3 1015 (D).

9.2.22. Fragment of *c*.1680–1730 with a poor burnish and a stem bore of 6/64". The rim has been bottered and milled. The inverted relief stamped mark reads WC (Die 2026). Park St. PSB01 1708 F700 Phase 3.2 (I).

9.2.23. Fragment of *c*.1670–1690 with a poor burnish and a stem bore of 8/64". The relief stamped mark reads MD (Die 268). Edgbaston St. BRB99 B 2016 cleaning Phase 3/4 (C).

9.2.24. Fragment of *c*.1670–1700 with an average burnish and a stem bore of 8/64". The relief stamped mark reads WE (Die 564). Park St. PSB01 1101 cleaning Phase 4/5 (U).

9.2.25. Fragment of *c*.1850–1920 with a good burnish and a stem bore of 5/64". The incuse stamped mark reads 'L.Fiolet à St. Omer Déposé' (Die 2013). Recovered from a deposit that most likely dates from *c*.1850–70. Edgbaston St. BRB97 Trans A 5107 (upper fill of brick culvert).

9.2.26. Fragment of *c*.1680–1720 with an average burnish and a stem bore of 7/64". The rim has been bottered and three-quarters milled. The relief stamped mark reads WF (Die 2027). Lettering very crudely executed. Park St. PSB01 1819 F761 Phase 3.1 (A).

9.2.27. Fragment of *c*.1710–1760 with an unburnished surface and a stem bore of 5/64". The relief stamped mark reads HH (Die 2046). Park St. PSB01 1938 F828 Phase 3.2.

9.2.28. Small bowl fragment of *c*.1730–1780 with an average burnish; the stem bore is unmeasureable. The rim has been cut. The relief stamped mark reads HH (Die 2044). Park St. PSB01 1125 F133 Phase 3.2 (G).

9.2.29. Fragment of *c*.1670–1720 with an average burnish and a stem bore of 6/64". The rim has been bottered and fully milled. The relief stamped mark reads IH (Die 324). Very highly fired – possibly a waster. Park St. PSB01 1738 cleaning Phase 4/5 (H).

9.2.30. Fragment of *c*.1690–1720 with an average burnish and a stem bore of 5/64". The rim has been bottered and three-quarters milled. The relief stamped mark reads II (Die 2028). The rim has squatted (deformed under its own weight) during firing. Park St. PSB01 1101 cleaning Phase 4/5 (D).

9.2.31. Fragment of *c*.1690–1720 with a good burnish and a stem bore of 5/64". The rim has been bottered and fully milled. The relief stamped mark reads II (Die 2029). Park St. PSB01 1708 F700 Phase 3.2 (S).

9.2.32. A spur bowl of *c*.1690–1720 with an average burnish, bottered and three-quarters milled rim, and stem bore of 6/64" was found with a poorly impressed mark that seems to read II. This appears to be very similar to or the same as Die 988, which is shown here to illustrate the mark type. The bowl is similar to the other II pipes described above (Figs 9.2.30–31). PSB01 A 1114.

9.2.33. Fragment of *c*.1680–1730 with an unburnished surface and a stem bore of 6/64". The rim has been bottered and fully milled. The bowl has a narrow slightly lozenge shaped tailed heel and the bowl form is almost identical to that illustrated in Fig. 9.2.34. The stem is oval in section and the inverted relief stamped mark reads IOHN IAMS (Die 2031). Park St. PSB01 1125 F133 Phase 3.2 (A).

9.2.34. Fragment of *c*.1680–1730 with an unburnished surface and a stem bore of 5/64". The rim has been bottered and fully milled. The relief stamped mark reads IOHN IAMS (Die 2030). The bowl has a joining stem (fresh break) giving a total length of 181mm from the back of heel. This stem is rather thin and waney in appearance. Park St. PSB01 1721 F702 Phase 3.1.

9.3.35. Fragment of *c*.1740–1790 with an average burnish and a stem bore of 4/64". The relief stamped mark reads THOS LEGG BROSELEY (Die 2047). Park St. PSB01 C 1827 rubble with Structure 5a Phase 4.

9.3.36. Chester stem fragment of *c*.1690–1715 with an average burnish and a stem bore of 7/64". The relief stamped mark reads ELIAS MASSEY (Die 1967) flanked by a pinacle and dot border (Die 1975). Park St. PSB01 1708 F700 Phase 3.2.

9.3.37. Fragment of *c*.1850–1910 with an unburnished surface and a stem bore of /64". There is an incuse moulded mark but only the first letter of the place-name (G...) and the last letter of the maker's name (...L) survives. This would, however, almost certainly have read McDOUGALL/ GLASGOW originally. This was one of the largest and most prolific of the Scottish firms, who operated from 1846–1967. The mouthpiece is coated with an orange/ brown lead glaze, which suggests that this piece dates to before *c*.1910, when the use of lead glazes on mouthpieces was discontinued. Park St. Intrusive in PSB01 1913 F816 Phase 3.

9.3.38. Fragment of *c*.1680–1730 with an unburnished surface and a stem bore of 7/64". The relief stamped mark reads GEORG POVEL (Die 595). Park St. PSB01 C U/S (C).

9.3.39. Fragment of *c*.1660–1690 with an unburnished surface and a stem bore of 6/64". The rim has been bottered and fully milled. The relief stamped mark reads IP (Die 2032). The mark has been placed at 90 degrees to the long axis of the pipe. Edgbaston St. BRB99 3000 cleaning Phase 3/ 4 (F).

9.3.40. Fragment of *c*.1730–1780 with an unburnished surface and a stem bore of 5/64". The rim has been internally trimmed and cut. The incuse stamped mark reads IP (Die 2045). Park St. PSB01 1139 F138 (E).

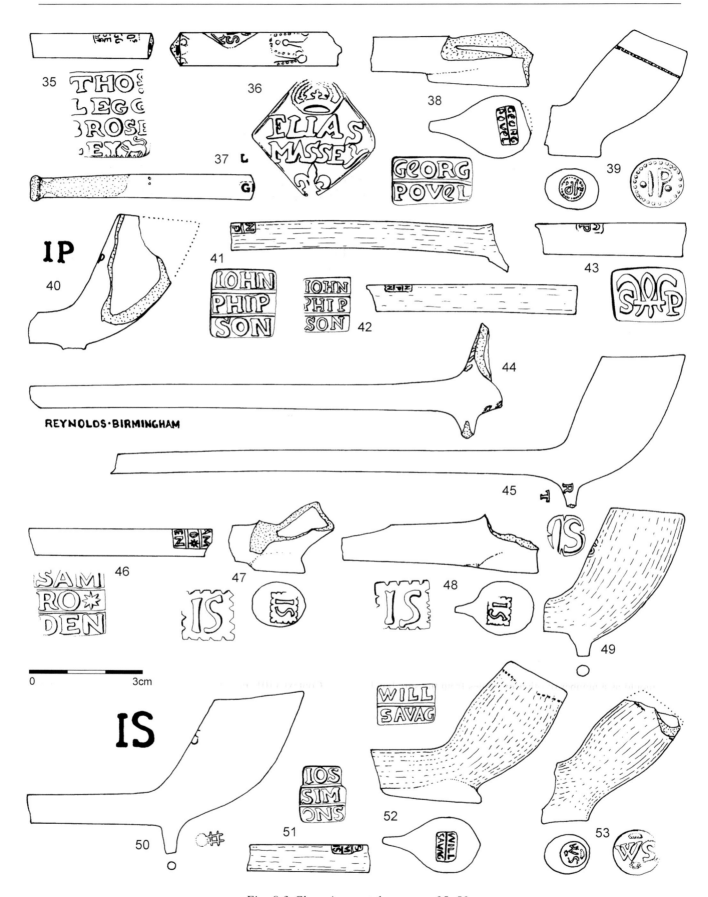

Fig. 9.3 Clay pipe, catalogue nos 35–53.

9.3.41. Fragment of *c*.1740–1800 with a burnt surface (so uncertain if it was burnished) and a stem bore of 5/64". The relief stamped mark reads IOHN PHIPSON (Die 885). The mark is on top of the stem *c*.60mm from the bowl and occurred in a deposit that may well date from before *c*.1760. Park St. PSB01 1512 F500 Phase 3.2 (A).

9.3.42. Fragment of *c*.1740–1780 with an unburnished surface and a stem bore of 5/64". The relief stamped mark reads IOHN PHIPSON (Die 2048). Park St. PSB01 1531 F510/F542. Phase 3.3.

9.3.43. Fragment of *c*.1690–1740 with an unburnished surface and a stem bore of 5/64". The relief stamped mark reads SP (Die 2049). Park St. PSB01 1512 F500 Phase 3.2.

9.3.44. Fragment of *c*.1850–1890 with an unburnished surface and a stem bore of 4/64". The incuse moulded mark reads REYNOLDS BIRMINGHAM. The pipe is only marked on the left-hand side of the stem using very crisp lettering, some of which appears white against the burnt surface of this fragment. This lettering was probably full of dirt and grime from heavy use when it was burnt, which protected it from discolouration. Traces of leaf decoration survive on the bowl seams. Recovered from a deposit that most likely dates from *c*.1850–70. Edgbaston St. BRB97 Transect A 5107 (upper fill of brick culvert) (E).

9.3.45. Fragment of *c*.1820–1860 with an unburnished surface and a stem bore of 4/64". The rim has been cut. The relief moulded mark reads TR. Edgbaston St. BRB99 1007 Phase 3/ 4 cleaning layer.

9.3.46. Fragment of *c*.1750–1790 with an unburnished surface and a stem bore of 5/64". The relief stamped mark reads SAM/ RO*/ DEN (Die 920). This was made by one of the various makers named Samuel Roden who worked in the Broseley area of Shropshire. Park St. PSB01 1505 Phase 4.

9.3.47. Fragment of *c*.1680–1730 with an unburnished surface and a stem bore of 6/64". The relief stamped mark reads IS (Die 2033). Park St. PSB01 1101 cleaning Phase 4/5 (S).

9.3.48. Fragment of *c*.1680–1730 with an unburnished surface and a stem bore of 7/64". The relief stamped mark reads IS (Die 2034). Edgbaston St. BRB99 3000 cleaning Phase 3/4 (D).

9.3.49. Fragment of *c*.1710–1740 with a good burnish and a stem bore of 5/64". The rim has been internally trimmed and bottered. The relief stamped mark reads IS (Die 882). This example appears to have been made using the same mould as a number of other examples from the site; bowl C from the same context, bowls B and C from context 1104 and bowl H context 1729. Park St. PSB01 1205 F180 Phase 3.2 (B).

9.3.50. Fragment of *c*.1740–1780 with an unburnished surface and a stem bore of 4/64". The rim has been internally trimmed and cut. The incuse stamped mark reads IS (Die 880). Long, thin, pointed spur that appears to have been flattened or trimmed at its tip. There is also an unusual internal bowl mark made of two vertical and two horizontal lines, like a noughts and crosses grid. Park St. PSB01 1505 Phase 4 (D).

9.3.51. Fragment of *c*.1720–1780 with an average burnish and a stem bore of 4/64". The relief stamped mark reads IOS SIMONS (Die 884). Another example of this mark is known from Birmingham. Park St. PSB01 1725 F705

Phase 3.3.

9.3.52. Fragment of *c*.1680–1730 with a good burnish and a stem bore of 6/64". The rim has been bottered and fully milled. The relief stamped mark reads WILL SAVAG (Die 1296). Park St. PSB01 1101 cleaning Phase 4/5 (P).

9.3.53. Fragment of *c*.1660–1680 with an average burnish and a stem bore of 6/64". The rim is chipped but has been fully milled. The relief stamped mark reads WS (Die 2035). Park St. PSB01 Eval. Tr. 3 1015 (I).

9.4.54. Fragment of *c*.1670–1690 with an average burnish and a stem bore of 6/64". The rim has been bottered and fully milled. The inverted relief stamped mark reads WT (Die 2037). Park St. PSB01 1702 cleaning Phase 4/5 (A).

9.4.55. Fragment of *c*.1670–1690 with an unburnished surface and a stem bore of 6/64". The rim has been bottered and three-quarters milled. The relief stamped mark reads WT (Die 466). Heart-shaped mark Park St. PSB01 1101 cleaning Phase 4/5 (A).

9.4.56. Fragment of *c*.1680–1730 with an average burnish and a stem bore of 7/64". The rim has been bottered and half milled. The relief stamped mark reads WT (Die 2038). Same mark as bowl C from this group, but different mould. Park St. PSB01 1738 cleaning Phase 4/5 (B).

9.4.57. Fragment of *c*.1680–1730 with an average burnish and a stem bore of 6/64". The relief stamped mark reads WT (Die 868). Mark upside down. Edgbaston St. BRB97 Tr. 1 5400 Demolition debris Transect D.

9.4.58. Fragment of *c*.1680–1730 with an average burnish and a stem bore of 5/64". The rim has been bottered. The inverted relief stamped mark reads WT (Die 947). Examples of pipes made in the same mould but marked with different stamps were recorded from the excavations; context 105 (bowls A, B, E and G); context 1101 (bowls Q and R) and context 1738 (bowl C). Park St. PSB01 1101 cleaning Phase 4/5 (R).

9.4.59. Fragment of *c*.1680–1730 with an unburnished surface and a stem bore of 6/64". The rim has been bottered and milled. The poorly impressed relief stamped mark reads WT (Die 869). Park St. PSB01 1725 F705 Phase 3.3 (D).

9.4.60. Fragment of *c*.1680–1730 with a good burnish and a stem bore of 5/64". The rim has been bottered and half milled. The relief stamped mark reads WT (Die 870). The excavations produced at least seven other bowls that distinctive flaws show were produced using the same mould. Three of these were stamped with the same die type; bowl E from this group and bowls Q and R from Context 1101. Four were made using the same mould but they had been stamped using different WT dies; bowls A (Fig. 9.4.61) and B from Context 1015, Bowl C from context 1738 and bowl A from context 1702. Park St. PSB01 Eval. Tr. 3 1015 (G).

9.4.61. Fragment of *c*.1680–1730 with an abraded surface (so uncertain if it was burnished) and a stem bore of 5/64". The rim has been bottered and three-quarters milled. The relief stamped mark is very crude and looks like LW because it has been stamped upside down. It can be shown, however, to be intended as a WT mark (Die 2039) because it occurs on the same mould type as seven other examples from the site, some of which are clearly marked WT. Some of the other marks are also inverted, showing that this was a particular characteristic of this maker. There is a second example of this mould and mark combination

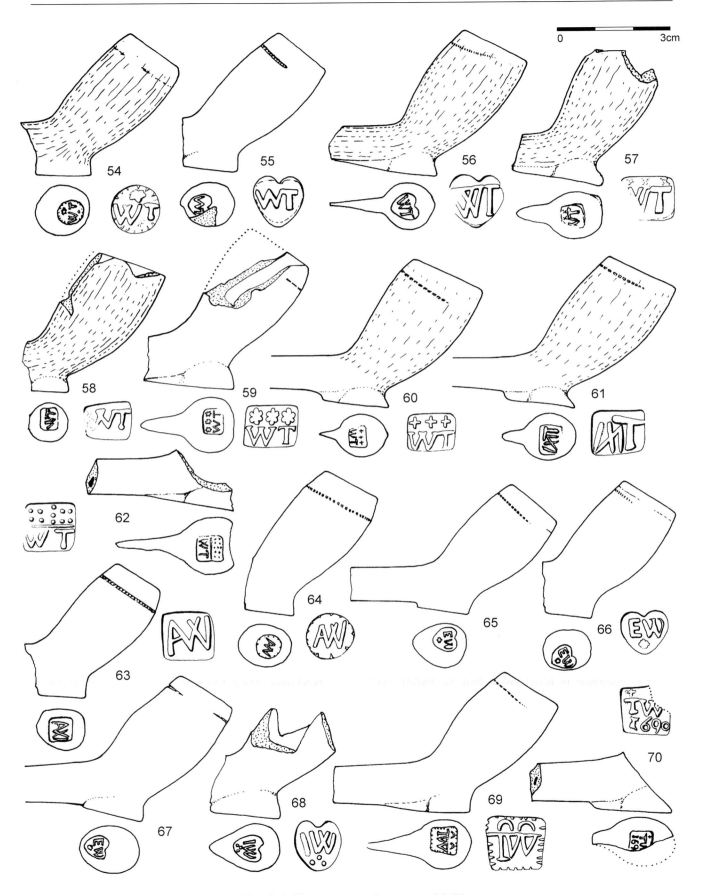

Fig. 9.4 Clay pipe, catalogue nos 54–70.

from this context (B) and six examples of this mould with other dies used on it; Context 1015 (E and G), Context 1788 (C), Context 1101 (Q and R) and Context 1702 (A). Park St. PSB01 Eval. Tr. 3 1015 (A).

9.4.62. Fragment of *c*.1680–1730 with an unburnished surface and a stem bore of 7/64". The relief stamped mark reads WT (Die 2040). Edgbaston St. BRB99 1066 F139 Phase 3 (B).

9.4.63. Fragment of *c*.1660–1680 with an unburnished surface and a stem bore of 5/64". The rim has been bottered and fully milled. The relief stamped ligatured mark reads AW (Die 2037). Edgbaston St. BRB99 3000 cleaning Phase 3/4 (G).

9.4.64. Fragment of *c*.1660–1680 with an abraded surface (so uncertain if it was burnished) and a stem bore of 6/64". The rim has been bottered and three-quarters milled. The relief stamped ligatured mark reads AW (Die 902). Park St. PSB01 1512 F500 Phase 3.2 (B).

9.4.65. Fragment of *c*.1670–1710 with an unburnished surface and a stem bore of 7/64". The rim has been bottered and half milled. The relief stamped mark reads EW (Die 900). Park St. PSB01 1101 cleaning Phase 4/5 (J).

9.4.66. Fragment of *c*.1670–1710 with a glossy but slightly abraded surface (so uncertain if it was burnished, but no burnishing lines visible) and a stem bore of 7/64". The rim has been bottered and half milled. The relief stamped mark reads EW (Die 900). Park St. PSB01 1101 cleaning Phase 4/5 (H).

9.4.67. Fragment of *c*.1680–1710 with an unburnished surface and a stem bore of 6/64". The rim has been bottered and had a plain groove around three-quarters of the rim. The relief stamped mark reads EW (Die 900). Park St. PSB01 1110 Phase 4/5(A).

9.4.68. Fragment of *c*.1680–1730 with an unburnished surface and a stem bore of 7/64". The relief stamped mark reads IW (Die 957). Park St. PSB01 1708 F700 Phase 3.2 (H).

9.4.69. Fragment of *c*.1680–1710 with an unburnished surface and a stem bore of 6/64". The rim has been bottered and three-quarters milled. The relief stamped mark reads TW Die 2041). Edgbaston St. BRB99 3000 cleaning Phase 3/4 (E).

9.4.70. Fragment of *c*.1690–1730 with an unburnished surface and a stem bore of 6/64". The relief stamped mark reads TW 1690 (Die 2042). The excavated example has the final digit of the date missing but it has been completed in the die detail drawing from another fragmentary example from elsewhere in Birmingham. Park St. PSB01 1819 F761 Phase 3.1(B).

9.5.71. Fragment of *c*.1620–1640 with an unburnished surface; the stem bore is unmeasurable. The rim has been bottered and three-quarters milled. The very edge of a relief stamped mark survives but not enough to identify any of the lettering. Edgbaston St. BRB99 F245 Phase 3 2179.

9.5.72. Fragment of *c*.1680–1730 with an unburnished surface and a stem bore of 5/64". Part of a relief stamped mark with the letter H survives, together with part of a tailed heel. The mark has been placed at nearly 90 degrees to the stem and it is unclear if the surviving letter (H) is the surname or Christian name initial. Park St. PSB01 Eval. Tr. 3 1015 (M).

9.5.73. Stem fragment with an unburnished surface and a stem bore of 5/64". The relief stamped mark reads ...OSLEY.

This is an unusual mark that probably just read 'BROSLEY' without any maker's name. This general style of mark dates from *c*.1780–1840 but this particular example was found in a well fill that most likely dates from *c*.1820–1840. A complete example of a similar 'BROSLEY' stamp has been found at Dudley Castle but that example comes from a different die with a serrated edge. Edgbaston St. BRB99 1026 Well F111 Phase 4.

9.5.74. Fragment of *c*.1640–1670 with an abraded surface (so uncertain if it was burnished). The relief stamped mark is a crude wheel type but it is too poorly impressed to define the die type. Concretion adhering to the fragment makes it difficult to measure the stem bore but it appears to be about 7/64". Park St. PSB01 1752 pit F720 Phase 4 (E).

9.5.75. Fragment of *c*.1640–1670 with an unburnished surface and a stem bore of 6/64". The rim has been bottered and fully milled and the pipe is stamped with a wheel mark with alternate straight and wavy spokes (Die 960). Park St. PSB01 1634 F510/ F532 Phase 3.3 (C).

9.5.76. Fragment of *c*.1660–1680 with an average burnish and a stem bore of 7/64". The rim has been bottered and three-quarters milled. The relief stamped mark is a wheel type with spikes between the spokes. Park St. PSB01 1126 F134 Phase 3.1 (B).

9.5.77. Fragment of *c*.1660–1680 with an unburnished surface and a stem bore of 6/64". The rim has been bottered and half milled. The relief stamped mark is a wheel type with spikes between the spokes. Edgbaston St. BRB99 3000 cleaning Phase 3/4 (H).

9.5.78. Fragment of *c*.1680–1730 with an unburnished surface and a stem bore of 6/64". The rim has been bottered and three-quarters milled. The large relief stamped wheel mark has distinctive dots between the spokes (Die 889). Park St. PSB01 1726 F706 Phase 3 (B).

9.5.79. Fragment of *c*.1680–1730 with an unburnished surface and a stem bore of 5/64". The rim has been bottered and fully milled. The large relief stamped wheel mark has distinctive dots between the spokes (Die 1154). Park St. PSB01 C 1726 F706 Phase 3 (C).

9.5.80. Fragment of *c*.1680–1730 with an average burnish and a stem bore of 7/64". The rim has been bottered and fully milled. The relief stamped wheel mark has spikes between the spokes. Park St. PSB01 1739 F713 Phase 3.2 (C).

9.5.81. Composite drawing of two fragments from the same mould and stamped with the same mark, dating from *c*.1660–1690. Both pieces have an average burnish on the bowl (only) and a stem bore of 6/64". The relief stamped hand mark is surrounded by a wreath (Die 961). Park St. PSB01 1126 F134 Phase 3.1 (C and D).

9.5.82. Fragment of *c*.1680–1730 with a fine burnish and a stem bore of 7/64". The rim has been bottered and has a groove around all the surviving rim. There is a crudely executed relief stamped hand mark flanked by dots (Die 2043). Edgbaston St. BRB99 3000 cleaning Phase 3/4 (C).

9.5.83. Stem fragment of *c*.1690–1740 with an unburnished surface and a stem bore of 5/64". The stem has been decorated with two stamped marks; an unusual series of incuse parallel diagonal lines mimicking a stem twist (Die 2012) and a griffin oval in the Chester style, which is too fragmentary to allocate a die number. Another fragment with this style of 'stem twist' mark was found in context

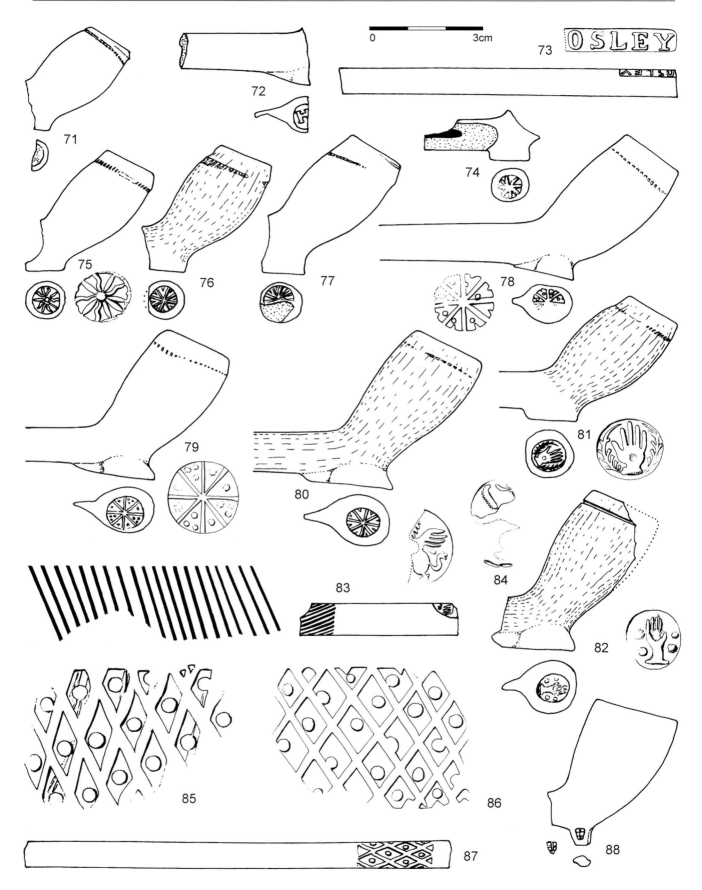

Fig. 9.5 Clay pipe, catalogue nos 71–88.

1634 in association with a bowl that may be from the same pipe (Fig. 9.7.109). Park St. PSB01 1646 F510/ F542 Phase 3.3.

9.5.84. Stem fragment (not illustrated) of *c.*1690–1740 with an unburnished surface and a stem bore of 5/64". The relief stamped mark across the stem comprises a rampant lion in an oval, but this is too fragmentary to allocate a die number. Park St. PSB01 1634 F510/ F542.

9.5.85. Stem fragment (not illustrated) of *c.*1690–1750 with an unburnished surface and a stem bore of 4/64". The stem is decorated with a relief roll-stamped lattice border (Die 2011). Park St. PSB01 1635 F510/ F542 Phase 3.3.

9.5.86. Stem fragment (not illustrated) of *c.*1690–1750 with an unburnished surface and a stem bore of 5/64". The stem is decorated with a relief roll-stamped lattice border (Die 897). This stem was originally bagged and catalogued as Context 1913 but fragment is clearly marked 1903, which has been used in the database. Park St. PSB01 1903 F809 Structure 2 Phase 3.

9.5.87. Stem fragment of *c.*1750–1780 with an unburnished surface and a stem bore of 5/64", decorated with a relief roll-stamped lattice border. This is similar to Die 2011 (Fig. 9.5.85), but this example is from a different die and the impression is too poor to draw in detail. This example comes from the fill of a tank dating from *c.*1780 and it is likely to be contemporary with this deposit. Park St. PSB01 1621 F510/ F542 Phase 3.3.

9.5.88. Fragment of *c.*1840–1900 with an unburnished surface and a stem bore of 5/64". The rim has been internally trimmed and wiped. There is a simple relief moulded mark on either side of the spur that appears to represent a simple shield. This fragment was originally bagged and as Context 1738 but the fragment is clearly labelled 1735, which is how it has been catalogued here. Park St. PSB01 1735 F711 Phase 4 drain (P).

9.6.89. Fragment of *c.*1640–1660 with an unburnished surface and a stem bore of 7/64". The rim has been bottered and is fully milled. Edgbaston St. BRB99 2004 cleaning Phase 3/4 (A).

9.6.90. Fragment of *c.*1640–1660 with an unburnished surface and a stem bore of 6/64". The rim has been bottered and is fully milled. Neat bowl, most likely a local product. Park St. PSB01 Eval. Tr. 3 1025.

9.6.91. Fragment of *c.*1650–1670 with an unburnished surface and a stem bore of 5/64". The rim has been bottered and is fully milled. Edgbaston St. BRB99 3009/ 3010 F304 Phase 3.

9.6.92. Fragment of *c.*1660–1690 with an unburnished surface and a stem bore of 6/64". The rim has been bottered and is fully milled. Moor St. MSB00 U/S.

9.6.93. Fragment of *c.*1660–1680 with a stem bore of 6/64". The rim has been bottered and is fully milled. Very glossy, smooth surface, but no obvious burnishing lines. Park St. PSB01 1153 F157 Phase 3 (A).

9.6.94. Fragment of *c.*1660–1680 with an unburnished surface and a stem bore of 7/64". The rim has been bottered and is fully milled. Park St. PSB01 1787 F745 Phase 3.3.

9.6.95. Fragment of *c.*1660–1680 with an unburnished surface and a stem bore of 7/64". The rim has been bottered and is fully milled. Edgbaston St. BRB99 1064 F141 Phase 3.

9.6.96. Fragment of *c.*1660–1690 with an unburnished surface and a stem bore of 6/64". The rim has been bottered and

is fully milled. Not a typically Birmingham area form; most likely from south Shropshire or Herefordshire area. Edgbaston St. BRB99 1020 F106 Phase 3 (A).

9.6.97. Fragment of *c.*1660–1680 with an average burnish on its surface and a stem bore of 6/64". The rim has been bottered and is fully milled. Park St. PSB01 1240 F193 Phase 3.3.

9.6.98. Fragment of *c.*1660–1680 with an unburnished surface and a stem bore of 7/64". The rim has been bottered and is fully milled. Park St. PSB01 1139 F138 Phase 4 (A).

9.6.99. Fragment of *c.*1660–1690 with an unburnished surface and a stem bore of 7/64". The rim has been bottered and three-quarters milled. Fine fabric with a glossy surface but not burnished. Park St. PSB01 1126 F134 Phase 3.1 (A).

9.6.100. Fragment of *c.*1660–1680 with an unburnished surface and a stem bore of 6/64". The rim has been bottered and three-quarters milled. Park St. PSB01 1101 cleaning Phase 4/5 (Y).

9.6.101. Fragment of *c.*1670–1690 with an unburnished surface and a stem bore of 6/64". The rim has been bottered and three-quarters milled. Park St. PSB01 1127 fill of drain F135 Phase 4 (A).

9.6.102. Fragment of *c.*1670–1690 with an unburnished surface and a stem bore of 6/64". The rim has been bottered and three-quarters milled. Park St. PSB01 1127 fill of drain F135 Phase 4 (B).

9.6.103. Fragment of *c.*1680–1720 with an unburnished surface and a stem bore of 5/64". The rim has been bottered but it has not been milled. Park St. PSB01 1738 cleaning Phase 4/5 (L).

9.6.104. Fragment of *c.*1700–1730 with an unburnished surface and a stem bore of 5/64". The rim has been bottered but it has not been milled. Park St. PSB01 1913 F816 Phase 3 (A).

9.6.105. Fragment of *c.*1680–1730 with an unburnished surface and a stem bore of 6/64". The rim has been bottered but it has not been milled. The tailed heel has not been trimmed. Park St. PSB01 1708 F700 Phase 3.2 (P).

9.6.106. Fragment of *c.*1710–1740 with a good burnish on its surface and a stem bore of 5/64". The rim has been bottered but it has not been milled. Park St. PSB01 1708 F700 Phase 3.2 (U).

9.6.107. Joining bowl and stem of *c.*1740–1770 with a good burnish on the surface and a stem bore of 5/64". The rim has been cut and is not milled. Park St. PSB01 1708 F700 Phase 3.2 (V).

9.6.108. Stem fragment of *c.*1660–1730 with an unburnished surface and a stem bore of 5/64". The stem has a gritty fabric and the edges of the thicker end have been slightly smoothed after the stem was broken. Park St. PSB01 Eval. Tr. 3 1015.

9.7.109. Fragment of *c.*1690–1730 with an average burnish on its surface and a stem bore of 5/64". The rim has been bottered and milled. The fabric colour and thickness of the stem in this example are similar to those of a stem decorated using a roll stamp of diagonal lines from the same context (similar to that shown in Fig. 9.5.83) and it is possible that this is the bowl from the same pipe. Park St. PSB01 1634 F5510/ F542 Phase 3.3 (E).

9.7.10. Fragment of *c.*1690–1720 with an average burnish on its surface and a stem bore of 5/64". The rim has been

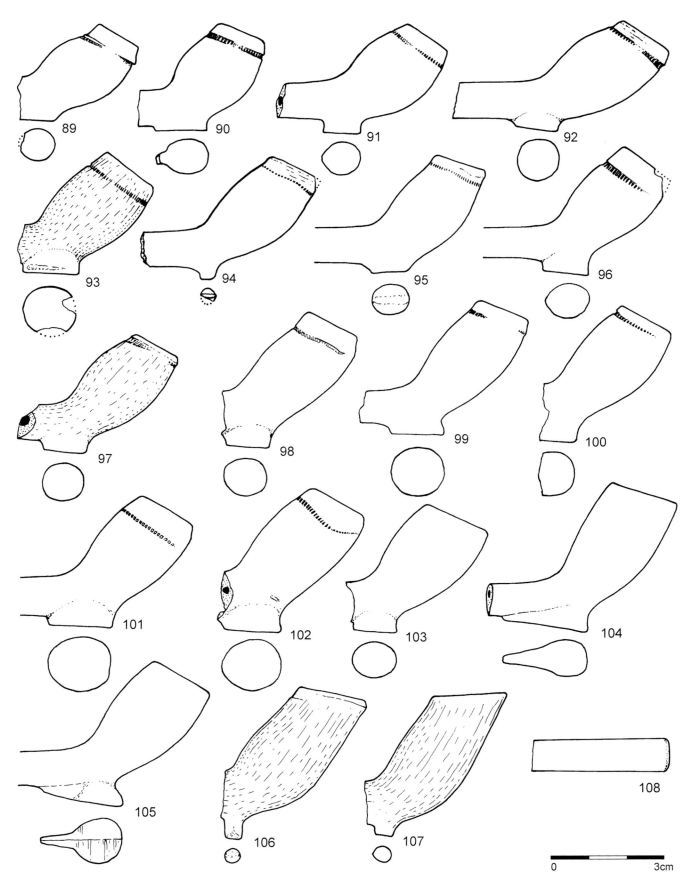

Fig. 9.6 Clay pipe, catalogue nos 89–108.

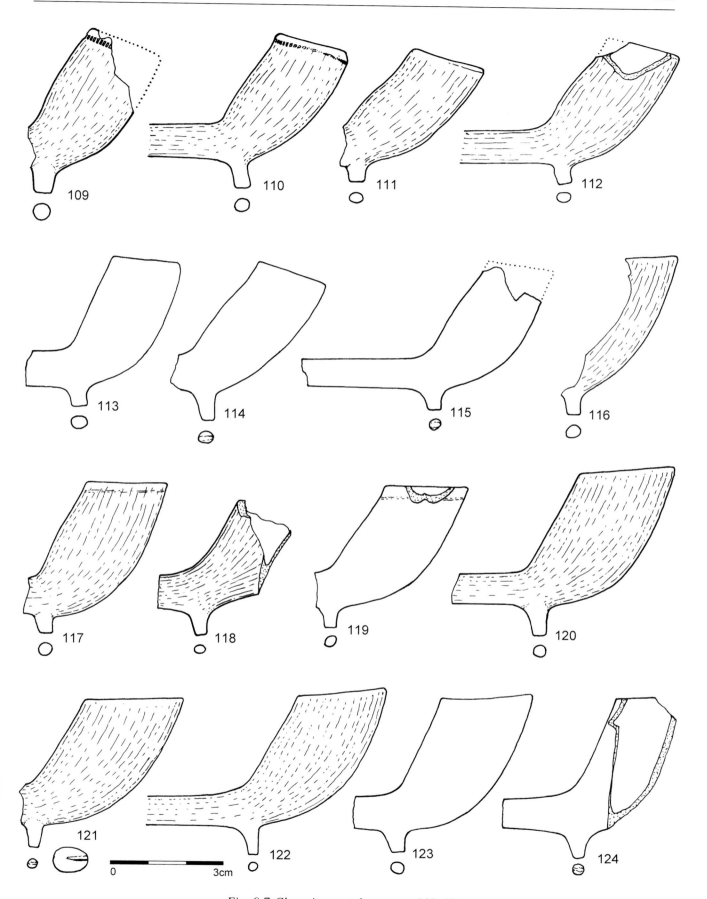

Fig. 9.7 Clay pipe, catalogue nos 109–124.

bottered and is half milled. PSB01 Eval. Tr. 3 1015 (J).

9.7.111. Fragment of *c.*1690–1720 with a good burnish on its surface and a stem bore of 5/64". The rim has been internally trimmed and wiped but it has not been milled. Park St. PSB01 1738 cleaning Phase 4/5 (M).

9.7.112. Fragment of *c.*1710–1740 with a good burnish on its surface and a stem bore of 5/64". The rim has been wiped but it has not been milled. Park St. PSB01 1101 cleaning Phase 4/5 (AE).

9.7.113. Fragment of *c.*1700–1740 with an unburnished surface and a stem bore of 5/64". The rim has been internally trimmed and bottered but it has not been milled. The base of the spur has been trimmed. Park St. PSB01 1521 F503/ F520 Phase 3.3.

9.7.114. Fragment of *c.*1700–1740 with an unburnished surface and a stem bore of 5/64". The rim has been bottered but it has not been milled. Park St. PSB01 1125 F133 Phase 3.2 (C).

9.7.115. Composite drawing of two bowl fragments from the same mould, dating from *c.*1710–1760. Both examples have unburnished surfaces and both have narrow stem bores of 4/64". Park St. PSB01 1125 F133 Phase 3.2 (D) and PSB01 1122 F131 Phase 3 (C).

9.7.116. Two joining fragments of *c.*1730–1790 from the same context (fresh break) with an average burnish. The rim has been cut and possibly wiped. Park St. PSB01 1125 F133 Phase 3.2 (E) and (J).

9.7.117. Fragment of *c.*1750–1790 with an average burnish on its surface and a stem bore of 5/64". The rim has been cut and internally trimmed but it has not been milled. Park St. PSB01 1101 cleaning Phase 4/5 (AH).

9.7.118. Fragment of *c.*1720–1780 with an average burnish on its surface and a stem bore of 4/64". The spur has been trimmed. Park St. PSB01 1512 F500 Phase 3.2 (D).

9.7.119. Fragment of *c.*1740–1800 with an unburnished surface and a stem bore of 4/64". The rim has been cut and is not milled. Traces of a mould line visible around the rim show that the mould has been repaired at some point. Park St. PSB01 1512 F500 Phase 3.2 (C).

9.7.120. Fragment of *c.*1750–1790 with an average burnish on its surface and a stem bore of 5/64". The rim has been cut and internally trimmed but it has not been milled. Spur trimmed. Park St. PSB01 over 1621 F510/ F542 Phase 3.3.

9.7.121. Fragment of *c.*1750–1790 with an average burnish on its surface and a stem bore of 5/64". The rim has been cut and internally trimmed but it has not been milled. Park St. PSB01 1621 F510/ F542 Phase 3.3 (C).

9.7.122. Fragment of *c.*1750–1790 with an average burnish on its surface and a stem bore of 5/64". The rim has been cut and internally trimmed but it has not been milled. Park St. PSB01 1634 F510/ F542 Phase 3.3 (G).

9.7.123. Fragment of *c.*1750–1790 with an unburnished surface and a stem bore of 4/64". The rim has been cut and internally trimmed but it has not been milled. The spur has been trimmed. Park St. PSB01 1621 F510/ F542 Phase 3.3 (B).

9.7.124. Fragment of *c.*1760–1840 with an unburnished surface and a stem bore of 5/64". The rim has possibly been wiped but it has not been milled. Park St. PSB01 B 1506 F505 Phase 3.3 (C).

9.8.125. Fragment from a well group of *c.*1820–40 with an unburnished surface and a stem bore of 5/64". The rim has been cut and is not milled. There are marks inside the bowl cavity (but not a regular cross or star pattern) that appear to have been created by deliberate marks on the stopper. Edgbaston St. BRB99 1026 Well F111 Phase 4 (E).

9.8.126. Bowl and joining stem fragment from a well group of *c.*1820–40 with an unburnished surface and a stem bore of 5/64". The rim has been cut and is not milled. This is one of four bowls from the same mould recovered from this context, another of which was also recovered from Context 1007. There is line visible near rim on the left hand side suggesting that the mould has been repaired. Edgbaston St. BRB99 1026 Well F111 Phase 4 (D).

9.8.127. Fragment of *c.*1820–1880 with an unburnished surface and a stem bore of 4/64". The rim has been cut and is not milled. The mould seams have been very poorly trimmed. Edgbaston St. BRB97 U/S.

9.8.128. Two joining fragments of *c.*1820–1860 with an unburnished surface and a stem bore of 4/64". The rim has been cut and is not milled. Traces of a mould line visible near rim indicate that mould may have been altered or repaired. Fairly crudely executed decoration on the bowl seams and a similar decorative motif on each side of the bowl. The pipe has been heavily smoked. Park St. PSB01 1139 F138 Phase 4 (G).

9.8.129. Two joining fragments of *c.*1810–1840 with an unburnished surface and a stem bore of 5/64". The rim has been cut and is not milled. The bowl has been very highly burnt resulting in slight a cracking and warping of the bowl together with slaggy concretions adhering its surface. Simply executed decoration on the seams and both sides of the bowl, apparently representing ears of corn (the same motif occurs on both sides). Park St. PSB01 1101 cleaning Phase 4/5 (F).

9.8.130. Fragment of *c.*1810–1850 with an unburnished surface and a stem bore of 4/64". The rim has been cut and is not milled. The bowl seams are decorated with simply executed leaves. Edgbaston St. BRB97 Tr. B 5200. demolition debris Transect B Phase 4.

9.8.131. Fragment of *c.*1820–1850 with an unburnished surface and a stem bore of 5/64". The rim has been cut and is not milled. The bowl seams are decorated with quite narrow leaves and there is a fairly crudely executed design on either side of the bowl representing nationalistic emblems of the British Isles. The left-hand side has a thistle in the centre with a rose leaf growing to its left and a shamrock leaf to its right. The right-hand side of the bowl depicts a rose. Edgbaston St. BRB97 Transect A 5108 lower fill of brick culvert.

9.8.132. Fragment of *c.*1820–1880 with an unburnished surface and a stem bore of 4/64". The rim has been cut and is not milled. Park St. PSB01 1101 cleaning Phase 4/5 (E).

9.8.133. Fragment of *c.*1820–1860 with an unburnished surface and a stem bore of 4/64". The rim has been cut and is not milled. Edgbaston St. BRB97 Transect A 5107 upper fill of brick culvert (D).

9.8.134. Bowl from a long-stemmed or 'churchwarden' type of pipe, of a type produced from *c.*1800–1960 (although this example came from a group most likely to date from *c.*1850–70). The bowl has an unburnished surface and a stem bore of 4/64". The rim has been cut and internally

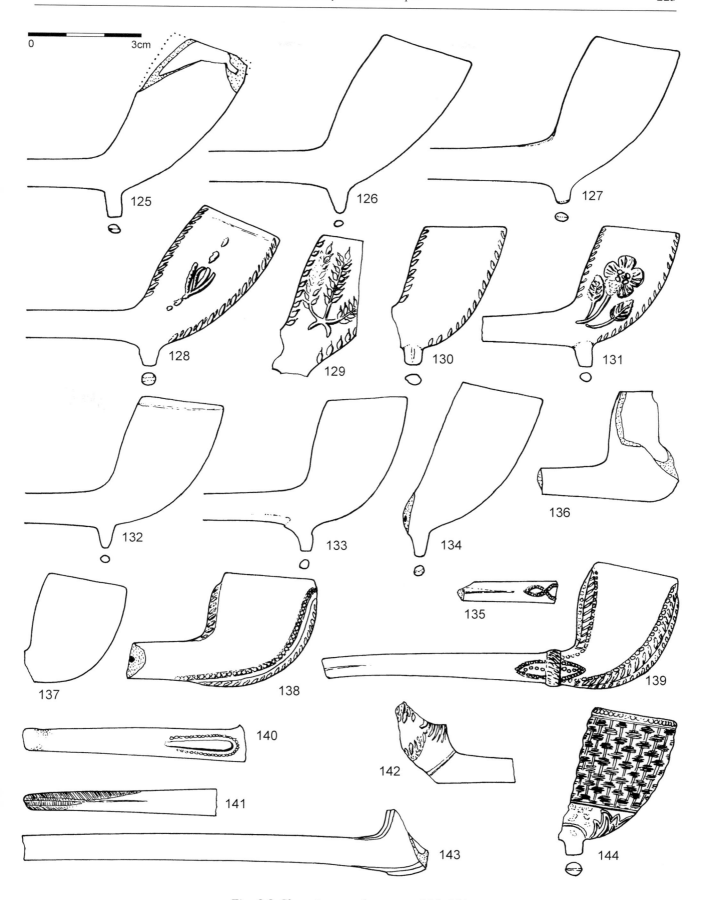

Fig. 9.8 Clay pipe, catalogue nos 125–144.

trimmed but it has not been milled. Most likely a product from Broseley. Park St. PSB01 1771 F836 Phase 4 (J).

9.8.135. Fragment from a deposit most likely dating from *c.*1850–70 (but this style produced *c.*1850–1910) with an unburnished surface and a stem bore of 4/64". There is part of a relief moulded beaded border on each side of the stem but no lettering survives. Park St. 1771 F836 Phase 4.

9.8.136. Fragment from a deposit most likely dating from *c.*1850–70 (but this style produced of *c.*1850–1910) with an unburnished surface and a stem bore of 4/64". The rim has been cut and is not milled. Park St. PSB01 1771 F836 Phase 4 (L).

9.8.137. Fragment from a deposit most likely dating from *c.*1850–70 (but this style produced of *c.*1850–1910) with an unburnished surface and a stem bore of 4/64". The rim has been cut and is not milled. Park St. PSB01 1771 F836 Phase 4 (K).

9.8.138. Fragment from a deposit most likely dating from *c.*1850–70 (but this style produced of *c.*1850–1910) with an unburnished surface and a stem bore of 5/64". The rim has been cut and is not milled. Same mould as bowl F from the same context. Park St. PSB01 1771 F836 Phase 4 (E).

9.8.139. Composite drawing of two fragments from a deposit most likely dating from *c.*1850–70 (but this style of pipe produced of *c.*1850–1910), both of which have an unburnished surface and a stem bore of 4/64". The rim has been cut and is not milled in the complete bowl (A). Two other fragments of pipes from the same mould were recovered from this context (C and D). Park St. PSB01 1771 F836 Phase 4 (A) and (B).

9.8.140. Stem fragment from a deposit most likely dating from *c.*1850–70 (but this style produced from *c.*1850–1910)

with an unburnished surface and a stem bore of 5/64". The same context produced a fragment of bowl decorated with a basket-weave pattern, which may possibly have come from this pipe. The broken stem end is of interest because it has become lightly rounded and has teeth marks where the pipe has clearly been reused in a broken state. Park St. PSB01 1771 F836 Phase 4.

9.8.141. Stem fragment from a deposit most likely dating from *c.*1850–70 (but this style produced from *c.*1850–1910) with an unburnished surface and a stem bore of 4/64". The stem originally terminated in a flattened, oval section, mouthpiece but this appears to have become chipped and the stem ground against a fairly coarse abrasive surface to produce a smoothed end for reuse. This re-working has produced a rather faceted and lop-sided end to the stem. Park St. PSB01 1771 F836 Phase 4.

9.8.142. Fragment from a deposit most likely dating from *c.*1850–70 (but this style produced from *c.*1820–1880) with an unburnished surface and a stem bore of 5/64". The bowl has been mould decorated in the form of a bearded man's head. Park St. PSB01 1771 F836 Phase 4 (I).

9.8.143. Fragment of *c.*1840–1900 from a long-stemmed pipe with an unburnished surface and a stem bore of 4/64". The bowl clearly had plain moulded ribs running up its seams. Park St. PSB01 1827 rubble within Structure 5a Phase 4.

9.8.144. Fragment of *c.*1850–1910 with an unburnished surface and a stem bore of 4/64". The rim has been cut and is not milled. The bowl has been badly burnt after use resulting in a discoloured surface and some slaggy concretion adhering to the stem break. Park St. PSB01 1871 Disturbed Phase 1 Ditch F799.

10 Metal-working Debris from Park Street

Matthew Nicholas

Historical background

One of the most important brass-related trades carried out in the 17th and 18th centuries involved the production of buckles. The buckle trade was introduced to the Birmingham area in the middle of the 17th century (Hamilton 1926). Fashion can be a brutal master, however, and the industry collapsed quickly in 1790 with the introduction of the 'effeminate shoe string' (Timmins 1866) or 'slovenly ribbon' (Bates 1860, quoting Freeth 1790). Such was the hardship caused by this change in style that in 1791 buckle makers petitioned the Prince of Wales to help the 'more than 20,000 persons who in consequence of the prevalence of shoe strings and slippers' were in dire straits and unemployed (Timmins 1866).

Trade directories can provide useful information about the location of particular industries. One of the earliest detailed directories for Birmingham was compiled at the beginning of the 19th century in 1818 (Wrightson 1869). The 63 brass founders listed in this directory mostly lived to the west, north and east of the city centre. This distribution closely follows the canals, which ring Birmingham's city centre. It is unclear if these industries had been established in these areas for some time or had been attracted by the construction of the canals. The professions listed for Park Street include brass founders and iron smiths.

Research aims and objectives

The research aim was to investigate the remains of medieval and later industrial activity.

Industrial activity was fundamental to the late medieval and post-medieval growth of the town yet little is known about the detail of specific industries. The Park Street assemblage offers an important opportunity to investigate post-medieval metal working in Birmingham during the start of its great expansion. The main objective was to determine the sorts of copper alloys that were being cast.

Visual assessment

A total of 92kg of material labelled as slag was visually assessed, noting its morphology, colour and weight using the principles and systems set out in Bayley *et al.* (2001). If required, qualitative X-ray fluorescence analysis (EDXRF) was carried out. Table 10.1 shows a breakdown of the results of the visual assessment (the full list is in Appendix 10.1).

Some types of slag are visually diagnostic, providing unambiguous evidence for a specific metallurgical process. Other debris is less distinctive and it is not possible to say from which metallurgical, or other high temperature process, it derives.

Explanation of slag classification

The diagnostic slag from Park Street comprised only a small percentage of the assemblage. However, this did include clear evidence of iron smithing (*i.e.* hot working) and copper alloy melting. There was no definite evidence that iron, or any other metal, had been smelted (reduced from the ore) on the site. As most of the diagnostic slag was produced by iron smithing, it is likely that the majority of the undiagnostic iron-working slag was also a by-product of smithing. Many pieces of slag and many of the smithing hearth bottoms contained varying sized fragments of coal, which must have been the fuel. Tap and run slag have a distinct shape resembling a flow of lava, and are a product of smelting. So little is present that it is not indicative of smelting on site. Vitrified hearth lining is clay from the hearth structure that has been exposed to high temperatures.

Smithing hearth bottoms have a distinctive shape, plano-convex to concavo-convex in section and circular or oval in plan. Sometimes (as is the case for Park Street) the upper surface has a depression produced by the air blast from the blowing hole. Hearth bottoms are the slag that collects in the base of the smith's hearth; they are unlikely to be confused with the waste products of smelting and are therefore considered to be diagnostic of iron smithing.

Hammerscale (see Appendix 10.2) is evidence of smithing and is produced when the oxidised surface of a hot iron object is struck. Concentrations of hammerscale can often indicate reasonably accurately where smithing took place on site. The majority of the hammerscale was recovered through environmental samples (mainly 20l soil samples). Floor deposits from within buildings used for iron smithing usually contain at least 10% hammer-

scale (Mills and McDonnell 1992) but the proportion of hammerscale from deposits in Park Street is relatively low.

Over a kilogram of vitrified ceramic material was present (Fig. 10.1, Table. 10.1), and was distinctly different from vitrified hearth lining. It is reduced fired; the outer surface is vitrified and the inner surfaces have up to three parallel indentations approximately 20mm wide. The surviving length is up to 140mm. A number of corners are present suggesting a cuboid structure. The exact function of this material is unknown, but it has been suggested that it may relate to the carburisation of iron objects. This is where iron objects are heated in a bed of charcoal, the carbon then entering the surface of the object and creating a steel shell.

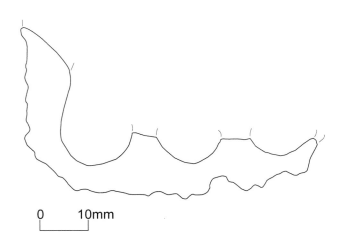

0   10mm

Fig. 10.1 Cross section of vitrified ceramic material.

Interpretation	Weight (g)
Run slag	18
Tap slag	130
Hammerscale	146
Smithing hearth bottoms	8866
Undiagnostic ironworking slag	80493
Vitrified hearth lining	148
Vitrified ceramic material	1375
Copper Slag	897
Vitrified tile	54
Vitrified building debris	460
Pot	2
Total	92589

Table 10.1 Metal-working debris; summary of the slag.

The evidence for copper alloy melting came from slag and vitrified tile as well as from the crucibles (see below). When analysed qualitatively by X-ray fluorescence the slag and tile both showed the presence of copper and zinc. The vitrified tile was probably part of the furnace structure. There was also vitrified building debris in the assemblage submitted for analysis. However, when analysed it was found to contain no copper, zinc or any other element indicative of a metallurgical use.

Spatial analysis

The metallurgical debris is split across the three areas as shown in Table 10.2 (the iron slag category includes smithing hearth bottoms, vitrified hearth lining and non-diagnostic slag). All of the copper alloy slag and the majority of the crucibles were recovered from Area A, whilst most of the iron slag came from Areas B and C. Interestingly, the hammerscale nearly all came from Area A, and was not always associated with iron slag deposits. This suggests that the iron slag was re-deposited in the contexts where it was found.

No industrial features were recorded on the site (with the exception of a kiln of unknown function assigned to Phase 2), and virtually all the metallurgical material came from the fills of the Phase 3 or Phase 4 pits. Pit F769 (Phase 3.2) in Area C was notable because of the large amount of slag and charcoal found in it (pers. comm. Catharine Patrick). As the inclusions within the slag were coal, the charcoal probably came from domestic sources, although the possible use of crushed glass and charcoal as a fluxing agent is noted below (see Discussion of crucible analysis, crucible 92). It is also possible that the charcoal was partially burnt wood rather than true charcoal. There were surprisingly few joins within the crucible assemblage and only a few of the crucibles appear to have failed whilst in the furnace, which suggests that metallurgical debris was not associated with brass founding within the excavated area, although documentary evidence from the trade directories of 1770 and 1781 list a Timothy Smith, brass founder, at No. 4 Park Street (see Rátkai, Chapter 4). It is possible that much of the evidence had been removed or dispersed

with the construction of three courts (Rátkai *ibid.*) in the late 18th and early 19th centuries.

Examination of crucibles (see Appendix 10.3 for catalogue)

A total of 130 fragments weighing a total of 15kg were recovered. Every crucible fragment was examined and weighed and its colour, position within the vessel body (*e.g.* base or rim) and vitrification noted. When a fragment was large enough the external diameter was measured. All were examined to see if any joins existed between the fragments. In total there are 17 base fragments, 41 rim fragments, and 71 side fragments and one possible lid. All the fragments were given a unique catalogue number.

Form

The Park Street crucibles (Fig. 10.2) are very similar to those from assemblages recovered from Legge's Mount, Tower of London (Bayley 1992, fig. 5) and Barnard Castle, County Durham (Bayley and Linton 1982). These crucibles tend to be deeper than they are wide; the walls are thick and near vertical or with a slight flare. Some of the rim fragments include a pinched-out lip. All the bases present are flat; in one case, crucible No. 29 (1634) F510/ F542 Phase 3.3, an entire base is preserved with no sides. That the crucibles were used in the melting and casting of copper alloys was confirmed by qualitative EDXRF. In a couple of instances, crucible Nos 45 (1167) F154 Phase 4 and 124 (1176) F159/ F138 Phase 4, the fragments contained layers of slag over 10mm thick. Large proportions of the crucibles show evidence of being wheel-thrown, as would be expected for this period (Bayley 1992, 5).

Not all the crucibles are of the deep, thick-walled style. Some sherds, *e.g.* crucible No. 25 (1708) F700 Phase 3.2, appear very similar to the thinner-walled crucibles also from Legge's Mount (Bayley 1992, fig. 6), including a similar style of pulled lip. There are no base fragments of this type present, but if they are similar to those from Legge's Mount, we could expect them to have a 'flower-pot' shape, everted walls and a flat base (Bayley 1992, 5).

	A	**B**	**C**
Crucibles (g)	12140	2087	857
Iron slag (g)	20013	9187	60939
Vitrified ceramic (g)	0	0	1375
Hammerscale (g)	121	25	0
Copper alloy slag (g)	897	0	0
Total (g)	33284	11312	63171

Table 10.2 Metal-working debris; distribution of types by weight across areas.

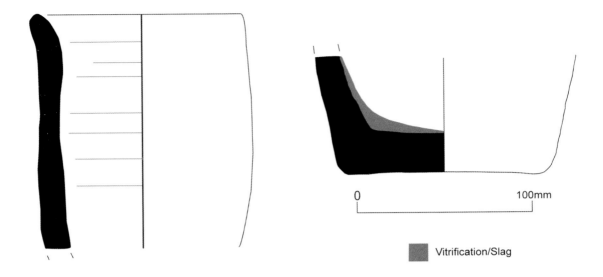

Fig. 10.2 Two sketches of typical crucibles from Park Street.

These also appear to be wheel-thrown.

Figure 10.3 shows a histogram of the wall thickness. The distribution appears to be bimodal; this is probably a reflection of the variability in wall thickness with height above the base (see Fig. 10.2). The outliers below the main group represent the thin-walled crucibles.

Figure 10.4 shows a histogram of diameters. The majority of crucibles have a diameter of 100–160mm. Those with small diameters are the thin-walled crucibles, with the exception of crucible No. 29, a complete base with no walls, which has the smallest diameter of all.

Fabric

The fabric of the crucibles appeared to be extremely uniform although there is a considerable variation in colour. Some pieces are a light brown whilst at the other end of the spectrum is a strong purple; the colour change usually occurs from the outside in, with darker colours towards the outside. This variability in appearance is likely to be a consequence of the differing amounts of usage each crucible had received at the time of its failure and/ or discard. A majority of the crucibles showed at least the beginning signs of some vitrification (where the heating of the crucible fabric has reached a point where the outer layers begin to change to a glassy or vitreous state, see Bayley *et al.* 2001). These crucibles have spent a long time at high temperatures.

In crucible No. 124, fused within the deposit on the inner surface, are two small lumps of coal. This implies that coal was being used as the fuel. With a few exceptions, *e.g.* crucible No. 88 (1176) F159/ F138 Phase 4, none of the crucibles appear to have failed whilst in the furnace. The vast majority of the breaks appear clean, suggesting that deposition occurred shortly after they were broken.

Selection of crucibles for analysis

Twenty-two fragments were analysed; 15 from Area A, two from Area B and five from Area C. It was hoped that the analysis would identify the alloys being melted so preference was given to fragments more likely to give positive results, such as those containing slag, which could potentially contain metallic droplets.

Sample preparation and method of analysis

Before sampling occurred, a digital photograph was taken of the inside, outside and edge of each crucible fragment. Samples were taken using a rock saw, then mounted in resin and polished to a 1-micron finish. Before carbon coating it was noted that two samples (crucible Nos 45 and 26) contained what appeared to be metallic droplets visible to the naked eye.

Examination and analyses were carried out using a scanning electron microscope (Leo Stereoscan 440) in backscatter mode. This provides an atomic number contrast image, allowing metallic droplets to be easily identified from the surrounding vitrified layers. The compositions of the crucibles, vitrified layers and metal droplets within the vitrified layers were determined using an energy dispersive spectrometer (with Germanium detector) attached to the scanning electron microscope. The spectra were collected at 25kV and 1.5nA for 50 seconds livetime and calibrated with a cobalt standard. The spectra were quantified using the Oxford Instruments SEMQuant software (ZAF correction procedure). Metal droplets were analysed using a small area (typically 10 by 20 microns). Some of these droplets had suffered from post-depositional corrosion; this could be seen in the levels of oxygen, sulphur and/ or chlorine detected. The results reported here include only those droplets which

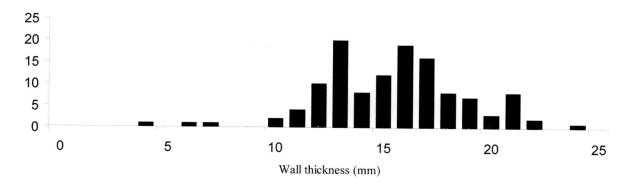

Fig. 10.3 Histogram of crucible wall thickness.

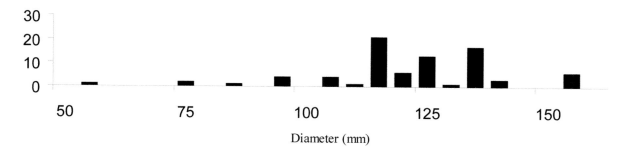

Fig. 10.4 Histogram of crucible diameters.

had suffered no post-depositional corrosion (Table 10.3). For the vitrified layers and crucible fabrics larger areas were analysed (typically 100 by 200 microns). The composition of the vitrified layers and crucible fabrics were calculated stoichiometrically as oxides. This involves making some assumptions about the oxidation state of some of the metals (*e.g.* iron). The vitrified layers and crucible fabrics displayed variable amounts of porosity and so the analytical results for these areas tended to give low totals (Table 10.4). To aid comparison between different vitrified layers and areas of crucible, the results were normalised to 100%. Other analytical work with this equipment and following the same procedures (*e.g.* Dungworth 2002) indicates that the results are accurate to within ±0.5% for minor elements or oxides (present but below ~5%) and ±1–2% for major elements or oxides.

Crucible No. 92 (1125) F133 Phase 3.2 was investigated in great detail in order to help establish analytical procedures for the others. Each crucible was analysed and recorded systematically. First the inner and outer sides of the sample were investigated for metallic droplets, then inner and outer vitrified layers, and lastly the fabric.

Discussion of crucible analyis

Vitrified layers and fabric
(see Appendices 10.5–10.7 for results)

As a case study, a detailed analysis was carried out across crucible No. 92 (Appendix 10.7). A series of small areas (typically 100–200 microns) was analysed across the width of the crucible between the inner and outer vitrified layers.

The inner vitrified surface of crucible No. 92, and also Nos 26 (1888) F810 Phase 3.1; 24 (1825) F769 Phase 3.2; 46 (1133) F139 Phase 4; 95 (1125) F133 Phase 3.2; and 118 (1133) F139 Phase 4, contained an unexpectedly high amount of soda. Figure 10.5 shows a plot of crucible No. 92; the inner vitrification has a high soda content that disappears once inside the fabric. This suggests the possibility that crushed glass was being used as a flux in combination with charcoal in order to prevent zinc diffusion (Higgins 1974). Indeed, many of the deposits inside the crucibles visually looked more like glass than slag.

Figure 10.6 shows the variation of copper and zinc throughout the fabric of crucible No. 92, from inner to outer vitrification. Zinc, as is discussed below, is highly

	Fe	Ni	Cu	Zn	As	Sn	Sb	Pb
MDL	<0.1	<0.1	<0.1	<0.1	<0.5	<0.5	<0.5	<0.5
Error	±0.1	±0.1	±0.1	±0.2	±0.2	±0.4	±0.4	±0.4

Table 10.3 Metal-working debris; minimum detection limits and errors for the metal droplets.

	Na$_2$O	MgO	Al$_2$O$_3$	SiO$_2$	P$_2$O$_5$	SO$_3$	K$_2$O	CaO
MDL	<1.0	<0.4	<0.5	<0.5	<0.2	<0.2	<0.2	<0.2
Error	±0.1	±0.5	±0.5	±0.5	±0.3	±0.3	±0.2	±0.3

	TiO$_2$	MnO$_2$	Fe$_2$O$_3$	CuO	ZnO	SnO$_2$	PbO
MDL	<0.2	<0.2	<0.2	<0.2	<0.2	<0.5	<0.5
Error	±0.1	±0.1	±0.1	±0.1	±0.1	±0.3	±0.5

Table 10.4 Metal-working debris; minimum detection limits and error for the fabric and vitrified layers.

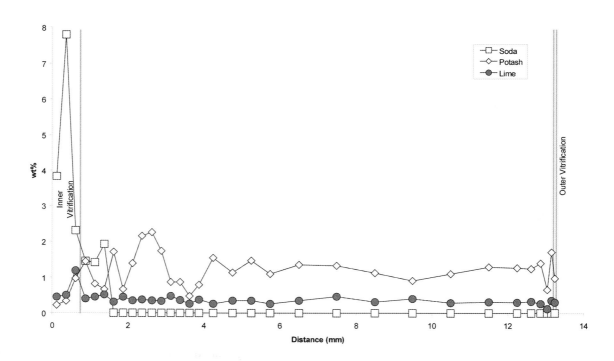

Fig. 10.5 Variation in composition across the thickness of crucible No. 92.

volatile so it is to be expected that crucibles used for brass would, on analysis, contain zinc, the amount decreasing steadily from inside to outside. This contrasts strongly with copper alloy working crucibles from Housesteads Roman Fort (Dungworth 2001), where the zinc had not diffused into the fabric as had been expected. Most likely this is due to different patterns of use. The Park Street crucibles were probably constantly in use while the crucibles from Housesteads would have had nowhere near the same frequency of employment.

For the crucibles as a whole, zinc is the metallic element most consistently present in the inner vitrified layers (average [mean] 12.3% ZnO). This is as to be expected due to zinc's high volatility; it has a boiling point of 907°C compared to copper's melting point of 1084°C. By the time copper has melted, zinc will be a

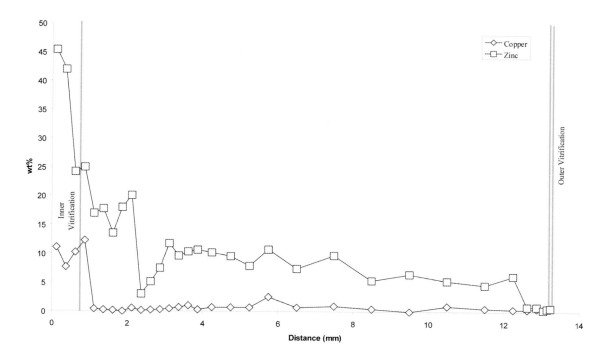

Fig. 10.6 Metal content across the thickness of crucible No. 92.

gas. Zinc is also more readily oxidised than copper, tin or lead (Dungworth 2000, table 2) and can act as glass-forming element, chemically binding it into the vitrified layer (pers. comm. J. Bayley).

The fabric of the majority of the crucibles is relatively uniform. Alumina is present at 23–30%, silica within the range of 62–70%. These high proportions ensure the fabric is refractory enough (can withstand high temperatures without vitrification; see Bayley *et al.* 2001) for use in a furnace. Other oxides that are consistently present are titania (TiO_2, approx. 1–1.5%), a trace of lime (CaO) and potash (K_2O), and approximately 2% iron oxide (Fe_2O_3). The best way of identifying an unusual fabric was when the titania dipped below 1%.

There was no clear evidence to help identify the reason for the purple coloration within the fabric. It is likely to be the product of a redox reaction possibly involving iron and manganese, but it is impossible to say using this analytical method as it provides no direct evidence for the oxidation state of elements present.

The vitrified surfaces of crucible No. 24 contained significant amounts of lead (inner 31.3%, outer 15.9%) and tin (inner 15%). There was no copper or zinc present. The composition of the vitrified surfaces of this crucible would have been fully molten at around 700°C (Molera *et al.* 1999) and so the crucible is unlikely to have been heated above this temperature. All this suggests that pewter was being melted.

Metallic droplets (see Appendix 10.4 for results)

Nine crucibles produced a total of 51 uncorroded droplets. The analyses can be divided into three categories: copper, brasses and gunmetals. There is considerable variation and overlapping within this classification.

The samples categorised as 'copper' contained between 95 and 98.9% copper and less than 1% of any other element. The majority of these droplets came from crucible No. 45 (1167) F154 Phase 4, and there were no droplets of any other composition from this sample. There are two possibilities: the metal once contained zinc and/ or tin/ antimony/ lead but this has been preferentially oxidised and hence lost, or the crucibles were sometimes used for melting unalloyed copper. On analysis, the slag in crucible No. 45 was found to be rich in zinc, strongly suggesting that the latter is unlikely. Copper alloys, probably some form of brass, were being melted in these crucibles.

The brasses are copper-zinc alloys that contain between 19 and 25% zinc. As has already been indicated, zinc is easily oxidised so there is a possibility that the droplets will have a lower zinc content than that of the brass originally melted (Dungworth 2000).

Gunmetals are copper alloys that contain significant amounts of both zinc and tin. There are three distinct groups within the gunmetals: those that contain antimony, those that contain lead, and those that contain neither (see Table 10.5).

Crucible no.			Fe	Ni	Cu	Zn	As	Sn	Sb	Pb
26	Mean		0.7	0.3	81.7	12.5	0.8	2.8	1.7	
	sd		0.3	0.1	2.2	2.8	0.2	0.9	0.9	
36	Mean		1.3		83.0	8.8		6.9		
	sd		0.1		1.0	1.4		2.5		
46	Mean			0.2	82.9	9.0		5.2		2.7
	sd			0.0	0.7	0.5		0.0		0.6
84	Mean		1.0	0.1	79.8	16.2		3.0		
	sd		0.6		6.3	7.0		1.2		

Table 10.5 Metal-working debris; mean composition and standard deviation for the gunmetals.

The addition of lead lowers the melting point of copper alloys and increases the fluidity (Dungworth 2001), making them easier and more economical to work when casting. Lead also affects the malleability when the alloy is solid and consequently makes it less suited to drawing, rolling and hammering.

The antimony gunmetal droplets all come from crucible No. 26 (1888) F810 Phase 3.1. This crucible had two vitrified layers on the inner surface: one contained the antimony gunmetals whilst the other contained a gunmetal with no antimony, but some lead in its place. In 1866 Samuel Timmins makes reference to a metal called Tutania 'which was said to take its name from one Tutin, the inventor', and was used primarily in the production of shoe buckles. Fleming and Honour (1977) give this definition: 'Tutania. An alloy of copper, calamine [zinc oxide], antimony and tin patented in 1770 by William Tutin whose Birmingham firm (Tutin and Haycroft) produced small domestic articles in it'. However an inquiry with the patent office elicited only one patent (No. 1019) by Mr Tutin in 1772 for a method of varnishing buckles.

The Oxford English Dictionary defines Tutania as being 'an earlier name for Britannia-metal [pewter]'. It then proceeds to give several 'recipes' for its production that contain considerable variation. However Bates (1860) suggests that Tutin's Tutania was originally named Tutinic (its main rival being the Chinese alloy Tutenac, a brass containing nickel). The introduction of Britannia metal from Sheffield led to the renaming of Tutinic to Tutania, enabling it to still indicate its paternity whilst imitating the new arrival.

There is also a Tutania song. Composed by Mr John Freeth (1790), who himself is recorded as a resident of Park Street in Sketchley's 1767 Directory of Birmingham, it is perhaps best viewed as a prototype advertising jingle rather than a work of art, and offers the following insights:

Some for Pinchbeck, some for Plated,
Some for Soft-White, some for Hard,

Everyone is overrated,
With Tutania, when compared.
All to one good soul must truckle,
He that does the rest eclipse,
Makes a Song and forms a Buckle,
Whilst a Pipe's between his Lips.

The 'Soft-White' and 'Hard' are most likely variants of pewter, whilst 'Pinchbeck' is a brass composed of approximately 83% copper and 17% zinc. It is possible that the antimony gunmetal detected in crucible No. 26 is Tutania. However, the pit F810 in which it was found is in Phase 3.1 which would be too early for Tutania. The pit is bereft of clay pipe or other datable finds and contained only residual medieval sherds. The pit did cut another much larger pit F808 securely phased to Phase 3.1 by clay pipe dating to 1650–1730. The quest for new non-ferrous alloys began in the early 18th century, although documentary details are scarce, and it is perhaps against this background that the presence of a metal alloy resembling Tutania in crucible No. 26, should be viewed. Whether antimony was added deliberately or not it, it helps us to define the purpose for which the alloy is used. Antimony increases the tenacity and hardness of copper, but if there is more than 0.2% present the metal will crack at the edges when rolled (Gowland 1921). The alloy that was being produced could therefore not have been intended for any use such as drawing or rolling, but would have been fit for casting purposes only.

Conclusion

The metal-working debris from Park Street represents a broad range of secondary metal working, including iron smithing and the casting of copper alloys. There was no indication of any primary activity, such as the smelting of either iron or copper, on the site. The majority of the crucibles were used in the melting of a range of copper alloys including brass and gunmetals. There were two exceptions, the 'Tutania' of crucible No. 26 and the pewter from crucible No. 24. All of the non-ferrous alloys melted in the Park Street crucibles would have most likely been used in the production of items such as buckles, spoons, buttons, skillets and other small- to medium-sized personal and household goods.

Although the sample is small, gunmetals appear more often in Phase 3.1 and 3.2 (see Appendix 10.4), the one exception being from the Phase 4 pit F139. The greater number of crucible fragments were from Phase 3 contexts and although it is not certainly provable, crucible fragments in Phase 4 features may also be largely residual, since most of the Phase 4 pits containing crucible fragments have a marked residual component in the pottery. However, the rate book of 1845 does list a Thomas Justin or Justen as owner of a smith's shop and

premises in what would be Area A (see Rátkai, Chapter 4).

The vitrified ceramic material recovered from Area C has no published parallels. The most likely suggestion is that it is related to the carburisation of iron objects. No industrial features were recorded on site and there were surprisingly few joins within the crucible assemblage. The suggestion remains that the Park Street metallurgical debris was not associated with iron smithing or brass-founding activity within the excavation area, although the documentary evidence suggests otherwise, but represents dumped or surface scatter material incorporated into later feature fills.

11   Human Bone Report

Rachel Ives

Introduction

Two articulated human burials (F743, F753) were recovered from the northeastern edge of Area C, along with a small quantity of disarticulated bone. The graves were cut through a large sub-circular pit (F746). The burials have been assigned to Phase 1 which has been given a broad medieval date from the 12th–14th centuries. More specifically, the burials cut layers 1761/ 1877 associated with pottery dated to the 13th century but which is likely to be residual (Rátkai, Chapter 7). The small number of burials may indicate the location of a burial ground from which burials had been removed at an earlier date, or alternatively, that burials may still exist under areas that were not disturbed in the archaeological excavations. However, the evidence for either of these is unconvincing (See Burrows *et al.* this volume, Chapter 4) and the two burials remain anomalous.

Medieval human remains were previously excavated from a rural abbey context in Redditch on the outskirts of Birmingham between 1969 and 1973 (Everton 1976) and at Sandwell Priory to the northwest of Birmingham in the Black Country (Flinn 1991). However, the recovery of medieval skeletons from an urban context within the West Midlands has not been a common occurrence. Therefore, the skeletons from Park Street do have some significance. It is of interest to question whether there were differences in health between individuals who lived in urban and rural, as well as between religious and non-religious contexts, in the past. Whilst tentative comparisons can be investigated, the small number of individuals and lack of secure context for the Park Street burials will necessarily limit detailed interpretation. The completeness, preservation and age and sex of each individual were determined together with possible diagnoses for pathological changes observed, and the results are presented in this report.

Methods

The state of bone preservation was graded following Behrensmeyer (1978) and assessment of skeletal completeness followed Buikstra and Ubelaker (1994). An inventory of all skeletal elements present was made. Degenerative changes at the pubic symphysis, auricular surface and sternal rib end determined adult age at death following Buikstra and Ubelaker (1994) and Bass (1995). Epiphyseal bone union was also assessed for individual F753 (Buikstra and Ubelaker 1994). Sex was determined based on the dimorphic aspects of the pelvis and skull (Buikstra and Ubelaker 1994; Bass 1995; Brothwell 1981). Metrical analysis followed Buikstra and Ubelaker (1994) and Brothwell (1981), with stature estimation calculated from long bone length (Trotter and Gleser 1952). Analysis of non-metric traits followed Brothwell (1981). Dental disease was recorded following Buikstra and Ubelaker (1994) and Brothwell (1981), with an assessment of tooth wear following Buikstra and Ubelaker (1994). Cranial and post-cranial pathological changes were also recorded.

Results

The results are summarised in Appendix 11.1 and discussed below.

Age and sex

The excavated remains were determined to be those of a middle-aged probable female (F743) and a young adult probable male (18–22 years) (F753). Both individuals were quite well preserved with the majority of all skeletal elements present. In general little fragmentation had occurred, although the skull of the young male was very broken.

Dental health

The dental health of the middle-aged female (F743) was relatively good, as only two of the large number of teeth present were affected by caries (2/19). In contrast, the majority of the teeth present in the young male (F753) were affected by caries (6/9), and in particular, the crowns of all left mandibular molars were destroyed by severe caries. At the hospital of St Mary's Spital, London, a high prevalence of caries existed in individuals buried in wealthier areas in the cemetery. This may indicate that a richer diet was consumed by wealthier individuals than was available to individuals buried in the main part of the cemetery (see Conheeney 1997, 226). Burials originating from a rural, medieval context from the Midlands, Sandwell Priory, also demonstrated high levels of this dental pathology. At this site both males and females were affected, as 37.5% of females and 30.4% of males with one or more teeth observable demonstrated one or more carious lesions (data determined from Flinn 1991; specific dental prevalence rates are not feasible). Without further evidence of the social, economic or religious status of the burials from Park Street, it is difficult to draw on any specific causative factor for the dental pathology, and a recent survey by Roberts and Cox (2003, 265) determined that caries and poor dental health frequently affected individuals during the medieval period in Britain.

Further evidence of poor dental hygiene and health was evident in the Park Street individuals, with moderate levels of calculus present throughout the dentition (see Appendix 11.1). High levels of calculus were reported in the Sandwell Priory burials (Flinn 1991), and were also consistently identified at St Mary's Spital, London, including examples on the teeth of young adults, similar to those of individual F753 from Park Street. As Conheeney (1997, 226) discusses, sugar was not common in the medieval diet. However, natural sugars found for example in honey, consumed together with a carbohydrate rich diet and combined with generally poor levels of oral hygiene, are factors likely to have resulted in poor dental health (Conheeney 1997, 225, 226; Roberts and Cox 2003, 243, 256).

Dental enamel defects were present in the Park Street dentition. The female skeleton (F743) displayed two teeth affected by both moderately severe linear and pit enamel defects (2/18 teeth affected). In contrast, the male skeleton (F753) displayed a large number of such markers in all but one of the remaining teeth (5/6 teeth affected). Whilst the etiology of these enamel defects is not certain, they are attributed to periods of non-specific 'stress' as a result of illness or nutritional inadequacy during childhood (Hillson 1996). The large number of defects apparent in the teeth of the young male suggests that a severe health insult, or a number of repeated insults, affected this individual during childhood. These findings are of interest as Duncan (2000, discussed in Roberts and Cox 2003,

279) found medieval British males to have had an inferior level of general health during childhood compared to females, manifest in part as a higher rate of enamel hypoplasia defects. Future analyses of medieval remains to compare such prevalences between the sexes are required to better understand the consistency of such trends. Extensive tooth wear was present in individual F743, with prominent cusp removal and large amounts of dentine exposure. Tooth wear in the young male was moderate compared to skeleton F743, as expected given the age difference. The extensive wear in the female is likely to be reflective of the quality of the diet at this time. Flinn (1991) noted high levels of tooth wear present in the sample from Sandwell Priory and attributed this to a diet containing coarse breads made from stone ground flour.

Pathology

A number of large Schmorl's nodes were present throughout the thoracic and lumbar vertebrae (T6–T8, T10–L3) of skeleton F753. These defects are attributable to displacement of the intervertebral disc, which penetrates into the vertebral body. Whilst these insults can become common in older individuals, presence in a young adult may be an indication of trauma or strain in the back and could indicate that this individual took part in some heavy manual labour. Degenerative joint disease in the spine was relatively common in the individuals observed from Sandwell Priory, but without Schmorl's nodes (Flinn 1991; calculation of prevalence data is not feasible). These changes may indicate a reaction to physical activity at the latter site, as was likely to have been undertaken in a rural setting, but are also likely to be a feature of the generally older age of the sample studied.

A small patch of focal, well-remodelled and striated periosteal new bone formation on the right tibia of the young male from Park Street is indicative of a minor trauma or infection, which resulted in localised inflammation (see Roberts and Manchester 2005, 172). Increased physical activity during manual labour could have resulted in minor trauma to the shin, and such lesions may have been exacerbated by a diet relatively low in ascorbic acid (vitamin C), which is necessary for wound healing (Mays 1991). The female from Park Street also exhibited a small (6mm by 6mm) round, button or ivory osteoma, a benign tumour, on the right-hand side of the frontal bone 3.4cm above the right orbit.

Disarticulated bone

A small amount of disarticulated bone was recovered from the site. This included a fragment of flat animal bone associated with burial F743. Context 1760 in Area C yielded a small number of human metatarsals (left 2nd, 3rd and 4th) and two middle phalanges, all quite weathered and broken. Human bone was also found in context 1780 from Area C and comprised a left talus and a fragment of left 5th metatarsal, both quite damaged.

Summary

Although the excavations at Park Street, Birmingham, only yielded two articulated skeletons, they have presented an interesting insight into medieval life in the city. The young male clearly suffered challenges to his health during childhood but survived to later develop poor dental health patterns similar to the older female and to other medieval individuals. The young male displayed evidence of minor trauma in the spine and tibia, which could indicate that he was involved in manual labour at some stage in his life. The older female also displayed poor dental health most likely related to diet and poor dental hygiene, as well as a childhood health insult, although this was markedly less severe than the male's.

12   The Plant Macroremains – Evidence of Domestic and Industrial Activities at Edgbaston Street, Moor Street, Park Street and The Row

Marina Ciaraldi

Introduction

The archaeological investigations at the four sites of Edgbaston Street, Moor Street, Park Street and 'The Row' offered a unique opportunity to examine aspects of the urban development of medieval and post-medieval Birmingham. This report looks at the plant remains recovered from the four excavations and discusses their contribution to the reconstruction of the urban environment and the industrial and domestic activities carried out in various parts of the town.

Although the archaeological evidence from the four excavations covers a period of eight centuries, from the 12th century to the 20th century, the plant assemblages discussed here were recovered exclusively from deposits of Phase 1 (12th–14th century), Phase 2 (15th–16th century) and Phase 3 (17th–18th century).

The research questions which shaped the sampling strategy during the excavation and the assessment of the biological remains (Ciaraldi 2002a and 2002b; Hall 2002; W. Smith 2002) are highlighted below and will be explored in detail in this report.

Sampling strategy and methodology

The excavation of the sites occurred at different times over a period of three years. This allowed the design of a sampling strategy that could take into account the preliminary results from earlier excavations. Such preliminary results provided useful guidance not only on the types of human activities carried out at the various sites but also on the preservation of the organic remains. Both waterlogged and charred biological remains were encountered on all three sites. Waterlogged remains were generally well preserved and often associated with ditches, watercourses or other deep features. Charred

deposits were rarer and their distribution often limited to particular areas of the excavations.

The priority research objectives addressed by the sampling strategy adopted for the four sites were as follows:

- determine the nature of the industrial processes and domestic or agricultural activities that took place on site during the medieval and post-medieval periods
- analyse the spatial patterning of the activities through time
- establish the presence of water on site and the general management of water resources in relation to the activities that took place
- reconstruct the environment surrounding the sites during their occupation.

This approach was implemented particularly during the excavation at Park Street as this was the last of the sites to be investigated and was the site from which the widest range of archaeological deposits was uncovered.

The archaeological features encountered during the excavation of the four sites included complex structures such as tanning pits, wood-lined tanks and kilns, together with ditches, pond-like features, pits and post-holes. These were sampled by considering how and whether the organic remains could best answer the research objectives highlighted above. Particular care was paid to avoid the sampling of deposits that were disturbed by later activity.

Samples of 20 litres were collected from non-waterlogged deposits, while samples of 30 litres were taken from waterlogged deposits. Smaller features, such as post-holes, were sampled entirely. The total number of samples collected from the three excavations was distributed between the sites as follows: 37 samples from Edgbaston Street, 22 samples from Moor Street, and 99 samples from Park Street. Waterlogged wood for dendrochronology and samples for residue analysis were also taken. Deeply stratified deposits (*e.g.* ditch fills) and large features (*e.g.* the wood-lined tanks) were generally multi-sampled. Kubiena tins were used to sample sections and to obtain sub-samples to reconstruct the pollen sequences. The criteria used to select the samples from the various excavations have been discussed in greater detail in the relevant assessment reports (Ciaraldi 2002a and 2002b; Hall 2002; W. Smith 2002).

Soil samples were processed according to the state of preservation of the biological remains present in the deposits. Most of the samples had a sandy matrix which facilitated easy processing, whereas some had a silty clayey matrix which hampered processing. The latter samples had to be soaked in a solution of hydrogen sodium carbonate and warm water before they could be processed further. Samples that were immediately identifiable as non-waterlogged were floated with a York flotation machine (indicated with 'f' in Tables 12.1–12.6). A sub-sample of one litre was taken from water-logged samples. This was wet sieved on a set of sieves, respectively with a 0.3mm, 0.5mm and 1mm mesh (indicated with 'ws' in Tables 12.1–12.6). The flots and the different waterlogged fractions were then sorted under a low-magnification stereomicroscope. The residue from the flotation was sorted by eye and scanned with a magnet in order to recover hammerscale (see Nicholas this volume).

The plant remains were identified with the help of the author's reference collection. Dr James Greig helped with some of the identifications, particularly with that of coral necklace (*Illicebrum verticillatum* L.). The Latin nomenclature follows Zohary and Hopf (2000) for the cereals and Stace (2000) for wild plants. Due to the limited time and resources available, the identification of fragments of hemp reed was undertaken only with the help of the stereomicroscope, which limited the accuracy of the identification.

Edgbaston Street

At Edgbaston Street, biological remains were mainly preserved by waterlogging. A few samples contained charred remains but none of these was recommended for further analysis in the assessment report (W. Smith 2002). The almost complete absence of charred remains from this site probably reflects its predominantly non-domestic nature.

The samples examined (Table 12.1) were collected from deposits belonging to Phases 1 and 3. Three types of context were represented: tanning pits ('TP'), organic layers ('OL'), and the primary fill of the watercourse ('WC').

The samples selected as having a good potential for the interpretation of the site were chosen mainly on the basis of the context type rather than the richness of the plant assemblage present (W. Smith 2002; Hall 2002).

Indeed, most of the samples yielded only small assemblages, even after larger than normal sub-samples were processed.

The watercourse vegetation

Samples 5043, 5401, 5110, 5402 and 5051 were collected from the lower or primary fills of the watercourse intercepted in Transects A–D of the excavation. All these samples were assigned to Phase 1. The watercourse ran approximately along the line of the later Smithfield Passage and joined the Lord of the Manor's Moat with the Parsonage Moat.

The five samples contained very similar taxa (Table 12.1). These included species typically found in ditches and watercourses, such as crowfoots (*Ranunculus* sp. subgen. BATRACHIUM), toad-rush (*Juncus bufonius* L.), sweet grass (*Glyceria* sp.), bristle club-rush (*Isolepis setacea* R.Br.), rushes (*Juncus* sp.) and club-rushes (*Scirpus* sp.). They also included numerous species typical of damp habitats, such as buttercups (*Ranunculus flammula/ reptans* and R. *bulbous/ acris/ repens*), bog stitchwort (*Stellaria uliginosa* Murray), ragged robin (*Lychnis flos-cuculi* L.), water pepper (*Persicaria hydropiper* Spach), pale persicaria (*Persicaria lapathifolium* L.) and sedges (*Carex* sp.). These represent the vegetation which grew in and around the watercourse or in waterlogged areas of the site.

A group of species typical of open/ disturbed habitats also appeared in the assemblage from the watercourse, including species such as brambles (*Rubus* sp.), common nettle (*Urtica dioica* L.), hemlock (*Conium maculatum* L.) and elder (*Sambucus nigra* L.). This group of plants is typical of urban areas where human activities are carried out.

Finally, the presence of bud scales of willow (*Salix* sp.) suggested the presence of this tree amongst the waterside vegetation. The tree boles identified during excavation support the presence of trees along this stretch of the watercourse.

The plant remains recovered from the watercourse deposits closely resemble those identified from some of the waterlogged deposits at Park Street (see below).

The tanning pits

Samples from the tanning pits were collected from deposits assigned to Phase 1 (F218/ 2087), Phase 2 (F209/ 2012), and Phase 3 (F338/ 3097, F300/ 3004, F323/ 3065, F325/ 3072, F347/ 3143 and F320/ 3058). Some of the samples are not listed in Table 12.1 as they contained very few or no plant remains.

The organic remains from Sample F218/ 2087, from a Phase 1 tanning pit (F218/ F232) in Area B, were very different from those found in the other samples from the tanning pits. It contained species mostly from wet and damp habitats similar to those identified in the deposits from the watercourse. Some food plants were also present, such as oats (*Avena* sp.) and hazelnut (*Corylus avellana*

	Area					B	C	C					
	Feature/Context		4032	F427/4063	4031	F218/2087	F338/3097	F320/3058	5043	5401	5110	5402	5051
	Flot / Wet Sieved		ws	ws	ws	ws	ws	ws	ws	ws	ws	ws	ws
	Mesh used (mm)		**0.3**	**0.3**	**0.3**	**0.3**	**0.3**	**0.3**	**0.3**	**0.3**	**0.3**	**0.3**	**0.3**
	Type of context		**OL**	**OL**	**OL**	**TP**	**TP**	**TP**	**WC**	**WC**	**WC**	**WC**	**WC**
	Phase		**1**	**3**	**4**	**2**	**3**	**3**	**1**	**1**	**1**	**1**	**1**
	Cereals												
oats	*Avena* sp.	g				x							
	Nuts												
hazelnut	*Corylus avellana* L	sh				x							
	Weeds – charred												
stinking chamomile	*Anthemis cotula* L.	s				x							
	Weeds – Waterlogged												
crowfoot	*Ranunculus* sp. sbgen. BATRACHIUM	s		x		x					x		
lesser/creeping spearwort	*Ranunculus flammula/reptans*	s	x		x				x				x
meadow/ceeeping/bulbous buttercup	*Ranunculus bulbosus/acris/repens*	s	x	x	x	xx			x		x		x
fumitory	*Fumaria* sp.	s				x							
common nettle	*Urtica dioica* L.	s	x		x	x					xx		x
hop	*Humulus lupulus* L.	s						x					
hemp	*Cannabis sativa* L.	s				x							
fat hen's goosefoot	*Chenopodium album* L.	s				x							
common orache	*Atriplex patula* L.	s				x							
blink	*Montia fontana* sbsp *fontana* L.	s	x		xxx								
common chickweed	*Stellaria media* Villars	s		x		x					x		
bog stitchwort	*Stellaria uliginosa* Murray	s	x	x	x	xx			x	x	xx	x	x
procumbent pearlwort	*Sagina procumbens* L.	s	x	x									
coral-necklace	*Illecebrum verticillatum* L.	s	x										
ragged robin	*Lychnis flos-cuculi* L.	s	x						x				
campions	*Silene* cf.	s				x							
water pepper	*Persicaria hydropiper* Spach	s	x			xx				x	x		x
pale persicaria	*Persicaria lapathifolium* L.	s				x							
knotweed/knotgrass	*Persicaria/Polygonum*	s											x
black	*Fallopia*	s				x							

Table 12.1 Edgbaston Street; list of taxa identified from contexts of various phase. Key: see overleaf.

common name	scientific name												
bindweed	*convolvulus* A. Love												
sheep's sorrel	*Rumex acetosella* L.	s				x							
dock	*Rumex* sp.	s		x									
St John's wort	*Hypericum* sp.	s	x										
bittercress	*Cardamine hirsuta/amara*	s				x							
cross-leaved heath	*Erica tetralix* L.	lf					x	x					
heath	*Erica* sp.	tw					x						
raspberry	*Rubus idaeus* L.	s				x							
bramble	*Rubus* sp.	s	x	x	x	x			x		x	x	
gorse	*Ulex* sp.	lf						x					
hemlock	*Conium maculatum* L.	s				x					x		
carrot family	Apiaceae	s									x		
nightshade	*Solanum* sp.	s				x							
white deadnettle	*Lamium* cf. *album.*	s				x					x		
common hemp-nettle	*Galeopsis tethrait* aggr	s				x							
bugle	*Ajuga reptans* L.	s				x							
deadnettle family	Lamiaceae	s			x	x							
greater plantain	*Plantago major* L.	s				x							
elder	*Sambucus nigra* L.	s	x	x		x					x		x
thistles	*Carduus/Cirsium*	s				x							
stinking chamomile	*Anthemis cotula* L.	s				x							
perennial sow-thistle	*Sonchus arvensis* L.	s				x							
sweet grass	*Glyceria* sp.	s			x	xx				x			
toad-rush	*Juncus bufonius* L.	s			xxx	x			x	xx			x
club-rush	*Juncus* sp.	s	xx	x					x	xx		x	x
club-rush	*Scirpus* sp.	s			x				x				
bristle club-rush	*Isolepis setacea* R.Br.	s	xx	x	xxx				x	x	x	x	x
sedges	*Carex* sp. flat	s			x	x			x	x			x
sedges	*Carex* sp. trigonous	s			x	x			x		x		x
grasses	Poacese medium	s								x			
grasses	Poaceae large	s		x		x							x
	Trees and other												
poplar	*Populus* sp.	bsc				x							
willow	*Salix* sp.	bd				x			x				
duckweed	*Lemna* sp.	s				xx							
	bud										x	x	
	leaf					x							
	sawdust						x	x					
	Decomposed leather					x							
	Bark sclereids					x							
	decomposed wood					x							

Key: a = awn, bd = bud, c = cone, d = ditch, f = flot, fl = flower, fr = fruit, g = grain, germ = germinated, l = layer, lf = leaf, p = pit, pd = pod, po = pond, s = seed, sh = shell, st = stone, stm = stem, th = thorn, tw = twig, wl = waterlogged, ws = wet sieved, x = 1–10, xx = 11–20, xxx = 21-30, xxxx = 31–40, >xxxx = more than 40

Table 12.1 continued.

L.), together with a few weeds, such as charred and waterlogged remains of stinking chamomile (*Anthemis cotula* L.) and waterlogged remains of common chickweed (*Stellaria media* Villars), common hemp-nettle (*Galeopsis tethrait* aggr.), and greater plantain (*Plantago major* L.). It is possible that some of the seeds were carried into the tanning pit by water taken from the watercourse.

Most important amongst the organic remains found in Sample F218/ 2087 were fragments of decomposed leather, decomposed wood and bark sclereids. Sclereids are stone-cells found in the support tissue of plants (schlerenchyma). Their occurrence in the fill indicates that degraded bark was present, a fact consistent with the production of tanning liquor. The contemporary presence of decomposed fragments of wood and leather as well as bark sclereids from Sample F218/ 2087 provides strong evidence for tanning activities (Cameron 1998; Ciaraldi *et al.* 2004; Hall 1997 and 2002). Oak bark was particularly suited to the tanning of leather because of its high tannin content, and the 'vegetable tanning' process involved soaking the hides in a liquor rich in tannins. This enabled the preservation of the hide and maintained a uniformity of colour (Thomson 1981). Evidence of tanning activity was also evident at Floodgate Street where abundant presence of leather offcuts, horncores, and the presence of organic-rich deposits containing large amount of animal hair were identified (Ciaraldi 2002c).

The presence of a single hemp seed (*Cannabis sativa* L.) could suggest that hemp retting was carried out on site, even though it is more likely an occasional find. Hemp seeds could have been transported by the water from other areas of the town (*e.g.* the Parsonage Moat, from which water was flowing into the site). A single hemp seed was also the only plant remain worth mentioning identified in Sample F209/ 2012, which was taken from a Phase 2 tanning pit, also in Area B.

The analysed samples from Phase 3 features were all collected from pits in Area C of the site. These pits may not have been used for tanning *per se* but are identified in the site narrative (Patrick and Rátkai, Chapter 2) as possible hide-curing pits, smaller than the tanning pits proper, and associated features. These pits contained a very small plant assemblage, which interestingly included heathland species, such as gorse (*Ulex* sp.) and cross-leaved heath (*Erica tetralix* L.). The pollen record also shows the presence of heather (Greig, Chapter 13), suggesting a more conspicuous presence on site, possibly because it was used as a bedding material or for thatching, or grew in the surrounding area. Pollen and macroremains of heather were also identified from the deposits from The Row (see below) Ciaraldi 2000; Greig 1980). A single seed of hop (*Humulus lupulus* L.) was also recovered.

The most important characteristic of the samples from these Phase 3 pits (F323/ 3065, F325/ 3072, F347/ 3143, F338/ 3097 and F320/ 3058) is that they were formed almost exclusively of small fragments of wood. No bark fragments or sclereids were observed. The most likely interpretation of this assemblage is that it represents waterlogged and un-decomposed sawdust, mainly of oak (*Quercus* sp.) (Hall 2000). While the use of bark, particularly oak bark, is well documented in the tanning process, the use of wood or sawdust is unknown to the author. Lenses of wood chips were found in what was interpreted as tanning pits in Dublin but it is also possible that sawdust could have been used for the curing of already tanned leather (see also Patrick and Rátkai, Chapter 2).

Organic deposits in Area D

Area D lay to the south of the watercourse. This area originally lay within one of the lord of the manor's hunting parks, Holme Park, and does not appear to have been developed until the 18th century when activities associated with the preparation of animal skins extended into the area. The area was low-lying and subject to waterlogging, no doubt in part due to the proximity of the adjacent watercourse.

A peaty, organic layer had formed across Area D which may be Phase 1 but probably more likely pre-dates the establishment of the town, and two samples from this layer were analysed (4031 and 4032). A further sample (F427/ 4063) was analysed from a Phase 3 linear gully. All three samples contained small plant assemblages with a very similar species composition. They included species from wet/ damp environments, such as crowfoots, buttercups, blink (*Montia fontana* L.), procumbent pearlwort (*Sagina procumbens* L.), coral necklace (*Illecebrum verticillatum* L.), knotgrasses, rushes and sedges. The soil matrix of the organic layer comprised a fine silt, which suggests deposition in a water environment, possibly as a result of periodic flooding by the nearby watercourse. The presence of a large percentage of tree pollen in a monolith sample equating to 4031 and 4032 (see Greig, Chapter 13) suggests the presence of fairly extensive woodland cover in the vicinity.

Moor Street

Only two of the 22 samples collected during the excavation at Moor Street contained well-preserved plant remains (Table 12.2). Both samples were dated to Phase 1 and were recovered from fills of the recut (F568) of the massive boundary ditch which formed the principal feature on the site. Sample F568/ 5188, from one of the lower fills of the ditch, produced a small waterlogged plant assemblage, whereas Sample F568/ 5184, from a fill much higher up in the ditch, contained mainly charred plant remains and a few waterlogged seeds.

Sample F568/ 5188 contained almost exclusively species from disturbed ground. Particularly abundant were seeds of common nettle (*Urtica dioica* L.) and elder (*Sambucus nigra* L.). Species of wet environments were

	Area		F568/ 5184	F568/ 5188
	Feature/ Context		**F568/ 5184**	**F568/ 5188**
	Flot / Wet Sieved		**f**	**ws**
	Mesh used (mm)		**0.5**	**0.3**
	Type of context		**charred**	**waterlogged**
	Cereals			
bread/club wheat	*Triticum aestivum-compactum*	g	4	
bread/club wheat	*Triticum aestivum-compactum* germinated	g	2	
barley	*Hordeum vulgare* L. indet.	g	1	
barley	*Hordeum vulgare* L. germinated	g	2	
? cultivated oats	*Avena* cf. *sativa*	g	40	
? cultivated oats	*Avena* cf. *sativa* germinated	g	18	
rye	*Secale cereale* L.	g	2	
cereals	Cereals	g	3	
	Chaff			
	Bulbils		xxx	
oats	*Avena* sp.	a	2	
cereals	Embryos		2	
	Weeds			
common nettle	*Urtica dioica* L.	s		>100
fat hen's goosefoot	*Chenopodium album* L.	s	34	
common orache	*Atriplex patula* L.	s	33	x
goosefoot/ orache	*Chenopodium/ Atriplex.*	s	21	
blink	*Montia fontana* sbsp *fontana* L.	s		x
bog stitchwort	*Stellaria uliginosa* Murray	s	1	
corn spurrey	*Spergula arvensis* L.	s	14	
ragged robin	*Lychnis flos-cuculi* L.	s	1	x
pale persicaria	*Persicaria lapathifolia* Gray	s	1	
water pepper	*Persicaria* cf. *hydropiper*	s	9	
black bindweed	*Fallopia convolvulus* A. Love	s	1	
sheep's sorrel	*Rumex acetosella* L.	s	3 + x	
docks	*Rumex* sp.	s	4	
bramble	*Rubus* sp.	s	x	x
vetch/tare	Vicia/Lathyrus	s	30	
hemlock	*Conium maculatum* L.	s		x
henbane	*Hyoscyamus niger* L.	s		x
nightshade	*Solanum* sp.	s	2	
common hemp-nettle	*Galeopsis tethrait* aggr.	s	20	
balm	*Melissa officinalis* L.	s		x
deadnettle family	Lamiaceae	s	4	
ribwort plantain	*Plantago Lanceolata* L.	s	11	
eyebright/ bartsias	Euphrasia/ Odontites	s	11	
elder	*Sambucus nigra* L.	s	13	>100

Table 12.2 Moor Street; list of taxa identified from Phase 1. Key: see Table 12.1.

narrow-fruited cornsalad	*Valerianella dentata* Pollich	s	4 + x	
nipplewort	*Lapsana communis* L.	s	85	
stinking chamomile	*Anthemis cotula* L.	s	150	
corn marigold	*Chrysanthemum segetum* L.	s	120	
mayweed	*Tripleurospermum* sp.	s	65	
daisy family	Compositae	fl	1	
grasses	Poaceae large	s	3	
grasses	Poaceae medium	s	11	
grasses	Poaceae small	s	40	
rush	*Juncus* sp.	s		x
bristle clubrush	*Isolepis setacea* R.Br.	s	1	x
sedges	*Carex* sp. flat	s	4	
sedges	*Carex* sp. trigonous	s	12 + x	x
	Other			
water flea	*Daphnia* sp. - ephippia			x

Table 12.2 continued.

also recorded, in particular some sedges (*Carex* sp.) and rushes (*Juncus* sp. and *Isolepis setacea* R.Br.). These species might have belonged to the vegetation which grew along and in the ditch.

The assemblage from F568/ 5184 was more diverse, and included many weeds and grassland species, as well as species of wet and disturbed ground. The substantial presence of grassland species is also mirrored by the pollen record from the site (Greig, Chapter 13).

Amongst the weeds there were narrow-fruited cornsalad (*Valerianella dentata* Pollich), stinking chamomile (*Anthemis cotula* L.), corn marigold (*Chrysanthemum segetum* L.) and mayweeds (*Tripleurospermum* sp.), all three present in great abundance (Table 12.2). Stinking chamomile is a cereal weed typically found on heavy soils, while corn marigold is an introduced species often found as a weed in cornfields. Unlike stinking chamomile, corn spurrey (*Spergula arvensis* L.) is a weed typical of sandy soils. The presence of two species indicative of differing soil types suggests that weeds of different crops were present in the assemblage, and that the two cereal crops were grown on different types of soils. Indeed, precisely these different types of soil were present in the vicinity of Birmingham town centre, with heavy clayey soils to the south and east, and lighter sandy soils to the north and west. Corn spurrey could be associated with rye, a cereal often cultivated on sandy soil and also present in Sample F568/ 5184.

Common hemp-nettle (*Galeopsis tethrait* agg.) is often found as a weed although it also grows on rough and damp ground. Indeed, species typical of disturbed ground are numerous, as is shown by the presence of common orache (*Atriplex patula* L.), fat hen goosefoot (*Chenopodium album* L.), and elder (*Sambucus nigra* L.).

Ribwort plantain (*Plantago lanceolata* L.), nipplewort (*Lapsana communis* L.) and the group of grasses belong to the category of grassland species. The presence of numerous charred bulbils of grasses suggests that they were present in great abundance in the deposit. A group of plants from wet/ damp habitats were also present in the assemblage. This included species also found in the archaeological deposits from Park Street (see below) and Edgbaston Street (see above), as well as in the other sample from Moor Street (F568/ 5188).

The assemblage from Sample F568/ 5184 also contained a substantial group of cereals. This, in fact, represents the largest cereal assemblage recovered from the three sites discussed here. Bread/ Club wheat (*Triticum aestivum-compactum*), barley (*Hordeum vulgare* L.), ?cultivated oat (*Avena* cf. *sativa*), and rye (*Secale cereale* L.) were all present in the assemblage. Several grains of all the species (with the exception of rye) had germinated, an indication that they may have been used for malting in the beer-making process or that they had been spoilt during storage and had therefore been used as fodder.

The presence of grassland species, together with the large number of oat grains and other germinated cereals, strongly indicates that the assemblage does, in fact, represent charred fodder. The weeds present may represent the waste from crop processing used as fodder as well. Interestingly, the pollen evidence also points towards the presence of fodder on the site (Greig, Chapter 13). A 16th-century reference describes the area around Moor Street and Park Street as follows: '...There were buildings only on the eastern end [of High Street]; several of them were barns or sheds' (Gill 1930, 128), suggesting a continuity of use over several centuries.

Park Street

The excavations at Park Street uncovered a large number of medieval and post-medieval features, including complex structures such as wood-lined tanks, together with ditches, pond-like features and numerous pits. The sampling strategy and the assessment of the samples were carried out in accordance with the research objectives highlighted above and are discussed in detail in the assessment report (Ciaraldi 2002b).

The plant remains discussed in this report include charred and waterlogged assemblages belonging to Phase 1, Phase 2 and Phase 3 (Tables 12.3–12.6).

Phase 1: Medieval period (12th to 14th centuries) (Tables 12.3 and 12.4)

The plant assemblage for the medieval period is by far the largest and, to simplify the discussion, the samples have been grouped according to their area of provenance. This approach also highlights spatial differences in the nature of the plant assemblage.

Area A (Table 12.3)

Eight samples from Area A dated to Phase 1 were studied. Of these, six derived from various fills of the large boundary ditch F174/ F201. Samples F174/ 1246 and F174/ 1213 were from the base of ditch section F174, with fill 1246 being the basal fill and 1213 the fill immediately above it. Samples F174/ 1197 and F174/ 1165 were from fills progressively higher up in this ditch section. Samples F201/ 1326 and F201/ 1325 were from lower fills of ditch section F201. Sample F195/ 1312 was the middle fill of the much slighter curvilinear ditch which abutted the large boundary ditch on its south-western side. The eighth sample (1239) was from a layer attributed to Phase 1.

The most important characteristic of the plant assemblage from Area A is that, unlike those from Areas B and C, it included numerous charred remains of cereals. The species present included bread/ club wheat (*Triticum aestivum-compactum*), barley (*Hordeum vulgare* L.), oats (*Avena* sp.), and rye (*Secale cereale* L.), a range of cereals quite characteristic of the medieval period and already identified in deposits of the same period from Moor Street (see above) as well as from deposits from the Hartwell site interpreted as remains of domestic refuse (Ciaraldi 2000). The presence of rye pollen (Greig, Chapter 13) suggests that this cereal was probably cultivated in the vicinity of the town.

The other species that formed the charred assemblage from Area A included grassland species and weeds, some of which were also present in the contemporary deposit at Moor Street (see above). Amongst the grassland species were ribwort plantain (*Plantago lanceolata* L.), nipplewort (*Lapsana communis* L.), some clover-type plant, mignonettes (*Reseda* cf. *luteola*) – a species found in non-acidic soils – and small-grain grasses. The weeds included stinking chamomile (*Anthemis cotula* L.), corn

spurrey (*Spergula arvensis* L.), and narrow-fruited cornsalad (*Valerianella dentata* Pollich). Heath (*Calluna vulgaris* Hull) and heath-grass (*Danthonia decumbens* DC) are species typical of heathlands and were also found at Moor Street. Heath-grass is known to have been an arable weed in the past, particularly of spelt (*Triticum spelta* L.) (Van der Veen 1988). It is possible that the presence of heath is associated with its use as a bedding or thatching material.

The presence of grassland species, together with a large quantity of culm internodes and culm bases of grasses (or Poaceae), suggests that the assemblage, as in the case of Moor Street, represents charred fodder, perhaps discarded in the ditch after routine cleaning of stables and barns. Evidence of fodder in towns is not unusual, as it is often associated with the presence of working animals in urban contexts. It is possible that, in this part of the site, there were stables or barns, as it is suggested also by the presence of fodder at the nearby site of Moor Street (see above).

The waterlogged plant assemblage was remarkably different from the charred one. It contained a smaller flora, with a large predominance of species typical of disturbed ground, such as greater celandine (*Chelidonium majus* L.), bramble (*Rubus* sp.), and elder (*Sambucus nigra* L.). It is possible that these plants grew next to areas where animals were kept. The same group of grassland species present in the charred assemblage is also present in the waterlogged one.

Many species are typical of wet/ damp environments, such as ragged robin (*Lychnis flos-cuculi* L.), water pepper (*Persicaria hydropiper* Spach), and the sedges (*Carex* sp.); or even of an aquatic environment, such as toadrush (*Juncus bufonius* L.) and watercress (*Rorippa nasturtium-aquaticum* Hayek). The plants indicative of an aquatic environment were found, not surprisingly, almost exclusively in the basal fills of the boundary ditch. The presence of bivalve and caddice fly cases from samples from ditch section F174 also suggests that the ditch must have been filled with water.

The presence of buds, seeds and cones of trees such as birch (*Betula* cf. *pubescens*), alder (*Alnus* sp.) and willow (*Salix* sp.) suggests that trees were growing in the area, a fact confirmed also by the pollen evidence (Greig, Chapter 13).

The plant assemblage from Area A contained a group of cultivated plants that are of particular importance. These included hemp (*Cannabis sativa* L.) and flax (*Linum usitatissimum* L.), two plants cultivated for their fibres, seeds and oil. It is possible that the presence of hemp and flax was related to their processing for the extraction of fibres (retting). More convincing evidence of hemp (and perhaps flax) retting was identified at Deritend Bridge (Ciaraldi 2002b), Digbeth and at The Row (see below) where fragments of hemp reeds and high concentrations of hemp pollen (Greig 1980) were present.

	Area		A	A	A	A	A	A	A	A
	Feature/ Context		F174 1165	F174 1197	F174 1246	F174 1213	F201 1326	F201 1325	F195 1312	1239
	Flot / Wet Sieved		f	f	ws	ws	f	ws	f	f
	Mesh used (mm)		0.5	0.5	0.3	0.3	0.5	0.3	0.5	0.5
	Type of context		D	D	D	D	D	D	D	L
			1	1	1	1	1	1	1	1
	Cereals									
bread wheat	*Triticum aestivum* sl	g								1
bread/club wheat	*Triticum aestivum-compactum*	g				1				
wheat	*Triticum* sp.	g				1			1	
barley	*Hordeum vulgare* L. indet.	g	1 tail	1				1	6	1
oats	*Avena* sp.	g					32		17	1
rye	*Secale cereale* L.	g	1	1		1 germ	2		2	
cereals	Cereals	g	6			1			15	1
	Chaff									
barley	*Hordeum vulgare* L.	ri	1 wl							
cereals	Culm bases/bulbils		13							14
cereals	Culm fragments		xxx				xxx			xx
	Fruits and nuts									
fig	*Ficus carica* L.	s	x			x			x	
grape	*Vitis vinifera* L.	s			x					
	Other cultivated									
hemp	*Cannabis sativa* L.	s		x			x			
hemp	*Cannabis sativa* L.	stm							x	
beet	*Beta vulgaris* L.	s				x				
flax	*Linum usitatissimum* L.	s				x				
	Weeds – charred									
fat hen's goosefoot	*Chenopodium album* L.	s								2
blink	*Montia fontana* sbsp *fontana* L.	s								1
corn spurrey	*Spergula arvensis* L	s								1
knotweed/ knotgrass	*Persicaria/ Polygonum*	s	1							
sheep's sorrel	*Rumex acetosella* L.	s	4							1
mignonette	*Reseda* cf. *luteola*	s								1
heather	*Calluna vulgaris* Hull	s								3
cinquefoil	*Potentilla* sp.	s					1			5
vetch/tare	*Vicia/Lathyrus*	s								
Fabaceae clover – type	*Medicago/Melilotus/ Trifolium*	s								2
nipplewort	*Lapsana communis* L.	s					1			
stinking chamomile	*Anthemis cotula* L.	s	1						1	2
sedges	*Carex* sp. flat	s								1
timothy grass	*Phleum pratensis* L.	s	3							
heath-grass	*Danthonia decumbens* DC.	s								7

Table 12.3 Park Street; list of taxa identified in the samples from Phase 1 from Area A. Key: see Table 12.1.

small grass	Poaceae small	s	7							5
	Weeds - Waterlogged									
buttercup	*Ranunculus* sp. *subgenus BATRACHIUM*	s		x						
lesser/ creeping spearwort	*Ranunculus flammula/ reptans*	s				x				
meadow/ creeping/ bulbous buttercup	*Ranunculus bulbosus/acris/ repens*	s		x						
greater celandine	*Chelidonium majus* L.	s	x			x	xx		>xxxx	x
fumitory	*Fumaria* sp.	s	x	x			x			x
common nettle	*Urtica dioica* L.	s	xxx	>100	>xxxx					
fat hen's goosefoot	*Chenopodium album* L.	s	x	>100			x			
common orache	*Atriplex patula* L.	s	x			x	xx			
blink	*Montia fontana* sbsp *fontana* L.	s	x							
three-nerved sandwort	*Moheringia trinervia* Clairv.	s				x				
common chickweed	*Stellaria media* Villars	s				xx				
lesser stitchwort	*Stellaria graminea* L.	s		x						
bog stitchwort	*Stellaria uliginosa* Murray	s			xx	x				
ragged robin	*Lychnis flos-cuculi* L.	s		x	x	xxx	xxx	>100		
water pepper	*Persicaria hydropiper* Spach	s		x	x	xxx	x			
knotgrass	*Polygonum aviculare* L.	s				x	x			
black bindweed	*Fallopia convolvulus* A. Love	s				x				
sheep's sorrel	*Rumex acetosella* L.	s		x						
dock	*Rumex* sp.	s				x	x	x		
sweet violet	*Viola odorata* L.	s				x		x		
watercress	*Rorippa nasturtium-aquaticum* Hayek	s			x					
bittercress	*Cardamine hirsuta/amara*	s			x					
mignonette	*Reseda* sp.	s		x						
raspberry	*Rubus idaeus* L.	s		xx	x					
bramble	*Rubus* sp.	s	xx	>100	xx	xx	x	xx	>xxxx	
sun spurge	*Euphorbia helioscopica* L.	s								x
dwarf spurge	*Euphorbia exigua* L.	s		x						
fool's parsley	*Aethusa cynapium* L.	s	x	x			x			
hemlock	*Conium maculatum* L.	s	xxx	xx			x	x		x
henbane	*Hyoscyamus niger* L.	s	x	>100			x			
nightshade	*Solanum* sp.	s		x						
forget-me-not	*Myosotis* sp.	s			x					
hedge woundwort	*Stachys sylvatica* L.	s							x	

Table 12.3 continued.

white deadnettle	*Lamium* cf. *album*	s	x	x						
common hemp-nettle	*Galeopsis tethrait* aggr.	s				x				
gypsywort	*Lycopus europaeus* L.	s				x				
deadnettle family	Lamiaceae	s				x			x	
eybright/ bartsias	Euphrasia/ Odontites	s	x							
elder	*Sambucus nigra* L.	s	>xxxx	>100	xx	xxx	xxx	>100	>100	xx
narrow-fruited cornsalad	*Valerianella dentata* Pollich	s				x				
dandelion	*Taraxacum* cf. *offcinalis*	s							x	
toadrush	*Juncus bufonius* L.	s			>xxxx			x		
bristle clubrush	*Isolepis setacea* R.Br.	s		x			x			
sedges	*Carex* sp. flat	s		x	x	x				
sedges	*Carex* sp. trigonous	s		x		x	x		>xxxx	
downy birch	*Betula* cf. *pubescens*	s			x					
alder	*Alnus* sp.	c					x			
willow	*Salix* sp. catkins				x					
	Liverwort	lf			x					
	leaf				x					
	Buds					x	x			
	Caddice fly cases			x		x			x	
	Bivalve			x						
	hammerscale									x

Table 12.3 continued.

A single beet seed (*Beta vulgaris* L.), one of fig (*Ficus carica* L.) and one of grape (*Vitis vinifera* L.) complete the list of food plants. The presence of beet seeds is important as it suggests cultivation in vegetable gardens, possibly present in this part of the town. Equally important was the presence of fig and grape as these represent exotic foodstuffs, probably imported from the Mediterranean area. Fig pips occur very often on sites of the medieval period, whereas grape is much rarer (Greig 1996). The presence of grape would suggest a rather high-status type of diet.

Areas B and C (Table 12.4)

In contrast to Area A, charred plant remains were absent from the samples from Areas B and C (Table 12.4). This probably reflects a difference in the nature of the activities carried out, with more evidence of domestic activity in Area A. In Areas B and C all the samples are derived from the waterlogged area to the rear of the Park Street plots, with samples both from the ditch defining the end of the plots (Area C) and from the adjacent area liable to flooding (Area B).

The two waterlogged samples from the water-lain deposits in Area B (1596 and 1652) were rather small but comprised a mixture of species from disturbed and wet/ damp environments. Hemp seeds were found in context 1596. The three samples from Area C (F760/ 1811, F776/ 1864 and F799/ 1871) all derived from the recut of the ditch (F760, F776, F799) that defined the rear end of the Park Street plots. This plant assemblage was larger and included most of the species from disturbed/ wet environments present in Area A and B. Some grassland species, such as self-heal (*Prunella vulgaris* L.), balm (*Melissa officinalis* L.), dandelion (*Taraxacus* cf. *officinalis*), and plantain, were also present, though not in a quantity sufficient to suggest that fodder was a major component of the deposit. A single seed of lupin (*Lupinus* sp.) was found in Sample F760/ 1811. This cultivated pulse could have been part of a fodder assemblage, although this species is also used as a decorative plant which could have been cultivated in nearby gardens. Melissa, self-heal and dandelion could perhaps also have been herb garden plants.

Many arboreal species were present, particularly in Sample F799/ 1871, where buds, seeds and twigs of willow, ?downy birch, poplar and holly (*Ilex aquifolium* L.) were found. Holly could have been used in hedges together with *Prunus* sp.

Hemp was present in samples from two of the ditch sections (F760/ 1811 and F799/ 1871), strengthening the view that hemp retting could have taken place here in the medieval period, particularly in features such as ditches, little streams and ponds. Food plants included waterlogged seeds of beet, fig, hazelnut (*Corylus avellana* L.), and Prunus sp.

	Area		B	B	B	C	C	C	C
	Feature/Context		1596	1652	F508 1585	F776 1864	F826 1935	F760 1811	F799 1871
	Flot / Wet Sieved		ws	ws	ws	ws	f	ws	ws
	Mesh used (mm)		0.3	0.3	0.3	0.5	0.5	0.3	0.3
	Type of context		L	L	P	D	P	D	D
	Phase		1?	1	1?	1	?	1	1
	Fruits and nuts								
hazelnut	*Corylus avellana* L	sh				x			
fig	*Ficus carica* L.	s							x
	Other cultivated								
hemp	*Cannabis sativa* L.	s	x		x			x	x
beet	*Beta vulgaris* L.	s/l							x
lupin	*Lupinus* sp.	s						x	
	Weeds – charred								
stinking chamomile	*Anthemis cotula* L.	s						1	
	Weeds – Waterlogged								
lesser/ creeping spearwort	*Ranunculus flammula/ reptans*	s						x	
meadow/ creeeping/ bulbous buttercup	*Ranunculus bulbosus/acris/ repens*	s	x		x			x	x
common nettle	*Urtica dioica* L.	s	x		xxx	x		>100	xxx
small nettle	*Uritca urens* L.	s		x					
fat hen's goosefoot	*Chenopodium album* L.	s							x
common orache	*Atriplex patula* L.	s			x			x	x
blink	*Montia fontana* sbsp *fontana* L.	s							
common chickweed	*Stellaria media* Villars	s	x				x	>100	x
lesser stitchwort	*Stellaria graminea* L.	s						x	
bog stitchwort	*Stellaria uliginosa* Murray	s						x	x
ragged robin	*Lychnis flos-cuculi* L.	s	x					xxx	x
water pepper	*Persicaria hydropiper* Spach	s	x				x	xx	x
knotweed/knotgrass	*Persicaria/ Polygonum*	s						x	
knotgrass	*Polygonum aviculare* L.	s	x				x		
black bindweed	*Fallopia convolvulus* A. Love	s						x	
sheep's sorrel	*Rumex acetosella* L.	s						x	
broad-leaved dock	*Rumex obtusifolium* L.	s						x	x
dock	*Rumex* sp.	s	x				x	x	
watercress	*Rorippa nasturtium-aquaticum* Hayek	s							x
bittercress	*Cardamine hirsuta/ amara*	s						x	x
mignonette	*Reseda* sp.	s						x	
pimpernel	*Anagallis* sp.	s						x	

Table 12.4 Park Street; list of taxa identified from contexts of Phase 1 from Areas B and C. Key: see Table 12.1.

bramble	*Rubus* sp.	s	x		x	x		xx	xx
agrimony	*Agrimonia eupatorium* L.	fr						x	
fenugreek type	*Trigonella* - type	pd							x
willowherb	*Epilobium* sp.	s						x	x
fool's parsley	*Aethusa cynapium* L.	s			x			x	x
hemlock	*Conium maculatum* L.	s						x	x
carrot family	Apiaceae	s						x	
nightshade	*Solanum* sp.	s						x	x
thornapple	*Datura stramonium* L.	s					x		
woundwort	*Stachys* sp.	s						x	
white deadnettle	*Lamium* cf. *album.*	s	x					x	
common hemp-nettle	*Galeopsis tethrait* aggr.	s			x	x		x	x
self-heal	*Prunella vulgaris* L.	s							x
balm	*Melissa officinalis* L.	s						x	x
gypsywort	*Lycopus europaeus* L.	s						x	
deadnettle family	Lamiaceae	s							x
bedstraw	*Galium aparine* L.	s							x
elder	*Sambucus nigra* L.	s	x		x			x	x
thistles	*Carduus/ Cirsium*	s						x	x
nipplewort	*Lapsana communis* L.	s						x	x
perennial sow-thistle	*Sonchus arvensis* L.	s						x	x
dandelion	*Taraxacum* cf. *offcinalis*	s							x
sweet grass	*Glyceria* sp.	s							xxx
toadrush	*Juncus bufonius* L.	s		x					
clubrush	*Scirpus* sp.	s						x	
bristle clubrush	*Isolepis setacea* R.Br.	s						x	
sedges	*Carex* sp. flat	s						x	
sedges	*Carex* sp. trigonous	s						x	x
	Trees and other								
downy birch	*Betula* cf. *pubescens*	s						x	
poplar	*Populus* sp.	bd				x		x	xx
poplar	*Populus* sp.	b sc							x
white poplar	*Populus alba*	tw							x
poplar/ willow	*Populus/Betula*	lf							x
willow	*Salix* sp. catkins								x
willow	*Salix* sp.	bd						x	x
holly	*Ilex aquifolium* L.	lf							x
duckweed	*Lemna* sp.	s						x	xx
	Sphagnum sp.						x		x
	mosses							x	
water flea	*Daphnia* sp. - ephippia							x	xx
	fungal spores		xx	xx					
	leaf							x	x
	Buds							x	
	Caddice fly cases								x

Table 12.4 continued.

Phase 2: Early post-medieval period (15th–16th centuries) (Table 12.5)

The plant assemblage from Phase 2 is very small and includes species mainly from wet and disturbed environments already observed in the plant assemblage from the previous period. Three samples were analysed, all from Area B. Two samples (F508/ 1508 and F508/ 1585) were taken from F508, a shallow clay-lined pit. The third sample (F561/ 1657) was taken from a rectangular pit or tank, F561/ F562. These two features formed part of a cluster of pond-like features at the bottom of the Park Street plots, interpreted as having been used primarily for the watering of animals. Although some scraps of leather-working waste were present, the absence of any

	Area		A	B	B
	Feature/		**F195**	**F500**	**F561**
	Context		**1245**	**1508**	**1657**
	Flot / Wet Sieved		**f**	**ws**	**ws**
	Mesh used (mm)		**0.5**	**0.3**	**0.3**
	Type of context		**D**	**P**	**P**
	Cereals				
bread wheat	*Triticum aestivum* sl	g	2		
cereals	Cereals	g	2		
	Fruits and nuts				
	nut				x
	Weeds – charred				
goosefoot/ orache	Chenopodium/ Atriplex	s	1		
knotgrass	*Polygonum* sp.	s	1		
sheep's sorrel	*Rumex acetosella* L.	s	2		
cinquefoil	*Potentilla* sp.	s	1		
vetch/tare	*Vicia/Lathyrus*	s	1		
Fabaceae clover –type	*Medicago/Melilotus/Trifolium*	s	1		
ribwort plantain	*Plantago lanceolata* L.	s	1		
narrow-fruited cornsalad	*Valerianella dentata* Pollich	s	1		
stinking chamomile	*Anthemis cotula* L.	s	11		
	Weeds – Waterlogged				
buttercup	*Ranunculus* sp. subgenus BATRACHIUM	s			x
meadow/ creeeping/ bulbous buttercup	*Ranunculus bulbosus/acris/ repens*	s		x	x
greater celandine	*Chelidonium majus* L.	s	x		
common nettle	*Urtica dioica* L.	s			>100
hop	*Humulus lupulus* L.				x
fat hen's goosefoot	*Chenopodium album* L.	s		x	
common orache	*Atriplex patula* L.	s			x
blink	*Montia fontana sbsp fontana* L.	s		xxx	
bog stitchwort	*Stellaria uliginosa* Murray	s		x	
ragged robin	*Lychnis flos-cuculi* L.	s		xxx	
dock	*Rumex* sp.	s			x
bramble	*Rubus* sp.	s		xxx	x
fool's parsley	*Aethusa cynapium* L.	s		x	x
hemlock	*Conium maculatum* L.	s		x	
henbane	*Hyoscyamus niger* L.	s		xx	
nightshade	*Solanum* sp.	s		x	
white deadnettle	*Lamium* cf. *album.*	s		x	
elder	*Sambucus nigra* L.	s	x	xxx	x
thistles	*Carduus/ Cirsium*	s			x
nipplewort	*Lapsana communis* L.	s		x	x
sedges	*Carex* sp. flat	s			x
sedges	*Carex* sp. trigonous	s			x
downy birch	*Betula* cf. *pubescens*	s		x	
willow	*Salix* sp.	bd		x	
	Lemna sp.	s			x
	Daphnia sp. ephippia			xx	xxx
	Buds			x	x
	Animal hair			xx	

Table 12.5 Park Street; list of taxa identified in the samples from Phase 2. Key: see Table 12.1.

other evidence of tanning, such as bark, lime pits, *etc.*, which were clearly present at Edgbaston Street, rules this out as a function for the pits. The near absence of pottery also suggests that there was no, or very limited, domestic occupation in Area B in Phase 2 and the use of the land for stock keeping and the various 'ponds' for watering livestock seem to fit the evidence most closely. Samples F508/ 1508 and F561/ 1657 contained duckweed seeds and ephippia of water fleas, indicating the presence of water in these two features. The sediment from F508 consisted of a fine, compacted silt, clearly deposited in a low-energy water environment (such as a pond). The presence of animal hair in F508 may lend credence to the interpretation of this feature as a pond or watering hole for stock. Although it is possible that the hair was part of butchery or tanning waste, the absence of any other definite corroborative evidence for these trades makes these interpretations less likely.

Phase 3: Post-medieval (late 16th–18th centuries) (Table 12.6)

The samples from Phase 3 were recovered from pits of various shapes and sizes scattered over the three excavated areas. The pits contained pottery, animal bone and other domestic refuse, as well as building debris and considerable quantities of slag and other metal-working debris. The fills of the pits thus derived from a range of domestic and industrial activities.

Area A

Three samples were analysed from Area A: two of these (F134/ 1126 and F187/ 1219) were from pits assigned to sub-phase 3.1, dating to the late 16th to early 18th centuries. Both pits were located close to the Park Street frontage. The third sample (F133/ 1125) was from a pit (F133/ F245) assigned to sub-phase 3.2 and dated to the mid-18th century. This pit contained a very rich and varied finds assemblage, including numerous crucible fragments used in the manufacture of copper alloy objects.

As in the case of the plant assemblages from the earlier phases, the presence of charred plant remains was limited to Area A. From the two earlier pits, the charred remains included a few cereal grains of barley, oats and rye and a few seeds of wild species. A large number of food plants were also present in the waterlogged assemblage from Area A. These included some vegetables typically grown in vegetable gardens, such as beet (present in large quantity) and turnip (*Brassica* cf. *rapa*). There were also several fruits, such as grape, fig, and plum (*Prunus domestica* sbsp. *domestica*). The presence of several nutlets of hop (*Humulus lupulus* L.) – a beer additive – in the 18th-century pit suggests that beer making may have occurred on site. A public house, at No. 3 Park Street (to which Area A/B forms the backplot), is mentioned in Sketchley's Birmingham Directory for 1767 and a brewhouse is listed in the same area in the 1801–2 Rate Book (see Rátkai, Chapter 4). The charred and water-

logged foodstuffs clearly derived from domestic refuse discarded in the pits.

The presence of species which would have been grown as decorative plants in the garden, such as rose (*Rosa* sp.) and violet (*Viola odorata* L.), also seems to point towards the fact that houses and gardens must have been present near by.

The wild species identified in the plant assemblage from Area A included numerous seeds of common nettle (*Urtica dioica* L.) and greater celandine (*Chelidonium majus* L.), both typically found in disturbed environments, often in the vicinity of houses. The rest of the waterlogged flora strongly resembled that from the previous period and included a mixture of species from disturbed and wet ground.

Amongst the cultivated plants present in Area A, particularly noteworthy was the high number of hemp seeds from Sample F133/ 1125. In the same context several hop seeds were also present. It also contained buds and leaves of cypress, poplar and willow.

Areas B and C

Two samples were examined from Area B, both of which dated to the end of the 18th century and were associated with a pottery dump possibly related to a house clearance (see Rátkai, Chapter 7). The first of the samples (F520/ 1580) derived from the wood-lined tank F503/ F520. It contained virtually no significant plant remains apart from fig and a single hemp seed. Sample F506/ 1519 was taken from the upper fill of the pond-like feature F506. Although 'pond' F506 appears to have been dug out in Phase 2, the pottery evidence demonstrates that its uppermost fill (1519) was deposited in the late 18th century. The sediment from this context was similar to that from F508 (1508) from Phase 2: a fine, compacted silt deposited in a low-energy water environment, containing many leaf imprints. The majority of the plants present in this sample were from wet and aquatic environments. Many of the taxa have already been identified in water-associated deposits from the previous phases, including the watercress.

The two samples from Area C were taken from two pits, F765 and F803, located at the rear end of the plot in what was generally a damp and waterlogged area. Both pits were dated to the 17th century (Phase 3.1), and variously contained pottery, building rubble, clay pipe, pieces of leather, and metal-working and bone-working debris. Samples F765/ 1822 and F803/ 1835 contained some interesting species. Hemp and parsnips (*Pastinaca sativa* L.) were the only cultivated plants present in the assemblage. Parsnips could have been cultivated in vegetable gardens. Some animal hair was found in Sample F765/ 1822, although given the rather varied nature of the finds assemblages from the pits this is more likely to represent general waste than evidence of any specific industry. Sediment with a high concentration of animal hair was also recorded at Floodgate Street (Ciaraldi 2000),

	Area		A	A	A	A	B	B	C	C
	Feature/ Context		F187/ 1219	F159/ 1176	F134/ 1126	F133/ 1125	F520/ 1580	F506/ 1519	F765/ 1822	F803/ 1835
	Flot / Wet Sieved		f	f	f	f	ws	ws	f	ws
	Mesh used (mm)		0.5	0.5	0.5	0.5	0.3	0.3	0.5	0.3
	Type of context		P	P	P	P	P (chair)	PO	P	P
	Phase		3	3	3	3	3	3	3	3
	Cereals									
barley	*Hordeum vulgare* L. indet.	g	3	1	1					
oats	*Avena* sp.	g	1		1					
rye	*Secale cereale* L.	g	2	1						
cereals	Cereals	g	7		1					
	Fruits and nuts									
hazelnut	*Corylus avellana* L	sh					x			
fig	*Ficus carica* L.	s	x		>xxxx	x	x		x	
plum	*Prunus domestica* sbsp domestica L.	st					x			
plums	*Prunus* sp.	st				x	x			
plums	*Prunus* sp.	th						x		x
strawberry	Fragaria vesca *L.*	s			x					
grape	*Vitis vinifera* L.	s	x			x	x			
	nut	sh							x	
	Other cultivated									
hemp	*Cannabis sativa* L.	s					xxx	x	x	x
hemp (from 77)	*Cannabis sativa* L.	stm								x
turnip	*Brassica* cf. *rapa*	s					xx			x
beet	*Beta vulgaris* L.	s				xxxx	x			
rose	*Rosa* sp.	s					x			
parsnip	*Pastinaca sativa* L.	s								x
	Weeds – charred									
ragged robin	*Lychnis flos-cuculi* L.	s			x					
dock	*Rumex* sp.	s			x					
vetch/tare	*Vicia/Lathyrus*	s				x				
Fabaceae clover –type	*Medicago/Melilotus/Trifolium*	s	x							
reastharrow/ greenweeds	*Ononis/ Genista*	s				x				
blue woodruff	*Asperula arvensis* L.	s				x				
carrot family	*Apiaceae*	s	x			x				
small grass	Poaceae small	s				x				
	Weeds – Waterlogged									
buttercup	*Ranunculus* sp. subgenus BATRACHIUM	s						x		x
meadow/ creeeping/ bulbous buttercup	*Ranunculus bulbosus/acris/ repens*	s			x		xxx	x	x	x
greater celandine	*Chelidonium majus* L.	s	x			xx				
fumitory	*Fumaria* sp.	s	x							
common nettle	*Urtica dioica* L.	s				>xxxx		x	>xxxx	>100
small nettle	*Urtica urens* L.	s					x			
hop	*Humulus lupulus* L.	s					x			
fat hen's goosefoot	*Chenopodium album* L.	s	xx	x			xx	x	x	

Table 12.6 Park Street; list of taxa from Phase 3. Key: see Table 12.1.

Common name	Species	Part								
common orache	*Atriplex patula* L.	s				x		x	x	x
orache	*Atriplex* sp.	s		x						
blink	*Montia fontana* sbsp *fontana* L.	s						x	xx	
common chickweed	*Stellaria media* Villars	s			x	xxx		x	xx	>100
lesser stitchwort	*Stellaria graminea* L.	s							x	
bog stitchwort	*Stellaria uliginosa* Murray	s			x	x		x		
ragged robin	*Lychnis flos-osculi* L.	s			x	x				
three-nerved sandwort	*Moheringia trinervia* Clairv.	s				x				
water pepper	*Persicaria hydropiper* Spach	s		x		x		x	x	x
knotweed/knotgrass	*Persicaria/ Polygonum*	s							x	
knotgrass	*Polygonum aviculare* L.	s				xx				
black bindweed	*Fallopia convolvulus* A. Love	s				x				
broad-leaved dock	*Rumex obtusifolium* L.	s								x
broad-leaved dock	*Rumex obtusifolium* L. pedicell									x
dock	*Rumex* sp.	s				x		x		
sweet violet	*Viola odorata* L.	s		x		x				
watercress	*Rorippa nasturtium – aquaticum* Hayek	s						x		
fieldpenny-cress	*Thlaspi arvense* L.	s							x	
mignonette	*Reseda* sp.	s				x				
pimpernel	*Anagallis* sp.	s								
raspberry	*Rubus idaeus* L.	s			xx	x				x
bramble	*Rubus* sp.	s	>xxxx	xxx	>xxxx	xx		x	xx	x
cinquefoil	*Potentilla* sp.	s				x				
hawthorn	*Crataegus* sp.	st		x		x		x		
willowherb	*Epilobium* sp.	s								x
sun spurge	*Euphorbia helioscopica* L.	s		x		x				
dwarf spurge	*Euphorbia exigua* L.	s								x
petty spurge	*Euphorbia peplus* L.	s		x		x				
greenweed/gorse	*Genista/Ulex*	s						x		
fool's parsley	*Aethusa cynapium* L.	s	xx	x		x	x			x
hemlock	*Conium maculatum* L.	s						x	x	x
henbane	*Hyoscyamus niger* L.	s			xxx	x				
nightshade	*Solanum* sp.	s							x	x
hedge woundwort	*Stachys sylvatica* L.	s							x	
white deadnettle	*Lamium* cf. *album.*	s			x	x		x	x	x
common hemp-nettle	*Galeopsis tethrait* aggr.	s				x			x	
balm	*Melissa officinalis* L.	s						x		
mint	*Mentha* sp.	s		x						
deadnettle family	Lamiaceae	s							x	
ribwort plantain	*Plantago Lanceolata* L.	s							x	
plantain	*Plantago major* L.	s						x		
small toadflax	*Chaenorhinum minus* Lange	s			x					
elder	*Sambucus nigra* L.	s	>xxxx	x	>xxxx	xx		x	xx	x
thistles	*Carduus/ Cirsium*	s				x				
bristly oxtongue	Picris echioides L.	s							x	
perennial sow-thistle	*Sonchus arvensis* L.	s				x			x	x
mayweed	*Tripleurospermum* sp.	s				x				
timothy	*Phleum pratense* L.	s				x				
sedges	*Carex* sp. flat	s				x		x		
sedges	*Carex* sp. trigonous	s		x	x	x		x	x	x

Table 12.6 continued.

	Trees and other								
cypress	*Cupressus* sp.	lf		x					
poplar	*Populus* sp.	bd		xx					
willow	*Salix* sp.	bd		x	xx	x			x
duckweed	*Lemna* sp.	s					xx		
	Sphagnum sp.			x		x			
	mosses					x			
water flea	*Daphnia* sp. – ephippia						xx	xx	few
	leaf					x			
	Buds			x		x			
	Animal hair						xx		

Table 12.6 continued.

where there was a clear association with tanning, but in this case the concentration was much higher.

The samples also contained a large quantity of common chickweed (*Stellaria media* Villars), as well as other species commonly found on waste or cultivated land, such as broad-leaved dock (*Rumex obtusifolium* L.) and field pennycress (*Thlaspi arvense* L.). Sample F765/ 1822 contained ephippia of *Daphnia* sp. and seeds of *Lemna* sp., suggesting that water was present in the pit.

An interesting waterlogged seed was recovered from an otherwise unremarkable post-hole, F826, at the northwest end of Area C, close to the Park Street frontage. It is a single seed of thornapple (*Datura stramonium* L.), recovered from Sample F826/ 1935. This is a poisonous plant native to the New World. It is believed that is was brought to Europe in the 16th century by the Spanish physician Francisco Hernandez (Starý 1998). It contains a high concentration of alkaloids (mainly scopolamine) and its medicinal properties are well attested (*ibid.*). The seed recovered from Park Street is the only example of thornapple so far recovered from an English archaeological site.

The Row

During the watching brief at The Row, Digbeth, four samples were collected from the section of the Birmingham Moat. Dating evidence for the construction of the moat and its subsequent infilling was poor. Pottery from the lowest moat levels was dated to the 12th–13th centuries (see Patrick, Chapter 5) and the final infilling of the moat may have begun in the late 18th century or have been contemporaneous with the construction of Smithfield Market in 1816 (see Patrick, Chapter 5). The samples described below were, however, medieval, being the equivalent of Watts Master Level 2.

The samples were assessed to establish if organic remains (in particular plant macroremains) were present and, if so, whether they could provide any insight into the water supply to the moat and the formation processes that occurred during the deposition of the moat's fill. The description of the soil profile and of the plant and insect assemblages recovered during earlier excavations

provided important comparative material (Greig 1980; Limbrey 1980; Osborne 1980). The sequence of deposits identified during the watching brief bears strong similarities with the stratigraphic sequence described by Limbrey (1980). The moat was cut into the natural sandstone. A first deposit of only few centimetres (SU 1010) consisted of a sandy/ silty layer with a darker grey colour compared to that of the natural sand through which the moat is cut. A thick deposit (*c*.50 cm) of dark brown decomposed organic matter lay at direct contact with this first layer (SU 1011, 1003 and 1005).

Samples 1011, 1003 and 1005 were all collected from the dark brown organic level. Sample 1011 was in direct contact with SU 1010, while SU 1003 was a band of charcoal observed within the main organic level.

Sample 1010 (No. 3)

This sample was taken from the bottom fill of the moat and it consisted of a fine sandy/ silt loam with lumps of darker organic material. The mineral component of this deposit prevails over the organic one. This bottom layer probably accumulated during the first periods of the existence of the moat. The plant remains present in this level consist mainly of fragments of waterlogged wood, well-preserved bud scales, and seeds. Some of the identified seeds belonged to plants associated with wet environments, such as duckweed (*Lemna* sp.) and rushes (*Juncus* sp.) or to plants associated with disturbed places, such as knotgrasses (*Polygonum* sp.), fat-hen (*Chenopodium album*), or common nettle (*Urtica dioica*). Fly pupae were observed in this sample although they were not abundant. The deposit also contained some caddis fly cases. These are generally associated with clean water, either still or flowing.

Sample 1011 (No. 4)

This sample was taken from the organic layer directly above sample 3 (SU 1010). It had a silty/ sandy matrix with a very compacted dark organic fraction that represents the predominant part of the deposit. Plant macroremains included mostly minute fragments of wood as well as larger pieces of waterlogged wood. A large quantity of stems of hemp (*Cannabis sativa* L.) were also identified. These were generally oriented horizontally and produced a lamellar pattern, a depositional pattern typical of sediments deposited in slow-flowing water environment, as one would have expected in a moat filled with water.

The hemp stems were identified only with a stereomicroscope and, therefore, their identification needs to be confirmed. However, the finding of hemp stems from other excavations in the areas (see above) and the presence of high percentages of Cannabinaceae pollen (Greig 1980) suggests that they could be the result of hemp retting. The retting of hemp in urban watercourses and canals was very common during this period and there are many references to the pollution caused by these activities (Ciaraldi *et al.* 2004).

The plant macroremains contained in this level were more abundant than in SU 1010 and contained species typical of wet and disturbed environments. A few insect remains were also observed.

Samples 1003 and 1005 (No. 1 and No. 2)
The nature of the deposit and the plant composition of the two samples closely resemble that of sample 1011, but contained a higher number of weed seeds: corncockle (*Agrostemma githago*), ragged-robin (*Lychnis flos-osculi*) and fairy flax (*Linum catharcticum*). The increased number of weeds could indicate either the proximity of cultivated fields or the presence of agricultural activities on the site. Of particular interest was the presence of some seeds of heather (*Erica* sp.). Heather appears also in the pollen sequence from the moat (Greig 1980). The finding of plant macroremains of heather, as well as pollen, confirms the presence of heather on site or in its immediate vicinity. Heather provides useful material for thatching and this could be one reason to explain its presence on site.

The plant assemblage recovered from samples 1, 2 and 4 (SU 1003, 1005, 1011) is similar to that recorded from the previous excavation (Greig 1980). It is, however, difficult to compare the two plant assemblages because of the absence of a stratigraphic reference in the previous work.

It is possible, however, to highlight some differences, in particular the absence in aquatic species such as pondweeds (*Potamogeton* sp.), bur-reeds (*Sparganium* sp.), and yellow water lilly (*Nuphar luteum*) in the deposit from The Row. The absence of these species could be either due to the small size of the sample examined or, more interestingly, to a real difference in the composition of the plant assemblage. If this was the case, it would indicate the existence of different environmental conditions in the two sections of the moat excavated, perhaps due to a different distance from the point where the water channel joined the moat.

Another important difference is the absence, in the new samples, of tree seeds. The pollen diagram from the old excavation seems to suggest the presence of close-by

trees (see Greig 1980). This difference, however, could also simply reflect the small size of the sample examined for the assessment.

Discussion

The picture of the centre of Birmingham during the medieval and post-medieval periods that emerges from the analysis of the plant macroremains is a complex one. During the period of time covered by this investigation (12th–18th centuries), important changes took place in social structure and in the organisation of urban spaces. The expansion of the town with its industrial activities and its commerce had a strong impact on the environment. Study of the plant remains from Egbaston Street, Moor Street, Park Street and The Row has provided some useful elements that contribute to the reconstruction of this picture.

Signs of industrial activity are already present in the archaeological deposits from Phase 1 (12th to 14th centuries). At Edgbaston Street, tanning activities are well attested, while at Park Street hemp retting may have been carried out in water-filled ditches. However, the emerging townscape still contained many open spaces, with trees and vegetation typical of disturbed ground. Working animals and animals destined for slaughter were probably kept in the town. The abundant supply of water would have been useful for watering the animals and the heather on all of the sites may have been derived from animal bedding or the thatching of byres and stables. Water, present in moats, ditches and ponds, must have attracted and favoured the establishment of industrial activities. Places such as Edgbaston Street and Park Street represented ideal locations for industries that required large amounts of water, such as tanning or hemp and flax retting. Gill refers to Digbeth during the 16th century. He notes 'the land hereabouts was much intersected by little streams, some of them natural but others cut artificially for use of the industry' (Gill 1930, 124). It is possible that a channel led from the postulated watercourse, identified as Hersum's Ditch (see Rátkai, Chapter 4), into the backplot boundary ditch at Park Street. The occurrence of water-based industrial activities at such a location must have been a typical strategy for the exploitation of wet environments, as the case of medieval Brewood also seems to attest (Ciaraldi *et al.* 2004). The use of ditches and moats for hemp retting (and possibly flax retting too) is also suggested in the centre of Birmingham by the late medieval deposits from the Manorial Moat at The Row (now Upper Dean Street) (Ciaraldi 2000; Greig 1980) and at Deritend Bridge, Digbeth (Ciaraldi 2002). The street name 'Rope Walk' in Digbeth, by the River Rea (Litherland 1995), is one of the few evidences left of the presence of this industry in Birmingham. Ropes, twines and linen must have been in great demand in the evolving and growing economy of medieval Birmingham. Documentary sources attest the cultivation of hemp and flax in Birmingham (see Hodder *et al.*, Chapter 16). The cultivation of hemp and flax is also suggested by the pollen evidence (Greig 1980 and this volume, Chapter 13).

Ditches and water features were surrounded by vegetation typical of damp and wet environments, with willows, poplars, rushes and sedges. Human habitations were located in close proximity to industrial activities. The presence of food debris in Area A at Park Street and at Moor Street suggests that houses must have been near by. Cereals were the most common food plants found, but there is also evidence for the consumption of figs, grapes, hazelnuts, plums and beet. The presence of grape suggests a high-status diet, even though it is difficult to imagine the presence of houses (and high-status ones!) in the vicinity of such insalubrious activities as tanning and retting, where the smell of degrading organic material must have been rather unpleasant. The presence of beet suggests that the cultivation of vegetables in plots and gardens was part of the daily life of the inhabitants of medieval Birmingham.

The plant evidence for Phase 3 is almost exclusively limited to Park Street. Evidence of human habitation still occurs in Area A. Food remains of cereals and fruits become even more varied, with the addition of new plants such as turnips. The increased variety of the food plants available must also reflect an intensification of trade activities. Hemp and flax are present in abundance (as also shown by pollen, Greig, Chapter 13) suggesting that hemp and flax retting may have continued to be important activities during this phase. Vegetation of wet environments and disturbed places is still predominant, however, with an increase in the number of arboreal species.

13   The Pollen

James Greig

Pollen analysis is especially useful for showing how wooded a past landscape was, whether cereals were being grown or processed in the vicinity, the status of some other crops such as peas, beans, hemp or buckwheat, and whether grassland or its remains were present. It can also detect sewage contamination and therefore the relative foulness of the deposits, in the form of parasite ova.

Summary

Pollen was generally abundant and well preserved in the material analysed, which was selected because of its organic appearance. Most of the samples showed much evidence of mature woodland, with oak, lime and elm, and of other woodland with birch, alder and holly, while hazel was present as an understorey of the woodland, or as scrub. Other trees present included hawthorn and willow. It seemed unusual that a settlement site should have so much evidence of woodland, but perhaps Birmingham was indeed founded in a wood. There is possible evidence of clearance of woodland, with smaller amounts being detected in samples of later date.

There was evidence of crops, such as cereals including rye and the cornfield weed cornflower, which are typical of the medieval and post-medieval periods. Other crops included broad bean, pea and buckwheat, a fairly unsophisticated selection. Flax was present, and may have been processed on the site to extract the linen fibres. Hemp was present in one feature, which may have been used for hemp processing.

Grassland or hay was also a feature of the deposits, which may be connected with the abundant signs of cattle, as well as being part of normal life at these times. A slight fouling of some of the deposits with parasite ova also provided evidence of town life.

Laboratory work, pollen analysis

The pollen samples were processed using the standard method: about 1 cm³ subsamples were dispersed in dilute NaOH and filtered through a 70-micron mesh to remove coarser material, which was then scanned under a stereo microscope. The finer organic part of the sample was concentrated by swirl separation on a shallow dish. Fine material was removed by filtration on a 10-micron mesh. The material was acetolysed to remove cellulose, stained with safranin and mounted on microscope slides in glycerol jelly. Counting was done with a Leitz Dialux microscope and several hundred pollen grains in each sample were counted. In addition, the slides were scanned so that rare but sometimes quite significant pollen types, such as flax, could be detected. Identification was achieved using the author's pollen reference collection, seen with a Leitz Lablux microscope. Standard reference works were used, notably Fægri and Iversen (1989) and Andrew (1984).

The pollen counts have been listed in taxonomic order in Tables 13.1–13.4. The nomenclature and order of the taxa in these lists follow Bennett (1994) and Kent (1992) respectively.

Edgbaston Street

Features with sediments that appeared organic in character were sampled during the excavations. All the samples and profiles selected for pollen analysis from the Edgbaston Street site related to the Phase 1 activity (12th to 14th centuries). The sample selected comprised a basal fill (1012) of the square Phase 1 pit F123/ F105 in Area A.

In addition, two profiles were collected as monoliths. The first, of 75cm depth, was collected by the excavation team from the fill of the ancient watercourse which once connected the Parsonage Moat with the Lord of the Manor's Moat. The profile encompassed layers 5056, a gleyed black clay, and 5057, a compacted peaty deposit, revealed in Trench 5 of the evaluation phase of the investigations. The pollen from three samples from this monolith has been analysed here.

The second monolith, of 50cm, was collected by the author from organic deposits overlying the natural gravel in Area D of the excavations. In the medieval period this area, immediately to the south of the watercourse, lay outside the town and within one of the lord of the manor's hunting parks, Holme Park. The profile encompassed layer 4031, an organic silt resting on gravel, and layer 4032, an organic silty clay overlain by more disturbed material with brick fragments. This monolith was subsampled at an interval of 5cm and the sub-samples stored in a fridge. Three subsamples from this monolith have been assessed here. In most of Area D the organic deposits were truncated by post-medieval features.

The watercourse (Table 13.1)

Pollen was well preserved and abundant at the bottom of the profile, but somewhat thin and sparse higher up.

Trees and shrubs, woodland

There was 17–20% tree and shrub pollen, which suggests no more than perhaps some hedgerows and a few trees growing here and there – common ones such as *Alnus* (alder), *Quercus* (oak), *Corylus* (hazel) and *Betula* (birch).

Crops and weeds

Some sign of human activity is shown by a small Cerealia (probably cereals) pollen record in the lower two samples. More interestingly, *Vicia faba* (broad bean) and Cannabaceae (possibly hemp) were found in the lowest sample. These are typical medieval crops, and hemp was widely used for making rope and canvas, while broad bean was eaten, possibly dried for storage.

Other herbs; weeds and grassland

Most of the pollen, about 50–65%, was from herbs which represent a range of grassland plants including characteristic ones such as *Plantago lanceolata* (ribwort plantain) and *Centaurea nigra* (knapweed). *Pteridium* (bracken) spores show the presence of the remains of this fern. The weeds include *Centaurea cyanus* (cornflower), a characteristic cornfield weed of the medieval and post-medieval period. This might not have grown near by, however, as its remains can also come from straw and from the processing and storage of cereals brought into the town. Other weeds are less diagnostic, but probably correspond with plants of the relevant taxa identified from macrofossils (see Ciaraldi, Chapter 12).

Wetland, marshland

Wet deposits usually have a high representation of aquatic and marsh plants. The 16% Cyperaceae (sedge) pollen probably comes from local sedges growing on the forming deposit, but have little to tell us of archaeological significance.

Sewage; parasite ova

One ovum of Trichuris (whipworm) was found. This is an intestinal parasite carried by many animals, especially pigs and humans. This provides a slight indication of sewage contamination.

Area D organic deposit (Table 13.2)

The pollen in the profile through this deposit was well preserved and abundant.

Woodland and scrub

The lowest layer shows considerable evidence of woodland, with 70% tree and shrub pollen, mainly *Alnus* (alder), with *Quercus* (oak), *Tilia* (lime) and *Ulmus* (elm). The upper layers had a much smaller amount of tree and shrub pollen (15–17%), as might be expected in an occupied landscape. *Sambucus nigra* (elder) seed was noted in the residue; it does not feature among the pollen results but then it does not disperse much pollen.

These results seem to show that the surroundings were rather wooded to start with, and were subsequently occupied, probably after clearance. Other samples from this area, as well as results from Metchley (Greig 2002), seem to show that what is now the city centre area and Edgbaston were once well wooded, with settlements making clearings and gradually reducing the wooded area.

Crops and weeds

A small amount of Cerealia (probable cereal pollen) was present throughout. Cannabaceae (probably hemp) was present in one sample (20cm), in which there was also a possible pollen grain of *Fagopyrum* (buckwheat). This last was a minor crop in the later medieval and post-medieval period, better known from pollen than macro-fossil remains. Buckwheat was grown, particularly on poor sandy soils on which it could be more productive than other crops.

Many pollen records are probably from weeds, including cornfield weeds such as *Centaurea cyanus* (corn-flower) (see above). Others included *Cirsium* type (thistle), *Arctium* (burdock), and *Chenopodiaceae* (goosefoot or orache), which indicate open habitats usually created by various human activities and, therefore, occupation of the site.

Grassland

At least some of the Poaceae (grass) pollen, although grasses grow in most habitats, is from wetland grasses growing on the spot, as shown by a record of Glyceria (sweet-grass) seen in the residue of the pollen preparation. More certain indicators of grassland include *Plantago lanceolata* (ribwort plantain) and *Centaurea nigra* (knapweed). The grassland part of the record might partly reflect local surroundings, but could just as easily have come from hay or dung that had been brought in from outside Birmingham.

depth in column from top	5 cm	30 cm	55 cm	
spores				
Pteridium	3	5	5	bracken
Polypodium	–	–	1	polypody
Sphagnum	9	8	–	sphagnum moss
Filicales	–	4	–	ferns, undifferentiated
pollen				
Pinus	1	4	-	pine
*Ranunculus*_tp.	-	-	1	buttercup, crowfoot
Thalictrum	–	–	1	meadow rue
*Cannabis*_tp.	–	–	1	hemp, hop
Quercus	5	5	11	oak
Betula	2	1	1	birch
Alnus	7	4	11	alder
Corylus	4	3	4	hazel
Chenopodiaceae	4	3	4	goosefoot
Caryophyllaceae	-	1	+	stitchwort family
*Persicaria bistorta*_tp.	2	-	-	bistort etc.
*Rumex*_tp.	1	–	–	docks and sorrels
Tilia	-	-	+	lime
Brassicaceae	1	1	–	brassicas
Ericales	–	2	2	heathers
cf. *Trifolium pratense*	2	1	-	red clover
Vicia faba	–	–	+	broad bean
Epilobium	–	1	–	willow herb
Plantago major/media	2	-	-	plantain
Plantago lanceolata	-	-	3	ribwort plantain
Dipsacaceae	–	1	1	scabiouses
*Cirsium*_tp	–	3	+	thistles
Centaurea cyanus	-	3	6	cornflower
Centaurea nigra	+	1	0	knapweed
Lactuceae	6	17	9	a group of composites
*Aster*_tp.	–	1	1	daisies etc.
Artemisia	1	1	–	mugwort
*Anthemis*_tp.	–	1	2	mayweeds etc.
Cyperaceae	22	19	24	sedges
Poaceae	40	32	64	grasses
Cerealia_tp.	–	–	4	probable cereals
total pollen	100	105	150	
non pollen				
charcoal	+	++	–	
Trichuris	-	1	-	whipworm (parasite ova)

Table 13.1 Edgbaston Street; pollen and spores from Trench 5, ditch or watercourse fill, 5057 and 5056.

depth in column	0cm	20cm	40cm	
spores				
Pteridium	–	–	7	bracken
Polypodium	–	–	1	polypody
Sphagnum	–	–	1	sphagnum moss
Filicales	–	–	2	ferns, undifferentiated
pollen				
Pinus	-	+	+	pine
*Ranunculus*_tp.	1	1	-	buttercup, crowfoot
Ulmus	-	-	2	elm
*Cannabis*_tp.	–	1	–	hemp, hop
Quercus	9	2	9	oak
Betula	3	3	5	birch
Alnus	6	7	49	alder
Corylus	1	4	5	hazel
Chenopodiaceae	1	2	-	goosefoot
Caryophyllaceae	1	2	+	stitchwort family
? *Fagopyrum*	–	+	–	possible buckwheat
*Rumex*_tp.	1	5	1	docks and sorrels
Tilia	1	1	6	lime
Brassicaceae	2	–	–	brassicas
Ericales	–	+	1	heathers
Filipendula	1	–	–	meadowsweet
Agrimonia	–	–	1	agrimony
Trifolium repens	-	1	-	white clover
Hedera	–	–	+	ivy
Apiaceae	–	–	1	umbellifers
Plantago lanceolata	-	4	6	ribwort plantain
Fraxinus	–	–	1	ash
Rubiaceae	–	–	+	bedstraws
Valeriana officinalis	–	+	–	valerian
Dipsacaceae	–	–	+	scabiouses
cf. *Arctium*	–	+	–	? burdock
*Cirsium*_tp.	1	1	–	thistles
Centaurea cyanus	1	-	+	cornflower
Centaurea nigra	1	1	-	knapweed
Lactuceae	12	6	1	a group of composites
*Aster*_tp.	2	6	1	daisies etc.
Artemisia	–	–	–	mugwort
*Anthemis*_tp.	–	–	2	mayweeds etc.
Cyperaceae	15	6	3	sedges
Poaceae	59	74	18	grasses
*Cerealia*_tp.	+	3	+	cereals
total pollen	118	130	113	
non pollen				
charcoal	++	++	–	
Trichuris	+	+	–	whipworm
diatoms	–	+	–	

Table 13.2 Edgbaston Street; pollen and spores from Area D, contexts 4031 and 4032.

Wetland and aquatic vegetation

Once again, the indications are of marshy conditions with Cyperaceae (sedges) and diatoms present, although without a big aquatic flora, suggesting that this was probably a small damp area rather than a big wet one.

Parasites

Trichuris (whipworm) ova were present in the middle and top sample, providing more evidence for a change from a rather natural, wooded, site to one becoming occupied and polluted.

Area A, medieval pit F123 (1012) Phase 1 (Table 13.3)

Trees and woodland

Abundant *Alnus* (alder), *Corylus* (hazel), *Betula* (birch) and *Quercus* (oak) pollen suggests wooded conditions in

sample number	6	22	23	
feature	F123	F265	F266	
context	1012	2225	2227	
spores				
Pteridium	26 (11)			bracken
Polypodium	2 (1)			polypody
Sphagnum	x			sphagnum moss
Filicales	5 (2)			ferns, undifferentiated
pollen				
Pinus	2 (1)			pine
Ranunculus tp.	+			buttercup, crowfoot
Ulmus	1 (+)			elm
Cannabis tp.				hemp, hop
Urtica	3 (1)			nettle
Quercus	15 (7)			oak
Betula	9 (4)			birch
Alnus	89 (39)			alder
Corylus	25 (11)			hazel
Chenopodiaceae	+			goosefoot
Caryophyllaceae	3 (1)			stitchwort family
? *Fagopyrum*				possible buckwheat
Persicaria bistorta tp.	1 (+)			bistort
Persicaria maculosa tp.	+			persicaria
Rumex tp.	2 (1)			docks and sorrels
Tilia	+			lime
Salix	6 (3)			willow
Brassicaceae				brassicas
Ericales	(+)			heathers
Filipendula	1 (+)			meadowsweet
Potentilla tp.	2 (1)			cinquefoils
Agrimonia				agrimony
Trifolium repens				white clover
Linum usitatissimum	+			flax
Hedera				ivy
Lamium tp.	1 (+)			dead-nettle
Apiaceae				umbellifers
Plantago lanceolata	3 (1)			ribwort plantain
Fraxinus	2 (1)			ash
Campanulaceae	1 (+)			bell flowers, rampion
Rubiaceae				bedstraws
Sambucus nigra	1 (+)			elder
Valeriana officinalis				valerian
Dipsacaceae				scabiouses
cf. *Arctium*				? burdock
Cirsium tp.				thistles
Centaurea cyanus	(2) 1			cornflower
Centaurea nigra	+			knapweed
Lactuceae	5 (2)			a group of composites
Aster tp.	1 (+)			daisies etc.
Artemisia	1 (+)			mugwort
Anthemis tp.				mayweeds etc.
Cyperaceae	1 (+)			sedges
Poaceae	47 (21)			grasses
Cerealia tp.	8 (3)			cereals
Secale	3 (1)			rye
total pollen	229			
non pollen				
charcoal				
Trichuris	1 (+)			whipworm
diatoms	+			

Table 13.3 Edgbaston Street; pollen and microfossils from Area A, F123, 1012 C12th–14th pit; F265, 2225 ditch and F266, 2227, C12th–14th pit.

James Greig

the surroundings. A range of other trees were also present, such as *Salix* (willow), *Ilex* (holly) and *Fraxinus* (ash), so that tree and shrub pollen is 64% of the total. So much sign of woodland is unusual for an occupied site, although this could represent woodland and scrub which grew after the area went out of use, if only temporarily. Although there is plenty of evidence that the surroundings were well wooded, it is possible that woodland products such as bark, which were evidently brought in to the site for use in the tanning process, could have brought in further tree pollen attached to them.

Crops and weeds
Cereal pollen, including some *Secale* (rye) and a single grain of *Linum usitatissimum* (flax), show a range of crops. The cornfield weed *Centaurea cyanus* was present. Quite a large range of weeds was also present, although the pollen cannot be exactly identified.

Grassland etc.
There are some signs of grassland plants such as *Plantago lanceolata* (ribwort plantain) and *Centaurea nigra* (knapweed), as well as grass pollen. The large amount of *Pteridium* (bracken) spores is striking, and could represent bracken brought in for some purpose, such as animal bedding. Polypodium spores were also present, from ferns growing on walls or tree trunks.

Wetland, aquatic
The signs of wet conditions are fairly few, with some records of plants of damp places such as *Filipendula* (meadowsweet). The presence of diatoms shows that the pit was probably filled with water, at least part of the time.

There were very few macrofossils in this material for comparanda. However, insect remains (Smith, Chapter 14) indicate human settlement waste and the presence of decaying vegetation and timbers. Smith (*ibid.*) also suggests that the water content of F123 may have been temporary.

Moor Street

Pollen analysis was undertaken on one sample from the Moor Street excavation. The sample was derived from a lower fill (5188) of the recut Phase 1 boundary ditch F568 dating to the first half of the 13th century. It contained plenty of well-preserved pollen (Table 13.4).

Trees and woodland, scrub
There is a large amount of tree pollen, mainly *Alnus* (alder), *Corylus* (hazel) and *Quercus* (oak), with a little *Betula* (birch), *Tilia* (lime), and *Ilex* (holly), amounting to 45% of the total pollen. It would seem that the area may have had woodland, or that woodland products with pollen such as firewood, tanning bark or brushwood were brought to the site. A small record of *Sambucus nigra* (elder) probably represents bushes growing in the occupied area; elder seeds were certainly numerous, but

there were no other signs of trees, which do not, however, show up very strongly from macrofossils (see Ciaraldi, Chapter 12). Pollen from *Ericales* (heathers) was quite abundant at 7%, and would seem to represent heathers which were brought to the site for some use such as roofing or making brooms.

Crops and weeds
Cerealia (mainly cereals), including *Secale* (rye), are the main crop, and the cornfield weed *Centaurea cyanus* (cornflower) would have been present with cereals and their processing products, whether as grain, corresponding with the numerous macrofossil finds of cereals and cornfield weeds (Ciaraldi, Chapter 12), or as other products such as straw, chaff or animal dung. They represent the normal background of medieval life, a time when rye was still one of the usual crops, especially grown on sandy soils where it, like buckwheat, does better than other cereals. *Linum usitatissimum* (flax) was also seen, a crop grown for its fibres and its seeds, which could be used for linseed oil or eaten. A large range of other weeds was present which probably correspond with macrofossil records, given in brackets; these include Chenopodiaceae (*Chenopodium*, *Atriplex*), Caryophyllaceae (*Stellaria*), Spergula (*Spergula arvensis*), and Rumex (*Rumex acetosella*). Some of these could have been cornfield weeds and brought in to the site, while others probably grew locally. *Spergula arvensis* and *Rumex acetosella* are characteristic of sandy soils.

Grassland, bracken
There was 30% *Poaceae* (grass) pollen, together with records of some grassland plants such as *Ononis* (restharrow), *Trifolium pratense* (red clover), *Centaurea nigra* (knapweed) and *Plantago lanceolata* (ribwort plantain), which could represent meadows or animal dung, or grassy ground growing on the site. There were also large numbers of *Pteridium* (bracken) spores, which could represent bracken brought into the town.

Wetland and aquatic
Cyperaceae (sedge) pollen and *Persicaria bistorta* (amphibious bistort) could represent the damp environment local to the ditch.

Other remains
Ova of the intestinal parasites Ascaris and Trichuris were present, and indicate a small level of sewage contamination, as might be expected in a ditch by a medieval settlement, but not enough to suggest that the ditch served as a latrine.

The picture from this deposit is rather consistent with that from the organic remains from other sites in Birmingham, with aspects of crops or their processing, and the waste products of every-day life being discovered. It adds to the picture of a settlement developing in the woods, at least to start with, and to the pattern of crops present.

spores	nr (%)		
Pteridium	30 (11)	bracken	open grassland; bracken brought to site?
Polypodium	6 (2)	polypody	tree trunks, walls, etc.
Sphagnum	2 (1)	sphagnum moss	
pollen			
Pinus	+	pine	woodland
Urtica	1 (+)	nettle	various overgrown habitats
Quercus	30 (11)	oak	woodland
Betula	10 (4)	birch	woodland and scrub
Alnus	40 (15)	alder	woodland
Corylus	34 (13)	hazel	woodland and scrub
Chenopodiaceae	4 (1)	goosefoot	weeds
Spergula	+	spurrey	weed, especially on sandy soils
Persicaria bistorta tp.	1 (+)	bistort etc.	wetland, marsh
Rumex tp.	1	docks and sorrels	many habitats; mainly weeds
Tilia	3 (1)	lime	woodland
Brassicaceae	1 (+)	brassicas	many habitats; weeds, some cultivated plants
Ericales	9 (7)	heathers	heathland; heather may have been brought in to site
Ononis sp.	1 (+)	restharrow	grassy places
cf. *Trifolium pratense*	1 (+)	red clover	grassland, meadow
Ilex aquifolium	2 (1)	holly	woodland, wood pasture
Linum usitatissimum	+	flax, linseed	cultivated crop, produces little pollen so small records are important
Plantago lanceolata	3 (1)	ribwort plantain	grassland
Sambucus nigra	2 (1)	elder	enriched waste ground
Dipsacaceae	+	scabiouses	various
Cirsium tp	+	thistles	
Centaurea cyanus	2 (1)	cornflower	weed of autumn-sown cornfields
Centaurea nigra	+	knapweed	grassland; hay meadow
Lactuceae	5 (2)	a group of composites	mainly grassland plants and some weeds
Aster tp.	3 (1)	daisies etc	mainly weeds
Cyperaceae	6 (2)	sedges	many habitats, mainly marshy
Poaceae	81 (30)	grasses	many habitats
Cerealia tp.	13 (5)	probable cereals	crop plant
Secale-tp.	+	rye	crop plant
total pollen	267 (100)		
non pollen			
charcoal	+		
Trichuris	1	whipworm	parasite ova
Ascaris	2		parasite ova

Table 13.4 Moor Street; pollen and other microfossils from Phase 1, F568 5018 ditch. Values given as '+' are pollen recorded during scanning of the slide, present as less than 1%.

Park Street

At Park Street, pollen analysis was undertaken on three samples from the major Phase 1 boundary ditch F174/F201, from a 17th-century (sub-phase 3.1) pit F803, and from a fill of F503/F520, one of the wood-lined tanks backfilled in the late 18th century (sub-phase 3.3). Park Street is the only one of the three sites where pollen analysis was undertaken on the deposits later than Phase 1, and this provided some opportunity to explore the changing environment of the town as reflected in the pollen record. The results are presented in Table 13.5.

Phase 1 boundary ditch F174/ F201

Three samples were analysed from three different fills of

this major Phase 1 boundary ditch in Area A. The samples were taken from ditch section F174. The samples were taken from 1246, the basal fill of the ditch dated post-1250 on the ceramic evidence, from the fill above it (1213), which contained possible pottery wasters, and from a middle fill of the ditch (1197), also containing possible pottery wasters. The results from the three samples are presented separately in Table 13.5 but are discussed together below.

Trees and woodland

The results show signs of woodland, as at the other sites, with *Alnus* (alder), *Quercus* (oak), *Betula* (birch), and *Corylus* (hazel). In the basal fill of the ditch (1246) tree pollen is 50%, increasing, perhaps surprisingly, to 68%

sample number	16	18	19	53	77	90	
feature	F174	F174	F174	F503	F803	F803	
context	1197	1213	1246	1580	1835	1835	
phase	1/2	1/2	1/2	1/2	3	3	
spores							
Pteridium	19 (8)	60 (27)	48 (42)	4 (2)	2 (1)	-	bracken
Polypodium	+	2 (1)	+	+	3 (1)	+	polypody
Sphagnum	-	-	-	-	+	1 (1)	sphagnum moss
pollen							
Pinus	+	+	+	2 (1)	7 (3)	6 (5)	pine
*Ranunculus*_tp.		1 (+)	-	2 (1)	-	-	buttercup, crowfoot
Ulmus	-	-	-	-	2 (1)	1 (1)	elm
*Cannabis*_tp.					12 (5)	2 (2)	hemp, hop
Urtica	-	1 (+)	1 (1)	-	-	-	
Fagus	-	-	+	-	+	-	beech
Quercus	40 (18)	44 (20)	9 (8)	13 (6)	21 (9)	13 (11)	oak
Betula	29 (13)	19 (9)	11 (10)	11 (5)	9 (4)	10 (9)	birch
Alnus	42 (19)	34 (15)	9 (8)	41 (19)	94 (38)	41 (35)	alder
Carpinus	-	-	-	-	1 (+)	-	hornbeam
Corylus	24 (11)	46 (21)	25 (22)	9 (4)	35 (14)	10 (9)	hazel
Chenopodiaceae	1 (+)	+	+	+	+	+	goosefoot
Caryophyllaceae	+	2 (+)	1 (1)	-	1 (+)	1 (1)	stitchwort family
Spergula	+	1 +)	2 (2)	-	-	-	spurrey
Fagopyrum esculentum	-	-	+	-	-	-	buckwheat
Fallopia convolvulus	1 (+)	-	-	-	-	-	black bindweed
*Persicaria maculosa*_tp.	+	-	+	-	-	1 (1)	persicaria
Persicaria bistorta tp.	-	-	-	-	+	-	amphibious bistort
*Rumex*_tp.	6 (3)	6 (3)	3 (3)	-	1 (+)	1 (1)	docks and sorrels
Tilia	1 (+)	1 (+)	+	2 (1)	3 (1)	1 (1)	lime
Populus	1 (+)	-	-	-	-	-	poplar
Salix	-	1 (+)	3 (3)	5 (2)	11 (4)	-	willow
Brassicaceae	1 (+)	+	2 (2)	-	1 (+)	1 (1)	brassicas
Ericales	1 (+)	13 (6)	+	2 (1)	+	-	heathers
Filipendula	2 (1)	1 (+)	+	-	-	-	meadowsweet
Potentilla tp.	-	1 (+)	-	-	-	-	cinquefoil
Crataegus	3 (1)	+	-	-	-	-	hawthorn
Pisum sativum	-	-	-	+	-	-	garden pea
Trifolium repens	-	-	-	1 (+)	-	1 (1)	white clover
cf. *Trifolium pratense*	-	-	-	8 (4)	-	-	red clover
Epilobium	-	-	+	-	-	-	willow herb
Ilex aquifolium	5 (2)	3 (1)	+	-	1 (+)	-	holly
cf. *Frangula alnus*	1 (+)	-	-	-	-	-	alder buckthorn
Hedera helix	-	1 (+)	-	-	-	-	ivy
Linum usitatissimum	+	-	+	-	-	-	flax
Plantago major/media	-	-	-	1 (+)	-	1 (1)	plantain
Plantago lanceolata	3 (1)	3 (1)	+	10 (5)	1 (+)	-	ribwort plantain
Fraxinus	-	1 (+)	-	3 (1)	-	1 (1)	ash
Galium tp.	-	-	-	1 (+)	-	-	bedstraws
Sambucus nigra	7 (3)	3 (1)	1 (1)	1 (+)	-	1 (1)	elder
Dipsacaceae	+	+	-	+	-	1 (1)	scabiouses
Arctium	-	-	-	-	+	-	burdock
*Cirsium*_tp	+	-	1 (1)	+	+	+	thistles
Centaurea cyanus	1 (+)	-	+	+	-	-	cornflower
Centaurea nigra	+	-	-	+	+	-	knapweed
Lactuceae	5 (2)	+	+	8 (4)	2 (1)	4 (3)	a group of composites

Table 13.5 Park St; pollen and spores from a medieval ditch and post-medieval and pits at Birmingham.

*Aster*_tp.	_	-	-	1 (+)	1 (+)	+	daisies etc
Artemisia	-	-	-	-	+	+	mugwort
*Anthemis*_tp.	2 (1)	1 (+)	+	-	-	-	mayweeds etc.
Cyperaceae	2 (1)	2 (1)	5 (4)	2 (1)	7 (3)	3 (3)	sedges
Poaceae	39 (8)	28 (13)	40 (35)	89 (41)	34 (14)	15 (13)	grasses
Cerealia_tp.	8 (4)	6 (3)	1 (1)	5 (2)	2 (1)	1 (1)	probable cereals
Secale tp.	-	1 (+)	+	-	+	+	rye
total pollen	225	221	113	219	245	116	
non pollen							
Trichuris	-	-	-	1 (+)	+	+	whipworm
Ascaris	2 (1)	-	-	-	-		(parasite ova)
diatoms	-	+	+	-	+	-	

Table 13.5 continued.

in the middle fill (1197). Other trees include *Ilex* (holly), which was probably more widespread than its pollen record would suggest, likewise *Crataegus* (hawthorn) and *Frangula alnus* (alder buckthorn), which might indicate woodland edge, scrub or hedgerow. *Sambucus nigra* (elder) indicates overgrown, nutrient-rich ground, while *Populus* (poplar) and *Salix* (willow) suggest damp ground. *Ericales* (heathers) were low except in 1213, where they reach 6%, perhaps from heathery material brought in.

Crops and weeds

There is a substantial Cerealia record of 3–4%, which could represent wheat, barley or oats; the first two were found as macrofossils (pers. comm. M Ciaraldi). *Secale* (rye) pollen was also supported by macrofossils, and pollen of *Centaurea cyanus* (cornflower). Pollen of *Linum usitatissimum* (flax) and of *Fagopyrum esculentum* (buckwheat) was also present, together with a possible pea. A large range of weeds was present, such as *Chenopodiaceae* (goosefoot), Aster type (daisies etc), *Cirsium* type (spear thistles), *Rumex* sp. (docks), and *Urtica* (nettle). *Spergula* (spurry) is characteristic of rather sandy soils.

Grassland

Grassland plants were present, including Poaceae (grasses), *Centaurea nigra* (knapweed) and *Plantago lanceolata* (ribwort plantain), together with a large number of *Pteridium* (bracken) spores. Grassland plants accounted for 42% of the pollen sum in 1246, the basal fill of the ditch, but accounted for only 8% in the later fill 1197 (with *Pteridium* spores not counted).

Wetland, other remains

There was little sign of any wetland or aquatic flora evident in the pollen from the ditch, apart from some Cyperaceae (sedge) pollen and some *Persicaria maculosa* tp., which includes a range of persicarias of damp and weedy habitats, and a record of *Filipendula* (meadowsweet).

Finally, only a single record of ova of the intestinal parasite Ascaris in 1197 seems to show relatively clean conditions, while diatoms from the basal fills (1246 and 1213) show that there was standing water at least part of the time.

Phase 3 pit F803 (1835)

This pit was located at the rear end of the plot in Area C, in the generally damp or waterlogged ground adjacent to the boundary ditch which defined the back of the Park Street plots. The pit contained domestic and building debris, as well as a small amount of metal-working slag and a piece of bone-working debris. The pottery from the pit suggested a 17th-century (Phase 3.1) date for its infilling. Two samples were analysed from fill 1835 of this pit.

In terms of the pollen, the assemblage was generally similar to those from the much earlier features described above, with more than 70% tree pollen. However, this was the only context with *Carpinus* (hornbeam) and *Fagus* (beech). Hornbeam is native mainly in southeast England although it has been widely planted elsewhere and grows well enough in the Midlands today, as shown by old hornbeam trees in the Edgbaston nature reserve. These trees could be a sign of later management and plantation.

An important difference from the other results is the presence of Cannabaceae pollen, with 5% in one of the samples from 1835. A macrofossil find of *Cannabis sativa* (hemp) suggests that the pollen record is also of hemp, rather than from hops. Hemp may have been processed in this pit but may also just have been part of the background of remains of crop plants that were around. A further difference is that there was rather little cereal pollen compared with most of the others.

Phase 3 wood-lined tank F503/ F520

This is one of two wood-lined tanks, of uncertain function, located in Area B, at the rear of the Park Street plots. The ceramic evidence suggests that the pits were infilled in late 18th century (sub-phase 3.3). The sample analysed was taken from 1580, one of the lower fills of the portion of the tank excavated as F520.

Similar finds to F174, with 40% tree pollen from a range of trees and shrubs, mainly alder, oak, birch and hazel, were found. Crops and weeds include cereal pollen, a record of pea and a range of weeds including cornflower. Grassland is also well represented by grasses, plantain and clover. A trace of whipworm shows some excrement.

General discussion of the evolution of the landscape and cityscape of Birmingham

A picture is gradually emerging of the development of the landscape of Birmingham, from results of various dates and from various sites, which seem to show that this was not a particularly good place to inhabit. Prehistoric evidence from beneath the Bronze Age burnt mound at Bournville shows that the prehistoric wildwood with lime and oak seems to have persisted there for longer than elsewhere, where woodland clearance on better land was already well advanced by this time (Greig 1982). A likely reason is that places with lighter and more easily tilled soil were much preferred for occupation, such as the Avon valley. This left the Birmingham plateau as a less favoured spot and major clearance and settlement in the West Midlands did not really occur until the Bronze Age in any case. Roman results from Metchley Fort seem to show that secondary woodland spread over an agricultural landscape after the fort was abandoned around AD 200; this seems to have lasted through the Anglo-Saxon/ early medieval period and the area was

only gradually reoccupied in the medieval period, before becoming part of Metchley Park (Greig 2002; 2005). This may reflect the general pattern of settlement of this area; the predominant signs of woodland with oak, elm and lime in some of the samples from the Birmingham city sites seem characteristic of mature woodland. Another medieval site with signs of thick woodland within a short distance of the settlement is Brewood, Staffordshire (Greig 2002), and it may be that in the case of Birmingham the settlement continued to grow, while others such as Brewood remained villages. Finally, the results from the previous excavation of the Birmingham moat (Watts 1980) show an occupied environment and evidence of cereals and probable hemp, which were probably being processed near by and possibly dated to the final fill of the moat, of post-medieval date. The signs of woodland were thought to represent trees actually overhanging the moat, as they probably were, but it now seems that early Birmingham was much more wooded overall. However, the presence of woodland may not indicate less occupation but may simply reflect landuse around the settled area. If, for example, the woodland represented wood pasture then it may indicate a bias towards stock rearing rather than arable farming. In this way the pollen and other environmental results from a number of suitable sites gradually fill in a picture of the evolving landscape which are of value for an understanding the development of the whole area.

14   The Insect Remains from Edgbaston Street and Park Street

David Smith

Introduction

It was hoped that the study of the insect remains from Edgbaston Street and Park Street might address the following questions:

- Can the insect remains from specific features help with the interpretation of these features?
- Do the insects present enable us to reconstruct the nature or processes of deposition within features?
- Do the insects suggest whether the contents of ditches or pits relate to the time of their use (*e.g.* as tanning pits) or do they represent activity occurring after the features had fallen out of use?
- Do the insects suggest the nature of the ground conditions adjacent to features?
- Do the insect remains support the conclusions drawn from the studies of the pollen and plant macrofossils?

The contribution of the results of the analysis of insect fauna to these research aims is discussed below.

Sample selection

The initial selection of samples for an assessment of their potential for insect remains was made on the basis of the security of the contexts and the dating of the individual deposits. An assessment of the potential of the various selected samples was presented in Mould *et al.* 2001b and Burrows *et al.* 2002. Selection of the samples for full analysis – the samples discussed here – was based on the quality of the insect faunas identified during the assessment stage. No suitable samples for full analysis were obtained from the Moor Street site.

Sample processing and analysis

The samples were processed using the standard method of paraffin flotation as outlined in Kenward *et al.* (1980). The weights and volumes of the samples processed are presented in Tables 14.3 and 14.4.

The insect remains present were sorted from the flots and stored in ethanol. The Coleoptera (beetles) present were identified by direct comparison to the Gorham and Girling Collections of British Coleoptera. The various taxa of insects recovered from the samples from Edgbaston Street are presented in Table 14.1 and those from Park Street are presented in Table 14.2. The taxonomy of both tables follows that of Lucht (1987).

Where applicable, each species of Coleoptera has been assigned to one or more ecological groupings and these are indicated in the second column of Tables 14.1 and 14.2. These groupings are derived from the preliminary classifications outlined by Kenward (1978). The classifications used here replicate those in Kenward and Hall (1995). The groupings themselves are described at the end of Table 14.1. The various proportions of these groups, expressed as percentages of the total Coleoptera present, are shown in Table 14.3 and Fig. 14.1 for Edgbaston Street, and Table 14.4 and Fig. 14.2 for Park Street.

Some of the Coleoptera have also been assigned codes based upon the extent of their synanthropy (dependence on human settlement). These codes are derived from those used by Kenward (1997). The author is grateful to Kenward for supplying him with a listing of the species in each grouping. The synanthropic groupings are described at the end of Table 14.1 and the individual codes for the relevant species are shown in column 3 of Table 14.1. The proportions of these synanthropic groupings, expressed as a percentage of the total fauna, is presented in Table 14.5 and Fig. 14.3 for Edgbaston Street, and Table 14.6 and Fig. 14.4 for Park Street.

The dipterous (fly) puparia were identified using the drawings in Smith (1973; 1989) and, where possible, by direct comparison with specimens identified by Peter Skidmore. The various taxa of insects recovered from these samples are presented in Table 14.1. The taxonomy follows that of Smith (1989) for the Diptera.

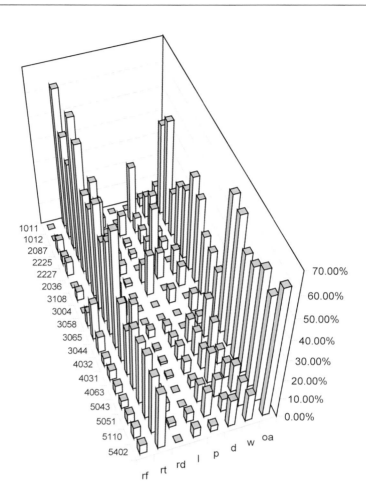

Fig. 14.1 Insect remains; proportions of the ecological groups for the Coleoptera present from Edgbaston Street.

The insect faunas recovered

The insect remains from Edgbaston Street

Area A
Two insect faunas were recovered from Area A. These came from the fill of the Phase 1 square-cut pit F123 (contexts 1011 and 1012).

Both faunas were relatively small (Tables 14.1 and 14.3) and the fragments recovered were quite eroded. The majority of the species are typical inhabitants of human settlement, such as *Omalium excavatum*, *Enicmus minutus*, *Monotoma*, the 'spider beetle' *Ptinus fur*, and the Cryptophagidae. These are all associated with a range of decaying and mouldering vegetation and other waste around human settlements. These species also form the core of the association of species that Kenward (Kenward and Hall 1995) has labelled the 'house fauna'. Also present in both samples is another species commonly associated with human settlement. This is the common woodworm *Anobium punctatum*. Sample 1011 also contained the 'powder post' beetle *Lyctus brunneus*. Both these species of insect are associated with decaying

prepared timbers.

Also present were small numbers of a range of water beetles such as Hydroporus, Agabus, Rhantus and Hydraena species. These are all associated with slow-flowing or still pools of water, which often are temporary (Friday 1988; Hansen 1997; Nillson and Holmen 1995).

The presence of these species may suggest that this pit was periodically flooded.

Area B
Four insect faunas were recovered from this area of the site. Three came from Phase 1 features: a tanning pit (F218, 2087), a gully (F265, 2225) and a pit (F266, 2227) also probably associated with tanning. A range of species that are commonly associated with rotting settlement waste dominated these three faunas (cf. Hall *et al.* 1983; Kenward and Hall 1995; Carrot and Kenward 2001). The ecological groups 'rt' and 'rd' in Table 14.3 and Fig. 14.1 represent this. These species are also predominantly synanthropic species (see Table 14.3 and Fig. 14.2). Examples of these are the Omalium species, *Xylodromus concinnus*, *Monotoma*, *Enicumus minutus*, *Corticaria* and *Cryptophagidae*. Sample 2225 also contained one

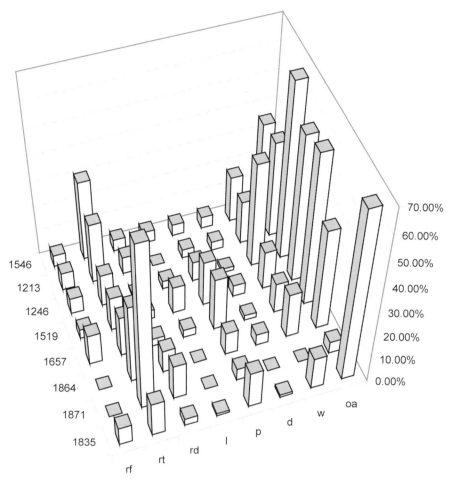

Fig. 14.2 Insect remains; proportions of the ecological groups for the Coleoptera present from Park Street.

individual of *Tenebrio obscurus*, a strongly synanthropic species which is particularly associated with human settlement (Kenward 1997).

Unfortunately, although it is clear that decaying settlement waste was present, there were no specific indicators for the nature of this material. It is also clear from the large number of Sepsis flies present that this material must have been fairly fluid and contained large amounts of dissolved organics. Today species of this genus are sometimes associated with human sewage but also often with cow and other domesticated mammal dung (Smith, K. G. V. 1986). Unfortunately, it was not possible to identify these puparia to species that would have enabled one to be more specific about the precise origin of this material. However, animal dung is sometimes used as part of the bating process in tanning (Hall and Kenward 2003). Despite this, it is not really clear from the insect faunas whether this material relates to the time of the use of the features or whether the material was waste thrown into the features once they had fallen out of use. However, recently Hall and Kenward (2003) have developed a clear 'indicator package' consisting of a

range of insect and plant remains that appear to be associated with tanning. In terms of insects, the scarabaeid beetle *Trox scaber* is seen as a key indicator for tanning. This species only occurs in low numbers at Edgbaston Street.

Also present were a relatively large proportion of species that probably came from the open areas around the features. These were mainly Carabidae 'ground beetles', the Chrysomelidae 'leaf beetles', and the Curculionidae 'weevils'. These taxa also made up the majority of ecological group 'oa' (Tables 14.1 and 14.3; Fig. 14.1). Most of the ground beetles present, such as the Trechus and Bembidion species, *Pterostichus strenuous*, and *P. melanarius* are associated with dry ground. Several of the weevils recovered from these deposits indicate that clover (the food plant of the Sitona species), docks (the food plant of *Apion hydrolapathi*) and ribwort plantain (the food plant of *Mecinus pyraster*) grew in the area. Certainly, the presence of such a high proportion of species associated with the 'external' environment suggests that these features may have remained open for a long period of time.

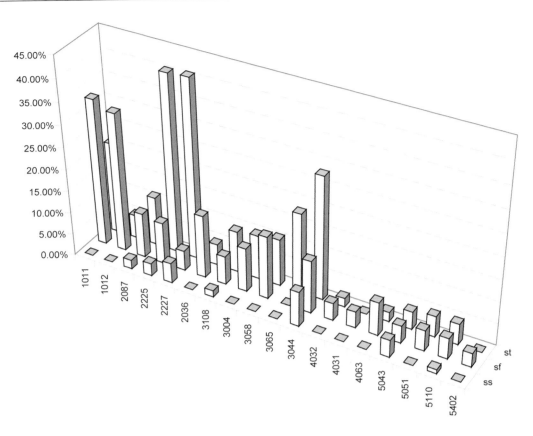

Fig. 14.3 Insect remains; percentages of the synanthropic fauna present at Edgbaston Street.

In addition there was a range of water beetles, which are similar to those seen in Area A. Once again, this suggests that the pits were periodically flooded or in the case of the gully (F265), that it held water. This conclusion is supported by the recovery of several species which are associated with waterside vegetation, such as Tanysphyrus lemnae, which is associated with duckweeds (*Lemna* sp.), and the Notaris species which are often associated with 'sweet grasses' (*Glyceria* sp.).

There were also a very small number of species that are normally associated with the bark or timber of trees. These included the scolytids 'bark beetles' *Dryocoetes villosus* and *Xyloborus dispar*, and the weevil, *Rhyncolus chloropus*. These species are usually found under the bark of a range of hardwood trees such as oak, beech and ash. They may have come either from vegetation around the site or from bark used during the tanning process.

One sample from Area B was associated with the water channel F256 (context 2036). Unfortunately the insect fauna recovered was very small. The majority of species present consisted of the species already mentioned above that are associated with decaying settlement waste. This suggests that the deposit sampled probably represents settlement waste dumped into the water channel.

Area C

Three of the insect faunas recovered from Area C came from Phase 3 tanning pits (F300/ 3004, F310/ 3044, F320/ 3058) and one from a Phase 3 pit (F323/ 3065). Unfortunately, all four of these faunas contained few individuals from a limited range of species. In the main these consisted of the same species as found in Areas A and B that were associated with settlement waste.

Context 3108, the bottom fill of Phase 3 water channel F337, however, produced a relatively large insect fauna. It is clear that the majority of species present in this deposit came from the channel itself or from the external environment around the site rather than representing deposits of urban waste (see Table 14.3 and Fig. 14.1). Unsurprisingly, a large part of this fauna consisted of a range of water beetles. This included species such as *Hydroporus palustris*, *Graptodytes granularis* and *Hydraena riparia*, which are commonly associated with shallow, slow-flowing and often muddy water. Several other species are associated with waterside vegetation, which probably grew within the ditch. For example, *Hydrophassa glabra* is often associated with the marsh buttercup and *Prasocuris phellandri* with aquatic species of cow parsley (Apiacae). The weevil *Notaris acridulus* is usually associated with the reed sweet grass *Glyceria maxima*. The presence of the pollen beetle *Brachypterus*

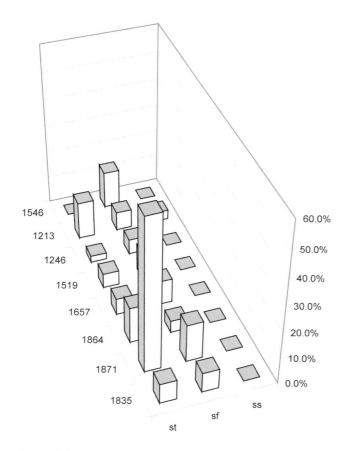

Fig. 14.4 Insect remains; percentages of the synanthropic fauna present at Park Street.

glaber and the weevil *Cidnorhinus quadrimaculatus* may suggest that stinging nettle (*Urtica* sp.) was present in the area.

However, there was again clear evidence for the presence of settlement waste, indicated by the same range of beetles encountered in Areas A and B (this is also reflected by the high proportions of ecological groups 'rt' 'rd' and 'rf' in Table 14.3 and Fig. 14.1).

Area D

Three insect faunas were recovered from this area of the site. Two (4031 and 4032) came from the peaty, organic layers overlying the subsoil, which may have pre-dated the establishment of the town. The third fauna derived from the fill (4063) of the Phase 3 linear gully F427. During Phase 1, this part of the site still lay within the lord's park to the south of the watercourse, while in Phase 3, activities associated with the tanning industry appear to have expanded across the line of the watercourse into Area D. The three faunas that were recovered were relatively large.

The faunas from 4031 and 4032 were dominated by species associated with the natural environment of the site (ecological group 'oa' in Tables 14.1 and 14.3, and Fig. 14.1). It was initially thought that these deposits,

which contained fragments of wood, might represent an area of waterlogged woodland that preceded the activity on the site. However, there were no species present that are specific to woodland. The majority of the ground beetles recovered are associated with open and disturbed ground rather than woodland. Classic indicators for this open environment are the various Bembidion, Nebria and Pterostichus species present. Similarly, several of the weevils present, such as the clover (*Trifolium* sp.) feeding Sitona and the ribwort plantain (*Plantago lanceolata*) feeding Gymnetron species, suggest an area of weedy ground beside the watercourse. It would therefore seem that this ground surface, if indeed it does represent the preserved remains of a woodland floor, had become more open in its nature by the time of the deposition of these insect faunas.

There is also clear evidence that this area may have been associated with a water channel or have been periodically flooded. Once again there were relatively large numbers of water beetles present (see ecological grouping 'oa-w' in Tables 14.1 and 14.3, and Fig. 14.1). In particular, there were numbers of species, such as *Coelostoma orbiculare* and *Chaetarthria seminulum*, which are associated with shallow, slow-flowing water (Friday 1988; Hansen 1986). The Dryops and several of the Staphylinid species, such as *Olophorum piceum*, also indicate similar rather muddy conditions. *Lathrimeam unicolor* and *Lesteva longelytrata* are also associated with the muddy edges of water bodies (Tottenham 1954).

There are also indicators for the presence of a stand of aquatic vegetation, perhaps associated with the nearby watercourse. This includes *Plateumaris braccata* which is associated with water reed (*Phragmites* sp.) and *Prasocuris phellandri*, which is associated with aquatic cow parsley (Apiacae) (Koch 1992).

In addition, there were numbers of the species discussed above which may be indicative of the presence of settlement waste. However, the species associated with dry settlement waste (ecological grouping 'rd'), which form the core of Kenward's 'house fauna', were present in far fewer numbers than they were in the material from Areas A and B. This may suggest that the contribution of waste directly from settlement or areas of human activity was limited.

The material from the Phase 3 linear feature F427 contained an essentially similar insect fauna to that recovered from Phase 1 of this part of the site. This suggests that an open environment, cut by water and rubbish-filled ditches, existed in both of these phases. The only major difference is that several species of plants indicative of waste ground seem to have been present in Phase 3. This included shepherd's purse (*Capsella bursa-pastoris*), indicated by *Ceutorhynchus erysmi*, and stinging nettle (*Urtica* spp.), indicated by *Cidnorhinus quadrimaculatus*. The local stands of waterside vegetation also appear to have contained sedges (*Carex* sp.) since this is the food plant of *Plateumaris sericea*.

Watercourse deposits

The last four samples from Edgbaston Street (contexts 5043, 5051, 5110 and 5402) came from the watercourse which linked the Manorial Moat with the Parsonage Moat. Context 5051 contained a sherd of possible 15th-century date.

A number of water beetles suggest the presence of slow-flowing or standing water. This evidence consisted of beetles belonging to the genera Hydroporus, Hydraena and Laccobus. There are also strong indicators of muddy water and bank sides, such as Coelostoma orbiculare, Cymbiodyta marginella and Chaetarthria seminulum, and the Dryops species. The plant-feeding species of leaf beetles and weevils, such as *Prasocuris phellandri* and *Notaris acridulus*, suggest that this ditch may, in places, have contained reeds, sedges and other aquatic plants. Duckweed (*Lemna* sp.) is also indicated by *Tanysphyrus lemnae*.

There is also a strong indication that grassland was present adjacent to the watercourse. There are reasonably large numbers of Aphodius dung beetles in these ditch deposits. These species are normally associated with animal dung lying in open grassland. Equally, many of species of weevil discussed above are also associated with weedy areas of open grassland. Taken together this might suggest that there was either pastureland nearby or a stocking yard in the area.

A range of beetles that are commonly associated with human settlement and housing in the archaeological record were also present in the watercourse fills. These include taxa such as some of the terrestrial Cercyons, the Oxytelus, Trogophloeus and Philonthus species that are commonly associated with wet and rather rotten rubbish, and other types of urban debris. Other species present, such as *Xylodromus concinnus*, the spider beetle (*Ptinus fur*) and woodworm (*Anobium punctatum*), are part of Harry Kenward's putative 'house fauna' (Kenward and Hall 1995), which is particularly associated with drier human housing and waste. It would therefore seem likely that a small quantity of domestic or settlement rubbish had become incorporated into the fill of this watercourse.

The insect remains from Park Street

The insect faunas recovered from Park Street were very similar in their nature to those recovered from Edgbaston Street.

Insect faunas from medieval ditch deposits

Four of the contexts examined from Park Street came from the two major Phase 1 boundary ditches identified on the site. Contexts 1246 and 1213 were respectively the bottom fill and the second-from-bottom fill of ditch F174/ F201, the massive east-west boundary ditch which defined the rear end of the plots fronting onto Digbeth. Contexts 1864 (F776) and 1871 (F799) were fills of the recut of the boundary ditch which defined the rear end of the plots fronting onto Park Street. With the exception of 1246 these contexts produced small insect faunas. The nature of the insect faunas from these ditch fills suggests that the ditches were infilled with dumped settlement waste and that at the time at which this waste was accumulating (presumably marking the disuse of the ditches) they contained standing water.

Context 1246 produced a relatively large insect fauna that was dominated by a range of water beetles typical of slow-flowing or standing water. These included relatively large numbers of Hydreanidae, such as the Hydraena and Limnebius species, and the individual of Haliplus recovered. A range of ground beetles, such as *Bembidion lampros*, *Bembidion obtusum*, and the Trechus, Harpalus and Calathus species, also indicate the presence of dry ground or grassy areas adjacent to the ditch. The plant-feeding species of weevil suggest that this waste or grassland contained clover (the food plant of *Sitona* spp.) and plantain (the food plant of *Gymnetron* spp.). A small number of individuals of the Aphodius dung beetles suggest that these areas may have been grazed.

Insect faunas from later features

Three faunas were examined that came from pits in the area of frequently waterlogged ground that lay to the rear of the Park Street plots, adjacent to the boundary ditch here. They comprise a fill (1657) of a largish Phase 2 pits or tank (F561/ F562) in Area B, the fill (1835) of a Phase 3.1 pit (F803) dating to the 17th century in Area C, and the uppermost fill (1519), dating to the late 18th century, of the 'pond' (F506) in Area B. Despite the difference in date of the three features, all three faunas were very similar in their nature. The faunas were dominated by a high proportion of species associated with the external environment (ecological groupings 'oa' 'oa-p', 'oa-w' and 'oa-d' in Table 14.4 and Fig. 14.2). In the main, this consisted of a range of water beetles typical of slow-flowing or still, muddy and often temporary waters. Good examples of species that prefer this kind of environment are Hydroporus palustris and the Hydraena, Octhebius and Helodidae species. Also present was a range of plant-feeding species that suggest that waterside plants such as duckweed (*Lemna* sp.), the host plant of *Tanysphyrus lemnae*, were present (see Table 14.7).

Of equal importance were the relatively high numbers of species associated with plants growing in open waste areas or grassland. A prime example of this is the range of species associated with stinging nettle (*Urtica* sp.) such as *Bracypterus glaber*, *Ceutorhynchus pollinarius* and *Cidnorhinus quadrimaculatus*. Other insects indicate the presence of classic waste ground plant species such as poppy (Papaveraceae), often the host plant of *Ceutorhyncus contractus*, docks (*Rumex* sp.), the host plant of *Gastroidea viridula*, clover (*Trifolium* sp.), the host plant of the Sitona and Hypera species, and ribwort plantain (*Plantago lanceolata*), often the host plant of *Ceutorhynchus troglodytes* and *Mecinus pyraster* (see

Table 14.7). Many of the Carabidae 'ground beetles' recovered are also typical of this kind of environment.

The other dominant aspect of the faunas recovered from these features was the range of species associated with decaying organic matter, usually associated with human activity (Tables 14.4 and 14.6, and Figs 14.2 and 14.4). It is not clear, however, when this material became incorporated, as the relatively large proportions of species associated with the external environment indicate that these features remained open for a period of time. The presence of numbers of water beetles suggests that this area of the site was either periodically flooded or was one in which pools of standing water occurred.

Discussion

The insect faunas from both Edgbaston and Park Street, regardless of whether they are from ditches, tanning pits or other features, appear to be essentially similar in their nature. In all cases there is abundant evidence from the range of water beetles for bodies of standing or slowly flowing water, whether these were associated with boundary ditches, that once may have served as watercourses, tanning pits or tanks/ ponds. Unfortunately, it is not clear from these faunas whether they developed during the primary use of these features or after they fell out of use. The different uses to which the Edgbaston Street, Moor Street and Park Street sites were put was not apparent in the insect faunas. This probably suggests that we are dealing with a range of urban rubbish and waste rather than materials specifically associated with the industries at the sites.

The synanthropic aspect of the insect faunas is typical of material from dense urban settlement in the archaeological record. The faunas are directly comparable to many aspects of the faunas from Roman and Anglo-Scandinavian York and a number of other towns (Hall and Kenward 1990; Kenward and Hall 1995). Unfortunately, the range of species recovered is very general. There are none of the specific species associations indicative of 'indicated groups' (*sensu* Kenward and Hall 1997) which could be used to identify the specific nature of materials involved. This would suggest that the settlement waste that became incorporated into these features was probably a rather random mix of material.

Comparison to other sites

In general, many aspects of the synanthropic insect faunas compare well with those seen at both Roman and Anglo-Scandinavian York (Hall and Kenward 1990; Kenward and Hall 1995) and also with the range of sites so far examined from Saxon and medieval London (Smith 1997; 1998; 2000; 2002; Smith and Chandler 2004). However, many of the faunas from these sites are essentially from urban housing and other settlement features. They tend, as a result, to be almost exclusively dominated by synanthropic species of beetle, particularly those belonging to Kenward's (Hall and Kenward 1990) 'house fauna' and his later (Carrot and Kenward 2001) 'Groupings A and B', which seem to be typical of housing with earthen floors.

Here, at the Edgbaston Street and Park Street sites, the insect faunas recovered do contain elements of this synanthropic fauna but in very much lower proportions than many other urban settlement sites (Table 14.3, Fig. 14.1, Table 14.4 and Fig. 14.2). When this is combined with the clear evidence for open grassy areas, animal dung and the presence of areas of standing water or flood wash, it suggests that these areas of Birmingham must have had a different use and aspect. It is probable that the insect faunas examined, and the local landscape reconstruction, reflect the use of these areas of the town for stalling animals, tanning and other associated practices. Whatever watercourses existed seem to have been the sites of the periodic dumping of settlement waste, a situation akin to the nature of deposition seen at Highgate, Beverley, East Yorkshire (Hall and Kenward 1980), and the Abbey ditch at Long Causeway, Peterbough (Smith 1996).

There has only been one previous set of insect faunas examined from this area of Birmingham (Osborne 1980). These came from the Birmingham Moat investigations undertaken in 1973–4. One of these deposits was clearly of glacial date and the other produced a limited fauna of insects thought to derive from the medieval fills of the moat itself. This latter fauna is essentially similar to those seen from the watercourses sampled during the present excavations. Osborne's faunas and the insects from the Bull Ring excavations are the only insect faunas so far recovered from urban contexts in the West Midlands. Perhaps, in terms of archaeological period and location, the nearest comparable site is a late medieval tenement at Stone, Staffordshire (Moffet and Smith 1996). However, in this case the insects are clearly derived from dense deposits of urban waste and possibly a collapsed roof.

Context number	Eco	Syn	1011	1012	2087	2225	2227	2036	3108	3004	3058	3065	3044	4032	4031	4063	5043	5051	5110	5402
Area			Area A		Area B				Area C					Area D			Watercourse deposits			
HEMIPTERA																				
Family, genus and spp. Indet.			-	-	-	-	-	-	-	-	-	-	-	-	-	+	-	-	-	-
COLEOPTERA																				
Carabidae																				
Nebria brevicollis (F.)	oa		-	-	-	-	-	-	-	-	-	-	-	1	-	1	-	-	-	1
N. salina Fairm. Lab.	oa		-	-	-	-	-	-	1	-	-	-	-	-	-	-	-	-	-	-
Notiophilus biguttatus (F.)	oa		-	-	-	-	-	-	-	-	-	-	-	1	-	-	-	-	-	1
Elaphrus spp.	Oa-d		-	-	-	-	-	-	-	-	-	-	-	-	1	-	-	-	-	1
Loricera pilicornis (F.)	oa		-	-	-	-	1	-	-	-	-	-	-	-	1	-	-	-	-	1
Clivina fossor (L.)	oa		-	-	1	-	-	-	-	-	-	-	-	1	1	-	-	-	1	-
Trechus secalis (Payk.)	Oa-d		-	-	-	-	-	-	-	-	-	-	-	-	-	-	-	-	-	1

Table 14.1 Edgbaston Street; the insect remains.

Ecological coding (Kenward and Hall 1995)
oa (& ob) – Species which will not breed in human housing.
w – aquatic species.
d – species associated with damp watersides and river banks.
rd – species primarily associated with drier organic matter.
rf – species primarily associated with foul organic matter often dung.
rt – insects associated with decaying organic matter but not belonging to either the rd or rf groups.
l – species associated with timber.
h – members of the 'house fauna' this is a very arbitrary group based on archaeological associations (Hall and Kenward 1990).

Synanthropic codings (Kenward 1997).
sf – faculative synanthropes – common in 'natural' habitats but clearly favoured by artificial ones.
st – typically synanthropes – particularly favoured by artificial habitats but believed to be able to survive in nature in the long term.
ss – strong synanthropes – essentially dependant on human activity for survival.

For non Coleoptera the following 'score' system has been used:
+   1–3 individuals
++   <5 individuals
+++   <10 individuals

T. quadristriatus (Schrk)/*T. obtusus* Er.	oa	-	-	-	-	1	-	1	-	1	1	1	-	1	-	-	-	-	-	-	-	-	-
Bembidion lampros (Hbst.)	oa	-	-	-	-	-	-	-	1	-	-	-	-	-	-	1	-	-	-	-	-	-	-
B. biguttatum (F.)	oa	-	-	-	-	-	-	-	-	-	-	-	-	1	-	-	-	-	-	-	-	-	-
B. guttula (F.)	oa	-	-	-	-	-	-	1	-	-	-	1	-	-	-	-	-	-	-	-	1	-	-
B. lunulatum (Fourcr.)	oa	-	-	-	-	1	-	-	-	-	1	-	-	-	-	-	-	-	-	-	-	-	-
B. spp.	oa	-	1	-	2	-	-	4	1	2	-	2	1	-	1	3	3
Patrobus atrorufus/(Ström)	oa	-	-	-	-	-	-	1	-	-	1	-	-	-	-	2	1
*P.*spp.	oa	-	-	1	-	-	-	-	-	1	-	-	-	-	-	-	-
Poecilus versicolor (Sturm)	oa	-	-	-	-	1	-	-	-	-	-	-	-	-	-	-	-
Pterostichus strenuus (Panz.)	oa	-	1	-	1	-	-	2	3	-	2	-	-	-	-	2
P. gracilis (Dej.)	oa	-	-	-	-	-	-	2	-	-	-	-	-	-	-	-
P. minor (Gyll.)	oa	-	-	-	-	-	-	-	2	5	-	-	-	-	-	-
P. melanarius (Ill.)	oa	-	1	-	-	1	-	-	-	4	-	2	1	-	-
C. melanocephalus (L.)	oa	1	-	-	-	-	-	-	-	-	-	-	-	-	1
C. spp.	oa	1	-	-	-	-	-	-	-	-	-	-	-	-	-
Platynus ruficornis (Goeze)	oa	-	-	-	1	-	-	-	-	1	-	-	-	-	-
Agonum thoreyi Dej.	oa-d	-	-	-	-	-	-	-	-	-	-	-	-	1
A. spp.	oa	-	-	-	1	-	-	2	1	-	-	-	-	-
Amara spp.	oa	-	-	-	-	-	-	-	1	-	-	-	1	1
Oodes helopioides (F.)	oa	-	-	-	-	-	-	-	-	-	-	-	-	1
Dromius spp.	oa-ws	-	1	-	-	-	1	-	-	-	-	-	-	-
Haliplidae														
Haliplus spp.		-	1	-	-	-	-	-	-	-	-	-	-	-
Dytiscidae														
Hydrophorus palustris (L.)	oa-w	-	-	-	-	3	-	-	-	-	-	-	-	-

Table 14.1 continued.

H. spp.	oa-w		-	1	1	1	-	-	1	-	1	-	1	-	-	-	2
Graptodytes granularis (L.)	oa-w		-	-	-	-	-	-	-	-	-	-	-	1	-	-	-
Agabus spp.	oa-w		1	1	-	-	-	-	1	-	-	-	-	1	-	-	-
Rhantus sp.	oa-w		-	-	-	-	-	-	-	-	-	-	-	-	-	1	-
Hydraenidae																	
Hydraena riparia Kug	oa-w		-	-	-	-	-	-	-	-	-	-	-	1	-	-	-
H. spp.	oa-w		2	3	1	-	-	2	4	-	-	-	-	1	-	1	-
Ochthebius spp.	oa-w		-	-	-	-	-	-	-	-	-	-	-	1	-	1	-
Limnebius spp.	oa-w		-	1	-	-	1	-	-	-	-	-	-	1	-	-	1
Helophorus spp.	oa-w		-	1	-	-	-	2	1	-	-	-	-	3	-	-	4
Hydrophilidae																	
Coelostoma orbiculare (F.)	oa-w		1	1	-	1	1	2	3	-	-	-	-	1	-	-	-
Sphaeridium lunatum F.	oa-rt		-	1	-	-	-	-	-	-	-	-	-	-	-	-	-
Cercyon impressus (Sturm)	rf	sf	-	2	-	-	3	1	2	-	-	-	-	-	-	-	1
C. haemorrhoidalis (F.)	rf	sf	-	-	-	-	-	-	-	-	-	-	-	-	-	1	2
C. atricapillus (Marsh.)	rf	st	-	1	-	-	-	-	-	-	-	-	-	-	-	-	2
C. analis (Payk.)	rt	sf	-	-	-	-	-	1	1	-	-	-	-	3	-	-	1
C. spp.	rt		-	-	-	1	-	-	-	-	-	-	-	-	-	1	-
Megasternum boletophagum (Marsh.)	rt		-	2	-	-	11	-	-	1	-	-	-	1	-	-	1
Cryptopleurum minutum (F.)	rf	st	-	-	-	-	-	-	-	-	-	-	-	1	-	-	-

Table 14.1 continued.

Taxon																									
Laccobius spp.	oa-w	-	-	1	-	-	-	-	1	1	-	-	-	-	-	-	1	-	-	-	-	-
Hydrobius fusipes (L.)	oa-w	-	-	1	1	-	2	-	1	1	1	-	-	-	-	-	1	-	-	-	-	-
Cymbiodyta marginella (F.)	oa-w	-	-	-	-	-	-	-	-	-	-	-	-	-	-	-	2	-	-	-	-	-
Chaetarthria seminulum (Hbst.)	oa-w	-	-	-	-	-	1	-	3	7	4	1	-	4	-	-	-	-	-	-	-	4
Histeridae																						
Acritus nigricornis (Hoffm.)	rt	st	-	-	-	-	-	2	-	-	2	-	-	-	-	-	-	-	-	-	-	-
H. cadaverinus Hoffm.	rt	sf	-	1	-	-	-	-	-	-	-	-	-	-	-	-	-	-	-	-	-	-
H. spp.	rt	sf	-	-	-	1	-	1	-	-	-	-	-	-	-	-	-	-	-	-	-	-
Silphidae																						
Silpha spp.	rt		-	-	-	-	-	-	-	-	1	-	-	-	-	-	-	-	-	-	-	-
Catopidae																						
Catops spp.			-	-	1	-	1	-	-	-	-	-	-	-	1	-	-	-	-	-	-	-
Scydmaenidae																						
Scydmaenidae Gen. & spp. indet.			-	-	-	-	-	1	-	-	-	-	1	-	-	-	1	-	-	-	-	-
Clambidae																						
Clambus spp.			1	-	-	-	-	-	-	-	-	-	-	-	-	-	-	-	-	-	-	-
Orthoperidae																						
Orthoperus spp.	rt		-	-	-	3	1	-	1	-	-	-	-	-	-	-	-	-	-	-	-	-
Ptiliidae																						
Ptiliidae Genus & spp. indet.	rt		1	-	1	1	-	1	-	-	-	-	-	-	-	-	-	-	-	-	-	-

Table 14.1 continued.

Table of column counts: this is a rotated wide data table (Table 14.1 continued). Species names with ecological codes are given at left; numeric abundance values follow across 14 sample columns.

Staphylinidae	code		1	2	3	4	5	6	7	8	9	10	11	12	13	14
Micropeplus staphylinoides (Marsh.)	rt		1	-	-	-	1	-	-	-	-	-	-	-	-	1
Megartharus depressus (Payk.)	rt		-	-	1	1	-	-	-	-	-	-	-	-	-	-
M. sinuatocollis (Boisd.Lacord.)	rt		-	-	-	-	2	-	-	-	-	-	-	-	-	-
M. spp.	rt		-	-	-	-	-	-	-	-	-	-	-	-	-	-
Eusphalerum sp.			-	-	-	-	-	-	-	-	1	1	-	-	-	-
Omalium riparium Thoms.	rt	sf	1	1	-	-	-	1	-	-	-	-	-	-	-	-
O. rivulare (Payk.)	rt		-	-	-	1	-	-	-	1	-	-	-	-	-	-
O. caesum Grav.	rt	sf	-	-	1	-	1	-	-	1	-	-	-	-	-	-
O. excavatum Steph.			1	2	-	-	1	1	-	-	1	-	-	-	1	1
O. spp.	rt		1	-	1	-	7	-	1	1	1	1	-	4	2
Xylodromus concinnus (Marsh.)	rt-h	st	-	2	2	1	-	-	-	-	-	-	-	-	-	-
Lathrimaeamunicolor (Marsh.)	oa-d		1	-	-	-	-	-	2	1	2	-	2	1	1
Olophrum piceum (Gyll.)	oa		-	-	-	-	-	1	4	2	2	1	2	2
Lesteva longelytrata (Goeze)	oa-d		4	3	3	3	11	2	1	1	-	3	4
L. spp.	oa-d		-	1	-	2	-	4	4	-	-
Coprophilus striatulus (F.)	rt	st	-	-	1	1	-	-	-	1	-
Trogophloeus bilineatus (Steph.)	rt	sf	1	-	-	1	-	2	-	2
T. corticinus (Grav.)	u	sf	-	-	-	1	1	-	-	1
T. spp.	u		2	1	1	1	1	-	-
Aploderus caelatus (Grav.)	rt		-	1	1	3	3	-	-
Oxytelus sculptus Grav.	rt	st	-	1	1	1	1	1	1
O. rugosus (F.)	rt		5	6	1	3	4	1	4	4	1	4	2	2	3	3
O. scupturatus Grav.	rt		-	-	-	-	-	-	-	-	1	1
O. nitidulus Grav.	rt-d		-	1	1	3	3	-	-
O. tetracarinatus (Block)	rt		-	-	-	1	-	-	-

Table 14.1 continued.

Taxon	Ecology																									
Platystethus arenarius (Fourc.)	rf	-	-	-	-	-	-	-	2	1	1	-	-	1	-	-	-	-	-	-	-	1	-	-	-
P. corntus (Grav.)	oa-d	-	-	-	-	-	-	-	-	1	1	-	1	-	-	-	-	1	-	-	-	-	-	-	-
Stenus spp.	u	5	7	2	3	7	11	10	1	1	1	5	1	-	-	-	5	1	-	-	-	1	-	1	-
Astenus spp.	rt	-	-	-	-	-	-	-	1	-	-	1	-	-	-	-	1	-	-	-	-	-	-	-	-
Stilicus orbiculatus (Payk.)	rt	-	1	-	-	-	1	-	-	1	-	-	-	-	-	-	-	-	-	-	-	-	-	-	-
Lithocharis spp.	rt	st	1	-	-	-	-	-	-	-	-	-	1	-	-	1	-	1	-	-	-	-	-	-	-
Lathrobium spp.	oa		2	-	2	2	2	3	1	1	1	-	-	1	1	-	2	-	2	1	-	1	-	-	-
Leptacinus spp.	rt	st	-	-	-	1	-	-	-	-	-	1	-	-	-	-	-	1	-	-	-	-	-	-	-
Gyrohypnus fracticornis (Müll.)	rt	st	1	-	1	2	1	-	-	-	1	2	-	2	1	-	1	-	-	-	-	-	-	-	-
Xantholinus spp.			1	4	-	4	4	2	2	1	1	-	1	1	-	-	-	-	-	-	-	-	-	1	-
Neobisnis spp.	rt		2	-	-	-	-	1	-	2	-	-	2	-	-	1	-	-	1	-	-	-	-	-	-
Gabrius spp.	rt		-	-	-	-	1	2	2	-	-	-	2	-	1	-	1	-	1	-	-	-	-	-	-
Philonthus spp.			2	-	1	-	3	-	-	2	-	-	2	-	-	1	-	3	-	1	-	-	-	-	-
Philonthus spp.			-	5	-	-	3	5	4	-	-	1	4	1	1	-	4	-	-	-	-	-	-	-	-
Tachyporus spp.			1	1	-	-	-	-	1	-	-	-	1	-	1	-	2	-	2	-	-	-	-	-	-
Tachinus rufipes (Geer.)			-	-	-	-	-	-	-	-	-	1	2	1	-	-	1	1	2	-	-	-	-	-	-
T. spp.			-	1	-	-	-	-	-	-	-	1	1	1	-	1	-	1	-	1	-	-	-	-	-
Aleocharinidae Genus & spp. Indet.			2	7	2	2	4	3	4	1	1	4	11	4	4	-	6	-	5	1	-	-	-	-	-
Pselpahidae																									
Bryaxis spp.			1	-	-	-	-	-	-	-	-	-	-	-	-	-	-	-	-	-	-	-	-	-	-
Brachygluta spp.			-	-	-	-	-	-	-	-	-	-	1	-	-	-	-	-	-	-	-	-	-	-	-
Reichenbachia spp.			1	1	-	-	1	1	-	-	-	-	-	-	-	-	-	-	-	-	-	-	-	-	-
Cantharidae																									
Cantharis sp.	oa		-	-	-	-	1	-	-	-	-	-	-	-	-	-	-	-	-	-	-	-	-	-	-
Melyridae																									
Haplocnemus nigricornis (F.)	1		-	-	-	-	-	-	-	-	-	-	1	-	-	-	-	-	-	-	-	-	-	-	-

Table 14.1 continued.

Elateridae																			
Agrotes spp.	oa-p		-	-	1	-	-	-	-	-	-	-	-	-	1	-	1	-	-
Athous haemorrhoidalis (F.)	oa-p		1	-	3	-	1	-	1	-	-	2	-	1	2	-	2	1	1
Helodidae																			
Helodidae Gen. & spp. Indet. (Cyphon?)	oa-w		2	-	2	-	-	-	1	-	-	1	-	1	-	-	3	-	-
Dryopidae																			
Dryops spp.	oa-w		-	-	-	-	-	-	1	-	2	4	-	-	2	-	1	-	2
Oulimnius spp.			-	-	1	-	-	-	-	-	-	-	-	-	-	-	-	-	-
Byrrhidae																			
Cytilus sericeus (Forst.)	oa-p	1	-	-	-	-	-	-	-	-	1	-	-	-	-	-	-	-	-
Nitidulidae																			
Brachypterus glaber (Steph.)	oa-p		-	-	1	-	-	-	-	-	-	-	-	-	-	1	-	-	-
Meligethes spp.	oa		-	-	1	-	-	-	-	1	-	1	-	-	1	-	-	-	-
Glischrochilus quadriguttatus (F.)			1	-	-	-	-	-	-	-	-	-	-	-	-	-	-	-	-
Cucujidae																			
Monotoma spp.	rt	sf	2	-	-	1	1	-	-	-	-	-	-	-	-	-	-	-	-
Cryptophagidae																			
Cryptophagus spp.	rd-h	st	3	1	2	1	2	-	-	1	-	-	3	-	-	-	-	-	-
Atomaria spp.	rd-h	st	2	-	2	-	2	-	-	-	-	-	2	-	1	-	1	-	-
Lathridiidae																			
Enicmus minutus (Group)	rd-h	st	2	-	30	10	4	1	-	-	-	-	-	-	-	1	-	1	-

Table 14.1 continued.

Corticaria/ corticarina spp.	rt	sf	2	2	1	5	-	2	1	1	-	-	-	-	1	1	4	1	-	1	1	1
Mycetophagidae																						
Typhaea stercorea (L.)	rd	ss	-	-	-	-	-	-	-	1	-	-	-	-	-	-	-	-	-	-	-	-
Endomychidae																						
Mycetaea hirta (Marsh.)	rd-h	st	-	-	-	2	-	1	-	-	-	-	-	-	-	-	-	-	-	-	-	-
Lyctidae																						
Lyctus brunneus (Steph.)	1	sf	1	-	-	-	-	-	-	-	-	-	-	-	-	-	-	-	-	-	-	-
Anobiidae																						
Anobium punctatum (Geer)	1	sf	1	1	1	2	1	2	1	-	-	-	1	1	-	-	-	2	-	1	2	1
Ptinidae																						
Ptinus fur (L.)	rd-h	sf	1	1	2	1	-	-	-	-	-	-	-	-	-	-	-	-	-	-	-	-
Anthicidae																						
Anthicus formicarius (Goeze)	rt	st	-	-	-	-	-	-	-	-	-	1	-	-	-	-	-	-	-	-	-	-
A. spp.	rt		-	-	-	-	-	1	-	-	-	-	-	-	-	-	-	-	-	-	-	-
Tenebrionidae																						
Tenebrio obscurus F.	rf	ss	-	-	-	1	-	-	-	-	-	-	-	-	-	-	-	-	-	-	-	-
Scarabaeidae																						
Trox scaber (L.)	rt	sf	-	1	1	1	1	-	-	-	-	-	-	-	-	-	-	-	-	-	-	-
Geotrupes spp.	oa-rf		-	-	-	-	-	-	-	-	-	-	-	-	-	-	-	-	-	1	-	-
Aphodius contaminatus (Hbst.)	oa-rf		-	-	-	2	-	2	-	2	-	-	1	-	-	-	-	-	-	1	-	2
A. sphacelatus (Panz.) or	oa-		-	-	-	-	-	-	-	-	-	-	1	2	-	-	-	2	-	2	2	-

Table 14.1 continued.

A. prodromus	rf	-	-	-	-	-	-	-	-	-	-	-	-	-	-	-	-	-
A. fimentarius (L.)	oa-rf	-	-	-	1	-	-	1	-	-	-	-	-	-	-	-	-	-
A. ater (Geer)	oa-rf	-	-	-	-	-	1	-	-	1	-	-	-	-	-	1	-	1
A. spp.	oa-rf	-	-	-	2	-	-	-	2	-	1	2	-	1	-	-	-	-
Phyllopertha horticola (L.)	oa-p	-	-	1	-	-	1	-	-	1	-	-	-	-	-	-	-	-
Chrysomelidae																		
Plateumaris braccata (Scop.)	oa-d	-	-	-	-	-	-	-	-	1	-	-	-	-	1	-	-	-
P. sericea (L.)	oa-d	-	-	-	-	-	-	-	-	-	-	-	1	-	-	-	-	-
Chrysomela hyperici Forst.	oa-p	-	-	-	1	-	-	-	-	1	-	-	-	-	-	-	-	-
Gastroidea viridula (Geer)	oa-p	-	-	-	-	-	-	-	-	-	-	-	-	-	-	-	-	-
Hydrothassa glabra (Hbst.)	oa-d	-	-	1	-	-	-	-	-	3	-	3	-	1	-	-	-	-
Prasocuris phellandri (L.)	oa-d	-	-	1	-	-	-	-	-	1	-	1	-	1	2	-	-	-
Phyllodecta vitellinae (L.)	oa-d	-	-	-	-	-	-	-	-	-	-	-	1	1	1	-	-	-
Phyllotreta spp.	oa	-	-	3	-	1	-	-	-	1	-	-	1	-	1	-	-	-
Haltica spp.	oa-l	-	-	-	-	-	-	-	-	-	-	-	1	-	-	-	-	1
Crepidodera spp.	oa	1	-	-	-	-	-	-	-	1	-	-	-	-	-	-	-	-
Chalcoides spp.	oa	-	-	-	-	-	-	-	-	-	-	-	1	-	1	-	-	-
Chaetocnema concinna (Marsh.)	oa	1	-	1	-	-	-	-	-	1	-	-	-	-	-	-	-	-
C. spp.	oa	-	-	-	-	-	-	-	-	1	3	1	1	-	-	-	-	-
Cassida spp.	Oa-p	-	-	-	-	-	-	-	-	-	-	-	1	-	1	-	-	-
Bruchidae																		
Bruchus spp.	oa	1	-	-	-	-	-	-	-	-	-	-	-	-	-	-	-	-
Scolytidae																		
Hylesinus oleiperda (F.)	oa-l	-	-	-	-	-	-	-	-	-	-	-	-	-	-	-	2	-

Table 14.1 continued.

Ptelobius vittatus (F.)	oa-l	-	-	-	-	-	-	-	-	-	-	-	-	-	-	1
Dryocoetes villosus (F.)	oa-l	-	-	-	1	-	-	-	-	-	-	-	-	-	-	-
Xyleborus dispar (F.)	oa-l	-	1	-	-	-	-	-	-	-	-	-	-	1	-	-
Cuculionidae																
Apion hydrolapathi (Marsh.)	oa-p	-	1	-	-	-	-	-	-	-	-	-	-	-	-	-
A. spp.	oa-p	3	1	-	1	-	3	-	1	-	1	-	3	1	-	6
Phyllobius sp.	oa-p	-	-	-	-	-	-	-	-	-	-	-	-	-	1	1
Barypeithes spp.		1	-	-	2	-	-	-	1	-	-	-	-	1	-	1
Sitona lineatus (L.)	oa-p	1	-	-	1	-	-	-	-	-	1	-	-	-	-	-
S. flavescens (Marsh.)	oa-p	-	-	-	1	-	-	-	-	-	-	-	-	-	-	1
S. hispidulus (F.)	oa-p	-	1	-	-	-	-	-	1	-	-	-	-	-	-	-
S. humeralis Steph.	oa-p	1	-	-	-	-	-	-	-	-	-	-	-	-	-	-
S. spp.	oa	2	2	-	2	-	2	-	1	-	1	-	-	-	-	-
Rhyncolus chloropus (L.)	oa-l	1	1	-	-	-	-	-	-	-	-	1	-	-	-	-
Bagous spp.	oa-d	-	-	-	-	-	-	-	2	-	-	-	-	-	1	-
Tanysphyrus lemnae (Payk.)	oa-w	3	-	-	-	-	-	-	-	-	-	1	-	-	-	1
Notaris acridulus (L.)	oa-d	-	-	-	2	-	2	-	4	7	2	1	-	-	1	-
N. spp.	oa-d	2	2	1	-	-	-	-	-	1	-	-	-	-	-	1
Hypera spp.	oa-p	-	-	-	-	-	-	-	-	1	-	-	-	-	1	-
Ceutorhynchus contratus (Marsh.)	oa-p	1	-	-	2	-	1	-	1	-	1	2	-	-	1	-
C. erysimi (F.)	oa-p	-	-	-	-	-	-	-	-	2	-	-	-	-	-	-
C. spp.	oa-p	3	1	1	-	-	-	-	-	1	-	-	-	-	-	-
Cidnorhinus quadrimaculatus (L.)	oa-p	-	-	-	1	-	-	-	1	-	-	-	-	-	1	-
Mecinus pyraster (Hbst.)	oa-p	-	-	-	-	-	-	-	-	-	-	-	-	-	-	-
Gymnetron spp.	oa-p	-	-	-	-	-	-	-	1	-	-	-	-	-	-	-
Rhynchaenus sp.	oa-l	-	-	-	-	-	1	-	-	-	-	-	-	-	1	-

Table 14.1 continued.

DIPTERA																	
SUBORDER NEMATOCERA																	
Family, genus & spp. indet.	-	-	-	-	-	-	-	-	-	-	-	-	-	-	+	-	-
SUBORDER CYCLORRHAPHA																	
Family, genus & spp. indet.	-	++	-	-	-	-	-	+	-	-	-	-	++	+	+	-	-
Sepsidae																	
Sepsis spp.	-	-	-	-	-	+	-	-	++	-	++	+	++	+	++	-	-
Calliphoridae																	
Calliphora spp.	-	-	-	-	-	-	-	-	-	-	-	-	+	-	-	-	-
TRICOPTERA																	
Genus and spp. Indet.	-	+	-	-	+	-	-	-	-	-	-	-	-	-	-	-	-
HYMENOPTERA																	
Formicoidea Family Genus and spp. indet.	-	++	+	-	+	-	++	+	-	-	-	-	-	-	-	-	-

Table 14.1 continued.

Context number			1546	1213	1246	1519	1657	1864	1871	1835
	Eco	Syn								
HEMIPTERA										
Family, genus and spp. Indet.			-	-	+	-	-	-	-	-
COLEOPTERA										
Carabidae										
Leistus spp.	oa		-	-	-	1	1	-	-	1
Nebria brevicollis (F.)	oa		-	-	-	-	1	-	-	-
Clivina fossor (L.)	oa		-	-	-	-	-	-	-	1
Trechus quadristriatus (Schrk)	oa		-	1	-	-	-	-	-	-
T. quadristriatus (Schrk) *T. obtusus* Er.	oa		-	1	1	-	1	1	-	2
Bembidion lampros (Hbst.)	oa		-	-	1	-	-	-	-	1
B. obtusum Serv.	oa		-	-	1	-	-	-	-	-
B. guttula (F.)	oa		-	1	-	1	-	-	-	-
B. spp.	oa		-	-	-	2	-	-	-	1
Patrobus spp.	oa		-	-	1	-	-	-	-	1
Harpalus spp.	oa		-	-	1	1	-	-	-	-
Bradycellus sp.	oa		-	-	1	-	-	-	-	-
Pterostichus strenuus (Panz.)	oa		-	-	-	-	1	-	-	1
P. nigrita (Payk.)	oa		-	-	-	-	-	-	-	1
P. melanarius (Ill.)	oa		-	-	-	2	1	-	-	6
Calathus fuscipes (Goeze)	oa		-	-	-	-	-	-	-	2
Platynus ruficornis (Goeze)	oa		-	-	1	-	1	-	-	-
Agonum spp.	oa		-	-	2	1	-	-	-	-
Amara spp.	oa		-	-	-	1	4	-	-	1
Haliplidae										
Haliplus spp.			-	-	1	-	-	-	-	-
Dytiscidae										
Hydrophorus palustris (L.)	oa-w		-	-	-	3	4	-	-	-
H. spp.	oa-w		-	-	3	2	-	-	-	-
Agabus spp.	oa-w		-	1	-	1	-	-	-	-
Colymbetes fuscus (L.)	oa-w		-	-	-	1	-	-	-	-
Hydraenidae										
Hydraena spp.	oa-w		1	1	7	1	-	-	-	2
Octhebius spp.	oa-w		-	-	2	-	-	-	-	-
Limnebius spp.	oa-w		1	2	15	2	-	-	-	2
Helophorus spp.	oa-w		1	1	15	2	4	1	-	5
Hydrophilidae										
Cercyon atricapillus (Marsh.)	rf	st	-	1	1	-	-	-	-	-

Table 14.2 Park St; the insect remains.

C. analis (Payk.)	rt	sf	-	-	-	2	1	-	1	1
C. spp.	rt		-	-	-	-	-	-	-	-
Megasternum boletophagum (Marsh.)	rt		1	1	1	-	1	1	1	-
Cryptopleurum minutum (F.)	rf	st	-	-	-	1	1	-	-	2
Laccobius spp.	oa-w		-	-	3	1	-	1	-	-
Hydrobius fusipes (L.)	oa-w		-	-	2	-	3	1	-	3
Chaetarthria seminulum (Hbst.)	oa-w		-	-	2	-	-	1	-	1
Histeridae										
Acritus nigricornis (Hoffm.)	rt	st	-	-	-	-	1	-	1	-
Hister cadaverinus Hoffm.	rt	sf	-	-	-	-	1	-	-	-
Ptiliidae										
Ptilidae Genus & spp. indet.	rt		-	-	1	-	1	-	-	-
Staphylinidae										
Micropeplus staphylinoides (Marsh.)	rt		1	1	-	1	-	-	-	-
Megartharus spp.	rt		-	-	-	2	2	-	-	1
Eusphalerum sp.			-	-	-	-	1	-	-	1
Omalium excavatum Steph.			-	1	-	-	-	-	-	-
O. spp.	rt		-	1	5	1	-	1	-	1
Lathrimeamunicolor (Marsh.)	oa-d		1	-	-	-	-	-	-	-
Olophrum piceum (Gyll.)	oa		-	-	2	-	-	-	-	-
Lesteva longelytrata (Goeze)	oa-d		-	1	2	3	-	1	-	-
Coprophilus striatulus (F.)	rt	st	-	-	-	-	-	-	-	1
Trogophloeus corticinus (Grav.)	u	sf	-	-	-	-	-	-	1	-
T. spp.	u		-	-	1	-	-	-	-	-
Aploderus caelatus (Grav.)	rt		-	-	-	-	-	1	-	-
Oxytelus sculptus Grav.	rt	st	-	1	-	-	1	-	-	-
O. rugosus (F.)	rt		3	-	-	3	2	1	1	2
O. nitidulus Grav.	rt-d		-	-	1	1	-	1	-	1
O. tetracarinatus (Block)	rt		-	-	1	-	-	-	-	-
Platystethus arenarius (Fourc.)	rf		-	-	2	1	6	-	-	1
Stenus spp.	u		1	1	5	2	3	1	-	3
Lithocharis spp.	rt	st	-	-	1	-	-	1	2	1
Lathrobium spp.	oa		-	-	1	-	2	1	-	1
Leptracinus spp.	rt	st	-	1	-	-	-	-	6	-
Gyrohypnus fracticornis (Müll.)	rt	st	-	-	-	1	-	-	-	1
Xantholinus spp.			1	-	2	4	1	1	-	-
Neobisnis spp.	rt		-	-	-	-	-	-	1	-
Gabrius spp.	rt		1	-	-	-	-	-	-	-
Philonthus splendens (F.)			-	-	-	1	-	-	-	-
P. spp.			-	2	4	1	2	1	1	6
Tachyporus spp.			-	1	2	1	1	-	-	1
Tachinus rufipes(Geer.)			-	-	-	3	-	-	-	-
T. spp.			1	1	2	-	-	-	-	1

Table 14.2 continued.

Aleocharinidae Genus & spp. Indet.			1	2	-	7	3	1	1	-
Cantharidae										
Cantharis sp.	oa		-	-	-	-	-	-	-	1
Malthinus sp.	oa		-	-	-	1	-	-	-	-
Elateridae										
Agroties spp.	oa-p		-	1	1	1	-	1	-	1
Athous haemorrhoidalis (F.)	oa-p		-	-	-	1	2	-	-	-
Throscidae										
Throscus sp.	oa-l		-	-	1	-	-	-	-	-
Helodidae										
Helodidae Gen. & spp. Indet. (*Cyphon?*)	oa-w		-	-	-	3	1	-	-	1
Dryopidae										
Dryops spp.	oa-w		1	-	1	-	-	-	-	-
Elmis aenea (Müll)	oa-w		-	-	1	-	-	-	-	-
Limnius volckmari (Panz.)	oa-w		-	-	1	-	-	-	-	-
Nitidulidae										
Brachypterus glaber (Steph.)	oa-p		-	-	-	1	1	-	-	3
Meligethes spp.	oa		-	-	-	-	2	-	-	1
Rhizophagidae										
Rhizophagus spp.	rt	sf	-	-	2	-	-	-	-	-
Cucujidae										
Monotoma spp.	rt	sf	-	-	3	-	3	-	-	2
Cryptophagidae										
Cryptophagus spp.	rd-h	st	-	-	1	-	1	1	3	-
Atomaria spp.	rd-h	st	-	-	-	1	1	-	-	1
Lathridiidae										
Enicmus minutus (Group)	rd-h	st	-	-	-	3	1	1	-	2
Corticaria/ corticarina spp.	rt	sf	1	1	1	3	3	1	1	4
Mycetophagidae										
Typhaea stercorea (L.)	rd	ss	-	1	-	-	-	-	-	-
Colydiidae										
Cerylon sp.	oa-l		-	-	1	-	-	-	-	-
Coccinellidae										
Coccidula rufa (Hbst.)	oa-p		-	-	1	-	-	-	-	-

Table 14.2 continued.

Scymnus sp.			-	-	1	-	-	-	-	-
Anobiidae										
Anobium punctatum (Geer)	l	sf	1	-	1	6	1	-	-	1
Ptinidae										
Ptinus fur (L.)	rd-h	sf	1	1	-	-	-	-	-	-
Anthicidae										
Anthicus formicarius (Goeze)	rt	st	-	1	-	-	-	-	-	-
A. spp.	rt		-	-	-	1	-	-	-	-
Scarabaeidae										
Aphodius rufipes (L.)	aa-rf		-	-	1	-	-	-	-	-
A. contaminatus (Hbst.)	oa-rf		-	-	1	1	1	-	-	1
A. sphacelatus (Panz.) or *A. prodromus*	oa-rf		-	-	2	1	3	-	-	4
A. fimentarius (L.)	oa-rf		1	1	1	-	1	-	-	-
Phyllopertha horticola (L.)	oa-p		-	-	1	-	1	-	-	-
Chyrsomelidae										
Gastroidea viridula (Geer)	oa-p		-	-	-	2	1	-	-	-
Phaedon spp.	oa-p		-	-	3	-	-	-	-	1
Hydrothassa glabra (Hbst.)	oa-d		-	-	-	1	-	-	-	-
Phyllodecta vitellinae (L.)	oa-d		-	-	-	-	1	-	-	-
Phyllotreta spp.	oa		1	-	1	4	4	-	-	3
Haltica spp.	oa-l		-	-	-	4	-	-	-	-
Chaetocnema concinna (Marsh.)	oa		-	-	-	-	-	-	-	2
Cassida spp.	oa-p		-	-	1	-	-	-	-	-
Scolytidae										
Phloeophthorus rhododactylus (Marsh.)	oa-l		-	-	-	-	1	-	-	-
Leperisinus varius (F.)	oa-l		-	-	-	2	1	-	-	-
Cuculionidae										
Rhynchites sp.	oa-l		-	-	1	-	-	-	-	-
Apion spp.	oa-p		1	-	-	6	2	-	1	2
Phyllobius sp.	oa-p		-	-	1	1	4	-	-	2
Barypeithes spp.			1	-	-	-	1	-	-	-
Sitona hispidulus (F.)	oa-p		-	-	-	-	8	-	-	4
S. humeralis Steph.	oa-p		-	-	-	2	-	-	-	2
S. spp.	oa		-	-	1	-	-	-	-	12
Tanysphyrus lemnae (Payk.)	oa-w		-	-	-	1	-	-	-	-
Notaris acridulus (L.)	oa-d		-	-	-	-	-	-	-	1
N. spp.	oa-d		-	-	-	1	1	-	-	-
Hypera spp.	oa-p		-	-	-	1	-	-	-	-
Ceutorhynchus contratus (Marsh.)	oa-p		-	-	1	1	1	-	-	1
C. pollinarius (Forst.)	oa-p		-	-	-	1	-	-	-	-

Table 14.2 continued.

Ceutorhynchidius troglodytes (F.)	oa-p	-	-	-	1	-	-	-	-
Cidnorhinus quadrimaculatus (L.)	oa-p	-	-	-	1	1	1	-	-
Mecinus pyraster (Hbst.)	oa-p	-	-	-	1	-	-	-	-
Gymnetron spp.	oa-p	-	-	1	-	-	-	-	-
Rhynchaenus sp.	oa-l								
SUBORDER CYCLORRHAPHA									
Family, genus & spp. indet.		-	-	+++	+	-	+	++	++
TRICOPTERA									
Genus and spp. Indet.		-	-	-	-	-	-	-	+
HYMENOPTERA									
Formicoidea Family Genus and spp. indet.		-	-	++	+	++	-	-	+

The key to the ecological groupings and the synanthropic groupings are given at the end of Table 14.1.

Table 14.2 continued.

Context number	1011	1012	2087	2225	2227	2036	3108	3004	3058
Weight (kg)	11.5	5.5	10	13	11	13	12.5	6	5
Volume (lt)	8	3	10	7	7	10	12	9	8
Total number of individuals	24	19	99	106	44	21	139	10	28
Total number of species	22	15	62	47	28	15	70	9	22
oa	8.33%	42.11%	48.48%	20.75%	29.55%	33.33%	44.60%	40.00%	28.57%
w	4.17%	10.53%	16.16%	3.77%	4.55%	0.00%	12.23%	10.00%	0.00%
d	0.00%	26.32%	7.07%	6.60%	6.82%	28.57%	12.95%	0.00%	7.14%
p	0.00%	0.00%	10.10%	1.89%	2.27%	0.00%	9.35%	20.00%	0.00%
l	8.33%	5.26%	3.03%	3.77%	4.55%	4.76%	1.44%	0.00%	0.00%
rd	16.67%	10.53%	9.09%	35.85%	31.82%	0.00%	6.47%	10.00%	7.14%
rt	62.50%	47.37%	40.40%	65.09%	59.09%	42.86%	42.45%	50.00%	39.29%
rf	0.00%	0.00%	6.06%	3.77%	6.82%	0.00%	4.32%	0.00%	7.14%

Context number	3065	3044	4032	4031	4063	5043	5051	5110	5402
Weight (kg)	6.5	6	6	7	10	4.8	6.4	4.5	5.9
Volume (lt)	12	9	7	6	10	6	5	5	8
Total number of individuals	11	25	101	81	92	25	21	105	64
Total number of species	11	18	53	42	40	18	17	58	40
oa	27.27%	24.00%	64.36%	61.73%	51.09%	52.00%	57.14%	52.38%	62.50%
w	9.09%	4.00%	19.80%	14.81%	7.61%	8.00%	14.29%	13.33%	14.06%
d	0.00%	0.00%	11.88%	12.35%	10.87%	16.00%	9.52%	6.67%	14.06%
p	0.00%	4.00%	4.95%	7.41%	6.52%	4.00%	9.52%	13.33%	3.13%
l	0.00%	4.00%	0.99%	1.23%	1.09%	0.00%	0.00%	4.76%	4.69%
rd	0.00%	20.00%	0.00%	0.00%	1.09%	4.00%	4.76%	1.90%	0.00%
rt	45.45%	56.00%	29.70%	23.46%	31.52%	32.00%	33.33%	30.48%	29.69%
rf	18.18%	8.00%	3.96%	4.94%	4.35%	4.00%	4.76%	5.71%	4.69%

Table 14.3 Edgbaston Street; the proportions of the ecological groups for the Coleoptera present.

	1546	1213	1246	1519	1657	1864	1871	1835
Weight (kg)	9.5	8.5	8	8	7	8.5	9	10.5
Volume (lt)	10	7	6	9	5	8	8	10
number of individuals	22	29	125	110	99	22	21	108
number of species	20	26	60	60	53	22	13	54
oa	36.36%	37.93%	68.80%	58.18%	60.61%	40.91%	4.76%	68.52%
w	18.18%	17.24%	41.60%	15.45%	12.12%	18.18%	0.00%	12.96%
d	4.55%	3.45%	1.60%	4.55%	2.02%	4.55%	0.00%	0.93%
p	4.55%	3.45%	8.00%	18.18%	21.21%	9.09%	4.76%	14.81%
l	4.55%	0.00%	3.20%	10.91%	3.03%	0.00%	0.00%	0.93%
rd	4.55%	6.90%	0.80%	3.64%	3.03%	9.09%	14.29%	2.78%
rt	31.82%	24.14%	12.80%	13.64%	16.16%	31.82%	66.67%	13.89%
rf	4.55%	6.90%	6.40%	3.64%	12.12%	0.00%	0.00%	7.41%

Table 14.4 Park Street; the proportions of the ecological groups for the Coleoptera present.

	1011	1012	2087	2225	2227	2036	3108	3004	3058
st	20.83%	5.26%	11.11%	40.57%	40.91%	4.76%	9.35%	10.00%	10.71%
sf	33.33%	31.58%	10.10%	9.43%	4.55%	14.29%	6.47%	10.00%	14.29%
ss	0.00%	0.00%	2.02%	2.83%	4.55%	0.00%	1.44%	0.00%	0.00%

	3065	3044	4032	4031	4063	5043	5051	5110	5402
st	18.18%	28.00%	1.98%	0.00%	2.17%	4.00%	4.76%	4.76%	0.00%
sf	0.00%	12.00%	3.96%	3.70%	7.61%	4.00%	4.76%	4.76%	3.13%
ss	0.00%	8.00%	0.00%	0.00%	0.00%	4.00%	0.00%	0.95%	0.00%

Table 14.5 Edgbaston Street; the percentages of the synanthropic fauna present.

	1546	1213	1246	1519	1657	1864	1871	1835
st	0.0%	13.8%	2.4%	5.5%	6.1%	13.6%	57.1%	7.4%
sf	13.6%	6.9%	5.6%	10.0%	9.1%	4.5%	14.3%	7.4%
ss	0.0%	3.4%	0.0%	0.0%	0.0%	0.0%	0.0%	0.0%

Table 14.6 Park Street; the percentages of the synanthropic fauna present.

Insect species	Host plant
Agroties spp.	On the roots of grass
Athous haemorrhoidalis (F.)	On the roots of grass
Plateumaris braccata (Scop.)	Phragmites australis (Cav.) (common reed)
P. sericea (L.)	Usually on Carex species (rushes)
Chrysomela hyperici Forst.	On Hypericum perforatum L. and H. maculatum Crantz (perforate and imperforate St John's Wort)
Gastroidea viridula (Geer)	Rumex species (Docks)
Hydrothassa glabra (Hbst.)	Ranunculus species (buttercups)
Prasocuris phellandri (L.)	On aquatic Apiacae (Umbellifers)
Phyllodecta vitellinae (L.)	On Salix species (Willow)
Haltica spp.	Usually on trees
Phloeophthorus rhododactylus (Marsh.)	Often on Cytisus species (Brooms)
Leperisinus varius (F.)	Mainly on Fraxinus (Ash)
Hylesinus oleiperda(F.)	Mainly on Fraxinus (Ash)
Ptelobius vittatus (F.)	Mainly on Ulmus (elm) occasionally on Fraxinus (Ash)
Dryocoetes villosus (F.)	On a range of hardwood trees
Xyleborus dispar (F.)	On a range of hardwood trees
Apion hydrolapathi (Marsh.)	On Rumex dock
Sitona lineatus (L.)	On Trifolium species (Clover)
Sitona hispidulus (F.)	On Trifolium species (Clover)
S. humeralis Steph.	On Trifolium species (Clover)
S. spp.	On Trifolium species (Clover)
Tanysphyrus lemnae (Payk.)	On Lemna species (Duck weed)
Notaris acridulus (L.)	Usually on Glyceria often G. maxima (Hartm.) Holmb. (Reed sweet grass)
Hypera spp.	On Trifolium species (Clover)
Ceutorhynchus contratus (Marsh.)	On Brassicaceae species sometimes on Papaveraceae (Poppies)
C. eryisimi (F.)	Often on Capsella bursa-pastoris (L.) (Shepard's Purse)
C. pollinarius (Forst.)	On Urtica dioica L. (Stinging neetles)
Ceutorhynchidius troglodytes (F.)	On Plantago lanceolata L. (ribwort plantain)
Cidnorhinus quadrimaculatus (L.)	On Urtica dioica L. (Stinging neetles)
Mecinus pyraster (Hbst.)	On Plantago species (Plantains)
Gymnetron spp.	On Plantago species (Plantains)

Ecological information from Koch (1992)
Plant nomenclature follows Stace (1997)

Table 14.7 The phytophage species of beetles and their host plants from the Birmingham sites.

15   The Mammal, Amphibian and Bird Bones

Ian L. Baxter

Introduction

The animal bones found at Edgbaston Street, Moor Street and Park Street are of particular importance at local, regional and national levels as the first assemblages of any size to be recovered from the city. They have considerable potential to aid in the elucidation of industrial processes and livestock improvement in the area during the medieval and post-medieval periods.

In general, preservation of animal bones was good, enabling the establishment of a corpus of measurements which should prove useful for comparative purposes with sites excavated in the future. However, information regarding stock-age profiles for any particular period at any site is limited in quantity. This analysis will, therefore, concentrate primarily on those aspects of the faunal assemblage for which evidence is abundant, and in particular the cattle and sheep, along with any industrial processes to which their products may have been subjected. Following the recommendations contained in the assessment reports only well-dated material was recorded, from Edgbaston Street Phases 1 (12th–14th centuries), 2 (15th–16th centuries), 3 (17th–18th centuries) and 4 (19th century); from Moor Street Phases 1 (12th–14th centuries) and 2 (15th–16th centuries); and from Park Street Phases 1/2 (12th–16th centuries) and 3 (17th–18th centuries). Numbers of identified specimens (NISP) for each site are shown in Tables 15.1–15.3.

Methods

All of the animal bones from the Bull Ring sites were hand-collected. Consequently an under-representation of bones from the smaller species is to be expected.

The mammal bones were recorded on an Access database following a modified version of the method described in Davis (1992) and Albarella and Davis (1994). In brief, all teeth (lower and upper) and a restricted suite of parts of the skeleton were recorded and used in counts. These are: horncores with a complete transverse section, skull (zygomaticus), atlas, axis, scapula (glenoid articulation), distal humerus, distal radius, proximal ulna, carpal 2+3, distal metacarpal, pelvis (ischial part of acetabulum), distal femur, distal tibia, calcaneum (sustenaculum), astragalus (lateral side), centrotarsale, distal metatarsal, proximal parts of the 1st, 2nd and 3rd phalanges. At least 50% of a given part had to be present for it to be counted.

The presence of large (cattle/ horse size) and medium (sheep/ pig size) vertebrae and ribs was recorded for each context, although these were not counted. 'Non-countable' elements of particular interest were recorded but not included in the counts. For birds, the following were always recorded: scapula (articular end), proximal coracoid, distal humerus, proximal ulna, proximal carpometacarpus, distal femur, distal tibiotarsus, distal tarsometatarsus.

The separation of sheep and goat was attempted on the following elements: horncores, dP3, dP4, distal humerus, distal metapodials (both fused and unfused), distal tibia, astragalus and calcaneum, using the criteria described in Boessneck (1969), Kratochvil (1969), Payne (1969 and 1985) and Schmid (1972). The shape of the enamel folds (Davis 1980; Eisenmann 1981) was used for identifying equid teeth to species. Equid postcrania were checked against criteria summarised in Baxter (1998).

Wear stages were recorded for all P4s and dP4s as well as for the lower molars of cattle, sheep/ goat and pig, both isolated and in mandibles. Tooth wear stages follow Grant (1982) and are listed in Appendix 15.1.

Measurements are listed in Appendix 15.2. These in general follow von den Driesch (1976). All pig measurements follow Payne and Bull (1988). Humerus HTC and BT and tibia Bd measurements were taken for all species as suggested by Payne and Bull (1988) for pigs. Measurements taken on equid teeth follow Payne (1991). Equid bones of uncertain specific attribution have been measured using the system of Eisenmann (1986) in

Taxon	Period						Total
	Phase 1/2 C12th–16th			Phase 3 C17th–18th			
	A	**B**	**C**	**A**	**B**	**C**	
Cattle (*Bos* f. domestic)	78	40	8	22	28	32	**208**
Sheep/ Goat (*Ovis/ Capra* f. domestic)	13	6	6	13	9	27	**74**
Sheep (*Ovis* f. domestic)	(7)	(2)	(-)	(2)	(3)	(13)	**(27)**
Pig (*Sus* f. domestic)			2	3	5	8	**18**
Horse (*Equus caballus*)	6	3	3	3	1	3	**19**
Dog (*Canis familiaris*)	1	1		+		1	**3**
Cat (*Felis catus*)	1	1		1	4	4*	**11**
Fallow Deer (*Dama dama*)				+			**+**
Deer (*Cervus/ Dama* sp.)				+			**+**
Rabbit (*Oryctolagus cuniculus*)				1		+	**1**
Domestic Fowl (*Gallus* f. domestic)	2					1	**3**
Goose (*Anser* f. domestic)	1		1		1	1	**4**
Duck (*Anas* f. domestic)					2		**2**
Anuran (*Bufo/ Rana* sp.)				7**			**7**
Total	**102**	**51**	**20**	**50**	**50**	**77**	**350**

'Sheep/ Goat' also includes the specimens identified to species. Numbers in parentheses are not included in the total of the period. '+' means that the taxon is present but no specimens could be 'counted' (see text).

*four bones from a partial skeleton
**ten bones from the partial skeletons of three individuals

Table 15.1 Park Street; number of identified specimens (NISP) by Area.

addition to that of von den Driesch. SD on dog long bones is measured as suggested by Harcourt (1974) and represents the midshaft diameter (msd).

Frequency of species

Exclusive of horncores, cattle fragments are most frequent at all sites with the exception of Edgbaston Street and Park Street in Phase 3 (17th–18th centuries), where sheep remains are more common. However, in view of the much larger carcass size, beef would have been the meat most frequently eaten in all periods. Pig is relatively infrequent on all the sites, accounting for no more that 6% of the major domestic mammals in any period. Horse and dog occur on all sites and cat at Edgbaston Street and Park Street. Rabbit bones are also found in the post-medieval deposits at Edgbaston Street and Park Street. Domestic fowl, goose and duck occur sporadically, and two turkey bones were found in a Phase 4 (19th-century) feature at Edgbaston Street. Occasional fallow deer fragments, mostly antler, were found in medieval/ earlier post-medieval deposits at Edgbaston Street and Moor Street, and a post-medieval feature at Park Street.

Cattle

Edgbaston Street Phase 1 (12th–14th centuries)
The only significant medieval cattle remains from Edgbaston Street consist of horncores. These are all from shorthorned beasts and are similar to those from Park Street (see below). Sex ratios, based on the criteria of Armitage and Clutton-Brock (1976), are 44% cows, 33% bulls (however see below), and 22% oxen.

Edgbaston Street Phase 2 (15th–16th centuries)
While most of the cattle from the earlier post-medieval period appear essentially similar to those from the medieval period, there is also some evidence for medium-horned cattle. Following the criteria established by Armitage (1982), mediumhorns are distinguished from smallhorns in having an outer horncore length in excess of 220mm and less than 360mm. Mediumhorns may be distinguished from longhorns through use of an index of length compared with circumference (L/C.100), where the value for mediumhorns is always less than 180 (*ibid.*). Female subadult and old adult mediumhorn cores occur in layer 2168 in Area B. Unlike the medieval assemblage, horncores do not form a disproportionate proportion of

Taxon	Phase 1 12th–14th				Phase 2 C15th–16th				Phase 3 C17th–18th				Phase 4 C18th–19th				Total
	A	B	C	D	A	B	C	D	A	B	C	D	A	B	C	D	
Cattle (*Bos* f. domestic)	14	2		2		37			19	51	4		1	1	2		133
Sheep/ Goat (*Ovis/ Capra* f. domestic)	3					5			10	7	24	6	1		7		63
Sheep (*Ovis* f. domestic)	(1)					(2)			(4)	(4)	(9)	(3)					(23)
Pig (*Sus* f. domestic)						3			2	1	1						7
Equid (*Equus* sp.)											1						1
Horse (*Equus caballus*)										3	9*						12
Dog (*Canis familiaris*)										1	23*						24
Cat (*Felis catus*)											+						+
cf. Fallow Deer (*Dama dama*)						+											+
Hare (*Lepus* sp.)						1									1		2
Rabbit (*Oryctolagus cuniculus*)										+							+
Turkey (*Meleagris gallopavo*)													2				2
Domestic Fowl (*Gallus* f. domestic)						2											2
Goose (*Anser/Branta* sp.)						1											1
TOTAL	17	2		2		49			31	63	62	6	4	1	10		247

Table 15.2 Edgbaston Street; number of identified specimens (NISP) by Area.

'Sheep/ Goat' also includes the specimens identified to species. Numbers in parentheses are not included in the total of the period. '+' means that the taxon is present but no specimens could be 'counted' (see text).

*six bones from a partial skeleton
**23 bones from two partial skeletons

Taxon	Period		Total
	Phase 1	**Phase 2**	
	C12th–14th	**C15th–16th**	
Cattle (*Bos* f. domestic)	34	11	**45**
Sheep/ Goat (*Ovis/ Capra* f. domestic)	8	4	**12**
Sheep (*Ovis* f. domestic)	-1	-2	**-3**
Pig (*Sus* f. domestic)	1		**1**
Equid (*Equus* sp.)	2	2	**4**
Horse (*Equus caballus*)	2	1	**3**
Dog (*Canis familiaris*)	+		**+**
cf. Fallow Deer (*Dama dama*)	1		**1**
Goose (*Anser/Branta* sp.)		+	**+**
Total	**48**	**18**	**66**

'Sheep/ Goat' also includes the specimens identified to species. Numbers in parentheses are not included in the total of the period. '+' means that the taxon is present but no specimens could be 'counted' (see text).

Table 15.3 Moor Street; number of identified specimens (NISP).

cattle remains in the earlier post-medieval deposits (Table 15.5a and Fig. 15.1). An occipital fragment with ante-mortem perforations was recovered from layer 2196 in Area B. Remains belonging to perinatal and unweened calves were found in 2061 and 2062 fills of Phase 2 tanning pit F223, and 2101 Phase 2 tanning pit F214. Both pits had clay linings. Unfortunately, the only cattle bone suitable for calculating a withers height recovered from Edgbaston Street came from fill (3129) of Phase 3 pit F346, connected with tanning or hide curing. This is a tibia belonging to a beast 121cm high at the shoulder, based on the multiplication factors of Matolcsi (1970).

Edgbaston Street Phase 3 (17th–18th centuries)
Horncores form a much greater proportion of the later post-medieval cattle assemblage than any other body element (Table 15.5b and Fig. 15.1). Although shorthorns are still present, out of 33 cores recorded 85% derive from mediumhorn beasts. Most of these were found in ditch F253 (2197). The horncores are generally attached to fronto-parietal fragments. One mediumhorn cranial fragment from 2197 has a flat frontal profile and a concave intercornual ridge, while a second specimen has a flat frontal profile and an intercornual low double arch. Like the shorthorned cattle, the mediumhorn cores curve downwards and forwards. Sex ratios for the medium-horned cores are 50% cows, 31% oxen and 19% bulls. The majority are adult and old adult beasts, although juveniles and sub-adults are also represented. One cranial fragment has an ante-mortem perforation and a meta-tarsal from 2177 the fill of Phase 3 drain F247 has an expanded distal epiphysis.

Moor Street Phase 1 (12th–14th centuries)
The horncores of shorthorned beasts form the largest proportion of cattle remains found in the medieval

features at Moor Street (Table 15.6 and Fig. 15.1). These are generally similar to those of the same period found at the other Bull Ring sites. Sex ratios are 39% cows, 33% bulls and 28% oxen although, in view of what is said below regarding the effect (or rather lack of effect) of late castration on male horncores, the high proportion of apparent 'bulls' may be illusory.

Park Street Phase 1/2 (12th–16th centuries)
Horncores and foot elements dominate the cattle assemblage at Park Street in the medieval and earlier post-medieval deposits (Fig. 15.1). All of the horncores recovered originate from shorthorned beasts, *i.e.* animals in which the outer length of the core is less than 220mm (Armitage 1982). The cores curve downwards and then forwards in similar fashion to those illustrated by Armitage and Clutton-Brock (1976, fig. 11). This horncore morphology is common for the period and well documented for other Midland sites, *e.g.* Hereford (Baxter 2000; Noddle 1985).

The cattle horncores were frequently left attached to fronto-parietal fragments and in three cases enough of the occipital region was present to enable morphological descriptions to be recorded using the system of Grigson (1976). All display differences, suggesting heterogeneity in the cattle population represented at the site during this period. Some, at least, of this heterogeneity may be due to the long period of time represented by this phase. An ox cranium from the Phase 1 boundary ditch F174/ F201 (1315) has a flat (very slightly convex) frontal profile and an intercornual high double arch.

A bull cranium from the 'pond' F506 (1519) has a pointed boss and high single arch. A cow cranium from the same context exhibits a convex frontal profile and an intercornual high double arch. Both of the crania from

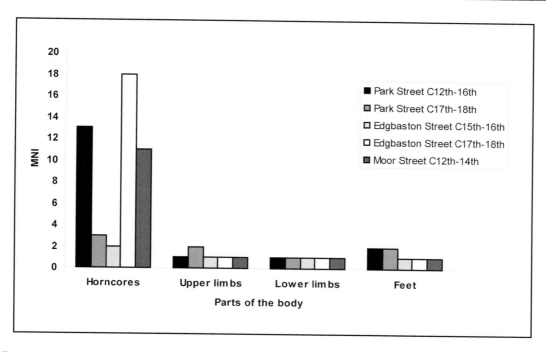

Fig. 15.1 Cattle MNI (based on NISP divided by expected number of bones in a complete carcass).

	Taxon			
Element	Cattle		Sheep/ Goat	
	NISP	%	NISP	%
Horncores	26	30	1	8
Upper limbs	7	8	5	42
Lower limbs	8	9	3	25
Feet	47	53	3	25

'Upper limbs' includes scapula, humerus, pelvis and femur
'Lower limbs' includes radius, ulna, tibia, carpal, astragalus and calcaneum
'Feet' includes metapodials and phalanges

Table 15.4a Park Street; Phase 1/2 (C12th–16th). Frequency by NISP of the main parts of the body of the main domestic mammals.

	Taxon			
Element	Cattle		Sheep/ Goat	
	NISP	%	NISP	%
Horncores	6	9	0	0
Upper limbs	10	15	21	64
Lower limbs	7	11	7	21
Feet	43	65	5	15

'Upper limbs' includes scapula, humerus, pelvis and femur
'Lower limbs' includes radius, ulna, tibia, carpal, astragalus and calcaneum
'Feet' includes metapodials and phalanges

Table 15.4b Park Street; Phase 3 (C17th–18th). Frequency by NISP of the main parts of the body of the main domestic mammals.

1519 have occipital perforations, a genetic trait of uncertain aetiology that is known to occur in populations of both wild and domestic bovids (Baxter 2002a; Manaseryan *et al.* 1999). Fill 1519 is the upper fill of the pond and has been interpreted as part of a late 18th-century house clearance (see Chapter 4) but the fill also contained residual material. Some small scraps of leather-working waste were found in the lower, Phase 2 fill of the pond and the balance of probabilities is that the two crania were associated with the Phase 2 disuse of the feature.

Two large juvenile horncores were found in an upper fill (1252) of the boundary ditch F174/ F201. Although due to their immaturity they cannot be accurately attributed to any particular type, from their size at this stage of development it is quite possible that they may originate from mediumhorned beasts *sensu* Armitage (1982) (see below).

Of the 22 horncores from deposits of this period that could be sexed with any degree of confidence, 36% belong to cows, and 32% each to bulls and oxen. The sexing of horncores is a qualitative procedure, dependant on fairly loose criteria and personal experience. In this case the criteria published by Armitage and Clutton-Brock (1976) were applied. The issue of sex is further complicated by the considerable differences displayed by ox horncores dependant on the age at castration. It seems highly probable that most of the 'bull' category actually represent oxen castrated after their first year, which would have little influence on the size or shape of the horns (*ibid.*, 332–3). Most of the horncores came from adult or old adult beasts. Juveniles and subadults were also represented.

Two metapodia with expanded distal epiphyses, suggestive of beasts used for traction (Bartosiewicz *et al.* 1997), were seen, from an upper fill (1252) of the boundary ditch F174/ F201 and from the fill (1642) of a probable pond (F552) in Area B. Both contexts are likely to be Phase 2. The only complete metapodial recovered derived from an animal 102cm high at the shoulder, based on the multiplication factors of Matolcsi (1970).

The limited information available from teeth and long bones relating to age at death also indicates that adult beasts were in a majority. The remains of younger animals were also present, including foetal foot bones in 1519 and a perinatal atlas fragment in the Phase 1 pit F714 (1706), which suggests that cattle were being kept in the immediate vicinity, a conclusion supported by the identification of several features at the site as possible water tanks for domestic stock.

Park Street Phase 3 (17th–18th centuries)
Cattle fragments exclusive of horncores are less frequent than those of sheep in Phase 3. The numbers of horncores are significantly reduced compared with the previous period, although the numbers of foot bones remain similar (Fig. 15.1). It is possible that some cattle were polled, although no evidence of this was seen, or that horncores

were generally disposed of elsewhere at this time. As with the previous period, shorthorns are in a majority. These appear to be essentially the same as those from the previous period. However, an incomplete horncore from a 17th-century pit (F765, 1818), from an old adult ox, suggests the presence of mediumhorned beasts. A shorthorned cranial fragment from pit F518 (1511) has a flat frontal profile and an intercornual ridge displaying a downward bow, which is different in morphology from those from the medieval deposits. This specimen has an occipital perforation (see above).

Complete metapodia derive from beasts ranging between 108cm to 123cm high at the shoulder (mean = 117cm). Most of the teeth and long bones recovered derive from adult beasts although younger animals are also present, including a perinatal scapula found in an 18th-century pit (F133/ 245, 1125).

Evidence of changes in cattle stock and husbandry
The shorthorned cattle of the medieval period show general similarities in horncore morphology at all sites. Cores with a more massive base, above the line in Fig. 15.3A, colour, probably belong to earlier castrated oxen. Indices of shape (Fig. 15.3C, colour) are fairly homogeneous and lie above the drawn line. However, cranial morphology appears to be fairly diverse suggesting the presence of several populations, types or 'breeds' (*sensu lato*). Plots of the measurable metapodials (Fig. 15.4, colour) indicate an increase in size of cattle during the later post-medieval period at Park Street. It is unlikely that this difference is one of sex but seems related to improved husbandry and/ or the introduction of improved stock. Mediumhorned cattle begin to appear at Edgbaston Street in the earlier post-medieval period and become the dominant type at that site in the later post-medieval. They have not been recorded at the other Bull Ring sites. Their horncores are quite distinct from those of short-horns in terms of both size and shape (Fig. 15.3A–C, colour, Appendix 15.3). However, unlike the later post-medieval cattle at Park Street, they do not appear to have been any larger in terms of body size than those of the medieval period (Fig. 15.4, colour).

Tanning, horn working or butchery?
The evidence for the exploitation of cattle, sheep and goats in the Midlands by tanners, tawyers and horn workers is the subject of a paper by Albarella (2002). He concludes that only when concentrations of horncores, with or without the frontal part of the skull, and foot bones are found together in primary contexts can we confidently attribute an assemblage to one of the activities associated with the leather trade. However, as there is independent evidence for tanning taking place at Edgbaston Street throughout the medieval to later post-medieval periods, the accumulation of mediumhorn horncores in the Phase 3 ditch F253 (2197) may be considered as most probably waste from these activities. No cattle foot bones were recovered in this assemblage,

92% of which consists of cattle horncores, but foot bones were not always left attached to skins (Serjeantson 1989, 141 and fig. 5). Also, mediumhorned cattle are otherwise unknown at the other Bull Ring sites and it may be that only the skins with horns and frontals attached were delivered to Edgbaston Street for processing. The possibility remains that the cache of horncores in 2197 derives from horn working, a trade allied to those of butchery and tanning, although the available evidence suggests that in most places this was more of an itinerant craft than a trade, and generally in decline by the post-medieval period (Albarella 2000). The cattle horncores found at the other Bull Ring sites may also comprise waste from activities associated with the leather-working trades; the proportions of cattle skeletal elements recovered at these sites in some periods is in marked contrast with those of sheep (compare Figs 15.1 and 15.2 and see below), but in general are more likely to be waste from primary butchery as here they are more mixed in with bones from other parts of the cattle skeleton and combined with elements of kitchen and other domestic waste.

Sheep

No remains identifiable as goat were found at any of the Bull Ring sites. The sheep/ goat assemblage is therefore best considered as exclusively composed of sheep. Unlike cattle, there are no disparities between expected and recovered sheep skeletal elements at any of the sites during any period, with the exception of an apparent preference for shoulder of mutton (a cheaper cut of meat)

at Park Street in the later post-medieval period (Table 15.4b and Fig. 15.2).

Some of the sheep were hornless. An artificially polled cranium found at Park Street in the Phase 1 ditch F174/ F201 (1213) has exostoses at the site of the horncore base. Another specimen found in the Phase 2 pit or tank F561/ F562 (1655) has a very rudimentary horncore. The only horncores recovered from any of the sites are small and belonged to ewes. There is insufficient data to provide an age profile for the sheep at any of the sites for any particular period, although most seem to have been adult. Evidence of the presence of younger animals include a perinatal metatarsal diaphysis found in Edgbaston Street Phase 2 layer 2196 and several juvenile metapodials found in Phase 4 layer 3001, including one perinatal specimen, and Phase 3 pit F300 (3002).

Several sheep bones, particularly metapodia, were sufficiently complete to provide withers heights based on the multiplication factors of Teichert (1975). At Park Street the three measurable specimens from the medieval and early post-medieval (Phase 1/2) deposits range from 52cm to 57cm. A single bone found in Edgbaston Street Phase 2 (15th–16th centuries) came from a similarly sized animal of 54cm. The later post-medieval (Phase 3) sheep at both Park Street and Edgbaston Street contain somewhat larger animals alongside others similar in size to those of the medieval period, suggesting some improvement in stock and/ or husbandry at this time. For Park Street the range is 56cm to 70cm (mean = 61cm, n = 6) and for Edgbaston Street 50cm to 70cm (mean = 60cm, n =11). Further evidence for sheep improvement during this period is illustrated by Fig. 15.5, colour, which

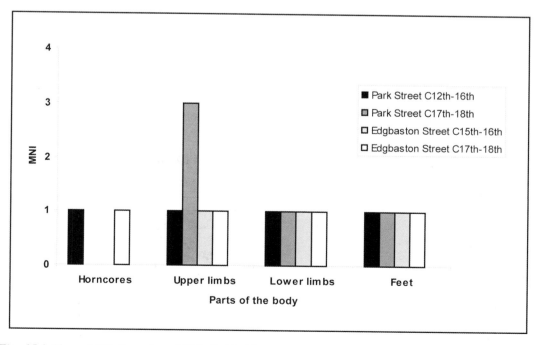

Fig. 15.2 Sheep MNI (based on NISP divided by expected number of bones in a complete carcass).

Element	Taxon Cattle		Sheep/ Goat	
	NISP	%	NISP	%
Horncores	4	18	0	0
Upper limbs	5	23	2	50
Lower limbs	6	27	1	25
Feet	7	32	1	25

'Upper limbs' includes scapula, humerus, pelvis and femur
'Lower limbs' includes radius, ulna, tibia, carpal, astragalus and calcaneum
'Feet' includes metapodials and phalanges

Table 15.5a Edgbaston Street; Phase 2 (C15th–16th). Frequency by NISP of the main parts of the body of the main domestic mammals.

Element	Taxon Cattle		Sheep/ Goat	
	NISP	%	NISP	%
Horncores	35	57	1	3
Upper limbs	2	3	5	13
Lower limbs	7	9	8	20
Feet	17	28	26	65

'Upper limbs' includes scapula, humerus, pelvis and femur
'Lower limbs' includes radius, ulna, tibia, carpal, astragalus and calcaneum
'Feet' includes metapodials and phalanges

Table 15.5b Edgbaston Street; Phase 3 (C17th–18th). Frequency by NISP of the main parts of the body of the main domestic mammals.

Element	Taxon Cattle	
	NISP	%
Horncores	21	78
Upper limbs	3	11
Lower limbs	1	4
Feet	2	7

'Upper limbs' includes scapula, humerus, pelvis and femur
'Lower limbs' includes radius, ulna, tibia, carpal, astragalus and calcaneum
'Feet' includes metapodials and phalanges

Table 15.6 Moor Street; Phase 1 (C12th–14th). Frequency by NISP of cattle body parts.

plots metacarpal condyle width against trochlea width after the manner of Payne (1969). The two metacarpals from Edgbaston Street Phase 3 are much larger in both dimensions than those from the earlier periods. The Phase 3 specimens from Park Street are also larger than the medieval examples from that site. That we are not here comparing sheep with goats is confirmed by the available indices of dorsovolar diameter of the peripheral trochlea compared with the parallel diameter of the verticillus (=

WT.100/DV) devised by Boessneck (1969), which confirms that we are dealing exclusively with sheep.
Two pathological specimens were seen from Edgbaston Street Phase 3: a metatarsal from pit F208 (2077) with a lump (haematoma) on the lateral shaft above the metaphysis, a well-healed old injury; and a metatarsal from well F327 (3063) with periostitis on the anterior proximal surface.

Discussion

As we have seen above, there is no evidence for the industrial processing of sheep/ goat products at any of the Bull Ring sites. Ovicaprid horncores are also poorly represented; in fact many of the sheep may have been hornless. If horning waste was a major contributor to the general animal bone assemblages we should expect to see high proportions of ram and goat horncores, both of which yielded more horn than those of shorthorned cattle. Medieval assemblages of this type have previously been documented elsewhere in the west Midlands, *e.g.* at Droitwich (Baxter 2002b). The sheep remains at the Bull Ring sites consist of butchery and kitchen refuse, and perhaps some natural mortalities. There is some evidence to suggest improvement in the breeding and husbandry of sheep leading to increased size during the later post-medieval period.

Other domestic mammals

Pig

Pig is not common at any of the sites during any period. It probably comprised an occasional element of diet and was kept locally.

Equids

While most of the equid remains found at the Bull Ring sites certainly belong to horses, some remains belonging to small animals found at Moor Street required further investigation to establish their specific identity. From the suitable bones available, these equids had a shoulder height of twelve hands based on figures published by Vitt (1952) and the multiplication factors of Kiesewalter (1888). The similarity of the proportion of their post-cranial bones to those of the domestic donkey necessitated further investigation. To date, the only donkey remains positively identified for the whole of the medieval period in England are a late Anglo-Saxon partial skeleton found at Westminster School in 1999 (Baxter 2002c), despite frequent mention of the species in the Domesday Book and subsequent documents.

The P3 from Phase 2 layer 5119, though small, belongs to a pony. The pli caballin is present, the interstylar surfaces are not particularly abrupt and the protocone is unreduced (Churcher and Richardson 1978). The radius from the same context is more problematic as the criteria for distinguishing horse and donkey published by Barone (1986) do not appear to be reliable (Baxter 1998) and methods based on the distal radius successfully used to distinguish hemiones from asses (Uerpmann 1991) are unable to distinguish between donkeys and ponies (Baxter 1998). In Phase 1 pit F550 (5141) the distal femur, metacarpal and first phalanx of small equids were recovered. While the metacarpal remains problematic, partly due to recent damage, the phalanx certainly belongs to a small pony. Plots of average dimensions of horses and donkeys compared with this specimen (based on Dive and Eisenmann 1991) confirm its caballine affinities (Fig.

15.6, colour). It seems most probable, therefore, that the small equid remains at Moor Street are those of ponies rather than donkeys.

Further horse remains found at the other sites include Park Street, where a metatarsal from a pony of 13 hands was found in a middle fill (1326) of the Phase 1 boundary ditch F174/ F201; a metacarpal from an animal over 15 hands in the Phase 2 large pit or pond F522 (1642); and a metacarpal from an animal of 14 hands in the Phase 3 upper fill (1519) of the 'pond' F506. There was also the partial skeleton of an animal of around 16 hands in the fill (3049) of the Phase 3 pit F315 at Edgbaston Street. The only butchery marks seen on horse bones were on a humerus from Park Street, which has two transverse cut marks on the posterior shaft lateral to and above the coronoid fossa. The bone was recovered from the fill (1863) of the massive Phase 3 pit F762, which appears to have been dug to remove a well.

Dog

Domestic dog remains are generally infrequent at the Bull Ring sites. The maxilla of a medium-sized animal was found in the Phase 1 boundary ditch F174/ F201 (1326) at Park Street, and an ulna fragment belonging to a similarly sized animal in the Phase 2 'pond' F506 (1584). A second medium-sized ulna fragment was found in Phase 3 pit F700 (1708), while an (uncounted) lumbar vertebra from a large animal found at Park Street Phase 3 pit F187 (1219) exhibits lipping by exostoses on the dorsal caudal centrum, symptomatic of spinal arthritis (Morgan *et al.* 1967; Harris 1977). At Edgbaston Street a 3rd metatarsal belonging to a dog approximately 28cm high at the shoulder (Clark 1995) was found in Phase 3 layer 2074. The partial skeletons of two perinatal puppies were found in Area C Phase 3 pit F316 (3050).

Perhaps most interesting is the cranium of an adult dog found in Area A which was unfortunately un-stratified. This animal was medium to large and male, based on the extent of sagittal cresting and basicranial morphology (The and Trouth 1976). There are at least two cut marks made with a sharp knife on the left bulla tympanica, and the occipital condyle has been chopped through. However, there are no cut marks on the maxilla, nasal bones or around the eyes, which would be expected if the animal had been skinned (Schmid 1972; Serjeantson 1989). The present author has seen a similar example of a complete dog skull from a 12th-century pit at the Leicester Forum site (unpublished), where the decapitating cut marks are also present on the posterior mandible. Although skinning remains a possibility, in neither case is an adequate explanation readily available.

Cat

Domestic cat remains were recovered from Park Street, from a middle fill (1197) of the Phase 1 boundary ditch F174/ F201, from the fill (1524) of the Phase 2 clay-lined pit or pond F512, from the Phase 3.1 (17th-century) pits F172 and F803 and from the fills of the Phase 3.3 (late

18th-century) wood-lined tank F510/ F542. They include a partial skeleton from the Phase 3.1 pit F803 (1835). At Edgbaston Street a single (uncounted) cat bone occurred in Phase 3 cleaning layer 3037. None of the bones seen bear cut marks and they probably represent the remains of domestic pets. In all cases the cat bones are significantly smaller than those of modern animals.

Wild mammals

Deer

All of the deer bones and antler fragments that could be identified to species belonged to fallow deer. These are uncommon and only occur sporadically at any of the sites. Isolated bones were found at Park Street Phase 3 (1111) and Moor Street Phase 1 (5158). A palmate antler tine was recovered from Edgbaston Street Phase 2 tanning pit F214, fill (2101), and a sawn red or fallow deer antler tine with chop marks was found in Park Street Phase 3.1 pit F172 (1190). The latter is evidence of craft working involving antler at the site during the 17th century.

Lagomorphs

Isolated teeth and bones of hare and rabbit occur sporadically in Phase 3 at Park Street and Phases 2–4 at Edgbaston Street, but never in such numbers as to suggest any particular affluence at these sites.

Birds

Bones of domestic fowl or chicken occur at Park Street in Phases 1/2 and 3, and Edgbaston Street Phase 2. Goose bones were found at Park Street in Phases 1/2 and 3, Edgbaston Street Phase 2 and Moor Street Phase 2. Most of these are fairly small and could equally belong to domestic or wild geese of Anser or Branta species. Duck bones of domestic size are relatively infrequent but were found in Phase 3 deposits at Park Street. Of interest is a femur and tibiotarsus belonging to turkey (*Meleagris gallopavo*) found in the Phase 4 (18th–19th-century) cellar at Edgbaston Street. The femur has distal jointing cuts, cat tooth punctures and gnawing marks (S. Hamilton-Dyer pers. comm.). The first record of the occurrence of this American bird in England is from 1541 (Crawford 1984).

Amphibians

The bones of anuran amphibians, *i.e.* frogs and toads, form occasional inclusions in the fills of features such as pits at the various sites. These would appear to be inadvertent 'pitfall' victims.

Summary and conclusion

The shorthorned cattle crania found in the medieval deposits at Park Street exhibit a morphological heterogeneity that suggests the presence of animals from different 'breeds' and/ or genetically distinct herds. This is perhaps not surprising given the proximity of the site to the historical market place and cattle may have been driven here from some distance. Several features on the site have been interpreted as 'ponds' or 'tanks' for the watering of beasts. The shorthorned medieval cattle from Edgbaston Street and Moor Street are essentially similar to those from Park Street. There is some evidence to suggest that the later post-medieval shorthorned cattle at Park Street were larger than their medieval forbears and represent improved beef stock. At Edgbaston Street in the post-medieval deposits, but not at the other sites, mediumhorned cattle make their appearance. In the later post-medieval period mediumhorned horncores dominate the assemblage at the site. As there is extensive evidence for tanning taking place at Edgbaston Street it is possible that many of the horncores found here are industrial waste. Unlike Park Street, there is no evidence of a corresponding increase in the size of cattle at Edgbaston Street in the later post-medieval period. It may be that only the skins, with frontals and horncores attached, arrived at the site for tanning.

The sheep, at all the sites during the medieval period, were the small animals common throughout England at this time. No significant accumulations of sheep or goat horncores were found at any of the Bull Ring sites, suggesting that the activities of horners were not a major agency of bone accumulation. There is limited evidence for size increase among the sheep stock during the later post-medieval period, doubtless due to an influx of improved breeds.

Pigs were kept locally and their flesh consumed during all periods but on a relatively low level. Domestic birds also formed a small, but important, dietary supplement and included turkey in the 18th and 19th centuries. Horse bones and teeth occur on all sites at all periods. These were doubtless pack animals employed by local traders. Some of the medieval and earlier post-medieval equines at Moor Street were small ponies. Dogs and cats were kept and their remains form occasional inclusions in the deposits of all periods. There is no firm evidence for commercial exploitation of their skins or fur.

16 Discussion

Michael Hodder, Catharine Patrick and Stephanie Rátkai

The information from archaeological excavations at the Bull Ring, some of which were extensive and all of which contained well-preserved deposits and features, has made it possible to construct a picture of the heart of medieval and post-medieval Birmingham in a way that would not have been possible just a few years ago, bringing the blurred picture from documentary sources more sharply into focus. The archaeological evidence provides new information on the origins of settlement in this part of Birmingham and its development from the 12th to the 19th centuries. It also indicates the existence, location, extent and date of particular industries and their relative importance.

The excavations have been particularly informative for many reasons, not least because they have completely overturned the accepted view that nothing much could possibly survive of Birmingham's past. This, coupled with the shortage of documentary evidence for the medieval and early post-medieval periods, and the demolition of medieval houses and handsome Georgian terraces and squares, has tended to relegate the city to the bottom of the historic towns' league regionally and nationally, especially in comparison to places such as Coventry and Warwick. The picture that has emerged is one of a thriving town, which was able to overcome the paucity of its immediate agricultural resources and turn to its advantage the ready availability of water, its position at the nexus of communications, and the exploitation of mineral resources from the Black Country. Whether the fortunes of the town, from the rather poor showing at Domesday, were in any way affected by the direct intervention of the de Birmingham family, can be argued either way. The fact remains that following the granting of the 12th-century market charter, Birmingham seems never to have looked back.

This discussion brings together the evidence from excavations at Park Street, Moor Street, Edgbaston Street, and The Row, which are the subject of this report, and related sites in the city centre – Wrottesley Street (Jones 2000), Masshouse, Hartwell Smithfield Garage, the Old Crown, Custard Factory, Floodgate Street, Park Street/ Bordesley Street (Tavener 2000) and High Street, Bordesley – and puts it into its wider context, in Birmingham and beyond (see Fig. 16.1, colour for site locations).

Landscape and origins

Perhaps the most difficult thing to appreciate from a modern perspective of Birmingham is the extremely wet nature of much of the historic heart of the city (Fig 16.2, colour). Visitors to the city in the 20th and 21st centuries would be unaware of the numerous springs (all now culverted), which even to this day result in basement flooding in many of the city-centre shops, and of the River Rea, which was in the past of sufficient size to merit a three-span bridge. The culverted Rea can today be glimpsed occasionally, but as a fairly insignificant watercourse. However, further upstream in the suburbs of Edgbaston and Kings Norton, the rapidity with which the Rea increases in volume during heavy or prolonged rain is remarkable. An understanding of the topography and development of Birmingham, therefore, cannot be understood without consideration of what could be euphemistically called its 'well-watered position'.

Pollen and seeds show that originally Birmingham lay in a well-wooded landscape. Much tree pollen was found in an organic layer at Edgbaston Street, which may pre-date the establishment of the town. However tree pollen was still abundant in the early fill of the large ditch at Park Street and Moor Street, and in the fill of the manor-house moat at The Row and the Wholesale Markets site. Buds, seeds, cones of birch, alder and willow were found in the ditch at Park Street. Lovers of damp environments, such as willow and poplar, were found at Park Street and Edgbaston Street. Trees such as willow and alder were often coppiced and this may indicate that the trees were part of managed woodland.

The establishment of the town may have brought about a reduction in the amount of woodland caused by the intensification of agriculture and the growth of industry. By the 14th century there was almost certainly something of a decline, a picture which is mirrored nationally. Although there is documentary evidence to suggest regeneration of Edgbaston Street after the Black Death at the instigation of Fulke de Birmingham (McKenna 2005), the later medieval period of reorganisation, with a greater focus on industry, resulted in a shift away from the old medieval core of the town further down into Digbeth and the valley floor of the River Rea, where the water supply was better. This would help account for the paucity of archaeological evidence of this period on both Moor Street and Park Street. High levels of tree pollen in a 17th-century pit on Park Street could suggest that in the face of the above reorganisation, perhaps allied with population and agricultural decline, there was some woodland regeneration within and around the town. A view of Birmingham, for example, in Dugdale's *Antiquities of Warwickshire* of 1656, shows dense woodland on the slopes above St Martin's and Park Street (Fig. 16.3). The rapid expansion of Birmingham from the later 17th century would have marked the beginning of the end for any woodland (Figs 16.4–6). However, although this picture is attractive there are caveats. Firstly, how representative is the fill of a single pit in determining the likely tree cover in the entire urban landscape? Secondly, James Greig (pers. comm.) notes that there is no body of evidence for the amount of tree pollen that is representative of an urban landscape with varying amounts of trees. Only when there is a sequence, as at Metchley Roman fort (Greig 2005), can clear changes in the treescape of Birmingham be seen with any certainty.

Considering the extent of the Bull Ring excavations, the tiny quantity of prehistoric worked flint found in them is remarkable. Had there been significant prehistoric activity, it would surely have been represented by objects occurring residually in later contexts, even if actual features did not survive because of the intensity of medieval and post-medieval activity. Elsewhere in the city centre, the only recorded discovery of a prehistoric object is a polished stone axe from Deritend (Sherlock 1957). Bronze Age burnt mounds, in particular, might be expected in the wetter areas. However, Bronze Age and Iron Age sites in this area might contain little pottery or other non-organic objects: for example, only a small quantity of pottery was found at the Iron Age farmstead at Langley Mill Farm in Sutton Coldfield (Booth 2002; Hodder 2004, 45–7) so, if structural remains did not survive, activity in these periods would be difficult to detect. The quantity of Roman pottery from the Moor Street and Park Street sites is small but locally significant and is sufficient to suggest the existence of a farmstead in the vicinity. This is the first discovery of Roman material other than coins in the city centre and is to be seen alongside the increasing number of Roman settlements now known elsewhere in Birmingham and its immediate surroundings (Hodder 2004, 63–70; Booth 2002). Roman coin hoards found some time ago in Dudley Street and Holliday Street (Birmingham City Council, Sites and Monuments Record) might also be related to settlements. Archaeologically, there is no evidence for a major settlement in this part of Birmingham until the 12th century. As with the prehistoric periods, any significant activity in the Anglo-Saxon period would surely have been visible as residual objects in such extensive controlled excavations even if no features survived. Four sherds, all from Park Street, could possibly have been Anglo-Saxon. Two may date to the early–middle Saxon period, a third may be Roman or late Anglo-Saxon, and a fourth from a spouted bowl is of late Anglo-Saxon or early post-Conquest date.

Fig. 16.3 View of Birmingham, from William Dugdale's Antiquities of Warwickshire, *1656.*

Town development and resources

The earliest feature located in the excavations was the large ditch, dated to the 12th century, which was found in Park Street and Moor Street (Fig 16.7) and interpreted as the division between the settlement and a deer park, Over Park. Twelfth-century pottery was found on Edgbaston Street, Moor Street and Park Street, although not in large quantities. This early pottery from Edgbaston Street probably marks occupation and development of Edgbaston Street after the granting of the Market Charter in the 12th century. Similarly dated pottery from Moor Street and Park Street is less easy to interpret and is probably not associated with development and occupation

on the streets themselves at such an early date but rather may derive from the occupation of backplots fronting onto the High Street and Digbeth, or may represent dumping of midden and similar material on the periphery of the town, in what may have been rather boggy unappealing land.

In its early years the town/ park ditch was wet, with fauna and flora typical of standing or slow-moving water. Given the slope of the ground, which would favour rather faster flowing water, it seems unlikely that the ditch could be classed as a permanent watercourse as such, especially since none of the finds from within the lower fills showed any sign of having been in water for long periods. A

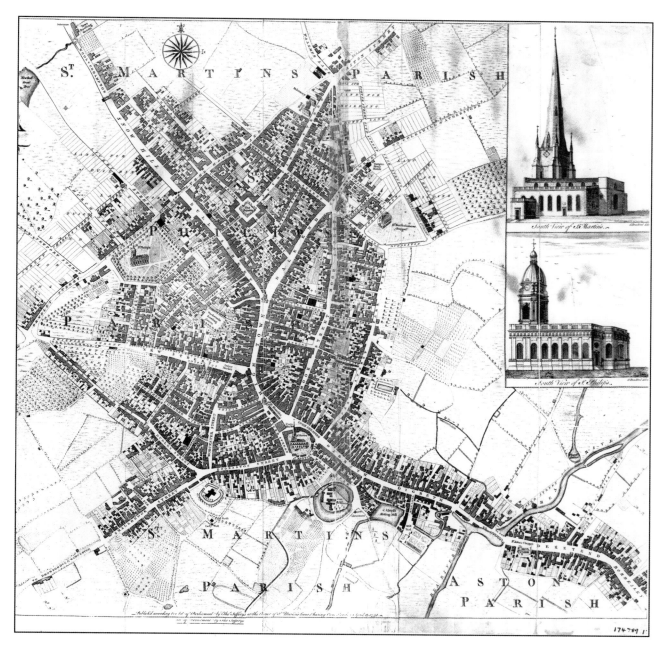

Fig. 16.4 Bradford's Map of Birmingham 1750.

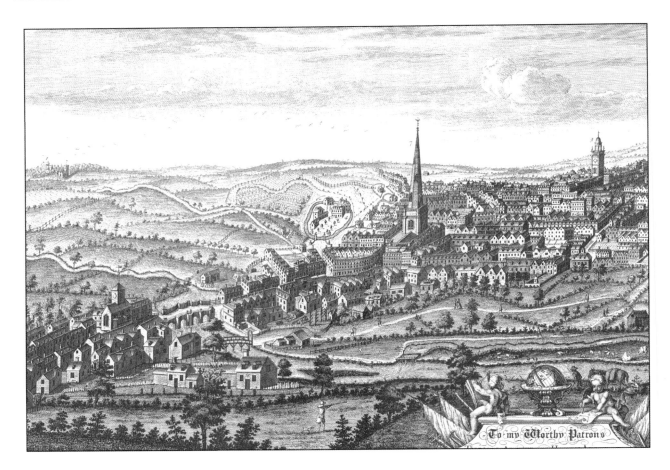

Fig. 16.5 Detail from Westley's East Prospect of Birmingham, *1732.*

Fig. 16.6 Nathaniels Buck's Prospect of Birmingham from the East, *1753.*

second medieval ditch, probably marking the backplot boundaries at Park Street, also contained water and may have been fed by a spring, although the evidence is uncertain. However, some supply of water in this general area is indicated by the alignment of Phase 1 and Phase 2 features, some possibly associated with tanning, along the edge of the ditch. In addition documentary evidence indicates that fish ponds were in the vicinity.

The third watercourse, which linked the Parsonage Moat and the Manorial Moat (see Westley's map Fig 2.2 and prospect Fig 16.5), was a more substantial water feature. Environmental information suggests that the area of the watercourse was well wooded and marshy probably before the establishment of the town. It seems most likely that the watercourse was originally a natural feature but later, with the establishment of the Parsonage and Manorial moats, was channelled to link the two moats and form a boundary to the backplots running back from Edgbaston Street. The junction of the watercourse with both moats, and of course the moats themselves, has been destroyed by later development so exactly how it functioned or was regulated is uncertain. The watercourse, from environmental evidence, contained flowing water and it is assumed that the Parsonage Moat was fed by a spring (or springs) and fed into the watercourse which then fed into the Manorial Moat and thence down to the River Rea. However the presence of both still and flowing water, evidenced by environmental remains, in two sections of the Manorial Moat which have been excavated, must surely indicate a system of sluices to control and moderate the flow of water. A further, presumed natural, watercourse was found at Edgbaston Street, running through Area B. Two other watercourses were located in Area C, which appeared to be associated with post-medieval tan- or skin-pits.

Further 12th-century activity, in the close vicinity of the excavations, is witnessed by St Martin's Church, where 12th-century architectural details were found during 19th-century restoration (Holliday 1874, 50) and the moated manor house, probably a ringwork, where 12th-century stone mouldings were found in the 1970s salvage recording (pers. comm. Richard Morris on the stones illustrated in Watts 1980, fig. 20).

Evidence of 13th-century domestic occupation on the Edgbaston Street frontage included a tile-floored oven. Dung beetles and weevils, associated with pollen and seed evidence for weedy open grassland from the watercourse joining Parsonage Moat with the Manor House Moat, suggest that cattle were pastured and watered at the back of Edgbaston Street. Plant and insect remains show that the large ditch at Park Street and Moor Street contained slow-flowing water or pools of standing water and that there was disturbed ground around it. The plant assemblage in the fill of this ditch has been interpreted as charred fodder, again indicating that stock was kept here. This early association of stock and Birmingham is interesting since it links with the

importance of droving and beast markets to the town (see Bradford's Map Fig 2.3 and 16.4) and the tanning industry. The plant remains indicate the use of heathland resources – heather, bracken and gorse – which could have been used for animal bedding, as a roofing material, or for brooms. These plants could have been obtained from Birmingham Heath to the west.

The first evidence for industries appears in the 13th century. In addition to its water resources, Birmingham had access to several sources of fuel. The date and appearance of Deritend pottery suggests that wood must have been the fuel used in pottery production. However, coal occurred in medieval contexts at all the Bull Ring sites. At Moor Street, it is in the fill of the deer park ditch. The very early dates for the presence of coal are significant and indicate Birmingham's exploitation of this resource from the 13th century. The coal must have come from the Black Country or the north Warwickshire coalfield and would therefore have been costly. Its apparently widespread use may have been in response to a shortage of wood for fuel, demonstrating the impact of the thriving town on the surrounding landscape, although this is not so apparent in the pollen data, and trees managed as a renewable resource by coppicing, which is not destructive, could have supplied wood for domestic fuel. Also, coal often burns quite dirtily, making it less desirable in a domestic setting, and is not very suitable for use on the typical medieval open domestic hearth. It is more likely, then, that the coal was used from an early period primarily for industrial processes, as it was in the Black Country (pers. comm. John Hunt), particularly since the iron and iron ore used in Birmingham's metal-working industries came from this area, as Leland notes (Toulmin-Smith 1964, V.96–7), albeit in the 16th century. The occurrence of coal with metal-working debris at Park Street in the post-medieval period is further evidence of its use as an industrial fuel.

Burnt peat found at Moor Street shows that this fuel was also used in medieval Birmingham. It was presumably dug from the turf pits on Birmingham Heath which are mentioned in Edward VI's Commissioner's Survey of the town in 1553. Peat was a fuel used by the poor in this area and peat was still being dug for fuel in Sutton Park in the 18th century (Incola 1762). The combination at Moor Street of peat and plant remains typical of heathland, *e.g.* heath, heather and rye, may be significant. Peat is generally thought of as a poor fuel, giving out little heat and of use only in a domestic setting. However, in areas where peat is the main or only fuel source, *e.g.* Shetland, it has been used for smelting and for turning into charcoal (pers. comm. Amanda Forster). However, the availability of other fuels in Birmingham may suggest that its presence at Moor Street may indicate rather poorer inhabitants or may be related to a specific function. Ciaraldi, Chapter 12, notes sprouted cereals, possibly associated with brewing, on Moor Street. The slow gentle heat, necessary for malting barley for

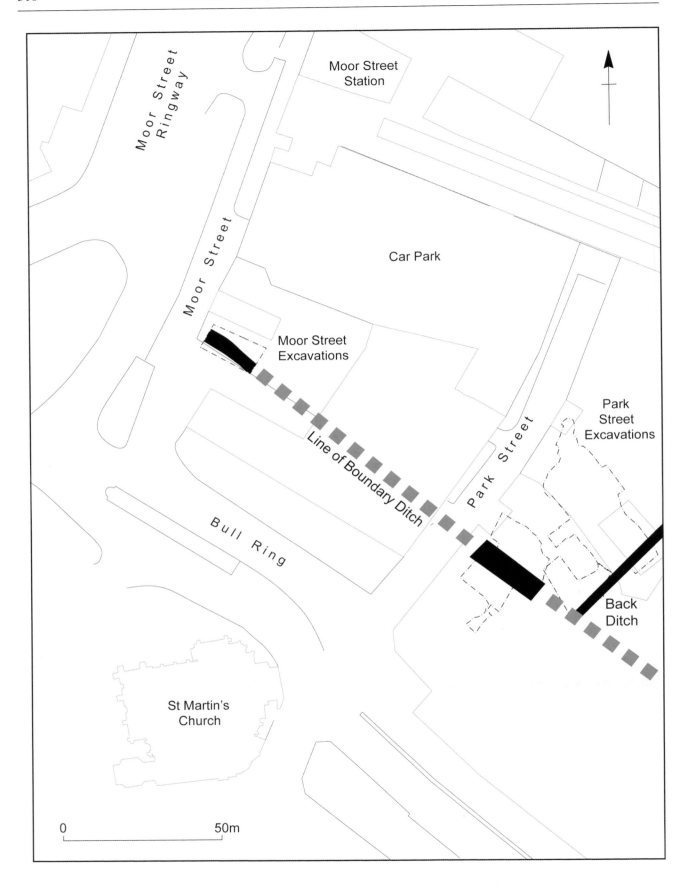

Fig. 16.7 Plan showing major boundary ditches at Moor Street and Park Street.

example, would have been obtainable from peat and may explain its presence here.

Evidence for the use of charcoal as a fuel was evidenced at Moor Street by a Phase 2 charcoal-rich layer probably associated with metal working. Both wood and charcoal for use as fuel could have been obtained from managed woodland in the town itself and in Over Park. The presence of trees which could be coppiced (see above) could in part be associated with charcoal-burning. Although no excavated evidence of charcoal-burning was found, it is probable that it was carried out in Over Park.

In the 13th and 14th centuries there was a planned expansion of the town to the north of St Martin's Church (the stone-lined wells outside St Martin's Church and on Moor Street may have been provided as public amenities at this time) within what had been the deer park, marked by the infilling of the major ditch to facilitate the construction of two new roads, Park Street and Moor Street. Some sort of 'unofficial' access to the deer park was probably already in existence quite early on, especially in view of the evidence of tan pits and the possibility of pottery manufacture on Park Street. This may have been little more than a plank or a small earthen causeway across the ditch. The formation of the Moor Street and Park Street burgage plots may have followed the wholesale infilling of the ditch but it was not necessarily essential to infill the whole ditch before it was possible to lay out the plots.

At Park Street, a ditch, containing water, running at right angles to the main deer park ditch, is probably associated with this expansion and marked the rear boundary of the plots. It was recut, possibly in the post-medieval period, and was subsequently followed by the back walls of Structures 7 and 8. Likewise, the main boundary ditch at Park Street was recut and its line also preserved by the wall of a late building. A medieval recut of the ditch at Moor Street was recorded but this seems to have been filled by c.1300 with no further recuts evidenced.

Fill material within the boundary ditches may have derived from the backplots fronting onto the High Street and Digbeth or from the newly created Moor Street and Park Street backplots. Plant and pollen evidence certainly shows a difference in activity levels between the lowest fills and the later fills where pottery is more abundant and evidence of crop processing and stock rearing appears. At Park Street the ditch was also a receptacle for pottery production waste. Although the evidence is somewhat scant, it is possible that the excavated area of Park Street, which lay within the ground bordered to the south by the town/ park ditch and to the north by Hersum Ditch, was utilised for pottery production and tanning and never really fully developed as 'normal' burgage plots. Certainly, a rather desolate air still seems to hang around the area in the 15th and 16th centuries.

No remains of medieval buildings were found during excavations in the Bull Ring. None of the excavations

extended as far as the presumed medieval street frontage, which, in any case, would have been unlikely to have survived because of cellaring or the insertion of services, or would have lain under modern roads or pavements. However, the finds from Edgbaston Street are typical of domestic occupation and it is unlikely that there were no house or houses associated with them. There is some evidence to suggest that Area A may have been abandoned in the 14th century and there was little evidence of medieval activity in areas C and D. The case regarding the excavated area of Park Street is somewhat different and it may not have been fully developed until the post-medieval period. The pottery, for example, is far from a typical urban assemblage and most of it covers a relatively short time span, with little apparently dating after the first quarter of the 14th century. It is hard not to see some set-back to the town in the 14th century. We know, for example, that Edgbaston Street was redeveloped after the Black Death, but worsening climatic changes earlier in the 14th century may have made some peripheral areas just too wet and boggy to be tolerable.

The footings of St Martin's Church, as revealed in the excavation of its graveyard, and the stone building discovered on the manor house site are obviously exceptional and, indeed, these are likely to have been the only stone buildings in the medieval town centre. A single *in situ* survival of a late medieval timber-framed building, the Old Crown, Deritend, dates to c.1500. The Old Crown in Deritend is possibly unrepresentative of other buildings in the town because of its date and because it is likely to have been built as a guildhall and school rather than as a dwelling or a workshop. However, old photographs reveal that there were a number of other good quality timber-framed buildings, probably dating to the 16th or early 17th century, such as the Golden Lion, High Street, Deritend (removed and reconstructed in Cannon Hill Park in 1911), Old Lamb House on the corner of Bull Street and High Street, and Assinder's Tripe House on Well Street, Digbeth, in the town centre. All three buildings had elaborate decorative framing and indicate a degree of affluence. Other buildings of a similar date were the Leather Bottle and Three Crowns public houses in Deritend. A small very dilapidated building is shown in a photograph of 1886 (Turner 1994, 37) which lay at the corner of Moor Street and Dale End and appears to have been brick-built and probably of 17th-century date.

Other evidence for buildings is largely circumstantial. Plant remains of alder, hazel and willow may have been used in wattle and daub construction. Osier pits are certainly shown to the south of the Manorial Moat-Parsonage Moat watercourse on Sherriff's map of 1808 (Fig 2.4) and they may be the final chapter of an industry stretching back to the medieval period. A basket maker was recorded on Edgbaston Street in Sketchley's 1770 directory and also on Upper Dean Street in the 19th century. The heather indicated by pollen and seeds may have been used for roofing. However, large quantities of ceramic roofing tile were found at Park Street and were also present at Edgbaston Street and Moor Street. Some of the flat roof tile was glazed and two glazed crested ridge tiles at Edgbaston Street suggest at least one building of quality. The roof tiles were almost certainly made in the city centre itself (a small amount of wastered roof tile was found on Moor Street), and in an urban setting tiles were used from the early 13th century. The somewhat hazardous nature of non-ceramic roofing material is evidenced by the 'great fire' of Birmingham in the late 13th or early 14th century (Razi 1978) and the wider use, if not the introduction, of tiled roofs in town-centre buildings could have been a response to this. However, roof tiles were already available and were used in the 13th-century oven at Edgbaston Street. This and the occurrence of loose roof tile in other medieval features indicate both the availability of roof tile and the existence of tiled roofs in the town centre by this time. The use of roof tile may have had a status value, judging by its occurrence on moated sites (see below), and its use in the excavated Bull Ring sites may indicate their status, as the glazed crested ridge tiles undoubtedly do. However, the presence of tiled hearths and ovens indicates that ceramic roof tile was also employed in a more pedestrian and practical way.

The town continued to expand in the post-medieval period. A 17th-century pit at the junction of Park Street and Bordesley Street (Tavener 2000) indicates that the settlement had extended this far by this period but on the opposite side of Park Street recent evaluation work on Freeman Street, which links Moor Street and Park Street, revealed considerable medieval deposits. Whether this represents a short-lived expansion of the town or represents dumps of town waste awaits clarification following full excavation. In contrast, expansion to the south of the Parsonage Moat-Manorial Moat watercourse did not really get underway until the 19th century.

Already by the later 17th century, tenements were being constructed. Early 18th-century prospects of Birmingham show a fairly dense patterning of tall buildings along the street frontages which may also reflect the boom in construction of quality properties in the late 17th and 18th centuries (Figs 16.5–6). The marble tiles or facing slabs recovered from Edgbaston Street may be a tantalising glimpse of this development. It is to this period that properties along Park Street seem mainly to belong. However, the spacious town houses, such as Nos 10 and 18 Park Street, seem to have quickly lost their purely domestic use and rapidly acquired a commercial or industrial one. The down-grading of some of these high quality buildings and the surge in Birmingham's population, led to the construction of courts containing dwellings, workshops and sheds. These had begun to be constructed by the early 18th century. The archaeological evidence for this process at Park Street is clear, although close dating is not possible. At Edgbaston Street, archaeological evidence for these processes was not recorded, although cartographic evidence shows it to have been the case, where the backyard industries included a skinyard, later Welch's Skinyard, and a glassworks, later the site of Glasshouse Court (Fig 2.4).

Pits on the Edgbaston Street frontage were filled in and the 17th-century tanning pits were filled with domestic debris by *c*.1725. However gardens also seem to have been a feature of the excavated Edgbaston Street backplots, which resisted encroachment and development until the 19th century. The presence of the gardens may in part account for the extensive 'dark earth' deposits across the site, although the environmental samples did not pick up evidence of them. However, at Park Street proof of the gardens, which from the cartographic evidence lay well to the rear of the plots, was seen in the environmental samples. Charred seeds, including a large quantity of beet together with turnip, strawberry and plum may represent locally cultivated plants.

By the 19th century all three excavated areas had become part of a dense cluster of low-grade housing and industry (Fig 16.8). The Parsonage-manor house water-course had been infilled and was subsequently covered by demolition debris, which contained information on other industries carried out in the locale. The late 18th- and 19th-century burials in St Martin's Churchyard (Brickley and Buteux *et al*. 2006) and St Philip's Churchyard (Patrick 2000) provide the earliest physical information on Birmingham people themselves, almost certainly including those who lived and worked on the other excavated sites.

Industries and crafts

An impressive range of industries and crafts is indicated or implied by the archaeological evidence, including some which are not known from documentary evidence: pottery and probably tile manufacture, leather tanning and presumably leather and skin working, metal working, including the smithing which was observed by Leland in the 16th century (Toulmin Smith 1964, V.96–7), and brass founding, cutlering, bone and ivory working, and possibly horn working, probable textile manufacture including linen and sack cloth, and, later, glass making and button manufacture.

In the medieval period, Birmingham appears to have had few Craft Guilds, unlike most medieval towns. This seems to have been beneficial rather than detrimental to the development of the trade and craft base, since craftsmen were pretty well unrestricted in the pursuance of their livelihoods. A certain amount of flexibility in working practice may well have developed early on and formed the basis of the post-medieval opportunism and flexibility evidenced in both the archaeological and documentary record.

Tanning and leather-working trades were long-lived industries, and Birmingham shoemakers were an impor-tant trade group in London in the 14th century (McKenna

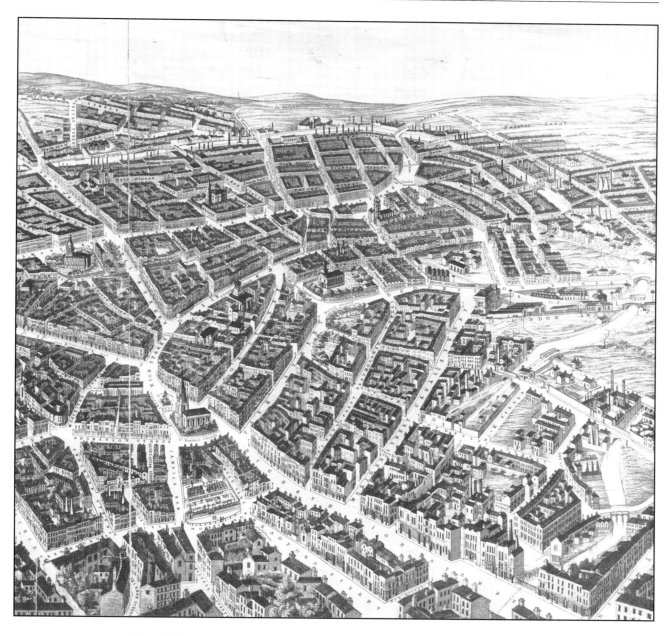

Fig. 16.8 Detail from Ackerman's Perspective View of Birmingham 1847.

2005). The importance of droving and the various beast markets to the development of the town should not be underestimated, since they provided not only food but the raw materials for tanners, leather workers, horn workers, bone workers etc. The references to tanners in the 16th century tend to be in locations in the low-lying ground south of the manor house and around the River Rea but the archaeological evidence shows that in the 13th century tanning was being undertaken near the parish church, manor house and market place. This noxious industry may have been tolerated in this location at this time because of its perceived economic significance to the town or simply because the town's medieval inhabitants were less sensitive to the smell than we might think.

Perhaps surprisingly, there was no archaeological evidence for the production of woollen cloth, also an important Birmingham industry, although there is evidence for hemp and flax retting. Since leather tanning and textile processing both required a water supply, it is not surprising to find them in close proximity to each other in Birmingham, as at Brewood (Ciaraldi *et al.* 2004), where there was hemp retting and leather tanning on the same site in the 12th and 13th centuries, and Leominster, where both flax debris and horncores were found in a medieval deposit in a wet area of the town (Buteux 1994).

The evidence for flax and hemp processing in Birmingham, as at these other places, has been obtained from the survival, sampling, and subsequent analysis of deposits in which their seeds and pollen have survived. Cloth manufacture was one of the three industries, together with leather-working and iron-working, which are known from documentary evidence to have been important in 16th-century Birmingham. The occurrence of craftsmen's names in medieval documents indicates that they were present earlier as well (VCH Warwickshire VII 1964, 78).

Hemp and flax occurs in late medieval and early post-medieval contexts in the Bull Ring and at Rea Street. Documentary evidence shows that both these crops were grown locally, for example in Yardley, where flax is mentioned in probate inventories between 1539 and 1559 (Skipp 1970), and in Wigginshill in Sutton Coldfield, where John Greasebrook's Probate inventory of 1671 mentions that he grew hemp (Lea 2002).

Flax and hemp retting could have taken place in the many natural and artificial watercourses in the Park Street area and seems to have taken place also in the Manor Moat. The manufacture of linen and hemp cloth, rope or thread presumably took place near by. In the third quarter of the 18th century, sacking weavers and thread makers are mentioned on Park Street and a thread maker and flax dresser worked on Edgbaston Street. It is perhaps no coincidence that several properties on Park Street were owned by Theophilus Merac, amongst other things a linen draper. It is also likely that dyeing was taking place in this area where there was ample water.

There was some evidence of metal working in the medieval period although it does not seem to have been a major concern in the areas excavated. This is probably misleading. An inventory of the possessions of the Master of the Order of Knights Templar in England on his arrest in 1308 includes 'Birmingham pieces' (Gooder 1988). The term 'Birmingham pieces' (from the context probably small metal items) appears without a gloss, suggesting that the term would have been familiar to the medieval reader. This not only indicates that good-quality metal work was being produced in Birmingham at this date but also that Birmingham products were familiar to those living in London.

Apart from tanning, the industry to leave the biggest archaeological mark on Birmingham was the production of pottery. There is no known documentary evidence for this industry in Birmingham. The previous archaeological evidence consisted of wasters found in a watching brief on the south side of High Street, Deritend, in the 1950s and wasters found in an evaluation in 1994 behind the Old Crown, on the north side of High Street, Deritend. Pottery manufacture used three of Birmingham's few raw materials, clay, water and wood, and possibly a fourth, sand, for temper. Water would have been readily available from the various watercourses in this area, and clay could be dug locally from Mercia Mudstone and drifts derived from it. The small quantities of non-local clay used by this industry were, significantly, white Coal Measure clay

from north Warwickshire or from the Black Country, the same area which provided Birmingham with its coal and iron. Above all else, the kilns would have required large quantities of wood as fuel. It may be significant that a surprisingly large amount of tree pollen was recovered from the middle fill of the town/ park boundary ditch at Park Street and it is possible that it was derived from fuel brought to the site to fire the kilns.

At Park Street a fire bar and wasters were found in the boundary ditch fills and further wasters in pits to the north of the boundary ditch. Possible wasters were also recovered from Moor Street. The presence of wasters in the northern pits at Park Street may be evidence for pottery production within what was effectively waste ground lying just inside the lord of the manor's deer park, consisting of a roughly triangular area defined by the main boundary ditch to the south, Hersum Ditch to the north and Park Street to the west. The ready availability of wood and water and the otherwise rather unprepossessing nature of the area, close to but outside the town, would seem an ideal location for such an industry. If so, then the establishment within Over Park of a further branch of a pottery industry, which stretched along Digbeth and Deritend, must have had the complicit agreement of the lords of Birmingham. That is not to say that their interest was anything other than pecuniary and need not be taken to indicate an active involvement in the promotion of crafts or trades in Birmingham.

A diverse range of pottery was produced which covered cooking and storage needs and table wares (vessels of consumption) such as jugs. The industry probably supplied much of Birmingham's needs in the 13th and early 14th centuries, although there was still a market for pottery manufactured outside the town.

The glazed Deritend jugs, particularly those with white slip decoration, are very similar to London ware jugs of the same period and it is hard not to see the influence of the latter on the former. This might tend to suggest reasonable amounts of contact between the two places, which the reference to Birmingham shoemakers in London and 'Birmingham pieces' (above) in the medieval period, and the trade in woollen cloth would also imply.

The distribution of Deritend ware also tells something about the contacts between Birmingham and the wider world. The mechanisms for pottery distribution can be complex. The simple model of purchase by local people at local markets (or direct from the potter) never quite explains all the distributions which are found. Other factors were at work, such as the transport of pottery amongst household baggage from one home to another. Another important factor could perhaps best be described as 'hidden trade'. In essence the pottery is picked up as an adjunct to trade in bulkier or more expensive goods. Alternatively, the pottery could be distributed as part of a two-way traffic. A late (19th-century) example of the latter (Young 1979) is provided by a Verwood potter who travelled from Hampshire to Somerset with a cart load of pottery for sale and returned with a number of cheeses, which could then be sold on when he returned to Hampshire.

The oxidised glazed jugs are most commonly found outside the town but the reduced cooking pots and jugs also travel. Deritend ware is found over most of Warwickshire (although rather surprisingly somewhat infrequently in Coventry), the Black Country and Staffordshire (as far north as Stafford), Worcester and Droitwich (although somewhat less common in the rest of Worcestershire). The distribution suggests a very wide area of contact, some clearly related to the acquisition of raw materials, *e.g.* iron and coal from the Black Country, some possibly associated with obtaining agricultural produce – *e.g.* the Warwickshire distribution – and salt (Droitwich and Worcester), and some from direct selling at Birmingham markets and fairs. If some of the Deritend pottery found outside Birmingham is an indication of outsiders coming to the town for other goods, then it could be taken to suggest that, overall, the range of goods for sale in Birmingham was either less easily obtainable or of a quality not found elsewhere.

The reasons for the end of Deritend ware production are obscure. The industry may have been short-lived because of the lack of easily available wood in sufficiently large quantities but the somewhat uncertain times of the 14th century may just as well have played their part. The shortage of excavated pottery from the later 14th–16th centuries in Birmingham makes the picture confusing and there is no way, at present, of knowing for certain whether pottery production ceased completely. Certainly by the 15th and 16th centuries there was competition from major production sites such as Wednesbury in the Black Country. However, it is not without interest that 18th-century wasters of black-glazed coarsewares and flower-pots were found during excavations at Floodgate Street and that a Luke Rogers, 'sackcloth weaver and potter', was listed at No. 1 Park Street in Sketchley's 1770 Directory. There is, therefore, the possibility of a continuity of pottery production from the medieval period. Pottery of the 15th and 16th centuries was rare across all the sites and its paucity merits some discussion. Although factors such as the truncation of deposits of this date and changes in the method of refuse disposal could affect the amount of pottery found, the hard evidence to support such an interpretation is lacking. Shaw notes that at The Green, Northampton, 'the main period of tanning activity coincided with a period of dereliction' (1996, 63). It is therefore possible that a similar situation pertained on Edgbaston Street at least.

In the case of Park Street, there is good reason to believe that the site was, at best, under-utilised in the medieval period and continued in this vein until the 17th century, when more intense domestic occupation probably began. The site appears to have been used for 'fringe activities', such as stock rearing and fish ponds, and there was some evidence for tanning or leather working.

However, what pottery there was, almost certainly derived from the Digbeth backplots, is perfectly in keeping with town dwellers of reasonable means, so a slump in the town's fortunes is not really indicated. This of course would tie in with the thriving town described by Leland and Camden (Toulmin Smith 1964, V.96–7; Camden 1586).

The importance of tanning in Birmingham in the 16th century and later is indicated by documentary sources. William Hutton described Birmingham as formerly being 'one vast tan-yard' but just one tanner remained by his time (Hutton 1783, 79–80). At least a dozen tanners are mentioned in the 1553 survey (VCH Warwickshire VII 1964, 81). Cattle hides would have come from cattle bought and sold in the market. Tanners were amongst the wealthiest of the town's inhabitants. Two leather sealers were appointed annually and there was a leather hall where business was transacted (Court 1938, 34). The tanning industry was in decline by the early 19th century – the leather hall had been removed and the leather trade restricted to the making of bellows and harnesses (Court 1938, 35; Hutton 1783). It has been suggested that, although they were certainly in existence at the time of his visit, the tanneries were not noted by John Leland because they were near watercourses behind street frontages, in contrast to the metal forges he observed and noted.

The location of tanneries was determined by the availability of water and hides. Cattle hides would have come from cattle bought and sold in the market. Documentary evidence shows that cattle came from Black Country towns such as Tipton and Wednesbury but also from further afield such as the Welsh Marches. The lime used as part of the tanning process and found stored in pits at Edgbaston Street, Park Street and Floodgate Street is also likely to be from this area, from limestone found at Rushall, Dudley Walsall or Wednesbury, and provides yet another link between Birmingham and the Black Country. It would also have been used in the mortar for St Martin's Church and the stone building at the manor house. The source of the oak bark used by Birmingham's tanners is unknown.

At Edgbaston Street tanning continued in the 15th–16th centuries, despite documentary sources and archaeological evidence from Floodgate Street which suggest that these industries were relocating closer to the River Rea. Here the absence of pottery of this date (although found residually) may reflect the removal of late medieval and early post-medieval deposits from nearer the frontage. The presence of 16th-century Rhenish stoneware does suggest that there were fairly prosperous people, or people with pretensions to good living, about. Gaimster notes the transformation of stoneware from 'the purely utilitarian to the social and symbolic spheres' and that 'The... archaeological evidence for stoneware in use serves to demonstrate its importance as an index of material comfort and social competition' (Gaimster 1997, 126).

The archaeological evidence for 17th-century tanning is in the southeastern part of the excavated area at Edgbaston Street and next to the River Rea in Floodgate Street, and there were 18th-century tanning pits at the Custard Factory site near the River Rea. Welch's Skinyard, in the southern part of the Edgbaston Street site by the early 19th century was probably a rather different process from the earlier tanyards here.

The archaeological evidence proves beyond doubt that tanning and, later, skin working was a more or less permanent fixture at Edgbaston Street from its inception. However, the shift towards the Rea is probably part of a refocusing of the heartland of the town, away from the higher ground, to areas well served by water power, which was used not only for tanning but in the numerous nail, blade making and allied trades for which Birmingham was already known. The cutlery trade was important in Birmingham even at the time of Leland (McKenna 2005, 18; Toulmin Smith 1964, V.96–7) and Birmingham was second only to Sheffield in the manufacture of cutlery in the post-medieval period. The occurrence, therefore, in the 17th century of handle waste, hearth bottoms and hammerscale in a single pit at Park Street is of great significance. Does the waste represent the debris from two unrelated industries and, if so, were the two practised at the same time on the site or is it more likely that the two industries were linked, *e.g.* in the hafting of knives and the cutlery trade? Knife hafter and iron worker were normally two separate and distinct occupations. A combination of the two skills might suggest embryonic or low-scale industry, or the type of minor industry which occurred in the suburbs or back streets away from the settlement centre. An example of this would be Cutler Street, London (pers. comm. Geoff Egan). Clearly, Park Street could not be classed as away from the settlement centre, although it is away from the industrial centre in the Rea valley. As such, the industry represented by the contents of the pit represents a move away from the metal-working heartland. If the debris from the pit does represent cutlery manufacture it may indicate the beginnings of the post-Restoration surge in industry mentioned by Hutton (1783) and the expansion of metal-working trades into other parts of the town.

Birmingham was a regular supplier of iron ware to London. An observer wrote in 1650 'all or most of the London ironmongers buy all or most of their nails and petty ironwork either from Birmingham...or at London as brought from thence' (quoted in Mckenna 2005, 22). By the time of the Civil War it was reported that Birmingham was producing as many swords as, and of equal quality to, those made in London. It was this (no doubt allied to Birmingham's pro-Parliamentary stance) which provoked Prince Rupert into his attack on the town. The Plague and the Great Fire of London provided further impetus to Birmingham's metal-working trades and the increasing demand for iron goods may explain the expansion of these trades away from the Rea.

The evidence from Park Street suggests that the first metal-working industries were probably associated with wrought iron objects and blades, since the earliest pits contain hammerscale. Subsequently, archaeological evidence indicates that brass founding was taking place. Documentary evidence supports this but also indicates that smithing was still being practised. The waste products from the burgeoning number of foundries in Birmingham are also linked to the occurrence of paths and working surfaces of clinker or cinder, essentially foundry waste products, paths and working surfaces, which are a feature of the 18th-century tan- and skinyards at Edgbaston Street.

There was some evidence of cutlering/ handle making at Edgbaston Street where a number of handle offcuts, similar to those from Park Street, were found. A section of sawn elephant tusk was also found on Edgbaston Street providing another indication of ivory-working. All this evidence seems to relate to the 17th century.

Some evidence of brush manufacture in the 18th or early 19th centuries was found at both Park Street and Edgbaston Street. Two brush makers were recorded for Edgbaston Street (Nos 24 and 51) in Sketchley's 1770 Directory, and one for Park Street (No. 16) and a late brush makers, adjacent to the excavated area, is shown on Park Street on the 1895 Goad Insurance Map.

A white metal button with a casting sprue still attached was found unstratified on Edgbaston Street and is the only definite evidence for the manufacture of metal buttons. Shell button blanks and waste were also associated with Edgbaston Street, and were concentrated in the backfills of a well in Transect A. The dating of this material is difficult since other finds from within the well suggest a period from the late 18th–late 19th century. The button-making waste could represent late 18th-century production. At least two button makers (William Fletcher and Edward Vincent) are listed on Edgbaston Street in Sketchley's 1770 directory, although only Vincent is recorded as a pearl button maker. A small amount of bone button-making waste was found at Park Street. William Pring, button maker, was living on Park Street outside the excavated area, at No. 13 Park Street in the 1790s but his property is probably too far away to account for the excavated finds. However, the artisans and craftsmen do seem to have quite often changed premises, for William Pring was formerly based in the 1780s in Snow Hill, the focus for button making in Birmingham. It is possible therefore that the Park Street button waste represented a short-lived venture, perhaps carried out in a small court workshop. Certainly, the presence of Luke Rogers, sackcloth weaver and potter (see above), and Martha Sheldon, 'bellows maker and sacking weaver' (Wrightson and Thomsons' 1812 Directory), suggests that the working population of Birmingham was versatile and could turn its hand to alternative crafts as the economic climate demanded.

Social and economic

The artefactual evidence, other than pottery, recovered from the Bull Ring sites, particularly for the earlier periods, is not plentiful and seems in the main to be connected with crafts and industries. Evidence for the domestic lives of the inhabitants is rare. However, a gaming token, marrow spoon and rock crystal seal from Park Street and vessel glass from Edgbaston Street and Park Street go some way to redress the balance. In fact, some of these finds, particularly the vessel glass but also the sword chape, loop-in-loop chain and fragment of decorated floor tile from Park Street and the glazed ridge tiles and marble tiles from Edgbaston Street, could be seen as pointers to relatively high-status dwellings and occupants. On the other hand, the medieval pottery (excluding the probable production waste) includes nothing out of the ordinary, whilst the small amount of pottery from the 15th and 16th centuries is consistent with urban assemblages and the relatively prosperous. The 17th–early 18th-century pottery was variable across the sites. However, there was a strong utilitarian component in most areas, made up of kitchen and storage wares. Table wares such as slipwares and drinking vessels were represented on all sites but there was very little to suggest occupation of a particularly high status. There was no apparent link between vessel function and the industrial activities being undertaken on the sites. The 18th-century (post-*c*.1730) pottery from Park Street is particularly interesting, since documentary research would suggest that it was associated with craftsmen and -women and their families. In this context, the near absence of tea wares and dining wares is significant. There is one exception to this, the dump of high-status pottery from the wood-lined tanks in Area B. The exact date of this deposit and its source is still something of a mystery.

Other than pottery, the best represented artefact class was clay pipe. The relatively large assemblage is of importance for many reasons, not least the absence of any published information for Birmingham. Although there is some evidence for the production of clay pipes in Birmingham itself, the most striking aspect of the assemblage is the domination of the market by the Much Wenlock and Broseley pipe makers. Clearly the strong links Birmingham forged with the northwest, from the medieval period onward, in the quest for raw materials, brought other commercial links in their wake.

The environmental evidence provides some idea of the diet of the inhabitants of Edgbaston Street, Moor Street and Park Street. Cereals associated with poorer soils, such as buckwheat (only present at Edgbaston Street) and rye, were consumed but oats, wheat and barley were also present. Vegetables were poorly represented so that only examples of broad bean and beet were found in the medieval period at Edgbaston Street and Park Street respectively and possible evidence of pea at Park Street.

Hazel nuts were found on all three sites and may well have been consumed as part of the human diet. The evidence thus far suggests an adequate but rather basic diet. Remains of watercress at Park Street may indicate that this formed part of the diet and melissa and dandelion could also have been consumed or, along with self-heal, used medicinally. Some exotica such as fig and grape were present at Park Street and although not well represented, are suggestive (particularly grape) of higher status occupation. Beef seems to have been the most frequently consumed meat – perhaps not so surprising in view of the importance of the cattle trade in Birmingham. Pig and sheep were not well represented and overall meat consumption was probably low. Skeletal evidence from the two internments at Park Street, however, suggests a poor diet, probably low in ascorbic acid, and a hard life of heavy manual labour.

In Phase 3 at Park Street, in addition to cereal crops, beet, turnip, pea, grape, strawberry, fig and plum were present. The numerous gardens shown in and around Birmingham in the 18th and early 19th centuries probably provided some of the fresh produce consumed. At least two orchards, commemorated by the name Cherry Street (McKenna 2005, 32), were within the town and yet another source of fresh produce. The presence of hops indicates that brewing was taking place. Wine bottles from the 17th–18th centuries were not common but were found on both Park Street and Edgbaston Street and suggest some pretension to good living. Fragments from a Spanish olive jar indicate that olives or olive oil were occasionally eaten and this is one of the few culinary indicators of high status. Meat consumption in Phase 3 was again dominated by beef but from the early post-medieval period a greater variety of meats was evidenced, such as rabbit, domestic fowl, geese and ducks and possibly also fallow deer. Although the evidence is slight, it does suggest an improvement and wider variety in the diet through time.

The Bull Ring excavations have also provided a unique opportunity to integrate documentary and cartographic evidence with the excavated remains. Thus not only has it been possible to learn something of the daily lives of the people of Birmingham but from the documentary evidence it has been possible, in part, to relate the dwellings, workshops and industrial remains, and the remnants of material culture to specific individuals and specific industries. This is a rich seam to be mined by further research.

The hinterland

Virtually all of the archaeological remains in the Bull Ring date from the 12th century onwards. The prehistoric and Roman periods are as yet poorly represented in the city centre, in contrast to the quantities of objects and structures from these periods that have been found in other parts of Birmingham (Hodder 2004, 21–80). The virtual absence of Anglo-Saxon material from the city centre reflects the situation in the city as a whole: this period in Birmingham is still largely a 'Dark Age' in archaeological terms.

In contrast with these earlier periods, the quantity of detailed archaeological evidence of medieval and post-medieval date from the Bull Ring excavations and other sites in the city centre provides an opportunity to compare its historic development with that represented by archaeological evidence from the surrounding area, which now comprises the City of Birmingham. Such evidence consists of excavated remains, earthworks and buildings, providing information on settlement form, status and chronology, and land management. Although some of the results of excavations undertaken some time ago may need re-interpreting in the light of current knowledge, and the dating of pottery and other finds from them may need to be reassessed, the archaeological evidence nonetheless allows a comparison independent of, but complementary to, the documentary record.

Archaeological evidence of 12th- to 14th-century date (defined as Phase 1 in the Bull Ring excavations) has been obtained from excavations in Sutton Coldfield town centre (Malim 2005), Kings Norton village (Jones *et al.* 2001), a hamlet at Minworth Greaves, several moated sites in south and east Birmingham (Hodder 2004, 103–18), and a 13th- or 14th-century ditched field system relating to assarting around Peddimore Hall in Sutton Coldfield, and from rural settlements investigated by fieldwalking (pers. comm. T. Jones). The sites investigated are part of a general expansion of settlement and population growth contemporary with activity recorded in the Bull Ring area at this time. Environmental evidence of medieval and post-medieval date is currently sparse outside the city centre. In Longbridge, pollen shows that between the 10th and 16th centuries mixed grassland and woodland alongside the River Rea became grassland alone. Pollen at Gannow Green in Frankley showed that woodland was cleared to construct the moated site but that cereals were being cultivated near by, and in Sutton Coldfield an oven contained charred rye grain. Status and access to markets is indicated by the sources of pottery in use at different sites, for example rural settlements such as Minworth Greaves used a much narrower range of pottery, from fewer and more local sources, than the excavated sites in the city centre or moated sites. The use of clay roof tiles on buildings at moated sites may, like the moats themselves, have been a status symbol.

The few sites hitherto excavated in the medieval town centre of Sutton Coldfield suggest a less dense occupation than that observed in the Bull Ring area, and there is as yet no evidence for industrial activity in either Sutton Coldfield or anywhere else in Birmingham's hinterland in this period, with the possible exception of parallel channels, located just outside the present city boundary in Walkers Heath, which went out of use in the 14th century, and were overlain by the ridge and furrow of

arable land. Clay tiles used on roofs and in hearths at some moated sites and in Kings Norton village may have been manufactured close to, and specifically for, the structures where they were used. Although the abundant water in the Bull Ring area was harnessed for industrial use, in the rural area, other than water-driven corn mills, water features such as moats and fish ponds were created as much for status as for practical use.

Denrochronology and architectural details show that Birmingham's oldest surviving secular buildings, including the Lad in the Lane (Erdington), the Old Smithy (Sutton Coldfield), the cruck-framed barn at New Shipton Farm, the Saracen's Head in Kings Norton, a barn at Minworth Greaves, Primrose Hill Farm, and the building whose timbers were reused at Monyhull Hall barn, were constructed in the 15th century, during Phase 2 at the Bull Ring. This may be a reflection of rural prosperity, resulting in increased investment, at the same time as the industries in the town centre were expanding and spreading. Excavations in Kings Norton indicated replanning around the Green. On the south side, a site occupied by a succession of buildings from the 12th to the 14th centuries became a garden in the 15th century, while, on the north side, 13th- to 14th-century buildings were replaced by the Saracens Head towards the end of the 15th century. There was another spate of rural building in the years around 1600, including Blakesley Hall and Stratford House, and this is mirrored in the town centre area by buildings which have unfortunately now disappeared such as Lamb House (see *Town development and resources* above). Some moated sites, including Kents Moat, Gannow Green moat, and probably Peddimore Hall, were occupied into the 15th century but abandoned thereafter. At other moats, houses outside the moated enclosure may have been built in this period to replace those within.

Rural industry is more apparent in this period. Water had been engineered, via leats and pools, to power corn mills before this but use of water power may have intensified (for example the construction of a mill leat on the Bourn Brook is radiocarbon-dated to the 15th to 16th centuries) and was applied to iron smelting at Aston Furnace and Perry, and to various forges, although none of these has yet been archaeologically investigated.

In Bull Ring Phase 3, 17th and 18th centuries, much new building took place, including 17th-century brick structures on a new site at Aston Hall and within the moated area, replacing earlier buildings, at Sheldon Hall and Peddimore Hall. At Aston Hall the great house and the service range were built in brick, the latter demonstrating confident building in this material on a difficult site. Peddimore Hall was accompanied by farm buildings which were timber-framed with brick nogging.

By the 18th century, increasing use of brick led to the development of a small-scale brick and tile industry in Woodgate Valley, represented by former clay pits and a kiln located by geophysical survey, and a brick and tile industry in Yardley. Use of water power may have intensified in the 17th and 18th centuries. Rebuilding occurred in this period at, for example, Edgbaston Mill, and long leats were constructed at several mills. Mathew Boulton's Soho Manufactory was established in a rural location at an existing water mill. The water engineering related to mills was of course on a small scale compared to that involved in the construction of canals, a major addition to Birmingham's landscape from 1769 onwards and a major influence on its subsequent industrial development.

It is difficult to make inter-site comparisons of domestic artefact assemblages for the post-medieval period since very few dwellings of this period have, as yet, been excavated in Birmingham but an 18th-century farm in Saltley was using fine mass-produced pottery just like that discarded in the disused tank at Park Street (Hodder 2004, 161). Indeed, the survival and significance of the post-medieval deposits from the Bull Ring sites, draws attention to the importance of the archaeological investigation, through excavation and through recording of surviving buildings, of settlements of this period elsewhere in Birmingham, which hitherto have been somewhat neglected.

Conclusions

The Bull Ring excavations have for the first time established Birmingham as a flourishing medieval and post-medieval town. An industrial base, in which tanning played a major role, was clearly established early on. Thirteenth-century tanning at both Edgbaston Street and Park Street show that this industry was spread across the town centre, and further excavation will probably provide yet more examples of medieval tanning within the historic centre. The sequence of medieval and post-medieval tanning pits in Areas B, C and D at Edgbaston Street is the most comprehensive in the West Midlands and is of

importance nationally. Pottery production was also spread widely through the town. Cloth production was probably also widespread but at present our knowledge is limited to plant and pollen remains of flax and hemp. Metal working was not especially well represented in the archaeology, although coal within the Moor Street ditch fills indicates that it was indeed taking place in the 13th century. There is clearly further scope for identifying evidence of other craft activities but also for expanding our knowledge of the relationship between Birmingham and its hinterland which provided the raw materials for industry. This is also true of the later medieval and early post-medieval periods when tanning and metal working were pre-eminent.

The later post-medieval evidence has been of importance not only in establishing the variety of crafts and industries taking place but also in demonstrating 'multiple-use' of plots, where different crafts and processes occurred simultaneously. The ingenuity, drive and flexibility of the people of Birmingham is as well demonstrated by the below-ground archaeology in the historic centre as it is in areas such as the Jewellery Quarter (Cattell *et al.* 2002) where the information has been primarily derived from standing buildings and documentary evidence.

The original research design for the project was concerned mainly with material pre-dating the 19th century. However, the survival, albeit rather truncated, of court buildings on Park Street and of associated assemblages of 19th-century pottery and artefacts, which could not on this occasion be examined in any detail, should open our eyes to the potential of an 'historical-archaeological' approach to this material in the future. In short, although the Bull Ring excavations have revealed much hitherto unknown information about Birmingham from the medieval period onwards, the potential for increasing our knowledge by future above- and below-ground archaeology is immense.

Appendix 7.1: A Note on Petrology of Medieval Pottery from the Bull Ring, Birmingham

David Williams

Thirteen sherds of medieval pottery from recent excavations at the Bull Ring site, Birmingham, were thin sectioned, allowing the individual fabrics to be studied under the petrological microscope. The purpose of this study is to characterise the various fabrics and, where possible, to suggest likely source areas. The dominant geology in the Birmingham area are the Triassic formations, mostly Mercia Mudstone (formerly known as Keuper Marl) and Bunter Sandstones, with Boulder Clays scattered about (Geological Survey 1-inch map of England no. 168).

Petrology

1) ?Olive Jar (Park Street (1531) and (1622) F542)

Large fragments of metamorphic rock, mostly quartz-mica-schist and phyllite dominate the clay matrix and can be clearly seen in the hand specimen. Also present are frequent flakes of mica, mostly muscovite, a little quartzite and a few discrete grains of subangular quartz.

2) Deritend cooking pot fabric, fabric Dertend cpj. (1314 F201)

All three sherds are similar in thin section, with a clay matrix containing fairly well-rounded quartz grains below 0.60mm in size, some small pieces of chert, the odd fragment of ferruginous sandstone, shreds of mica and some opaque iron oxide.

3) Reduced Deritend ware, fabric DertendR. Edgbaston Street (2043) and (3020), Park Street (1314) F201

i) DeritendR (fabric variant RSb)
Fairly frequent, generally well-sorted and on the whole fairly well-rounded grains of quartz, normally below 0.60mm across, set in a fairly clean clay matrix. Also present are a few grains of quartzite and a little opaque iron oxide.

ii) DeritendR (fabric variant RSc)
A groundmass of closely packed silt-sized quartz grains with a scatter of larger, fairly well-rounded quartz grains below 0.60mm in size. Also present are a few pieces of siltstone and chert, some small shreds of mica and a little opaque iron oxide.

iii) Deritend R (fabric variant RS01)
A somewhat similar fabric to 3.ii above.

4) Wastered Deritend ware jug sherd (from jug Fig. 7.1.11)

Similar in thin section to 3.ii above.

5) Fabric cpj12

i) Moor Street (5158)
This is a heterogeneous fabric containing ill-sorted quartz grains, well-rounded mudstone, quartzite, chert, sandstone and opaque iron oxide.

ii) Park Street (1588)
This sample shows a micaceous clay matrix containing ill-sorted quartz grains, some pieces of well rounded mudstone and opaque iron oxide.

6) Fabric cpj13 Edgbaston Street (2103)

A moderate scatter of well-rounded quartz grains, a few pieces of siltstone, shreds of mica and a little opaque iron oxide.

7) Fabric cpj14 Park Street (1761)

A moderate groundmass of silt-sized quartz grains and shreds of mica. Scattered throughout are ill-sorted grains of well rounded quartz with some quartzite, ferruginous sandstone and finer grained sandstone.

322 *David Williams*

Discussion

Two of the sherds (Sample 1), quite possibly belonging to the same vessel, are in a very distinctive micaceous fabric, which contains large fragments of quartz-mica-schist and discrete flakes of silver mica, both easily seen in the hand-specimen. This is clearly a non-local fabric, and the vessel, coarse and wide-mouthed, must have been imported from some distance away. Geologically, the nearest possible British source would seem to be the Welsh schist formations. However, on archaeological grounds this seems rather unlikely and in this case a continental origin may be more probable. A Spanish olive jar has been suggested as a possibility, though the fabric of the Bull Ring vessel is noticeably different from that normally associated with the typical range of olive jars made in the Guadalquivir Valley in southern Spain (Williams 1984). An Andalusian origin is still possible, since there are large metamorphic formations in the region, especially in the area of the Andalusian Mountains.

Of the remaining sherds the three sherds from Sample 2, all thought to have been made in the region of the find site, contain well-rounded grains of quartz probably derived from the local Triassic. So do Samples 3.i–iii, which suggest the use of fairly similar raw materials. Sample 4, Deritend Ware is similar in composition and texture to Sample 3.ii. Samples 5.i and 5.ii contain mudstone inclusions which are probably derived from the local Keuper Marl. However the varied range and texture of the other non-plastic inclusions in Sample 5.i might suggest Boulder Clays.

Appendix 9.1: Clay Pipes, Recording System

David Higgins

A detailed catalogue of all the fragments recovered has been prepared for the site archive.

This has been compiled on an Excel spreadsheet using columns and codes based on those developed for a pipe recording system at the University of Liverpool in 1994, a copy of which is provided below.

Draft guidelines for using clay tobacco recording sheets

Introduction

This system has been designed to allow groups of pipes to be recorded in a standard manner. It has been conceived to deal primarily with excavated assemblages although it can easily be adapted for mixed or unstratified collections. The object has been to produce a flexible system that includes all of the main categories of information commonly recorded by pipe researchers. Not all of these categories will necessarily be relevant to any given group but, when they are used, they allow quick and easy comparison of material both within and between sites.

An A3 format has been adopted for the recording sheets since this allows all the relevant data to be collected on one line. The information is, as far as possible, symbol coded in columns. There are three advantages to this. It is quick to compile, easy to scan for information and can be simply computerised. Three different types of sheet are used to build up the record for each site:

– the group summary sheet
– the clay tobacco pipe record sheet
– the clay tobacco pipe summary sheet

These sheets are intended to provide a detailed catalogue of the individual fragments present from each site or collection for archive and research purposes. This record may be supplemented by additional notes and drawings that collectively will form the basis for a synthesised written report. Each of these three types of sheet is described below, followed by an explanation of the categories of information collected and the codes used for recording.

The group summary sheet

Only one of these sheets is completed for each group. It acts as a guide to the record which has been made and defines the way in which the record has been arrived at. The sheet sets out basic information about the material such as who has commissioned the work, where the material is from and exactly what the record consists of. It also gives details of how the record was compiled and by whom. Most of the categories are self explanatory and do not need further clarification. The main thing to note is that flexibility in the recording system has been built in by allowing specific recording elements to be defined. For example, the bowl form typology or fabric types can be set on this sheet to define the codes used on the recording forms. The 'notes' section allows free text which can be used to further define way in which the material has been studied and recorded.

The clay tobacco pipe record sheet

The second sheet is used to list, in context order, the individual fragments making up each group. The site and total number of sheets completed is recorded at the top of the sheet. Each line is used to record an individual fragment or a group of fragments if their attributes are all the same. For each different context the bowls, stems and mouthpieces should be listed, in that order, with marked or decorated pieces coming before the plain examples within each category. The symbols /, 0 or - are used to mean 'yes', 'no' or 'can't tell' respectively. The following classes of information can then be recorded:

Identification

The context number and any individual small find or bag number for the piece(s) are recorded in the first two columns. Normally all the numbers actually written on each pipe are included here.

Fab

This column is used for recording fabric differences, where these can be seen. This might simply differentiate coarse, gritty, 'local' fabrics (L) from fine 'imported' clays (I). Where more detailed divisions can be made the codes used should be defined on the Group Summary Sheet.

B S M

The number of bowl (B), stem (S) and mouthpiece (M) fragments recovered from each context are entered in these three columns. As entries on the right-hand side of the sheet must relate to <u>all</u> of the fragments entered in these first columns, a number of different lines are usually required to build up a complete record of each context group.

The numbers of fragments entered are the numbers as excavated. Two or more joining pieces which have clearly damaged during recovery or handling are counted as one piece. Reconstructed fragments which were damaged before deposition are counted individually, being listed in their appropriate columns but on the same line. A note of any such joins or of other cross context joins should be placed in the final column.

If an unbroken pipe is recovered it is counted under the bowl column and an arrow (>) drawn across the stem and mouthpiece columns. The fact that the pipe is complete noted in the 'comments' column where details of the stem length, mouthpiece form and finish can be given. In this way details of the pipe can still be found on the form without distorting the count of fragments recorded in the columns.

Bowls (B)

A bowl fragment is defined as any fragment with part of the base of the heel or spur surviving or with enough of the bowl to show its thickness (*i.e.* with any part of the internal bowl cavity surviving). The length of any surviving stem is irrelevant and is not counted separately in the stem column. This does not apply to reassembled fragments of stem which have been joined to a bowl fragment. These should be counted under the stem column on the same line.

Stems (S) A stem is any fragment with neither bowl nor mouthpiece surviving.

Mouthpieces (M) A mouthpiece is any piece with some or all the mouthpiece surviving.

MN

Minimum number. The minimum number of pipes represented. Where this column is completed the methodology used should be stated on the group summary sheet.

B/64

This records the stem bore(s) of the fragments listed on each line in 64ths of an inch, '7', for example, representing a fragment with a bore of 7/64". The means by which the bore has been measured should be stated on the Group Summary Sheet (*e.g.* ruler, butt end of imperial drill bit, travelling microscope). Where the stem bore at either end of a fragment varies only the smaller measurement should be recorded. For mouthpieces only the broken end is to be measured.

BUR

Records burnishing on the fragments(s). This can either be a yes tick (/) where burnishing is present or it can be further graded as fine (F), good (G), average (A) or poor (P). A fine (F) burnish is when the polishing lines are so closely spaced and even that there are no gaps between and a fine very glossy surface is created. A good (G) burnish is well applied with close, even strokes. An average (A) burnish will have gaps of roughly equal width to the burnish lines and may be light and uneven. A poor (P) burnish is very scrappy and irregularly applied. Burnishing on the stem is usually less well applied than that on the bowl and can often only be noted as being present rather than being graded. Great care must be taken on the identification of burnishing, especially where naturally glossy fabrics are used. Burnished pipes exhibit the slight facets caused by polishing and, usually, an alternating surface of glossy and matt strips.

TIP

These two columns describe the tip or mouthpiece of the pipe. They record the type of mouthpiece (T) and finish (F) applied to it.

T The types of mouthpiece are coded as follows:
C = Cut: the mouthpiece is formed by a simple cut end to the stem and no other moulded shape is present.
R = Rounded: the mouthpiece is formed in the mould as a simple rounded end.
N = Nipple: a circular sectioned stem which terminates with a moulded nipple.
D = Diamond shaped: the stem ends with a diamond-shaped cross section but without a nipple.
DN = Diamond nipple: where the stem takes on lozenge or sharply oval section in shape directly before the nipple.
FO = Flattened Oval: the stem takes on a flat, oval, section at the tip, without a nipple.

F The types of finish are coded as follows:
0 = No visible finish.
RW = Red Wax.
GW = Green Wax.
GG = Green Glazed; often thin and light in colour.
YG = Yellow Glaze.
CG = Clear Glaze.
* = Other; specify under 'comments'.

BOWL

Four columns deal with various attributes of the bowl. These are:

X Internal bowl crosses. The most common marks found on the internal base of a bowl are crosses. When viewed with the stem pointing down these can either appear as '+' or 'x'. These symbols should be used to indicate which type is present. If some other symbol or letter is found enter * and describe it in the comments section.

M/4 Milling. The amount of milling around the rim is estimated to the nearest quarter of a complete circumference so, for example, a half-milled pipe is entered as 2. If no milling is present a 0 is entered, if milling is present but the rim damaged a / is entered, if no rim survives a − is entered.

RIM Rim finish. The way in which the rim has been treated is coded:

C = Cut: the rim is formed by just a single horizontal knife cut.
B = Bottered: the rim has been smoothed with a bottering tool giving a rounded profile.
I = Internal knife cut: a knife has been used to cut clay from the inside of the bowl to make a thinner, finer rim.
W = Wiped: the rim has been wiped or smoothed (as opposed to being bottered).

These codes may be used together. Thus CW is a rim which has been cut and wiped or IB is a rim which had been internally knife cut and bottered. These last two techniques are often very difficult to distinguish where they occur together and any results should be regarded cautiously, looking for general trends rather than exact figures. As a general rule bottering produces a smooth, rounded and 'wiped' appearance near the rim as opposed to knife trimming which produces less even and deeper marks within the bowl with a fresher 'scraped' appearance to the surface.

FORM

The type number of the bowl form from a recognised typology which should be entered on the status sheet. If the bowl falls between two forms these should both be entered (*e.g.* 25/27) and if the bowl is not a very good match it should be noted as a 'variant' of the basic form using the letter 'v' (*e.g.* 25v).

MARK

The next five columns deal with any maker's mark. A sketch or transcription of the mark is written under MARK.

CAT NO =

The National Catalogue number of any stamped mark. This is intended to relate specifically to the National Stamp Catalogue which is being compiled at the University of Liverpool. Any alternative numbering system should be defined on the Group Summary Sheet.

POS =

Position the position/style of mark. The codes are:

H : On the base of the heel.
SP: On the base of the spur.
BB: Beneath the bowl where a pipe has neither heel nor spur.
SH: On the sides of the heel.
SS: On the sides of the spur.
BF: On the bowl facing the smoker.
BL: On the bowl, on the left-hand side as smoked.
BR: On the bowl, on the right-hand side as smoked.
BA: On the bowl facing away from the smoker.
SX: On the top of the stem, reading across it.
SL: On the stem, reading along it.
SM: Multiple individual stamps right around the stem, as a band or pattern.
RS: Roll-stamped stem, a continuous band or zone around the stem. This may be plain or decorated but does not include milled decoration.
ST: Stem twist, a specific form of roll stamp forming a spiral of shallow grooves around the stem.

TYPE

The type of mark is recorded:

I: The primary pattern or motif is incuse.
R: The primary pattern or motif is in relief.
A: Applied mark formed of some medium other than clay such as a rubber stamp, transfer print or hand written mark.

METHOD

The method by which the mark was formed:

M : Moulded mark.
S : Stamped mark.
I : Ink stamp (rubber stamp).
TP: Transfer printed mark.
HW: Hand written mark.
* : Other, specify the exact type under comments.

DECORATION

Describe or sketch any decorative treatment of the pipe.

DATE

The date range for the piece(s) recorded. This is an estimate of the likely period during which the pieces were made.

DR

Drawing. Any letter or numeric code used to identify drawn examples. If both record sketches and full publication drawings are made these should be differentiated.

COMMENTS

Any comments or notes on the pipe(s) recorded. Particular note should be made to expand any column where * or an arrow has been entered and to note features such as cross context joins.

Context summary sheet

The third sheet is the context summary sheet which tabulates the cumulative information from the record sheets. It acts as an index as well as a summary and is of particular value for the excavator or finds assistant since it shows the overall date range for each context and the number of fragments upon which that date is based.

CONTEXT
The context number.

PHASE
The site phase or period to which the context belongs.

B S M
Totals of Bowl, Stem and Mouthpiece recovered from that context.

TOT
The total number of fragments from that context.

DATE RANGE
The overall date range of all the fragments recovered. If a more precise date for deposition can be suggested, for example where some material is likely to be either residual or intrusive, the date can be asterisked and further details given in the comments section.

BURNISH
The total number of burnished bowl, stem and mouthpiece fragments is entered in the first column and then the ratio of burnished pieces, expressed as a percentage, in the second. This provides an indication of the 'quality' of the deposit since burnishing increased the price of a pipe.

MILLING INDEX
The milling index is calculated by adding the figures for each complete rim in a context, which will range from 0–4, and dividing by the sum of the number recorded. This gives the average quantity of milling, measured in units of 1/4 of the circumference of the rim, for the pipes in that deposit. Since it cost more for fully milled pipes the closer the average approaches 4.0 the higher the 'quality' of the pipes.

STAMPED
The total number of stamped marks.

MOULDED MARKS
The total number of moulded marks.

DECORATED
The total number of decorated pipes.

ILLUSTRATIONS
The drawing numbers of all drawn pieces.

KILN
The total number of pieces considered to be kiln wasters is entered. This will often represent only the minimum number present since actual damage or discoloration occurs on a small percentage of all kiln waste.

COMMENTS
Brief comments on pieces of particular importance or the group as a whole.

Appendix 9.2: Clay Pipes, Context Summary

David Higgins

This appendix provides a summary of the clay tobacco pipe evidence from the site. The context number is given first (Cxt) followed by the number of bowl (B), stem (S) or mouthpiece (M) fragments recovered from that context and the total number of pipe fragments from the context as a whole (Tot). The suggested deposition date of the context, based on the pipe fragments, is then given (this is based on the latest dates for the pipe fragments recovered, or the dates that best fit all the pipe evidence, not the overall range of pipe fragments present). The date is followed by a summary of the marked or decorated pieces from each context and the figure numbers of any illustrated examples (Figs). Bowl fragments, especially if they are marked, are much more closely datable than stem fragments. For this reason, the number and type of fragments present should be taken into account when assessing the reliance that can be placed on the suggested context dates given here.

Code	Cxt	Other	B	S	M	Tot	Range	Deposit	Marks	Decoration	Figs	Comments
BRB97	1006			2		2	1650-1820	1720-1820				Two very small plain stem fragments.
BRB97	3006			1		1	1800-1900	1800-1900				Thin and highly fired plain stem with a small bore.
BRB97	5004			1		1	1750-1850	1750-1850				Single plain stem fragment.
BRB97	5012			3		3	1680-1820	1720-1820				Three plain stem fragments of mixed date. Appears to have been 'kicked' around.
BRB97	5024			4		4	1750-1850	1750-1850				Group of very small scrappy plain stem fragments.
BRB97	5039			3		3	1640-1850	1750-1850				Small group of plain stems of mixed date.
BRB97	5040			2		2	1720-1820	1720-1820				Two plain stem fragments.
BRB97	5102			1		1	1690-1790	1690-1790				Reasonably long fragment of plain stem (98mm).
BRB97	5105			3		3	1720-1820	1720-1820				Small plain stem fragments.
BRB97	5107		5	13	1	19	1800-1920	1850-1890	REYNOLDS BIRMINGHAM stem mark X1; FIOLET X1	Leaf dec seams X1	25, 44, 133	Coherent 19th-century group. The three small bowl fragments appear to be from churchwarden style bowls from the first half of the 19th century. The nipple mouthpiece would not be expected before c.1840. All of the plain stems appear to be from long-stemmed pipes and are most likely to be contemporary with the bowl fragments in this group. The nipple mouthpiece and the Reynolds fragment in this group would suggest a deposition date of c.1850–1890.
BRB97	5108		1			1	1820-1850	1820-1850		Thistle/rose + leaf dec seams	131	
BRB97	5112			14		14	1780-1880	1780-1880				Group of plain stems, all in fine white fabric.
BRB97	5117			10	1	11	1780-1880	1780-1880				Group of plain stems, all in fine white fabric.
BRB97	5118			3		3	1780-1880	1780-1880				Group of plain stems, all in fine white fabric.
BRB97	5200		1			1	1810-1850	1810-1850		Leaf dec seams	130	
BRB97	5202		1			1	1750-1790	1750-1790				
BRB97	5400		1	2		3	1680-1850	1750-1850	WT x1		57	Late 17th- to early 18th-century bowl; two plain stems in a fine white fabric, almost certainly late 18th or early 19th century.
BRB97	U/S		1			1	1810-1910	1810-1910			127	Single bowl with a freshly broken stem.
BRB99	1006			2		2	1720-1820	1720-1820				Two plain stems; one fragment found bagged with Context 1007.

Code	Cxt	Other	B	S	M	Tot	Range	Deposit	Marks	Decoration	Figs	Comments
BRB99	1007		1			1	1820-1860	1820-1860	TR moulded mark X1		45	Single bowl. See also 1007 below.
BRB99	1007	F. 102	1	5		6	1650-1810	1760-1810				Single late 17th- or early 18th-century stem fragment, that appears to have been burnt, may be residual. Remaining stems are all long fresh-looking pieces which have been given a broad date bracket of 1710–1820 but there is no reason why they could not be contemporary with the single bowl fragment (*i.e.* 1760–1810). See also 1007 above.
BRB99	1013		4			4	1640-1670	1640-1670				Four joining fragments from a single bowl.
BRB99	1020		3	4		7	1620-1700	1650-1700			96	A small but coherent group from the late 17th century. The most complete of the bowls (Fig. 96) is not a Midlands type but is very similar to the forms found in south Shropshire or north Herefordshire. All four stems are plain and may well be contemporary with the bowl fragments, although one of the stem fragments has a very large bore (8/64").
BRB99	1022			1		1	1620-1720	1620-1720				Single plain stem.
BRB99	1026		6	32	10	48	1780-1840	1790-1840	(BR)OSLEY stem mark X1	Internal bowl mark	73, 125, 126	Very good contemporary group with long fresh-looking fragments. Most of the bowls are from the same mould and they may well have had long curved stems with red wax or green-glazed mouthpieces. One bowl has five or six unusual internal 'ribs' extending 2/3 of the way up the bowl sides. Marked bottles from this deposit (a well fill) further refine the date, suggesting this group can be dated at *c.*1820–40.
BRB99	1030			2		2	1650-1850	1750-1850				Two plain stems. One appears to be 17th or early 18th century, whilst the other is clearly late and may well be 18th or early 19th.
BRB99	1031			2		2	1650-1730	1650-1730				Late 17th- or early 18th-century plain stems.
BRB99	1033		1	1		2	1640-1700	1640-1700				Very small heel fragment and a single plain stem. Both are clearly 17th century.
BRB99	1038		1			1	1620-1660	1620-1660				Very small rim fragment.
BRB99	1045			2		2	1650-1730	1650-1730				Two plain stem fragments.
BRB99	1049			3		3	1650-1780	1690-1780				Three plain stem fragments, two of which look most likely to be 17th century, but could be early 18th. The third stem is almost certainly 18th century.
BRB99	1050		1	5	1	7	1640-1700	1640-1670	Wheel X1			With the exception of one stem fragment from this group all would appear to be contemporary with the bowl (*i.e.* 1640–1670). The one remaining stem has quite a small bore and is made from a finer fabric suggesting it may be early 18th century, however it does have quite a marked taper which is a 17th-century feature.
BRB99	1050/6?			4		4	1640-1700	1640-1700				Small scrappy pieces of 17th-century stem.
BRB99	1058		1	3		4	1640-1700	1640-1660				Single Civil War period bowl and three plain stems. Although a broader date range has been given for the stems, there is no reason why all the fragments from this group could not be contemporary (*i.e.* 1640–1660).
BRB99	1061		1	2		3	1650-1750	1660-1700				A single spur fragment and two plain stems all of which could be contemporary.

Code	Cxt	Other	B	S	M	Tot	Range	Deposit	Marks	Decoration	Figs	Comments
BRB99	1062			3		3	1650-1730	1650-1730				Plain stems
BRB99	1064		1	1		2	1660-1730	1660-1680			95	A single bowl and small plain stem fragment. Although a wide date range has been given for the stem fragment there is no reason why it could not be contemporary with the bowl.
BRB99	1066		2	1	1	4	1640-1780	1680-1730	WT X1		62	Very small group with rather scrappy fragments making it difficult to suggest a deposition date. The latest closely datable piece is a heel stamped WT, which dates from c.1680-1730.
BRB99	1070			1		1	1680-1730	1680-1730				Single plain stem.
BRB99	2001			2		2	1650-1750	1650-1750				Plain stem fragments.
BRB99	2002		5	13		18	1620-1850	1660-1700				With the exception of a single, very small piece of 18th- or 19th-century stem, all the remaining fragments appear to be mid–late 17th century. It is possible that the later stem fragment is intrusive.
BRB99	2003	F201		1		1	1620-1720	1620-1720				Single plain stem.
BRB99	2003	F202	2			2	1660-1710	1680-1710	EW X1			Two bowls. One earlier spur type from c.1660-1680 and one slightly later marked EW (c.1680-1710).
BRB99	2004		3	3		6	1630-1730	1680-1730*	MICH BROWN x1		89	These pipes came in two separate bags – both labelled as being from the same context. However, the first bag contained two bowl fragments and three stems all dating from the mid-17th century while the second bag contained a single, later bowl marked MICH BROWN, which dates from c.1680-1730.
BRB99	2005		1	17	1	19	1650-1730	1670-1690				Single bowl dating from c.1670-1690 and a group of contemporary looking plain stems, together with a single mouthpiece. A couple of the stems have smaller bores and may be late 17th or early 18th century but, equally, there is no real reason why they could not be contemporary with the bowls.
BRB99	2016		4	6		10	1650-1820	1720-1820	MD x1; Wheel X1		23	Small group. All the bowls in this group fall within a date range of c.1650-1690. Although the plain stems have been given a fairly wide date bracket four of the six could be contemporary with the bowls. The remaining two stems, however, are clearly 18th century.
BRB99	2021			1		1	1620-1700	1620-1700				Single 17th-century stem.
BRB99	2028		1			1	1650-1690	1650-1690				Small spur fragment.
BRB99	2029		1			1	1650-1670	1650-1670				Single bowl – not a Midlands form.
BRB99	2074			1		1	1750-1850	1750-1850				Single plain stem.
BRB99	2138			1		1	1650-1750	1650-1750				Single plain stem.
BRB99	2179		1			1	1620-1640	1620-1640	Unident X1		71	Bowl fragment with the partial remains of a stamped mark.

Code	Cxt	Other	B	S	M	Tot	Range	Deposit	Marks	Decoration	Figs	Comments
BRB99	3000		9	10	1	20	1660-1730	1680-1730	Unident gauntlet X1; IS X1; TW X1; IB X1; AW X1; MICH BROWNE X1; wheel x1		13, 39, 48, 63, 69, 77, 82	Good coherent group with all the bowls, stems and mouthpiece fragment falling within a reasonably tight date range. All fragments are quite fresh and do not appear to have been 'kicking' around.
BRB99	3005		1			1	1680-1720	1680-1720				Single bowl. See also 1007 below.
BRB99	3037		1	7		8	1650-1730	1680-1730				Fragment of a tailed heel and a number of plain stems; one in a very white fabric that has been well burnished.
BRB99	3040			1		1	1710-1800	1710-1800				Small 18th-century stem fragment.
BRB99	3044			1		1	1680-1750	1680-1750				Single 17th- or early 18th-century stem.
BRB99	3054			1		1	1680-1730	1680-1730				Single 17th- or early 18th-century stem.
BRB99	3061			1		1	1680-1730	1680-1730				Single 17th- or early 18th-century stem.
BRB99	3062		1	1		2	1650-1730	1680-1720	Wheel X1			Single bowl and stem fragment. Wide date range given for the plain stem but there is no reason why it could not be contemporary with the bowl of c.1670–1700.
BRB99	3063		1	5		6	1680-1780	1740-1780				Three of the five plain stems appear to be late 17th/ early 18th century in date and may therefore be residual. The remaining two stem fragments and single bowl fragment are most likely to be contemporary and to date from c.1740–1780.
BRB99	3064		1	1		2	1640-1690	1640-1670				One bowl and a single stem fragment. Plain stems are often difficult to date, therefore a wide date range has been given, however there is no reason why it could not be contemporary with the bowl of c.1640–70.
BRB99	3073			4		4	1620-1730	1680-1730				Small pieces of plain stem. Three of the fragments are quite thin stems but they have large bores suggesting that they could date from as early as 1620 through until the beginning of the 18th century. The fourth stem fragment, however, is much thicker and is burnished and bears very close resemblance to fragments associated with large bowls of the period 1680-1730.
BRB99	3093			3		3	1620-1850	1750-1850				Three very small fragments that are difficult to date. Two of the stem fragments are rather thin but have large bores suggesting that they could be as early as c.1620 but their fine fabric could suggest a later date. The third fragment comes from the bowl/ stem junction of a bowl but not enough of it survives to determine the form. The size of the bore on this third fragment would suggest a later 18th- or even 19th-century date.
BRB99	3094		1			1	1680-1720	1680-1720				Single bowl. See also 1007 below.
BRB99	3095		2	2		4	1650-1730	1680-1730	Wheel X1			Small group of rather scrappy bits. The tailed heel fragment is particularly heavily iron stained.

Code	Cxt	Other	B	S	M	Tot	Range	Deposit	Marks	Decoration	Figs	Comments
BRB99	3106		2	1		3	1620-1690	1660-1690				Only one substantially complete bowl from this group dating from c.1660–1680. The other fragments include a rim from a bowl with milling quite low down the side of the bowl and a short piece of plain stem with an unusually large bore (10/64").
BRB99	3009 / 3010		1	7		8	1650-1700	1650-1700			91	Only a single diagnostic fragment from this context, but also some fresh and reasonable long pieces of plain stem (longest fragment 96mm). All the plain stems are mid–late 17th or just into the early 18th century in date, but there is no reason why they could not be contemporary with the bowl (i.e. 1650–1670).
BRB99	3113			4		4	1620-1730	1640-1730				Four pieces of plain stem all of which are 17th or early 18th century in date.
BRB99	3118		1	4		5	1640-1730	1680-1730				A single bowl and four stems. A wide date range has been given for the stems but it is possible that they are contemporary with the bowl (i.e. 1680–1730).
BRB99	3125			1		1	1640-1730	1640-1730				Mid-17th–early 18th-century stem fragment — very short piece.
BRB99	3131		1	5		6	1620-1730	1680-1730	unident X1			Small group of very scrappy fragments. On the tailed heel fragment the bottom border of a heel stamp is just visible but not enough survives to identify the maker. The other fragments are very small pieces of plain stem.
BRB99	3132			1		1	1640-1730	1640-1730				Splinter of plain stem.
BRB99	4000			3		3	1620-1730	1640-1730				Three pieces of plain stem.
BRB99	4001			1		1	1750-1850	1750-1850				Plain stem fragment.
BRB99	4019			2		2	1640-1730	1640-1730				Two plain stem fragments.
BRB99	4035			1		1	1750-1850	1750-1850				Plain stem fragment.
BRB99	4051		2	5		7	1640-1850	1770-1800				The two bowl fragments in this group are clearly late 18th century. The spur fragment in particular, with its trimmed spur, would not date any later that c. 1800. Four of the five plain stems are more problematic. All have bores of between 6/64" and 7/64" and have the general appearance of fragments from the 17th century. They do not appear to be round enough, or parallel sided enough to be mid–late 18th-century pieces although they could date from just into the 18th century.
BRB99	4054			1		1	1720-1820	1720-1820				Single plain stem fragment.
BRB99	4060			1		1	1750-1850	1750-1850				Single plain stem fragment.
BRB99	6009			1		1	1720-1820	1720-1820				Single plain stem fragment.
BRB99	7002		1	1		2	1640-1790	1750-1790				Stem clearly 17th century in date due to size of the bore and overall finish. The bowl fragment appears to be the front part of a large 18th-century bowl.
BRB99	Bk Fill	Tr. 2		4		4	1640-1850	1750-1850				Bag labelled 'backfill of original at TR2'. Four plain stem fragments of mixed date.
BRB99	U/S		1			1	1670-	1670-	EW X1			Single bowl. See also 1007 below.

Code	Cxt	Other	B	S	M	Tot	Range	Deposit	Marks	Decoration	Figs	Comments
MSB00	1313		2	6		8	1700; 1700-1820	1700; 1720-1820				Small group of plain stems and two very small 18th-century bowl fragments. Very difficult to date accurately.
MSB00	1314			1		1	1680-1730	1680-1730				Plain stem fragment.
MSB00	1316			2		2	1620-1820	1720-1820				Two small stem fragments. One clearly 17th the other 18th or early 19th century.
MSB00	1317			1		1	1750-1850	1750-1850				Plain stem fragment.
MSB00	1501			1		1	1620-1720	1620-1720				Plain stem fragment.
MSB00	5030			1		1	1650-1750	1650-1750				Plain stem fragment.
MSB00	5119		1			1	1680-1730	1680-1730				Tailed heel fragment.
MSB00	5130			1		1	1620-1720	1620-1720				Plain stem fragment.
MSB00	5131			5		5	1680-1910	1840-1910				Three residual stem fragments of late 17th- or 18th-century date. The two later fragments are most likely from a cutty style pipe; one shows traces of the start of a nipple style mouthpiece.
MSB00	5200			1		1	1750-1850	1750-1850				Plain stem fragment.
MSB00	6000		6	28		34	1650-1750	1690-1720				Reasonably large group but all the pipes are very small and fragmentary. The most complete bowl dates from c.1690-1730. All other bowl fragments too small to determine a form although the thickness of the bowl walls suggests a 17th-century rather than 18th-century date. All the stems are plain with quite large bores and appear to range from mid 17th to mid-18th century in date.
MSB00	6001			1		1	1750-1850	1750-1850				Plain stem fragment.
MSB00	6016			1		1	1750-1850	1750-1850				Plain stem fragment.
MSB00	U/S		1			1	1660-1690	1660-1690			92	Single bowl. See also 1007 below.
PSB01	1015	Eval (f.101)	2	12		14	1650-1820	1720-1820				Rather small group most of which would fall quite happily into the first part of the 18th century. There is a slightly later bowl fragment, but this is rather difficult to date. It could be contemporary with the other fragments (*i.e.* first half of the 18th century) but equally could be a little later.
PSB01	1015	Eval Tr. 3, F 104	1			1	1710-1740	1710-1740	IB bowl mark X1		5	Small bowl fragment only. See also 1015 below.

Code	Cxt	Other	B	S	M	Tot	Range	Deposit	Marks	Decoration	Figs	Comments
PSB01	1015	Tr. 3, F 104	16	77	11	104	1660-1730	1680-1720	TC X1; ?C/G X1; ?H X1; WS X1; WT X4		21, 53, 60, 61, 72, 108, 110	Good group with quite tight date range. Large number of late 17th-/ early 18th-century bowls. No obvious residual material. Most likely that all could have been deposited during the period 1680–1720. See also 1015 above.
PSB01	1017		1	6		7	1640-1720	1660-1700				Small group. Bowl fragment very small which is most likely to be 17th century but could be early 18th. All the stems are quite thick with large bores suggesting a 17th-century date. Therefore likely deposition date given as 1660–1700.
PSB01	1025		1	3		4	1640-1700	1640-1660			90	Very small but coherent group. Nice neat mid-17th-century bowl (1640–1660), possibly a local form. The three plain stems are clearly 17th century and may well be contemporary with the bowl.
PSB01	1026	Eval Tr. 3	1			1	1680-1730	1680-1730				Small abraded bowl fragment.
PSB01	1031	Eval Tr. 5		2		2	1620-1720	1620-1720				Two plain stems.
PSB01	1033	Eval Tr. 5		1		1	1700-1800	1700-1800				Very abraded stem, possibly 18th century.
PSB01	1059	Eval Tr. 5		2		2	1620-1820	1720-1820				Two small, plain pieces of stem – one 17th, one 18th century.
PSB01	1101		48	124	2	174	1640-1880	1820-1840	EB X1; BRITTEN stem X1; MICH BROWN X6; TC X1; WE X1; II X1; WI X1; IS X1; WILL SAVAG X1; WT X2; EW X3; Wheel motif X1	Leaf dec seams X1; Wreath with LDS X1	2, 8, 11, 17, 24, 30, 47, 52, 55, 58, 65, 66, 100, 112, 117, 129, 132	Large mixed group dating from 17th through to the 19th century. Most likely date of deposition being 1820–1840.
PSB01	1104		6	38		44	1650-1740	1710-1740	IS X2; ME/B? X1			The majority of this group dates from late 17th to early 18th century with a likely deposition date of 1710–1740.
PSB01	1105			5		5	1640-1800	1700-1800				Small group of plain stems, four of which appear to be 18th century.

Code	Cxt	Other	B	S	M	Tot	Range	Deposit	Marks	Decoration	Figs	Comments
PSB01	1108		3	8		11	1660-1730	1680-1730				Small but coherent group of pipe fragments. All the bowls and stems appear to be contemporary with each other. Suggested deposition date of 1680-1730 .
PSB01	1110		2	1		3	1660-1850	1750-1850	EW X1		67	Very small group, only three fragments. The latest piece is a rather small spur fragment that appears to be late 18th-mid-19th century.
PSB01	1111		3	8		11	1650-1800	1680-1750				The early date of 1650 in this date range is provided by three plain 17th-century stems. It is possible, however, that these may be contemporary with the bowls in this group, which date to c.1680-1730. There are three plain stems that are almost certainly 18th century. It is difficult to date plain stems very closely, but given the bowl fragments and other stems in this group a deposition date of 1680-1750 is suggested.
PSB01	1114		1	12		13	1650-1820	1750-1820				Apart from one residual stem all of these fragments appear to be very consistent and are most likely to have been deposited c.1750-1820.
PSB01	1115		2	6		8	1660-1850	1760-1820				Apart from one residual stem all of these fragments appear to be very consistent and are most likely to have been deposited c.1760-1820.
PSB01	1116		2	7		9	1650-1820	1730-1800	MICH BROWN X1			Small group possibly with residual mid-17th-century stem fragment. Five stems and a bowl fragment date from c.1740-1820 therefore a mid-late 18th-century date is suggested for deposition.
PSB01	1122		5	3		8	1650-1760	1670-1730	MICH BROWN X1		115	Rather small group with quite wide date range. Four of the eight fragments clearly late 17th century whilst the remaining four are of early 18th-century date.
PSB01	1125	A (3)	6	13		19	1620-1850	1700-1850				Small group of very small and scrappy fragments of mixed date, which appears to be the result of sieving a soil sample. Two of the bowl fragments are from bowls with tailed heels (c.1680-1730) but all the other bowl fragments are too small to attribute to a particular form. The stems are plan and of mixed date but they generally appear to be 18th century with the latest pieces probably being early 19th century.
PSB01	1125		10	18	1	29	1680-1850	1800-1850	JOHN JAMES X1; HH bowl mark X1		28, 33, 114, 115, 116	Mixed group. Some residual 17th century material, but this is rather abraded. Majority of the stems are of a fine white fabric with a small bore suggesting a mid-late 18th-century date. Large fragments of late 18th-century bowl, one with fresh breaks, and one bowl that probably dates from the first half of the 19th century.
PSB01	1126		9	18		27	1650-1730	1660-1690	Hand X2; Wheel X1		76, 81, 99	Good late 17th-century group. All the bowl fragments would fit happily within the date range 1660-1690. Bowls include a spur fragment from a rather chunky, forward leaning bowl that is most likely contemporary with the other heel bowls in this group.
PSB01	1127		2	1		3	1660-1700	1670-1690			101, 102	Two bowls of c.1670-1690 type and one plain 17th-century bowl, almost certainly contemporary with bowls.
PSB01	1130		1	14		15	1650-1820	1750-1820				Fragment of a tailed heel bowl, which may be residual. Rest of the group all plain stems. Majority late 17th or early 18th century but three that are highly fired and with a small bore possibly dating late 18th/ early 19th century, date of deposition therefore suggested as being c.1750-1820.
PSB01	1133		5	7	1	13	1680-1850	1750-1850				Small group of very small and scrappy fragments of mixed date. This appears to be the result of sieving a soil sample. The bowl fragments are, in four of the five cases, too small to attribute to a form,

Code	Cxt	Other	B	S	M	Tot	Range	Deposit	Marks	Decoration	Figs	Comments
PSB01	1136		1	3		4	1710-1820	1720-1820				Small group with one bowl fragment and just three stems. The bowl fragment is quite forward leaning with a wiped rim and appears to be of a type dating to c.1710–1740. The stems could be later 18th century or even early 19th. Date of deposition suggested at 1720–1820.
PSB01	1137		2	3		5	1620-1800	1720-1800				Small group with small fragments of bowls and plain stems. Earliest fragment is a burnished stem with a large bore, possibly early–mid-17th century. The latest stem fragment could date from late 18th or even the early 19th century. The two bowls are rim fragments only but appear to be c.1660–1730. Date of deposition is difficult with such a small group but most likely to be late 18th (or later).
PSB01	1139		8	28		36	1660-1860	1820-1860	IP X1	Floral motif inc LDS X2	40, 98, 128	Mixed group. Some residual 17th-century material, but majority mid-18th to mid-19th century.
PSB01	1153		3	5		8	1660-1800	1680-1750			93	Small group. All but one stem fragment would fall within the date range 1660–1700. The one later plain stem is 18th century in date. It has a small bore but is most likely to date from the first half of the century. Suggested deposition date of 1680–1750 is therefore given.
PSB01	1167		2	6		8	1680-1860	1820-1860	WE X1	Tassels on a stem fragment X1	9	Small group of mixed date. Latest fragment is a stem with traces of moulded decoration in the form of tassels on either side of the stem dating from c.1820–1860. Most likely date of deposition therefore early to mid 19th century.
PSB01	1175		4	2		6	1660-1730	1680-1730	MICH BROWN X1			Small but coherent group of pipe fragments. All the bowls and stems appear to be contemporary with each other. Suggested deposition date of 1680–1730.
PSB01	1176		5	11		16	1660-1840	1780-1840	HH stem stamp X1			Group comprising a number of fragmentary pieces from 17th through to 19th century – some with fresh breaks. Earlier material most likely to be residual. The later plain stems are all in a fine fabric and are highly fired giving them a distinctive 'tinkly' sound. Most likely date of deposition early 19th century.
PSB01	1178		4	5		9	1640-1730	1680-1730	MICH BROWN X2; WE X1			Small but coherent group of pipe fragments. Includes one ?waster/ badly burnt bowl fragment with two joining stems (freshly broken). Heel form of this ?waster very similar to a Broseley Type 2 dating from c.1660–1680 (Higgins 1987a), but could be later.
PSB01	1180		1	5		6	1620-1800	1700-1800				Very small group comprising a fragment of a burnished bowl and short pieces of stem, one of which is quite abraded. Three of the stems appear to be 17th century and two are almost certainly 18th century. The bowl fragment is very small and could be either late 17th or early 18th. Date of deposition therefore suggested as 18th century.
PSB01	1187		1	9		10	1680-1850	1750-1850	MICH BROWN X1			Only bowl from this group is marked with a Michael Browne stamp and may well be residual. All the stems are plan. Majority date to the 18th century, but one has a rather small bore and may well be early 19th. Date of deposition therefore suggested as late 18th or early 19th century.
PSB01	1189		1			1	1680-1730	1680-1730	MICH BROWN X1			Single bowl dating 1680–1730.
PSB01	1192		4	10		14	1640-1780	1720-1780	Roll stamp border X1			Mixed group of very small fragments suggesting that the pieces have be 'churned' around. Nothing in the group appears to be later than c.1780.

Code	Cxt	Other	B	S	M	Tot	Range	Deposit	Marks	Decoration	Figs	Comments
PSB01	1193			4		4	1640-1800	1700-1800				Small group of stems including a lattice stem border dating from c.1690-1750. This particular fragment is quite fresh and does not appear to have been 'kicking around'. The other fragments, however, are quite small with the latest piece (c.1700-1800) having been burnt. Deposition date is difficult, but most likely at some point during the 18th century.
PSB01	1199		1	1		2	1670-1800	1700-1800				Two fragments – one bowl one stem.
PSB01	1203		1	2		3	1640-1720	1680-1720				Very fragmentary group.
PSB01	1204			1		1	1650-1750	1650-1750				Single abraded stem fragment.
PSB01	1205		4	7		11	1640-1800	1710-1740	IS bowl marks X2; MICH BROWN x1		49	A couple of residual 17th-century fragments in this group. The remaining stems and bowl fragments, however, would appear to date from the first half of the 18th century.
PSB01	1210		1			1	1670-1710	1670-1710	E?W X1			Single heel fragment with a partial mark, most likely EW in a heart.
PSB01	1219		3	1		4	1680-1750	1680-1730	MICH BROWN with date X1		12	Three joining bowl fragments from a bowl bearing a dated Michael Brown mark, unfortunately the final digit of the date is missing – 168? The only other fragment from this group is a very small plain stem. It is not very thick but has a large bore and may be contemporary with the bowl.
PSB01	1231		2	6		8	1660-1850	1810-1840		Leaf dec seams X2		Group includes a 17th-century stem, which may well be residual. Other stems and two bowl fragments (both with crude leaf decorated seams) could be contemporary and date from the first half of the 19th century.
PSB01	1233		1	5		6	1650-1850	1700-1850				Small group of fragments, nothing very diagnostic apart from the fragment of a tailed heel which could date from c.1660-1730. The rest of the group are plain stems. Four of these are nicely burnished suggesting a late 17th- or early 18th-century date. The remaining two stems are highly fired in a fine white fabric. They are rather thin with small bores suggesting a late 18th- or early 19th-century date.
PSB01	1234		2	4		6	1650-1750	1680-1730				Small group of late 17th- to early 18th-century material. The smallest of the stem fragments has been given a rather wide date range (1650-1750) but it is possible that it may be contemporary with the bowl fragments and other stems. Therefore a suggestion deposition date of 1680-1730 has been given.
PSB01	1235			3		3	1720-1780	1720-1780				Three stem fragments in a fine white fabric. They do not join but are almost certainly from the same long-stemmed pipe.
PSB01	1240		1	5		6	1620-1720	1660-1700			97	Single bowl from this group date to c.1660-1680. The plain stems are most likely to be 17th century in date. Dating of plain stems is difficult – one is finely burnished which could be first half of the 17th century, whilst the others could date as late as the first quarter of the 18th century. Most likely date of deposition there given as 1660-1700.
PSB01	1241			3		3	1650-1820	1720-1800				A small group with just three plain stems. Two are almost certainly 17th or early 18th century – the thicker of the two has a marked curve. The third stem is in a much white and finer fabric, almost certainly 18th century.
PSB01	1243			2		2	1650-1850	1750-1850				Two plain stem fragments. One clearly 17th century but appears to be residual the other is in a very gritty fabric but appears to be either 18th or 19th century in date.

Code	Cxt	Other	B	S	M	Tot	Range	Deposit	Marks	Decoration	Figs	Comments
PSB01	1297			1		1	1650-1750	1650-1750				Single plain stem, burnished.
PSB01	1310			1		1	1620-1720	1620-1720				Single plain stem, burnished.
PSB01	1367		1	3	1	5	1650-1800	1700-1800				Small group. Bowl is almost certainly from the first half of the 18th century, but the dating of the plain stems is more problematic. Most like date of deposition is therefore given as 18th century.
PSB01	1381			2		2	1620-1720	1620-1720				Two plain stem fragments.
PSB01	1505		5	29		34	1620-1850	1760-1800	IS bowl mark X1; SAM RO*DEN stem mark X1		46, 50	All of the fragments in this group are rather small and give the impression of having been 'kicked around'. The plain stems are of rather mixed date with some burnished 17th–century fragments that could be quite early. Some of the later stems, however, could be late 18th or even early 19th century in date. With the exception of one 17th-century heel fragment, the other bowls and the single marked stem date from the end of the 18th century. The suggested date of deposition is therefore given as 1760–1800.
PSB01	1506		3	18		21	1650-1850	1760-1840	IB bowl mark X1		6, 124	Very small and scrappy pieces of plain stem. The two earlier pieces of plain stem also have the appearance of having been 'kicked around' for some time. The third bowl fragment is damaged and is difficult to date. The rim finish and angle suggests a late 18th-century date, but it could equally be early 19th century.
PSB01	1507			3		3	1650-1750	1680-1750				Three plain stem fragments one of which has traces of what may be the end of a tailed heel. The remaining two fragments are much thinner and may well be 18th century in date.
PSB01	1508		1	1		2	1650-1750	1650-1750				Very scrappy fragments – part of a 17th- or early 18th-century bowl and a splinter from a thick burnished stem.
PSB01	1512		16	242	12	270	1660-1850	1740-1800	BRITTEN stem X1; SP stem X1; JOHN PHIPSON stem X5, AW X1; unident. Stem X1; IP bowl mark X1		7, 41, 43, 64, 118, 119	With the exception of one 1660–1680 bowl, which appears to be residual, all the material from this context would sit quite happily in the 18th century. Interesting group of Phipson stem marks, four out of five of which have been badly burnt. All remaining bowl fragments appear to be of a mid–late 18th-century type.
PSB01	1514		2			2	1740-1780	1740-1780				Two joining bowl fragments.
PSB01	1515		1	25		26	1650-1700	1650-1700	IC/G? X1			Although all of the fragments in this group appear to be of a similar date, *i.e.* 1650–1700, they are all very small and scrappy.
PSB01	1519			1		1	1720-1820	1720-1820				Single plain stem, of 18th- or early 19th-century date.
PSB01	1520	505	1	5		6	1650-1750	1680-1750				Small group. Bowl is a Broseley Type 5 (Higgins 1987a), dating *c.*1680–1730, the plain stems are more difficult to date but could be contemporary with the bowl.
PSB01	1520	507		1		1	1690-1750	1690-1750				Single plain stem. Very thin but has a very large bore. Difficult to date but likely to be late 17th or early 18th century.

Code	Cxt	Other	B	S	M	Tot	Range	Deposit	Marks	Decoration	Figs	Comments
PSB01	1521		1	3		4	1680-1750	1700-1740			113	Bowl has a trimmed spur and is bottered suggesting a date of c.1700–1740. The plain stems are more difficult to date and may be late 17th or early 18th, however there is no reason why they could not be contemporary with the bowl.
PSB01	1522		2	4		6	1690-1800	1740-1780	SP stem mark X1			Stamped stem appears to be slightly earlier than the rest of this group and may, therefore, be residual. The plain stems are of a standard 18th-century type but there is no reason why they could not be contemporary with the later bowl fragments (*i.e.* 1740–1780).
PSB01	1526			1		1	1680-1730	1680-1730				Short length of plain stem.
PSB01	1530		1	1		2	1680-1730	1680-1730	TA X1			Bowl fragment and single plain stem. They do not join, but appear to be contemporary. Mark damaged but same mould and die as two examples from 1739.
PSB01	1531		1	10		11	1650-1800	1740-1800	IOHN PHIPSON stem mark X1		42	Very small and scrappy pieces of stem and a single bowl fragment all of which are late 17th or early 18th century in date. The single marked stem, however, is a much fresher looking fragment.
PSB01	1580		1	1		2	1680-1750	1680-1750	MP/B x1			A very small group with a single bowl and stem fragment. The stem has a fresh break at one end. This is a very neat stem with a fine white fabric. Most likely to be 18th century but no real reason why it could not be contemporary with the bowl.
PSB01	1621 (over)		1			1	1750-1790	1750-1790			120	Single bowl.
PSB01	1621		7	21		28	1650-1800	1760-1780	Lattice stem mark X1; IOHN IAMS X1		87, 121, 123	Late 17th-century bowl with a IOHN IAMS mark and four plain stems – all rather scrappy – are most likely to be residual. The rest of the group is very coherent with a number of large 18th-century bowls and fresh pieces of stem, including one with a lattice roll stamp border. The marked stem measures 111mm in length. One burnished stem from this group, with a freshly broken end, joins a stem fragment from Context 1622.
PSB01	1622		1	7		8	1650-1800	1760-1790				Small group with a number of freshly broken pieces. Two of the plain stems appear to be late 17th or early 18th century in date. The single bowl and remaining stem fragments appear to be contemporary and are late 18th century in date with the most likely date of deposition being c.1760–1790. One of the burnished stems from this group, with a freshly broken end, joins a stem fragment from Context 1621.
PSB01	1632		1	1		2	1650-1800	1750-1800				Single bowl fragment from the 18th century and a single stem fragment from late 17th or early 18th century.
PSB01	1634		7	18	1	26	1640-1800	1750-1800	Wheel X1; diagonal lines RS mark X1; Rampant lion X1; IB bowl mark X1		75, 84, 109, 122	Mixed group with quite a wide overall date range. Some earlier residual pieces from the second half of the 17th century through in to the early 18th. Two interesting stem marks similar in style to Chester stems but clearly not products of that centre. Date of deposition most likely to be towards the end of the 18th century.
PSB01	1635			3		3	1650-1750	1690-1750	lattice stem mark X1		85	One marked stem in this very small group. Two remaining stems are plain and of either late 17th- or early 18th-century date – no reason why all three stems should not be contemporary.
PSB01	1643		1	1		2	1690-1800	1700-1800			83	Fragment of a spur bowl that dates from c.1690–1740. The two plain stems are certainly 18th century in date.

Code	Cxt	Other	B	S	M	Tot	Range	Deposit	Marks	Decoration	Figs	Comments
PSB01	1643			1		1	1690-1730	1690-1730	diagonal lines and oval X1			Single marked stem with diagonal lines mimicking a stem twist and also an oval. In the Chester style but clearly not a Chester product.
PSB01	1646			1		1	1690-1740	1690-1740				
PSB01	1655			1		1	1650-1730	1650-1730				Single battered stem.
PSB01	1678			1		1	1650-1730	1650-1700				Single stem, most likely from second half of the 17th century.
PSB01	1701		2			2	1680-1790	1750-1790				Two bowls the later of which is covered in heavy iron concretion.
PSB01	1702		2			2	1670-1730	1680-1730	WT X1; MICH BROWN X1		54	Two marked bowls.
PSB01	1705			1		1	1660-1720	1660-1700				A single stem fragment with a very large bore (8/64").
PSB01	1708			1		1	1600-1800	1600-1800				A single stem fragment covered in a very thick layer of slaggy material. It is impossible to see any of the outer surface of the stem itself. The size of the bore is measurable (6/64") and would suggest either a 17th- or early 18th-century date.
PSB01	1708		32	29		61	1660-1770	1740-1770	MB X1; MICH BROWN X 4; TC X2; WC/G X 1, II X1; ELIAS MASSEY stem X1; IW X1; I/EW X1; Wheel X1		10, 20, 22, 31, 36, 68, 105, 106, 107	Reasonably large group with lots of bowl fragments but unusually low number of associated stem fragments. The majority of the bowls date from the end of the 17th or beginning of the 18th century, but it is the later fragments of bowl that set the deposition date of mid-18th century. Good range of heel marks and one nice stem fragment from the Chester maker Elias Massey.
PSB01	1710			2		2	1680-1730	1680-1730				Two late 17th-/ early 18th-century stems – both burnished. One has been freshly broken.
PSB01	1721		1	13		14	1680-1750	1680-1730	IOHN IAMS X1		34	Single bowl with a long length of stem surviving. A number of other plain stem fragments, most of which could be contemporary with the bowl, i.e. 1680-1730. There are two slightly thicker and earlier looking stem fragments, which may be residual.
PSB01	1725		9	23		32	1660-1790	1750-1790	unident X2; IS bowl mark X1; IOS SIMONS stem mark X1; wheel X1		51, 59	Mixed group of fragments, some of which appear abraded and are clearly residual.
PSB01	1726		4	26	2	32	1660-1790	1720-1790	Wheel X3		78, 79	Small group of pipe fragments. The three most complete bowls, all 1680-1730 in date, have wheel marks. The stems are all plain and are more difficult to date. The majority are contemporary with the three marked bowls, however there are one or two that are clearly later in date, and one bowl fragment of c.1710-90 (most likely to be late 18th century).

Code	Cxt	Other	B	S	M	Tot	Range	Deposit	Marks	Decoration	Figs	Comments
PSB01	1727			1		1	1720-1780	1720-1780				Single piece of 18th century stem. Neatly finished and well burnished – has a fresh break at one end. Survives to a length of 68mm.
PSB01	1735		1	1		2	1650-1900	1840-1900			88	One piece of stem, quite short with a large bore, likely to be either late 17th or early 18th century in date, and a 19th-century bowl fragment.
PSB01	1738		18	65	3	86	1650-1880	1800-1880	IB bowl mark X1; MICH BROWN X4; TC X1; IH X 1; IS bowl mark X1; WT X2; EW X1; moulded shield X1		3, 15, 18, 29, 56, 103, 111	Large mixed group. The majority of the material dates from the period 1680-1730 but there are one or two 19th-century fragments amongst it. Interestingly there is nothing earlier than c.1660 and this could be a good group of c.1680-1740 with odd intrusive contamination.
PSB01	1739		9	9		18	1650-1850	1740-1780	TA X2; W? X1; wheel X2		1, 80	Small group. Eight of the nine bowls are of a Broseley Type 5a (Higgins 1987a), dating from c.1680-1730. The remaining bowl fragment, however, is clearly mid- to late 18th century. Most of the stems would be contemporary with the late 17th-/ early 18th-century bowls but one is much later and may well be late 18th or early 19th. As with many of the groups the material has a number of fresh breaks. TA pipe from the same mould and die in 1530.
PSB01	1752		5	10		15	1620-1900	1800+	TC x1; wheel X1		19, 74	Small bowl fragment and single stem are clearly 19th century in date but neither are diagnostic enough to date more accurately. Date of deposition is therefore suggested after 1800.
PSB01	1755			1		1	1750-1850	1750-1850				Single plain stem. Very thin but has a very large bore. Difficult to date but likely to be late 17th or early 18th century.
PSB01	1757			2		2	1720-1820	1720-1820				Two plain stems.
PSB01	1768			16	1	17	1620-1850	1750-1850				Plain stems and a single mouthpiece fragment of mixed date.
PSB01	1769		1	5		6	1680-1840	1790-1840				Small group. All the stems are thick, burnished 17th-century examples but the single bowl fragment is clearly late 18th or early 19th century in date.
PSB01	1770			10	2	12	1650-1910	1840-1910		Moulded ribs X1		A group of stems of mixed date. One of the 17th-/ 18th-century pieces is stuck in a block of mortar. The latest stem fragment in this group is very crudely finished and appears to have come from a short stemmed 'cutty' style pipe. The ends of moulded ribs, which would have run up the sides of the bowl, can be seen.
PSB01	1771		15	27	4	46	1660-1910	1850-1870		Bowls = basket X1; large leaves X4; head x1; beaded seams x 3; flutes? X1. Stems = beaded border x1; enclosed 'ovals' x1.	134, 135, 136, 137, 138, 139, 140, 141, 142	Large group of mainly mid-19th-century material but with one or two residual stem fragments from the end of the 17th century. The group includes a high proportion of mould-decorated pipes, some of which were made in the same mould. Several of these mould-decorated bowls are quite crudely made.

Code	Cxt	Other	B	S	M	Tot	Range	Deposit	Marks	Decoration	Figs	Comments
PSB01	1785		1			1	1700-1900	1700-1900				A single very small 'flake' from a bowl. Very difficult to date although the thickness might suggest either 18th or 19th century.
PSB01	1787		1	10		11	1620-1820	1720-1820			94	Single bowl dating c.1660-1680. Over half of the stems could be contemporary. There are, however, four later stems that appear to be either 18th or early 19th century in date.
PSB01	1798		1	1		2	1680-1820	1720-1820				Single bowl and stem. Bowl has been 'kicked' around but dates from c.1680-1730. The single stem fragment is clearly early 18th century but could be as late as early 19th century.
PSB01	1814			1		1	1680-1730	1680-1730				Single plain stem. Very thin but has a very large bore. Difficult to date but likely to be late 17th or early 18th century.
PSB01	1815		2	7	1	10	1650-1730	1680-1730	MICH BROWNE X1			A small but coherent group from the late 17th or early 18th century, although none of the pieces are particularly fresh.
PSB01	1819		2	8		10	1650-1730	1690-1730	TW x1; WF x1		26, 70	Small but coherent group.
PSB01	1820		2	2		4	1650-1750	1680-1730	Hand? X1			Two late 17th-/ early 18th-century bowls one of which is only part of a heel with traces of a mark. One of the two plain stems is rather thick but has a small bore suggesting a mid- to late 18th-century date, although there is no reason why it should not be contemporary with the bowls (i.e. 1680-1730).
PSB01	1825		3	19	1	23	1650-1730	1680-1730	Unident X1; MICH BROWNE X1			Very coherent group with all fragments dating from end of the 17th or early 18th century. Some of the unburnished plain stems may be a little earlier but there is no real reason why they could not be contemporary with the bowl fragments and majority of the other stems.
PSB01	1826		1	4		5	1650-1750	1680-1730				Tailed heel fragment and a plain stem.
PSB01	1827		1	7	1	9	1720-1900	1840-1900	THOS LEGG X1	Moulded ribs X1	35, 143	A small and mixed group. The Thomas Legg stem stamp looks quite fresh but there are later fragments in this group (i.e. nipple mouthpiece and moulded bowl), which pushes the date of deposition into the second half of the 19th century.
PSB01	1832			2		2	1650-1820	1720-1820				Two plain stems.
PSB01	1833			1		1	1720-1820	1720-1820				Single plain stem. Very thin but has a very large bore. Difficult to date but likely to be late 17th or early 18th century.
PSB01	1839		1	8		9	1650-1750	1680-1730	MICH BROWN X1		16	Small but coherent group.
PSB01	1841			4		4	1650-1820	1650-1820				Four very small and scrappy plain stems of mixed date.
PSB01	1842			1		1	1720-1820	1720-1820				Single plain stem - very white, fine fabric.
PSB01	1851		1			1	1680-1730	1680-1730				Bowl fragment.
PSB01	1853			1		1	1680-1730	1680-1730				Plain stem.
PSB01	1860			3		3	1650-1750	1650-1750				Plain stems.

Code	Cxt	Other	B	S	M	Tot	Range	Deposit	Marks	Decoration	Figs	Comments
PSB01	1871		1			1	1850-1910	1850-1910		Basket X1	144	Single mould decorated bowl, which has been over fired/burnt.
PSB01	1872			1		1	1720-1820	1720-1820				Single stem fragment that has been highly fired – possibly a waster – with lumps of slaggy concretion adhering.
PSB01	1872			4		4	1650-1750	1650-1750				Four plain stems.
PSB01	1876	785	1	1		2	1620-1730	1680-1730	Unident X1			Single tailed heel fragment and a small piece of plain stem.
PSB01	1876	791		1		1	1720-1820	1720-1820				Plain stem.
PSB01	1878		1	3		4	1650-1900	1800-1900				A small group of mixed date – all fragments very small and scrappy. A single abraded stem that could be mid-17th to mid-18th century in date, but the spur fragment and the two remaining plain stems appear to be 19th century.
PSB01	1902			2		2	1650-1730	1650-1730				Two plain burnished stems.
PSB01	1903			3		3	1690-1850	1750-1850	lattice stem X1		86	Two plain stems and one with lattice decoration (originally catalogued as 1913).
PSB01	1908			4		4	1750-1850	1750-1850				Group of plain stems all but one are heavily iron stained.
PSB01	1913		10	34	4	48	1650-1967	1850-1910	McDougall / Glasgow? X1		37, 104	Reasonably large group of mixed date. The presence of a 19th-century mould decorated bowl fragment and the McDougall stem, however, pushes the suggested date for deposition into the second half of the 19th century (McDougall's only closed in 1967, but the marked stem is more likely to be of 19th-century date).
PSB01	1916			2		2	1650-1750	1680-1750				Two plain stems, one burnished.
PSB01	1918			1		1	1620-1720	1620-1720				Single plain stem. Very thin but has a very large bore. Difficult to date but likely to be late 17th or early 18th century.
PSB01	1930			1		1	1620-1720	1620-1720				Single plain stem – burnt.
PSB01	1938		1	13		14	1650-1760	1710-1760	HH stem stamp X1		27	Small group. A single late 17th- or early 18th-century stem may well be residual. The remaining stems, including one marked HH, and the bowl fragment could all be contemporary (c.1710–1740).
PSB01	U/S	Area A	2		1	3	1690-1750	1710-1740	IS bowl mark X1; IB bowl mark X1		4, 14	
PSB01	U/S*	Area B		1		1	1620-1700	1620-1700				Single piece of 17th-century stem. NB. Fragment is not marked but is in a bag labelled with the context label 1505 as well as U/S (unstratified).
PSB01	U/S	Area C	7	17	2	26	1620-1860	1800-1860	MICH BROWN x2; wheel X1; GEORG POVEL X1		38	Group of mixed date including a mouthpiece with either red wax or some form of red paint on the tip.
		Totals	458	1643	67	2168						

Appendix 9.3: Clay Pipes, Summary of Marked Pipes

David Higgins

This appendix provides a summary of the marked clay tobacco pipes recovered from the site. A transcription of the mark is followed by the unique die number that identifies that particular mark, as allocated by the author from the national catalogue that he is compiling. This is followed by the number of examples recovered from the excavations and the position or type of mark represented (BF = stamped mark on the bowl facing the smoker; H = stamped mark on the base of the heel; M = moulded mark (various locations); RS = roll-stamped mark running around the stem; S = stamped mark on the base of the spur; SL = stamped mark along the stem; SX = stamped mark across the stem). The figure number of the illustrated example is then followed by the date, suggested maker and suggested origin of the mark.

Mark	Die	No	Pos	Fig	Date	Suggested Maker	Suggested Origin	Comments
TA	2001	3	H	1	1680–1730	Thomas Andrews	Coventry	Probably a Shropshire maker working in Coventry.
EB	136	1	H	2	1680–1730		Much Wenlock area	
IB (crowned)	959	1	BF	3	1710–1740		Birmingham / Coventry area	Possibly one of the Britten family from Wednesbury.
IB	2003	2	BF	4	1710–1740		Birmingham / Coventry area	Possibly one of the Britten family from Wednesbury.
IB	2016	1	BF	5	1710–1740		Birmingham / Coventry area	Possibly one of the Britten family from Wednesbury.
IB (crowned)	2002	1	BF	6	1710–1740		Birmingham / Coventry area	Possibly one of the Britten family from Wednesbury.
IOHN BRITTEN	246	1	RS	7	1720–1770	John Britten	Wednesbury?	
(THOMAS?) BRITTEN	-	1	SX	8	1720–1780	(Thomas?) Britten	Wednesbury?	
MB	2017	3	H	9	1680–1730	Michael Brown	Much Wenlock	
MB	248	3	H	10	1680–1730	Michael Brown	Much Wenlock	
MICH BROUN	2018	1	H	11	1670–	Michael Brown	Much Wenlock	

Mark	Die	No	Pos	Fig	Date	Suggested Maker	Suggested Origin	Comments
					1690			
MICH BROWN	2020	5	H	16	1680–1730	Michael Brown	Much Wenlock	
MICH BROWN	2019	8	H	13	1690–1730	Michael Brown	Much Wenlock	
MICH BROWN 1688	251	2	H	12	1688–1700	Michael Brown	Much Wenlock	
MICH BROWNE	250	13	H	14	1680–1730	Michael Brown	Much Wenlock	
MICHAELL BROWN	871	1	H	15	1680–1730	Michael Brown	Much Wenlock	
TC	2023	1	H	17	1670–1690	Thomas Clark	Broseley area	
TC	2021	1	H	18	1670–1690	Thomas Clark	Broseley area	
TC	2022	1	H	19	1670–1690	Thomas Clark	Broseley area	
TC	2025	2	H	20	1680–1730	Thomas Clark	Broseley area	
TC	2024	1	H	21	1680–1730	Thomas Clark	Broseley area	
WC	2026	1	H	22	1680–1730		West Midlands area	Mark inverted on the heel.
MD	268	1	H	23	1670–1690	Morris Deacon	Much Wenlock / Broseley area	
WE	564	2	H	24	1670–1700	William Evans	Wellington	
L. Fiolet / à St. Omer / Déposé	2013	1	SX	25	1850–1920	Louis Fiolet	St Omer, France	Incuse stem stamp reading 'L. Fiolet / à St. Omer / Déposé'.
WF	2027	1	H	26	1680–1720		West Midlands area	
HH	2046	2	SX	27	1710–1760		West Midlands area	The only other known example is from the Stourbridge area.
HH	2044	1	BF	28	1730–1780		West Midlands area	
IH	324	1	H	29	1670–1720		Broseley area	Various known makers with these initials.
II	2028	1	S	30	1690–1720		Broseley area	Possibly either John James or John Jones.
II	2029	1	S	31	1690–1720		Broseley area	Possibly either John James or John Jones.
II	988?	1	S	32	1690–1720		Broseley area	Possibly either John James or John Jones. Poor example, possibly die type 988.
IOHN IAMS	2031	1	H	33	1680–1730	John James	Broseley area	
IOHN IAMS	2030	1	H	34	1680–1730	John James	Broseley area	
THOS LEGG BROSELEY	2047	1	SX	35	1740–1790	Thomas Legg	Broseley	Four line stamp reading 'THOS/LEGG/BROSE/LEY'.
ELIAS MASSEY	1967	1	SX	36	1690–1715	Elias Massey	Chester	Mark associated with pinnacle and dot border (Die 1975).
McDOUGALL GLASGOW	-	1	M	37	1850–1900	McDougall	Glasgow	Moulded stem mark with just '...L / G...' surviving. McDougall's operated from 1846–1967.
GeORG POVeL	595	1	H	38	1680–	George Powell	Much Wenlock area	

Mark	Die	No	Pos	Fig	Date	Suggested Maker	Suggested Origin	Comments
					1730			
IP	2032	1	H	39	1660–1690		Kingswinford / Stourbridge area?	Perhaps made by a member of the Phipson family, who are thought to have worked in the Kingswinford / Stourbridge area.
IP	2045	2	BF	40	1730–1780	John Phipson?	Kingswinford / Stourbridge area?	Contemporary with John Phipson stem marks and most likely the same maker.
IOHN PHIPSON	885	5	SX	41	1740–1800	John Phipson	Kingswinford / Stourbridge area	Maker not yet located in documentary sources.
IOHN PHIPSON	2048	1	SX	42	1740–1800	John Phipson	Kingswinford / Stourbridge area	Maker not yet located in documentary sources.
SP	2049	2	SX	43	1690–1740		Kingswinford / Stourbridge area?	Perhaps made by a member of the Phipson family, who are thought to have worked in the Kingswinford / Stourbridge area.
SAM RODEN	920	1	SX	46	1750–1790	Samuel Roden	Broseley area	Mark reads 'SAM/RO*/DEN'.
REYNOLDS BIRMINGHAM	-	1	M	44	1850–1900	Reynolds	Birmingham	Moulded stem mark made by one of the various members of the Reynolds family, who worked in Birmingham from c.1864–92.
TR	-	1	M	45	1820–1860	Thomas Reynolds	Birmingham	Moulded spur mark – probably a Thomas Reynolds piece.
IS	2033	1	H	47	1680–1730	Joseph Simmons?	Wilnecote	
IS	2034	1	H	48	1680–1730	Joseph Simmons?	Wilnecote	
IS	882	7	BF	49	1710–1740	Joseph Simmons?	Wilnecote	
IS	880	1	BF	50	1730–1770	Joseph Simmons?	Wilnecote	
IOS SIMONS	884	1	SX	51	1720–1780	Joseph Simmons	Wilnecote	
WILL SAVAG	1296	1	H	52	1680–1730	William Savage	Much Wenlock	
WS	2035	1	H	53	1660–1680	William Savage	Much Wenlock	
WT	2037	1	H	54	1670–1690		Birmingham area	
WT	466	1	H	55	1670–1690		Birmingham area	
WT	2038	2	H	56	1680–1730		Birmingham area	
WT	868	1	H	57	1680–1730		Birmingham area	
WT	947	1	H	58	1680–1730		Birmingham area	
WT	869	2	H	59	1680–1730		Birmingham area	
WT	870	3	H	60	1680–1730		Birmingham area	
WT	2039	2	H	61	1680–1730		Birmingham area	
WT	2040	1	H	62	1680–1730		Birmingham area	

Mark	Die	No	Pos	Fig	Date	Suggested Maker	Suggested Origin	Comments
AW	2037	1	H	63	1660–1680		Birmingham area	AW, EW and IW might have been members of the same local pipemaking family; perhaps TW as well.
AW	902	1	H	64	1660–1680		Birmingham area	AW, EW and IW might have been members of the same local pipemaking family; perhaps TW as well.
EW	900	10	H	65–67	1670–1710		Birmingham area	AW, EW and IW might have been members of the same local pipemaking family; perhaps TW as well.
IW	957	1	H	68	1680–1730		Birmingham area	AW, EW and IW might have been members of the same local pipemaking family; perhaps TW as well.
TW	2041	1	H	69	1680–1730		Birmingham area	Perhaps an incorrectly cut WT die, or perhaps another member of the 'W' family.
TW 1690	2042	1	H	70	1690–1730		Birmingham area	Perhaps an incorrectly cut WT die, or perhaps another member of the 'W' family.
…OSLEY	-	1	SL	73	1770–1840		Broseley	May have just been a place-name stamp reading 'BROSELEY'.
Wheel	-	13	H	74, 76, 77, 80	1640–1730		Regional types	Various die types represented in this general group with representative examples illustrated.
Wheel	960	1	H	75	1640–1670		West Midlands area	
Wheel	889	2	H	78	1680–1730		West Midlands area	
Wheel	1154	2	H	79	1680–1730		West Midlands area	
Hand	961	3	H	81	1660–1690		Birmingham area	
Hand	2043	1	H	82	1680–1730		West Midlands area	
Spiral Border	2012	2	RS	83	1690–1740		Birmingham area	One example associated with a griffin oval.
Griffin oval	-	1	SX	83	1690–1740		West Midlands area	Associated with a spiral border (Die 2012).
Rampant lion	-	1	SX	84	1690–1740		West Midlands area	
Lattice and dot	2011	2	RS	85	1690–1750		West Midlands area	
Lattice and dot	897	1	RS	86	1690–1750		West Midlands area	
Lattice and dot	-	1	RS	87	1750–1800		West Midlands area	Too poor an impression to allocate a unique die number.
Pinnacle & Dot	1975	1	RS	36	1690–1715	Elias Massey	Chester	Border associated with an Elias Massey lozenge (Die 1967).
Shields	-	1	M	88	1840–1900		West Midlands area	Moulded symbol mark on the spur of a plain bowl.

Appendix 10.1: Catalogue of Slag (weight in grams)

Matthew Nicholas

Context	Smithing Hearth Bottoms	Non Diagnostic	Cu Slag	Vitrified ceramic material	Other	Crucibles	Area	Feature	Phase
1030							A		
1101		1592	399			956	A		
1103						135			
1104		1159					A		
1108			106			186	A		3 or 4
1110			72			87	A	F123	3 or 4
1111		3					A	F124	3
1115						139			
1116		145					A	F128	3
1118		305					A		4
1125	763	2982	320			6277	A	F133	3
1126		181					A	F134	3
1130							A	F137	3
1132		262				91	A	F138	3
1133		8				133	A	F139	4
1139					VHL 28	1221	A	F138	3
1143					TAP 38		A		3 or 4
1153		43					A		
1157		34					A	F148	3 or 4
1158		413					A		
1162	494	926					A	F157	1 or 2
1165		8					A	F174	1 or 2
1166		510					A	F234	4
1167	846	113			VHL 120	989	A	F154	3
1175		2754					A	F158	3
1176	227					1523	A	F159	3
1177		320					A	F160	1 or 2
1187		29				323	A		
1197		6					A	F174	1 or 2

Key:
Run – Run slag   VHL – Vitrified hearth lining
Tap – Tap slag   VBD – Vitrified building debris

Context	Smithing Hearth Bottoms	Non Diagnostic	Cu Slag	Vitrified ceramic material	Other	Crucibles	Area	Feature	Phase
1203		117					A	F183	3
1204		191					A	F182	3
1205		579					A	F180	1 or 2
1210		23					A		4
1213		517					A	F174	1 or 2
1219		13					A	F187	3
1220		61			18 RUN		A	F188	1 or 2
1225		21					A	F170	3
1234		8					A	F194	3
1239	2742	33					A		1 or 2
1240		76					A	F193	3
1241		114					A	F194	3
1243						60	A		
1252		730					A	F201	1 or 2
1297		311					A	F233	
1312		6					A	F196	
1326		11					A	F201	
1367		133					A	F245	
1381		3					A	F233	
U/S						36	A		
1505		118					B		
1505		503			92 TAP		B		
1506		211					B	F503	3
1512		474					B	F500	3
1515	1074	2132					B	F504	
1519		468					B	F506	1 or 2
1520		119				39	B		3 or 4
1521		19				180	B	F503	3
1522		21				35	B	F509	3
1526		142					B	F511	3
1530		75					B	F520	3
1531		374				20	B	F510	3
1580						634			
1596		197					B		1 or 2
1621		765				848	B	F542	3
1622		60					B	F542	3
1631		87					B		1 or 2
1632		41					B	F546	1 or 2
1634	1027	731				333	B	F542	3
1635		342					B	F542	3
1646						33			
1659		44					B	F562	1 or 2
1690		87					B		1 or 2
1708		23				419	C	F700	3

Context	Smithing Hearth Bottoms	Non Diagnostic	Cu Slag	Vitrified ceramic material	Other	Crucibles	Area	Feature	Phase
1711						50			
1721		42179					C	F702	3
1725		110					C	F705	3
1726		38					C	F706	3
1727						58			
1738		1329				147	C		
1739						VBD 460	C	F713	3
1772		39					C	F752	1
1784	1368						C	F746	1 or 2
1787		7					C	F745	3
1795		55					C	F775	3
1798				18			C	F749	3
1807		28					C	F759	4 or 5
1818		3					C	F765	3
1819		138					C	F761	3
1820		450	7				C	F762	3
1825		591				3	C	F769	3
1826		6896					C	F789	3
1827		159					C		
1834		19					C		
1839		676					C	F773	3
1841		1647					C		1 or 2
1842		8					C	F775	3
1851		171					C	F782	3 or 4
1857		96					C	F783	3
1872		210				11	C	F789	3
1888		6				27	C	F810	3
1908		2143		434			C	F811	3
1913		955		652			C	F816	3
1916				20	Vitrified tile 54		C	F808	3
1918				78			C	F816	3
1920		5					C	F829	1 or 2
1930		3					C	F823	3
1931		160				126	C	F824	3
1938	325	474		136			C	F828	3
1941		171		30			C	F828	3

Key:
Run – Run slag   VHL – Vitrified hearth lining
Tap – Tap slag   VBD – Vitrified building debris

Appendix 10.2: Catalogue of Hammerscale (weight in grams)

Matthew Nicholas

Context	Weight	Area	Feature
1176	36		F159
1312	1	A	F195
1144	11	A	F144
1141	1	A	F141
1219	8	A	F187
1175	14		F158
1157	5	A	F148
1030	1		
1220	4	A	F188
1133	6	A	F139
1126	9	A	F134
1213	1	A	F174
1367	3	A	F245
1033	2		
1175	19	A	F158
1515	25	B	F504

Appendix 10.3: Catalogue of Crucibles (weight in grams)

Matthew Nicholas

Context	Area	Feature	Phase	Crucible No.	Sampled	Position	Weight	Width (side, mm)	Width (base mm)	Diam (mm)
1101	A			18		Side	223	15		120
1101	A			61		Side	125	17		
1101	A			62	Y	Rim	74	16		120
1101	A			63		Lid?	109	28		
1101	A			64		Side	85	19		
1101	A			65		Base	154	18	20	124
1101	A			66		Side	89	17		140
1101	A			67		Side	27	13		
1101	A			68	Y	Side	70	16		140
1103	A			39		Side	135	21		120
1108	A		3 or 4	38		Base	186	16	21	144
1110	A		4 or 5	41	Y	Side	87	35		
1115	A	F127		48		Side	81	16		130
1115	A	F127		50		Side	58	18		124
1125	A	F133	3	69	Y	Side	153	15		142
1125	A	F133	3	70		Side	273	20		124
1125	A	F133	3	71		Side	182	19		
1125	A	F133	3	72		Rim	128	15		130
1125	A	F133	3	73		Rim	236	13		124
1125	A	F133	3	74		Rim	87	13		
1125	A	F133	3	75		Base	104	16	9	100
1125	A	F133	3	76		Rim	127	15		130
1125	A	F133	3	77		Side	160	17		
1125	A	F133	3	78		Side	121	19		120
1125	A	F133	3	79		Base	121	18	20	
1125	A	F133	3	80		Rim	130	15		
1125	A	F133	3	81	Y	Rim	72	13		120
1125	A	F133	3	82		Rim	93	13		110

Context	Area	Feature	Phase	Crucible No.	Sampled	Position	Weight	Width (side, mm)	Width (base mm)	Diam (mm)
1125	A	F133	3	83		Rim	155	13		110
1125	A	F133	3	84	Y	Side	76	13		120
1125	A	F133	3	85		Side	186	20		
1125	A	F133	3	86		Rim	75	15		120
1125	A	F133	3	87		Rim	134	14		140
1125	A	F133	3	88		Rim	90	15		120
1125	A	F133	3	89		Side	73	14		140
1125	A	F133	3	90		Rim	89	13		120
1125	A	F133	3	91		Rim	174	12		130
1125	A	F133	3	92	Y	Side	58	12		128
1125	A	F133	3	93		Side	174	19		140
1125	A	F133	3	94		Base	93	22	30	
1125	A	F133	3	95	Y	Side	197	21		120
1125	A	F133	3	96		Rim	122	13		160
1125	A	F133	3	97	Y	Rim	82	14		140
1125	A	F133	3	98		Side	98	12		148
1125	A	F133	3	99		Side	94	13		140
1125	A	F133	3	100		Base	168	21	21	
1125	A	F133	3	101		Side	251	21		110
1125	A	F133	3	102		Side	120	18		124
1125	A	F133	3	103		Side	248	16		128
1125	A	F133	3	104		Rim	329	17		160
1125	A	F133	3	105	Y	Rim	57	14		120
1125	A	F133	3	106		Rim	102	14		136
1125	A	F133	3	107		Rim	135	12		130
1125	A	F133	3	108		Rim	168	13		140
1125	A	F133	3	127		Side	416	21		140
1125	A	F133	3	128		Rim	326	17		
1132	A	F138		17	Y	Side	56	16		
1132	A	F138		52		Rim	35	15		130
1133	A	F139		46	Y	Side	24	15		
1133	A	F139	4 or 5	47		Rim	93	16		120
1139	A	F139	3	109		Base	219	18	23	100
1139	A	F139	3	110		Base	228	19	16	
1139	A	F139	3	111		Rim	188	15		112
1139	A	F139	3	112		Side	23	14		120
1139	A	F139	3	113		Side	215	22		120
1139	A	F139	3	114		Rim	96	16		120
1139	A	F139	3	115		Side	12	12		160
1139	A	F139	3	116		Side	37	13		140
1139	A	F139	3	117		Rim	99	16		128
1139	A	F139	3	118	Y	Side	65	16		

Context	Area	Feature	Phase	Crucible No.	Sampled	Position	Weight	Width (side, mm)	Width (base mm)	Diam (mm)
1139	A	F139	3	119		Side	39	12		120
1139	A	F139	3	123		Side	16	11		
1167	A	F154	4	45	Y	Side	482	16		
1167	A	F154	4	53		Base	160	21	22	
1167	A	F154	4	54		Side	20	17		144
1167	A	F154	4	55		Side	73	16		
1167	A	F154	4	56		Base	254	21	26	140
1176	A	F159	3	1		Side	47	16		100
1176	A	F159	3	57		Side	170	13		120
1176	A	F159	3	58		Side	69	18		148
1176	A	F159	3	59		Side	100	15		132
1176	A	F159	3	60		Rim	183	18		
1176	A	F159	3	120		Side	260	21		120
1176	A	F159	3	121		Side	140	18		140
1176	A	F159	3	122		Rim	200	14		110
1176	A	F159	3	124	Y	Side	103	17		
1176	A	F159	3	125		Rim	92	13		128
1176	A	F159	3	126		Side	159	17		120
1187	A	F176	3	32		Side	59	14		
1187	A	F176	3	33		Rim	161	12		160
1187	A	F176	3	49		Side	103	20		
1243	A			43		Rim	60	11		
1520	B	F505		2		Side	39	17		128
1521	B	F503	3	3		Side	69	13		140
1521	B	F504	3	40		Rim	111	16		
1531	B	F510	3	4	Y	Side	20	10		90
1580	B	F520	3	5		Base	276	24	26	80
1580	B	F520	3	6		Base	358	17	30	
1621	B	F542	3	7		Base	50	12	17	116
1621	B	F542	3	19		Side	374	19		160
1621	B	F542	3	23	Y	Side	42	19		140
1621	B	F542	3	34		Side	136	16		140
1621	B	F542	3	35		Rim	246	18		124
1634	B	F542	3	8		Rim	48	17		
1634	B	F542	3	29		Complete base	285		31	60
1646	B		3 or 4	9		Side	33	17		
1708	C	F700	3	10		Side	24	15		
1708	C	F700	3	11		Rim	101	13		140
1708	C	F700	3	13		Side	46	16		130
1708	C	F700	3	14		Side	37	17		
1708	C	F700	3	15		Side	17	17		80

Context	Area	Feature	Phase	Crucible No.	Sampled	Position	Weight	Width (side, mm)	Width (base mm)	Diam (mm)
1708	C	F700	3	16		Side	20	13		
1708	C	F700	3	25		Side	10	6		
1708	C	F700	3	31		Side	48	11		
1708	C	F700	3	36	Y	Base	16	12	10	
1708	C	F700	3	37	Y	Base	65	13	14	
1711	C		4	12		Side	50	17		
1727	C	F707	3	28		Base	58	13	13	100
1738	C			21		Rim	107	13		148
1738	C			44		Side	40	No measurable dimensions		
1825	C	F769		24	Y	Side	3	7		
1872	C	F789	3	30	Y	Rim	11	4		
1888	C	F810	3	26	Y	Side	27	11		
1931	C	F824	3	27		Rim	126	12		130
Over cleaning area 1621		22		Side	51	17		160		
1205	A			129		Side	13			
1104	A			130		Side	79			
1125	A	F133	3	131		Rim	21			
1580	B	F520	3	132		Side	13			
U/S	A			20		Rim	36	1		116

Appendix 10.4: Analyses of Metal Droplets found within the Park Street Crucibles

Matthew Nicholas

Crucible No.	S	Fe	Ni	Cu	Zn	As	Sn	Sb	Pb	Alloy type
68	<0.2	0.2	<0.1	99.8	<0.1	<0.5	<0.5	<0.5	<0.5	Copper
68	<0.2	<0.1	<0.1	100.0	<0.1	<0.5	<0.5	<0.5	<0.5	Copper
68	<0.2	<0.1	<0.1	100.0	<0.1	<0.5	<0.5	<0.5	<0.5	Copper
68	<0.2	0.2	<0.1	99.8	<0.1	<0.5	<0.5	<0.5	<0.5	Copper
105	<0.2	0.5	0.2	98.2	0.7	<0.5	<0.5	<0.5	<0.5	Copper
105	<0.2	0.8	0.2	95.0	<0.1	2.3	0.7	0.9	<0.5	Copper
84	<0.2	0.6	0.1	84.3	11.2	<0.5	3.8	<0.5	<0.5	Gunmetal
84	<0.2	1.4	<0.1	75.3	21.1	<0.5	2.1	<0.5	<0.5	Gunmetal
17	<0.2	0.8	<0.1	75.1	21.5	<0.5	1.1	<0.5	1.5	Brass
17	<0.2	0.2	<0.1	99.8	<0.1	<0.5	<0.5	<0.5	<0.5	Copper
17	<0.2	0.3	<0.1	98.3	<0.1	1.0	<0.5	<0.5	<0.5	Copper
46	<0.2	0.2	<0.1	99.8	<0.1	<0.5	<0.5	<0.5	<0.5	Copper
46	<0.2	0.1	<0.1	97.2	0.5	<0.5	2.1	<0.5	<0.5	Copper
46	<0.2	0.1	<0.1	98.5	0.5	<0.5	0.9	<0.5	<0.5	Copper
46	<0.2	0.2	<0.1	97.9	1.1	<0.5	0.5	<0.5	<0.5	Copper
46	<0.2	<0.1	0.1	83.2	8.6	<0.5	5.1	<0.5	3.0	Gunmetal
46	<0.2	<0.1	0.2	83.5	8.9	<0.5	5.2	<0.5	2.0	Gunmetal
46	<0.2	<0.1	<0.1	82.1	9.5	<0.5	5.2	<0.5	3.2	Gunmetal
45	0.8	<0.1	0.2	97.7	<0.1	<0.5	1.2	<0.5	<0.5	Copper
45	<0.2	<0.1	<0.1	99.2	<0.1	<0.5	0.7	<0.5	<0.5	Copper
45	<0.2	0.4	<0.1	98.8	<0.1	<0.5	<0.5	0.6	<0.5	Copper
45	<0.2	0.1	<0.1	99.9	<0.1	<0.5	<0.5	<0.5	<0.5	Copper
45	<0.2	<0.1	0.2	99.8	<0.1	<0.5	<0.5	<0.5	<0.5	Copper
45	<0.2	<0.1	0.1	98.2	<0.1	0.6	0.5	0.6	<0.5	Copper
45	<0.2	0.5	0.2	96.4	<0.1	1.6	<0.5	0.8	<0.5	Copper
45	<0.2	0.1	<0.1	97.6	<0.1	1.4	<0.5	<0.5	<0.5	Copper
45	<0.2	0.1	<0.1	99.0	<0.1	0.9	<0.5	<0.5	<0.5	Copper
45	<0.2	0.2	<0.1	98.4	<0.1	0.9	0.5	<0.5	<0.5	Copper

Crucible No.	S	Fe	Ni	Cu	Zn	As	Sn	Sb	Pb	Alloy type
45	<0.2	<0.1	0.2	98.4	<0.1	0.9	<0.5	<0.5	<0.5	Copper
124	<0.2	1.2	<0.1	76.0	19.8	<0.5	3.0	<0.5	<0.5	Brass
124	<0.2	1.7	<0.1	74.0	20.9	<0.5	3.4	<0.5	<0.5	Brass
124	<0.2	1.3	<0.1	71.7	25.3	<0.5	1.7	<0.5	<0.5	Brass
36	<0.2	1.2	<0.1	81.9	7.2	<0.5	9.7	<0.5	<0.5	Gunmetal
36	<0.2	1.2	<0.1	83.7	9.5	<0.5	5.6	<0.5	<0.5	Gunmetal
36	<0.2	1.4	<0.1	83.6	9.8	<0.5	5.2	<0.5	<0.5	Gunmetal
26	<0.2	0.3	<0.1	81.1	17.8	<0.5	<0.5	<0.5	0.5	Brass
26	<0.2	0.6	<0.1	80.2	17.8	<0.5	<0.5	<0.5	0.9	Brass
26	<0.2	0.3	0.1	80.2	19.2	<0.5	<0.5	<0.5	<0.5	Brass
26	<0.2	0.3	<0.1	80.1	19.3	<0.5	<0.5	<0.5	<0.5	Brass
26	<0.2	1.3	0.1	78.1	13.8	<0.5	5.4	<0.5	1.0	Gunmetal
26	<0.2	0.3	0.3	86.0	8.4	<0.5	3.8	1.2	<0.5	Gunmetal (Sb)
26	<0.2	0.4	0.4	82.3	8.7	<0.5	4.5	3.8	<0.5	Gunmetal (Sb)
26	<0.2	0.2	0.2	84.9	9.5	0.8	2.1	1.8	<0.5	Gunmetal (Sb)
26	<0.2	0.5	0.3	81.3	11.7	0.7	3.4	2.0	<0.5	Gunmetal (Sb)
26	<0.2	0.7	0.3	81.7	11.9	<0.5	3.2	2.2	<0.5	Gunmetal (Sb)
26	<0.2	0.7	0.3	80.0	12.5	0.7	3.2	2.6	<0.5	Gunmetal (Sb)
26	<0.2	0.7	0.3	80.6	14.2	<0.5	2.7	1.5	<0.5	Gunmetal (Sb)
26	<0.2	0.8	0.3	79.4	14.5	1.1	2.5	1.4	<0.5	Gunmetal (Sb)
26	<0.2	1.0	<0.1	81.1	15.7	<0.5	1.6	0.6	<0.5	Gunmetal (Sb)
26	<0.2	1.0	0.4	78.8	16.9	<0.5	1.8	1.0	<0.5	Gunmetal (Sb)
26	<0.2	0.8	<0.1	82.3	13.1	<0.5	2.0	0.8	1.0	Gunmetal (Sb)

Appendix 10.5: Analyses of the Vitrified Layers

Matthew Nicholas

Crucible No.	Description	Notes	Na$_2$O	MgO	Al$_2$O$_3$	SiO$_2$	P$_2$O$_5$	SO$_3$	K$_2$O	CaO	TiO$_2$	MnO$_2$	Fe$_2$O$_3$	CuO	ZnO	SnO$_2$	PbO	Total
4	Inner vitrification		<1.0	<0.4	13.6	50.9	<0.2	<0.2	1.2	2.5	0.5	0.4	16.1	0.2	13.6	<0.5	<0.5	98.9
17	Outer vitrification		4.5	<0.4	20.7	39.1	1.2	<0.2	4.0	1.2	0.9	<0.2	3.8	5.4	14.6	3.6	0.9	100.0
23	Inner vitrification		<1.0	<0.4	34.0	60.4	<0.2	<0.2	0.6	0.7	1.4	<0.2	2.4	<0.2	0.3	<0.5	<0.5	99.8
24	Inner vitrification		3.3	2.1	2.3	33.4	<0.2	<0.2	5.0	5.5	<0.2	<0.2	1.4	<0.2	<0.2	15.7	31.3	100.0
24	Outer vitrification		2.3	1.5	4.2	52.3	1.2	<0.2	3.9	3.9	0.2	0.4	3.2	<0.2	<0.2	8.6	15.9	97.6
26	Inner vitrification	Layer 1 (Tutania)	3.1	1.2	10.9	48.7	1.0	0.4	3.4	2.5	0.6	<0.2	12.5	15.4	<0.2	<0.5	<0.5	99.7
26	Inner vitrification	Layer 2 (brass)	5.9	2.5	1.7	31.6	4.3	0.3	0.8	6.4	<0.2	0.4	2.6	2.5	40.8	<0.5	<0.5	99.8
30	Inner vitrified surface		1.9	<0.4	34	52.4	<0.2	<0.2	5.6	1.0	1.5	<0.2	1.3	0.3	1.6	<0.5	<0.5	99.6
30	Outer vitrified surface		<1.0	0.8	37.4	36.2	1.3	<0.2	0.3	11.5	1.5	<0.2	8.6	0.4	1.4	0.5	<0.5	99.9
36	Inner vitrification		<1.0	0.9	18.7	60.8	1.3	<0.2	2.9	4.2	1.0	0.2	5.4	2.1	2	<0.5	<0.5	99.5
36	Outer vitrification		<1.0	0.4	20.4	60.4	0.5	<0.2	1.7	3.0	1.0	0.3	5.3	4.3	2.3	0.5	<0.5	100.1
37	Inner vitrification		1.8	<0.4	24.4	54	<0.2	<0.2	0.2	<0.2	0.8	<0.2	1.7	<0.2	17.3	<0.5	<0.5	100.2
37	Outer vitrification		1.3	<0.4	10.4	64.7	0.6	<0.2	0.2	0.5	0.5	<0.2	13.6	<0.2	7.9	<0.5	<0.5	99.7
37	Rim vitrification		<1.0	0.6	3	20.4	3.9	<0.2	0.3	2.5	<0.2	<0.2	0.9	5.2	3.7	53.8	2.2	96.5
41	Outer vitrification		1.7	<0.4	22.6	56.2	<0.2	<0.2	0.9	0.3	0.8	<0.2	1.8	<0.2	15.7	<0.5	<0.5	100.0
42	Inner vitrification		<1.0	8.2	8.1	73.8	<0.2	<0.2	2.4	2.9	0.6	<0.2	3.2	0.3	0.4	<0.5	<0.5	99.9
45	Slag	Bulk	3.5	0.6	18.1	42.6	0.9	<0.2	1.0	4.8	0.6	<0.2	10.7	1.9	13.9	<0.5	0.7	99.1
46	Vitrified surface		5.8	0.4	15.3	20.1	<0.2	<0.2	0.3	<0.2	0.3	<0.2	0.9	9.0	44.6	1.4	1.1	99.1
62	Outer vitrification		<1.0	<0.4	21.3	46.6	0.4	<0.2	0.3	0.6	0.7	<0.2	4.3	16.7	1.4	7.8	<0.5	100.1
68	Inner vitrification		<1.0	<0.4	22.2	59.9	<0.2	<0.2	0.9	<0.2	1.6	<0.2	4.4	<0.2	10.9	<0.5	<0.5	99.9
69	Outer vitrification		8.5	0.7	24.8	49.5	0.7	<0.2	0.8	2.9	1.3	<0.2	9.3	<0.2	1.3	<0.5	<0.5	99.8

Crucible No.	Description	Notes	Na_2O	MgO	Al_2O_3	SiO_2	P_2O_5	SO_3	K_2O	CaO	TiO_2	MnO_2	Fe_2O_3	CuO	ZnO	SnO_2	PbO	Total
84	Inner vitrification		1.5	<0.4	16.8	40.3	<0.2	<0.2	1.3	1.0	0.5	<0.2	1.7	16.3	19.6	0.6	<0.5	99.6
92	Inner vitrification		6.4	<0.4	3.2	25.3	<0.2	<0.2	<0.2	<0.2	<0.2	<0.2	0.8	9.7	54.0	<0.5	0.6	100.0
92	Outer vitrification		1.5	1.5	15.8	47.5	4.8	<0.2	2.4	4.1	1.9	<0.2	5.0	2.8	9.9	<0.5	0.9	98.1
95	Inner vitrification		7.2	<0.4	7.5	21.6	<0.2	<0.2	0.1	0.5	0.3	0.2	2.6	2.8	54.6	0.7	1.0	99.1
95	Outer vitrification		<1.0	0.9	31.2	51.9	0.9	<0.2	1.2	2.7	1.4	<0.2	6.8	1.2	0.8	0.8	<0.5	100.0
97	Inner vitrification		<1.0	<0.4	11.4	42.6	<0.2	<0.2	0.9	0.3	0.7	<0.2	2.4	22.3	16.1	<0.5	3.3	100.0
97	Outer vitrification		<1.0	0.8	22.6	55.7	1.4	<0.2	1.4	1.0	1.0	0.8	10.0	1.0	3.0	<0.5	1.4	100.1
105	Vitrified surface		2.7	0.5	10.4	36.6	<0.2	<0.2	0.9	0.6	1.0	0.2	4.7	8.6	27.8	5.3	1.1	100.3
118	Outer vitrification		10.5	0.6	17.6	39.0	0.5	<0.2	0.3	2.1	1.2	20.6	0.9	6.6	<0.2	<0.5	<0.5	99.9
118	Inner vitrification		11.9	<0.4	7.4	55.4	<0.2	0.3	0.7	1.5	0.4	6.1	<0.2	16.4	<0.2	<0.5	<0.5	100.1
124	Outer vitrification		2.7	0.5	16.3	48.6	0.5	<0.2	2.1	2.9	0.8	<0.2	5.4	2.8	13.6	1.4	<0.5	97.6

Appendix 10.6: Analyses of the Crucible Fabric

Matthew Nicholas

Crucible no.	Na_2O	MgO	Al_2O_3	SiO_2	P_2O_5	SO_3	K_2O	CaO	TiO_2	Fe_2O_3	CuO	ZnO	PbO	Total
4	<1.0	<0.4	21.3	64.3	<0.2	0.2	0.7	0.5	1.2	2.5	<0.2	7.5	<0.5	98.3
17	1.1	0.5	27.4	62.3	0.3	<0.2	1.4	0.3	1.6	2.4	<0.2	2.3	<0.5	99.6
23	<1.0	<0.4	27.0	66.7	<0.2	<0.2	1.0	0.3	1.3	2.6	0.3	0.5	<0.5	99.7
24	<1.0	1.6	17.0	55.0	1.4	<0.2	0.8	16.8	0.8	6.7	<0.2	<0.2	<0.5	100.0
26	<1.0	<0.4	23.4	70.8	<0.2	0.3	0.7	0.3	1.2	2.1	0.2	0.6	<0.5	99.6
30	<1.0	1.1	28.8	61.9	<0.2	<0.2	1.2	0.3	1.5	1.8	<0.2	2.7	<0.5	99.3
36	<1.0	0.4	26.6	68.3	<0.2	<0.2	0.6	0.2	1.3	2.1	0.2	0.3	<0.5	100.0
37	<1.0	<0.4	26.5	67.9	<0.2	<0.2	0.7	0.3	1.1	1.9	<0.2	0.7	<0.5	99.2
41	<1.0	<0.4	25.6	51.1	<0.2	<0.2	0.3	0.2	1.0	1.8	<0.2	20.0	<0.5	100.0
42	<1.0	9.3	17.6	54.3	0.3	<0.2	3.6	4.1	0.8	9.5	0.3	0.3	<0.5	100.1
45	<1.0	<0.4	22.1	61.3	<0.2	<0.2	0.5	0.4	1.3	2.2	<0.2	11.0	<0.5	98.7
46	<1.0	<0.4	23.0	73.3	<0.2	<0.2	0.4	0.1	1.0	1.3	<0.2	0.9	<0.5	100.0
51	<1.0	0.9	11.4	79.5	<0.2	<0.2	2.8	0.4	0.6	4.1	<0.2	<0.2	<0.5	99.5
62	<1.0	1.0	23.4	69.4	<0.2	<0.2	0.9	0.2	1.4	2.4	0.7	1.0	<0.5	100.3
68	<1.0	1.1	23.5	67.7	<0.2	<0.2	0.9	0.3	1.1	2.0	2.6	0.5	<0.5	99.6
69	2.9	0.9	26.9	64.1	<0.2	<0.2	0.8	0.3	1.4	1.5	<0.2	0.4	<0.5	99.1
81	<1.0	1.0	25.6	63.5	<0.2	<0.2	1.0	0.4	1.2	4.2	1.9	0.9	<0.5	99.7
84	<1.0	0.9	23.1	67.5	<0.2	<0.2	0.9	0.3	1.3	2.9	<0.2	2.7	<0.5	99.5
92	1.5	<0.4	17.1	38.2	<0.2	<0.2	1.4	0.4	0.7	2.6	12.4	25.0	0.8	100.0
95	<1.0	<0.4	26.7	60.8	<0.2	<0.2	1.3	0.4	1.1	3.3	0.2	5.5	<0.5	99.3
97	1.1	1.3	26.5	55.0	<0.2	<0.2	1.2	0.4	1.3	3.3	0.7	8.6	<0.5	99.5
105	<1.0	1.1	27.8	61.6	<0.2	<0.2	1.3	0.3	1.2	4.7	0.6	1.5	<0.5	100.0
118	<1.0	<0.4	28.7	60.9	<0.2	<0.2	1.8	0.3	1.5	2.4	<0.2	4.4	<0.5	100.0
124	<1.0	1.2	26.5	61.3	<0.2	<0.2	1.2	0.4	1.3	3.2	0.8	3.1	<0.5	98.8

Appendix 10.7: Crucible No. 92, Line Trace Data

Matthew Nicholas

Description	Na$_2$O	MgO	Al$_2$O$_3$	SiO$_2$	K$_2$O	CaO	TiO$_2$	Fe$_2$O$_3$	CuO	ZnO	SnO$_2$	PbO	Total
Inner vitrification	3.8	<0.4	8.4	23.4	0.2	0.5	0.3	3.0	11.1	45.4	0.8	1.4	98.2
Inner vitrification	7.8	<0.4	6.8	30.4	0.3	0.5	<0.2	1.7	7.8	41.9	0.0	1.0	98.2
Inner vitrification	2.3	<0.4	21.2	26.6	1.0	1.2	0.6	5.1	10.3	24.1	0.6	2.3	95.2
Crucible	1.5	<0.4	17.1	38.2	1.4	0.4	0.7	2.6	12.4	25.0	0.0	0.8	100.0
Crucible	1.4	<0.4	24.5	52.0	0.8	0.5	0.8	2.2	0.4	17.0	0.0	0.0	99.6
Crucible	1.9	0.4	26.3	48.5	0.7	0.5	1.1	2.3	0.3	17.8	<0.5	<0.5	99.9
Crucible	<0.1	<0.4	27.9	52.4	1.7	0.3	1.4	1.8	0.2	13.6	<0.5	<0.5	99.3
Crucible	<0.1	<0.4	17.9	58.8	0.7	0.4	1.1	2.4	0.0	18.1	<0.5	<0.5	99.2
Crucible	<0.1	<0.4	23.4	47.7	1.4	0.4	1.2	3.8	0.6	20.1	<0.5	<0.5	98.7
Crucible	<0.1	0.4	31.8	58.4	2.2	0.4	0.9	2.9	0.2	3.0	<0.5	<0.5	100.1
Crucible	<0.1	0.4	29.6	58.1	2.3	0.4	1.0	2.6	0.2	5.2	<0.5	<0.5	99.7
Crucible	<0.1	<0.4	27.6	58.6	1.7	0.3	1.1	2.1	0.4	7.5	<0.5	<0.5	99.4
Crucible	<0.1	<0.4	22.8	53.3	0.9	0.5	4.6	3.7	0.5	11.9	<0.5	<0.5	98.0
Crucible	<0.1	<0.4	19.8	63.3	0.9	0.4	1.1	3.2	0.7	9.7	<0.5	<0.5	99.0
Crucible	<0.1	0.5	20.3	58.1	0.5	0.3	1.0	6.4	1.1	10.4	<0.5	<0.5	98.5
Crucible	<0.1	0.7	24.0	53.5	0.8	0.4	1.8	6.5	0.4	10.8	<0.5	<0.5	98.8
Crucible	<0.1	0.5	25.5	56.0	1.5	0.3	1.0	3.2	0.8	10.2	<0.5	<0.5	99.0
Crucible	<0.1	0.9	26.9	55.2	1.1	0.3	1.1	3.1	0.7	9.6	<0.5	<0.5	99.0
Crucible	<0.1	<0.4	24.5	60.0	1.5	0.3	1.3	2.8	0.7	7.9	<0.5	<0.5	99.1
Crucible	<0.1	<0.4	25.0	53.1	1.1	0.3	0.9	4.3	2.6	10.8	<0.5	<0.5	98.0
Crucible	<0.1	<0.4	24.9	59.6	1.4	0.4	0.9	2.8	0.7	7.5	<0.5	<0.5	98.1
Crucible	<0.1	<0.4	23.7	58.5	1.3	0.5	1.1	3.7	1.0	9.8	<0.5	<0.5	99.5
Crucible	<0.1	<0.4	23.9	63.7	1.1	0.3	1.1	2.6	0.5	5.4	<0.5	<0.5	98.7
Crucible	<0.1	<0.4	27.2	60.1	0.9	0.4	1.3	3.3	0.0	6.5	<0.5	<0.5	99.6
Crucible	<0.1	<0.4	27.3	57.2	1.1	0.3	1.2	5.0	1.0	5.3	<0.5	<0.5	98.3
Crucible	<0.1	<0.4	26.3	62.2	1.3	0.3	1.1	2.7	0.6	4.6	<0.5	<0.5	99.0
Crucible	<0.1	<0.4	24.5	62.4	1.3	0.3	1.2	3.1	0.4	6.2	<0.5	<0.5	99.3
Crucible	<0.1	0.4	20.3	73.1	1.2	0.3	1.4	1.9	0.4	0.9	<0.5	<0.5	99.9
Crucible	<0.1	<0.4	23.9	69.0	1.4	0.3	1.4	2.1	0.6	0.9	<0.5	<0.5	99.5
Crucible	<0.1	<0.4	15.3	80.6	0.7	0.1	0.7	1.3	0.4	0.3	<0.5	<0.5	99.5
Crucible	<0.1	0.5	32.9	59.0	1.7	0.3	1.5	2.6	0.6	0.6	<0.5	<0.5	99.6
Outer vitrification	<0.1	<0.4	37.5	56.3	1.0	0.3	0.9	2.5	0.7	0.7	<0.5	<0.5	99.7

Appendix 11.1: Catalogue of Human Burials, Park Street, Birmingham

Rachel Ives

Key: Good   Little taphonomic alteration, overall good preservation
       Fair   Minor weathering or damage
       Poor   Significant damage or poor preservation
       Weathering stages as classified by Behrensmeyer (1978)
       /   tooth lost postmortem
       x   tooth lost antemortem
       z   congenitally absent
       —   jaw and teeth not present
       c   caries
       a   abscess
       ca   calculus
       eh   enamel hypoplasia

HB F743
Orientation: east–west
Age: middle adult (36–50 years)
Sex: probable female
Stature: 152cm
Preservation: good overall, some damage and weathering of vertebrae and feet (stage 2).
Completeness: 50–75%
Bones present: all except nasal bones, lacrimals, palatines, vomer, ethomoid, hyoid, cricoid, thyroid, 7 ribs, some thoracic and lumbar vertebrae, those present are fragmentary. Both pubes are missing as well as the right patella, sternum, coccyx and some small hand and foot bones.
Additional bones: small fragment of a flat animal bone.
Dentition:

	ca	ca			ca					ca	ca	ca	ca	ca	
Z	2	3	/	/	6	/	/	/	z	11	12	13	14	15	---
32	31	x	/	28	27	26	25	24	23	22	21	20	x	X	/
Ca	ca			ca (eh)	ca	ca	ca	ca	ca	ca	c	c (ca, eh)			

Dental pathology: caries (2/19), calculus (18/18), periodontal disease (15/15), enamel hypoplasia linear (1/18), pit (1/18).
Non-metric traits: left parietal foramen, bilateral mastoid foramen exsutural, bilateral double superior atlas facets.
Skeletal pathology: minor joint enlargement of several superior and inferior apophyseal joints. Only 2/9 joints affected displayed porosity. Four rib fragments display flattened and slightly enlarged rib tubercules, no corresponding changes could be identified on the fragmentary thoracic vertebrae. A small button osteoma is present on the right-hand side of the frontal bone, 3.4cm above the right orbit. The osteoma comprises smooth, dense cortical bone with clearly demarcated edges measuring 0.6cm (SI) by 0.6cm (ML). The endocranium was not affected.

HB F753

Orientation: northwest to southeast

Age: older sub-adult – young adult (18–22 years)

Sex: probable male

Stature: 168cm

Preservation: good

Completeness: 75%+, although the skull is quite fragmentary.

Bones present: all except maxillae, nasal bones, zygomatics, lacrimals, palatines, frontal, vomer, ethmoid, cricoid, thyroid, 2 ribs, left ischium and pubis, coccyx and some small hand and foot bones.

Additional bones: none.

Dentition:

32	31	30	29	28	27	26	/	/	---	---	---	20	x	Z	z
---	---	---	---	---	---	---	---	---	---	---	---	---	---	---	---
c	c	c	c	ca	ca	ca						c			c
			ca	eh	eh	eh						ca			ca
			eh									eh			

Dental pathology: caries (6/9), calculus (6/6), enamel hypoplasia (5/6 affected, linear 1/5, pit 5/5).

Non-metric traits: none.

Skeletal pathology: Schmorl's nodes (9/25 surfaces available), supranumerary vertebra L6 present displaying incomplete sacralisation from cranial shifting of the lumbosacral border (Barnes 1994, 113). Focal patch of periostitis on the right proximal tibia displaying slight swelling surmounted by well remodelled, healed, striated new bone.

Appendix 15.1: Animal Bones; mandibular wear stages for the main species

Ian L. Baxter

Mandibular wear stage

Tooth wear stages for cattle, sheep/goat and pig follow Grant (1982). Mandibular wear stages for cattle and pig follow O'Connor (1988), for sheep/goat follow Crabtree (1989). Only mandibles with M3 and/or two or more teeth (with recordable wear stage) in the dP4/P4–M3 row are given.

TAXA

B cattle
OVA sheep
O sheep/goat
S pig

Cattle & Pig:		
J	Juvenile	M1 not in wear
I	Immature	M1 in wear, M2 not in wear
S	Sub-adult	M2 in wear, M3 not in wear
A	Adult	M3 in wear
E	Elderly	M3 at j+

Sheep/Goat:			Payne (1973) equivalent
A	*c.*0–6 months	M1 unworn	A–B
B	*c.*6–12 months	M2 unworn	C
C	*c.*1–2 years	M3 unworn	D
D	*c.*2–4 years	M3 coming into wear	E–F
E	*c.*4–8 years	M3 in full wear	G–H
F	*c.*8–10 years	M3 in heavy wear	I

Site periods

Site:	Park Street (PS)	Phase	Edgbaston Street (ES)		Moor Street (MS)
Phase					Phase
1/2	C12th–16th	1	C12th–14th		1
3	C17th–18th	2	C15th–16th		2
		3	C17th–18th		
		4	C18th–19th		

Mandibular wear stages

Site	Phase	Taxon	P4	dP4	M1	M2	M3	Mandibular wear stage
PS	1/2	B					j	E
PS	3	B					a	S
PS	3	B	g		k			A
ES	2	B		c	E			J
ES	2	B		f	E			J
ES	2	B					k	E
ES	3	B					g	A
ES	3	B	a		C			J
ES	3	B					k	E
MS	1	B	h		l	k	k	E
MS	1	B					g	A
MS	1	B	f		k			A
PS	3	OVA		f	E			A
PS	3	OVA		f	U			A
PS	3	OVA		f	E			A
PS	1/2	O	h		l	g	g	E
PS	1/2	O	e		g	f	d	D
PS	1/2	O	h		g	g	d	D
PS	1/2	O					d	D
PS	1/2	O					f	D
PS	3	O			l	g	g	E
PS	3	O					e	D
PS	3	O					g	E
PS	3	O	g		g	g	g	E
ES	1	O					e	D
ES	2	O				m	j	F
ES	3	O					e	D
ES	3	O					c	D
ES	3	O	g		g	g		E
MS	1	O				f	U	C
MS	1	O	g		g	g		E
MS	1	O	h		h	g	g	E
PS	3	S			e	a	C	I
ES	2/3	S		g	a	C		J

Appendix 15.2: Measurements of Animal Bones and Teeth

Ian L. Baxter

Measurements of animal bones and teeth, arranged by taxon, part of the skeleton and period. All measurements are in tenths of a millimetre. See text for an explanation of how measurements are taken. Measurements are given in the following order: horncores, teeth, postcranial bones.

Key

Taxa are coded as follows:

B	Bos (cattle)
OVA	Ovis (sheep)
O	Ovis/Capra (sheep/goat)
S	Sus (pig)
EQ	Equidae (equid)
EQC	Equus caballus (horse)
CAF	Canis familiaris (dog)
FEC	Felis catus (cat)
LE	Lepus sp. (hare)
ORC	Oryctolagus cuniculus (rabbit)
GAG	Gallus gallus (domestic fowl)
ANA	Anas (duck)
MEG	Meleagris gallapavo (turkey)

The presence/absence of a spur on a bird tarso-metatarsus is coded as follows:

A	absent
P	present
S	scar

Approximate measurements are designated:

c – within 0.2 mm
e – within 0.5 mm

Parts of skeleton (Element) are coded as follows:

AS	astragalus
CA	calcaneum
HU	humerus
MC1	complete distal metacarpal
MC2	half distal metacarpal
MT1	complete distal metatarsal
MT2	half distal metatarsal
PE	pelvis
RA	radius
FE	femur
TI	tibia (tibiotarsus in birds)
TMT	tarsometatarsus

Epiphyseal fusion/age is coded as follows:

F	fused
H	fused/fusing
G	fusing
UM	unfused diaphysis
UE	unfused epiphysis
UX	unfused diaphysis+epiphysis

Horncore measurements

Taxon	Site	Period	L	Width max (mm)	Width min (mm)	C	Index (L/C.100)
B	ES	1		377	327		
B	ES	1		306	260		
B	ES	1	900	314	269		
B	ES	1		522	405		
B	ES	1		487	443		
B	ES	1	850	306	263		
B	ES	1		399	299		
B	ES	1	1290	405	312		
B	ES	1		393	319		
B	MS	1		411	330		
B	MS	1	1230	473	404		
B	MS	1		540	413		
B	MS	1		438	343		
B	MS	1		382	306		
B	MS	1		385	348		
B	MS	1		313	297		
B	MS	1		552	453		
B	MS	1		340	293		
B	MS	1			484		
B	MS	1		373	324		
B	MS	1		524	368		
B	MS	1		339	261		
B	MS	1		431	278		
B	MS	1		452	363		
B	MS	1		316	246		
B	MS	1		541	414		
B	MS	1		437	375		
B	PS	1/2	950	360	272		
B	PS	1/2	800	361	250		
B	PS	1/2	850	334	252		
B	PS	1/2	1040		257		
B	PS	1/2		381	280		
B	PS	1/2		380	290		
B	PS	1/2	900	325	264		
B	PS	1/2	e800	282	249		
B	PS	1/2		595	485		
B	PS	1/2	1200	471	379		
B	PS	1/2		479	369		
B	PS	1/2		576	455		
B	PS	1/2		480	404		
B	PS	1/2		528	407		
B	PS	1/2		594	438		
B	PS	1/2		312	237		
B	PS	1/2			389		
B	PS	1/2		543	396		
B	PS	1/2	1290	419	347		
B	PS	1/2	1000	407	307		
B	PS	1/2		324	277		

Taxon	Site	Period	L	Width max (mm)	Width min (mm)	C	Index (L/C.100)
B	PS	1/2		394	316		
B	PS	1/2		388	305		
B	ES	2	2240	555	515	1640	137
B	ES	2		479	450		
B	ES	2		402	377		
B	MS	2	900	435	323		
B	PS	3		503	376		
B	PS	3	1440	445	393		
B	PS	3	740	316	218		
B	PS	3	1170	330	274		
B	PS	3		600	480		
B	ES	3		592	462		
B	ES	3	1530	526	412		
B	ES	3		600	527		
B	ES	3		770	594		
B	ES	3		559	469		
B	ES	3		608	489		
B	ES	3		640	545		
B	ES	3		614	550		
B	ES	3		609	488		
B	ES	3		720	558		
B	ES	3	2530	600	492	1800	141
B	ES	3	2420	623	469	1770	137
B	ES	3		576	392		
B	ES	3		553	472		
B	ES	3		571	466		
B	ES	3		629	464		
B	ES	3		577	518		
B	ES	3	2070	588	533	1870	111
B	ES	3		418	355		
B	ES	3		495	409		
B	ES	3		607	445		
B	ES	3		628	479		
B	ES	3		780	630		
B	ES	3		629	449		
B	ES	3		554	492		
B	ES	3		605	502		
B	ES	3		522	402		
B	ES	3		536	436		
B	ES	3	2900	646	518	1900	153
B	ES	3	2300	515	501	1620	142
B	ES	3		478	450		
B	ES	4		332	268		
OVA	MS	1		328	218		
OVA	PS	1/2	730	269	171		
OVA	ES	3	690	260	185		

Upper tooth measurements

Taxon	Site	Period	Tooth	OL	Be	Bapf	LP	CH
EQC	MS	2	P3	231	228	0	95	390
EQC	PS	1/2	P4					550
EQC	PS	3	P3					591

Upper tooth measurements

Taxon	Site	Period	M3L	M3W
B	MS	1	312	136
B	MS	1	352	129
B	ES	2	377	161
B	ES	3		147

Taxon	Site	Period	Tooth	CH
EQC	PS	1/2	M1	449

Bone measurements

Cranium										
Taxon	Site	Period	I	II	III	IV	IX	X	XI	XII
CAF	ES	U/S	2109	1153	1028	1112	1039	655	651	404

Taxon	Element	Site	Period	GLl	Bd	Dl
B	AS	ES	2	643	408	343
B	AS	PS	3	701	454	402
B	AS	ES	3		368	
OVA	AS	PS	3	283	187	159

Taxon	Element	Site	Period	GH	GB	BFd	LmT
EQC	AS	PS	1/2	528	550	480	516

Taxon	Element	Site	Period	Fusion	GL
B	CA	PS	1/2	F	1179
B	CA	PS	3	F	1609
B	CA	ES	3	F	1290
OVA	CA	PS	3	F	526

Taxon	Element	Site	Period	Fusion	GL	GLl	GLC	BT	HTC	SD	Dp	Bd
B	HU	MS	1	F				615	257			
B	HU	MS	1	F				701				
B	HU	PS	3	F				763	348			
B	HU	ES	3	F				681	329			
OVA	HU	PS	1/2	F				266	138			
OVA	HU	PS	1/2	F					133			
OVA	HU	PS	1/2	F				279	142			
OVA	HU	ES	2	F				269	132			
OVA	HU	ES	2	F				269	138			
OVA	HU	PS	3	F				261	133			
OVA	HU	PS	3	F				290	152			
OVA	HU	PS	3	F				321	169			
OVA	HU	PS	3	F				294	154			
OVA	HU	PS	3	F				264	130			
OVA	HU	PS	3	F				267	137			
OVA	HU	PS	3	F				257	128			
OVA	HU	ES	3	F				303	155			
OVA	HU	ES	3	F				294	161			
S	HU	MS	1	F				322	223			
S	HU	ES	2	F				328	209			
S	HU	PS	3	UX				378	246			
S	HU	PS	3	F				401	254			
EQC	HU	PS	3	F				794	430			
EQC	HU	PS	3	F				724	377	348		
EQC	HU	ES	3	F	3154	3100		802	401	374		849
CAF	HU	MS	1	F							368	
FEC	HU	PS	1/2	F	725		711	102	49	47	138	136
FEC	HU	PS	3	F	850			129	60	60		

Taxon	Element	Site	Period	Fusion	GL	Bd	3	SD	BatF	a	b
B	MC1	PS	1/2	F	1648	474	242	231	438	227	222
B	MC1	PS	1/2	F		517	227		460	251	248
B	MC1	PS	1/2	F		502	252		468	243	234
B	MC1	PS	1/2	F		630	286		529	328	278
B	MC1	PS	1/2	UE		602	237			289	284
B	MC1	PS	1/2	F		611	283		544	287	290
B	MC1	MS	2	F		528	272		490	258	246
B	MC1	MS	2	UE		518	390			243	237
B	MC1	PS	3	F		631	313		595	291	297
B	MC1	PS	3	F		632	321		607	299	292
B	MC1	PS	3	F		582	275		578	280	260
B	MC1	PS	3	F		566	290		527	248	252
B	MC1	PS	3	UE		582	286			278	267
B	MC2	PS	3	F	1740		244	271		225	
B	MC1	PS	3	F	1947	569	281	332	526	281	266
B	MC1	PS	3	F	1990	600	295	356	366	290	271
B	MC1	PS	3	F		582	295	317	552	279	269
B	MC1	ES	3	F		536	267		497	256	250
B	MC1	ES	3	UE		561	294			273	262
B	MC1	ES	3	F		546	283		505	264	253

Taxon	Element	Site	Period	Fusion	GL	Bd	SD	WC	WT	DV	Index (WT.100/DV)
OVA	MC1	PS	1/2	F	1055	230	126	100	95		
OVA	MC2	PS	1/2	F				108	98		
OVA	MC1	MS	2	F	1360	234	136	103	93		
OVA	MC1	PS	3	F	1180	258	135	117	106	157	68
OVA	MC1	PS	3	F		257		114	103		
OVA	MC1	ES	3	F	1177	229	143	103	100		
OVA	MC1	ES	3	F	1324	268	149	128	128	181	71
OVA	MC1	ES	3	F	1102	242	131	111	102	146	70
OVA	MC1	ES	3	F	1248	284	152	126	128	180	71

Taxon	Element	Site	Period	Fusion	GL	Ll	Bd	SD	Dd
EQ	MC1	MS	1	F	1895		376	264	302
EQC	MC1	PS	1/2	F			468		
EQC	MC1	PS	1/2	F	2250	2230	494	326	376
EQC	MC1	PS	1/2	F	2470	2430	572	384	

Taxon	Element	Site	Period	Fusion	1	3	4	10	11	12	13	14
EQ	MC1	MS	1	F	1895	264	195	362	376	301	245	248

Taxon	Element	Site	Period	Fusion	GL	Bd	3	SD	BatF	a	b
B	MT1	PS	1/2	F		450	254		401	222	206
B	MT1	PS	1/2	F		506	242		477	248	231
B	MT1	PS	1/2	F		500	260		474	235	233
B	MT1	PS	1/2	F		445	248		414	219	204
B	MT1	PS	1/2	UX		534	273		504	253	241
B	MT1	PS	1/2	UE		539	257			270	253
B	MT1	PS	1/2	F		528	272		486	250	242
B	MT1	PS	1/2	F		500	265		467	244	232
B	MT1	ES	2	F		488	258		460	238	225
B	MT1	PS	3	F		546	298		521	260	249
B	MT1	PS	3	F		515	267		500	245	236
B	MT1	PS	3	F		529	278		543	251	239
B	MT1	PS	3	F		548	294		536	262	251
B	MT1	PS	3	F		535	282		501	252	249
B	MT1	PS	3	F		582			549		
B	MT1	PS	3	F		572	281		512	282	267
B	MT1	PS	3	F		590	297	323	608	270	268
B	MT2	PS	3	F	2110					275	
B	MT1	PS	3	F		511	275	266	518	243	237
B	MT1	PS	3	F		592		296	560	263	276
B	MT1	ES	3	F		591	296		587	274	273
B	MT1	ES	3	F		495	242		456	234	232
B	MT1	ES	3	F		523	272		492	232	241
B	MT1	ES	3	F		488			465	234	216
B	MT1	ES	3	F		474	266		447	228	212
B	MT1	ES	3	F		454	249		428	219	207

Taxon	Element	Site	Period	Fusion	GL	Bd	SD	WT	DV	Index (WT.100/DV)
OVA	MT2	PS	1/2	F	1239		116			
OVA	MT1	PS	3	F	1551	260	149	106	173	61
OVA	MT1	PS	3	F	1261		126			
OVA	MT2	ES	3	F	1209			89	135	66
OVA	MT1	ES	3	F		237		95	145	66
OVA	MT1	ES	3	F	1546	294	158	122	188	65
OVA	MT1	ES	3	F	1259	230	112	99	153	65
OVA	MT1	ES	3	F	1425	273	150	117	172	68
OVA	MT1	ES	3	F	1429	268	141	116	187	62
OVA	MT1	ES	3	F	1254	237	119	103	160	64

Taxon	Element	Site	Period	Fusion	GL	Ll	Bd	SD	Dd
EQC	MT1	PS	1/2	F	2480			281	
CAF	Mt.II	ES	3	F	390		61	44	
FEC	Mt.III	PS	3	F	389		51	45	

Taxon	Element	Site	Period	Fusion	LA	LAR	Rim height	
B	PE	PS	1/2	F			120	dip
B	PE	PS	3	F	707		111	no dip
B	PE	PS	3	F	629		100	dip
B	PE	ES	3	F			105	no dip
OVA	PE	ES	2/3	F	268			
OVA	PE	PS	3	F	291			
OVA	PE	PS	3	F	318			
OVA	PE	ES	3	F	253			
EQC	PE	PS	3	F		729		
EQC	PE	ES	3	F		733		
LE	PE	ES	2	F		122		

Taxon	Element	Site	Period	Fusion	GL	Ll	Bp	SD	Bd
OVA	RA	PS	1/2	F	1407			159	
OVA	RA	ES	2	F	1348			144	
OVA	RA	PS	3	F	1382			144	
OVA	RA	ES	3	F	1252			139	
EQ	RA	MS	2	F	e2860	e2800		296	
EQC	RA	ES	3	F	3650	3520		400	
FEC	RA	PS	3	F	840			55	
FEC	RA	PS	3	F	813			50	

Taxon	Element	Site	Period	Fusion	1	2	3	7	8	9	10	11
EQ	RA	MS	2	F	e2860	e2800	296	590	501	302	210	112

Taxon	Element	Site	Period	Fusion	8
EQ	FE	MS	2	F	682

Taxon	Element	Site	Period	Fusion	GL	Ll	Bd
B	TI	PS	1/2	F			652
B	TI	PS	1/2	F			592
B	TI	ES	1/2	F	3510		599
B	TI	ES	2	F			555
B	TI	ES	2	F			540
B	TI	PS	3	F			620
B	TI	PS	3	F			603
B	TI	ES	3	F			594
B	TI	ES	3	F			552
OVA	TI	PS	1/2	F			287
OVA	TI	PS	3	F			239
OVA	TI	PS	3	F			312
OVA	TI	PS	3	F			300
OVA	TI	ES	3	F			291
OVA	TI	ES	3	F			259
OVA	TI	ES	3	F			268
OVA	TI	ES	3	F			251
OVA	TI	ES	3	F			231
EQC	TI	MS	1	F			655
EQC	TI	PS	1/2	F			667
EQC	TI	ES	3	F	3580	3250	714
FEC	TI	PS	3	F	969		130
ORC	TI	PS	3	F	924		127

Taxon	Element	Site	Period	Fusion	GL	BFd	Dd	SD
EQC	P1	MS	1	F	606	335	200	261

Taxon	Element	Site	Period	Fusion	1	2	3	5	6	7	8	9	10	11	12	13	14
EQC	P1	MS	1	F	606	598	261	286	353	362	351	539	458	476	111	111	335

Taxon	Element	Site	Period	GL	Bd	SC
GAG	HU	PS	3	716	156	74

Taxon	Element	Site	Period	GL	Bd	Dd	SC	Lm
MEG	FE	ES	4	1133		211	114	

Taxon	Element	Site	Period	GL	Bd	Dd	SC	La
GAG	TI	PS	1/2		107	114	58	
ANA	TI	PS	3		104	115	54	
MEG	TI	ES	4	1785	208	188	108	1764

Taxon	Element	Site	Period	GL	Bd	SC	Spur
GAG	TMT	ES	2	710	127	55	A

Appendix 15.3: Discriminant Function Analysis of Cattle Horncones

Ian L. Baxter

Obs	Length (mm)	Width max (mm)	Width min (mm)	Site
Obs 1	900	314	269	Edgbaston1
Obs 2	850	306	263	Edgbaston1
Obs 3	1290	405	312	Edgbaston1
Obs 4	950	360	272	Park1/2
Obs 5	800	361	250	Park1/2
Obs 6	850	334	252	Park1/2
Obs 7	900	325	264	Park1/2
Obs 8	800	282	249	Park1/2
Obs 9	1200	471	379	Park1/2
Obs 10	1290	419	347	Park1/2
Obs 11	1000	407	307	Park1/2
Obs 12	730	269	171	Park1/2
Obs 13	1440	445	393	Park3
Obs 14	740	316	218	Park3
Obs 15	1170	330	274	Park3
Obs 16	1530	526	412	Edgbaston3
Obs 17	2530	600	492	Edgbaston3
Obs 18	2420	623	469	Edgbaston3
Obs 19	2070	588	533	Edgbaston3
Obs 20	2900	646	518	Edgbaston3
Obs 21	2300	515	501	Edgbaston3
Obs 22	690	260	185	Edgbaston3

Discriminant analysis (DA)

Within-class covariance matrices are assumed to be equal
Prior probabilities are taken into account
Significance level (%): 5
Model selection: Forward
Threshold value to enter: 0.05

Summary statistics

Variable	Categories	Frequencies	%
Site	Edgbaston1	3	13.636
	Edgbaston3	7	31.818
	Park1/2	9	40.909
	Park3	3	13.636

Variable	Observations	Obs. with missing data	Obs. without missing data	Minimum	Maximum	Mean	Std. deviation
L	22	0	22	690.000	2900.000	1334.091	670.548
Wmax	22	0	22	260.000	646.000	413.727	121.503
Wmin	22	0	22	171.000	533.000	333.182	111.768

Correlation matrix

Variables	L	Wmax	Wmin
L	1.000	0.941	0.938
Wmax	0.941	1.000	0.962
Wmin	0.938	0.962	1.000

Discriminant analysis

Means by class

Class \ Variable	L	Wmax	Wmin
Edgbaston1	1013.333	341.667	281.333
Edgbaston3	2062.857	536.857	444.286
Park1/2	946.667	358.667	276.778
Park3	1116.667	363.667	295.000

Sum of weights, prior probabilities and logarithms of determinants for each class

Class	Sum of weights	Prior probabilities	Log (Determinant)
Edgbaston1	3.000	0.136	11.780
Edgbaston3	7.000	0.318	13.517
Park1/2	9.000	0.409	10.721
Park3	3.000	0.136	12.544

Multicolinearity statistics

Statistic	L	Wmax	Wmin
Tolerance	0.100	0.062	0.065
VIF	9.977	16.054	15.334

Between-classes SSCP matrix

	L	Wmax	Wmin
L	5519055.628	922111.688	838249.351
Wmax	922111.688	156508.173	140655.139
Wmin	838249.351	140655.139	127479.622

Pooled within-class SSCP matrix

	L	Wmax	Wmin
L	3923276.190	687662.857	638034.286
Wmax	687662.857	153512.190	133672.952
Wmin	638034.286	133672.952	134853.651

Total-sample SSCP matrix

	L	Wmax	Wmin
L	9442331.818	1609774.545	1476283.636
Wmax	1609774.545	310020.364	274328.091
Wmin	1476283.636	274328.091	262333.273

Between-classes covariance matrix

	L	Wmax	Wmin
L	334488.220	55885.557	50802.991
Wmax	55885.557	9485.344	8524.554
Wmin	50802.991	8524.554	7726.038

Within-class covariance matrix for class Edgbaston1

	L	Wmax	Wmin
L	58033.333	13241.667	6438.333
Wmax	13241.667	3024.333	1468.667
Wmin	6438.333	1468.667	714.333

Within-class covariance matrix for class Edgbaston3

	L	Wmax	Wmin
L	545257.143	88780.476	80012.381
Wmax	88780.476	17196.810	14770.048
Wmin	80012.381	14770.048	14613.238

Within-class covariance matrix for class Park1/2

	L	Wmax	Wmin
L	35800.000	10755.000	10689.167
Wmax	10755.000	4282.750	3720.917
Wmin	10689.167	3720.917	3721.444

Within-class covariance matrix for class Park3

	L	Wmax	Wmin
L	124633.333	21228.333	29785.000
Wmax	21228.333	5010.333	6174.000
Wmin	29785.000	6174.000	7987.000

Pooled within-class covariance matrix

	L	Wmax	Wmin
L	217959.788	38203.492	35446.349
Wmax	38203.492	8528.455	7426.275
Wmin	35446.349	7426.275	7491.869

Total covariance matrix

	L	Wmax	Wmin
L	449634.848	76655.931	70299.221
Wmax	76655.931	14762.874	13063.242
Wmin	70299.221	13063.242	12492.061

Summary of the variables selection

No. of variables	Variables	Variable IN/OUT	Status	Partial R²	F	Pr > F	Wilks' Lambda	Pr < Lambda
1	L	L	IN	0.585	8.440	0.001	0.415	0.001

Box test (chi-square asymptotic approximation)

-2Log(M)	5.736
Chi-square (Observed value)	4.948
Chi-square (Critical value)	7.815
DF	3
p-value	0.176
alpha	0.05

Test interpretation:
H0: The within-class covariance matrices are equal.
Ha: The within-class covariance matrices are different.
As the computed p-value is greater than the significance level alpha=0.05, one should accept the null hypothesis H0.
The risk to reject the null hypothesis H0 while it is true is 17.57%.

Box test (Fisher's F asymptotic approximation)

-2Log(M)	5.736
F (Observed value)	1.666
F (Critical value)	2.639
DF1	3
DF2	265
p-value	0.175
alpha	0.05

Test interpretation:
H0: The within-class covariance matrices are equal.
Ha: The within-class covariance matrices are different.
As the computed p-value is greater than the significance level alpha=0.05, one should accept the null hypothesis H0.
The risk to reject the null hypothesis H0 while it is true is 17.48%.

Kullback's test

K (Observed value)	2.868
K (Critical value)	7.815
DF	3
p-value	0.412
alpha	0.05

Test interpretation:
H0: The within-class covariance matrices are equal.
Ha: The within-class covariance matrices are different.
As the computed p-value is greater than the significance level alpha=0.05, one should accept the null hypothesis H0.
The risk to reject the null hypothesis H0 while it is true is 41.25%.

Mahalanobis distances

	Edgbaston1	Edgbaston3	Park1/2	Park3
Edgbaston1	0	5.054	0.020	0.049
Edgbaston3	5.054	0	5.716	4.108
Park1/2	0.020	5.716	0	0.133
Park3	0.049	4.108	0.133	0

Generalized squared distances

	Edgbaston1	Edgbaston3	Park1/2	Park3
Edgbaston1	0	5.054	0.020	0.049
Edgbaston3	5.054	0	5.716	4.108
Park1/2	0.020	5.716	0	0.133
Park3	0.049	4.108	0.133	0

Fisher distances

	Edgbaston1	Edgbaston3	Park1/2	Park3
Edgbaston1	0	3.145	0.014	0.022
Edgbaston3	3.145	0	6.669	2.556
Park1/2	0.014	6.669	0	0.088
Park3	0.022	2.556	0.088	0

p-values for Fisher distances

	Edgbaston1	Edgbaston3	Park1/2	Park3
Edgbaston1	1	0.054	0.998	0.995
Edgbaston3	0.054	1	0.004	0.092
Park1/2	0.998	0.004	1	0.965
Park3	0.995	0.092	0.965	1

Wilks' Lambda test (Rao's approximation)

Lambda	**0.415**
F (Observed value)	8.440
F (Critical value)	3.160
DF1	3
DF2	18
p-value	0.001
alpha	0.05

Test interpretation:
H0: The means vectors of the four classes are equal.
Ha: At least one of the means vector is different from another.
As the computed p-value is lower than the significance level alpha=0.05, one should reject the null hypothesis H0, and accept the alternative hypothesis Ha.
The risk to reject the null hypothesis H0 while it is true is lower than 0.10%.

Unidimensional test of equality of the means of the classes

Variable	**Lambda**	**F**	**DF1**	**DF2**	**p-value**
L	0.415	8.440	3	18	0.001
Wmax			3	18	
Wmin			3	18	

Pillai's trace

Trace	**0.585**
F (Observed value)	8.440
F (Critical value)	3.160
DF1	3
DF2	18
p-value	0.001
alpha	0.05

Test interpretation:
H0: The means vectors of the four classes are equal.
Ha: At least one of the means vector is different from another.
As the computed p-value is lower than the significance level alpha=0.05, one should reject the null hypothesis H0, and accept the alternative hypothesis Ha.
The risk to reject the null hypothesis H0 while it is true is lower than 0.10%.

Hotelling-Lawley trace

Trace	**1.407**
F (Observed value)	8.440
F (Critical value)	3.160
DF1	3
DF2	18
p-value	0.001
alpha	0.05

Test interpretation:

H0: The means vectors of the four classes are equal.

Ha: At least one of the means vector is different from another.

As the computed p-value is lower than the significance level alpha=0.05, one should reject the null hypothesis H0, and accept the alternative hypothesis Ha.

The risk to reject the null hypothesis H0 while it is true is lower than 0.10%.

Roy's greatest root

Root	1.407
F (Observed value)	8.440
F (Critical value)	3.160
DF1	3
DF2	18
p-value	0.001
alpha	0.05

Test interpretation:

H0: The means vectors of the four classes are equal.

Ha: At least one of the means vector is different from another.

As the computed p-value is lower than the significance level alpha=0.05, one should reject the null hypothesis H0, and accept the alternative hypothesis Ha.

The risk to reject the null hypothesis H0 while it is true is lower than 0.10%.

Eigenvalues

	F1
Eigenvalue	1.407
Discrimination (%)	100.000
Cumulative %	100.000

Eigenvectors

	F1
L	0.001
Wmax	0.000
Wmin	0.000

Canonical correlations

F1
0.765

Canonical discriminant function coefficients

	F1
Intercept	-2.858
L	0.002
Wmax	0.000
Wmin	0.000

Standardized canonical discriminant function coefficients

	F1
L	1.000
Wmax	0.000
Wmin	0.000

Functions at the centroids

	F1
Edgbaston1	-0.687
Edgbaston3	1.561
Park1/2	-0.830
Park3	-0.466

Classification functions

	Edgbaston1	Edgbaston3	Park1/2	Park3
Intercept	-4.348	-10.907	-2.950	-4.853
L	0.005	0.009	0.004	0.005
Wmax	0.000	0.000	0.000	0.000
Wmin	0.000	0.000	0.000	0.000

Prior and posterior classification, membership probabilities, scores and squared distances

Observation	Prior	Posterior	Pr(Edgbaston1)	Pr(Edgbaston3)	Pr(Park1/2)	Pr(Park3)	F1	D^2(Edgbaston1)	D^2(Edgbaston3)	D^2(Park1/2)	D^2(Park3)
Obs 1	Edgbaston1	Park1/2	0.196	0.021	0.602	0.181	-0.930	4.044	8.494	1.798	4.200
Obs 2	Edgbaston1	Park1/2	0.196	0.017	0.611	0.177	-1.037	4.107	9.039	1.831	4.311
Obs 3	Edgbaston1	Park1/2	0.180	0.127	0.492	0.201	-0.094	4.336	5.031	2.328	4.123
Obs 4	Park1/2	Park1/2	0.196	0.027	0.592	0.185	-0.823	4.003	7.972	1.788	4.112
Obs 5	Park1/2	Park1/2	0.195	0.013	0.619	0.172	-1.144	4.194	9.607	1.886	4.445
Obs 6	Park1/2	Park1/2	0.196	0.017	0.611	0.177	-1.037	4.107	9.039	1.831	4.311
Obs 7	Park1/2	Park1/2	0.196	0.021	0.602	0.181	-0.930	4.044	8.494	1.798	4.200
Obs 8	Park1/2	Park1/2	0.195	0.013	0.619	0.172	-1.144	4.194	9.607	1.886	4.445
Obs 9	Park1/2	Park1/2	0.188	0.086	0.526	0.200	-0.287	4.145	5.706	2.082	4.017
Obs 10	Park1/2	Park1/2	0.180	0.127	0.492	0.201	-0.094	4.336	5.031	2.328	4.123
Obs 11	Park1/2	Park1/2	0.195	0.034	0.582	0.189	-0.716	3.986	7.473	1.801	4.047
Obs 12	Park1/2	Park1/2	0.195	0.009	0.630	0.166	-1.294	4.353	10.441	2.003	4.671
Obs 13	Park3	Park1/2	0.160	0.233	0.417	0.191	0.227	4.820	4.070	2.904	4.465
Obs 14	Park3	Park1/2	0.195	0.010	0.629	0.167	-1.273	4.328	10.319	1.984	4.636
Obs 15	Park3	Park1/2	0.189	0.075	0.536	0.199	-0.351	4.097	5.948	2.016	3.998
Obs 16	Edgbaston3	Park1/2	0.142	0.319	0.361	0.177	0.420	5.210	3.593	3.349	4.769
Obs 17	Edgbaston3	Edgbaston3	0.004	0.983	0.007	0.007	2.562	14.539	3.291	13.290	13.149
Obs 18	Edgbaston3	Edgbaston3	0.006	0.971	0.012	0.011	2.326	13.063	2.875	11.747	11.778
Obs 19	Edgbaston3	Edgbaston3	0.029	0.864	0.061	0.046	1.576	9.108	2.290	7.577	8.155
Obs 20	Edgbaston3	Edgbaston3	0.001	0.997	0.001	0.001	3.354	20.316	5.506	19.293	18.576
Obs 21	Edgbaston3	Edgbaston3	0.010	0.950	0.021	0.019	2.069	11.580	2.548	10.191	10.409
Obs 22	Edgbaston3	Park1/2	0.194	0.008	0.636	0.162	-1.380	4.465	10.937	2.090	4.820

Centroids

	F1
Edgbaston1	-0.687
Edgbaston3	1.561
Park1/2	-0.830
Park3	-0.466

Confusion matrix for the estimation sample

from\ to	Edgbaston1	Edgbaston3	Park1/2	Park3	Total	% correct
Edgbaston1	0	0	3	0	3	0.00%
Edgbaston3	0	5	2	0	7	71.43%
Park1/2	0	0	9	0	9	100.00%
Park3	0	0	3	0	3	0.00%
Total	0	5	17	0	22	63.64%

Cross-validation: Prior and posterior classification, membership probabilities, scores and squared distances

Observation	Prior	Posterior	Edgbaston1	Edgbaston3	Park1/2	Park3
Obs 1	Edgbaston1	Park1/2	0.190	0.025	0.603	0.182
Obs 2	Edgbaston1	Park1/2	0.184	0.020	0.617	0.180
Obs 3	Edgbaston1	Park1/2	0.150	0.136	0.508	0.206
Obs 4	Park1/2	Park1/2	0.195	0.031	0.589	0.185
Obs 5	Park1/2	Park1/2	0.196	0.016	0.613	0.174
Obs 6	Park1/2	Park1/2	0.196	0.020	0.607	0.178
Obs 7	Park1/2	Park1/2	0.195	0.025	0.599	0.181
Obs 8	Park1/2	Park1/2	0.196	0.016	0.613	0.174
Obs 9	Park1/2	Park1/2	0.190	0.093	0.515	0.202
Obs 10	Park1/2	Park1/2	0.186	0.135	0.473	0.206
Obs 11	Park1/2	Park1/2	0.194	0.039	0.578	0.189
Obs 12	Park1/2	Park1/2	0.198	0.011	0.621	0.170
Obs 13	Park3	Park1/2	0.168	0.246	0.438	0.149
Obs 14	Park3	Park1/2	0.206	0.010	0.666	0.118
Obs 15	Park3	Park1/2	0.188	0.082	0.534	0.196
Obs 16	Edgbaston3	Park1/2	0.153	0.269	0.386	0.192
Obs 17	Edgbaston3	Edgbaston3	0.004	0.980	0.008	0.008
Obs 18	Edgbaston3	Edgbaston3	0.007	0.966	0.014	0.013
Obs 19	Edgbaston3	Edgbaston3	0.032	0.846	0.071	0.051
Obs 20	Edgbaston3	Edgbaston3	0.000	0.998	0.001	0.001
Obs 21	Edgbaston3	Edgbaston3	0.012	0.940	0.025	0.022
Obs 22	Edgbaston3	Park1/2	0.188	0.000	0.683	0.128

Confusion matrix for the cross-validation results

from\ to	Edgbaston1	Edgbaston3	Park1/2	Park3	Total	% correct
Edgbaston1	0	0	3	0	3	0.00%
Edgbaston3	0	5	2	0	7	71.43%
Park1/2	0	0	9	0	9	100.00%
Park3	0	0	3	0	3	0.00%
Total	0	5	17	0	22	63.64%

Bibliography

Abbreviations

WMRRFA www.arch-ant.bham.ac.uk/wmrrfa West Midlands Regional Research Framework for Archaeology

References

Adamson D. (ed.) (1996) *John Byng, Viscount Torrington; rides round Britain.* London, Folio Society.

Albarella, U. and Davis, S. (1994) *The Saxon and Medieval Animal Bones Excavated 1985–1989 from West Cotton, Northamptonshire.* London, English Heritage AML Report 17/94.

Albarella, U. (2002) Tanners, tawyers, horn working and the mystery of the missing goat. In P. Murphy and P. Wiltshire (eds) *The Environmental Archaeology of Industry.* Oxford, Oxbow Books.

Allan, J. P. (ed.) (1984) *Medieval and Post-Medieval Finds from Exeter, 1971–1980.* Exeter Archaeological Reports: Volume 3. Exeter City Council and the University of Exeter.

Alvey, R. C., Laxton R. R. and Paeschter, G. F. (1979) Statistical analysis of some Nottingham clay tobacco pipes'. In P. Davey (ed.) *The Archaeology of the Clay Tobacco Pipe, I,* 229–53.

Andrew, R. (1984) *A Practical Pollen Guide to the British Flora.* Quaternary Research Association, Technical Guide 1. Cambridge.

Anon (1987) Alphabetical list of pipemakers in Scotland. In P Davey (ed.) *The Archaeology of the Clay Tobacco Pipe, X. Scotland.* British Archaeological Reports No. 178, 337–350. Oxford, British Archaeological Reports.

Armitage, P. L. (1982) A system for aging and sexing the horn cores of cattle from British post-medieval sites (17th to early 18th century) with special reference to unimproved British Longhorn cattle. In R. Wilson, C. Grigson and S. Payne (eds) *Ageing and Sexing Animal Bones from Archaeological Sites.* British Archaeological Reports, British series 109, 37–54. Oxford, British Archaeological Reports.

Armitage, P. L. and Clutton-Brock, J. (1976) A system for classification and description of the horn cores of cattle from archaeological sites. *Journal of Archaeological Science* 3, 329–348.

Bailey, G. (2000) *Finds Identified.* Essex, Greenlight Publishing.

Baker, N. J. (1995) A town-plan analysis of the Digbeth Economic Regeneration Area and Cheapside Industrial Area. In S. Litherland *An Archaeological Assessment of the Digbeth Economic Regeneration Area and Cheapside Industrial Area.* Birmingham University Field Archaeology Unit Report 337.

Baren, M. (1998) *Victorian Shopping: how it all began.* London, Michael O'Mara.

Barker, D. (1985) The Newcastle-under-Lyme clay tobacco pipe industry. In P. Davey (ed.) *The Archaeology of the Clay Tobacco Pipe, IX,* 237–289.

Barker D. (1986) *North Staffordshire Post-Medieval Ceramics – A Type Series. Part Two: Blackware.* Staffordshire Archaeological Studies, Museum Archaeological Society Report, New Series No. 3. Stoke-on-Trent City Museum & Art Gallery, Stoke-on-Trent.

Barker, D. (1991) *William Greatbatch, a Staffordshire Potter.* London, Jonathan Horne.

Barker, D. and Barker, B. (1984) A late 18th century pit group from Haregate Hall, Leek, Staffordshire, *Staffordshire Archaeological Studies* 1, 87–136.

Barley, M. W. (ed.) (1975) *The Plans and Topography of Medieval Towns* (Council for British Archaeology Research report 14). York, Council for British Archaeology.

Barnes, E. (1994) *Developmental Defects of the Axial Skeleton in Paleopathology.* Colorado, University Press of Colorado.

Barone, R. (1986) *Anatomie comparée des mammifères domestiques.* Volume 1 Osteologie. Paris, Vigot Freres.

Bartosiewicz, L., Van Neer, W. and Lentacker, A. (1997) *Draught Cattle: their osteological identification and history.* Koninklijk Museum voor Midden-Afrka, Tervuren, België, Annalen Zoölogische Wetenschappen/ Annales Sciences Zoologiques, Musée Royale de l'Afrique Centrale. Tervuren, Belgium.

Bass, W. M. (1995) *Human Osteology: a laboratory and field manual.* 4th edition. Columbia, Mo, Missouri Archaeological Society.

Bates, W. (1860) Sept 15 'Tooth and Egg' metal, *Notes and Queries* 10, 2nd series (246), 214.

Baxter, I. L. (1998) Species identification of equids from Western European archaeological deposits: methodologies, techniques and problems. In S. Anderson (ed.) *Current and Recent Research in Osteoarchaeology,* 3–17. Proceedings of the third meeting of the Osteoarchaeological Research Group. Oxford, Oxbow Books.

Baxter, I. L. (2000) *Report on the Animal Bones from 16–18 Harrison Street, Hereford.* Unpublished report prepared for Archenfield Archaeology.

Baxter, I. L. (2002a) Occipital perforations in a Late Neolithic probable aurochs (*Bos primigenius Bojansus*) cranium from Letchworth, Hertfordshire, U.K. *International Journal of Osteoarchaeology* 12, 142–143.

Baxter, I. L. (2002b) Animal bone. In J. Bretherton, D. Hurst, I. Baxter, L. Jones and L. Pearson. Excavation of a multi-period site at Worcester Road, Droitwich. *Transactions of the Worcestershire Archaeological Society* 18, 25–51.

Baxter, I. L. (2002c) A donkey (*Equus asinus* L.) partial skeleton from a Mid–Late Anglo-Saxon alluvial layer at Deans Yard, Westminster, London SW1. *Environmental Archaeology* 7, 89–94.

Bayley, J. (1992) Metalworking ceramics. *Medieval Ceramics* 16, 3–10.

Bayley, J., Dungworth, D. and Paynter, S. (2001) *Archaeo-metallurgy*. Centre for Archaeology Guidelines. London, English Heritage.

Bayley, J. and Linton, R. (1982) *Technological Samples from Barnard Castle, Co Durham*. Ancient Monuments Laboratory Report 3810. London, English Heritage.

Behrensmeyer, A. (1978) Taphonomic and Ecological Information from Bone Weathering. *Paleobiology* 4, 150–162.

Bennett, K. D. (1994) *Annotated Catalogue of Pollen and Pteridophyte Spore Types of the British Isles*. Unpublished report.

Bevan, L. (2001) Other finds. In C. Mould (2001a) *The Custard Factory*.

Bevan, L. (2006) Jewellery and other personal items. In M. Brickley and S. Buteux *et al.*, *St. Martin's Uncovered*, 279–186.

Bickley, W. B. and Hill, J. (1891) *A Survey of the Borough and Manor or Demesne of Birmingham made in 1553*. Birmingham.

Biddle, M. (ed.) (1990) *Object and Economy in Medieval Winchester: artefacts from medieval Winchester*. Winchester Studies Volume 7.2 (two volumes). Oxford, Clarendon Press.

Biddle, M. and Hinton, D. A. (1990) Decorative bone casket-strips. In M. Biddle (ed.) *Object and Economy in Medieval Winchester*, 781–787.

Birmingham City Council (2004) *Archaeology Strategy Supplementary Planning Guidance*. Birmingham.

Blakeman, A. (2000) *Antique Bottle Collector's Encyclopaedia*. Barnsley, BBR Publishing.

Boessneck, J. (1969) Osteological differences between sheep (*Ovis aries Linne*) and goat (*Capra hircus Linne*). In D. R. Brothwell and E. Higgs (eds) *Science in Archaeology*, 331–359. London, Thames and Hudson.

Booth, P. (2002) *The Medieval Pottery recovered from the Birmingham Northern Relief Road*. Assessment reports for Oxford-Wessex Unit, ed. P. Booth.

Boothroyd, N. and Higgins, D. (2005) An inn-clearance group, *c*1800, from the Royal Oak, Eccleshall, Staffordshire. *Post-Medieval Archaeology*, 39/1, 197–203.

Brickley M., Buteux, S., Adams, J. and Cherrington, R. (2006) *St. Martin's Uncovered. Investigations in the churchyard of St. Martin's-in-the-Bull Ring, Birmingham, 2001*. Oxford, Oxbow.

Brothwell, D. (1981) *Digging Up Bones*. 3rd edition. Cornell University Press, New York.

Brown, D. (1990) *Games and Toys*. In Biddle, M. (ed.) *Object and Economy in Medieval Winchester*, 692–706.

Brunskill, R. W. (1997) *Brick Building in Britain*. London, Gollancz.

Buikstra, J. and Ubelaker, D. (eds) (1994) *Standards for Data Collection from Human Skeletal Remains. Proceedings of a seminar at the Field Museum of Natural History*. Arkansas, Arkansas Archaeological Survey Research Series 44.

Burrows, B. and Martin, H. (2002) *Park Street, Birmingham City Centre. Archaeological investigations 200. Post-excavation assessment and research design*. Birmingham University Field Archaeology Unit Report, Project Number 776.

Burrows, R., Dingwall, L. and Williams, J. (2000) *Further Archaeological Investigations at Hartwell Smithfield Garage Site, Digbeth, Birmingham, 2000*. Birmingham University Field Archaeology Unit Report No. 638.

Burrows, R. and Mould, C. A. (2000a) *Historic Town-Plan Analysis and Archaeological Evaluation of Manzoni Gardens, Birmingham City Centre*. Birmingham University Field Archaeology Unit Report No. 703.

Burrows, R. and Mould, C. A. (2000b) *Historic Town-Plan Analysis and Archaeological Evaluation of the Open Markets, Birmingham City Centre*. Birmingham University Field Archaeology Unit Report No. 704.

Buteux, S. (2003) *Beneath the Bull Ring: the archaeology of life and death in early Birmingham*. Studley, Brewin Books.

Buteux, V. (1994) *Watching Brief at the Hop Pole, Leominster (HWCM 21465)*. Hereford and Worcester County Archeological Service Internal Report 290 December 1994.

Butler, R. and Green, C. (2003) *English Bronze Cooking Vessels and their Founders 1350–1830*. Somerset, Acanthus Press Ltd.

Camden, W. (1586) *Britannia* (1789 edition ed. R. Gough).

Cameron (1998) *Leather and Fur*. London, Archetype Publications.

Carrott, J. and Kenward, H. K. (2001). Species associations amongst insect remains from urban archaeological deposits and their significance in reconstructing the past human landscape. *Journal of Archaeological Science* 28, 887–905.

Cattell, J., Ely, S. and Jones, B. (2002) *The Birmingham Jewellery Quarter*. London, English Heritage.

Charleston, R. J. (1990) Vessel glass of the late medieval to modern periods. In M. Biddle (ed.) *Object and Economy in Medieval Winchester*, 934–947.

Churcher, C. and Richardson, M. (1978) Equidae. In V. J. Maglio and H. B. S. Cooke (eds) *Evolution of African Mammals*, 379–422. Cambridge (Mass.) and London, Harvard University Press.

Ciaraldi, M. (2000) Plant remains. In Patrick, C. *The Row Birmingham City Centre, West Midlands. An archaeological watching brief*. Birmingham University Field Archaeology Unit Report No. 635, 7–8.

Ciaraldi, M. (2002a) The plant remains. In C. Mould *An Archaeological Evaluation and Excavation at Moor Street, Birmingham City Centre 2000. Post-excavation assessment and research design*. Birmingham University Field Archaeology Unit Report No. 687, 24–26.

Ciaraldi, M. (2002b) The charred and waterlogged plant remains. In B. Burrows and H. Martin *Park Street, Birmingham City Centre: archaeological investigations 2001. Post-excavation assessment and research design*. Birmingham University Field Archaeology Unit Report No. 776, 29–39.

Ciaraldi, M. (2002c) The plant remains: evidence of tanning. In J. Williams *Floodgate Street, Birmingham City Centre. Archaeological investigations 2002. Post-excavation assessment and research design.* Birmingham University Field Archaeology Unit Report 909.

Ciaraldi M., Cuttler R., Dingwall, L. and Dyer, C. (2004) Medieval tanning and retting at Brewood, Staffordshire: archaeological excavations 1999–2000. *Transactions of the Staffordshire Archaeological and Historical Society* 40, 1–55.

Clark, K. M. (1995) The later prehistoric and protohistoric dog: the emergence of canine diversity. *Archaeozoologia* 7 (2), 9–32.

Conheeney, J. (1997) The human bone. In C. Thomas, B. Sloane, and C. Phillpotts *Excavations at the Priory and Hospital of St. Mary's Spital, London.* Museum of London Archaeology Service Monograph 1. London, Museum of London Archaeology Service, Medieval Monasteries Series.

Cook, M. and Rátkai, S. (1995) *Excavation at 131–148 High Street, Bordesley, Birmingham.* Hereford and Worcester County Archaeological Service Report 1179.

Court, W. H. B. (1938) *The Rise of the Midland Industries.* London, Oxford University Press.

Cowell, M. R. (1993) Ceramic building materials. In S. Margeson *Norwich Households*, 163–168.

Crabtree, P. (1989) *West Stow, Suffolk: Early Anglo-Saxon animal husbandry.* East Anglian Archaeology 47.

Crawford, R. (1984) Turkey. In I. Mason *Evolution of Domesticated Animals*, 325–334. London, Longman.

Crossley, D. W. (1981) *Medieval Industry* (Council for British Archaeology Research Report 40). York, Council for British Archaeology.

Cuddeford, M. J. (1994) *Identifying Metallic Small Finds.* Ipswich Suffolk, Anglia Publishing.

Cullum, P. H. (1993) St. Leonard's Hospital York: the spatial and social analysis of an Augustinian Hospital. In R. Gilchrist and H. Mytum (eds) *Advances in Monastic Archaeology.* British Archaeological Reports, British Series 227. Oxford, British Archaeological Reports.

Davey, P. (ed.) (1979) *The Archaeology of the Clay Tobacco Pipe, I.* British Archaeological Reports, British Series No. 63, 255–278. Oxford, British Archaeological Reports.

Davey, P. (ed.) (1985) *The Archaeology of the Clay Tobacco Pipe, IX. More pipes from the Midlands and Southern England.* British Archaeological Reports, British Series No 146(i), 237–289. Oxford, British Archaeological Reports.

Davis, S. J. M. (1980) Late Pleistocene and Holocene equid remains from Israel. *Zoological Journal of the Linnean Society* 70 (3), 289–312.

Davis, S. J. M. (1992) *A Rapid Method for Recording Information About Mammal Bones From Archaeological Sites.* London, English Heritage AML report 19/92.

Demidowicz, T. (1994) *Back to Back in Birmingham.* Birmingham, Birmingham City Council.

Demidowicz, G. (2003) The Hersum Ditch, Birmingham and Coventry: a local topographical term? *Transactions of the Birmingham and Warwickshire Archaeological Society* 106 for 2002, 143–150.

Department of the Environment (1990) *PPG 16: Planning Policy Guidance: Archaeology and Planning.*

Diderot, D. (1772) *Encyclopédie, ou Dictionnaire raisonné des Sciences, des Arts et des Métiers, par une société de gens de lettres.* Geneva.

Diderot, D. (1993) *A Diderot Pictorial Encyclopedia of Trades and Industry*, Volume 2. New York, Dover Publications.

Dive, J. and Eisenmann, V. (1991) Identification and discrimination of first phalanges from Pleistocene and modern *Equus*, wild and domestic. In Meadow and Uerpmann (eds) *Equids in the Ancient World*, Volume 2, pp. 278–333.

Dodds N. and Rátkai S. in prep *Park Street, Birmingham in the 18th and 19th centuries: an historical-archaeological study.*

Driesch, A., von den (1976) *A Guide to the Measurement of Animal Bones from Archaeological Sites.* Harvard, Peabody Museum Bulletin 1, Cambridge Mass., Harvard University.

Duncan, C. (2000) *The Comparative Paleopathology of Males and Females in English Medieval Skeletal Samples in its Social Context.* Unpublished Ph.D. thesis, University of Leicester.

Dungworth, D. (2000) A note on the analysis of crucibles and moulds. *Historical Metallurgy* 34, 83–87.

Dungworth, D. (2001) *Metal Working Evidence from Housesteads Roman Fort, Northumberland.* Centre for Archaeology Report 109/2001. London, English Heritage.

Dungworth, D. B. (2002) *Analysis of Post-Medieval Lead-Tin Alloy, Copper Alloy and Glass Artefacts from Southwark, London.* Centre for Archaeology Report 64/2002. London, English Heritage.

Dyer, A. (1981) Urban housing: a documentary study of four midland towns 1500–1700. *Post-Medieval Archaeology* 15, 207–218.

Eapinoza, E. O. and Mann, M-J. (1991) *Identification Guide for Ivory and Ivory Substitutes.* CITES 1999 online reprint http://www.cites.org/eng/resources/publications.shtml

Edwards H. G. M., Farwell, D. W., Holder, J. M. and Lawson E. E. (1998) Fourier Transform-Raman spectroscopy of ivory: a non-destructive diagnostic technique. *Studies in Conservation* 43, No. 1, 9–16.

Egan, G. (1998a) *Medieval Finds from Excavations in London 6: The Medieval Household, daily living c. 1150 – c. 1450.* London, Stationery Office.

Egan, G. (1998b) Weighing apparatus. In G. Egan (1998) *Medieval Finds from Excavations in London 6: The Medieval Household, daily living c. 1150 – c. 1450*, 301–329. London, Millennium.

Egan, G. and Henig, M. (1984) In Hassall, T.G., Halpin, C.E. and Mellor, M. 1984, 229.

Egan, G. and Pritchard, F. (1991) *Medieval Finds from Excavations in London: 3. Dress Accessories c. 1150–c. 1450.* London, Stationery Office.

Eisenmann, V. (1981) Étude des dents jugales inferieures des *Equus* (Mammalia, Perissodactyla) actuels et fossiles. *Palaeovertebrata* 10, 127–226.

Eisenmann, V. (1986) Comparative anatomy of modern and fossil horses, half-asses and asses. In R. H. Meadow and H-P. Uerpmann (eds) *Equids in the Ancient World*, Volume I, 67–116.

Ellis, S. E. and Moore, D. T. (1990) Sharpening and grinding stones. In M. Biddle (ed.) *Object and Economy in Medieval Winchester*, 868–881.

Elville E. M. (1961) *The Collector's Dictionary of Glass.* London, Country Life publication.

English Heritage (1991) *Exploring Our Past: strategies for the archaeology of England.* London, English Heritage.

Everton, R. (1976) Human bones. In P. Rahtz and S. Hirst *Bordesley Abbey, Redditch, Hereford-Worcestershire: first report on excavations 1969–1973.* British Archaeological

Reports, British Series 23, 216–221. Oxford, British Archaeological Reports.

Fægri, K. and Iversen, J. (1989) *Textbook of Pollen Analysis* (4th edition). Chichester, Wiley.

Fleming, J. and Honour, H. (1977) *The Penguin Dictionary of Decorative Arts.* London, Viking.

Flinn, R. (1991) The human remains. In M. Hodder, Excavations at Sandwell Priory and Hall 1982–1988. *South Staffordshire Archaeological and Historical Society Transactions* 31, 115–136.

Ford, D. A. (1995) *Medieval Pottery in Staffordshire, AD800– 1600: a review.* Staffordshire Archaeological Studies No. 7.

Freeth, J. (1790) *The Political Songster; or a touch on the times &c.* Birmingham, T. Pearson.

Friday L. E. (1988) A key to the adults of the British water beetles. *Field Studies* 7.

Friendship-Taylor, D. (1993) Leather. In S. Margeson *Norwich Households,* 60–61.

Gaffney, V., White, R. and Buteux, S. (forthcoming) Wroxter, Rome and the Urban Process. Final report on the work of the Wroxeter Hinterlands Survey 1994–99.

Gaimster, D. (1997) *German Stoneware 1200–1900.* London, British Museum Press.

Gault, W. R. (1979) Warwickshire, in R. A. Alvey and W. R. Gault, *County lists of clay tobacco-pipe makers,* 392–408. In P. Davey (ed.) The Archaeology of the Clay Tobacco Pipe, I, 363–411.

Gill, C. (1930) *Studies in Midlands History.* Oxford, Clarendon Press.

Gill, C. (1952) *History of Birmingham. 1. Manor and Borough to 1865.* London, Oxford University Press.

Godden, G. (1964) *Encyclopaedia of British Pottery & Porcelain Marks.* London, Herbert Jenkins.

Gooder, E. A. (1978) Birmingham Pieces. *Transactions of the Birmingham and Warwickshire Archaeological Society* 88 for 1976–77, 135.

Gowland, W. (1921) *The Metallurgy of the Non-Ferrous Metals.* London, Charles Griffin.

Grant, A. (1982) The use of tooth wear as a guide to the age of domestic ungulates. In R. Wilson, C. Grigson and S. Payne (eds) *Ageing and Sexing Animal Bones from Archaeological Sites.* British Archaeological Reports, British Series 109, 91–108. Oxford, British Archaeological Reports.

Green, C. (1999) *John Dwight's Fulham Pottery: excavations 1971–1979.* London, English Heritage.

Greig, J. (1980) *The plant remains.* In Watts, L. (1980), 66– 72.

Greig, J. (1982) Past and present lime woods of Europe. In M. Bell and S. Limbrey (eds) *Archaeological Aspects of Woodland Ecology.* British Archaeological Reports, International Series 146, 23–55. Oxford, British Archaeological Reports.

Greig, J. (1996) Archaeobotanical and historical records compared. *Circea* 12(2) (1996 for 1995), 211–247.

Greig, J. (2002) When the Romans departed. Evidence of landscape change in Birmingham from Metchley Roman fort, Edgbaston, Birmingham. *Acta Palaeobotanica* 42(2) (Festschrift for Krystyna Wasylikowa), 177–184.

Greig, J. (2005) Pollen and waterlogged seeds. In A. Jones (ed.) Roman Birmingham 2. Metchley Roman Forts excavations 1998–2000 and 2002. The eastern and southern annexes and other investigations. *Transactions of the Birmingham and Warwickshire Archaeological Society* 108 for 2004, 75–80.

Grew, F. (1984) Small finds. In Thompson, A., Grew, F. and Schofield, J. (1984) Excavations at Aldgate, 1974. *Post-Medieval Archaeology* 18, 91–129.

Grigson, C. (1976) The craniology and relationships of four species of *Bos.* 3. Basic craniology: *Bos taurus* L. sagittal profiles and other non-measurable Characters. *Journal of Archaeological Science* 3, 115–136.

Hall, A. (1997) *Rapport Sur un Échantillon de Matière Végétale Trouvé Dans une Cuve en Bois du 16e/17e siècle à Chartres (Eure-et-Loire), France.* Reports from the Environmental Archaeology Unit, York 97/6.

Hall, A. (2000) *Comments on Plant Remains from Some Samples from Medieval and Post-Medieval 'Tan Pits' at a Site in the Bull Ring, Birmingham.* Reports from the Environmental Archaeology Unit, York (Rep. 2000/31).

Hall, A. (2002) Plant remains from medieval and post-medieval 'tanning pits'. In C. Mould *Land to the South of Edgbaston Street, Birmingham City Centre. Archaeological investigations 1997–1999. Post-excavation assessment and research design.* Birmingham University Field Archaeology Unit report No. 473, 29–32.

Hall, A. R. (forthcoming) Plant remains from medieval and post-medieval 'tanning pits'. In C. A. Mould *Land to the South of Edgbaston Street, Birmingham City Centre. Archaeological investigation 1997–1999. Post-excavation assessment and research design,* 29–32.

Hall, A. R. and Kenward, H. K. (1980) An interpretation of biological remains form Highgate, Beverley. *Journal of Archaeological Science* 7, 33–51.

Hall, A. R. and Kenward, H. K. (1990) *Environmental Evidence from the Collonia* (The Archaeology of York 14/6). London, Council for British Archaeology.

Hall, A. and Kenward, H. K. (2003) Can we identify biological indicator groups for craft, industry and other activities? In P. Murphy, and P. E. J. Wiltshire (eds) *The Environmental Archaeology of Industry* (Symposia of the Association for Environmental Archaeology 20), 114–30. Oxford, Oxbow.

Hall, A. R., Kenward, H. K, Williams, D. and Greig, J. R. A. (1983) *Environment and Living Conditions at Two Anglo-Scandinavian Sites* (The Archaeology of York 14/4). London, Council for British Archaeology.

Halsted, J. (2006) *Tameside Park, Perry Barr, Birmingham: an archaeological evaluation 2006 Birmingham.* Birmingham Archaeology Report No. 1395.

Hammond, P. J. (1988) *Registered and Patented Clay Tobacco Pipes.* Privately published.

Hammond, P. J. (1991) Another Political Union pipe. *Society for Clay Pipe Research Newsletter* 29, 25.

Hansen, M. (1987) The hydrophiloidea (Coleoptera) of Fennoscandia and Denmark. *Fauna Entomologica Scandinavica.* Volume 18. Leiden and Copenhagen, Scandinavian Science Press.

Harcourt, R. A. (1974) The dog in prehistoric and early historic Britain. *Journal of Archaeological Science* 1, 151–175.

Harris, S. (1977) Spinal arthritis (Spondylosis Deformans) in the red fox, *Vulpes vulpes,* with some methodology of relevance to zooarchaeology. *Journal of Archaeological Science* 4, 183–195.

Hartley, D. (1985) *Food in England.* London, Futura.

Hassall, T. G., Halpin, C. E. and Mellor, M. (1984) Excavations in St Ebbes, Oxford 1967–76: Part II: Post-medieval domestic tenements and the post-dissolution site of the Greyfriars. *Oxoniensia* 49, 175–265.

Hayes, L. (2006) *City Park Gate, Birmingham. Report on an archaeological evaluation.* Gifford report no. 13510.

Hayfield, C. and Greig, J. (1989) *Excavation and salvage work on a moated site at Cowick, South Humberside 1976.* Yorkshire Archaeological Journal 61, 41–70.

Hedges, A. A. C. (1996) *Bottles and Bottle Collecting.* Princes Risborough, Shire Publications.

Heighway, C. M. (ed.) (1972) The Erosion of History: archaeology and planning in towns (Council for British Archaeology, Urban Research Committee).

Higgins D. A. (1985) Leicester clay tobacco pipes. In P. Davey (ed.) *The Archaeology of the Clay Tobacco Pipe, IX,* 291–307.

Higgins, D. A. (1986) The clay tobacco pipes. In D. Barker and M. Holland, Two post-medieval pit groups from Stafford, *Staffordshire Archaeological Studies,* New Series No. 3, Stoke-on-Trent City Museum and Art Gallery, 101–117.

Higgins, D. A. (1987a) *The Interpretation and Regional Study of Clay Tobacco Pipes: a case study of the Broseley district.* Unpublished Ph.D. thesis, University of Liverpool.

Higgins. D. A. (1987b) The clay tobacco pipes. In M. J. Kershaw, An 18th century pit group from Stafford. *Staffordshire Archaeological Studies,* New Series No. 4, 60–85.

Higgins, D. A. (1988) The Brittain family of pipemakers. *Society for Clay Pipe Research Newsletter* 20, 9–11.

Higgins, D. A. (1996) Clay tobacco pipes. In C. Mould, Archaeological excavations at the former Hanson's Brewery Site, High Street, Dudley. *Transactions of the Worcestershire Archaeological Society,* 3rd Series 15, 334–338 (317–342).

Higgins, D. A. and Davey, P. J. (1994) Draft Guidelines for using the clay tobacco pipe record sheets. Appendix 4 in S. D. White (2004) *The Dynamics of Regionalisation and Trade: Yorkshire Clay Tobacco Pipes c.1600–1800.* British Archaeological Reports, British Series 374. Oxford, Archaeopress.

Higgins, R. A. (1974) *Engineering Metallurgy 2. Metallurgical process technology.* London, Edward Arnold (Hodder and Stoughton).

Higham, C. F. W. (1969) The metrical attributes of two samples of bovine limb bones. *Journal of the Zoogical Society of London* 157, 63–74.

Hillson, S. (1996) *Dental Anthropology.* Cambridge, Cambridge University Press.

Hinton, D. A. (1990) Chapes. In M. Biddle (ed.) *Object and Economy in Medieval Winchester,* 1082–1083.

Hinton, P. (ed.) (1988) *Excavations in Southwark 1973–1976 and Lambeth 1973–79.* Joint Publication No. 3. London and Middlesex Archaeological Society and Surrey Archaeological Society.

Hodder, M. A. (1992) Excavations in Wednesbury, 1988 and 1989. The medieval and post-medieval settlement, and the 17th century pottery industry. *Transactions of the South Staffordshire Archaeological and Historical Society* 32, 96–115.

Hodder, M. A. (2004) *Birmingham: the hidden history.* Stroud, Tempus Publishing.

Hodder, M. A. and Glazebrook, J. (1987) Excavations at

Oakeswell Hall, Wednesbury, 1983. *Transactions of the South Staffordshire Archaeological and Historical Society* 27, 64–77.

Holt, R. (1985) *The Early History of the Town of Birmingham 1166–1600.* Dugdale Society Occasional Paper 30.

Holt, R. (1995) The historical background. In S. Litherland *An Archaeological Assessment of the Digbeth Economic Regeneration Area and Cheapside Industrial Area.* Birmingham University Field Archaeology Unit Report No. 337.

Hope, A. (1990) *Londoner's Larder: English cuisine from Chaucer to the present.* Edinburgh, Mainstream Publishing.

Hovey, J. (1999) *An Archaeological Evaluation at The Row Market, Edgbaston Street, Birmingham City Centre.* Report No. 603.

Howes, F. N. (1953) *Vegetable Tanning Agents.* London, Butterworths.

Hunt, J. and Klemperer, W. (2003) Staffordshire in the medieval period, WMRRFA Seminar 5. www.arch-ant.bham.ac.uk/wmrrfa

Hurst, D. (1992) Pottery. In S. Woodiwiss (ed.) *Iron Age and Roman Salt Production and the Medieval Town of Droitwich: reports of excavations at the Old Bowling Green and Friar Street* (Council for British Archaeology Research Report No. 81), 132–157. London, Council for British Archaeology.

Hurst, D. (2003) Medieval industry in the West Midlands, WMRRFA Seminar 5. www.arch-ant.bham.ac.uk/wmrrfa

Hurst, J. G. (1957) Saxo-Norman Pottery in East Anglia: Part II. Thetford Ware. *Proceedings of the Cambridge Antiquarian Society* 50, 29–60.

Hutton, W. (1783) *History of Birmingham* (2nd edition). Birmingham.

IGI, The International Genealogical Index, internet version consulted (2004–2005).

'Incola' (1762) The Natural History of Sutton Coldfield. *Gentleman's Magazine* 32, 403–404.

Jackson, R. and Rátkai, S. (1995) *Evaluation at 131–148 High Street, Bordesley, Birmingham.* Hereford and Worcester County Archaeological Service Report 1082. Hereford and Worcester County Council.

Jackson, W. A. (1999) *The Victorian Chemist.* Princes Risborough, Shire Publications.

Jennings, S. (1981) *Eighteen Centuries of Pottery from Norwich.* East Anglian Archaeology 13.

Jones, A. E. (1993) *High Street, Bilston, Wolverhampton. An archaeological evaluation.* Birmingham University Field Archaeology Unit Report No. 266.

Jones, G. C. (2000) *Archaeological Observation at Wrottesley Street, Birmingham.* Warwickshire Museum Report.

Jones, L., Rátkai, S. and Ellis, P. (2001) Excavations at No.15, The Green, Kings Norton, 1992. *Transactions of the Birmingham and Warwickshire Archaeological Society* 104 for 2000, 101–102.

Kent, D. H. (1992) *List of Vascular Plants of the British Isles.* London, Botanical Society of the British Isles.

Kenward, H. K. (1978) *The Analysis of Archaeological Insect Assemblages: a new approach* (The Archaeology of York, 19/1). Council for British Archaeology for York Archaeological Trust.

Kenward H. K. (1997) Synanthropic insects and the size, remoteness and longevity of archaeological occupation sites:

applying concepts from biogeography to past 'islands' of human occupation. *Quaternary Proceedings*. 5, 135–152.

Kenward, H. K., Engleman, C., Robertson, A. and Large, F. (1985) Rapid scanning of urban archaeological deposits for insect remains. *Circaea* 3, 163–72.

Kenward, H. K. and Hall, A. R. (1995) *Biological Evidence from Anglo-Scandinavian Deposits at 16–22 Coppergate* (The Archaeology of York 14/7). York, Council for British Archaeology.

Kenward, H. K. and Hall, A. R. (1997) Enhancing bio-archaeological interpretation using indicator groups: stable manure as a paradigm. *Journal of Archaeological Science* 24, 663–673.

Kenward, H. K., Hall, A. R. and Jones, A. K. G. (1980) A tested set of techniques for the extraction of plant and animal macrofossils from waterlogged archaeological Deposits. *Scientific Archaeology* 22, 3–15.

Kershaw, M. (1987) An 18th century pit group from Stafford. *Staffordshire Archaeological Studies* 4, 60–85.

Kiesewalter, L. (1888) *Skelettmessungen an Pferden als Beitrag zur theoretischen Grundlage der Beurteilungslehre des Pferdes*. Leipzig. Dissertation.

Kilmurry, K. (1980) *The Pottery Industry of Stamford, Lincs., A.D. 850–1250*. British Archaeological Reports, British Series 84. Oxford, British Archaeological Reports.

Koch, K. (1992) *Die Kafer Mitteleuropas. Okologie*. Band 3. Goeke and Evers, Krefeld.

Kracowicz, R. and Rudge, A. (2004) *Masshouse Circus, Birmingham City Centre, Arcaheological recording 2002*. Birmingham Archaeology project number 923.

Kratochvil, Z. (1969) Species criteria on the distal section of the tibia in *Ovis ammon* F. *aries* L. and *Capra aegagrus* F. *hircus* L. *Acta Veterinaria* (Brno) 38, 483–490.

Langford, J. A. (1868) *A Century of Birmingham Life; or, a chronicle of local events, from 1741 to 1841* (2 volumes). Birmingham.

Lea, E. (2001) *Park Street Clay Tobacco Pipes: an analysis*. M.A. in Practical Archaeology Project, University of Birmingham.

Lea, R. (2002) *The Story of Sutton Coldfield*. Stroud, Sutton Publishing.

van Lemmen, H. (2000) *Medieval Tiles*. Princes Risborough, Shire Publications.

Limbrey, S. (1980) The moat sediment. In Watts, L. (1980), 66.

Linnane, S. (2004) *Archaeological Excavation, 4–6 Ardee Street, The Coombe*. Archaeological Consultancy Services Ltd Internal Report, Ref 03_28.

Litherland, S., Jones, L., Holt, R. and Baker, N. J. (1995) *An Archaeological Assessment of the Digbeth Economic Regeneration Area and Cheapside Industrial Area, Birmingham*. Birmingham University Field Archaeology Unit Report No. 337.

Litherland, S. and Moscrop, D. (1996) *Hartwell (Smithfield) Garage Site, Digbeth, Birmingham: an archaeological evaluation*. Birmingham University Field Archaeology Unit Report project number 336.02.

Litherland, S. and Mould, C. A. (1997) *An Archaeological Desk-Based Assessment of the Proposed Martineau Galleries Development, Birmingham City Centre*. Birmingham University Field Archaeology Unit Report No. 479.

Litherland, S., Mould, C. A. and Rátkai, S. (1994) *The Old Crown Inn Deritend: an archaeological evaluation*. Birmingham University Field Archaeology Unit Report No. 310.

Litherland, S. and Watt, S. (2000) *An Archaeological Desk-Based Assessment of Land at Upper Dean Street, Birmingham City Centre*. Birmingham University Field Archaeology Unit Report 730.

de Lotbiniere, S. (1977) The study of the English gunflint, some theories and queries. *Journal of Arms and Armour Society* 9, 18–53.

Lucht, W. H. (1987) *Die Käfer Mitteleuropas. Katalog*. Krefeld, Goecke and Evers.

Macey, E. (2002) The tile. In B. Burrows and H. Martin *Park Street, Birmingham City Centre: archaeological investigations 2001. Post-excavation assessment and research design*. Birmingham University Field Archaeology Unit Report No. 776, 21–22.

MacGregor, A. (1984) *Bone Antler Ivory and Horn. The technology of skeletal materials since the Roman period*. London, Croom Helm.

McKenna, J. (2005) *Birmingham: the building of a city*. Stroud, Tempus.

McKenna, J. (2006) *Central Birmingham Pubs, Volume II* (Images of England Series). Stroud, Tempus.

Malim, C. (2005) Medieval and post-medieval structures at Coleshill Street, Sutton Coldfield. *Transactions of the Birmingham and Warwickshire Archaeological Society* 109 for 2005, 55–73.

Manaseryan, N. H., Dobney, K. and Ervynck, A. (1999) On the causes of perforations in archaeological domestic cattle skulls: new evidence. *International Journal of Osteoarchaeology* 9, 74–75.

Margeson, S. (1993) *Norwich Households: the medieval and post-medieval finds from Norwich Survey Excavations 1971–1978*. East Anglian Archaeology Report No. 58. The Norwich Survey/Norfolk Museums Service, University of East Anglia.

Martin, H. (2004) *170 High Street Deritend, Birmingham: archaeological evaluation 2004*. Birmingham Archaeology project number 1143.

Martin, H. (2005) *149–159 High Street Bordesley, Birmingham: an archaeological desk-based assessment and field evaluation, 2005*. Birmingham Archaeology project number 1285.

Martin, H. and Rátkai, S. (2005) 'The Dirty Brook': excavations at Dean House, Upper Dean Street, Birmingham. *Transactions of the Birmingham and Warwickshire Archaeological Society* 109 for 2005, 75–84.

Matolcsi, J. (1970) Historische Erforschung der Körpergröße des Rindes auf Grund von ungarischem Knochenmaterial. *Zeitschrif für Tierzüchtung und Züchtungsbiologie, Hamburg* 87, 89–137.

Matthews, K. (1999) Familiarity and contempt. In S. Tarlow and S. West (eds) *The Familiar Past*, 155–178. London, Routledge.

Matthews, L. G. (1971) *Antiques of Pharmacy*. London, G. Bell and Sons.

Mayes, P. and Scott, K. (1984) *Pottery Kilns at Chilvers Coton Nuneaton*. Society for Medieval Archaeology Monograph Series 10.

Mays, S. (1991) *The Medieval Blackfriars from the Blackfriars*

Friary, Ipswich, Suffolk (excavated 1983–1985). Ancient Monuments Laboratory Report, 16/91.

McKenna, J. (1979) *Birmingham as it was*. Birmingham, Birmingham Public Libraries.

Meadow, R. H. and Uerpmann H-P. (eds) (1986–91) *Equids in the Ancient World*, 2 volumes, Beheifte zum Tübinger Atlas des Vorderen Orients, Reihe A (naturwissenschaften) 19/1 and 19/2, Wiesbaden, Dr Ludwig Reichert Verlag.

Megaw, J. V. S. (1984) The bone objects and miscellaneous small finds. In J. P. Allan (ed.) *Medieval and Post-Medieval Finds*, 349–352.

Mellor, M. (1994) Oxfordshire pottery: a synthesis of middle and late Saxon, medieval and early post-medieval pottery in the Oxford region. *Oxoniensia* 59, 17–217.

Melton, N. (1990) Birmingham Political Union pipes. *Society for Clay Pipe Research Newsletter* 28, 17–21.

Melton, N. (1991) The Brittain family at Wednesbury – some further notes. *Society for Clay Pipe Research Newsletter* 30, 1–4.

Melton, N. D. (1997) *Clay Tobacco Pipes and Pipemaking in Northern Warwickshire*. Unpublished M.Phil. thesis, University of Liverpool.

Miller, G. L. (1980) Classification and economic scaling of 19th century ceramics. *Historical Archaeology* 14, 1–40.

Miller, G. L. (1987) The origin of Josiah Wedgwood's pearlware. *Northeast Historical Archaeology* 16, 80–92.

Miller, G. L. (1991) A revised set of CC index values for classification & economic scaling of English ceramics from 1787–1880. *Historical Archaeology* 25, 1–25.

Mills, A. and McDonnell, J. G. (1992) *The Identification and Analysis of the Hammer Scale from Burton Dasset, Warwickshire*. Ancient Monuments Laboratory Report 47/92. London, English Heritage.

Mitchell, W. (2005) *Archaeological Excavation at the Former Tally Ho! Site, Edgbaston*. Ironbridge Archaeology Series Report No. 164.

Moffett, L. C. and Smith, D. N. (1996) Insects and plants from a late medieval tenement in Stone, Staffordshire. *Circaea* 12(2), 157–175.

Molera, J., Pradell, T., Salvadó, N. and Vendrell-Saz, M. (1999) Evidence of tin oxide recrystallization in opacified lead glazes. *Journal of the American Ceramics Society* 82, 2871–2875.

Molyneux (1984) *29–30 Park Street, Birmingham*. Unpublished report, held at Birmingham Museums and Art Gallery.

Moore, S. (1999) *Cutlery for the Table: a history of British table and pocket cutlery*. Sheffield, Hallamshire Press.

Morgan, J. P., Ljunggren, G. and Read, R. (1967) Spondylosis deformans (vertebral osteophytosis) in the dog. *Journal of Small Animal Practice* 8, 57–66.

Mould, C. A. (1998) *An Archaeological Watching Brief of the Proposed Martineau Galleries Development, Birmingham City Centre*. Birmingham University Field Archaeology Unit Report.

Mould, C. A. (1999) *An Archaeological Desk-Based Assessment of Part of the Digbeth Millennium Quarter, Birmingham City Centre*. Birmingham University Field Archaeology Unit Report No. 575.

Mould, C. A. (2001a) *The Custard Factory, Phase Two, Digbeth, Birmingham. Archaeological excavation 2000, post-excavation assessment and research design*. Birmingham Archaeology Report No. 664.

Mould, C. A. (2001b) *Land to the South of Edgbaston Street, Birmingham City Centre. Archaeological investigations 1997–1999. Post-excavation assessment and research design*. Birmingham Archaeology Report No. 473.

Mould, C. A. (2001c) *Martineau Galleries Development Phases 1 and 2: Lower Bull Street/Corporation Street Birmingham City Centre*. Summary Statement for Archaeological Observation and Recording.

Mould, C. A. and Litherland, S. (1995a) *A Preliminary Archaeological Assessment of the Area of Moor Street, Bull Ring and Park Street, Birmingham City Centre*. Birmingham Archaeology Report No. 353.

Mould, C. A. and Litherland, S. (1995b) *A Preliminary Archaeological Assessment of the Area of Edgbaston Street, Pershore Street, Upper Dean Street and Moat Lane, Birmingham City Centre*. Birmingham Archaeology Report No. 354.

Moxam, A. (2002) *Time, Please: a look back at Birmingham's pubs*. Smethwick, Crown Cards.

Muldoon, S. (1979) Marked clay pipes from Coventry. In P. Davey (ed.) *The Archaeology of the Clay Tobacco Pipe, I*, 255–278.

Nichol, K. and Rátkai, S. (2004) *Archaeological Excavation on the North Side of Sandford Street, Lichfield, Staffs, 2000*. Birmingham Archaeology Report No. 644.

Nilsson, A. N. and Holmen M. (1995) The aquatic Adephaga (Coleoptera) of Fennoscandia and Denmark. II. Dytiscidae. *Fauna Entomologica Scandinavica*, Volume 32.

Noddle, B. A. (1985) The animal bones. In R. Shoesmith *Hereford City Excavations. Volume 3. The Finds*, 84–95 (Council for British Archaeology Research Report no. 56). London, Council for British Archaeology.

O'Connor, T. P. (1988) *Bones from the General Accident Site, Tanner Row* (The Archaeology of York 15/2). London, Council for British Archaeology.

Office of the Deputy Prime Minister (2005) *Planning Policy Statement 1: Delivering sustainable development*. London, HMSO.

Orton, D. (2001) *A Report on the Glass Finds from Excavations at the Bull Ring, Birmingham, 1997–99*. Unpublished project for MA in Practical Archaeology 2001. University of Birmingham.

Osborne, P. J. (1980) Report on the insects from two organic deposits on the Smithfield Market site, Birmingham. In Watts, L (1980), 63–66.

Oswald, A. (1951) Finds from the Birmingham Moat. *Transactions of the Birmingham and Warwickshire Archaeological Society* 67, 79–80.

Oswald, A. H. (1962) Interim report on excavations at Weoley Castle 195–60. *Transactions of the Birmingham and Warwickshire Archaeological Society* 78, 61–85.

Oswald, A. (1964) Excavation of a thirteenth-century wooden building at Weoley Castle, Birmingham, 1960–61. *Medieval Archaeology* 6–7, 109–134.

Oswald, A. (1975) *Clay Pipes for the Archaeologist*. British Archaeological Reports 14. Oxford, British Archaeological Reports.

Oswald, A. and James, R. E. (1955) Tobacco pipes of Broseley, Shropshire – Part II, *Archaeological Newsletter* 1955 (April), 22–25.

Palliser, D. M. (1993) The topography of monastic houses in Yorkshire towns. In R. Gilchrist and H. Mytum (eds)

Advances in Monastic Archaeology, 3–9. British Archaeological Reports, British Series 227. Oxford, Tempus Reparatum.

Palmer, N. (2003) Warwickshire (and Solihull) – the medieval period, WMRRFA Seminar 5. www.arch-ant.bham.ac.uk/wmrrfa

Patrick, C. (2000) *The Row, Birmingham City Centre, West Midlands. An archaeological watching brief*. Birmingham University Field Archaeology Unit Report No. 635.

Payne, S. (1969) A metrical distinction between sheep and goat metacarpals. In P. Ucko and G. Dimbleby (eds) *The Domestication and Exploitation of Plants and Animals*, 295–305. London, Duckworth.

Payne, S. (1985) Morphological distinctions between the mandibular teeth of young sheep, *Ovis*, and goats, *Capra*. *Journal of Archaeological Science* 12, 139–147.

Payne, S. (1991) Early Holocene equids from Tall-I-Mushki (Iran) and Can Hasan III (Turkey). In R. H. Meadow and H-P. Uerpmann (eds) *Equids in the Ancient World. Volume 2*, 132–164.

Payne, S. and Bull, G. (1988) Components of variation in measurements of pig bones and teeth, and the use of measurements to distinguish wild from domestic pig remains. *Archaeozoologia* 2, 27–65.

Peacock, P. (1996) *Discovering Old Buttons*. Princes Risborough, Shire Publications.

Pearce, J. E., Vince, A. G. and Jenner, M. A. (1985) *A Dated Type Series of London Medieval Pottery. Part Two: London-Type Ware*. London and Middlesex Archaeological Society Special Paper No. 6.

Pearce, J. E., Vince, A. G. and White, R. (1982) A dated type series of London medieval pottery. Part One: Mill Green Ware. *Transactions of the London and Middlesex Archaeological Society* 33, 266–298.

Pelham, R. A. (1950) The growth of settlement and industry c. 1100 – c. 1700. In R. H. Kinvig *Birmingham and its Regional Setting. A scientific survey*, 135–158. Birmingham, British Association for the Advancement of Science.

Penniman, T. K. (1952) *Pictures of Ivory and other Animal Teeth, Bone and Antler*. Occasional Paper on Technology 5, Pitt Rivers Museum, Oxford.

Ramsey, E. (2000) *An Archaeological Watching Brief at The Row Market, Edgbaston Street, Birmingham City Centre*. Birmingham Archaeology Report No. 603.01.

Ramsey, E. (2004) *25–27 Heath Mill Lane, Deritend, Birmingham. Archaeological evaluation 2004*, Birmingham Archaeology project number 1168.

Raphaël, M. (1991) *La Pipe en Terre son Périple à Travers la France*. France, Editions Aztec.

Rátkai, S. (1987) *The Post-Medieval Coarsewares from the Motte and Keep of Dudley Castle*. Staffordshire Archaeological Studies, Museum Archaeological Society Report, New Series No. 4, 1–11.

Rátkai, S. (1990) The medieval pottery. In S. Cracknell, Bridge End, Warwick: archaeological excavation of a medieval street frontage. *Transactions of the Birmingham and Warwickshire Archaeological Society* 95 for 1987–8, 17–72.

Rátkai, S. (1992a) Medieval pottery. In S. Cracknell and M. W. Bishop, Excavations at 25–33 Brook Street, Warwick 1973. *Transactions of the Birmingham and Warwickshire Archaeological Society* 97 for 1991–92, 8–22.

Rátkai, S. (1992b) Medieval pottery. In S. Cracknell, 'Bards Walk', Wood Street, Stratford-upon-Avon. Medieval structures excavated in 1989. *Transactions of the Birmingham and Warwickshire Archaeological Society* 97 for 1991–92, 62–73.

Rátkai, S. (1994a) Pottery. In S. Cracknell, Archaeological excavation at the Minories, Stratford-upon-Avon. *Transactions of the Birmingham and Warwickshire Archaeological Society* 98 for 1993–94, 67–69.

Rátkai, S. (1994b) Medieval pottery. In S. Cracknell and C. Mahany (eds) *Roman Alcester: southern extramural area. 1964–66 excavations*, Roman Alcester Series Volume 1 (Council for British Archaeology Research Report 96–97), 154–156. York, Council for British Archaeology.

Rátkai, S. (1994c) Potters at Deritend, Birmingham. *West Midlands Pottery Research Group Newsletter* 19.

Rátkai, S. (1996) Medieval pottery (Gas House Lane and Gateway Supermarket). In S. Cracknell (ed.) *Roman Alcester: defences and defended area*. Roman Alcester Series Volume 2 (Council for British Archaeology Research Report 97). York, Council for British Archaeology.

Rátkai, S. (2000a) The pottery. In R. Burrows and C. Mould *An Archaeological Evaluation at Smithfield Hartwells Garage, Digbeth, Birmingham 1999*. Birmingham University Field Archaeology Unit Report No. 336.

Rátkai, S. (2000b) The pottery. In R. Burrows, L. Dingwall and J. Williams *Further Archaeological Investigations at Hartwell Smithfield Garage, Digbeth, Birmingham 2000*, 5. Birmingham University Field Archaeology Unit Report No. 638.

Rátkai, S. (2001a) The pottery. In L. Jones, S. Rátkai and P. Ellis, Excavations at No 15, The Green, Kings Norton 1992, 112–118. *Transactions of the Birmingham and Warwickshire Archaeological Society* 104 for 2000, 101–121.

Rátkai, S. (2001b) Explosion Site: medieval pottery. In P. Booth and J. Evans *Roman Alcester: northern extramural area, 1969–1988 excavations*, 232 and M2:D7). Roman Alcester Series Volume 3 (Council for British Archaeology Research Report 127). York, Council for British Archaeology.

Rátkai, S. (2001c) The pottery. In K. Pack *Archaeological Watching Brief of Land at Minworth Greaves Farm, Sutton Coldfield*. LP Archaeology Internal Report 2001.

Rátkai, S. (2002a) The pottery. In J. Williams *Floodgate Street, Deritend Island, Digbeth, Birmingham; archaeological excavations 2002: post-excavation assessment and updated research design*. Birmingham Archaeology Report No. 909.

Rátkai, S. (2002b) Medieval and post-medieval pottery. In P. Booth (ed.) *M6 Toll 2000–2 Proposals for Archaeological Post-Excavation Analysis and Publication of Results*. Unpublished report by Oxford Wessex Archaeology for CAMBBA, October 2002, Document Ref 49001.1, 143–156.

Rátkai, S. (2003) *Medieval Material Culture in the West Midlands* WMRRFA Seminar 5. www.arch-ant.bham.ac.uk/wmrrfa

Rátkai, S. (2004) The pottery. In K. Nichol and S. Rátkai, Archaeological excavation on the north side of Sandford Street, Lichfield, Staffs, 2000. *Transactions of the Staffordshire Archaeological and Historical Society* 40, 58–121.

Rátkai, S. (2005) The medieval and later pottery. In C.

Woodfield *The Church of Our Lady of Mount Carmel and some Conventual Buildings at the Whitefriars, Coventry*. British Archaeological Reports, British series 389, 315–325. Oxford, Archaeopress.

Rátkai S. (2007) The medieval and early post-medieval pottery. In I. Soden (ed.) *Stafford Castle: survey, excavation and research 1978–1998. Volume II – the excavations 1978–1991*. Stafford Borough Council, Stafford 57–118.

Rátkai, S. (2008) The medieval pottery. In P. Booth, A. D. Crockett, A. P. Fitzpatrick, A. B. Powell and K. E. Walker *The Archaeology of the M6 Toll, 2000–2002*. Oxford Wessex Archaeology Monograph No. 2, 491–500.

Rátkai, S. (forthcoming a) The pottery. In N. Palmer *Burton Dassett; a deserted medieval settlement in SE Warwickshire*. Society for Medieval Archaeology Monograph.

Rátkai, S. (forthcoming b) The pottery. In C. Coutts *Excavations at Park House, Warwick*.

Rátkai, S. and Soden, I. (1998) *Warwickshire Medieval and Post-Medieval Ceramic Type Series*. Unpublished manuscript held by Warwickshire Museum Archaeological Field Services.

Razi, Z. (1978) The 'big fire' of the town of Birmingham. *Transactions of the Birmingham and Warwickshire Archaeological Society* 88 for 1976–1977, 135.

Redknap, M. (1985) Twelfth and thirteenth century Coventry Wares. *Medieval Ceramics* 9, 65–78.

Redknap, M. (1996) Earlier medieval pottery. In M. Rylatt and M. Stokes *The Excavations at Broadgate* East, Coventry 1974–5. Coventry Museums Monograph Series 537–42.

Roberts, C. and Cox, M. (2003) *Health and Disease in Britain. From Prehistory to the Present Day*. Stroud, Sutton Publishing.

Roberts, C. and Manchester, K. (2005) *The Archaeology of Disease* (3rd edition). Stroud, Sutton Publishing.

Rutter, J. and Davey, P. (1980) Clay pipes from Chester. In P Davey (ed.), *The Archaeology of the Clay Tobacco Pipes, III*, British Archaeological Reports, British Series 78, 41–272. Oxford, Archaeopress.

Salaman, R. A. (1986) *Dictionary of Leather-Working Tools, c.1700–1950 and the Tools of the Allied Trades*. New Jersey, Astragal Press.

Saltzman, L. F. (1952) *Building in England down to 1540: a documentary history*. Oxford, Clarendon Press.

Schmid, E. (1972) *Atlas of Animal Bones for Prehistorians, Archaeologists and Quaternary Geologists*. Amsterdam, London and New York, Elsevier.

Selby, J. (ed.) (1998) *The Recollections of Sergeant Morris*. Moreton-in-Marsh, Windrush Press.

Serjeantson, D. (1989) Animal remains and the tanning trade. In D. Serjeantson and T. Waldron (eds) *Diet and Crafts in Towns*. British Archaeological Reports, British Series 199, 129–146. Oxford, British Archaeological Reports.

Shaw, M. (1996) The excavation of a late 15th–17th century tanning complex at The Green, Northampton. *Post-Medieval Archaeology* 30, 63–127.

Sherlock, R. J. (1957) Excavations at Deritend. *Transactions of the Birmingham and Warwickshire Archaeological Society* 73, 109–114.

Shoesmith, R. (1985) *Hereford City Excavations. Volume 3, The Finds* (Council for British Archaeology Research Report No. 56), London, Council for British Archaeology.

Singh, R. R. (in prep.) *Characterisation of Asian and African elephant ivory using various morphometric and analytical techniques*.

Skipp, V. (1970) *Medieval Yardley*. Chichester, Phillimore.

Smith, D. N. (1996) The insect remains. In A. Jones *25/26 Long Causeway, Peterborough, Cambridgeshire. An archaeological evaluation 1994*. Birmingham University Field Archaeology Unit Report No. 317.

Smith, D. N. (1997). The insect fauna. In C. Thomas, B. Sloane, and C. Philpotts (eds) *Excavations at the Priory and Hospital of St. Mary Spital, London*, 245–247. Museum of London Archaeology Service Monograph 1. London, Museum of London Archaeology Service.

Smith, D. N. (1998). *The Insect Remains from Saxon and Medieval Deposits at Ball Wharf, London*. Unpublished report to Museum of London Archaeology Service.

Smith, D. N. (2000). The insect remains from one Poultry, London. *The University of Birmingham Environmental Archaeology Services*. Report 13.

Smith, D. N. (2002). The insect remains. In B. Barber and C. Thomas *The London Charterhouse*. London, Museum of London Archaeology Service.

Smith, D. N. (2007) The insect remains. In D. Seeley, C. Phillpotts and M. Samuel (eds) *Winchester Palace: excavations at the Southwark residence of the bishops of Winchester*. Museum of London Archaeology Service Monograph 31. London, Museum of London Archaeology Service.

Smith, D. N. and Chandler, G. (2004) Insect remains. In B. Sloane and G. Malcolm (eds) *Excavations at the Priory of the Order of the Hospital of St John of Jerusalem, Clerkenwell, London*. Museum of London Archaeology Service Monograph 20. London, Museum of London.

Smith, K. G. V. (1973) *Insects and Other Arthropods of Medical Importance*. London, British Museum (Natural History).

Smith, K. G. V. (1986) A *Manual of Forensic Entomology*. London, Trustees of the British Museum.

Smith, K. G. V. (1989) *An Introduction to the Immature Stages of British Flies. Handbooks for the identification of British Insects*. Volume 10 part 14. London, Royal Entemological Society of London.

Smith, W. (2002) Charred plant remains; waterlogged plant remains. In C. Mould *Land to the South of Edgbaston Street, Birmingham City Centre. Archaeological investigations 1997–1999. Post–excavation assessment and research design*, 26–29 and 32–39. Birmingham University Field Archaeology Unit Report No. 473.

Society for Post-Medieval Archaeology (1988) *Research Priorities for Post-Medieval Archaeology*.

Stace, C.A. (2000) *New Flora of the British Isles*. 2nd edition (1st edition 1992). Cambridge, Cambridge University Press.

Starý, F. (1998) *Medicinal Herbs and Plants*. Twickenham, Tiger Books International.

Stockton, J. (1981) *Victorian Bottles: a collectors guide to yesterday's empties*. David and Charles, Newton Abbott.

Symons, D. (1984) Birmingham (West Midlands) Deritend. *West Midlands Archaeology* 27, 56.

Talbot, O. (1974) The evolution of glass bottles for carbonated drinks. *Post-Medieval Archaeology* 8, 29–62.

Tavener, N. (2000) Land on the southern corner of Park Street and Bordesley Street, Digbeth, Birmingham. A report on an archaeological evaluation, *Marches Archaeology Series* 111.

Teichert, M. (1975) Osteometrische Untersuchungen zur Berechnung der Widerristhöhe bei Schafen. In A. T. Clason (ed.) *Archaeozoological Studies*, 51–69. Amsterdam and Oxford, North-Holland Publishing.

The, T. L. and Trouth, C. O. (1976) Sexual dimorphism in the basilar part of the occipital bone of the dog (*Canis familiaris*). *Acta Anatomica* 95, 565–571.

Thompson, A., Grew, F. and Schofield, J. (1984) Excavations at Aldgate, 1974. *Post-Medieval Archaeology* 18, 1–148.

Thomson, R. (1981) Leather manufacture in the post-medieval period with special reference to Northamptonshire. *Post-Medieval Archaeology* 15.

Thursfield, T. H. (1907) Early Salopian pipes. *Transactions of the Shropshire Archaeological and Natural History Society*, 3rd Series 7, 160–165.

Timmins, S. (1866) The industrial history of Birmingham. In S. Timmins (ed.) *Birmingham and the Midland Hardware District* (Cass Library of Industrial Classics No. 7). London, Robert Hardwicke (reprint 1967. London, Frank Cass).

Tottenham, C. E. (1954) *Coleoptera Staphylinidae. Section (a) Piestinae to Euaesthetinae*. Handbooks for the Identification of British Insects 4/8 (a). London, Royal Entomological Society of London.

Toulmin Smith, L. (1964) *The Itinerary of John Leland in or about the years 1535–1543, Part V* (London, Centaur Press).

Townend, P. (1988) Bone working industry. In P. Hinton (ed.), *Excavations in Southwark*, 409–412.

Trotter, M. and Gleser, G. C. (1952) Estimation of stature from long bones of American whites and negroes. *American Journal of Physical Anthropology* 10, 46–514. Reproduced in W. M. Bass *Human Osteology: a laboratory and field manual*.

Turner, K. (1994) *Central Birmingham 1870–1920* (The Old Photographs Series). Stroud, Tempus.

Turner, J. (1866) *The Birmingham Button Trade. Birmingham and Midland hardware district*. Birmingham.

Twist, M. (2001) *Images of England: Saltley, Duddeston and Nechells*. Stroud, Tempus.

Uerpmann, H-P. (1991) Equus africanus in Arabia. In Meadow and Uerpmann (eds) *Equids in the Ancient World*. Volume 2, 12–33.

VCH Warwicks VII (1964) *A History of the County of Warwick. Volume VII: The City of Birmingham*, ed. W. B. Stephens. Oxford, Oxford University Press.

van der Veen, M. (1988) *Crop Husbandry Regimes*. Sheffield Archaeological Monographs 3. Sheffield.

Vince, A. G. (1983) Medieval white slipped pottery. *London Archaeology* 14, No. 12.

Vitt, V. (1952) Loshadi Pezyryksich kurganov. *Sovetskaja Archeologija* 16, 163–205.

von den Driesch, A. (1976) *A Guide to the Measurement of Animal Bones from Archaeological Sites*, Peabody Museum Bulletin 1, Harvard University.

Wakefield, H. (1982) *Nineteenth Century British* Glass (2nd edition). London, Faber and Faber Ltd.

Watts, L. (1980) Birmingham Moat: its history, topography and destruction. *Transactions of the Birmingham and Warwickshire Society* 89 for 1978–79, 1–77.

Watt, S. (2001) *Floodgate Street/Milk Street, Digbeth, Birmingham City Centre: an archaeological desk-based assessment*. Birmingham University Field Archaeology Unit Report No. 768.

White, D. P. (1977) The Birmingham button industry. *Post-Medieval Archaeology* 2, 67–79.

Williams, D. F. (1984) The petrology of the olive jars and Merida-type wares. In J. P. Allen *Medieval and Post-Medieval Finds from Exeter, 1971–80*.

Williams, J. (2001) *Floodgate Street, Digbeth, Birmingham: an archaeological evaluation*. Birmingham University Field Archaeology Unit Report No. 787.

Williams, J. (2002) *Floodgate Street, Deritend Island, Digbeth, Birmingham; Archaeological Excavations 2002: post-excavation assessment and updated research design*. Birmingham University Field Archaeology Unit project number 909.

Williams, J. (2003) *Deritend Bridge, Birmingham: an archaeological evaluation*. Birmingham University Field Archaeology Unit project number 1007.

Willmott, H. (2002) *Early Post-Medieval Vessel Glass in England* (Council for British Archaeology Research Report 132). York, Council for British Archaeology.

Wills, G. (1974) *English Glass Bottles for the Collector*. Edinburgh, John Bartholomew and Son.

Woodfield, C. (1981) Finds from the Free Grammar School at the Whitefriars, Coventry c.1545–1557/58. *Post-Medieval Archaeology* 15, 81–159.

Woodfield, P. (1966) Yellow glazed wares of the seventeenth century. *Transactions of the Birmingham and Wawickshire Archaeological Society* 81, 78–87.

Woodland, R. (1981) The pottery. In J. E. Mellor and T. Pearce *The Austin Friars, Leicester* (Council for British Archaeology Research Report 35), 81–129. Leicester, Leicester County Council.

Wrightson, R. (1869) *Wrightson's Triennial Directory of Birmingham: 1818*. Facsimile reprint of 1st edition, Birmingham. Newcastle upon Tyne, Graham.

Yarwood, D. (1979) *The English Home*. London, Batsford.

Zohary, D. and Hopf, M. (1994) *Domestication of Plants in the Old World: the origin and spread of cultivated plants in West Asia, Europe, and the Nile Valley* (2nd edition). Oxford, Clarendon Press.

Trade Directories (in date order)

Sketchley 1767 Sketchley's Birmingham, Wolverhampton and Walsall Directory.

Sketchley 1770 Sketchley's Birmingham, Wolverhampton and Walsall Directory.

Pearson and Rollason 1781 The Birmingham, Wolverhampton, Walsall, Dudley, Bilston and Willenhall Directory.

Pye 1787 The Birmingham Directory for the Year 1787.

Pye 1791 The Birmingham Directory for the Year 1791.

Pye 1797 The Birmingham Directory for the Year 1797.

Chapman 1801 Chapman's Birmingham Directory or alphabetical list of the merchants, tradesmen and principal inhabitants of the Town of Birmingham.

Chapman 1803 Chapman's Birmingham Directory or alphabetical list of the merchants, tradesmen and principal inhabitants of the Town of Birmingham.

Wrightson and Thomson 1812 New Triennial Directory of Birmingham.

Wrightson 1815 Triennial Directory of Birmingham.

Wrightson 1818 Triennial Directory of Birmingham.

Wrightson 1821 Triennial Directory of Birmingham.

Wrightson 1831 Wrightson's Annual Directory of Birmingham.
Post Office Directory of Birmingham 1856.
Robson 1839 Birmingham and Sheffield Directory: Birmingham, Coventry, Dudley, Wolverhampton and their immediate environs.

Kelly's Directories Ltd. *Kelly's Directory of Birmingham* for the years: 1861, 1863, 1868, 1869, 1875, 1878, 1880, 1886, 1892, 1895, 1899, 1902 and 1906.
Kelly's Directories Ltd. *Kelly's Post Office Directory of London* for the years: 1881 and 1887.

Index

Colour Plates

Fig. 2.6 Area A, Edgbaston St. under excavation.

Fig. 2.9 Deritend ware cooking pot, Area A, Edgbaston St.

Fig. 2.10 Area A, Edgbaston St.; tiled oven base F109.

Fig. 2.11 Area B, Edgbaston St., during excavation.

Fig. 2.18 Area C, Edgbaston St., after excavation, showing skin pits in foreground.

Fig. 2.24 Area A, Edgbaston St.; under excavation.

Fig. 2.30 Area D, Edgbaston St., during excavation.

Fig. 3.2 Photograph showing excavated ditch sections and major features, Moor St.

Fig. 3.7 Area A, Moor St.; photograph of ditch section F537, F538.

Fig. 3.11 Trench 8c, Moor St.; medieval well.

Fig. 4.2 Park St.; general view during excavation looking west towards Moor St.

Fig. 4.3 Park St; general view during excavation, looking south.

Fig. 4.6 Area A, Park St.; photograph through Phase 1 town/ deer park boundary ditch, F201.

Fig. 4.7 Area A, Park St.; photograph through Phase 1 town/ deer park boundary ditch, F174.

Fig. 4.8 Area C, Park St.; sections through southeastern boundary ditch (F800, F760 and F766), Phase 1.

Fig. 4.9 Area C, Park St.; section through southeastern boundary ditch (F715), Phase 1.

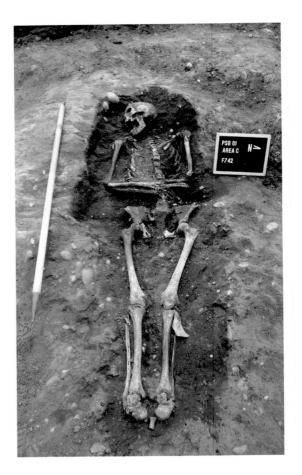

*Fig. 4.11 Area C, Park St.; section through tanning pit
F714 after removal of F803.*

Fig. 4.13 Area C, Park St., F742 female burial.

Fig. 4.14 Area B, Park St.; tank/ pond F506, Phase 2.

Fig. 4.15 Area C, Park St.; kiln F768, Phase 2.

Fig. 4.21 Area B, Park St.; tanks F503/F520 during excavation Phase 3.3.

Fig. 4.22 Area B, Park St.; section showing organic fill of F503/ F520, Phase 3.3.

Fig. 4.23 Area B, Park St.; tank F503/ F520 showing wooden chair in situ, *Phase 3.3.*

Fig. 4.24 Area B, Park St.; tank F510/ F542 under excavation, Phase 3.3.

Fig. 4.25 Area B, Park St.; tank F510/ F542 showing detail of timber lining Phase 3.3.

Fig. 4.26 Area B, Park St.; tanks F503/ F520 and F510/ F542 after excavation Phases 3.3.

Fig. 4.27 Area A, Park St.; pit F124 Phase 3.1/ 3.2.

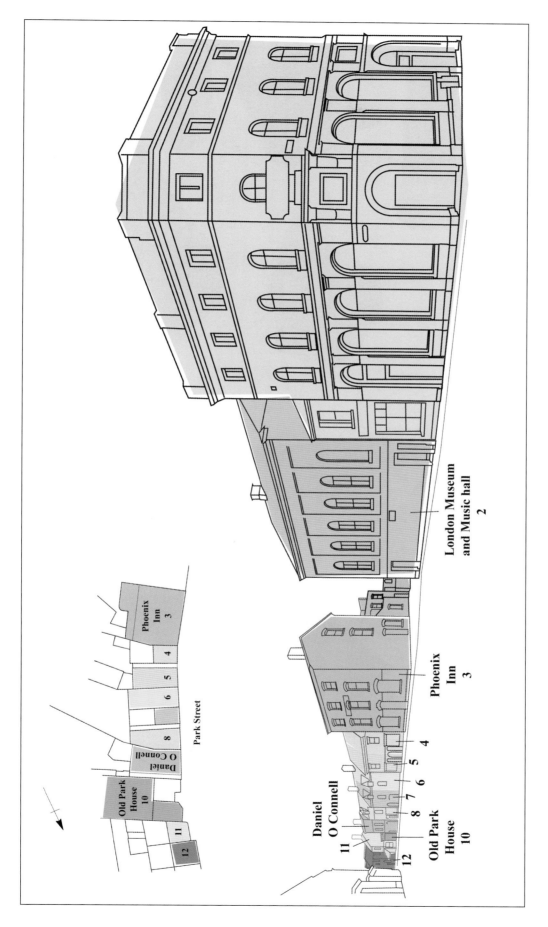

Fig. 4.35 Suggested reconstruction of buildings on Park Street based on photographs and engravings (colour).

Fig. 7.15 Deritend ware (13th–early 14th centuries).

CM

1

2

3

4

Fig. 7.16 Boarstall-Brill ware.

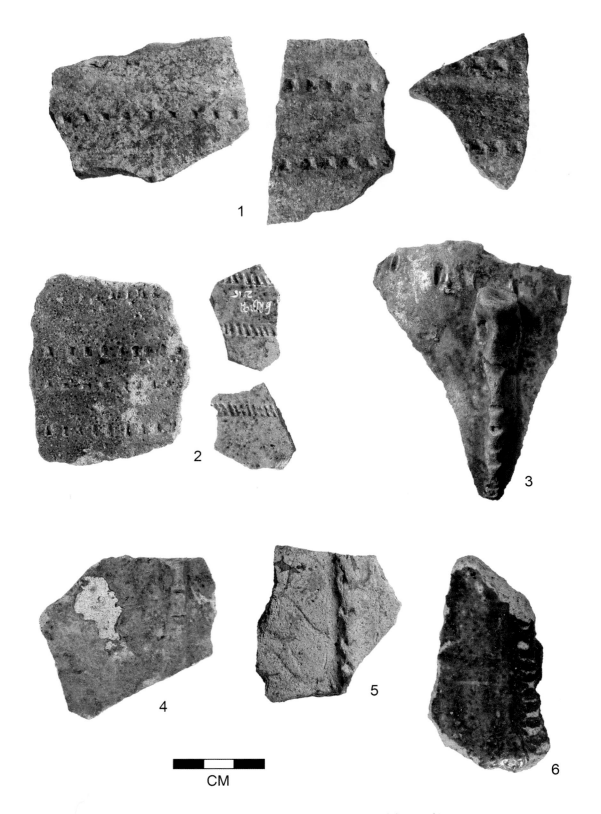

CM

Fig. 7.17 Decorated iron-poor ware (fabric ip2).

Fig. 7.18 Miscellaneous glazed wares.

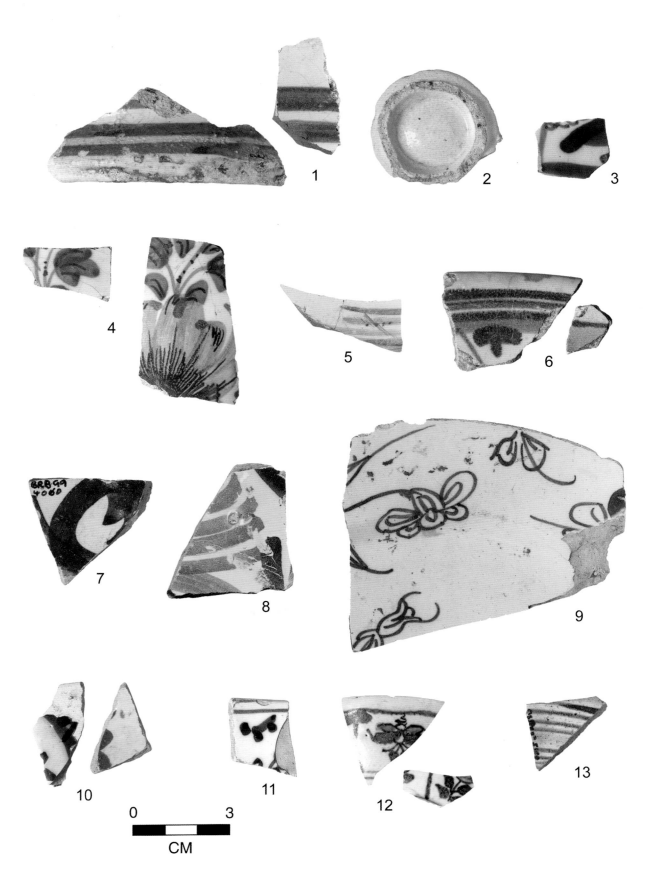

Fig. 7.19 Tin-glazed earthenwares.

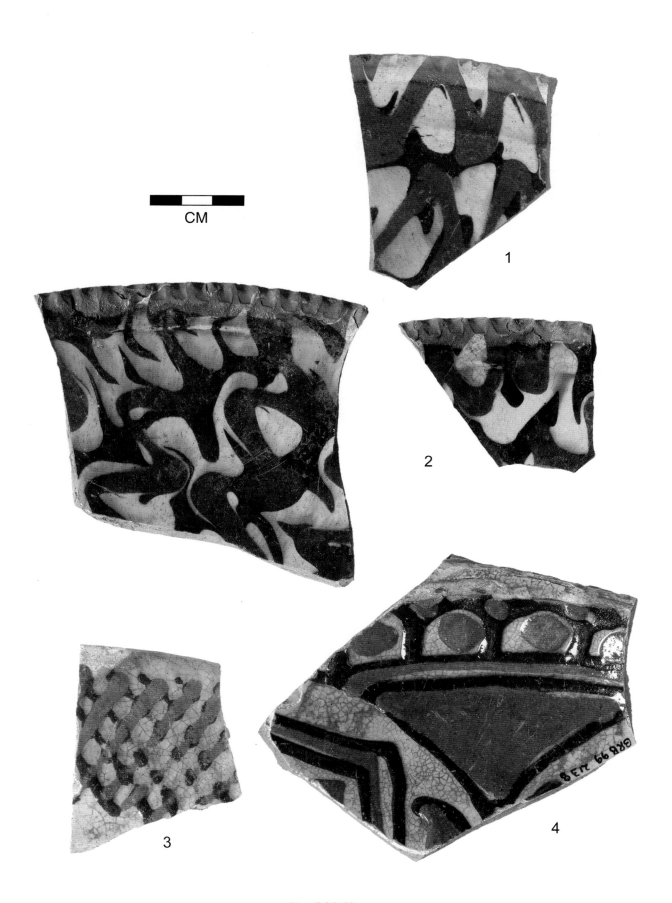

Fig. 7.20 Slipware.

Fig. 7.21 Slipware.

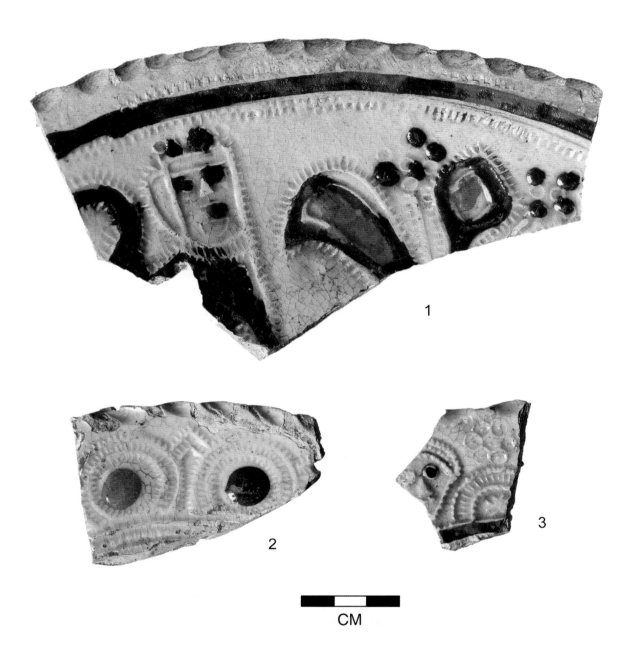

Fig. 7.22 Slipware.

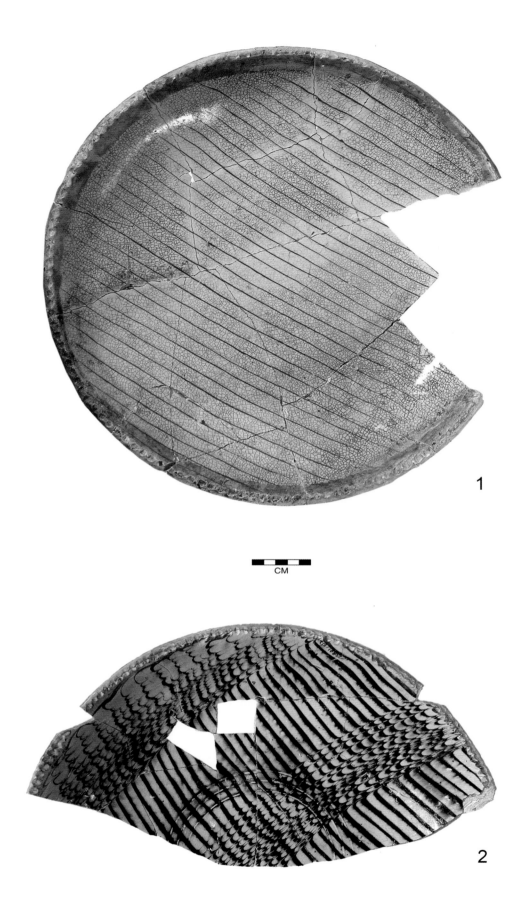

1

CM

2

Fig. 7.23 Slipware.

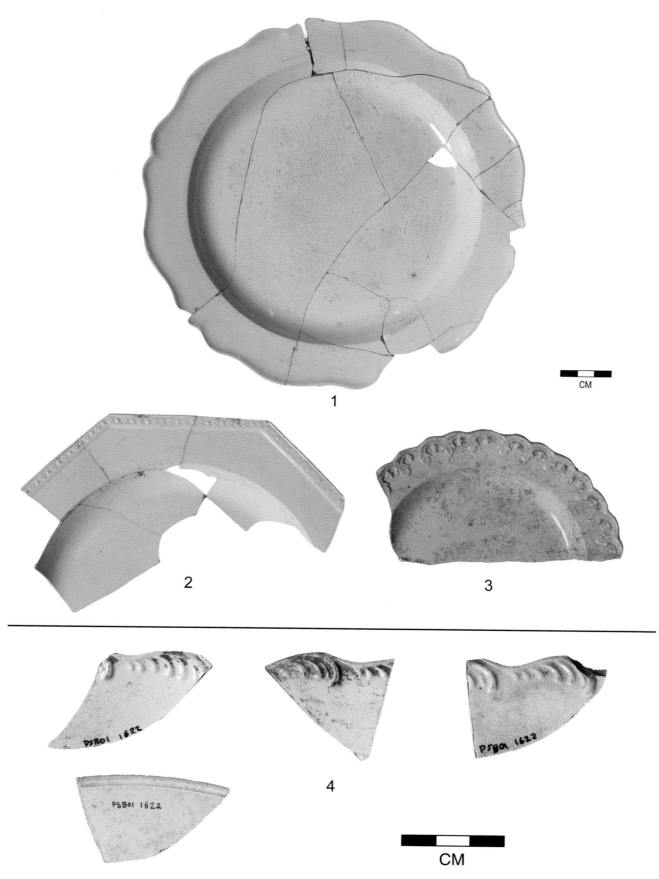

CM

1

2

3

4

CM

Fig. 7.24 Creamware (c.1760–1780).

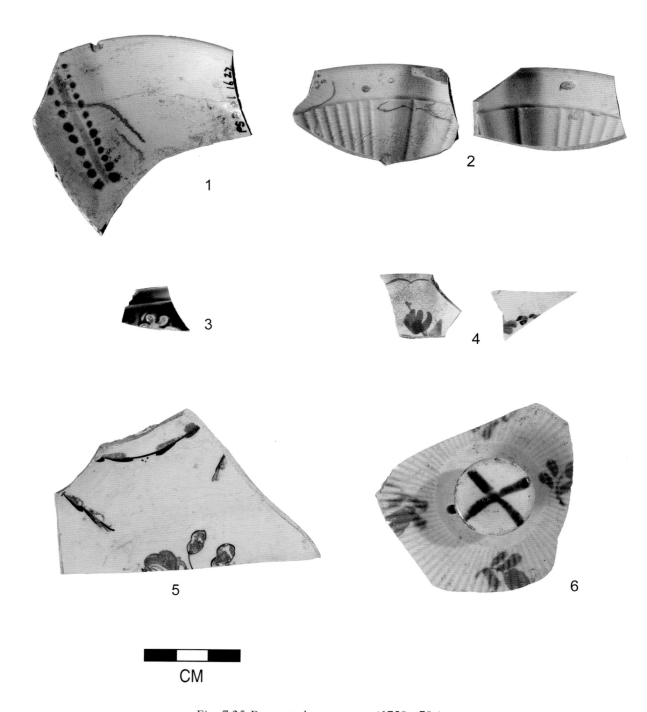

Fig. 7.25 Decorated creamware (1750s–70s).

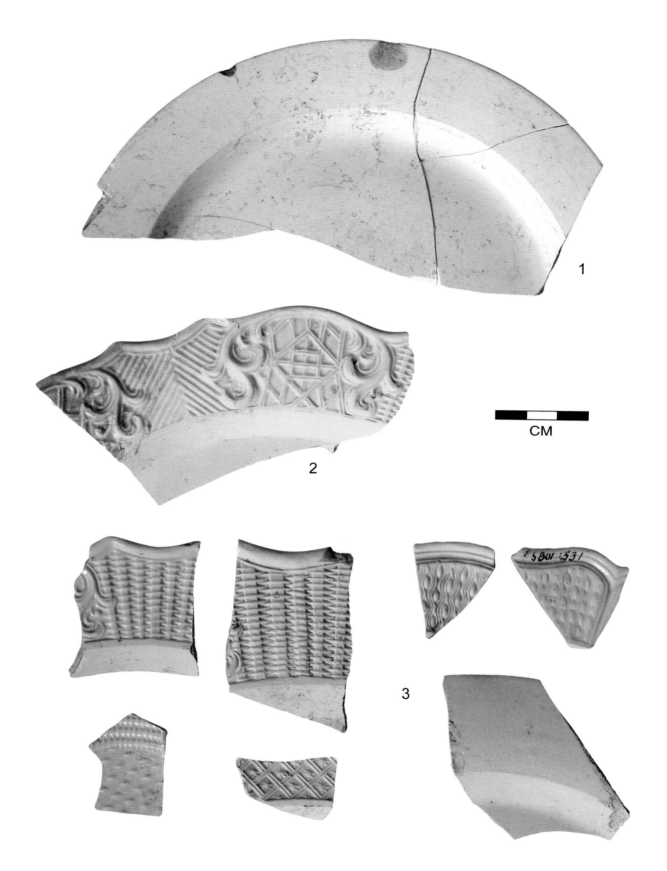

Fig. 7.26 White salt-glazed stoneware (c.1720–60).

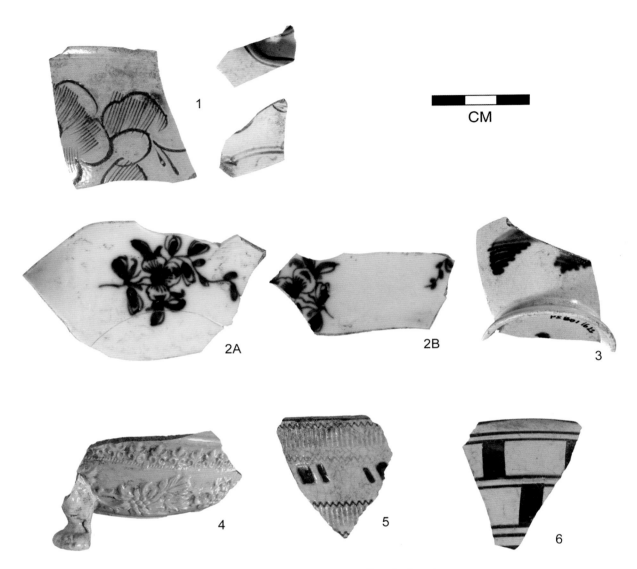

Fig. 7.27 Miscellaneous post-medieval glazed wares.

Fig. 8.2 Mid-17th century wooden chair from infill of tank F503.

1

2

3

4

cm

Fig. 8.4 Cu Alloy objects; 8.4.1 hoop earring, 8.4.2 clothing hook, 8.4.3 terminal with thread, 8.4.4 button.

Fig. 8.6 Lead, crystal and glass; 8.6.1 lead weight, 8.6.2 wine glass stem, 8.6.3 crystal seal.

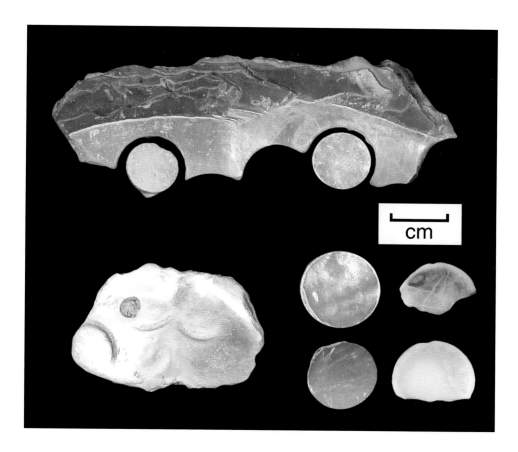

Fig. 8.7 Button making waste.

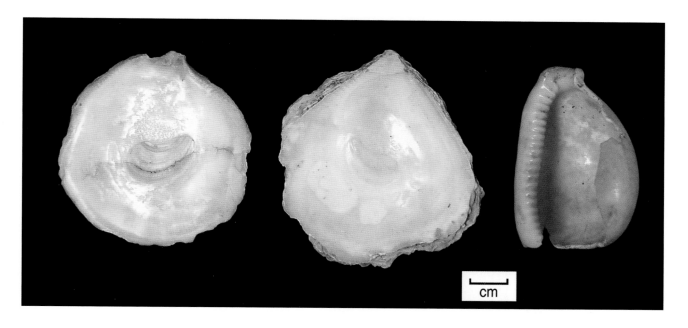

Fig. 8.8 Oyster and cowrie shells.

2

3

4

CM

5

6

1

CM

7

CM

Fig. 8.9 (opposite) Bone, ivory, horn and antler artefacts, Edgbaston St; 8.9.1 sawn elephant tusk, 8.9.2 tapered handle, 8.9.3 apple corer or cheese scoop, 8.9.4 comb fragment, 8.9.5 bone handle fragment, 8.9.6 hairbrush, 8.9.7 bone handle-working debris.

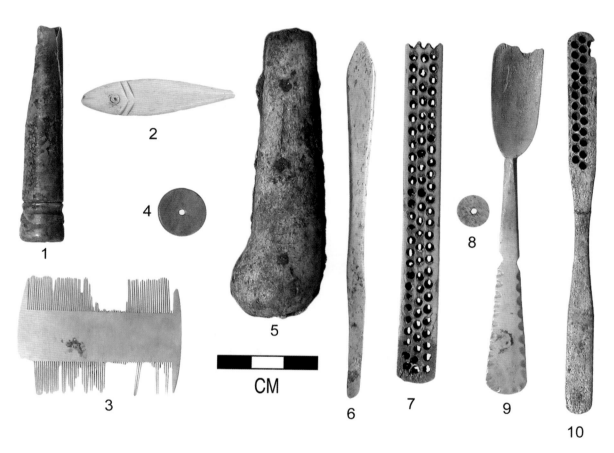

Fig. 8.10 Bone, horn and antler artefacts, Park St; 8.10.1 handle, with turned decoration, 8.10.2 carved fish, 8.10.3 comb, double sided, 8.10.4 circular button, 8.10.5 pistol-grip knife handle, 8.10.6 brush, 8.10.7 brush, 8.10.8 circular button, 8.10.9 spoon, 8.10.10 brush.

Fig. 8.11 Bone and ivory handle manufacturing, Park St; 8.11.1 tapering bone handle fragment, 8.11.2 unfinished handle terminal, 8.11.3 handle fragment, with incised cross-hatch decoration, 8.11.4 handle, 8.11.5 tapering piece of ivory, 8.11.6 unfinished handle, with curved outer face, 8.11.7 debris from the manufacture of ivory handles.

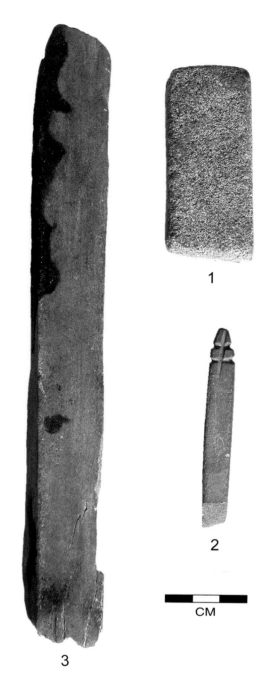

Fig. 8.12 Worked stone artefacts; 8.12.1 whetstone or rubbing stone, 8.12.2 whetstone, with a carved terminal, 8.12.3 whetstone or rubbing stone.

CM

Fig. 8.14 Ceramic tile.

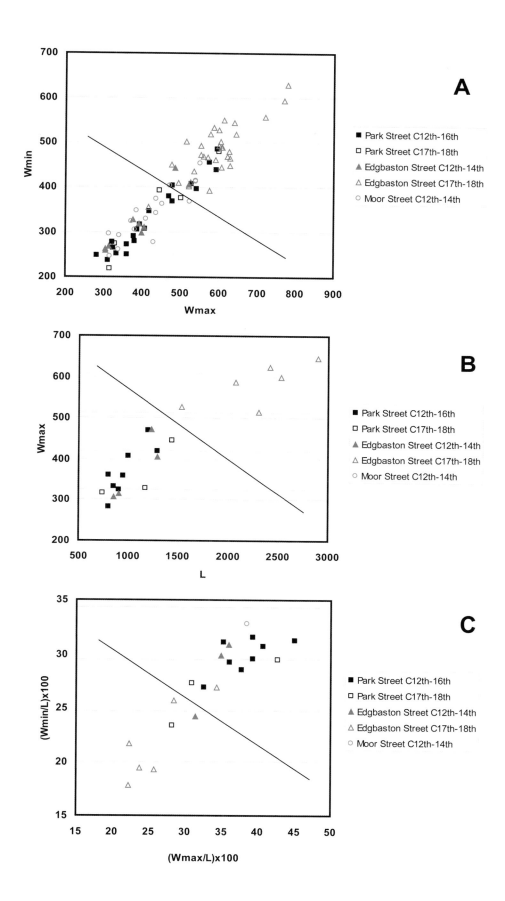

Fig. 15.3 Size (A and B) and shape (C) of cattle horncores.

Metacarpals

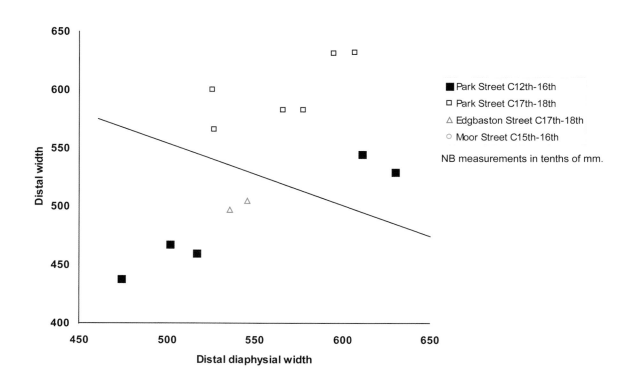

Metatarsals

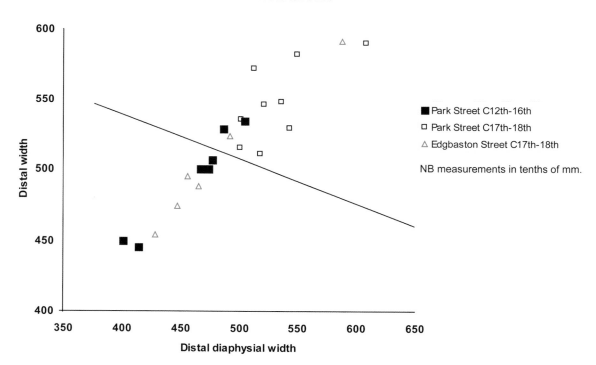

Fig. 15.4 Size of cattle metapodials (based on Higham 1969).

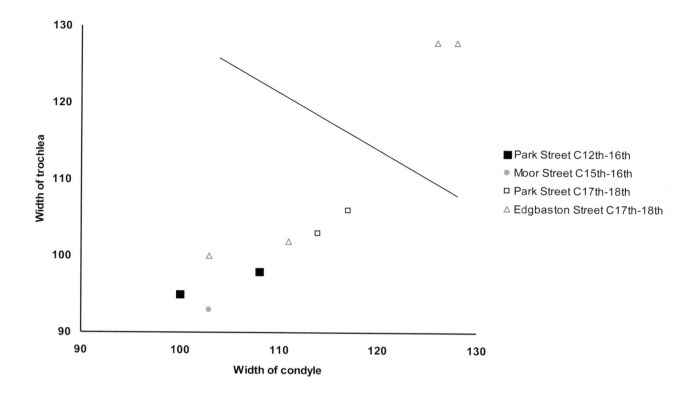

Fig. 15.5 Sheep metacarpals (based on Payne 1969 and Boessneck 1969). Numbers next to symbols refer to Index: WT.100/DV.

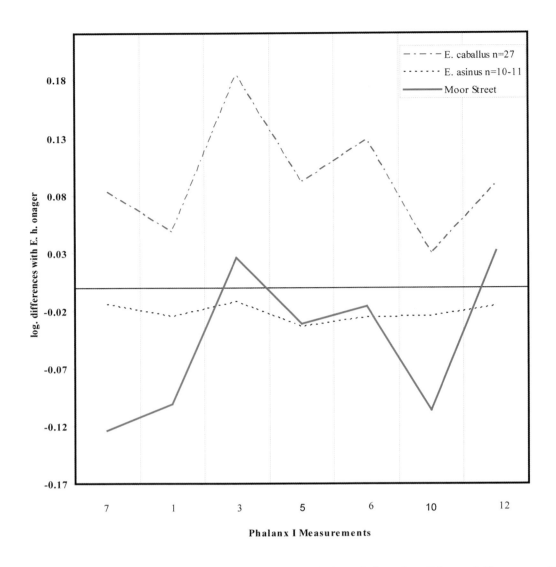

Fig. 15.6 Ratio diagrams of mean values for equid anterior phalanx 1 (based on Dive and Eisenmann 1991).

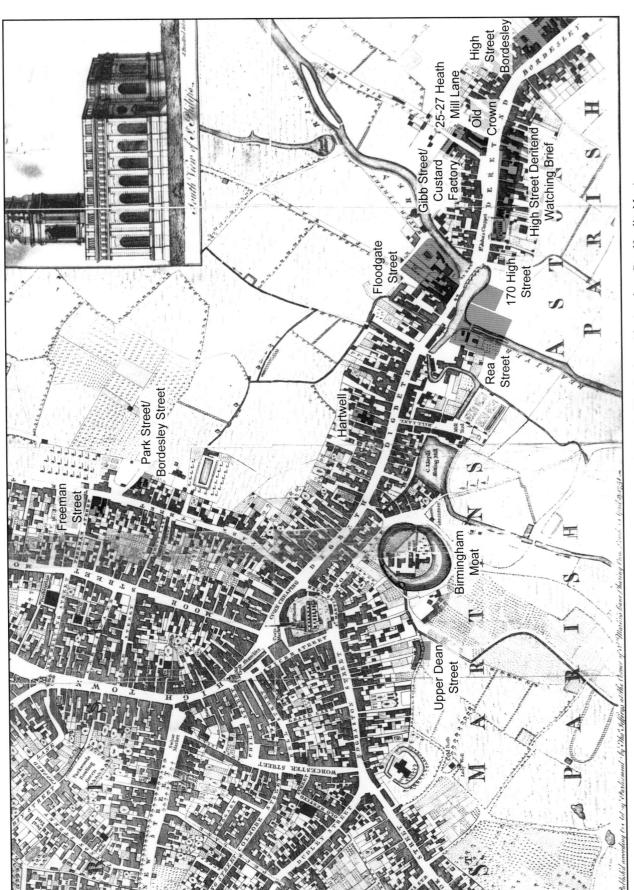

Fig. 16.1 Map illustrating the location of excavated sites in Birmingham (depicted on Bradford's Map).

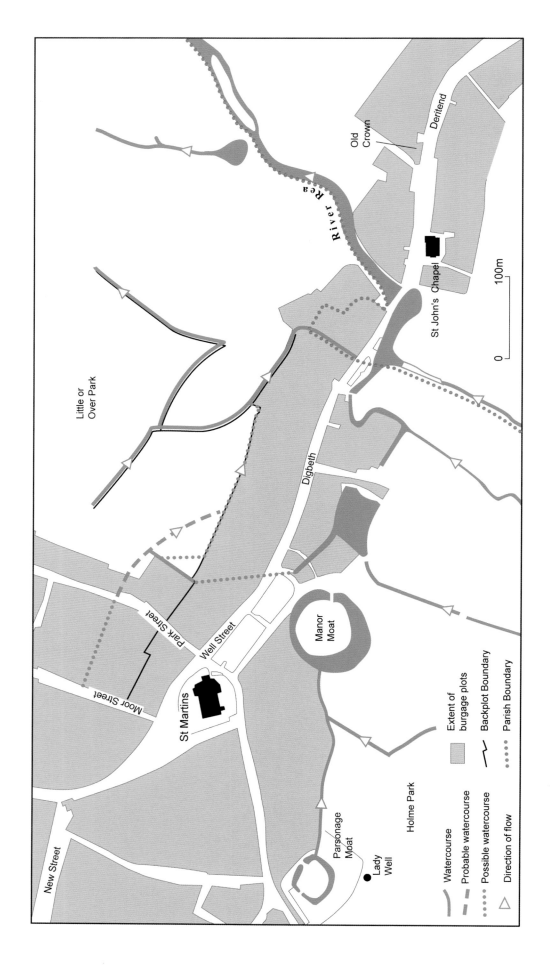

Fig. 16.2 Map illustrating the location of watercourses and watermills in Birmingham.

River Rea

Old Crown

Deritend

St John's Chapel

Little or Over Park

Digbeth

Manor Moat

Well Street

Park Street

Moor Street

St Martins

New Street

Parsonage Moat

Lady Well

Holme Park

0   100m

Watercourse

Probable watercourse

Possible watercourse

Direction of flow

Extent of burgage plots

Backplot Boundary

Parish Boundary